Selected Writings on Grace
and Pelagianism

Augustinian Heritage Institute
www.augustinianheritage.org

THE WORKS OF SAINT AUGUSTINE
A Translation for the 21st Century

**Selected Writings on Grace
and Pelagianism**

THE WORKS OF SAINT AUGUSTINE

A Translation for the 21st Century

Selected Writings on Grace and Pelagianism

translation, notes and introduction by
Roland Teske, S.J.

edited by
Boniface Ramsey

New City Press
Hyde Park, New York

Published in the United States by New City Press
202 Comforter Blvd., Hyde Park, NY 12538
www.newcitypress.com
©2011 Augustinian Heritage Institute

Cover design by Leandro De Leon
Cover illustration:
Add. Ms. 15815, f. 54
Padova, 1500

Library of Congress Cataloging-in-Publication Data:

Augustine, Saint, Bishop of Hippo.
    [Selections. English. 2011]
    Selected writings on grace and Pelagianism / translation, notes, and
introduction by Roland Teske ; edited by Boniface Ramsey.
        p. cm.
Includes bibliographical references.
ISBN 978-1-56548-372-9 (pbk. : alk. paper)
1. Grace (Theology) 2. Pelagianism. I. Teske, Roland J., 1934- II. Ramsey, Boniface. III. Title.
BR65.A52E6 2011
273'.5—dc22   2011006440

2nd printing September 2012
3rd printing March 2013

Printed in the United States of America

Contents

The Spirit and the Letter

Nature and Grace

The Predestination of the Saints

The Gift of Perseverance

General Introduction

Augustine of Hippo is arguably the greatest of the Western Doctors of the Church, and his writings on grace have rightly earned him the title Teacher of Grace. His teaching on grace is partly found in his account of the workings of the grace of Christ in his own life in his *Confessions*, written about ten years after his conversion to Catholicism and his baptism in Milan at the hands of Saint Ambrose at the Easter vigil in 387. But it is also found in the work he wrote for Simplician, Ambrose's successor as bishop of Milan, in his many works written in his long controversy with the Pelagians, and in his writings for the monks of Hadrumetum and of Provence.

Augustine's explicit teaching on the need for grace, even for the beginning of one's faith in Christ, anticipated the outbreak of the Pelagian controversy by almost fifteen years. For, in the second part of his *Miscellany of Questions in Response to Simplician*, a work written in 396 for Ambrose's successor as bishop of Milan and a man who had played a significant role in Augustine's conversion to Catholic Christianity in 386–387, Augustine's understanding of the role of grace in human life took a decisive turn, which has been labeled his third conversion after his conversion to Manichaeism in Carthage and his conversion to Catholicism in Italy.[1]

Augustine's third conversion was a conversion to grace or to theology. It was a conversion to grace in the sense that he came to realize that our salvation was not up to us but was a gratuitous gift of God, including even the first steps of faith in God. It was a conversion to theology, that is, the understanding of faith, in the sense that previously he had understood religious faith as simply a reasonable

---

1. See François Masai, "Les conversions de saint Augustin et les débuts du spritualïsme en Occident," *Le Moyen Âge* 67 (1961) 1–40. Masai rightly sees Augustine's first conversion as that to Manichaeism when he was a young man, his second as that to Catholicism in 387, and his third as that to grace at the time of the *Confessions* and the work for Simplician. On the multiplicity of Augustine's conversions also see J.-M. Le Blond, *Les conversions de saint Augustin* (Paris 1950), and Leo Ferrari, *The Conversions of Saint Augustine*=The Saint Augustine Lecture 1982 (Villanova 1984). For a contrary view, see Carol Harrison, *Rethinking Augustine's Early Theology: An Argument for Continuity* (Oxford 2006). I have argued the case for discontinuity in "Augustine's Third Conversion: A Case for Discontinuity," *Proceedings of the Jesuit Philosophical Association* 2007, ed. Joseph Koterski, 19–38.

assent to the word of another, as we believe our mother regarding the identity of our father, to give one example, with the understanding that without such trust society could not survive.[2] François Masai has put it well: "From this time on faith is for him, as it will be for the whole of later Latin theology, a theological virtue, a gratuitous gift of God, in other words 'grace.' On the contrary, up to the *Miscellany of Questions in Response to Simplician,* the bishop of Hippo thought that faith was a human assent."[3]

Hence, the second part of the work for Simplician rightly belongs among Augustine's principal writings on grace and anticipates the later great works on grace written in the Pelagian controversy.[4] After all, in *The Predestination of the Saints* 4, 8, he recalls his struggle over the roles of free choice and grace in his work for Simplician and says, in discussing God's choice of Jacob rather than Esau, that "I worked hard in defense of the free choice of the human will, but the grace of Christ conquered." Grace did not conquer in the sense that it did away with free choice but in the sense that the initiative in our salvation was seen to lie in the grace of God and not in our own will. In *The Predestination of the Saints* 3, 7, Augustine clearly admits that he was previously "mistaken, thinking that the faith by which we believe in God is not a gift of God, but that we have it from ourselves...." Ands he admits that he had earlier said in his *Commentary on Some Statements in the Letter to the Romans* 53, "For it is up to us to believe and to will, but it is up to [God] to give to those who believe and who will the ability to act well through the Holy Spirit...."[5]

The Pelagian controversy itself is divided into two phases. The first phase began in 411, when Pelagius and his disciple Caelestius arrived in Africa along with a number of Roman aristocrats who were fleeing from the Vandals after the fall of Rome to Alaric in August 410. This first phase ended with the condemnation of the teachings of Pelagius and Caelestius in 418 by Pope Zosimus, the Emperor Honorius, and the Council of Carthage. The first two works of this phase of the controversy, *The Merits and Forgiveness of Sins and the*

---

2. See *The Advantage of Believing* 12, 26.
3. F. Masai, "Les conversions," p. 34; my translation.
4. See James Wetzel, "Pelagius Anticipated: Grace and Election in Augustine's *Ad Simplicianum*." in *Augustine: From Rhetor to Theologian,* ed. Joanne McWilliam (Waterloo Ontario 1992) 121–132.
5. *The Predestination of the Saints* 3, 7, where Augustine cites *Some Statements in the Letter to the Romans* 53.

Baptism of Infants and *The Spirit and the Letter* were written without any mention of Pelagius or Caelestius, for Augustine did not want to mention them by name until he had written proof of their error, in the hope that they might not be offended but come to see the truth. He wrote these works at the request of Marcellinus, the prefect of Africa, who had reported to Augustine some of the disturbing things that were being said by the followers of Pelagius in Carthage. It was only in 417, with *Nature and Grace*, which Augustine wrote after obtaining a copy of Pelagius's work, *Nature*, that he began to cite his name. Since Pelagius's work was written as early as 405 when he was still in Rome, it is hardly true that Augustine badgered him into heresy, as has been suggested.[6] Besides these three works, which are contained in this volume, the first phase of the controversy saw the appearance of three other works of Augustine. In *The Perfection of Human Righteousness*, Augustine explains for Marcellinus how it is possible for a human being to be sinless, although no one has ever been such. In *The Deeds of Pelagius*, after having obtained the record of Pelagius's trial in Palestine, he shows that Pelagius was acquitted by the episcopal court in Palestine only because he denied propositions that he in fact held. And in *The Grace of Christ and Original Sin*, written after the condemnation of Pelagius's teaching in 418, Augustine explains the Catholic position on grace and original sin in contrast to the teaching of Pelagius.[7]

The second phase of the Pelagian controversy began in 418 and centered around Julian, the bishop of Eclanum, who along with eighteen other bishops refused to submit to the condemnation of Pelagian doctrine by Pope Zosimus. The struggle with Julian, who was Augustine's most persistent, articulate, and intelligent opponent on the question of grace, occupied Augustine during much of the last years of his life. His writings against Julian are *Marriage and Desire*, the *Answer to Two Letters of the Pelagians*, the *Answer to*

---

6. On the dating of Pelagius's work see Yves-Marie Duval, "La date du 'De natura' de Pélage: Les premières étapes de la controverse sur la grâce," *Revue des études augustiniennes* 36 (1990) 257–283. On the accusation that Augustine pushed Pelagius into heresy, see "Pelagius: A Reluctant Heretic," in B. R. Rees, *Pelagius: Life and Letters* (Rochester 1998).

7. *The Nature and Origin of the Soul*, which has been published in the first volume of *Answer to the Pelagians* is not part of the Pelagian controversy, although it touches upon a related issue, namely, the transmission of original sin, given the diverse opinions on the origin of individual souls after those of Adam and Eve.

Julian, and the huge *Unfinished Work in Answer to Julian*, which was left incomplete at Augustine's death in 430. No writings from this second phase of the controversy are included in the present volume, because they advance the general lines of Augustine's theology of grace only a little, while they are filled with many misunderstandings, bitter wrangling, and unresolved controversies. For Augustine's initial information about what Julian held was fragmentary and based on excerpts and alleged misquotations. It is also likely that Julian never had the chance to read any of Augustine's works in answer to him while he was exiled in the East.

The final two works in the present volume do not belong to the Pelagian controversy at all, since they were written for Catholic monks of Provence who, like their African counterparts, the monks of Hadrumetum, had found difficulty with Augustine's teaching on grace. For the monks of Hadrumetum Augustine wrote *Grace and Free Choice* and *Rebuke and Grace*, while for the monks of Provence he wrote *The Predestination of the Saints* and *The Gift of Perseverance*. In the first work for the African monks Augustine argued that grace does not do away with free choice, just as free choice does not eliminate grace. In the second work he answered the claim that, if everything is up to the grace of God, a superior ought not to rebuke a monk who misbehaves but should simply pray for his improvement. For the monks of Provence Augustine wrote the final two works contained in the present volume, *The Predestination of the Saints* and *The Gift of Perseverance*, which were originally two books of a single work.

It was only in the sixteenth century that Augustine's opponents in Provence were labeled "Semi-Pelagians,"[8] a title that incorrectly implied that the monks were heretics or half-heretics, and that was certainly not true. Some of them in fact, such as John Cassian, the abbot of Lérins, who was the spiritual leader of the monks of Provence, were then regarded as holy men and are now regarded as saints of the Church. If some teachings of the Gallic monks eventually came

---

8. The label "Semi-Pelagian" was, it seems, first applied to the Jesuits, who stressed a more active role for the human will, at least in the eyes of their opponents, who were more firmly rooted in the Augustinian tradition on the role of grace. Despite the incorrectness of applying the term to the monks of Provence, it is hard to uproot it from the tradition. See Alex Hwang's discussion of alternative labels for the position taken by these monks in *Intrepid Lover of Perfect Grace: The Life and Thought of Prosper of Aquitaine* (Washington 2009) 2–6.

under condemnation by the Council of Orange in 529, that certainly did not make them heretics retroactively.[9]

The views of the monks of Provence were brought to Augustine's attention by Prosper of Aquitaine and his friend Hilary, who were initially outraged at the monks' opposition to Augustine's teaching on grace. However, later in his life, after the deaths of Augustine and Cassian and after becoming a friend and secretary to Pope Leo, Prosper wrote *The Calling of All the Nations* around the year 450, which was the first work that emphasized the universal salvific will of God, contrary to the teaching of Augustine in his later years, and which marked a step away from the teaching on predestination found in Augustine's works for the monks of Provence.[10]

The Council of Orange in 529 settled the earlier dispute about grace and predestination for a time, but another form of the controversy arose again in the ninth century when Gottschalk of Orbais taught a double predestination, of the elect to eternal salvation and of the reprobate to eternal damnation, and claimed Augustine as his source for that doctrine.[11] The predestination controversy again loomed large in the Reformation, when both Martin Luther and John Calvin claimed Augustine for their views on grace and predestination.[12] Hence, the two works of the monks of Provence had and continue to have an afterlife in the Christian churches, which certainly makes their inclusion in this volume worthwhile and important for students of Augustine's teaching on grace.

Roland J. Teske, S.J.

---

9. Augustine himself defended Cyprian, the bishop and martyr of Carthage, against such a charge because of his views on the repetition of baptism. See my "Augustine's Appeal to Tradition," in *Tradition and the Rule of Faith in the Early Church*, ed. Ronnie J. Rombs and Alexander Y. Hwang (Washington 2010) 153–172, esp. 159–162.

10. See the introduction to *Prosper: De Vocatione Omnium Gentium*, ed. Roland Teske and Dorothea Weber (Vienna 2009).

11. For Gottschalk's teaching on predestination, see *Gottschalk and a Medieval Predestination Controversy: Texts Translated from the Latin*=Medieval Philosophical Texts in Translation 47, ed. Victor Genke and Francis X. Gummerlock. (Milwaukee 2010).

12. See Carl Andressen's "Vorwort, zugleich eine Einführung," in *Zum Augustin-Gespräch der Gegenwart* I, ed. Carl Andressen (Darmstadt 1975) 31, where he cites both Luther's and Calvin's claim to Augustine's teaching on grace and predestination.

Miscellany of Questions
in Response to Simplician I

Introduction

In *Revisions* II,1,1 Augustine identifies the Simplician of this work's title as the bishop of Milan who succeeded Ambrose in 397. Paulinus of Milan, the author of Ambrose's biography, indicates that he was to all intents hand-picked by Ambrose himself for the position, despite his advanced age.[1] Simplician had been instrumental in the conversion to Catholic Christianity of the famous Roman rhetor Marius Victorinus in the 350s and in that of Ambrose as well in 374.[2] Years after his death, which occurred about 400, Augustine spoke of him in *The City of God*[3] as a "saintly old man" and used him as a reference regarding the doctrine of the Incarnation. It is clear that Simplician was a man capable of making an enduring impression. But, as one author observes, he is "better known by what we hear of his influence over others more famous than himself, than by any writings of his own," and this influence, "which was very great, was shewn more in drawing forth their thoughts than in recording his own."[4] Certainly Simplician's letter to Augustine, now lost, which he wrote sometime in the mid-390s in order to request answers to eight questions on scripture, succeeded in drawing forth from his addressee some thoughts of considerable consequence.

We know from *Revisions* II,1,1 that the *Miscellany of Questions in Response to Simplician* was the first work that Augustine wrote as a bishop. Since he was ordained to the episcopacy in Hippo in 395, the treatise is dated to the period 396-398. Not possessing Simplician's letter of request to Augustine, we know nothing other than what the *Miscellany* tells us of his questions. Their order, which Augustine probably did not alter, is slightly unusual in that the first book is devoted to two questions on the Epistle to the Romans while the second, which is not included in this volume, goes back to the Old Testament and covers six questions from the Books of Kings (specifically 1 and 2 Samuel and 1 Kings).

---

1. See *Life of Saint Ambrose* 46.
2. See Augustine, *Confessions* VIII,2,3-5.
3. X,29.
4. William Smith and Henry Wace, eds., *A Dictionary of Christian Biography* IV (London 1887) 688, 689.

From Augustine's own treatment of the *Miscellany* in his *Revisions* it is obvious that the first book overshadows the second in importance: in particular he dwells at some length on the meaning of the first book's second question and calls attention to its significance, while he deals quite conventionally with the six questions contained in the second book. And the excerpts from *The Predestination of the Saints* and *The Gift of Perseverance* that are included in this volume make it even more evident how much of a turning point in his theological development the second question in the first book represents.

Augustine had already written two works on Paul's Epistle to the Romans—the *Commentary on Some Statements in the Epistle to the Romans* and the *Unfinished Commentary on the Epistle to the Romans*—and had interpreted three passages from it in his *Miscellany of Eighty-three Questions* 66-68 when, in response to Simplician's request, he once more addressed himself to this crucial New Testament text, which would in fact continue to preoccupy him for the rest of his life.

The topic of the first question is a lengthy passage from the seventh chapter of this epistle, in which Paul, while insisting that the Old Testament law is good, points to the interior struggle that its very existence inspires or at least throws into relief. Augustine follows Paul closely and, like him, emphasizes the law's goodness. Although Simplician had asked for an explanation of Rom 7:7-24, Augustine begins and ends his exegesis with the preceding verse, which distinguishes between the spirit and the letter of the law. This verse is the key to the lines that follow, for the spirit of the law is the love that frees from the letter that kills.

In the course of this first question, however, as in his *Commentary on Some Statements in the Epistle to the Romans,* Augustine takes two positions that he will later disavow.[5] The first position, which he states at the outset of the question,[6] is that Paul is speaking in this passage not in his own person but in that of someone under the law other than himself. Twenty years later, in his writings against

---

5. See *Revisions* I,23,1.3, where he blames himself for having held in the *Commentary* the two views that will be discussed. The first, regarding the person of Paul, is in section 41 but is not glaring. The second, concerning grace, comes across very clearly in section 61: "It is ours to believe and to will, but [God's] to give to those who believe and will the faculty of doing good through the Holy Spirit."

6. See I,1,1. See also I,1,9.

the Pelagians, Augustine repudiates this view as characteristically Pelagian and asserts that Paul himself was no more removed from the struggle with sin than was any other human being.[7] The second of these two positions is that the very beginnings of the life of grace are within the scope of human ability. As Augustine says in I,1,11, "willing itself is in our power," even though accomplishing the good that one has willed is impossible. And in I,1,14 he states: "What in fact is left to free choice (*libero arbitrio*) in this mortal life is not that a person may fulfill righteousness when he wants to but that by suppliant piety he may turn to him by whose gift he may be enabled to fulfill it." In other words a person may turn to God by his own initiative, although it is only God himself who gives the power to act rightly once the turn has been made. The notion that the human will could at least on occasion anticipate the action of divine grace was later espoused by John Cassian in the famous thirteenth of his twenty-four *Conferences* and came to be referred to as semi-Pelagianism or, more recently and probably more correctly, as semi-Augustinianism. Having initially entertained this notion in responding to Simplician's first question, Augustine goes on to reject it in his answer to the second.

In this question, at Simplician's request, Augustine interprets the text of Rom 9:10-29, in which Paul works out a theology of human merit and divine grace based upon the Genesis narrative of Jacob and Esau. Augustine tells us in *Revisions* II,1,2 that "in answering this question I in fact strove on behalf of the free choice of the human will, but God's grace conquered...." He had not expected, he seems to be saying, that his response to Simplician would turn out as it did. Perhaps at the time, despite his account thirty years later in the *Revisions* and elsewhere, he did not even appreciate how greatly the second question was at variance with the first. For why, after having said what he did in the second, did he not immediately return to the first and revise it from the perspective of his new insight? In any event, only the conclusion that he came to in his second question could make sense of the words that Paul wrote elsewhere, which cast light on the text from Romans: *What do you possess that you have not received? But if you have received, why do you boast as if you had not received?* (1 Cor 4:7)

---

7. See, e.g., *The Grace of Christ and Original Sin* I,39,43; *Answer to the Two Letters of the Pelagians* I,8,13-11,24.

If the passage from Romans that Augustine had interpreted in the first part of the first book of his *Miscellany* left an opening for the human will to make a salvific decision without the assistance of grace, Paul's meditation on the story of Jacob and Esau allowed for no such opening. For Paul made it clear—at least to Augustine—that nothing good whatsoever, whether will or merit, whether faith or work, precedes the influence of grace. Neither Jacob nor Esau, who were conceived at the same moment and born only moments apart and who seemed to be morally identical, had done anything to merit that one should serve the other or that one should be loved by God and the other, in the hyperbolic language of scripture, be hated by him. The reason why one was chosen and the other rejected lies in God's mysterious purpose (*propositum*), which cannot be explained away by suggesting that he made his choice (*electio*) based on his foreknowledge of Jacob's future faith and good works and of Esau's future evil will and misdeeds: this would only make God's foreknowledge and grace dependent upon human activity.[8]

Once he has settled the issue of the absolute primacy of grace, Augustine turns to the distinction that is made in Mt 20:16: *Many are called, but few are chosen.* It is one thing for a person to be the object of God's call (*vocatio*) and quite another for him to be chosen. As Augustine would explain it, to have been called is to have been visited by grace, but not all who have been visited by grace are moved by it; only those who have been moved constitute "the few" who have been chosen. This is the basis for what theologians would later refer to as the distinction between "operating" or "sufficient" grace on the one hand and "cooperating" or "efficacious" grace on the other.

Why are some called and others not? And why, even among those who are called, are some chosen and others not? The response can only be that, since Adam's transgression, the whole human race is "a kind of single mass of sin (*una quaedam massa peccati*)," as Augustine describes it in I,2,16, and as such is deserving of punishment in its entirety. If God allows some of the "mass of sin" to pay the debt of punishment that is owed him but forgives the same debt of others, so that they may experience being made righteous (*justificatio*), no one may reasonably object. "It should be maintained with unflinching

---

8. This was the solution to the problem of the interaction of grace and free will offered by Augustine's greatest predecessor, Origen. See his *On Prayer* 6,2-5.

faith," he says in I,2,17, "that there is no injustice with God, who either forgives or exacts what is owed him, and neither can the one from whom he rightly exacts it complain of his injustice nor ought the other to whom it is forgiven boast of his own merits. For the one only repays what is owed while the other has only what he has received."

Augustine must find a place for free will here, and toward the end of the question he emphasizes it—only to cast its ultimate value into doubt by adding a qualification inspired by Rom 7:14: "The free choice of the will (*liberum voluntatis arbitrium*) counts for a great deal, to be sure. But what does it count for in those who have been sold under sin?" (I,2,21)

As he approaches his conclusion Augustine wonders rhetorically what sort of person might be chosen by God. Would it be someone whose sins were few and who had, in addition, useful learning, intelligence, mental refinement? Yet people with unlikely backgrounds, prostitutes and actors among others, are converted and enjoy a sudden inrush of virtue that could not have been anticipated. What preparation did Paul himself have for the conversion that conquered his "rabid, raging, blind will" (I,2,22)? And so Augustine's final words on the subject are an appeal to recognize the inscrutability of God's judgments and to join in the canticle of praise that should ever greet those judgments—an appeal to which, it may be noted, only the chosen would respond.

This first book of the *Miscellany of Questions in Response to Simplician*, then, shows that Augustine's view of grace, free will and predestination was in place well before the appearence of Pelagianism. It was the actual battle with Pelagianism, however, that transformed this view into the one that, more than any other, would define forever Augustine's impact on Western culture.

The Text and Translations

The critical Latin text for this translation was published in 1970 by A. Mutzenbecher in CCSL XLIV, 7-56. An earlier edition of the Latin text appears in Migne, PL XL, 101-128; it is reproduced in Bibliothèque Augustinienne X, 410-509, along with a French translation by J. Boutet. There is an English translation by John H. S. Burleigh in *Augustine's Earlier Writings* = Library of Chrisitan Classics VI (London 1953) 376-406.

Revisions II,1

1. The first two books that I worked on as a bishop are addressed to Simplician, bishop of the church of Milan, who succeeded the most blessed Ambrose, on a miscellany of questions. Two of them I took from the epistle of the apostle Paul to the Romans and put in the first book.

2. The first of these is on what is written: *What, then, shall we say? That the law is sin?* (Rom 7:7) up to the point where it says: *Who will liberate me from the body of this death? The grace of God through Jesus Christ our Lord.* (Rom 7:24-25) In it I explained those words of the Apostle—*The law is spiritual, but I am fleshly* (Rom 7:14), and so forth, by which the flesh is shown to struggle with the spirit—in such a way as to see humankind described as being *still under the law* and *not yet under grace* (Rom 6:14). For it was not until long afterwards that I realized that those words can as well—and this is more likely—pertain to the spiritual person.

3. The second question in this book is from the place where it says: *As well as that* [i.e., Sarah's story], *there is also Rebecca, who from a single act of intercourse conceived from our father Isaac* (Rom 9:10) up to the point where it says: *Unless the Lord of hosts had left us offspring, we would have become like Sodom, and we would have been like Gomorrah* (Rom 9:29). In answering this question I in fact strove on behalf of the free choice of the human will, but God's grace conquered, and otherwise I would have been unable to arrive at understanding what the Apostle said with the most evident truthfulness, *For who sets you apart? What do you possess that you have not received? But if you have received, why do you boast as though you had not received?* (1 Cor 4:7) The martyr Cyprian also, wishing to demonstrate this, summed it all up with this very title when he said, "No one must boast of anything since nothing is ours."[1]

---

1. *Testimonies* III,4, also referred to by Augustine in *The Predestination of the Saints* 3,7. Cyprian of Carthage (200?-258) is often cited by Augustine as an authority of high standing.

4. Other questions are treated in the second book and answered in accordance with whatever ability we had. They all concern the so-called Books of Kingdoms.[2]

5. The first of these is on what is written: *And the spirit of the Lord came over Saul* (1 S 10:10), inasmuch as it is said elsewhere: *And there was an evil spirit of the Lord in Saul* (1 S 16:14). In explaining this I said, "Although it is in a person's power to will something, nonetheless it is not in his power to be able to do it." I said this because we do not say that something is in our power unless what we will happens. The first and most important thing is the willing itself. Without any hiatus whatsoever the will itself is present when we will. But we also receive the power from on high for living a good life when our will is prepared by the Lord.[3]

6. The second question asks how it was said: *I regret having made Saul king* (1 S 15:11).

7. The third is on whether the unclean spirit that was in the necromancer was able to bring it about that Samuel was seen by Saul and spoke with him.[4]

8. The fourth is on what is written: *King David went up and sat before the Lord* (2 S 7:18).

9. The fifth is on what Elijah said: *O Lord, witness of this widow, with whom I am living in her home, you have acted badly by killing her son* (1 K 17:20).

10. This work begins thus: "[In sending me your questions, Father Simplician, you have shown me] the clearly most welcome and delightful [honor]."

---

2. What Augustine knew as the four books of Kingdoms are now divided into two books of Samuel and two books of Kings.

3. See Prv 8:35 LXX.

4. See 1 S 28:7-19.

The Predestination of the Saints 4,8[1]

You certainly see what I believed then about faith and works, even though I tried to emphasize the grace of God. I see now that such is the view that those brothers of ours hold because, as they did not make an effort to read my books, they did not advance along with me in them.[2] For, if they had made an effort, they would have found that question answered in accordance with the truth of the divine scriptures in the first of the two books that I wrote at the very beginning of my episcopate to Simplician of blessed memory, the bishop of the church of Milan and the successor of Saint Ambrose. Perhaps, on the other hand, they were unaware of them. In that case, see to it that they are aware of them. I spoke first of the first of those two books in the second book of the *Revisions.* My words there are as follows:

"The first two books that I worked on as bishop are addressed to Simplician, bishop of the church of Milan, who succeeded the most blessed Ambrose, on a miscellany of questions. Two of them I took from the epistle of the apostle Paul to the Romans and put in the first book.

"The first of these is on what is written: *What, then, shall we say? That the law is sin?* (Rom 7:7) up to the point where it says: *Who will liberate me from the body of this death? The grace of God through Jesus Christ our Lord.* (Rom 7:24-25) In it I explained those words of the Apostle—*The law is spiritual, but I am fleshly* (Rom 7:14), and so forth, by which the flesh is shown to struggle with the spirit—in such a way as to see humankind described as being *still under the law* and *not yet under grace* (Rom 6:14). For it was not until long afterwards that I realized that those words can as well—and this is more likely—pertain to the spiritual person.

"The second question in this book is from the place where it says: *As well as that* [i.e., Sarah's story], *there is also Rebecca, who from*

---

1. Written in 428-429 and addressed to Prosper of Aquitaine and a certain Hilary.

2. The brothers to whom Augustine refers were monks of southern Gaul, centered in Marseilles, whose understanding of grace was the same as that of Augustine himself in the *Miscellany of Questions in Response to Simplician* I,1. Whereas he had revised his thinking, however, in the second half of the first book of the *Miscellany*, they still clung to a view of grace that on occasion allowed human initiative to precede divine action.

a single act of intercourse conceived from our father Isaac (Rom 9:10) up to the point where it says: *Unless the Lord of hosts had left us offspring, we would have become like Sodom, and we would have been like Gomorrah* (Rom 9:29). In answering this question I in fact strove on behalf of the free choice of the human will, but God's grace conquered, and otherwise I would have been unable to arrive at understanding what the Apostle said with the most evident truthfulness, *For who sets you apart? What do you possess that you have not received? But if you have received, why do you boast as though you had not received?* (1 Cor 4:7) The martyr Cyprian also, wishing to demonstrate this, summed it all with this very title when he said, 'No one must boast of anything since nothing is ours.' "[3]

This is why I previously said that, when I thought otherwise about this matter, I myself had also been convinced in particular by this testimony of the Apostle.[4] God revealed this to me in the answer to the question that, as I said, I was writing to Simplician. This testimony of the Apostle, then, when he said, in order to check human boastfulness, *For what do you possess that you have not received?* does not permit any of the faithful to say, "I have faith that I have not received." This utterly prideful response is completely checked by these words of the Apostle. Not even this much can be said: "Although I do not have a perfect faith, still I have the beginning of it, thanks to which I first believed in Christ." For the response here as well is: *But what do you possess that you have not received? But if you have received, why do you boast as though you had not received?*

---

3. *Testimonies* III,4.
4. See 1 Cor 4:7.

The Gift of Perseverance 20,52; 21,55[1]

But they say, "It was not necessary that the hearts of so many
persons of little intelligence be disturbed by the uncertainty of this
kind of discussion, since the Catholic faith has been upheld no less
advantageously over the course of so many years without this definition of predestination, occasionally against others but especially
against the Pelagians, thanks to the books that we already have, both
by Catholics and by others."[2] I am quite surprised that they say this
and do not consider that those books of ours (to say nothing here
of others) were written and published before the Pelagians came
upon the scene, and that they do not notice in how many places in
them, without our even having been aware of it, we cut to pieces the
future Pelagian heresy by extolling the grace by which God frees us
from our wicked errors and behavior, which he does in accordance
with his own gratuitous mercy and apart from any antecedent merits of ours. I began to understand this more fully in the treatise that
I wrote at the beginning of my episcopate to Simplician of blessed
memory, the bishop of Milan, when I realized and affirmed that the
beginning of faith is God's gift....

Let them see, I say, whether in the final sections of the first book
of the two that I wrote at the beginning of my episcopate, before
the Pelagian heresy came upon the scene, to Simplician, the bishop

---

1. Written in 428-429 as a sequel to *The Predestination of the Saints* and likewise addressed to Prosper and Hilary.
2. Augustine is quoting a letter from Hilary to him, which is included in Augustine's own
correspondence. See Letter 226,8. Hilary is in turn citing the position of those who say
that Augustine's definition of predestination is confusing and inopportune. Augustine's
response in both excerpts from *The Gift of Perseverance* that are reproduced here is
that his theology of grace was ultimately not reactive to Pelagius (whose understanding of grace was diametrically opposed to Augustine's) but had already existed in all
its principal elements, implicitly including final perseverance and predestination, by
the time of the composition of the *Miscellany of Questions in Response to Simplician*
I,2, well before Pelagius came to Augustine's attention. In her *Rethinking Augustine's
Early Theology: An Argument for Continuity* (Oxford 2006) 142-154, esp. 150-154,
Carol Harrison argues that Augustine's characteristic theology of grace predated even
the *Miscellany* and that in I,1 he was merely experimenting with the notion of grace that
he presents there, to see whether he could maintain some small role for human freedom.
See Chad Tyler Gerber's sympathetic but critical review of Harrison's thesis in *Journal
of Early Christian Studies* 15 (2007) 120-122.

of Milan, anything remains that might call into doubt the fact that God's grace is not given in accordance with our merits; whether I did not make it clear that even the beginning of faith is God's gift; and whether, from what was said there, it does not plainly follow—even if it is not openly expressed—that final perseverance is not given except by him who has predestined us for his kingdom and glory.

Letter 37, to Simplician

To Simplician, his most blessed lord and father, who deserves to be reverently embraced with most sincere love, Augustine sends greetings in the Lord.

1. I have received the letter that was sent at the behest of Your Holiness. It is full of pleasant joys because I hold a place in your memory and you love me as you always have, and because whatever gifts of his the Lord has deigned to confer upon me—not by my own merits but by his mercy—are a source of gladness for you. In it, my most blessed Lord, who deserves to be reverently embraced, I drank from your most kindly heart a not unexpected and new fatherly feeling towards me, but I claimed it as something evidently proven and known.

2. But how is it that our literary exertions, which have engaged our efforts in the writing of some books, have had such good fortune as to be read by Your Honor? It must be that the Lord, to whom I have submitted my soul, wished my troubles to be assuaged and to release me from the concern, which is my ineluctable preoccupation in such labors, that, being perhaps somewhat ignorant and rash, I might cause offense anywhere even while on the most level plain of truth. For if my writing pleases you, I know whom [else] it pleases, since I know who dwells within you. Indeed, the same one who distributes and bestows every spiritual gift has confirmed my obedience through your judgment. For whatever those writings possess that is worthy of your admiration, it was God who, in my ministry, said, "Let it be done," and it was done, but it was in your approval that God saw that it was good.[1]

3. Even if I were hindered by my own obtuseness and did not understand the questions that you deigned to command me to elucidate, I would approach them with the assistance of your merits. This alone I seek—that you beseech God on behalf of my weakness and, whether in these matters in which you have desired to occupy me in kindly and fatherly fashion or in others when something of ours may perhaps fall into your holy hands, that, inasmuch as I recognize my own errors as well as I do God's gifts, you not only exercise a reader's care but also provide a critic's judgment.

---

1. See Gn 1:3-4.

Miscellany of Questions in Response to Simplician

Book One

In sending me your questions, Father Simplician, you have shown me the clearly most welcome and delightful honor, and I would consider myself not only insolent but also ungrateful if I did not attempt to reply to them. And in fact the things that you proposed should be answered with regard to the apostle Paul had already been discussed by us to some degree or other and had been committed to writing.[1] But still I am not satisfied with my previous research and explanation, since I may have negligently overlooked something pertinent, and I have gone through the Apostle's words and the sense of his statements more carefully and attentively. For, if it were a quick and easy matter to understand them, you would not consider that they should be investigated.

First Question

1,1. You have wished us to elucidate the first question—from the place where it is written: *What, then, shall we say? That the law is sin? Of course not!* (Rom 7:7) up to the place where it says: *The law, then, is good for me when I am willing* (Rom 7:21), and I believe what remains as far as: *Wretched man that I am! Who will liberate me from the body of this death? The grace of God through Jesus Christ our Lord.* (Rom 7:24-25) In this text it seems to me that the Apostle has put himself in the place of someone who is under the law, whose words he speaks in his own person. He had said a little before, *We are rid of the law, in which imprisonment we were dead, so that thus we may serve in the new way of the spirit and not in the old way of the letter* (Rom 7:6). But because he could thus seem as it were to have rebuked the law by these words, he immediately added,

---

1. Augustine is undoubtedly referring to his *Commentary on Some Statements in the Letter to the Romans* 37-46, 60-65 and to the *Miscellany of Eighty-three Questions* 66, 68.

*What, then, shall we say? That the law is sin? Of course not! But I
did not know sin except through the law, for I did not know about
covetousness* (concupiscentiam) *except that the law said, You shall
not covet* (concupisces). (Rom 7:7)

1,2. Here again there is something striking: If the law is not sin
but implants sin, it is nonetheless censured in these words. This is
why it must be understood that the law was given not that sin might
be instilled nor that it might be extirpated but only that it might be
made manifest. In this way it would make the human soul, seemingly
secure in its innocence, guilty by the very manifestation of sin so
that, inasmuch as sin could not be conquered apart from the grace of
God, [the soul] would be turned by its uneasy awareness of guilt to
a receptivity to grace. And so he does not say, "I did not commit sin
except through the law," but, *I did not know sin except through the
law*. Nor, again, does he say, "For I did not have covetousness except
that the law said, You shall not covet," but, *I did not know about
covetousness except that the law said, You shall not covet*. From this
it is clear that covetousness was not instilled by the law but made
manifest by it.

1,3. But the consequence was that, since grace had not yet been
received and the human person could not resist covetousness, it was
even increased, because this covetousness grew even more, since,
when by acting even against the law it is joined to the offense of
transgression (*crimine praevaricationis*), it takes on greater strength
than it would have done had there been no law forbidding it. And
so [Paul] adds what follows: *But, having seized the occasion,
sin brought about every kind of covetousness in me through the
commandment* (Rom 7:8). For it also existed before the law, but it
was not all-encompassing when the offense of transgression was still
lacking. Hence he says in another place, *For where there is no law
there is no transgression* (Rom 4:15).

1,4. To this he adds, *For without the law sin was dead* (Rom 7:8).
It was as though he said that it was hidden—that is, it was thought
to be dead. Shortly thereafter he says more clearly, *But once I lived
without the law* (Rom 7:9)—that is, I was unafraid of death from
sin because it had not appeared when there was no law. *But with the
coming of the commandment sin came back to life* (Rom 7:9)—that
is, it made its appearance. *But I died* (Rom 7:10)—that is, I knew
that I was dead for the reason that the guilt of transgression threatens

me with the certain punishment of death. Clearly, when he said, *Sin came back to life with the coming of the commandment,* he indicated in this way that sin once lived—that is, that it was known, in my opinion, at the transgression of the first man, because he himself had also received a commandment.[2] For in another place he says, *But the woman, once seduced, fell into transgression* (1 Tm 2:14); and again, *In the likeness of the transgression of Adam, who is the form of the one who is to come* (Rom 5:14). For unless [sin] was once alive it cannot come back to life. But it was dead—that is, hidden—when mortal men who were born without the law's commandment lived in pursuit of the covetous desires of the flesh without any knowledge, because there was no prohibition. Therefore he says, *Once I lived without the law,* and in this way he demonstrates that he is speaking not just for himself but for human beings in general. *But with the coming of the commandment sin came back to life. But I died, and the commandment, which was for life, turned out to be death for me.* (Rom 7:9-10) For if one is obedient to the commandment, life is certainly there. But it turns out to be death as long as the commandment is contravened, so that it not only becomes sin, which was committed even before the commandment, but becomes it in a more widespread and pernicious fashion, such that sin is now committed by a knowing transgressor.

1,5. *For,* he says, *having seized the occasion, sin deceived me through the commandment, and in this way it killed me* (Rom 7:11). Sin, using the law unlawfully, grew more desirable because of its prohibition and became sweeter, and so it deceived. For deception is a sweetness that is followed by more and greater bitter punishments. Since, then, it is quite reasonably admitted by those who are not yet in possession of spiritual grace that there is a prohibition, sin deceives by a false sweetness; but because the guilt of transgression is also present, it kills.

1,6. *And so, to be sure, the law is holy, and the commandment is holy and righteous and good* (Rom 7:12), for it enjoins what should be enjoined and prohibits what should be prohibited. *Has, then, what is good become death for me? Of course not!* (Rom 7:13) There is vice in using a thing badly, not in the commandment itself, which is good, *because the law is good if a person uses it lawfully* (1 Tm 1:8). But a person uses the law badly if he does not submit to God with

---

2. See Gn 2:16-17.

devout humility so that the law may be fulfilled through grace. And so he who does not use it lawfully receives it for no other purpose than that his sin, which before its prohibition lay hidden, may begin to appear through transgression, and to appear without limit, because now it is not only a matter of committing sin but also of contravening the commandment. He continues, therefore, and adds, *But sin, in order to appear as sin, worked death in me through what was good, so that the sinner and the sin might, thanks to the commandment, be without limit* (Rom 7:13). From this it is evident what he meant when he said previously, *For without the law sin was dead,* not because it did not exist but because it was not manifest, and how it was said, *Sin came back to life,* not that it might be just what it was before the law but that it might be made manifest inasmuch as it contravened the law, since he says in this place, *But sin, in order to appear as sin, worked death in me through what was good*; for he does not say "in order to be sin" but *in order to appear as sin.*

1,7. Then he gives the reason why this is so: *For we know that the law is spiritual, but I am fleshly* (Rom 7:14). In saying this he clearly indicates that the law cannot be fulfilled except by spiritual persons, who do not become such apart from grace. For a person becomes that much more conformed to the spiritual law—that is, he rises all the more to a spiritual disposition—the more he fulfills it, because he takes that much more delight in it when he is no longer worn down by its burdensomeness but energized by its light. For the precept of the Lord is lucid and enlightens the eyes,[3] and the law of the Lord is unsullied, transforming souls.[4] By grace he forgives sins and pours out the spirit of love, which is why practicing righteousness is no longer burdensome but indeed joyful.

Although he plainly said, *But I am fleshly,* what he meant by *fleshly* must be clarified. For even those who are already living in grace, who have already been redeemed by the blood of the Lord[5] and renewed by faith, are referred to as fleshly to a certain degree. To them the same Apostle says, *And I, brothers, have not been able to speak to you as to spiritual persons but as to fleshly ones. Since you are little children in Christ, I have given you milk to drink, not solid food.* (1 Cor 3:2) By saying this he shows that those who were

3. See Ps 19:8.
4. See Ps 19:7.
5. See 1 Pt 1:18-19.

little children in Christ and had to be given milk to drink have in fact already been reborn through grace, and yet he still refers to them as fleshly. The person who is not yet under grace but under the law is fleshly in that he has not yet been reborn from sin but is *sold under sin* (Rom 7:14), because he willingly accepts the sweet price of the deathly pleasure by which he is being deceived and also delights in contravening the law, since the less it is allowed the more attractive it is.[6] This sweetness he cannot enjoy as the price of his condition unless he serves his appetites like a bought slave. For he who is prohibited and knows that he is justly prohibited and nonetheless does the deed is aware that he is the slave of the desire that masters him.

1,8. *For,* he says, *I know not what I do* (Rom 7:15). He does not say *I know not* here as though he did not know that he was sinning. For that contradicts what he said [previously], *But sin, in order to appear as sin, worked death in me through what was good,* and what came before that, *I did not know sin except through the law.* For how is it made manifest or how did he know what he did not know? But he said this in the same way that the Lord will say to the wicked, *I do not know you* (Mt 25:12). For there is nothing that is hidden from God, since *the face of the Lord is over those who do wickedness, to destroy their memory from the earth* (Ps 34:16). But we are sometimes said not to know what we do not approve of. It is in that sense, then, that he says, *I know not what I do*—that is, "I do not approve of it." This he shows in what follows, when he says, *For I do not do what I want, but I do what I hate* (Rom 7:15). When he says, *I hate,* it means "I do not know," because, regarding those to whom the Lord will say, *I do not know you,* it is also said to him, *Lord, you hate all who do evil* (Ps 5:5).

1,9. *But if I do what I do not want, I consent to the law because it is good* (Rom 7:16), for neither does the law want it, since the law forbids it. He consents to the law, then, not insofar as he does what it prohibits but insofar as he does not want to do what he does. He is overcome, not yet having been liberated by grace, although through the law he already both knows that he is doing wrong and does not want to do it. But the next thing that he says is: *It is no longer I that do it but the sin that dwells in me* (Rom 7:17). He does not say this because he does not consent to committing sin, although he consents

---

6. "Since the less it is allowed the more attractive it is": *cum tanto magis libet, quanto minus licet.*

to the law that disapproves of it (for he is still speaking in the person of someone who is living under the law and not yet under grace,[7] who is actually drawn to do wrong under the mastery of covetousness and by the deceptive sweetness of forbidden sin, although he disapproves of this by reason of his knowledge of the law), but he says, *It is not I that do it*, because he has been overcome. It is in fact desire (*cupiditas*) that does it, to whose victory he surrenders. But it is grace that sees to it that there is no surrender and that a person's mind is fortified against desire. Of this he will speak later.

1,10. *For I know,* he says, *that good does not dwell in me—that is, in my flesh* (Rom 7:18). As regards what he knows, he consents to the law; but as regards what he does, he surrenders to sin. Perhaps someone would ask, "Whence comes it that he says that good does not dwell in him, meaning that sin does?" What would the answer be except that it comes from the passing on of mortality and the constant repetition of sensual pleasure? The former derives from the punishment for the original sin,[8] the latter from the punishment for repeated sin; with the former we are born into this life, while the latter we augment over the course of our lives. These two things, which we may call nature and habit, create a very strong and unconquerable covetousness once they have been joined together, which [Paul] refers to as sin and says dwells in his flesh—that is, possesses a certain sovereignty and rule, as it were. This is why the psalm says, *I have preferred to be cast down in the house of the Lord than to dwell in the tents of sinners* (Ps 84:10)—as though he who has been cast down, wherever that may be, is not dwelling, although he is there. And so he suggests that "dwelling" is to be understood with a note of mastery. But if what he says in another place should happen to us through grace—that sin should not rule in our mortal body to make us obey its desires[9]—it is no longer properly said to dwell there.

---

7. In the *Revisions* Augustine qualifies his position here by saying: "It was not until long afterwards that I realized that those words can as well—and this is more likely—pertain to the spiritual person."

8. "The original sin": *originalis peccati*. This is Augustine's first use of a term that would probably be more closely associated with him than any other, although at this point he is not yet using it in the sense of an inherited sin. For its first use in that sense see *The Punishment and Forgiveness of Sin and the Baptism of Little Ones* I, 9, 9. "Original sin" is translated here with the article "the" in order both to emphasize that it is in fact Adam's sin in its origin and to suggest that it is not yet a popular expression, which not using the article might connote.

9. See Rom 6:14, 12.

1,11. *For to will the good is close at hand, but the doing of it is not* (Rom 7:18). To those who do not correctly understand he seems with these words to be abolishing free choice. But how can he be abolishing it when he says, *To will is close at hand*? For willing itself is in our power since it is close at hand, but the fact that doing the good is not in our power is part of the deserts of the original sin. For nothing remains of this first nature of humankind but the punishment of sin, through which mortality itself has become a kind of second nature, and it is from this that the grace of the creator frees those who have submitted to him through faith. But those are the words of a person who lives now under the law and not under grace. For he who is not yet under grace does not do the good that he wants but he does the evil that he does not want,[10] thanks to the domination of covetousness, which is strengthened not only by the bond of mortality but also by the millstone of habit. But if he does what he does not want, it is no longer he that does it but the sin that dwells in him, as was stated and explained previously.

1,12. *I find it, therefore, to be a law,* he says, *that, when I want to do good, evil is close at hand* (Rom 7:21)—that is, I find the law to be a good thing for me when I want to do what the law maintains, because evil is close at hand and hence easy to do, since what he said previously, *To will is close at hand,* he said with reference to its being easy. For what is easier for a person living under the law than to will good and to do evil? For the one he wills without difficulty, although he does not do with such ease what he easily wills, and the other, which he hates, he easily possesses, although he would not will it. It is like someone who, once having been pushed, easily continues to fall, even though he does not want to and hates what is happening. I have said this in light of the expression that he uses—*is close at hand.* A person who is living under [the law] and who has not yet been freed by grace bears witness that the law is good. It certainly bears witness to him, inasmuch as he restrains himself from contravening the law and finds that it is a good thing for him even when he wills to do what it enjoins and is unable to do so because covetousness has overwhelmed him. And thus he sees that he is caught up in the guilt of transgression, so that he must beg for the grace of the liberator.

---

10. See Rom 7:19.

1,13. *For I am delighted,* he says, *with the law of God according
to the inner person* (Rom 7:22), and certainly with the law that says,
You shall not covet. But, he says, *I see another law in my members,
opposing the law of my mind and making me captive under the law
of sin that is in my members* (Rom 7:23). He refers to the law in his
members as the very burden of mortality, under which we groan
who are burdened by it.[11] *For the body that is corruptible weighs
down the soul* (Wis 9:15). Because of this it often happens that what
is impermissible is ineluctably delightful. Therefore he refers to
the law as an oppressive and burdensome weight, because it was
assigned as punishment by divine judgment and imposed by him
who warned the man when he said, *On the day you eat you shall
die* (Gn 2:17). This law opposes the law of the mind, which says,
You shall not covet, and in which one delights according to the inner
person. And, before someone is under grace, [this law] opposes [the
law of the mind] in such a way that it also holds [its subject] captive
under the law of sin—that is, under itself. For, when he says *that is
in my members* (Rom 7:23), he indicates that this is the same as that
of which he had spoken earlier: *I see another law in my members.*

1,14. But all of this is said in order to make it clear to humankind,
which is held captive, that it must not presume on its own strength.
This is why [Paul] reproved the Jews who boasted proudly of what
they thought were their works of the law, although they were drawn
by covetousness to whatever is unlawful, since the law about which
they boasted says, *You shall not covet.* Humankind vanquished, condemned and held captive, which even after having received the law
is not victorious but rather a transgressor, must humbly say, must
humbly cry out, *Wretched man that I am, who will liberate me from
the body of this death? The grace of God through Jesus Christ our
Lord.* (Rom 7:24-25) What in fact is left to free choice in this mortal
life is not that a person may fulfill righteousness when he wants to
but that by suppliant piety he may turn to him by whose gift he may
be enabled to fulfill it.

1,15. In respect to this whole ensemble of the apostolic text that
we have been treating, whoever holds that the Apostle thought that
the law was bad—because he says, *The law entered in so that wrongdoing might abound* (Rom 5:20); and, *The administering of death*

---

11. See 2 Cor 5:4.

written in letters of stone (2 Cor 3:7); and, *The power of sin is the law* (1 Cor 15:56); and, *You have died to the law through the body of Christ, so that you might belong to another, who has risen from the dead* (Rom 7:4); and, *The passions of sin, which are through the law, were at work in our members, so that they bore fruit for death, but now we are rid of the law, in which imprisonment we were dead, so that thus we may serve in the new way of the spirit and not in the old way of the letter* (Rom 7:5-6); and other things along these lines which we have found that the Apostle said—should consider that these things were said in view of the fact that the law increases covetousness because of its prohibitions and, because of transgression, binds the guilty person, since it enjoins what human beings in their weakness cannot fulfill unless in piety they turn to God's grace. And for that reason those over whom it rules are said to be under it; it rules over those whom it punishes, and it punishes all transgressors. But those who have received the law transgress it unless through grace they arrive at the possibility of doing what it enjoins. Thus it comes about that it no longer rules over those who were at one time condemned under the fear of it but who now, under grace, are fulfilling it through love.

1,16. For if what was said causes anyone to think that the Apostle found fault with the law, what are we to make of his saying, *For I am delighted with the law of God according to the inner person?* In saying this he certainly praises the law. When those persons hear this, they reply that in this passage the Apostle is referring to another law—that is, the law of Christ, not that which was given to the Jews. If we ask them, then, what law he is speaking about when he says, *The law entered in so that wrongdoing might abound,* they will doubtlessly reply, "That which the Jews received." See, then, whether that is the one of which it is said, *Having seized the occasion, sin brought about every kind of covetousness in me through the commandment.* What does *brought about every kind of covetousness in me* mean if not *so that wrongdoing might abound?* See also whether these words are consistent: *So that the sinner and the sin might, thanks to the commandment, be without limit.* For what this means is that sin might become limitless—that is, that sin might abound. If we have shown, then, that the commandment is good from which, *having seized the occasion, sin has brought about every kind of covetousness* so that it might be without limit, let us also show that the law is good which *entered in so that wrongdoing might abound—* that is, so that sin might bring about every kind of covetousness and become limitless. Let them listen to the same Apostle, then, when he says, *What, then, shall we say? That the law is sin? Of course not!* This, they say, was said of the law of Christ; this refers to the law of grace. Let them respond, therefore, as to how they understand what follows: *But I did not know sin except through the law, for I did not know about covetousness except that the law said, You shall not covet. But, having seized the occasion, sin brought about every kind of covetousness in me through the commandment.* The very phrasing makes it clear enough about what law he said, *That the law is sin? Of course not!* He was speaking, namely, about that [law] through whose commandment an occasion was given to sin, so that it might bring about every kind of covetousness—about that [law], therefore, which entered in so that wrongdoing might abound, and which they think is evil. But what is plainer than what he says a little later: *And so, to be sure, the law is holy, and the commandment is holy and righteous and good?* This, they say again, was said not of the law that was given to the Jews but of the gospel. For so unspeakably blind is this perversity of the Manicheans![12] For they pay no heed to what follows, which is very plain and clear: *Has, then, what is good become death for me? Of course not! But sin, in order to appear as sin, worked death in me through what was good, so that the sinner and the sin might, thanks to the commandment, be without limit—*that is, through the holy and righteous and good commandment, which nonetheless entered in so that sin might abound, that is, so that it might be without limit.

1,17. Why, then, if the law is good, is it referred to *as the administering of death?* Because *sin, in order to appear as sin, worked death in me through what was good.* You should not be surprised when it is said of the very preaching of the gospel: *We are the good odor of Christ in those who are to be saved and in those who are perishing—for some, indeed, the odor of life unto life, while for others the odor of death unto death* (2 Cor 2:15-16). For in regard to the

---

12. Here it becomes clear that the Manicheans are the ones who are denying that the Old Testament law is good and who, when Paul refers to the law's goodness, claim that he means the law of Christ. The Manicheans, whose name comes from the Persian religious figure Mani (216-277), rejected the Old Testament in its entirety. Much of Augustine's earliest polemical work is directed against them. On the point that he makes here see also the *Answer to Faustus, a Manichean* XV,8; XIX,7. (The Manichean Faustus' view of the law is given in his own words ibid. XIX,1-6.)

Jews, for whom it was even written in stone because of their hardness, the law is called *the administering of death*, but not in regard to us, who fulfill the law through love. *For love is the fulfillment of the law* (Rom 13:10). For the law itself, which is written in letters of stone, says, *You shall not commit adultery, you shall not kill, you shall not steal, you shall not covet* (Ex 20:14.13.15.17), and so forth. The Apostle states that this law is fulfilled through love when he says, *The one who loves his fellow human being has fulfilled the law. For you shall not commit adultery, you shall not kill, you shall not steal, you shall not covet, and any other commandment that there is, is summed up in this phrase: You shall love your neighbor as yourself* (Rom 13:8-9), because this too is written in the same law.

Why is the law the power of sin if the law is good? Because sin worked death through what was good, so that it might be without limit—that is, so that it might acquire still greater strength from transgression.

Why have we died to the law through the body of Christ if the law is good? Because we have died to a law that was dominating us and were liberated from that disposition which the law punishes and condemns. For the law is very commonly referred to in the context of warning and instilling fear and punishing. And so the same precept is law for the fearful and grace for those who love. Hence it says in the gospel, *The law was given through Moses, but grace and truth were brought about through Jesus Christ* (Jn 1:17). This very same law, which was given through Moses in order to inspire fear, became grace and truth through Jesus Christ in order to be fulfilled. Therefore it was said, *You died to the law* (Rom 7:4) as though to say that you died to the law's punishment, *through the body of Christ* (Rom 7:4), through which the sins have been forgiven that were under the constraint deserving of lawful punishment.

Why do the passions of sin stem from the law if the law is good? Because he [i.e., the Apostle] wanted them to be understood here as the passions of sin that have already been frequently spoken of, an increase of covetousness resulting from prohibition and the guilt of punishment resulting from transgression —that is, because *it worked death through what was good, so that the sinner and the sin might, thanks to the commandment, be without limit.*

Why *are we freed from the law, in which imprisonment we were dead, so that thus we may serve in the new way of the spirit and not in the old way of the letter*, if the law is good? Because the law *is* the letter for those who do not fulfill it through the spirit of love, which is the domain of the New Testament. And so those who have died to sin are freed from the letter in which are imprisoned the wrongdoers who do not fulfill what is written. For what is the law other than a letter, pure and simple, for those who know how to read it but are unable to fulfill it? For it is not unknown to those for whom it was written, but, inasmuch as it is known only to the extent that it is read as a piece of writing and not to the extent that it is fulfilled as an object of love, it is nothing but a letter for such persons. This letter is not a help to its readers but rather a witness against sinners. Those who are renewed through the spirit, then, are freed from its condemnation so that they are no longer bound to the punishment of the letter but are united to its understanding through righteousness. This is why it says, *The letter kills, but the spirit gives life* (2 Cor 3:6). For the law, if it is only read but not understood and not fulfilled, does indeed kill; it is then that it is called "the letter." But the spirit gives life, because the fullness of the law is the love which *has been poured into our hearts through the Holy Spirit who has been given to us* (Rom 5:5).

Second Question

2,1. But now, in my opinion, it is time to pass on to the second question that you posed. It is a matter of discussing the entire text from where it is written: *As well as that* [i.e., Sarah's story], *there is also Rebecca, who from a single act of intercourse conceived from our father Isaac. For when they were not yet born and had not done anything good or evil* (Rom 9:10-11) up to the point where it is written: *Unless the Lord of hosts had left us offspring, we would have become like Sodom, and we would have been like Gomorrah* (Rom 9:29). This is exceedingly obscure. But I know for a certainty that, because of your feelings in my regard, you could not request me to interpret these words unless you had interceded with the Lord that I could do so. Having been reassured by this help, I proceed.

2,2. And in the first place I shall seize upon the Apostle's main thought, which is evident throughout the epistle that I am going to consider. Now this is that no one should boast of the merits of his works. The Israelites dared to boast of them on the grounds that they had observed the law that had been given to them[13] and so had received the grace of the gospel as though it were due them for their merits, because they observed the law. Hence they did not want that same grace to be given to the gentiles, whom they saw as unworthy, unless they took up the Jewish sacraments[14] (which is an issue that, when it arose, was dealt with in the Acts of the Apostles[15]). For they did not understand that the grace of the gospel is not dependent on works; otherwise grace is no longer grace.[16]

And in many places [the Apostle] frequently testifies that grace comes before works not in order to do away with works but in order to show that works do not precede but follow upon faith—in other words, so that a person may not think that he has obtained grace because he has done good works but that he cannot do good works unless he has obtained grace through faith.[17] But a person begins to obtain grace when he begins to believe in God, having been moved to faith by either an internal or an external urging.[18]

Now it is important to know if grace is poured out more fully and more manifestly at certain moments of time or at the celebration of the sacraments. For catechumens do not lack belief; if they do, then Cornelius, to whom an angel was sent, did not believe in God when he was making himself worthy through his almsgiving and prayers.[19] But in no way would he have done these things unless he had believed beforehand; in no way would he have believed, however, unless he had been called by secret urgings that his mind or spirit could perceive or by more evident ones coming to him through his bodily senses.[20] But in certain persons, like catechumens and like Cornelius himself, before he was incorporated into the Church by participating in the sacraments, the grace of faith, as great as it is, is insufficient to attain to the kingdom of heaven;[21] but in others it is so great that they are already counted as belonging to the body of Christ and to the holy temple of God. *For the temple of God is holy,*

---

13. See Rom 2:17-23.
14. "Sacrament" was a term that was very broadly understood in Christian antiquity. Here of course the word refers to Old Testament rituals and observances.
15. See Acts 15.
16. See Rom 11:6.
17. See Rom 5:2.
18. See Rom 10:14.
19. See Acts 10:1-4.
20. See Rom 10:14.
21. See Acts 10:44-48.

[the Apostle] says, *which you are* (1 Cor 3:17). And the Lord himself says, *Unless a person has been born of water and the Holy Spirit he shall not enter the kingdom of heaven* (Jn 3:5). Certain beginnings of faith, therefore, are like conceptions. Yet, in order to arrive at eternal life, one must not only be conceived but also be born. But none of this is without the grace of God's mercy, because even if works that are good follow that grace, as they say, they do not precede it.

2,3. The Apostle wishes to emphasize this, because as he says in another passage, *It is not because of us but is a gift of God; it is not because of works, lest perhaps anyone be inflated* (Eph 2:8-9). Therefore he provided proof by referring to those who had not yet been born. For no one could say that Jacob, who was not yet born, had been meritorious before God on account of his works, so that it might be said as divinely inspired: *The older shall serve the younger* (Gn 25:23). Therefore he says, *It was not only Isaac who was promised* (Rom 9:10) when it was said, *At this time I will come and Sarah shall have a son* (Rom 9:9). [Isaac] had certainly not been meritorious before God on account of any works so that a promise would be made that he was to be born, so that the seed of Abraham would be named in Isaac[22]—that is, that they would share in the lot of the saints, which is in Christ, understanding that they were children of the promise[23] and not boasting of their own merits but attributing the fact that they were co-heirs in Christ[24] to the grace of their calling.[25] For, when it was promised that they would exist, they who did not yet exist had been deserving of nothing. [And he continues:] *But also Rebecca, who from a single act of intercourse conceived from our father Isaac* (Rom 9:10). He says with great precision, *from a single act of intercourse*. For it was twins who were conceived. Otherwise it might be attributed to the father's merits, and someone could say that such and such a son was born because his father was influenced in a particular way at the time when he sowed him in his mother's womb, or his mother was influenced in a particular way when she conceived him. For he sowed both at the same time and she conceived both at the same time. [Paul] says *from a single act of intercourse* in order to emphasize that there is no room for astrologers here or rather

22. See Rom 9:7.
23. See Rom 9:8.
24. See Rom 8:17.
25. See Rom 9:12.

for those whom they call *genethliaci,* who make conjectures about
behaviors and destinies on the basis of people's birthdays.[26] For they
have no idea what to say when the one conception occurs at one
precise moment, when the heavens and the stars are arranged in a
particular way so that no differences whatsoever in this respect can
be discerned with regard to either of the twins, and [yet] there is a
great difference between them. And, if they wish, they can easily see
that the oracles which they sell to wretched people come not from a
familiarity with any scientific theory but from fortuitous inklings.[27]

But (to speak rather of the matter at hand) these things are recalled
for the purpose of smashing and overturning the pride of persons
who are unthankful for the grace of God and who dare to boast of
their own merits. *For when they were not yet born and had not done
anything good or evil, not because of their works but because of him
who called them it was said to her that the older would serve the
younger* (Rom 9:11-12). Grace, then, comes from him who calls, but
good works come as a consequence from him who receives grace;
they do not beget grace but are begotten by grace. For a fire does not
heat *in order* to burn but *because* it burns, nor does a wheel run well
in order to be round but *because* it is round. Thus no one does good
works *in order* to receive grace but *because* he has received it. For
how can a person live righteously who has not been made righteous?
In the same way that a person cannot live holily who has not been
made holy or live at all if he has not been given life. It is grace that
makes righteous,[28] so that one who has been made righteous can
live righteously. Grace, therefore, comes first, and good works are
second. As [the Apostle] says in another passage, *To a person who
works, wages are owed not as a grace but as a debt* (Rom 4:4). A
case in point would be if immortality following upon good works
were demanded as a debt. In the words of the same [Apostle]: *I have
fought the good fight, I have finished the race, I have kept the faith.
For the rest there remains for me a crown of righteousness which the*

---

26. *Genethliaci*: the Latin form of a Greek word meaning "pertaining to the day of one's
    birth."
27. The case of twins with different life histories was a classic objection to the claims
    of astrologers that the arrangement of the heavens at the time of conception or birth
    was determinative of a person's life course. Augustine, who emphasizes the single
    moment of Jacob and Esau's conception, often avails himself of this objection. See
    Confessions VII,6,8-10; *Teaching Christianity* II,22,33-34; *The City of God* V,1-6.
28. See Rom 3:24.

Lord, the just judge, will render me on that day. (2 Tm 4:7-8) For, perhaps because he said *will render (reddet),* it is a matter of debt. But when he ascended on high and led captivity captive, he did not render but *gave (dedit)* gifts to men.[29] For how would the Apostle himself presume that a debt, as it were, was being rendered to him if he had not first received a grace that was not owed him, by which, as one who had been made righteous,[30] he could fight the good fight? For he had been a blasphemer and a persecutor and a reviler, but he obtained mercy, as he himself testifies,[31] believing in him who makes righteous not the one who is upright but the one who is wicked, so that he may make him upright by making him righteous.[32]

2,4. *Not because of their works,* he says, *but because of him who called them it was said to her that the older would serve the younger* (Rom 9:12). To this pertains what was said, *For when they were not yet born and had not done anything good or evil* (Rom 9:11), so that it could be said, *Not because of their works but because of him who called them.* This is why a person may ask why he said, *That God's purpose would abide in accordance with his choice* (Rom 9:11). For how is a choice righteous or of any quality at all when there is no distinction [between persons]? For if Jacob, who was not yet born and had not yet done any works, was not chosen on account of any merit, he could not have been chosen in any sense of the word when there was no difference [between him and his brother] on the basis of which he might be chosen. Likewise, if Esau, who also was not yet born and had not yet done any works, was not rejected on account of any merit when it was said, *And the older shall serve the younger,* how can his rejection be called righteous? Based on what act of discernment and on what equitable judgment are we to understand what follows: *I loved Jacob but I hated Esau* (Rom 9:13)? This was, to be sure, written in a prophet, who long afterwards prophesied how they were born and died.[33] Yet that phrase, *And the older shall serve the younger,* seems to have been used both before they were born and before they did any works. How could this or any other choice be made if, since they were not yet born and had not yet done any works, they

---

29. See Eph 4:8.
30. See Rom 3:24.
31. See 1 Tm 1:13.
32. See Rom 4:5.
33. See Mal 1:2-3.

had no opportunities for merit? Were they perhaps somehow of different natures? Who could claim this, inasmuch as they had the same father and the same mother, came from a single act of intercourse and had the same creator? As the same creator brought forth from the same earth different living and self-reproducing beings,[34] did he from the same union and embrace of [two] human beings bring forth different offspring in twins, one whom he loved and another whom he hated? There would be no choice, therefore, until there was something to be chosen. For if Jacob was made good so that he would be pleasing, how was he pleasing before he was made, so that he would be made good? And so he was not chosen in order to be made good but, once made good, he was able to be chosen.

2,5. Is it *in accordance with his choice* that God, knowing all things in advance, would see future faith in Jacob, who was not yet born? Thus, although a person does not merit to be made righteous because of his works, since in fact he cannot do good works unless he is made righteous, yet, inasmuch as God makes the pagans righteous by faith[35] and no one believes except by free will, did God foresee this very future will to believe and in his foreknowledge choose someone who was not yet even born in order to make him righteous? If a choice is made through foreknowledge, then, and God foreknew Jacob's faith, how do you prove that he did not also choose him because of his works? If it was the case, then, that they had not yet been born and had not yet done anything either good or evil, it was also the case that neither of them had yet believed. But foreknowledge sees who will believe. Thus foreknowledge could see who would do works, so that, as one person may be said to have been chosen because of a future faith that God foreknew, another could say that he, for his part, was chosen because of future works that God likewise foreknew. How, then, does the Apostle show that these words, *The older shall serve the younger*, were not said on account of works? Because if they were not yet born, it applied not only to works but also to faith, since those who were not yet born lacked both. He did not want it to be understood, therefore, that it was the result of foreknowledge that the younger was chosen with a view to his being served by the older. For he wanted to show that this did not

---

34. See Gn 1:24.
35. See Gal 3:8.

happen because of works, and so he added the words, *For when they were not yet born and had not done anything good or evil*; otherwise it could have been said to him, "But God already knew who was going to do what." The question, therefore, is just how that choice was made. Because if it was not based on works, which did not exist in those who were not yet born, nor based on faith, because that itself did not exist, how then did it happen?

2,6. Must it be said that there would have been no choice had there not been some difference in their mother's womb, whether of faith or of works or of some kind of merits, whatever they might have been? But it is said that *God's purpose would abide in accordance with his choice*, and so we try to discover why it was said. Perhaps this sentence should be construed in a different way—so that we would not understand the words, *so that God's purpose would abide in accordance with his choice,* as following on from *not because of their works but because of him who called them was it said that the older would serve the younger* but rather as referring to the example given of persons yet unborn, who have not yet accomplished any works, so that no choice [based on works] could be understood here. *For when they were not yet born and had not done anything good or evil, so that God's purpose would abide in accordance with his choice*—that is, *they had not done anything good or evil* which would allow for some choice to be made of a person who had something good, based on that very action. Since, therefore, no choice was made of someone who had done something good, on account of which God's purpose would abide, it was *not because of their works but because of him who called them* that *it was said to her that the older would serve the younger*. In other words, it was because of him who, by calling the wicked to faith, makes him righteous by grace.[36]

God's purpose, therefore, does not abide on account of a choice, but the choice results from the purpose—that is, it is not because God discovers in human beings good works that he chooses, and that therefore his plan of making righteous abides, but because it abides in order to make righteous those who believe, and that therefore he discovers works that he may now choose for the kingdom of heaven. For unless a choice were made there would be no chosen ones, nor would it correctly be said, *Who will accuse God's chosen ones?*

---

36. See Rom 4:5.

(Rom 8:33) Yet it is not making a choice that precedes making righteous but making righteous that precedes making a choice. For no one is chosen unless he is already entirely different than a person who is rejected. Hence I do not see how these words, *God chose us before the foundation of the world* (Eph 1:4), could have been said if not with foreknowledge. But what he says here, *Not because of their works but because of him who called them it was said to her that the older would serve the younger*, he wanted to be understood not of a choice based upon merits, which occur after a person has been made righteous by grace, but of the generosity of God's gifts, lest anyone be inflated because of his works. *For by God's grace we have been saved. And this is not because of us but is a gift of God; it is not because of works, lest perhaps anyone be inflated.* (Eph 2:8-9)

2,7. Now the question is whether faith merits humankind's being made righteous. Do faith's merits precede God's mercy, or should even faith itself not be numbered among the gifts of grace? For in the passage where he said, *Not because of their works*, he did *not* say, "Because of their faith it was said to her that the older would serve the younger," but he *did* say, *But because of him who called them.* For no one believes who is not called. But it is a merciful God who calls, bestowing this [gift] when there are no merits of faith, because the merits of faith follow the call rather than precede it. For *how will they believe him whom they have not heard? And how will they hear without a preacher?* (Rom 10:14) If God's mercy does not precede by way of a call, therefore, a person cannot believe, so that from this he may begin to be made righteous and to receive the capacity to do good works. Before every merit, then, there is grace, since Christ died for the wicked.[37] Hence it was not because of any merits of his own, but because of him who called, that the younger received [the grace] to be served by the older. This also explains the phrase, *I loved Jacob*, which was because of God who called and not because of Jacob's works.

2,8. What then of Esau? On account of what evil deeds of his did he merit to serve his younger [brother] and to have it written [of him]: *I hated Esau?* For neither had *he* been born yet or done anything good or evil when it was said, *And the older shall serve the younger.* Is it perhaps that, just as that was said of Jacob, who had no merits for any

---

37. See Rom 5:6.

good deed, so Esau was hated, who had no merits for any evil deed? For, if God predestined him to serve his younger [brother] because he foreknew his future evil works and predestined Jacob as well, so that his older [brother] would serve him, because he foreknew his future good works, what he says now is false: *Not because of their works.* But if it is true that this did not occur because of their works and that [God] approves of this, inasmuch as it is said of persons who were not yet born and had not yet done any works, and that it was not done because of faith either, which similarly did not exist in persons not yet born, on the basis of what merit was Esau hated before he was born? For there is no doubt that God loves what he has made. But if we say that he hated what he made, it contradicts another text of scripture that says, *You did not create anything in hatred, but you hate nothing that you have made* (Wis 11:24). For by what merit was the sun made the sun? Or how did the moon offend, that it is so inferior to it? Or how did it merit to be created so much brighter than the other stars? But all of these were created good, each in its own kind.[38] For God would not say, "I loved the sun but I hated the moon," or, "I loved the moon but I hated the stars," as he *did* say, *I loved Jacob but I hated Esau.* But he loved all those things, even though they were placed in different ranks of excellence, because God saw that they were good when he created them by his word.[39] But it is unjust that he would have hated Esau when there was no unrighteousness to merit it. If we grant this, then Jacob begins to be loved because of the merit of righteousness. If this is true, then it is false that it is not because of works. Was it perhaps because of the righteousness of faith? How do these words, *For when they were not yet born*, support your position, then, when in fact there could not have been any righteousness of faith in someone who was not yet born?

2,9. And so the Apostle saw what effect his words could have on the mind of his hearer or reader, and he immediately added, *What, then, shall we say? Is there injustice with God? Of course not!* (Rom 9:14) And as if teaching how absurd this is, he says, *For Moses says, I will have mercy on whom I will have mercy, and I will show compassion to whom I will be compassionate* (Rom 9:15). With these words he solves the problem—or, rather, complicates it

---

38. See Gn 1:16-18.
39. See Gn 1:16-18.

further. For this is the very thing that is so disturbing: if he will have mercy on whom he will have mercy and show compassion to whom he will be compassionate, why was this compassion lacking in regard to Esau, so that by it he might have been good, just as by it Jacob became good? Or was this said, *I will have mercy on whom I will have mercy, and I will show compassion to whom I will be compassionate,* because God will have mercy on a person in order to call him, will be merciful to him so that he may believe, and will show compassion to him to whom he is compassionate—that is, will make him compassionate, so that he may also do good works? From this we are warned that it is not right for anyone to boast or to be inflated even because of his works of mercy, [saying] that he is deserving of God [by claiming God's works] as if they were his own, when in fact he who will show compassion to whom he will be compassionate showed him the very compassion that he was to have. If a person boasts that he has merited this by believing, he should know that [God], who by inspiring faith has mercy on whom he is merciful, has shown it to him in order to communicate his call to one who was without faith up until that moment. For the one with faith is already differentiated from the wicked. *For what do you have,* he says, *that you have not received? But if you have received, why do you boast as if you had not received?* (1 Cor 4:7)

2,10. Well said! But why was this compassion withdrawn from Esau? Why was he not called in such a way that, once called, he would be inspired with faith and, as a believer, become compassionate, so that he might do good works? Was it perhaps because he did not will to? If, then, Jacob believed because he willed to, God did not bestow faith on him, but he conferred it upon himself by an act of will, and he had something that he did not receive. Is it the case that, because no one can believe unless he wills to and no one can will to unless he is called, but no one can confer it upon himself to be called, God, by calling, also confers faith, because no one can believe without being called, although no one believes unwillingly? *For how will they believe him whom they have not heard? And how will they hear without a preacher?* And so no one believes who has not been called, but not everyone who has been called believes, *for many are called, but few are chosen* (Mt 20:16); these are the ones who have not disdained him who calls but, by believing, have followed him. Without doubt, however, they have believed willingly. What is this, then, that follows: *It is not a matter of willing or of running, therefore, but of a merciful God* (Rom 9:16)? Can we not will unless we are called, and does our willing count for naught unless God helps to bring it to completion? It is necessary, then, to will and to run, for it was not without purpose that it was said, *Peace on earth to men of good will* (Lk 2:14), and, *Run in such a way that you may seize the prize* (1 Cor 9:24). Yet *it is not a matter of willing or of running but of a merciful God* that we obtain what we will and arrive where we will. Esau did not will, therefore, and did not run. But, if he had both willed and run, he would have arrived with the help of God, who would also have bestowed willing and running upon him by calling him if he had not, by disdaining the call, made himself disapproved. For in one way God bestows so that we may will, and in another he bestows what we have willed. For he has willed that our willing be both his and ours—his by calling and ours by following. He alone bestows, however, what we have willed—that is, the ability to act well and to live blessedly forever. But Esau, who was not yet born, could neither will nor not will anything. Why, then, was he disapproved when he was in the womb? This brings us back to those difficulties which are all the more complex by reason of both their obscurity and also our frequent repetition.

2,11. For why was Esau, who was not yet born, disapproved, when he was unable to have faith in him who called him or to disdain his call or to do anything either good or evil? If God foreknew his [i.e., Esau's] future evil will, why was Jacob not also approved through God's foreknowledge of his future good will? If you but once concede that a person could have been either approved or disapproved on the basis of what was not yet in him but because God foreknew what was going to be in him, it follows that he could also have been approved on the basis of the works that God foreknew were going to be in him, although he had not yet done any works, and the fact that they were not yet born when it was said, *The older shall serve the younger,* will not support your position at all, since you must then show that this was not said because of works, inasmuch as he had not yet done any works.

2,12. If you also pay close attention to these words, *It is not a matter of willing or of running, therefore, but of a merciful God,* the Apostle will be seen to have said this because it is not only by God's help that we attain to what we will but also in the context of that effort to which he refers in another text: *Work out your salvation with fear and trembling. For it is God who, for the sake of a good will, works in you both the willing and the working.* (Phil 2:12-13) Here he shows clearly that even a good will itself comes about in us through God's working. For if it is only said that it is not a matter of willing but of a merciful God, because the human will does not suffice for us to live in rectitude and righteousness unless we are aided by God's mercy, it can therefore also be said that it is not a matter of a merciful God but of human willing, because God's mercy alone does not suffice unless our will's consent is joined to it. But it is evident that we will to no avail unless God is merciful. I do not know how it may be said, on the other hand, that God is merciful to no avail unless we will. For if God is merciful, we also will. It pertains to the same mercy, in fact, that we will, *for it is God who, for the sake of a good will, works in us both the willing and the working.* For if we asked whether a good will was God's gift, it would be strange if someone dared to deny it. For, since it is not a good will that precedes a call but a call that precedes a good will, it is rightly ascribed to God who calls that we will what is good, but it cannot be ascribed to us that we are called. It must not be thought, then, that these words, *It is not a matter of willing or of running but of a merciful* God, were said because without his aid we cannot attain to what we will but rather because without his call we do not will.

2,13. But if this call brings about a good will in such a way that everyone who has been called follows it [i.e., the call], how is it correct that *many are called, but few are chosen* (Mt 20:16)? If this is correct and the one who has been called does not follow and submit to the call, because it is built into his will not to submit, it can also rightly be said that it is not a matter of God's being merciful but of man's willing and running, because the mercy of him who calls is insufficient unless there follows the obedience of the one who has been called. What if those who have been called in this way do not consent? Could they, if called in another way, accommodate their will to faith? Thus this would be correct: *Many are called, but few are chosen*, so that, although many have been called in one way, yet, because not all have been touched in one way, only they would follow the call who are found fit to grasp it. And this would be no less correct: *It is not a matter of willing or of running, therefore, but of a merciful God*, who called in a way that was appropriate for those who followed the call. The call has indeed reached others, but because it was such that they could not be moved by it and were not suited to grasp it, they could indeed be said to have been called but not chosen, and it is no longer similarly correct that it is not a matter of God's being merciful but of man's willing and running. For the effectiveness of God's mercy cannot be in man's power, so that he would be merciful to no avail if man were unwilling, because, if he should will to have mercy even on those persons [who were mentioned shortly before], he could call them in such a way as would be appropriate for them, so that they would be moved and would understand and would follow. This, then, is correct: *Many are called, but few are chosen.* For the chosen are those who have been called in an appropriate way, whereas those who did not consent and were not obedient to the call are not chosen, because they did not follow even though they were called. Likewise this is correct: *It is not a matter of willing or of running but of a merciful God,* because, even if he calls many, he still has mercy on those whom he calls in such a way as is appropriate for them to be called so that they may follow. It is incorrect, however, if anyone says that it is not a matter of God's being merciful but of man's willing and running, because God has mercy on no one in vain. But the person on whom he has mercy he calls in such a way as he knows is appropriate for him, so that he may not reject him who calls.

2,14. At this point someone will say, "Why, then, was Esau not called in such a way that he would will to obey?" For we see that others have been moved to faith when these same things have been shown or signified. For example, Simeon, when the Spirit revealed it to him, recognized our Lord Jesus Christ when he was still a tiny infant and believed in him.[40] Nathanael, when he had heard one sentence of his, *Before Philip called you, when you were under the fig tree, I saw you* (Jn 1:48), responded, *Rabbi, you are the Son of God, you are the king of Israel* (Jn 1:49). When Peter confessed this much later, he merited to hear that he was blessed and that the keys of the kingdom of heaven would be given to him.[41] When the miracle was performed at Cana in Galilee that the evangelist John mentions as the first of his signs, when water was turned into wine, his disciples

---

40. See Lk 2:25-35.
41. See Mt 16:16-19.

believed in him.[42] When he spoke he invited many to faith, but there were many who did not believe when he raised the dead.[43] Even the disciples were terrified by his cross and death and wavered,[44] yet the thief believed when he saw him not as one more excellent in his deeds but as his equal in the fellowship of the cross.[45] After his resurrection one of the band of disciples believed not so much because of his living members as because of his fresh wounds.[46] There were many from the number of those by whom he was crucified who saw him performing miracles and disdained him, but they believed his disciples when they preached him and did similar things in his name.[47]

Since, therefore, one person is moved to faith in one way while another is moved in another way, and frequently the same thing said to one person at one time moves him but said to another at another time does not move him, and it moves one and does not move another, who would dare to say that God lacked that way of calling by which Esau as well could have applied his mind and joined his will to that faith in which Jacob was made righteous?

If the resistance of a person's will can be so great that a mental revulsion hardens him against any manner of calling, it may be asked whether this very hardening comes from a divine punishment, when God has abandoned a person by not calling him in such a way that he will be moved to faith. For who would say that the manner in which he might be persuaded to have faith was lacking to the Almighty?

2,15. But why do we ask this? For the Apostle himself adds, *For in scripture* [God] *says to Pharaoh, It was for this that I raised you up, so that I might display my power in you and so that my name might be made known throughout the earth* (Rom 9:17). The Apostle appended this statement, however, in order to prove what he had said before: *It is not a matter of willing or of running, therefore, but of a merciful God.* For as though he were being asked what the source of his teaching was, he declares, *For in scripture* [God] *says to Pharaoh, It was for this that I raised you up, so that I might display my power in you and so that my name might be made known throughout the earth.*

---

42. See Jn 2:1-11.
43. See Lk 16:13.
44. See Mt 26:56.
45. See Lk 23:40-42.
46. See Jn 20:27-29.
47. See Acts 2:37-41; 5:12-16.

In this way he shows that *it is not a matter of willing or of running but of a merciful God*, and he concludes as follows, *Therefore he has mercy on whom he wills, and whom he wills he hardens* (Rom 9:18), since neither had been mentioned previously. For these words, *It is not a matter of willing or of running but of a merciful God*, are not said in the same way that these others are: "It is not a matter of being unwilling or of disdaining but of a God who hardens." From this it becomes clear that what [the Apostle] previously said, *Therefore he has mercy on whom he wills, and whom he wills he hardens*, can fit in with the previous phrase [i.e., *It is not a matter of willing or of running but of a merciful God*] so that [it is understood that] God's hardening is an unwillingness to be merciful. Thus he imposes nothing whereby a person may become worse, but nothing is given to the person whereby he may become better. If this occurs when there is no difference in merits, who would not burst out into those words that the very Apostle uses against himself: *And so you say to me, Why is there still complaint? For who resists his will?* (Rom 9:19) For God often complains of human beings, as is clear from countless passages of scripture, because they are unwilling to believe and to live uprightly. Hence those who are faithful and carry out God's will are said to live *without giving rise to complaint* (Lk 1:6), because scripture does not complain of them. But why is there complaint, he asks, *for one who resists his will* (Rom 9:18), when *he has mercy on whom he wills, and whom he wills he hardens?* Yet let us consider what was said previously, and on that basis let us, to the degree that the Lord himself assists, shape our own perspective.

2,16. For he said shortly before, *What, then, shall we say? Is there injustice with God? Of course not!* Let this, then, be something fixed and settled in minds that are devoutly serious and steadfast in faith—that there is no injustice with God. And thus this very thing—that God *has mercy on whom he wills, and whom he wills he hardens*, which means that he has mercy on whom he wills and does not have mercy on whom he does not will—may be believed with utter tenacity and firmness as pertaining to a kind of justice that is hidden from that which is sought and must be observed in our human affairs and earthly agreements. Unless we held fast there to certain clearly marked vestiges of eternal justice, our frail efforts would never aim at and long for the holiest and purest resting place and sanctuary of spiritual precepts. *Blessed are those who hunger and thirst for justice, for they shall be satisfied* (Mt 5:6). In the aridity of our life and of this mortal condition, therefore, unless there were a sprinkling from on high of, so to speak, the slightest mist of justice, we would wither away more quickly than we thirst. Hence, since it is by giving and receiving that human society is bound together, while it is things either owed or not owed that are given and received, who would not see that no one—and certainly not he who would willingly forgive what is owed him—can be accused of injustice who exacts what is owed him, and that this [i.e., whether a debt should be exacted or not] falls under the judgment not of those who owe the debt but of the one to whom the debt is owed? This thought or vestige (as I said above) has been clearly marked upon the affairs of men from the highest summit of justice.

Therefore, all human beings—since, as the Apostle says, *all die in Adam* (1 Cor 15:22), from whom the origin of the offense against God spread throughout the whole human race—are a kind of single mass of sin owing a debt of punishment to the divine and loftiest justice, and whether [the punishment that is owed] be exacted or forgiven, there is no injustice. They are debtors, however, who proudly judge from whom it should be exacted and by whom it should be forgiven, like those who, having been brought to that vineyard, were unjustly angered when precisely as much was gifted to the others as was paid to them.[48] And so the Apostle beats back this impudent question in this way: *O man, who are you that you talk back to God?* (Rom 9:20) For he talks back to God when it displeases him that God complains of sinners, as if God would compel someone to sin, although he himself compels no one to sin but only does not bestow on certain sinners the mercy of being made righteous by him, and for that reason it is said that he hardens certain sinners because he does not have mercy on them, not because he forces them to sin. But to those to whom he is not merciful he judges, with a most secret justice that is far removed from human understanding, that mercy must not be shown. For *inscrutable are his judgments and unfathomable his ways* (Rom 11:33). Justly, however, does he complain of sinners as one who does not force them to sin. And likewise [he complains] so that those to whom he shows mercy may possess a call [to grace] as well. Thus, as God complains of sinners, their hearts may be pricked and they may turn to his grace. Justly and mercifully, then, does he complain.

---

48. See Mt 20:1-12.

2,17. But if it is disturbing that no one resists his will, because whom he wills he sustains and whom he wills he abandons, since both the one whom he sustains and the one whom he abandons come from the same mass of sinners and, although both owe a debt of punishment, yet it is exacted from one and forgiven another—if it is disturbing, *O man, who are you that you talk back to God?* For I think that the meaning of *man* is the same here as in the passage, *Are you not men and do you not walk as men do?* (1 Cor 3:3) For by this term they are designated as fleshly and animal persons, as when it is said to them, *I have not been able to speak to you as to spiritual persons but as to fleshly ones* (1 Cor 3:1); and, *You were not able, and you are still not able, for you are still fleshly* (1 Cor 3:2); and, *The animal man, however, does not grasp the things that are of God's Spirit* (1 Cor 2:14). To these, therefore, it is said, *O man, who are you that you talk back to God? Does what has been fashioned say to the one who fashioned it, Why did you make me thus? Or does the potter not indeed have the power to make from the same lump of clay one vessel for honor and another for reproach?* (Rom 9:20-21) With those very words he seems to show with sufficient clarity that he is speaking to fleshly man, because the mire itself alludes to that from which the first man was formed.[49] And since, as I have already noted, according to the same Apostle, *all die in Adam*, he says that there is a single lump for all. And although one vessel is made for honor and another for reproach, nonetheless even the one that is made for honor has to begin in fleshly fashion and from there rise up to spiritual maturity, since they had already been made for honor and already been reborn in Christ. Yet, because he is addressing little children, he also refers to them as fleshly when he says, *I have not been able to speak to you as to spiritual persons but as to fleshly ones. Since you are little children in Christ, I have given you milk to drink, not solid food. For you were not able, and you are in fact still not able, for you are still fleshly.* (1 Cor 3:1-2) Although he says that they are fleshly, then, still they have already been born in Christ and are little children in him and must drink milk. And what he adds—*you are in fact still not able*—indicates that it will be possible for them to make progress because grace had already begun in them when they were spiritually reborn. These, therefore, were vessels made for honor, to

---

49. See Gn 2:7.

whom it may still rightly be said, *O man, who are you that you talk back to God?* And if this is rightly said to such as them, it is much more rightly said to those who either have not yet been regenerated in this way or have even been made for reproach. Only it should be maintained with unflinching faith that there is no injustice with God, who either forgives or exacts what is owed him, and neither can the one from whom he rightfully exacts it complain of his injustice nor ought the other to whom it is forgiven boast of his own merits. For the one only repays what is owed while the other has only what he has received.

2,18. But at this point we must strive to see, with the Lord's assistance, how both these statements are true: *You hate nothing that you have made* and *I loved Jacob but I hated Esau.* For if he hated Esau because he was a vessel made for reproach, and it was the same potter who made one vessel for honor and another for reproach, how is it that *you hate nothing that you have made?* For obviously he hates Esau, because he made him a vessel for reproach. This problem is solved if we understand that God is the maker of all creatures. But every creature of God is good,[50] and every human being, insofar as he is a human being and not insofar as he is a sinner, is a creature. God, therefore, is the creator of the human body and soul. Neither of these is evil and neither is hated by God, for he hates nothing that he has made. The soul, however, is more excellent than the body, but God, the author and creator of each, is more excellent than both soul and body, and he hates nothing in the human being other than sin. Sin, however, is a disorder and a perversion in the human being—that is, a turning away from the creator, who is more excellent, and a turning to created things, which are inferior.[51] God, therefore, does not hate Esau the human being, but God does hate Esau the sinner, as is said of the Lord: *He came unto his own, and his own did not accept him* (Jn 1:11). To these he himself says, *You do not hear me because you are not of God* (Jn 8:47). How are they his own and how are they not of God if not because the one thing is said of human beings whom the Lord himself made while the other is said of sinners whom the Lord himself was rebuking? Yet the same persons are themselves both human beings and sinners—but human beings by God's doing and sinners by their own will.

---

50. See 1 Tm 4:4.
51. "A turning away ... a turning to": *aversio ... conversio.* This definition of sin is notable for its brevity and its breadth.

As far as his loving Jacob is concerned: was he not a sinner? But he loved in him not the guilt that he did away with but the grace that he bestowed. For Christ also died for the wicked[52]—yet not that they might remain wicked but that, having been made righteous, they might be changed from their wickedness and believe in him who makes the wicked righteous. For God hates wickedness. And so in some he punishes it by condemning them, while in others he removes it by making them righteous, just as he himself judges by his inscrutable judgments[53] must be done in their regard. And, because he makes vessels for reproach from the number of the wicked whom he does not make righteous, he does not hate in them the fact that he makes them, for they are accursed insofar as they are wicked, but insofar as they are made vessels they are made for a certain use, so that, by way of the punishments that have been decreed for them, the vessels that are made for honor may advance [in holiness]. And so God does not hate them insofar as they are human beings, nor insofar as they are vessels—that is, [he does not hate] what he does in them in creation nor what he does in them by his decree. For he hates nothing that he has made. Yet, in that he makes them vessels of perdition to use in correcting others, he hates the wickedness in them that he himself did not make. For as a judge hates theft in a person but does not hate the fact that he is sent to the mines[54]—for a thief does the former and a judge the latter—neither does God hate what he makes because out of a lump of the wicked he makes vessels of perdition—that is, a work decreed by him for the punishment owed to those who are perishing, in which those on whom he has mercy discover their opportunity for salvation. Thus it was said to Pharaoh: *It was for this that I raised you up, so that I might display my power in you and so that my name might be made known throughout the earth.* This manifestation of God's power and the making known of his name throughout the earth are of benefit to those for whom such a calling is fitting so that they may be fearful and correct their ways. Accordingly he says as follows, *But if God, who is willing to display his wrath and to manifest his power, has borne with great patience the vessels of wrath that have been produced for perdition* (Rom 9:22). The implication is: *Who are you that you talk back to God?* When we

52. See Rom 5:6.
53. See Rom 11:33.
54. Laboring in the state-controlled mines was a standard form of criminal punishment.

join this text to the previous words, this is the meaning: If God, who is willing to display his wrath, has borne with the vessels of wrath, who are you that you talk back to God? He is willing, however, not only to display his wrath and to manifest his power, having borne with great patience the vessels of wrath that have been produced for perdition, but also, as in the words that follow, *to reveal the riches of his glory for the vessels of mercy* (Rom 9:23). For what profit is there to the vessels produced for perdition in God's patiently enduring them when, in accordance with his decree, he destroys and uses them as a means of salvation for those others on whom he has mercy? But it does indeed profit those for whose salvation he thus uses them, so that, as it is written, the righteous hand may wash in the blood of the sinner[55]—that is, that it may be cleansed of evil works through the fear of God, when it sees the punishments of sinners. That he is willing to display his wrath and has borne with the vessels of wrath, therefore, contributes to a beneficial fear to which others must be exposed and to the making known of the riches of his glory to the vessels of mercy, *which he has prepared for glory* (Rom 9:23). And indeed that hardening of the wicked demonstrates two things—both what should be feared, so that through goodness a person may be converted to God, and what great thanks are owed to the mercy of God, who shows in the punishment of the ones what he forgives in the others. But if what he exacts of the ones is not a just punishment, then nothing is forgiven the others, from whom he does not exact it. But because it is just and there is no injustice with God when he punishes, who can give adequate thanks to him who remits what, if he willed to exact it, no one would rightly say he did not owe?

2,19. *Us whom he also called, not only from the Jews but also from the gentiles* (Rom 9:24)—that is, *the vessels of mercy which he has prepared for glory.* For those [who are called] are not all Jews, but they are *from* the Jews; nor are they absolutely all the peoples of the gentiles, but they are *from* the gentiles. For from Adam has come a single mass of sinners and wicked persons; it is far from God's grace, and both Jews and gentiles belong to the one lump of it. For if from the same lump the potter makes one vessel for honor and another for reproach, and if it is obvious that from the Jews, as from the gentiles, some vessels are for honor and some are for

---

55. See Ps 58:10.

reproach, it follows that they should all be understood to belong to one lump.

Then he begins to offer prophetic testimonies to individual cases in reverse chronological order. For he had spoken first of the Jews and afterwards of the gentiles, but [now] he submits testimony on behalf of the gentiles first and then on behalf of the Jews. Thus: *As Hosea says, I will call a people that was not mine, my people, and that was not loved, loved, and in the place where it was said, You are not my people, there they shall be called the children of the living God* (Rom 9:25-26). This is understood to have been said of the gentiles, because they did not have a single place designated for sacrifices as did the Jews in Jerusalem. But apostles were sent to the gentiles so that those *to whom he gave the power to become children of God* (Jn 1:12) would believe, each of them in their own place, and so that wherever they had come to faith they would also offer there a sacrifice of praise.[56]

But Isaiah, he says, *cries out for Israel* (Rom 9:27). Lest, on the other hand, all the Israelites be believed to have fallen into perdition, he also teaches there that some vessels have been made for honor and others for reproach. *If,* he says, *the number of the children of Israel were like the sands of the sea, a remnant will be saved* (Rom 9:27). The remaining vessels, then, are the throng that has been produced for perdition. *For the Lord,* he says, *will carry out his brief and swift word upon the earth* (Rom 9:28)—that is, in order to save those who believe[57] through grace by the simplicity of their faith, not through the innumerable observances by which that multitude was burdened and oppressed as though they were slaves. Through grace he carried out his brief and swift word upon the earth for us when he said, *My yoke is easy, and my burden is light* (Mt 11:30). And shortly thereafter this is said: *The word is near you, in your mouth and in your heart—that is, the word of faith that we preach. Because if you confess in your mouth that Jesus is Lord and believe in your heart that God has raised him from the dead, you shall be saved. For with the heart there is belief unto righteousness, while with the mouth confession is made unto salvation.* (Rom 10:8-10) This is the brief and swift word that the Lord has carried out upon the earth. By its brevity and swiftness the thief was made righteous who, with all his members fastened to the cross but with these two [members]

---

56. See Ps 50:14.
57. See 1 Cor 1:21.

unhindered, believed with his heart unto righteousness and confessed with his mouth unto salvation, and immediately he deserved to hear:[58] *Today you shall be with me in paradise* (Lk 23:43). For his good works would have followed had he, upon receiving grace, lived for a long time among men. Yet they had not come in advance so as to merit the same grace by which he who was fastened to the cross as a thief was borne away from the cross to paradise.

And, he says, *as Isaiah predicted, Unless the Lord of hosts had left us offspring, we would have become like Sodom, and we would have been like Gomorrah* (Rom 9:29). What he says here, *had left us offspring*, appears elsewhere as *a remnant will be saved*. But others who owed the debt of punishment perished as vessels of perdition. And the fact that not all would perish as at Sodom and Gomorrah was not due to anything that they had merited; it was rather the grace of God leaving a seed from which another harvest would spring throughout the whole earth. A little later he also says this: *And so, therefore, at this time as well a remnant exists that was chosen by grace. But if by grace, then not by works; otherwise grace is no longer grace. What then? What Israel was seeking it did not find. The chosen found it, however, while the rest were blinded.* (Rom 11:5-7) The vessels of mercy found it but the vessels of wrath were blinded; yet, like all the gentiles, they are from the same lump.

2,20. There is a certain passage of scripture that is very pertinent to the matter at hand, which provides marvelous proof of what has been explained. It is in the book that is called Jesus Sirach by some and Ecclesiasticus by others, and in it there is written as follows: *All human beings come from the ground, and from the earth Adam was created. In the abundance of discipline the Lord separated them and changed their ways. Some he blessed and exalted, and these he sanctified and brought to himself. Some he cursed and humbled and turned to dissension. Like clay in a potter's hand, for shaping and forming all its ways according to his plan, so is man in the hands of the one who made him, the one who deals with him according to his judgment. In contrast to evil there is good, and opposed to death there is life; in the same way the sinner is opposed to the righteous man. Look thus upon the work of the Most High, in twos, one opposed to the other.* (Sir 33:10-15)

---

58. See Lk 23:32-43.

The first thing that is mentioned here is God's discipline. *In the abundance of discipline,* it says, *the Lord separated them*—from what if not from the blessedness of paradise?—*and changed their ways* (Sir 33:11), so that they would now live as mortals. Then a single mass was made of all of them, which came from the transmission of sin and the punishment of mortality, although, thanks to God's forming and creating them, they are good. For in all people there is a beauty and cohesion of body with such harmony among its members that the Apostle used this to illustrate how charity should be maintained;[59] in all people there is also a vital spirit that gives life to their earthly members; and the whole nature of the human person is regulated in marvelous fashion by the mastery of the soul and the servitude of the body. But the fleshly desire that results from the punishment for sin has, because of the original guilt, cast abiding confusion into everything, and now it presides over the whole human race as one complete lump. But there also follows: *Some he blessed and exalted, and them he sanctified and brought to himself. Some he cursed and humbled and turned to dissension.* (Sir 33:12)

As the Apostle says, *Or does the potter not have the power to make from the same lump of clay one vessel for honor and another for reproach?* (Rom 9:21) And so the passage that has been cited uses the same imagery: *Like clay in a potter's hand,* it says, *for shaping and forming all its ways according to his plan, so is man in the hands of the one who made him* (Sir 33:13-14). But the Apostle says, *Is there injustice with God?* Notice, therefore, what is added here: *He deals with him according to his judgment* (Sir 33:14). But although just punishments are assigned to those who have been condemned, yet, because this very thing is turned to the advantage of those to whom mercy is shown so that they may advance [in holiness], pay attention to what remains: *In contrast to evil there is good, and opposed to death there is life; in the same way the sinner is opposed to the righteous man. Look thus upon all the work of the Most High, in twos, one opposed to the other.* (Sir 33:15) Thus, from the conjunction of two bad things, better things emerge and advance [in holiness]. Yet, because they are better through grace, it is as though [the writer] were saying, *A remnant will be saved.* Speaking in the person of that remnant, he goes on to say, *And I have been*

---

59. See 1 Cor 12:12-27.

the last to keep watch, like someone who gleans after the vintagers (Sir 33:16). And where is the proof that this is not the result of merits but of God's mercy? *In the blessing of the Lord,* he says, *I myself have hoped, and like one who gathers the vintage I have filled the winepress* (Sir 33:17). For although he was the last to keep watch, nevertheless, because, as is said, the last shall be first,[60] the people of Israel, which has been gleaned from the rest[61] and which hopes in the Lord, has filled its winepress from out of the abundance of the vintage, which has flourished throughout the world.

2,21. The main thought of the Apostle, then, as well as of those who have been made righteous, through whom an understanding of grace has been given to us, is none other than that whoever boasts should boast in the Lord.[62] For would anyone question the works of the Lord, who from the same lump condemns one person and makes another righteous? The free choice of the will counts for a great deal, to be sure. But what does it count for in those who have been sold under sin?[63] *The flesh,* [the Apostle] says, *lusts against the spirit, the spirit against the flesh, so that you do not do the things that you want* (Gal 5:17). It is commanded that we live uprightly, and in fact this reward has been offered—that we merit to live blessedly forever. But who can live uprightly and do good works without having been made righteous by faith?[64] It is commanded that we believe so that, having received the gift of the Holy Spirit through love, we may be able to do good works. But who can believe without being touched by some call—that is, by the evidence of things? Who has it in his power for his mind to be touched by such a manifestation as would move his will to faith? Who embraces in his heart something that does not attract him? Who has it in his power either to come into contact with what can attract him or to be attracted once he has come into contact? When, therefore, things attract us whereby we may advance towards God, this is inspired and furnished by the grace of God; it is not obtained by our own assent and effort or by the merits of our works because, whether it be the assent of our will or our intense effort or our works aglow with charity, it is he who gives, he who bestows it.

---

60. See Mt 20:16.
61. See Jer 6:9.
62. See 2 Cor 10:17.
63. See Rom 7:14.
64. See Rom 5:1.

We are ordered to ask so that we may receive, and to seek so that we may find, and to knock so that it may be opened to us.[65] Is not this particular prayer of ours sometimes so lukewarm, or rather cold and practically non-existent, indeed, sometimes so utterly non-existent, that we do not notice this in ourselves without sorrow? Because if this actually makes us sorry, we are already praying. What else, then, is being shown to us than that it is he who orders us to ask and seek and knock who enables us to do these things? *It is not a matter of willing or of running, therefore, but of a merciful God*, since in fact we could neither will nor run if he did not move and rouse us.

2,22. If there is some choice that is made here, such as we understand from the words, *A remnant that was chosen by grace* (Rom 11:5), the choice is not of those who, for the sake of eternal life, have been made righteous. It is, rather, that those are chosen who are to be made righteous, and this choice is so very hidden that it can by no means be discerned by us who are in the same lump. Or, if it is discernible to some, I for my part acknowledge my incompetence in the matter. For, if in my thoughts I am allowed some insight into this choice, I cannot see how persons are chosen for the grace of salvation apart from either greater endowments or lesser sins or both. We may also add, if you wish, learning that is good and useful. Whoever, then, has been ensnared in and sullied by only the very least sins—for who could be without *any*?—and is endowed with intelligence and has been refined by the liberal arts seems as if he must have been chosen for grace. But when I arrive at this conclusion, he who has chosen the weak things of the world to confound the strong, and the foolish things of the world to confound the wise,[66] laughs at me in such a way that, as I gaze upon him and am checked by shame, I myself begin to make fun of many who are more chaste than certain sinners and better speech-makers than certain fishermen.[67] Do we not notice that many of us who are faithful and who walk in God's way by no means possess endowments comparable not only, I would say, to those of

---

65. See Mt 7:7.
66. See 1 Cor 1:27.
67. These lines bear a remarkable resemblance to a scene recounted in *Confessions* VIII,11,27, in which Continence, appearing to Augustine in a kind of vision and bringing before his mind's eye a throng of the chaste of every condition (analogous to the many who are weak and foolish in the view of the world), mocks him because he fears that he cannot be chaste himself, whereupon he blushes. The present work and the *Confessions* were written at most within a year or two of each other.

some heretics but even to those of actors? On the other hand, do we not see some persons of both sexes living peacefully in married chastity, who are nonetheless heretics or pagans or even members of the true faith and the true Church and who are so lukewarm that we marvel at how they are surpassed not only by the patience and temperance but even by the faith, hope and charity of prostitutes and actors who have experienced sudden conversions?

The upshot, then, is that wills are chosen. But the will itself, unless it comes into contact with something that attracts and beckons the soul, can by no means be moved. But that it may come into contact with this is not in a person's power. What did Saul want to do but attack, seize, enchain and kill Christians? What a rabid, raging, blind will![68] Yet at a single voice from heaven he fell prostrate and, having had such an experience that his mind and will, broken by savagery, were turned about and directed toward faith, he was at once transformed from a famous persecutor of the gospel to its still more famous preacher.[69]

And yet *what shall we say? Is there injustice with God*, who exacts from whom he pleases and gives to whom he pleases but who never exacts what is not owed him and never gives what is not his? *Is there injustice with God? Of course not!* Yet why is one person treated one way and another person another way? *O man, who are you?* If you do not repay what is owed, you have reason to be grateful; if you do repay it, you have no reason to complain. Let us only believe, even if we cannot understand, that he who made and established the whole of creation, spiritual and corporeal, arranges everything according to number and weight and measure.[70] But *inscrutable are his judgments and unfathomable his ways* (Rom 11:33). Let us say "Alleluia" and join in the canticle, and let us not say "Why this?" or "Why that?" For all things have been created in their own time.[71]

---

68. See Acts 8:3; 9:1-2.
69. See Acts 9:3-22.
70. See Wis 11:20.
71. See Sir 39:21. This and the preceding allusion to Wis 11:20, which is one of Augustine's favorite verses, is intended to hint at the order that governs creation, even though it may not always be immediately apparent.

The Punishment and Forgiveness of Sins
and the Baptism of Little Ones

Introduction

Historical Background

Augustine began his first work against the Pelagians, *The Punishment and Forgiveness of Sin and the Baptism of Little Ones*,[1] soon after Caelestius, the disciple of Pelagius, was condemned by the Council of Carthage in the late fall of 411 or early in 412. As the opening paragraph tells us, the immediate occasion of the work was a letter from the tribune, Flavius Marcellinus, asking Augustine to answer a series of questions. Though the letter from Marcellinus has not been preserved, the first paragraph of Book Three indicates that Marcellinus' chief concern was with the baptism of little ones and that this concern led him to ask Augustine to answer those who held (1) "that, even if he had not sinned, Adam would have died," (2) "that nothing passed to his descendants as a result of his sin by the process of generation," and (3) "that in this life there are and have been and will be human beings who have absolutely no sin."

In Book One Augustine responds to the first two propositions, while he spends all of Book Two on the third proposition, to which he returns in *The Spirit and the Letter*, because Marcellinus found it baffling that Augustine had maintained both that it is possible that human beings be completely free from sin and that apart from Christ there is no example of such human sinlessness. The second proposition reported to Augustine by Marcellinus obviously denies any inherited sin contracted from Adam by generation such that even newly born infants require baptism for the forgiveness of sins. The third proposition, which Augustine distinguishes into four separate

---

1. Because of the length of the title, I will hereafter use in this introduction the short title, *The Punishment and Forgiveness of Sins* (*De peccatorum meritis et remissione*), which Augustine himself used to refer to the work in his *Revisions* II, 59 (33). He also referred to it as *The Books on the Baptism of Little Ones* (*Libri de baptismo parvulorum*) in Letter 139, 3 and in *The Grace of Christ and Original Sin* II, 21, 24. He also called it *The Works on the Baptism of Little Ones and the Perfection of Human Righteousness* (*Opuscula de baptismo parvulorum et de perfectione iustitiae hominis*) in *The Spirit and the Letter* 1, 1. Possidius used the title *Two Books on the Baptism of Little Ones for Marcellinus and a Letter to Him on the Punishment and Forgiveness of Sins* (*De baptismo parvulorum ad Marcellinum libri duo et epistola ad ipsum de peccatorum meritis et remissione*) in his *Operum sancti Augustini elenchus* (MA II, 149-233, here 171).

questions, also denies any inherited sin, at least insofar as it maintains that there actually have been, are, or will be people who have no sin whatsoever at any time in their lives.

In the months following the fall of Rome to Alaric's Goths on 24 August 410, Pelagius passed through North Africa on his way from Rome to Jerusalem, landing at Hippo and soon leaving for Carthage. Augustine mentions in *The Deeds of Pelagius* 22, 46 that he saw him several times from a distance, but the two apparently never met. Pelagius' disciple, Caelestius, however, remained in Carthage where he disturbed many with his ideas about the abilities of human nature to avoid sin. When he asked to be ordained, he was accused of heresy by the deacon, Paulinus of Milan, formerly secretary to St. Ambrose—a fact of no small interest, since it clearly indicates that the doctrine of original sin did not originate with Augustine, as some historians of theology have maintained.[2]

Caelestius was brought before an episcopal tribunal, where Augustine reports that he refused to condemn those who say "that the sin of Adam harmed him alone and not the human race and that at their birth infants are in that state in which Adam was before his transgression."[3] Under questioning by Paulinus, Caelestius said that he was in doubt about the transmission of sin and claimed that the question was open to debate among Catholics. He could, however, offer only the name of Rufinus, a Roman priest, as one who shared this view with him. This priest was Rufinus the Syrian, whose *Profession of Faith* (*Liber de fide*) Augustine cites almost verbatim, though without mentioning the author, in *The Punishment and Forgiveness of Sins* I, 18, 23 and who was reported by Marius Mercator as having introduced this heresy in the Roman Church during the pontificate of Anastasius (399-402).[4] Indeed, by some, Rufinus is regarded as the real founder of Pelagianism.[5] This first Council of Carthage concerned with the Pelagians,

2. See, for example, J. Gross, *Geschichte des Erbsündendogmas. Ein Beitrag zur Geschichte des Problems vom Ursprung des Übels. I. Entstehungsgeschichte des Erbsündendogmas von der Bibel bis Augustinus* (München und Basel, 1960), 375: "Augustinus ist somit im Vollsinn des Wortes der Vater des Erbsündendogmas."
3. *The Grace of Christ and Original Sin* II, 2, 2.
4. Marius Mercator, *Liber subnotationum in Acta conciliorum oecumenicorum*, ed. E. Schwartz (Berlin, I, v, 5. "Under the supreme pontiff of the Roman Church, Anastasius, of holy memory, Rufinus, formerly Syrian in nationality, first introduced this question which is foolish and no less hostile to the true faith...."
5. For the role of Rufinus in the development of Pelagian thought, see Gerald Bonner, "Rufinus the Syrian and African Pelagianism," *Augustinian Studies* 1 (1970) 31-47,

which took place after September of 411 and at the latest in January of 412, condemned Caelestius' teaching and excommunicated him.[6] Augustine himself was not present at it, and though he reviewed the acts of the council during a later stay in Carthage,[7] he does not seem to have been familiar with them at the time he wrote the first two books of *The Punishment and Forgiveness of Sins.*

In *The Deeds of Pelagius* 11, 23, Augustine listed the propositions of Caelestius that were condemned at Carthage after they had been raised as charges against Pelagius at the Council of Diospolis in 415. These propositions which formed the core of the Pelagian teachings are: "Adam was created mortal so that he would die whether he sinned or did not sin." " The sin of Adam harmed him alone and not the human race." "The law leads to the kingdom just as the gospel does." "Before the coming of Christ there were human beings without sin." "Newly born infants are in the same state in which Adam was before his transgression." "The whole human race does not die through the death or transgression of Adam, nor does the whole human race rise through the resurrection of Christ."

Though Caelestius left Africa after being condemned, his followers and those of Pelagius continued to present a problem for the church of Carthage—so much so that Marcellinus wrote to Augustine with a plea for help and by his plea brought him into the controversy against Pelagius and his followers as a writer, though he states in the *Revisions* II, 33 (60) that he and others had previously combatted the heresy in sermons and conferences.

Marcellinus, the brother of the proconsul Arpingius, had been sent to North Africa in the winter of 411-412 by the emperor Honorius to convoke and preside over a conference between the Catholics and the

---

as well as his *Augustine and Pelagianism in the Light of Modern Research.* The Saint Augustine Lecture, 1970 (Villanova: Villanova University Press, 1972); both are reprinted in *God's Decree and Man's Destiny. Studies on the Thought of Augustine of Hippo* (London: Variorum Reprints, 1987). See also Bonner's "Pelagianism and Augustine," *Augustinian Studies* 23 (1992) 33-51 and 24 (1993) 27-47.

6. See F. Refoulé, "Datation du premier concile de Carthage contre les Pélagiens et du *Libellus fidei* de Rufin," *Revue des études augustiniennes* 9 (1963) 41-49. This important article not merely established the date of the Council of Carthage, but showed that Rufinus' *Liber de fide* was the work Augustine refuted in the first thirty-four chapters of *The Punishment and Forgiveness of Sins* and that the so-called Augustinian concept of original sin antedated Augustine and was already widely known in the Church at the end of the fourth century.

7. See *The Deeds of Pelagius* 11, 23.

Donatists and, in general, to supervise ecclesiastical affairs. During the conference with the Donatists held at Carthage in June of 411 Marcellinus had come to know Augustine. Indeed, through their common efforts at Church unity in preparation for and during the conference, a warm friendship grew up between the two men. In a letter written after Marcellinus' execution on 13 September 413, Augustine described him at length in highly laudatory terms; a short excerpt from the letter is sufficient to indicate Augustine's high opinion of his friend: "He lived as a religious man—a Christian in his heart and in his life. This reputation preceded him so that he arrived with it in the cause of the Church; this reputation stayed with him after his arrival. What moral goodness he had, what loyalty in friendship, what zeal for learning, what sincerity in religion! He was chaste in marriage, restrained as a judge, patient toward enemies, warm toward friends, humble toward the saints, loving toward all. He was quick to bestow favors, slow to ask for them; he loved good deeds and was saddened by sins."[8]

Marcellinus appealed for help to Augustine in the winter of 411-412, because, as Augustine recalled, "Many of our weak brothers were being disturbed by these questions and by the assertion of these opinions which are now fiercely argued and heatedly debated everywhere."[9] Indeed, Augustine tells us that Marcellinus was daily enduring the troublesome arguments of those raising these questions so that he consulted the bishop of Hippo by letter,[10] the letter which brought Augustine to write the first of his works against the Pelagians.

Thus, Augustine came to write *The Punishment and Forgiveness of Sins*, the first in the long list of works against "the enemies of the grace of God" that ultimately earned for him the title *Doctor gratiae*, Teacher of Grace. This letter was not, however, the only influence Marcellinus had on Augustine's writing career. His difficulties with Augustine's position in *The Punishment and Forgiveness of Sins* evoked Augustine's second book against the Pelagians, *The Spirit and the Letter*, and it was again Marcellinus who by another letter to Augustine induced him to write the twenty-two books of his great work, *The City of God*. Hence, it was a deep personal loss for Augustine when Marcellinus and his brother were executed for their alleged connection with the uprising of Heraclian.

---

8. Letter 151, 8.
9. *The Deeds of Pelagius* 11, 25.
10. Ibid.

Augustine wrote *The Punishment and Forgiveness of Sins* after the Council of Carthage, hence, after September 411, its earliest possible date.[11] In Letter 139 to Marcellinus, written before 28 February 412, Augustine said, "I have forgotten why, after I sent the volume to Your Excellency, I received back from you the books on the baptism of little ones, unless I perhaps found them defective, when I looked at them, and wanted to correct them, but I have still not done so, as I have been incredibly busy. You should know that the letter, which I was also to write for you and add to these, has progressed slightly, but is still unfinished, though I had already begun to dictate it, when I was there [i.e., at Carthage]."[12]

Hence, the first two books of *The Punishment and Forgiveness of Sins* were completed—except for final emendations, which may have been extensive—early enough for Augustine to have sent them to Marcellinus, received them back from him, and supposedly forgotten why he received them back by the end of February 412.[13] The third book, which was written as a letter and added to the other two books by reason of its content, was still unfinished at the time of Letter 139. Between the completion of the first two books and the writing of the third, Augustine obtained a copy of Pelagius' *Expositions of the Letters of Saint Paul*,[14] which contained an interpretation of Romans 5:12 of which Augustine had not been previously aware. Realizing that it required its own refutation, Augustine produced the third book of *The Punishment and Forgiveness of Sins*.[15]

The Structure and Contents of the Work

Book One first argues against the claim that Adam would have died, even if he had not sinned (sections 2-8); then it defends the transmission of original sin to Adam's descendants by generation (sections 9-20); finally, it takes up the principal concern of Marcellinus,

---

11. See F. Refoulé, "Datation du premier concile de Carthage," 41-49.
12. Letter 139, 3: CSEL 44, 152.
13. In his *The Origin of the Soul in Saint Augustine's Later Works* (New York: Fordham University Press, 1987), pp. 104-115 and 198-200, Robert J. O'Connell argues for a later date for the completion of the work, largely on the basis of Augustine's rejection of prenatal sin in this work, a view which, according to O'Connell, Augustine came to only some years later.
14. Pelagius' work is extant: *Expositiones XIII Epistularum Pauli Apostoli*, ed. A. Souter (Cambridge, 1926); reprinted in PLS I, 1110-1374.
15. See *The Punishment and Forgiveness of Sins* III, 1, 1.

namely, the purpose of infant baptism (sections 21-61). The question
of infant baptism leads Augustine to muster the scriptural texts that
show that Christ is the savior and redeemer of the newborn (sections
33-38) and that all human beings need Christ's redemption (sections
39-61). The work is heavily laden with scriptural citations; in fact,
approximately one fourth of the words in the first book are direct
quotations from the Bible.

Augustine rejects in sections 2-8 the Pelagian claim that Adam
would have died, even if he had not sinned, as contrary to the clear
statements of scripture. He does not deny that Adam had a mortal
body, but claims that his mortal body would not have aged and
suffered death, if he had remained obedient to God's commandment.

Marcellinus had reported to Augustine that those people who
had aroused his concern had distorted the sense of Romans 5:12, but
he did not indicate how they had interpreted the text. In section 9,
Augustine explains that he has tried to discover how they interpreted
the passage and suggests that they held that Paul was referring to the
death of the soul that is sin itself and that they maintained that sin was
passed on to all human beings, not by propagation, but by imitation.
Pelagius had, in fact, written in his commentary on Romans, "As
by the example of Adam's disobedience many sinned, so too by the
obedience of Christ many are justified."[16] In opposition to the view
that Adam's sin has been transmitted to all of Adam's descendants
by imitation, Augustine sets out to prove that sin has passed to all
by generation. It is here that Augustine uses for the first time in his
writings the expression "original sin" to refer to the sinful condition
in which human beings are born as the result of Adam's sin.

His Old Latin version of Rom 5:12 omitted the word "death" so
that "sin" was understood as the subject of "was passed on to all human beings." Hence, in Rom 5:12 Augustine believed that he had a
clear statement of sin's transmission to all human beings. Furthermore, his Latin text seemed to say that all sinned either in Adam or in
Adam's sin, though neither reading is accepted by modern exegetes.

In sections 12-20 Augustine continues his explanation of Rom 5,
clarifying the roles of the law, of sin, and of grace, a theme to which
he will return again and again and to which he devoted the whole of
The Spirit and the Letter. The fact that all human beings are born
with the guilt of Adam's sin explains the need for baptism for the for-

16. Pelagius, *Expositio in epistolam ad Romanos* 5:19.

giveness of sins, even in the case of newly born infants. In section 21 Augustine states that infants who die without baptism will be subject to condemnation, though theirs will be the mildest punishment of all. Augustine is adamant (section 22) in his denial that infants have any personal sins for which they need baptism. He cites in section 23 a passage almost verbatim from Rufinus the Syrian's *Liber de fide*, in which Rufinus claimed that infants are baptized, not so that their sins might be forgiven, but so that they might be spiritually created in Christ and attain a share in the kingdom of heaven.[17] Augustine indicates in section 24 that some appealed to the Lord's statement in Mt 19:14 that the kingdom of heaven belongs to the little ones. Though Augustine wavers between taking these little ones as an example of humility and seeing them as already made righteous by baptism, he insists in accord with Lk 5:32 that Christ either did not come to call them or that they were sinners. Just as they cannot as yet profess the faith in their own words but are counted as believers by reason of the words of their parents or sponsors, so they express their repentance by reason of the words of those who make the renunciations for them (section 25).

The Pelagians wanted to grant to unbaptized infants salvation and eternal life, even though they accepted the Lord's words in Jn 3:3.5 which excluded them from the kingdom of God or of heaven. Against this view Augustine appeals in sections 26-27 to the words of the Lord, *Unless you eat my flesh and drink my blood, you will not have life in you* (Jn 6:54), and maintains that those words apply to little ones, since in Augustine's time little ones received the Eucharist at their baptism, as is still the practice in Eastern churches. So too, in sections 28-29 he appeals to Jn 3:35-36, arguing that either the little ones are to be counted as believers in the Son or they will not have life, but the anger of God will remain over them. Yet, when it comes to the question of why one infant dies after baptism and another dies without it, Augustine can only point to Paul's cry, *O the depth of the riches of the wisdom and knowledge of God* (Rom 11:33). To the Pelagian complaint that it is unjust to deprive unbaptized little ones of both the kingdom and eternal life, Augustine asks them how it is just in their view to deprive an unbaptized infant of the kingdom of heaven (section 30).

---

17. Refoulé's article, "Datation du premier concile de Carthage," has shown that Augustine was refuting this work of Rufinus throughout the first thirty-four chapters of *The Punishment and Forgiveness of Sins*.

An alternative explanation of the fact that human beings are born sinful claimed that preexistent souls sinned in their heavenly dwelling and, as punishment, came down to bodies appropriate to their merits. Such was the view attributed to Origen, and such was the view that Augustine himself seems at some point to have held.[18] In section 31 Augustine flatly rejects any prenatal sin on the basis of Rom 9:11-12, in which Paul repudiates as an explanation of the election of Jacob and rejection of Esau their having done anything either good or bad before they were born.[19] Augustine points out that the appeal to prenatal sin does not, in any case, solve the mystery of divine election and that its proponents are left to cry out, *O the depth*, when confronted with a good person who lives where he is unable to receive baptism, while a sinner is baptized and dies. In section 32 Augustine produces examples meant to counter the theory that souls are more heavily weighed down by earthly bodies in proportion to the gravity of their prenatal sin; he points, for example, to the simple-minded whose affliction should, according to the theory, have been due to their grave prenatal sin, but who are baptized and live good Christian lives.

Hence, Augustine urges the Pelagians to assent to the authority of scripture (section 33) which proclaims Christ as physician, as savior, and as redeemer for little ones as well as for adults. He points to the practice of Punic Christians who refer to baptism as salvation and who call the Eucharist life (section 34), again insisting that they are salvation and life for little ones as well as for adults and that, if little ones were not sinners, they would not need salvation and life.

Christ came as light so that everyone who believes in him might not remain in the darkness, according to Jn 12:46; hence, Augustine argues that, if the little ones are not numbered among believers, they remain in that darkness. Some people, Augustine tells us in sections 36-38, interpret Jn 1:19 as implying that every human

---

18. See Orosius' *Consulation or Memorandum to Augustine on the Error of the Priscillianists and Origenists* 3 and Augustine's *To Orosius in Refutation of the Priscillianists and Origenists* 8, 9, for the attribution of this error to Origen and its refutation by Augustine. For the ablest argument that Augustine himself held the doctrine of the fall of the soul into mortal bodies, see the many books of R. J. O'Connell.
19. See R. J. O'Connell's *The Origin of the Soul in St. Augustine's Later Works* (New York: Fordham University Press, 1989), pp. 179-200, where O'Connell argues for a later dating of *The Punishment and Forgiveness of Sins* on the grounds that Augustine did not come to see Rom 9:11 as excluding all prenatal sin until late 417 or spring of 418.

being is enlightened by the true light at birth, though they admit that we still need baptism in order to attain the kingdom of God. After distinguishing various meanings of enlightenment, Augustine insists that the enlightenment of the gift of faith is given only in baptism, by which the little ones become believers.

In sections 39-56, Augustine amasses a series of scripture texts on Christ as redeemer and our participation through baptism in the salvation and redemption he has brought. The transmission of original sin through generation leads him to distinguish in section 57 between the good use of sexual desire in marriage for the procreation of children and concupiscence itself, which is an evil. In sections 58-62 he returns to scripture and develops the theology of baptism and union with Christ found in the crucial third chapter of John's gospel. He points out in section 63 that the very form of baptism with its exorcism, renunciations, and profession of faith indicates that a little one is baptized for the forgiveness of sins. Well aware that not all those against whom he is arguing hold the same views, Augustine notes in section 64 that some in the Pelagian camp maintain that infants are sinless so that baptism for the forgiveness of sin is a fraud, while others hold that sins are forgiven, but claim that infants have committed personal sins. Augustine regards the supposition that infants sin in their own lives immediately after birth as absurd and describes the darkness of their ignorance in sections 65-69. Finally, in section 70 he concludes the first book with the claim that, though all sins are forgiven in baptism, concupiscence remains. The fact that concupiscence remains leads into the question of the second book.

At the beginning of Book Two, Augustine turns to the third point raised by Marcellinus' letter, namely, whether there has been, is now, or will be anyone in this life, apart from Christ, who has no sin whatsoever. In section 2 he indicates that the words of the Lord's Prayer, *And bring us not into temptation* (Mt 6:13), point to our need for God's help if we are to overcome temptation. The Pelagians correctly see that we do not sin unless we will to, but they fail to see that we need the full strength of the will if we are to avoid sin. However, concupiscence remains, Augustine insists, in section 4, in the body of this death. Though its guilt is removed when infants are baptized, it remains as something against which we must struggle in this life until death is swallowed up in victory. Hence, we pray for the forgiveness of our sins and ask not to be brought into temptation, because we have lost our strength and need to be healed from the wounds of sin. As a result, Augustine claims in sections 5-6 that we cannot do what is right without God's help and need to pray that God will grant what he commands. Otherwise, we would be like the Pharisee who thought he had already attained perfection and did not ask for God's help to grow in righteousness.

Augustine then turns in section 7 to the principal topic of Book Two: whether human beings can attain or have attained sinlessness (*impeccantia*). He divides the topic into four questions: (1) Can human beings be sinless in this life? (2) Is there actually someone without sin? (3) Why are no human beings without sin, though a sinless life is possible? and (4) Can or could there be a human being who has had or will have absolutely no sin?

To the first question Augustine answers in section 7 that human beings can be without sin in this life "by the grace of God and free choice." He insists, however, that our free choice is God's gift, not merely insofar as it exists, but insofar as it is good. Augustine's answer to the second question (sections 8-25) is considerably longer. Two scripture texts, *No living person will be found righteous in your sight* (Ps 142:2) and *If we say that we have no sin, we deceive ourselves, and the truth is not in us* (1 Jn 1:8), lead Augustine to a negative answer. The Pelagians, however, appealed to the apparently contrary text, *Those who have been born of God do not sin and cannot sin, because his seed remains in them* (1 Jn 3:9). In response, Augustine cites many scripture texts to show that our renewal in the Spirit, begun by the full forgiveness of sins in baptism, is at present only partial and needs to be completed as we are renewed from day to day until we attain the fullness of our redemption at the resurrection of our bodies. Thus he is able to counter the objection (section 11) that a righteous person ought to produce a righteous child, just as sinners give birth to sinners, since human beings bear children, not insofar as they are children of God, but insofar as they are still children of this world.

In sections 12-21, Augustine turns to a list of women and men whom scripture describes as righteous: Noah, Daniel, Job, Elizabeth and Zechariah, all figures to whom the Pelagians appealed.[20]

---

20. See, for example, Pelagius' letter, "To Demetrias" 5, 1-6, 3, in R. B. Rees, *The Letters of Pelagius and his Followers* (Woodbridge: Boydell Press, 1991), pp. 29-70. The letter, written in 413, illustrates the Pelagian appeal to scriptural models of righteousness.

Augustine grants that they were righteous and beyond reproach, but argues that they were not sinless. Even Paul, in fact, had not attained perfection. Though we are commanded to be perfect as our heavenly Father is perfect, no one actually attains perfect sinlessness in this life. In section 22 Augustine shows from Paul that Christians can in this life be perfect in one respect and yet lack perfection in another. He argues in section 23 that God commands us to be sinless, though he foreknows that we will sin, just as he gave Adam and Eve the commandment about not eating the fruit of the tree, though he foreknew they would sin. Even Paul, who fought the good fight, ran the race, and kept the faith, had not yet attained perfect sinlessness; rather, because of his firm hope he spoke as though he had attained what still lay ahead. Hence, in section 25, Augustine concludes this section by granting that there were many outstandingly holy women and men, but none of them were sinless.

In section 26 Augustine turns to the third question: Why are no human beings in this life without sin, though they can be when God's grace helps their will? Augustine gives a brief answer: Because they do not will to be without sin. But the answer becomes long when the question shifts to the more profound one of why human beings do not will to be without sin. His answer points to their ignorance and weakness: either they do not know what is right or they find no delight in it. For we will something with greater strength in proportion to our certainty about its goodness and our delight in that goodness. In this work, as in others prior to 418, Augustine explains the influence of grace upon the human will in terms of God's providing knowledge and causing delight in the known good, not in terms of his acting directly upon the will.[21] Thus, in section 27 he says, "Hence, at one moment a person has the knowledge to undertake, perform, and complete a good deed; at another he does not. At one moment a person finds delight in this; at another he does not." Whatever good we human beings have, we have received, Augustine insists following 1 Cor 4:7. Yet, we must not "defend grace in such a way that we

---

21. This change in the functioning of grace in Augustine's theology is one of the major points made in J. Patout Burns, *The Development of Augustine's Doctrine of Operative Grace* (Paris: Etudes Augustiniennes, 1980). On p. 9, he says, "The explanation of the mode of divine control over the human will in the process of conversion changed in 418 from the original theory of a manipulation of the environment of choice to an assertion of direct influence on the will through an interior grace."

seem to destroy free choice" and must not "stress free choice in such a way that we are judged ungrateful to the grace of God ..." (section 28). If we attribute to God whatever good will we have, just because he has given us our existence, without which the good will could not exist, then we would be forced to attribute our bad will to him for the same reason (section 29). Hence, we must attribute to God not only the natural good of free choice, which we can misuse, but the good will, which we cannot misuse (section 30).

Though we can turn away from God by our own evil will, we cannot turn back to him except by a good will which we cannot have without his help (section 31). Yet, why God turns back to himself some and not others lies hidden in his plan (section 32). When we pray for God's help to do what is right, we ask "that he disclose what was hidden and that he make attractive what was not pleasing" (section 33). Even God's holy people are at times healed of their defects more slowly so that "the good attracts them less than suffices for accomplishing what is right, whether it remains hidden from them or it is already clearly seen" (section 33).

At last, Augustine turns in section 34 to his fourth question: whether there can or could ever be a completely sinless human being. Augustine's first question had asked about the possibility of human sinlessness as something that could be brought about in this life by the help of God's grace. The present question asks whether any human beings could be absolutely free from sin in their whole lives so that they were not merely free from all personal sins but also from original sin. Hence, since all human beings apart from the one mediator between God and human beings enter this world with original sin, the question can only be answered in the negative.[22]

In sections 35-36 Augustine turns to the story of the fall and stresses that the sin of Adam and Eve was a sin of disobedience and that, as a result of their disobedience, they came to experience the disobedience of their flesh, which Augustine sees most clearly exemplified in involuntary sexual arousal. Augustine argues (section 37) that

---

22. In *Nature and Grace* 36, 42, Augustine finds the Virgin Mary at the end of Pelagius' list of righteous men and women from the scriptures. Pelagius said, "Piety demands that we admit that she was without sin." Augustine says, "Let us then leave aside the holy Virgin Mary; on account of the honor due to the Lord, I do not want to raise here any question about her when we are dealing with sins. After all, how do we know what wealth of grace was given her in order to conquer sin completely, since she merited to conceive and bear the one who obviously had no sin?"

from their sinful flesh our sinful flesh is born that needs purification by the sacrament of Christ. He was born, not in sinful flesh, but in the likeness of sinful flesh, so that we who are born in sinful flesh might be reborn as children of God (section 38).

In sections 39-40 Augustine argues that even a child of baptized parents needs to be baptized, fending off the claim that children of baptized parents receive baptism in their parents' bodies, as Levi received tithes from Melchizedek in the loins of Abraham. So too, Augustine argues against the interpretation of 1 Cor 7:14 as implying that children of believers have a cleanness and holiness that replaces the need for baptism; he shows that there are various kinds of sanctification, such as that conferred by the imposition of hands upon a catechumen, which do not dispense from the need for baptism (sections 41-42). Again, Augustine tries to explain the need for children of the baptized parents to be baptized, insisting in section 43 that the sacrament of rebirth presupposes birth, so that unborn children cannot be reborn in their baptized parents. Augustine struggles to explain why, despite the fact that parents receive the full forgiveness of their sins in baptism, they beget offspring with the guilt of original sin (section 44). Again, he explains in section 45 that concupiscence remains in the baptized, not as something that needs forgiveness, but as something to be overcome with the help of grace and eventually destroyed in the resurrection of the body. But from the moment of Adam's sin until the end of this carnal generation, no human being is entirely free from all sin apart from the one mediator, and he is the one savior of both little ones and adults (sections 47-48).

Augustine turns in section 49 to another Pelagian objection, namely that, if Adam's sin caused us to die, then those who believe in Christ should not die, since Adam's sin did not produce more harm than Christ's coming produced good. He replies that Adam's sin has indeed brought about bodily death for all, but that Christ has brought us redemption and resurrection to endless life. Christ could have exempted believers from bodily death, but that would have removed from faith its challenge and its merit (sections 50-51). So too, the Lord performed miracles when faith was in its infancy, but faith is stronger to the extent that it does not rely on such things (section 52).

A similar objection argues that, if death came from sin, we should no longer die once we have our sins forgiven in baptism (section 53). Augustine answers that, though the guilt of sin has been removed, some of the penalties of sin remain to try us in the struggle of life. Death remains for us so that through faith we can conquer the fear of death (section 54). After their dismissal from paradise, the sinful flesh of Adam and Eve needed to be taught obedience through labors, even though their sin was forgiven (section 55). The fact that David suffered punishment for his sin, even though the sin was forgiven, confirms the same point (section 56).

Hence, Augustine urges his reader in section 57 to hold to the rule of faith that only Christ was born without any sin and to cling to the middle path, neither claiming to be without sin nor simply abandoning oneself to sin. Augustine brings the book to a close by pointing out that the Pelagian concession that little ones need redemption should really lead the Pelagians to see that even little ones have sin and therefore need Christ's salvation and redemption.

The work had originally ended with the second book. However, no sooner had Augustine completed the first two books than he came upon Pelagius' *Exposition of Saint Paul's Letter to the Romans*, as he explains to Marcellinus in the beginning of the third book. In it he found a new argument against the transmission of sin. Hence, Augustine adds the third book as a letter to Marcellinus; his sole objective in it is the refutation of the interpretation of Rom 5:12, which Pelagius reports as the thought of those who oppose the transmission of sin, not as his own position. Here Pelagius is for the first time mentioned by name, though Augustine refers to him as "a holy man" (section 1) and "a fine and praiseworthy man, as those who know him say" (section 5).

The new argument found in Pelagius' work sets out to reduce to absurdity the idea that Adam's sin harmed those who did not themselves sin; it claims that, if Adam's sin harmed those who did not sin, then Christ's righteousness ought to benefit even those who do not believe (section 2). It is, however, clear that Christ's righteousness does not benefit those who do not believe. Hence, the objectors would have us conclude that Adam's sin did not harm those who did not themselves sin, especially since the grace of Christ by far surpasses Adam's sin, as Paul assures us in Rom 5:15.

In his reply Augustine latches onto the argument's concession that Christ's righteousness does benefit baptized little ones. He appeals to the Pelagians' Christian faith that Christ's righteousness can benefit only believers. Hence, he concludes that little ones must be included among believers. "Just as by the responses of those through whom they are reborn the Spirit of righteousness gives them a faith which they could not have by their own will, so the sinful flesh of those through whom they are born gives them a guilt which they have not yet contracted in their own life" (section 2). However, since Mk 16:16 is clear that those who do not believe and are not baptized will be condemned, little ones could not be justly condemned if they did not have original sin, since they have no personal sin (section 3).

In sections 5-6 Augustine is careful to note that Pelagius merely reports the views of others in his commentary on Romans and does not present these arguments in his own name. Augustine tries to put the best interpretation he can on Pelagius' procedure, so he does not at this point condemn him personally, though he clearly sees that the opinions and views Pelagius reports are opposed to the Christian faith.

In the face of the reported claims that Rom 5:12 is not clear, Augustine insists that texts that one finds unclear should be interpreted in the light of those which are perfectly clear (section 7) and appeals to Jn 3:5, Mt 1:21, and Mt 9:12 as texts that clearly show the need for baptism and the roles of Jesus as savior and physician (section 8). On the other hand, he is unwilling to concede that there is anything ambiguous in the passage from Romans except for Rom 5:14, in which Adam is said to be the form of what is to come—a text which both he and Pelagius interpreted in different ways.

In sections 10-14 Augustine offers several citations from Cyprian's Letter 64, as well as from two of Jerome's writings, to show that it is the ancient tradition of the Church that infants are to be baptized for the forgiveness of sins, which in their case can only be the sin inherited from Adam, since they are obviously incapable of personal sin. Since Jerome is a contemporary, the proof from the Church's ancient tradition really amounts to the letter of Cyprian alone. It was not until 418 that Augustine appealed to Ambrose in support of his view on original sin.[23] On the other hand, Augustine is confident that, if he only had the opportunity to question a man of immense learning like Jerome, he would have been able to supply further evidence. In any case the canonical books are clear and authoritative; Rom 5:12 states that all sinned in Adam, "when they were all still that one man

---

23. See *The Grace of Christ and Original Sin* II, 41, 47.

in virtue of that power implanted in his nature by which he was able to beget them." Through this presence of the whole race in Adam when he sinned, Augustine explains that little ones share in Adam's guilt, even though they were not yet living their own lives.

In sections 15-18 Augustine turns to a series of three objections drawn from Pelagius' *Exposition of Saint Paul's Letter to the Romans*. The first objection argues that, if God forgives personal sins, he surely will not hold one person guilty of the sin of another, i.e., of Adam's sin. Augustine answers that what was once Adam's sin becomes ours when we are born. The second objection argues that baptized parents cannot pass on to their children the sin they no longer have. Along with complaints about the ignorance of those who ask such questions, Augustine appeals to a pair of analogies: in the first, the son of a circumcised father is born uncircumcised, and in the second, wheat grown from grains from which the chaff has been removed grows with chaff. Augustine says that, if he were arguing against people who rejected the necessity of baptism, he would use such arguments to show the need for baptism. But since the Pelagians with whom he is arguing grant the necessity of baptism, though not for the forgiveness of sins, he argues that even they must admit that the children of Christian parents are not born Christians. The third objection drawn from Pelagius argues that, if the soul of the newborn did not come from Adam by generation, it is unjust that the soul bears the sin of Adam. Augustine notes the wariness of the objector with regard to the difficult question of the soul's origin and replies with an equal wariness, challenging the objector to show the justice in a newly born child's suffering bodily pains and torment from demons. And finally, in sections 19-23, he offers a summary of the whole work and brings it to an end. He emphasizes the centrality of three passages from Paul, namely, Rom 5:12, 1 Cor 15:21-22, and 1 Cor 15:54-56, for showing that our being subject to bodily death is punishment for Adam's sin and that the sinfulness with which we are born is the inherited result of Adam's sin. Hence, even newly born infants need Christ's baptism for the forgiveness of sin, and there exists no human being—apart from Jesus Christ—who has been, is, or will be completely sinless.

The Pelagian Sources

In I, 34, 63, Augustine refers to "a brief memo" (*libellus brevissimus*) which contains the view that infants receive redemption from baptism, if not the remission of sin. Scholars generally agree that this "memo" is the document which Caelestius submitted in his own defense to the Council of Carthage in 411 or 412. Once Augustine cites almost verbatim the *Liber de fide* of Rufinus the Syrian,[24] who has been called the real founder of Pelagianism. F. Refoulé has also pointed out a series of verbal parallels between statements from this work by Rufinus and the positions to which Augustine replies in the first thirty-four chapters of Book One. By the time of the third book Augustine obviously had come upon Pelagius' *Expositions of the Letters of Saint Paul* which he cites frequently.

The Text and Translations

The text translated is that of C. F. Urba and J. Zycha in CSEL LX (Vienna 1913) 3-151. I have also at times adopted the emendations to the text suggested in the ALG edition. The work has been previously translated into English by P. Holmes in NPNF I/5 (New York 1887; repr. 1971) 15-78. In the present century it has also been translated into Spanish by V. Capánaga in BAC LXXIX (Madrid 1952) 200-439; into German by A. Fingerle in ALG I (Würzburg 1964) 54-301; and into Italian by I. Volpi in NBA XVII/1 (Rome 1981) 15-239.

---

24. See *The Punishment and Forgiveness of Sin and the Baptism of Little Ones* I, 18, 23.

Revisions II, 33(60)

An urgent concern also arose which forced me to write against the new Pelagian heresy. Earlier we were opposing it, when there was need, not in writing, but by sermons and conferences, as each of us was able and ought to have. After there had been sent to me from Carthage some questions of theirs which I was to resolve by written reply, I first wrote three books, the title of which is *The Punishment and Forgiveness of Sins.*

In them the discussion focused principally on the baptism of little ones on account of original sin and on the grace of God by which we are justified, that is, become righteous, even though in this life none so observe the commandments enjoining righteousness that they have no need to say in prayer for their own sins, *Forgive us our debts* (Mt 7:12). With views opposed to all of these, they founded a new heresy.

In these books I still thought that I should not mention their names, in the hope that they could be more easily corrected. In fact, in the third book, which is a letter, but included among my books on account of the two to which I thought it should be joined, I mentioned the name of Pelagius with a certain amount of praise, because many spoke well of his life, and I refuted those statements which he did not set forth in his writings in his own name, but which he presented as what others were saying. Yet later, when he had become a heretic, he defended these ideas with a strong streak of stubbornness. On account of such statements, however, Caelestius, his disciple, had deserved excommunication before the episcopal tribunal at Carthage, at which I myself was not present.

In the second book, I said in a certain place that it will be granted to some people in the end that they will not feel death because of a swift transformation, for I was saving room for a more careful examination of this matter. After all, either they will not die, or by passing from this life to death and from death to eternal life by a very swift transformation, as in the blink of an eye, they will not feel death.

This work begins: "We are pressed on all sides by the worries and the concerns we have."

The Punishment and Forgiveness of Sins and the Baptism of Little Ones

Book One

1, 1. We are pressed on all sides by the worries and concerns we have over sinners who abandon God's law,[1] though we count them as punishments for our own sins. I did not, nonetheless, want to be and, to tell you the truth, I could not endure to be any longer indebted to your zeal, Marcellinus, for it makes you very dear and pleasing to us. We are, in fact, compelled either by the love which makes us one in the immutable One, as we are being transformed for the better, or by the fear of offending God in you. For he has given you this desire, and by serving you I serve him who has given it to you. I am so compelled, as I said, so pulled and drawn, to solve as best I can, given my modest abilities, these questions which you posed, when you wrote to me.[2] In fact, this matter has presently driven all the others from my mind, until I produce something that proves that I have been of service, if not sufficiently, at least obediently, to your good desire and that of those who are worried about these matters.

If Adam Had Not Sinned, He Would Not Have Died

2, 2. These people say, "Adam was created so that he would die, even if he did not sin, not as a punishment for his guilt, but by the necessity of his nature."[3] They, of course, try to take the words of

---

1. Aside from the continued concerns of a pastor for his flock, Augustine surely had in mind the controversy with the Donatists. Though a conference of the Catholic and Donatist bishops held at Carthage in June of 411 under the supervision of Marcellinus and at the order of the emperor, Honorius, ended with a victory for the Catholics and with stronger legal measures against the Donatists, the schism continued to occupy Augustine's time and energy.

2. The letter from the tribune, Marcellinus, to Augustine is lost. At the beginning of the third book Augustine summarizes the points about which Marcellinus had asked him to reply, namely, that, even if Adam had not sinned, he would have died, that as a result of his sin nothing was passed on to his descendants by generation, especially on account of infant baptism, and that there have been, are, and will be human beings who have no sin at all.

3. Caelestius, the disciple of Pelagius, who was in fact in Carthage at this time, taught this doctrine. See *The Deeds of Pelagius* 2, 23 and *The Grace of Christ and Original Sin* II, 2, 12, for Caelestius' thesis.

the law, *On the day that you eat, you will surely die* (Gn 2:17), as referring not to the death of the body but to the death of the soul that occurs when one sins. The Lord indicated that unbelievers had died the latter sort of death, when he said of them, *Let the dead bury their dead* (Mt 8:22; Lk 9:60). What reply, then, will they make, when they read that, by way of rebuke and condemnation, God also said to the first man after his sin, *You are earth, and you will return to earth* (Gn 3:19). After all, it was obviously his body that was earth, not his soul, and it was by the death of that body that he was going to return to earth. He was surely earth in terms of his body and bore the animal body in which he was created; nonetheless, if he had not sinned, he was going to be changed into a spiritual body and pass into the state of incorruption,[4] which is promised to believers and saints, without suffering the punishment of death. We not only experience in ourselves a desire for that state, but we also acknowledge it because of the apostle's statement. He says, *In this body we groan, longing to be clothed with our heavenly dwelling, if only we might be found clothed and not naked. We who are in this present dwelling groan in our distress, for we do not want to be stripped, but to be clothed over with immortality and incorruption, so that what is mortal might be swallowed up by life.* (2 Cor 5:2-4) Accordingly, if Adam had not sinned, he was not going to be stripped of his body; rather, he was going to be clothed over with immortality and incorruption so that what was mortal might be swallowed up by life, that is, that he might pass from an animal to a spiritual body.

3, 3. There was, after all, no need to fear that, if he lived here in his animal body for a long time, he would be burdened by old age and gradually come to die by growing old. God kept the clothes and shoes of the Israelites from wearing out during those many years.[5] Why should we be surprised if the power of the same God would grant to the first man, if he remained obedient, that, though he had an animal, that is, a mortal body, he would enjoy in it a state that would allow him to live for many years without any diminishment? And then at the time God willed, he would pass from mortality to immortality

---

4. See 1 Cor 15:44. Augustine uses Paul's terms, "animal" and "spiritual," to describe the mortal and the risen body. He holds that Adam's body was mortal, though, if he had not sinned, he would not have died, since bodily death is, according to scripture, a punishment for Adam's sin. The Pelagian position claimed that death was natural and would have occurred whether or not Adam sinned.

5. See Dt 29:5.

without death intervening. For, just as this flesh which we now have is not invulnerable, simply because it need not suffer a wound, so Adam's flesh was not immortal, simply because it did not need to die. In my opinion, those who were taken from this life without dying were granted such a condition while still in their animal and mortal body. Henoch and Elijah, after all, have not during their long life deteriorated by reason of old age, and I do not believe that they were transformed into that spiritual sort of body that we are promised at the resurrection, because the Lord was the first to have that sort of body. Perhaps they have no need of these earthly foods which restore us as they are consumed, but from the time that they were carried off, they continue to live and are satisfied, just as Elijah was during those forty days when he survived on a cup of water and a piece of bread.[6] Or, if there was need of earthly foods, these men are perhaps fed in paradise, as Adam was before he deserved to leave there because of his sin. As I see it, he received refreshment against deterioration from the fruits of the trees and stability against old age from the tree of life.[7]

Adam's Sin Is the Cause of Bodily Death

4, 4. I do not know how the words, *You are earth, and you will return to earth* (Gn 3:19), can be interpreted except as referring to bodily death. But besides this passage which the Lord spoke while imposing punishment, there are other testimonies which make it perfectly clear that the human race earned death, not merely death of the spirit, but also death of the body. The apostle says to the Romans, *But if Christ is in you, the body is indeed dead on account of sin, but the spirit is life on account of righteousness. If then the Spirit of him who raised Jesus from the dead dwells in you, he who raised Christ Jesus from the dead will bring to life even your mortal bodies through his Spirit dwelling in you.* (Rom 8:10-11) I do not believe that so clear and so obvious a statement needs anyone to interpret it; it merely needs someone to read it. He says, *The body is dead*, not on account of its earthly frailness, because it has been made from the dust of the earth, but *on account of sin* (Rom 8:10). What more could we want? He was most careful not to say "mortal" but "dead."

---

6. See 1 K 19:6-8.
7. See Gn 2:9.

5, 5. After all, the body could be mortal without being destined to die, before being changed into that state of incorruption which is promised to the saints at the resurrection.[8] So too, this body of ours can be, so to speak, liable to illness,[9] without being destined to become ill. After all, is there anyone who has flesh that cannot become ill, even if in a particular case the person dies before becoming ill? So too, that body was already mortal. The transformation into the state of eternal incorruption would have swallowed up this mortality, if righteousness, that is, obedience, had lasted in the man, but the mortal body experienced death only on account of sin. That transformation in the future resurrection is not only not going to have any death, for death came about on account of sin; it is also not going to have any mortality of the sort that the animal body had before sin. Hence, Paul did not say, "He who raised Christ Jesus from the dead will also bring to life your dead bodies," though he had said "dead body" above. Rather, he said, *He will bring to life even your mortal bodies* (Rom 8:11). That is, he will not only make them to be not dead, but not mortal, when the animal body rises as spiritual and this mortal body dons immortality and what is mortal is swallowed up by life.[10]

6, 6. I am amazed that anyone wants something clearer than this clear statement. But perhaps one should listen to what they say in opposition to this clarity. They say that we should understand that the body is dead in the sense in which scripture said, *Put to death your earthly members* (Col 3:5). In this sense, however, the body is put to death on account of righteousness, not on account of sin. After all, we put to death our earthly members in order that we might act with righteousness. Or, they might suppose that *on account of sin* was added, so that we might understand not "because sin was committed" but "so that sin might not be committed." Then scripture would mean that the body is dead so that we do not commit sin. But then what did he mean, when after adding, *but the spirit is life*, he went on to say, *on account of righteousness*? (Rom 8:10) After all, it was enough to mention the life of the spirit, so that one would understand here, too, "so that sin might not be committed." Then we would understand that each of them has a single purpose: both the body is dead and the spirit

---

8. See 1 Cor 15:52.

9. Augustine here coins the term *aegrotabile*, which literally would be something like "sicken-able."

10. See 1 Cor 15:44.53-54.

is life so that sin might not be committed. Thus, even if he wanted merely to say, *on account of righteousness*, that is, on account of acting righteously, each of them could refer to this. That is, both the body is dead and the spirit is life on account of acting righteously. But he in fact said that the body is dead on account of sin and the spirit is life on account of righteousness, assigning different recompenses to different things: to the body of death the punishment of sin, but to the life of the spirit the reward of righteousness. Hence, it is beyond doubt that *the spirit is life on account of righteousness* (Rom 8:10), that is, as a reward of righteousness. How else then ought we or can we understand the words, *the body is dead on account of sin*, except as the punishment of sin, unless, of course, we are going to try to twist and distort the perfectly clear meaning of scripture as we choose? The following words also throw light on this. In describing the grace of the present era, he said that the body was indeed dead on account of sin, because the punishment of sin, that is, the necessity of death, remains in the body which has not yet been renewed by the resurrection. But the spirit is life on account of righteousness, because, although we are still burdened *by the body of this death* (Rom 7:24), we already breathe more easily *in terms of the interior human being* (Rom 7:22), since we have begun to be renewed in the righteousness that comes from faith. Nonetheless, so that human ignorance might not be without any hope for the resurrection of the body, he says that the very body which he called dead in the present world on account of the punishment of sin will be brought to life in the world to come on account of the reward of righteousness. And it will be brought to life, not merely in the sense that it will become alive after being dead, but in the sense that it will become immortal after being mortal.

7, 7. I am afraid that an explanation may simply obscure something that is quite clear, but pay attention to the light found in the apostle's words. He says, *But if Christ is in you, the body is indeed dead on account of sin, but the spirit is life on account of righteousness* (Rom 8:10). He said this so that people would not suppose that they had little or no benefit from the grace of Christ, since they were necessarily going to die a bodily death. They ought, of course, to be aware that the body still bears the punishment of sin, because it is subject to death, but that the spirit has already begun to live because of the righteousness of faith, even though the spirit itself had in human beings been extinguished by a sort of death stemming from unbelief. Therefore, you should not, he said, suppose that you have received a small gift by reason of the fact that Christ is present in you, because your spirit lives on account of righteousness in the body that is dead on account of sin. Nor should you give up hope for the life of the body either. *For if the Spirit of him who raised Christ from the dead dwells in you, he who raised Christ from the dead will bring to life even your mortal bodies through his Spirit dwelling in you* (Rom 8:11). Why does the fog of bickering continue to block out such a strong light? The Apostle cries out, *The body is indeed dead* in you *on account of sin,* but even your mortal bodies will be brought to life on account of righteousness. On account of that righteousness the spirit is already life, and all of this will be brought about through the grace of Christ, that is, *through his Spirit dwelling in you.* And yet they cry out against this! Paul even says how it will come about that life will transform death into life by putting it to death. *Therefore, my brothers and sisters,* he says, *we owe nothing to the flesh so that we should live according to the flesh. For if you live according to the flesh, you will die, but if you put to death the works of the flesh, you will live.* (Rom 8:12-13) What else does this mean but this: If you live according to death, the whole of you will die, but if you put death to death by living according to life, the whole of you will live?

8, 8. Similarly, how can the words, *Death came through a man, and the resurrection of the dead came through a man* (1 Cor 15:21), be understood otherwise than as referring to the death of the body? For he said this when he was speaking of the resurrection of the body, and he was arguing for it with great insistence and passion. He said, *Death came through a man, and the resurrection of the dead came through a man. For, just as all die in Adam, so too all will be brought to life in Christ.* (1 Cor 15:21-22) What was he saying to the Corinthians in this passage but what he also said to the Romans: *Through one man sin entered the world, and through sin death* (Rom 5:12). Those people want to interpret this death, not as the death of the body, but as the death of the soul. They imply that he was saying something else to the Corinthians by the words, *Death came through a man.* Here they certainly may not understand the death of the soul, because the passage is dealing with the resurrection of the body, which is just the opposite of the death of the body. He mentioned there only the death that came about through a man and not sin, precisely because he was not dealing with the righteousness which is the opposite of sin, but with the resurrection of the body, which is the opposite of the death of the body.

All Share in Adam's Sin by Generation, Not Merely by Imitation

9, 9. You have intimated in your letter that they try to twist into a new and different meaning the testimony of the Apostle in which he says, *Through one man sin entered the world, and through sin death* (Rom 5:12). But you have not mentioned what meaning it was that they derived from those words. As far as I have been able to find out from others, this is what they think of that text: The death mentioned in that passage is not the death of the body which they deny Adam merited by sinning; it is, rather, the death of the soul which occurs in the sin itself, and this sin passed from the first man to other human beings not by propagation, but by imitation.[11] Hence, they refuse to believe that in the case of little children original sin[12] is removed by baptism, since they maintain that there is no sin at all in newborns. But if the Apostle had wanted to mention the sin that entered this world, not by propagation, but by imitation, he would have called its originator not Adam, but the devil. Of the latter scripture says, *The devil is a sinner from the beginning* (1 Jn 3:8). We also read regarding him in the Book of Wisdom, *By the hatred of the devil, death entered the world* (Wis 2:24). After all, this death came to human beings from the devil, not because they came from him by propagation, but because they imitated him. Hence, it immediately added, *Those who belong to him imitate him* (Wis 2:25). Thus, when the Apostle mentioned the sin and the death that passed from the one to all by propagation, he made their originator the one from whom the propagation of the human race took its beginning.

10. Of course, all those who through disobedience transgress God's commandment imitate Adam. But it is one thing for him to be an example for those who sin by their will; it is something else for him to be the origin of those born with sin. After all, the saints also imitate Christ in the pursuit of righteousness. For this reason the same Apostle says, *Be imitators of me, as I am of Christ* (1 Cor

---

11. Augustine offers no source for this Pelagian thesis.
12. Here Augustine uses for the first time the term "original sin" to refer to the sin of Adam which has been passed on to the whole human race.

11:1). But apart from this imitation his grace also produces within us our enlightenment and justification by that action of which this same preacher says, *Neither the one who plants nor the one who waters is anything; it is, rather, God who gives the increase* (1 Cor 3:7). By this grace he brings into his body even infants who are baptized, and they are certainly unable to imitate him. Apart from his having offered himself as an example of righteousness to those who imitate him, the one in whom all are brought to life[13] also gives to the faithful the most hidden grace of his Spirit, and he also bestows this grace upon little ones in a hidden manner. So too, apart from his being an example for those to imitate who willingly transgress the commandment of the Lord, the one in whom all die also infects in himself with the hidden corruption of his carnal concupiscence all those who are to come from his lineage. For this reason and none other, the apostle says, *Through one man sin entered the world, and through sin death, and thus it*[14] *was passed on to all human beings in whom all have sinned*[15] (Rom 5:12). If I were to state this, these people would resist and cry out that I speak incorrectly and think incorrectly. They would, of course, find in these words no other meaning, regardless of who spoke them, than the meaning which they refuse to find in the apostle. But because they are the words of one to whose authority and teaching they yield, they accuse us of being slow to understand, while they try to twist a perfectly clear statement into some other meaning. Paul said, *Through one man sin entered the world, and through sin death.* This means by propagation, not by imitation; otherwise, he would say, "through the devil." He is speaking of the first man, who was called Adam, a point which no one doubts. *And thus,* he says, *it was passed on to all human beings.*

---

13. See 1 Cor 15:22.
14. The Vulgate has: *Et ita in omnes homines mors pertransiit*: "and thus death was passed on to all human beings." Augustine's Old Latin version omits the subject, *mors* (death), following some ancient Greek manuscripts. Thus, according to Augustine's text, it is sin that was passed on to all human beings. Hence, Augustine believed he had in this text a clear scriptural proof of the transmission of Adam's sin to all his descendants.
15. The relative pronoun in the clause, "in whom all have sinned," *in quo omnes peccaverunt*, is subsequently in this passage interpreted as referring both to the sin and to Adam. In English one has to choose between "in which" and "in whom." Neither interpretation is accepted by modern exegetes. In his *Answer to Two Letters of the Pelagians* IV, 4, 7, Augustine came to see that the relative pronoun could not have referred to sin, since the Greek word is feminine, while the relative pronoun is masculine.

10, 11. Then, note the carefulness, the propriety, the clarity with which the next clause is stated, *in whom all have sinned* (Rom 5:12). For if you have here understood the sin that entered the world through the one man in which sin all have sinned, it is certainly clear that personal sins of each person by which they alone sinned are distinct from this one in which all have sinned, when all were that one man. But if you have understood not the sin but that one man in which one man all have sinned, what could be clearer than that clear statement? For we read that those who believe in him are justified in Christ on account of the hidden communication and inspiration of spiritual grace,[16] which makes whoever clings to the Lord one spirit.[17] Even though his saints also imitate him,[18] I would like to find something of the sort said of those who have imitated his saints. Has anyone been said to have been justified in Paul or in Peter or in anyone else of those who have an eminent authority among the people of God? We are, of course, said to be blessed in Abraham in accord with God's words to him, *All the nations will be blessed in you* (Gn 12:3; Gal 3:8), on account of Christ who is called his offspring according to the flesh.[19] This is stated more clearly, when the same idea is put as follows, *All the nations will be blessed in your offspring* (Gn 22:18). I doubt that anyone will find it stated in the words of God that someone has sinned or sins in the devil, though all sinful and evil persons imitate him. But with regard to the words of the Apostle concerning the first man, *in whom all have sinned*, they continue to resist the propagation of sin and raise in objection the idea of imitation to cloud over the issue.

The Roles of Sin, the Law, and Grace

12. Notice the words that follow. For, after he said, *In whom all have sinned*, he went on to say, *For before the law there was sin in the world* (Rom 5:12-13), that is, because the law could not take away sin. After all, it came so that sin might be more abundant.[20] This holds both for the natural law under which each person with the use

---

16. See Rom 4:5; Gal 2:16.
17. See 1 Cor 6:17.
18. The editors of the CSEL edition linked the preceding clause with the last sentence. I have followed the emendation of the German translators in ALG in linking it with the following sentence.
19. See Gal 3:16.
20. See Rom 5:20.

of reason begins to add personal sins to original sin and for the written law given to the people by Moses. *For, if a law had been given which could give life, righteousness would, of course, come from the law. But scripture has enclosed all things under sin so that on the basis of faith in Jesus Christ the promise might be given to those who believe* (Gal 3:21-22). *But sin was not imputed, when the law did not exist* (Rom 5:13). What does *was not imputed* mean but that in their ignorance people did not know it was sin? Nor did the Lord God regard sin as non-existent, since scripture says, *Those who have sinned apart from the law will perish apart from the law* (Rom 2:12).

11, 13. He said, *But death reigned from Adam until Moses* (Rom 5:14), that is, from the first man right up to the law which God promulgated, since even the law could not remove the reign of death. For the reign of death means that the guilt of sin lords it over human beings in such a way that it does not permit them to attain eternal life, which is true life, but draws them to the second death,[21] which is eternal punishment. In any human being this reign of death was destroyed only by the grace of the savior. That grace was also at work in the saints of old, all those who, before Christ came in the flesh,[22] had recourse to his helping grace, not to the letter of the law, which can only command, but cannot provide help. This was hidden in the Old Testament in accord with God's perfectly just plan for the different times, but it has now been revealed in the New Testament. Hence, *death reigned from Adam until Moses* in all human beings who were not helped by the grace of Christ so that the reign of death in them was destroyed. Hence, it reigned in those *who did not sin in the likeness of the transgression of Adam*, that is, in those who did not sin, as he did, by their own personal will, but contracted original sin from him *who is the pattern of what was to come* (Rom 5:14). For in him the pattern of condemnation was established for his posterity yet to come who would come into being from his lineage. Thus, from the one man all are born destined for a condemnation,[23] from which only the grace of Christ sets them free.[24] I know, of course, that most Latin manuscripts read as follows: *Death reigned from Adam until Moses in those who sinned in the likeness of the transgression*

21. See Rv 20:14.
22. See 1 Jn 4:2; 2 Jn 7.
23. See Rom 5:18.
24. See Ti 2:11.

of Adam (Rom 5:14), and those who have this reading give it the same interpretation. They understand that those who sinned in Adam sinned in the likeness of his transgression so that they are born like him. Just as they are human beings from a human being, so they are sinners from a sinner, persons destined to die from one destined to die, and persons under condemnation from one under condemnation. But all or nearly all the Greek manuscripts from which the Latin translation was made have the text as I first cited it.

14. He goes on to say, *But the gift is not completely like the sin. For, if on account of the sin of one man many have died, the grace of God and the gift in the grace of the one man, Jesus Christ, has been much more abundant for many* (Rom 5:15). It has not been abundant for many more, that is, for many more human beings, for there are not more who are justified than are condemned, but it has been much more abundant. Adam fathered many who were guilty as a result of his single transgression, but Christ destroyed and forgave by his grace even those sins human beings committed by their own will and added to the original sin in which they were born. He stated this more clearly in what follows.

12, 15. Consider more carefully his statement that on account of the sin of one man many have died. After all, why did he say *on account of the sin of one man* and not rather "on account of their own personal sins," if we are to understand this passage as speaking of imitation and not propagation? Notice what follows: *But the gift does not come in the same way as sin came through the one who sinned. For judgment starts from the one and leads to condemnation, but grace starts from many sins and leads to justification.* (Rom 5:16) Let them state at this point how imitation has any place in these words. He says, *From the one and leads to condemnation.* From one what, if not from one sin? He explains this when he adds, *But grace starts from many sins and leads to justification.* Why then does judgment start from one sin and lead to condemnation, but grace starts from many sins and leads to justification? If there is no original sin, would it not be true not only that grace leads human beings to justification from many sins, but also that judgment leads them to condemnation from many sins? After all, grace pardons many sins, and judgment also condemns many sins. If people are brought to condemnation as the result of the one sin, because all the sins which are condemned were committed in imitation of that one sin, there is the same basis for understanding that they are led to justification from the one sin, since all the sins which are forgiven for those who have been justified have been committed in imitation of that one sin. Yet that is not, of course, what the apostle understood when he said, *Judgment starts from the one sin and leads to condemnation, but grace starts from many sins and leads to justification.* But let us understand the Apostle and see that he said that judgment starts from the one sin and leads to condemnation, because it would be sufficient reason for condemnation, even if there were only original sin in human beings. The condemnation of those who added personal sins to original sin is more severe, and more severe for individuals in proportion to the gravity of each person's sins. But that sin alone which was contracted from our origin separates people from the kingdom of God. Even little ones who have died cannot enter that kingdom without having received the grace of Christ, as this person admits. But that sin also keeps them from salvation and eternal life. For there is no salvation and eternal life apart from the kingdom of God into which one is brought only by the community of Christ.

13, 16. Thus we have contracted from Adam, in whom we have all sinned, not all our sins, but only original sin. But from Christ, in whom we are all justified, we obtain the forgiveness not only of that original sin, but also of the other sins which we have added to it. Therefore, *the gift does not come in the same way as the sin came through the one who sinned* (Rom 5:16). For judgment coming from the one sin, that is, from original sin, if it is not forgiven, can lead to condemnation, but grace starting from many sins that have been forgiven, that is, not from original sin alone, but also from all the rest, leads to our justification.

17. *For, if on account of the sin of one man, death reigned through the one man, far more shall those who receive an abundance of grace and righteousness reign in life through the one Jesus Christ* (Rom 5:17). Why did death reign through the one man on account of the sin of the one man, if not because, in that one man in whom all sinned, they were held bound by the chain of death, even if they did not add personal sins? Otherwise, death did not reign on account of the sin of the one man through the one man, but on account of the many sins of many through each one who sins. For, if the rest are dead on account of the sin of another, precisely because they followed after and imitated the one who preceded them in sinning, then Adam has for a much better reason died on account of the sin of another. For the devil sinned before him in order to persuade him to sin as well. But Adam did not try to persuade those

who imitate him, and many who are called his imitators have either not heard or do not believe that he existed or committed such a sin. How much more correctly, as I said, would the Apostle have made the devil the originator! Then he could say that sin and death passed from him to all,[25] if he had wanted in this passage to teach not propagation, but imitation. It makes much more sense, after all, to call Adam the imitator of the devil who persuaded him to sin, if we can call people imitators of Adam, though Adam did not try to persuade them to sin or was utterly unknown to them. What does the phrase mean, *who receive an abundance of grace and righteousness*? It surely means that they were given the grace of forgiveness, not only for that sin in which all sinned, but also for those sins which they added to it, and that human beings received such righteousness that, though Adam consented to sin when he was enticed, they do not yield even when pressured. Since the kingdom of death draws many more into eternal punishments, what can it mean that they will *reign in life* far more, unless we understand that both passages are speaking of those who have passed from Adam to Christ, that is, from death to life? For they will reign without end in eternal life far more than death reigned in them for a time and with an end.

18. *And so, just as the sin of one led to the condemnation of all human beings, so the justification of one leads to righteousness of life for all human beings* (Rom 5:18). If we have imitation in mind, this sin of the one will be that of the devil. But since it is clear that the text is speaking of Adam and not of the devil, we are left to understand not imitation, but the propagation of sin.

14. For his words concerning Christ, *the justification of one*, express this better than if he said, "the righteousness of one man." He is speaking, of course, of that justification by which Christ makes the sinner righteous.[26] He does not set this justification before us as an example to be imitated; rather, it is something that he alone can do. The Apostle could, of course, say with correctness, *Be imitators of me, as I am of Christ* (1 Cor 11:1), but he would never say, "Be justified by me, as I am justified by Christ." There can be, there are, and there have been many righteous human beings for us to imitate, but Christ alone is righteous and justifies others.[27] For this reason scripture says, *For those who believe in him who justifies sinners, faith is*

---

25. See Rom 5:12.
26. See Rom 4:5.
27. See Rom 3:26.

credited to them as righteousness (Rom 4:5). If anyone, then, would dare to say, "I justify you," it would follow that this person should also say, "Believe in me." But no holy person could say that except *the Holy of Holies* (Dn 9:24). He says, *Believe in God, and believe in me* (Jn 14:1), so that, because he makes the sinner righteous, the faith of one who believes in him may be counted as righteousness.

15, 19. For, if imitation alone produces sinners through Adam, why does imitation alone not produce righteous persons through Christ? For *just as the sin of one led to the condemnation of all human beings, so the justification of one leads to righteousness of life for all human beings.* In accord with such a view, those two individuals should not have been Adam and Christ, but Adam and Abel. For many sinners have gone before us in this life, and those who sinned at a later time imitated them. These people, nonetheless, would have it that scripture mentioned Adam alone as the one in whom all would sin[28] by imitation, because he was the first human being to sin. On such grounds Abel ought, likewise, to be called the one in whom human beings are justified by imitation, since he was the first human being to live righteously. Or, if it was on account of the crucial moment of time marking the beginning of the New Testament that Christ was proposed as the head of those who are righteous by imitation, then Judas, who betrayed him, ought to be made the head of sinners. On the other hand, if Christ is the one in whom all are justified, because it is not merely imitation of him that makes persons righteous, but the grace that gives them rebirth through the Spirit, then Adam is the one *in whom all have sinned*, because it is not merely imitation of him that makes them sinners, but the penalty that gives them birth through the flesh. This is the reason that it says "all" both times. For not all who are born through Adam are reborn through Christ. But the statement is correct, because, as no one is born in the flesh except through Adam, so no one is born spiritually except through Christ. For if some human beings could be born in the flesh other than through Adam and some could be born[29] in the Spirit other than through Christ, "all" would not have a clear meaning in either this passage or the other one. Scripture later refers to the same "all" as

---

28. The CSEL text has *peccaverunt* (sinned) in accord with a minority of the older mss. I have followed ALG.
29. The CSEL text has *regenerari* (reborn) in accord with a minority of the older mss. I have followed the reading in ALG.

"many." In a particular case, a few can be all there are. But many are born in the flesh and many are born spiritually, though not as many are born spiritually as are born in the flesh. Nonetheless, as birth in the flesh includes all human beings, so spiritual birth includes all the righteous. For, as no one is a human being apart from birth in the flesh, so no one is a righteous human being apart from spiritual birth, and there are many in each group. *For just as by the disobedience of one man many were made sinners, so by the obedience of one man many will be made righteous* (Rom 5:19).

20. *But the law entered in so that sin might abound* (Rom 5:20). This was the sin that human beings added to original sin by their own will, not through Adam. This sin is also taken away and healed through Christ. For, *where sin abounded, there grace was even more abundant so that, as the reign of sin led to death*—including the sin which human beings did not inherit from Adam, but added by their own will—*so the reign of grace might through righteousness lead to eternal life* (Rom 5:20-21). But there is no righteousness apart from Christ, as there are some sins apart from Adam. Hence, after he said, *as the reign of sin led to death*, he did not at this point add, "through one man" or "through Adam," because it said above that, when the law entered in, sin abounded, and this sin is not that which comes from our origin, but that which comes from our own will. But when he said, *so the reign of grace might through righteousness lead to eternal life*, he added, *through Jesus Christ, our Lord* (Rom 5:21). For only original sin is contracted through birth in the flesh, but through rebirth in the Spirit we have forgiveness, not only of original sin, but also of voluntary sins.

Little Ones Who Die without Baptism Are Condemned

16, 21. Accordingly, one can correctly say that little ones who leave the body without baptism will be under the mildest condemnation of all. But one who preaches that they will not be under any condemnation misleads others very much and is himself very mistaken. For the apostle says, *Judgment starts from one sin and leads to condemnation,* and a little later, *The sin of one led to the condemnation of all human beings.* Hence, even though Adam's body was animal and mortal, when he sinned by not obeying God, his body lost the grace which made it completely obedient to his soul. At that moment there came into being that animal arousal of which human beings are rightly ashamed and which caused Adam to be embarrassed by his nakedness. At that moment too, they contracted a disease from an unexpected and deadly corruption. The result for them was that they lost the stability of the life in which they were created and began to move toward death through ages subject to change. Thus, although they lived for many years after this, they began to die on that day on which they received the law of death by which they began to age and grow old. For time does not stand still even for a moment. Rather, it unceasingly slips past, and everything involved in constant change gradually moves, not toward an end that perfects, but toward one that destroys. In that sense God's words, *On the day that you eat, you will surely die* (Gn 2:17), have been fulfilled. As a result, then, of this disobedience of the flesh, as a result of this law of sin and death, all who are born in the flesh need to be reborn spiritually, not only so that they may come to the kingdom of heaven, but also so that they may be set free from the condemnation of sin. Thus they are born in the flesh, subject to both the sin and the death of the first human being, and they are reborn in baptism, joined to both the righteousness and the eternal life of the second. In accord with this, we find in Sirach, *The beginning of sin was brought about by the woman, and we all die by reason of her* (Sir 25:24). Whether it says "by the woman" or "by Adam," both belong to the first human being, because, as we know, the woman came from the man and both had one flesh. Hence, we have the words of scripture, *And they will be two in one flesh. Therefore, they are no longer two*, says the Lord, *but one flesh* (Mt 19:5-6).

17, 22. Hence, it will not take a great effort to refute those who say that little ones are baptized in order to be forgiven the personal sin which they have contracted in this life, not the sin which they inherited from Adam. For, when they reflect a little by themselves, without wanting to be argumentative, on how absurd and unworthy of discussion their claim really is, they will immediately change their position. But if they refuse to do so, we should not place so little hope in the human mind that we fear that they will persuade anyone of their position. These people were themselves driven to say this, unless I am mistaken, as a result of some other position they previously adopted. That is, they must admit that sins are forgiven in baptism, and they refuse to admit that there is a sin derived from Adam which they concede that the little ones are forgiven. Hence, they are forced to accuse infants of sin, as if they are safer in accusing infants by the very fact that the accused cannot speak in their own defense. But, as I said, let us leave these people aside. After all, words or proofs are superfluous for establishing the innocence of infants in the life which they live in their own persons immediately after their birth, if the human mind fails to recognize it, unaided by the help of any argument.

18, 23. On the other hand, those people do raise a question and seem to offer something worth consideration and discussion. They claim that little ones newly born from their mothers' wombs do not receive baptism on account of the forgiveness of sin, but so that, through spiritual procreation, they might be created in Christ and become partakers of the kingdom of heaven, and in the same way children and *heirs of God, coheirs with Christ* (Rom 8:17).[30] But when we ask them whether those who are not baptized and have not become coheirs with Christ and sharers in the kingdom of heaven will have at least the benefit of eternal salvation at the resurrection of the dead, they find themselves in serious difficulties and see no way out. After all, will any Christian tolerate hearing that someone can attain eternal salvation without being reborn in Christ? He willed that this rebirth be brought about by baptism back when he was about to institute such a sacrament for those who needed to be reborn for the hope of eternal life. For this reason the Apostle said, *Not as a result of the works of righteousness which we performed, but in accord with his mercy, he saved us through the bath of rebirth* (Ti 3:5). He stated that this salvation is a matter of hope, while we live this life, when he said, *For we are saved in hope. But hope that is seen is not hope; after all, why should one hope for what one already sees? But if we hope for what we do not see, we look forward to it with patience.* (Rom 8:24-25) Who then would dare to claim that little ones can attain eternal salvation without this rebirth, as if Christ did not die for them? After all, *Christ died for sinners* (Rom 5:6). But, if they are not held by any bond of sinfulness stemming from their origin, how did Christ, who died for sinners, die for these infants who obviously

---

30. This passage comes close to being a direct quotation from Rufinus the Syrian's *Profession of Faith* (*Libellus de fide*) 40: "Infants, therefore, do not receive baptism on account of sins, but so that through spiritual procreation, they might be created in Christ and become partakers of the heavenly kingdom, as blessed Paul teaches in this way: *If one is in Christ, one is a new creature* (1 Cor 3:17), and again, *But if sons and heirs, heirs of God, coheirs with Christ* (Rom 8:17).

have done nothing sinful in their own lives? If they are not afflicted by the disease of original sin, why do those caring for[31] them bring them out of a holy fear to Christ the physician, that is, to receive the sacrament of eternal salvation? Why are they not told in church, "Take these innocents away; *it is not those who are in good health who need a physician, but those who are sick* (Mt 9:12); Christ did not come *to call the righteous, but sinners*" (Lk 5:32)? No one ever said, no one ever says, and no one ever will say something as false and contrived as that in the Church of Christ!

19, 24. No one should think[32] that little ones should be brought to baptism, because, just as they are not sinners, so they are not righteous. Why, given that opinion, do some mention that the Lord praised the goodness of this age, when he said, *Let the little ones come to me, for to such belongs the kingdom of heaven* (Mt 19:14)? For if he said this, not on account of the likeness to humility, since humility makes people little, but on account of the praiseworthy life of children, they are, then, righteous as well. After all, one could not be correct otherwise in saying, *To such belongs the kingdom of heaven* (Mt 19:14), since it can only belong to the righteous. But perhaps it is not wrong to say that the Lord praised the life of little ones, when he said that the kingdom of heaven belongs to them, because the interpretation is correct that found a likeness of humility in that young age. On the other hand, perhaps one should maintain the interpretation I mentioned, that little ones should be baptized, because, as they are not sinners, so they are not righteous. But after he said, *I have not come to call the righteous*, as if he received the reply, "Whom then have you come to call?" he immediately added, *but sinners to repentance* (Lk 5:32). And thus, just as he did not come to call them if they are righteous, so he did not come to call them if they are not sinners, for he said, *I have not come to call the righteous, but sinners*. Accordingly, they seem to rush, not only pointlessly, but also wrongly, to his baptism, though he does not call them. Heaven forbid that we hold such a view! The physician, then, calls them; he is not needed by those who are in good health, but by those who are sick, and he has come, not to call the righteous, but sinners, to

---

31. The manuscripts have *currentium* (those running); the CSEL editors have plausibly suggested *curantium* (those caring for).
32. Though the editors of the ALG text suggest *Ac si quis existimet* (And if anyone thinks), I have followed PL and CSEL, which read: *Ac ne quis existimet.*

repentance. And since they are not yet held guilty of any sins from their own lives, the illness stemming from their origin is healed in them by the grace of him who saves them through the bath of rebirth.

25. Someone will say, "How, then, are they called to repentance? Can such little ones repent of anything?" To this we answer: If they should not be called repentant, because they do not yet have a mind capable of repentance, they should not be called believers, because they likewise do not yet have a mind capable of believing. But if they are correctly called believers, because they in some sense profess the faith by the words of their parents,[33] why should we not also first regard them as repentant, since we see that they renounce the devil and this world by the words of these same parents? All of this takes place in hope by the power of the sacrament and of the divine grace which Christ has given to the Church. Moreover, is there anyone who does not know that, if baptized infants, upon coming to the age of reason, do not believe and do not refrain from illicit desires, they derive no benefit from what they received as children? If, nonetheless, they depart from this life, after receiving baptism, the guilt to which they were held subject by reason of their origin has been removed, and they will be made perfect in that light of the truth. While remaining unchangeable for eternity, that light enlightens those who have been made righteous by the presence of the Creator. For sins alone produce the separation between human beings and God, and they are removed by the grace of him through whom we are reconciled, when he *makes the sinner righteous* (Rom 4:5).

There Is No Eternal Life apart from the Kingdom of God

20, 26. These people stand in awe of the statement of the Lord, *Unless one has been born again, one will not see the kingdom of God* (Jn 3:3). When he explained it, he said, *Unless one has been reborn of water and the Spirit, one will not enter the kingdom of heaven* (Jn 3:5). Hence, they try to ascribe salvation and eternal life to unbaptized little ones as a recompense for their innocence. But, by a novel and strange hypothesis, they try to exclude them from the kingdom of heaven, because they were not baptized, as if there could

---

33. Augustine uses the term *gestantium* (those who bear them). The editors of the ALG text suggest that the term includes those to whom we refer as "godparents" or "sponsors."

be the eternal salvation of eternal life apart from the inheritance of Christ, apart from the kingdom of heaven. They do, of course, have a place in which to take refuge and hide, because the Lord did not say, *Unless one has been reborn of water and the Spirit,* one will not have life, but said, *one will not enter the kingdom of heaven.* For if he had said the former, no doubt could arise on this point. Let the doubt, then, be removed; let us, I say, listen to the Lord, not to the suspicions and conjectures of mortals. Let us listen to the Lord, I say, as he speaks, not about the sacrament of the holy bath, but of the sacrament of his holy table which no one approaches properly unless he is baptized. The Lord says, *Unless you eat my flesh and drink my blood, you will not have life in you* (Jn 6:54). What more are we looking for? What answer can anyone make to this, unless stubbornness turns its feisty muscles against the firmness of the clear truth?[34]

27. Or will anyone dare to say that this statement does not hold for little ones and that they can have life in themselves without sharing in this body and blood? For he did not say, "Unless one has eaten," as he said regarding baptism, *Unless one has been reborn*; rather, he said, *Unless you eat,* as if he were addressing those who were able to hear and understand him, something that little ones, of course, cannot do. But one who says this fails to notice this point: Unless the statement includes all people so that, without the body and blood of the Son of Man, they cannot have life, adults would have no reason to be concerned about it. After all, if you consider not the intent but the words of the speaker, it can seem that they were addressed only to those people to whom the Lord was then speaking, since he did not say, "Unless one has eaten," but *Unless you eat.* What happens to his statement in the same passage, where he says, *The bread which I shall give is my flesh for the life of the world* (Jn 6:52)? In accord with this statement, then, we see that this sacrament includes us as well, who did not yet exist at the time when he was saying these words. For we cannot say that we do not belong to the world for the life of which Christ gave his flesh. Who is going to doubt that the term "world" refers to human beings who come into this world by birth? For, in another passage, he said, *The children of this world are born and beget children* (Lk 20:34). Accordingly, his flesh, which was given for

---

34. The strength of Augustine's argument rests upon the fact that at his time infants received the Eucharist at baptism, a practice that is still found in some Eastern Churches.

the life of the world, was also given for the life of the little ones, and if they have not eaten the flesh of the Son of Man, they will not have life either.

28. For this reason we also have the statement, *The Father loves the Son and has placed all things in his hand. One who believes in the Son has eternal life, but one who does not believe in the Son will not have life. Rather, the anger of God remains over him.* (Jn 3:35-36) In which of these classes, then, are we to put infants? Among those who believe in the Son, or among those who do not believe in him? "In neither of them," someone will say, "because they cannot as yet believe, and they should not be counted as unbelievers." That is not what the rule of the Church indicates, for it includes baptized infants among the faithful. Moreover, if those who are baptized are counted among the faithful on account of the power and the celebration of this great sacrament, although they do not in their heart and on their lips do what belief and profession imply,[35] then those who lack the sacrament should be regarded as among those who do not believe in the Son. Hence, if they leave the body without this grace, they will meet with what scripture says: They will not see life. Rather, the anger of God remains over them. And, since it is clear that they do not have personal sins, what is the reason for this, if they are not held subject to original sin?

21, 29. It was correct not to say, "*The anger of God* will come over him, but *remains over him.*" This is the anger by which we are all under the power of sin; the Apostle says of it, *For we were once by nature children of anger, just as the others* (Eph 2:3). From this anger nothing sets us free except *the grace of God through Jesus Christ, our Lord* (Rom 7:25). Why this grace comes to one person and does not come to another can have a hidden but not an unjust cause. *Is there injustice in God? Heaven forbid!* (Rom 9:14) But we must first bend our necks before the authorities of the holy scriptures so that through faith each of us may come to understanding. Scripture did not, after all, say without a reason, *Your judgments are like a great abyss* (Ps 36:7). As if he were gasping at the depth of this abyss, the apostle cried out, *O the depth of the riches of the wisdom and knowledge of God!* (Rom 11:33) He has prefaced this with a statement of amazing depth, when he said, *For God has enclosed all in unbelief so that he might have mercy upon all* (Rom

---

35. See Rom 10:10.

11:32). As if struck with horror at this depth, he says, *O the depth of the riches of the wisdom and knowledge of God! How inscrutable are his judgments and unsearchable his ways! Who has known the mind of the Lord? Or who has been his counselor? Who first gave something to him so that he will be repaid? For all things are from him and through him and in him. To him be glory forever and ever. Amen.* (Rom 11:33-36) Thus we have a very limited mind for investigating the righteousness of God's judgments, for investigating his gratuitous grace. This grace is not unjust despite the lack of previous merits; it does not disturb us so much when it is offered to the unworthy as when it is denied to others who are equally unworthy.

30. For these people think it unjust that little ones who leave the body without the grace of Christ are deprived not only of the kingdom of God, into which they admit that they cannot enter unless they are reborn by baptism, but also of eternal life and salvation. They ask how it can be just that one person is set free from original sinfulness and another is not, though both share the same condition. Let them respond in terms of their own view how it is just that baptism is offered again and again to one person so that he enters the kingdom of God and is not offered to another, though the case of each of them is on a par. They are disturbed over the reason why from these two, though both were equally sinners in terms of their origin, the one to whom baptism is granted is freed from this bond and the other to whom this grace is not granted is not freed. Why, then, are they not equally disturbed that, from two who are innocent in terms of their origin, one received baptism and can enter the kingdom of God and another did not receive it and cannot approach the kingdom of God? In each case we, of course, come back to that exclamation, *O the depth of the riches!* (Rom 11:33) Why from among the baptized little ones is one of them taken *so that evil would not change its mind* (Wis 4:11) and another lives on to be evil? Would not both enter the kingdom of heaven, if both were taken? And yet there is no injustice in God.[36] Why? Who is not troubled? Who is not forced to exclaim at such a great depth,[37] when some little ones are afflicted by an unclean spirit,[38] and others suffer nothing of the sort, when some,

36. See Rom 9:14.
37. See Rom 11:33.
38. See Lk 6:18.

like Jeremiah, are made holy in the wombs of their mothers,[39] though, if there is original sin, all are equally guilty and, if there is not, they are equally innocent? What is the source of this great diversity, if it is not that his judgments are inscrutable and his ways unsearchable.

The Rejection of the Preexistence of Souls

22, 31. Or are we perhaps supposed to hold that exploded and rejected theory that souls first sin in their heavenly dwelling and gradually and slowly come down to bodies corresponding to their merits and suffer more or less bodily afflictions for the life they previously lived? Holy scripture clearly contradicts this opinion and says, while commending grace, *They were not yet born and had done nothing either good or bad, but in order that God's plan might remain in accord with his choice, scripture said that the older would serve the younger, not because of any works, but because of the one who calls* (Rom 9:11-12). Those who hold this position do not, nonetheless, escape the difficulty of this question; rather, they are trapped by it and are stuck there. And, just as we are, they are forced to exclaim, *O the depth!* Why does it happen that some who are from youth on quite modest, talented, and temperate, who to a large extent conquer sexual desires, hate greed, and detest luxury, and who develop into persons much inclined toward and suited for the other virtues, live, nonetheless, in a place where the grace of Christ cannot be preached to them? *For how will they call upon him in whom they have not believed? Or how will they believe in him of whom they have not heard? And how will they hear of him without someone to preach?* (Rom 10:14) Yet other persons who are slow of wit, given to sexual desires, buried deep in crimes and wrongdoing, are so guided by providence that they hear the word, believe, are baptized and then taken by death—or, if they are kept in this life, live in a praiseworthy manner. Where have these two different kinds attained such diverse merits—I do not mean so that the latter believe, while the former do not believe, which comes from the individual will, but so that the latter hear what they believe while the former do not hear, for this does not fall within the individual's power? Where, I ask, have they attained such diverse merits? If they lived another

39. See Jer 1:5.

life in heaven, so that in accord with their actions they are driven
or fall to earth and are held in bodily containers suited to the life
they previously lived, we must believe that the former lived a better
life prior to this mortal body, since they merited not to be weighed
down by it very much. Thus they had fine talents and were driven by
milder desires of the body, which they could easily overcome. Yet
they did not merit that grace be preached to them, though it alone
could set them free from the destruction of the second death.[40] But
the other, in accord with worse merits, as they suppose, became attached to heavier bodies. And, for this reason, they were dull of heart
and were overcome by the allurements of the flesh with its burning
desire. Moreover, by a life of great sinfulnesss, they added on earth
worse sins to those previous sins by which they merited to come here.
Nonetheless, they either heard on the cross, *Today you will be with me
in paradise* (Lk 23:43), or they attached themselves to some apostle
and, transformed by his preaching, were saved by the bath of rebirth,[41]
so that, where sin abounded, grace might be even more abundant.[42]
I simply cannot see what answer those people might make; in their
desire to defend the righteousness of God by human conjectures and
in ignorance of the depth of his grace, they have composed myths
lacking any probability.

32. Many things can be said about the marvelous vocations of human beings which we have read about or encountered ourselves. These
destroy the opinion of those who believe that the souls of human beings
lived lives of their own prior to these bodies of theirs so that by those
lives they came to these bodies in accord with their different merits to
meet with different experiences, either good or bad, in this life. But my
concern to bring this work to a close does not allow me to delay any longer on them. Yet I will not pass over one remarkable point among many
which I have found. These people suppose that souls are weighed down
more or less by earthly bodies as a result of the merits of the previous
life they lived in the heavenly regions prior to this body. In accord with
this opinion of theirs, who would not claim that those people sinned
more wickedly and more seriously before this life who merited to lose
the light of their mind to such an extent that they are born with a mind

40. See Rv 20:6.
41. See Ti 3:5.
42. See Rom 5:20.

close to that of animals? I do not mean those who are slow-witted—for we use that expression of others—but those who are so stupid that, even with hair curled to incite laughter, they provide the intelligent with the entertainment of their simplemindedness. The common people call them by the term "morons" (*moriones*), which is derived from a Greek word. One of these persons, nonetheless, was so Christian that, though he patiently endured all the injuries done to him with an amazing simplicity, he could not tolerate an injury done to the name of Christ or, in his own person, to the religion in which he had been instructed. He would not cease pursuing with stones blasphemers—intelligent people, of course—who said these things to provoke him, and on such grounds he would not spare even his masters. I think that such persons were predestined and created so that those who can might understand that the grace of God and the Spirit, who *breathes where he wills* (Jn 3:8), do not on this account leave out any kind of natural talent from the children of mercy. And, likewise, they do not leave out any kind of natural talent from the children of hell. And so, *Let him who boasts boast in the Lord* (1 Cor 1:31; 2 Cor 10:17). But what response can those people make who claim that for the merits of a previous life individual souls receive different earthly bodies by which some are weighed down more and others less? They claim that human natural abilities differ in accord with the same merits so that some are more quick-witted and others more dull and that divine grace is bestowed to set human beings free in accord with the merits of the previous life. How are they going to ascribe to that man both a terrible previous life so that he was born simpleminded and so meritorious a life that he was, for that reason, preferred to many very clever people in terms of the grace of Christ?

33. Let us then yield and give our assent to the authority of holy scripture which can neither deceive nor be deceived. And as we believe that those who have not yet been born have done nothing good or bad to make a difference in their merits,[43] so we have not the slightest doubt that all are subject to the sin which entered the world through one human being and has been passed on to all human beings.[44] And from that sin only *the grace of God through our Lord Jesus Christ* (Rom 7:25) sets us free.

---

43. See Rom 9:11-12.
44. See Rom 5:12.

Christ Is the Physician, Savior, and Redeemer for Little Ones

23. It is not those who are in good health, but those who are sick, who need his coming as a physician, for he did not come to call the righteous, but sinners.[45] Only one who has been born again of water and the Spirit[46] will enter into his kingdom, and no one will attain eternal life apart from his kingdom, since those who have not eaten his flesh[47] and do not believe in the Son will not have life,[48] but the anger of God remains over them. Only the physician who came, not on account of those who are in good health, but on account of those who are sick, only *the Lamb of God who takes away the sins of the world* (Jn 1:29), only the savior of whom the human race was told, *Today a savior has been born for you* (Lk 2:11), only the redeemer whose blood wipes away our transgression, sets people free from this sin, from this illness, from this anger of God. Even if they do not have personal sin because of their age, those who carry with them original sin are by nature children of this anger.[49] Who will be so bold as to say that Christ is not the savior and redeemer of infants? But from what does he save them, if they do not have the disease of original sin? From what does he redeem them, if they were not sold through their origin from the first human being to the power of sin?[50] In our judgment, then, apart from Christ's baptism, no eternal salvation is promised to infants except that promised by the divine scripture, which we should prefer to all the powers of the human mind.

24, 34. Punic Christians are perfectly correct in calling baptism "salvation" and in calling the sacrament of Christ's body "life." What is their basis for doing this, if it is not, as I believe, the ancient and apostolic tradition? That tradition leads them to regard it as a mark of the Church of Christ that without baptism and participation in the Lord's table no human being can attain either to the kingdom of God or to salvation and eternal life. After all, scripture also testifies to this as we have stated above. For what else do those who call baptism "salvation" hold but what scripture says, *He saved us through the bath of rebirth* (Ti 3:5), and what Peter said, *So too, baptism has saved*

---

45. See Lk 5:31-32.
46. See Jn 3:5.
47. See Jn 6:54.
48. See Jn 3:36.
49. See Eph 2:3.
50. See Rom 7:14.

you in a similar manner (1 Pt 3:21)? What else do those who call the sacrament of the Lord's table "life" say but what scripture says: *I am the living bread who have come down from heaven*, and *The bread which I shall give is my flesh for the life of the world*, and *Unless you eat the flesh of the Son of Man and drink his blood, you will not have life in you* (Jn 6:51-52.54)? If, then, as so many and such great testimonies of God agree, no one can hope for either salvation or eternal life without baptism and the body and blood of the Lord, there is no reason to promise either salvation or eternal life to little ones without these. Moreover, if only sins separate one from salvation and eternal life, it is the guilt of sin that is removed in little ones by these sacraments. Scripture says that none are free from that guilt, *even if their lives last but a single day* (Jb 14:5 LXX).[51] For this reason there is also this passage in the psalms, *For I was conceived in iniquity, and amid sins my mother fed me in the womb* (Ps 51:7). Either this was said in the name of human beings in general, or, if David said this of himself personally, he was certainly not born out of wedlock, but from a lawful marriage. Hence, we should have no doubt that Christ's blood was also shed for infants who were to be baptized. Before that blood was shed, it was given and entrusted to us in the sacrament, so that he said, *This is my blood which will be poured out for many for the forgiveness of sins* (Mt 26:28). But these people deny that those human beings are set free, who they do not want to admit are under the power of sin. After all, from what are they set free, if they are not held captive in slavery to sin?

35. He said, *I came into the world as light so that everyone who believes in me does not remain in darkness* (Jn 12:46). By saying this, what did he show but that everyone who does not believe in him remains in darkness and, by believing, one brings it about that one does not remain in darkness. What do we take this darkness to be but sins? But however else one may interpret this darkness, one who does not believe in Christ will in any case remain in it, and it is certainly a punishment, not like the darkness of night that is needed to provide rest for animals.

25. Hence, if little ones do not enter the number of believers by the sacrament which God established for this purpose, they will certainly remain in this darkness.

---

51. Augustine's Old Latin version follows the Septuagint, but the Hebrew text has no reference to the newly born.

36. And yet some believe that they are enlightened as soon as they are born.[52] They interpret in that sense the text of scripture, *He was the true light that enlightens every human being that comes into this world* (Jn 1:9). But if that is so, it is very puzzling why, after having been enlightened by the only Son, since he was the Word in the beginning, God with God,[53] they are not admitted to the kingdom of God and are not *heirs of God, coheirs with Christ* (Rom 8:17). For even those who hold this view admit that they receive this latter only through baptism. Hence, if those who have been already enlightened are not fit to attain the kingdom of God, they ought at least to be happy to receive the baptism by which they become fit for it. And yet we see them resist it with much weeping, and we pay no attention to their ignorance at that age so that we perform for them, even as they resist, the sacraments which we know are of benefit to them. After all, why does the apostle say, *Do not have minds like children* (1 Cor 14:20), if their minds have already been enlightened by that true light which is the Word of God?[54]

37. Hence, the gospel says, *He was the true light that enlightens every human being that comes into this world* (Jn 1:9). The gospel said this, because no human being is enlightened save by that light of the truth which is God. Thus none should suppose that they are enlightened so as to learn by someone from whom they hear something. And I do not mean merely if one happens to have as a teacher some great human being, but not even if one happens to have an angel. The word of truth is externally presented by means of a bodily voice; nonetheless, *neither the one who plants nor the one who waters is anything; it is, rather, God who gives the increase* (1 Cor 3:7). A human being hears someone speaking, either another human being or an angel, but in order that he might see and know that what is said is true, that light which remains eternally, but also *shines in the darkness* (Jn 1:5), is interiorly shed upon the mind. But as this sun in our sky is not seen by the blind, though it in a sense clothes them with its rays, so this light is not grasped by the darkness of folly.[55]

---

52. The text of ALG, contrary to the Maurists and the CSEL edition, takes the previous text which is a dependent clause in the Latin with the following sentences. I have made it into an independent sentence.
53. See Jn 1:1.
54. See Jn 1:9.
55. See Jn 1:5.

38. But why, after saying, *that enlightens every human being*, did it add, *that comes into this world* (Jn 1:9)? This is the source of the idea that he enlightens the minds of little ones as they are born right at their bodily emergence from the womb of their mother. Although the Greek reads so that one could understand the light itself as coming into this world, nonetheless, if we must interpret it as speaking of every human being coming into this world, I see two possibilities. Either, like many things we find in the scriptures, the phrase was simply stated in such a way that, even if it is removed, nothing is lost from the meaning. Or, if we are to believe that this was added to indicate some distinction, it may have been said to differentiate spiritual enlightenment from this bodily enlightenment which brings light to the eyes of the body, whether by the sources of light in the heavens or by any fire. In that case, it spoke of the interior human being coming into this world, since the exterior human being is bodily, as this world is. Then it would equivalently say: He enlightens every human being coming into a body, in accord with the words of scripture, *I obtained a good soul, and I have entered a body that has been defiled* (Wis 8:19-20). If, then, that he *enlightens every human being that comes into this world* was stated in order to make some distinction, it was either stated in such a way as to convey that he enlightens every interior human being. For, when the interior human being becomes truly wise, it is enlightened only by that which is the true light. Or it intended to call reason itself enlightenment, like the creation of the interior eye. For it is from reason that the human soul is called rational, and this reason remains hidden, as if at rest and asleep, but still present and implanted, as it were, in little ones. In this case one should not oppose the idea that the enlightenment took place when the soul was created, and it is not absurd to understand that this occurs when a human being comes into the world. Even though this eye has been created, it must, nonetheless, remain in darkness, if it does not believe in him who said, *I came into the world as light so that everyone who believes in me does not remain in darkness* (Jn 12:46). Mother Church has no doubt that this takes place in little ones by means of the sacrament; she offers them her maternal heart and lips so that they may be initiated in the sacred mysteries, because they cannot yet believe unto righteousness with their own heart or make profession with their own lips unto salvation.[56] And no believer

---

56. See Rom 10:10.

hesitates to call them believers—a name which is, of course, taken from believing. And yet, it was not these little ones themselves, but others who made the responses for them during the sacred rites.

The Scriptures Speak of Christ as the Redeemer

26, 39. It would take far too long, if we were to discuss the individual testimonies from scripture in this way. Hence, I think it is more appropriate to bring together the many testimonies that come to mind or that seem sufficient, which make it clear that the Lord Jesus Christ came in the flesh[57] and that he took the form of the servant and became obedient unto the death of the cross for no other reason than the following.[58] It was so that, by the dispensation of his grace filled with mercy, he might bring to life all those of whom he is the head, when they have become members inserted in his body. It was so that he might save them, set them free, redeem them, and enlighten them for the attainment of the kingdom of heaven. For they were previously situated in the death, illness, slavery, captivity, and darkness of sins, under the power of the devil, the prince of sinners. It was so that he would be the mediator between God and human beings.[59] And, it was so that, after he had by the peace of his grace brought to an end the hostilities stemming from our godlessness, we would through him be reconciled to God,[60] having been rescued for eternal life from the eternal death that awaited us. Once this point has been made abundantly clear, it will follow that those who do not need life, salvation, liberation, redemption, and enlightenment cannot belong to this dispensation of Christ's grace which was brought about by this lowliness he assumed. And since this dispensation of grace includes the baptism by which they are buried with Christ[61] so that they might be incorporated in him as his members, that is, as believers in him, they certainly do not need baptism, since they have no need of that benefit of forgiveness and reconciliation which comes about through the mediator. In any case, those people grant that little ones should be baptized, because they cannot stand up against the authority, which

---

57. See 1 Jn 4:2; 2 Jn 7.
58. See Phil 2:7-8.
59. See 1 Tm 2:5.
60. See Rom 4:10.
61. See Rom 6:4; Col 2:12.

was, beyond any doubt, given to the whole Church through the Lord and the apostles. They should, then, also grant that they need these benefits of the mediator so that, washed by the sacrament and love of the faithful and thus incorporated into Christ's body, which is the Church, they might be reconciled to God. Thus they would become in him living, saved, set free, redeemed, and enlightened. From what, save from the death, failings, guilt, subjection, and darkness of sins? And since they committed at that age no sins in their own life, there remains only original sin.

27, 40. This argument will be stronger when I have mustered the many testimonies I promised. We have already cited above, *I have not come to call the righteous, but sinners.* So too, when he entered the home of Zacchaeus, he said, *Today salvation has come to this house, since this man too is a son of Abraham. For the Son of Man has come to seek and to save that which was lost.* (Lk 19:9-10) He made the same point concerning the lost sheep which was sought after and found, while the ninety-nine were left untended; he made the same point concerning the one coin out of ten that was lost.[62] For this reason, *It was necessary*, as he said, *that repentance and the forgiveness of sins be preached in his name to all nations, beginning from Jerusalem* (Lk 24:46.47). At the end of his gospel, Mark testifies that the Lord said, *Go into the whole world and preach the good news to every creature. Those who believe and are baptized will be saved, but those who do not believe will be condemned.* (Mk 16:15-16) But who does not know that for infants to believe means to be baptized and not to believe means not to be baptized? Although we have already quoted some passages from the Gospel of John, note these as well. John the Baptist said of him, *Behold the Lamb of God; behold the one who takes away the sins of the world* (Jn 1:29). And the Lord says of himself, *Those who belong to my sheep hear my voice; I know them, and they follow me. And I give them eternal life, and they will not perish for eternity.* (Jn 10:27-28) Since little ones begin to belong to his sheep only by baptism, they will certainly perish, if they do not receive it, for they will not have the eternal life which he will give to his sheep. So too, in another passage he says, *I am the way, the truth, and the life; no one comes to the Father except through me* (Jn 14:6).

---

62. See Lk 15:3-10.

41. The apostles accepted this teaching. Observe the great solemnity with which they proclaim it. In his first letter, Peter says, *Blessed be God, the Father of our Lord, Jesus Christ. In accord with the abundance of his mercy, he gave us a new birth for the hope of eternal life through the resurrection of Jesus Christ, for an immortal, untarnished, unfading inheritance that is kept in heaven for you who live in God's truth through faith in the salvation that has been made ready to be revealed in the last times.* (1 Pt 1:3-5) A little later he says, *May you be found destined for the praise and glory of Jesus Christ whom you once did not know, but in whom you now believe, though you do not see him. But when you see him, you will rejoice with an indescribable joy and with a glorious joy as you receive the inheritance of the faith, the salvation of your souls.* (1 Pt 1:7-9) So too, in another passage, he says, *But you are a chosen race, a royal priesthood, a holy nation, a people he has adopted, so that you may announce the great deeds of him who has called you out of darkness into his wonderful light* (1 Pt 2:9). Again he says, *Christ has suffered for our sins, a righteous man for the unrighteous, so that he might bring us to God* (1 Pt 3:18). Likewise, when he recalled the eight persons saved in Noah's ark, he said, *So too, baptism has saved you in a similar manner* (1 Pt 3:21). Little ones are strangers to this salvation and light, and they will remain lost and in darkness, unless they are joined by adoption to the people of God and hold onto Christ, who suffered as a righteous man for the unrighteous so that he might bring them to God.

42. From the Letter of John the following passages came to mind which I thought indispensable for this question. He says, *But if we walk in the light, as he too is in the light, we have fellowship with one another, and the blood of Jesus, his Son, will cleanse us from every sin* (1 Jn 1:7). Likewise, he says in another passage, *If we accept human testimony, the testimony of God is greater, because this is the testimony of God. Those who believe in the Son of God have the testimony in themselves. Those who do not believe God make him a liar, because they do not believe in the testimony which he gave concerning his Son. And this testimony is that God has given us eternal life, and this life is in his Son. Those who have the Son have life; those who do not have the Son do not have life.* (1 Jn 5:9-12) Little ones, then, will not only not have the kingdom of heaven, but will not even have life, if they do not have the Son, and they can have him only through baptism. So too, in another passage, he says, *The*

Son of God has been revealed for this purpose, that he might destroy the works of the devil (1 Jn 3:8). Little ones, then, will not share in the grace of the revelation of the Son of God, if he does not destroy the works of the devil in them.

43. Now pay attention to the testimonies of the apostle Paul on this topic. They are, of course, more numerous, since he wrote more letters and took greater care to emphasize the grace of God in confrontation with those who were proud of their works. Not knowing God's righteousness and wanting to establish their own righteousness, they were not subject to the righteousness of God.[63] In the Letter to the Romans, he says, *The righteousness of God for all who believe; for there is no distinction. For all have sinned and lack the glory of God. They have been gratuitously justified by his grace through the redemption that is in Christ Jesus. God made him a sacrifice of atonement in his own blood through faith in order to show his righteousness with respect to the sins committed earlier during the time of God's patience in order that he might reveal his righteousness in the present time, that he is righteous and justifies those who have faith in Jesus.* (Rom 3:22-26) In another passage he also says, *For one who works, recompense is not counted as a grace, but as something owed. But for one who does not work, but believes in him who justifies sinners, faith is credited to him as righteousness. In that way David also declared blessed the person whom God accepts and to whom he grants righteousness without works: Blessed are they whose iniquities have been forgiven and whose sins have been covered over. Blessed are they to whom God has not imputed sin.* (Rom 4:4-8) So too, he says a little later, *Scripture did not say that faith was credited to him on his account alone, but on our account. For it will be credited to us who believe in him who raised up Christ Jesus, our Lord, from the dead. He was betrayed on account of our sins, and he rose on account of our justification.* (Rom 4:23-25) Shortly afterward, he says, *When we were still weak, Christ died for sinners at the proper time* (Rom 5:6). Elsewhere he says, *We know that the law is spiritual, but I am carnal, sold under the power of sin. I do not know what I do, for I do not do what I want; rather, I do what I hate. But if I do what I do not want, I agree that the law is good. Now it is not I who do this, but the sin that dwells in me.*

---

63. See Rom 10:3.

For I know that the good does not dwell in me, that is, in my flesh. I can will the good, but I cannot do it. I do not do the good that I want, but I do the evil that I do not want. But if I do what I do not want, then it is no longer I who do it, but the sin that dwells in me. I find it, then, to be a law that, when I want to do good, evil lies at hand for me. For I delight in the law of God in terms of the interior human being, but I see another law in my members that resists the law of my mind and holds me captive in the law of sin which lies in my members. Wretched man that I am! Who will set me free from the body of this death? The grace of God through Jesus Christ, our Lord. (Rom 7:14-25) Let those who can claim that human beings are not born in *the body of this death* so that they can also claim that they do not need the grace of God through Jesus Christ to be set free *from the body of this death.* A little later he says, *For what the law could not do inasmuch as it was weakened by the flesh God has done; he sent his own Son in the likeness of sinful flesh, and by sin he condemned sin in the flesh* (Rom 8:3). Let them claim, if they dare, that Christ would have had to be born in the likeness of sinful flesh, if we were not born in sinful flesh.

44. Similarly, he writes to the Corinthians, *First of all, I handed on to you what I myself received, that Christ has died for our sins according to the scriptures* (1 Cor 15:3). So too, he says to the same Corinthians in his Second Letter, *The love of Christ compels us, for we believe that one has died for all. Hence, all have died, and he has died for all so that those who live might no longer live for themselves, but for him who has died for them and has risen. At present, then, we know no one in terms of the flesh, and if we did know Christ in terms of the flesh, we now no longer know him in that way. If, then, any are in Christ, they are a new creation; what is old has passed away; see, everything has been made new. But all this comes from God who has reconciled us to himself through Christ and has given us the ministry of reconciliation. How did he do that? God was in Christ reconciling the world to himself, not holding their sins against them and entrusting to us the message of reconciliation. We function, then, as ambassadors of Christ, and God speaks words of encouragement through us. On behalf of Christ we beg you to be reconciled to God. For him who did not know sin, he made sin on our behalf, so that in him we might be the righteousness of God. As your fellow workers, we beg you not to receive God's grace in vain. For he says, At a favorable*

moment I have heard you, and on the day of salvation I have helped
you. Look, this is the favorable moment, this is the day of salvation
(2 Cor 5:14-6:2). If little ones have no need for this reconciliation and
salvation, who is going to try to bring them to Christ's baptism? But if
they do, they are among the dead for whom Christ has died, and they
cannot receive reconciliation and salvation from him unless he does not
hold against them the sins that have been forgiven.

45. Likewise, he writes to the Galatians, *May grace and peace
be yours from God the Father and the Lord, Jesus Christ, who gave
himself up for our sins in order to remove us from this present evil
age* (Gal 1:3-4). And in another passage he says, *The law was given
for the sake of transgression until the offspring should come to whom
the promise pertains; it was decreed by angels through the hand
of a mediator. But a mediator implies more than one, and God is
one. Is the law, then, opposed to what God has promised? Heaven
forbid! For, if a law had been given which could give life, righteousness would, of course, come from the law. But scripture has enclosed
all things under sin so that on the basis of faith in Jesus Christ the
promise might be given to those who believe.* (Gal 3:19-22)

46. He also writes to the Ephesians, *You were dead because of
the transgressions and sins in which you once lived in accord with
the age of this world, in accord with the prince of the power of the
air, that spirit which is now at work in the children of disbelief. We
all once lived among them in the desires of our flesh, doing the will
of the flesh and of its inclinations, and we were by nature children of
anger, just like the others. But God who is rich in mercy, on account
of the great love with which he loved us, even when we were dead
by sins, brought us to life with Christ, by whose grace we have been
saved.* (Eph 2:1-5) Shortly afterward he says, *You have been saved
by grace through faith. This does not come from you; rather, it is
God's gift. It is not the result of works, so that no one may be filled
with pride. We are, after all, the result of his workmanship, created
in Christ Jesus for the good deeds which God prepared, so that we
might live our lives in them.* (Eph 2:8-10) A little later he says, *You
were then without Christ, separated from the community of Israel
and strangers to the covenants and the promise. You had no hope and
were without God in this world. But now in Christ Jesus you who
were once distant have become near in the blood of Christ. For he is
our peace; he has made the two one, removing the wall of stone, the*

hostility, dividing us. He has in his flesh rendered powerless the law with the decrees of its commandments so that he might, while bringing about peace, form in himself a new human being from the two and through the cross transform both of them into one body for God, slaying in himself the hostility. He came and proclaimed the good news of peace to you who were distant and the good news of peace to those who were near, for through him we both have access in the one Spirit to the Father. (Eph 2:12-18) Elsewhere he writes, *As the truth is present in Jesus, lay aside the old human being in accord with your former way of life. Be renewed, rather, in the spirit of your mind, and put on the new human being, the one who was created unto God in righteousness and holiness.* (Eph 4:21-24) And in another passage he says, *Do not sadden the Holy Spirit of God with whom you have been sealed for the day of redemption* (Eph 4:30).

47. He writes as follows to the Colossians, *Give thanks to the Father who makes us capable of sharing the heritage of the saints in the light. He has snatched us from the power of darkness and brought us into the kingdom of his beloved Son, in whom we have redemption through the forgiveness of sins.* (Col 1:12-14) Elsewhere he says, *You have been made full in him who is the head of every principality and power. For in him you have been circumcised by a circumcision that has not been made by hand through the removal of flesh from the body, but by the circumcision of Christ you were buried with him in baptism. In him you have also risen through faith in the action of God who raised him from the dead, and though you were dead in your sins and in your uncircumcised flesh, he brought you to life along with him. He forgave all our sins, and he wiped out the record of our debts that stood against us, removing it and fixing it to the cross. He stripped himself of the flesh and made a public spectacle of the principalities and powers, triumphing over them in himself.* (Col 2:10-15)

48. And to Timothy he wrote, *It is a message full of mercy and worthy of complete acceptance that Christ Jesus came into this world to save sinners. Of them I am the first. I have obtained mercy so that in me first of all Christ might display his complete patience for the instruction of those who are going to believe in him unto eternal life.* (1 Tm 1:15-16) Likewise he says, *For God is one; one too is the mediator between God and human beings, the man Christ Jesus, who gave himself up as redemption for all* (1 Tm 2:5-6). In his Second Letter to the same Timothy he says, *Do not, then, be ashamed of the testimony of our Lord or of*

me, *a prisoner on account of him. Rather, work with me for the gospel in accord with the power of God who is saving us and calling us with his holy vocation, not in accord with our deeds, but in accord with his plan and the grace which has been given to us in Christ Jesus before endless ages, but has now been revealed through the coming of our Lord, Jesus Christ. He has stripped death of its power and through the gospel has brought light to life and incorruption.* (2 Tm 1:8-10)

49. He also wrote to Titus, *Awaiting that blessed hope and the revelation of the great God and our savior, Jesus Christ, who gave himself for us that he might redeem us from all iniquity and cleanse us for himself as a people great in number and zealous for good works* (Ti 2:13-14). In another passage he said, *But when the kindness and mercy of the savior, our God, appeared, not because of the works of righteousness which we performed, but in accord with his mercy, he saved us through the bath of rebirth and renewal in the Holy Spirit, which he poured out in great richness upon us through Jesus Christ, our savior, so that, having been justified by his grace, we might become heirs in accord with the hope of eternal life* (Ti 3:4-7).

50. Some people regard the Letter to the Hebrews as uncertain. Yet I have read that some who hold views contrary to this position of ours concerning the baptism of little ones have wanted to use it as evidence for certain of their views. I myself am moved more by the authority of the eastern churches which includes it among the canonical books. Hence, one should note how many testimonies it contains in favor of our side. In its beginning we read, *Gradually and in many ways God spoke in former times to our forefathers through the prophets; finally, in the present time he has spoken to us through his Son, whom he made heir of all things, through whom he also made all ages. He is the reflection of his glory and the image of his substance; he also rules all things by his powerful word. He has brought about the purification from sins and has taken his seat at the right hand of the majesty on high.* (Heb 1:1-3) And shortly thereafter he said, *For if the message proclaimed by the angels had such force that every transgression and act of disobedience received its just recompense, how are we going to escape, if we disregard this great salvation?* (Heb 2:2-3) In another passage he says, *For this reason the children shared the same flesh and blood, and in a like fashion he shared in theirs so that he might through death destroy the one who had power over death, that is, the devil, and might set free those who were held in servitude to him*

through their whole life out of fear of death (Heb 2:14-15). A little later he says, *Hence, he had to be like his brothers in every respect so that he might be the merciful and trustworthy high priest in those things which have to do with winning God's forgiveness for the sins of the people* (Heb 2:17). Elsewhere he said, *Let us cling to our confession, for we do not have a priest who is unable to share our weaknesses with us. He has, in fact, experienced everything, just like us, apart from sin.* (Heb 4:14-15) And in another passage, he said, *He has an unsurpassable priesthood. Hence, he can bring about the salvation of those who come to God through him, for he lives forever to make intercession for them. It was fitting, after all, that we have a high priest of this sort: righteous, without malice, undefiled, removed from sinners, raised above the heavens, who does not have the daily need, as the high priests did, to offer sacrifice first for his own sins, then for the people. For he did this once for all when he offered himself.* (Heb 7:24-27) In another passage he said, *For Christ did not enter a sanctuary made by hand, which resembled the true one; rather, he entered heaven itself to appear on our behalf before the face of God. He did not offer himself many times, as the high priest enters the sanctuary once a year with the blood of another. Otherwise, he would have had to suffer many times from the creation of the world, but now he has appeared once at the end of the ages for the forgiveness of sin through his sacrifice. Just as it is determined for human beings that they die only once and, after that, face judgment, so Christ was offered once in order to bear the sins of many. He will appear a second time without sins for the salvation of those who await him.* (Heb 9:24-28)

51. The Revelation of John bears witness that these praises are offered to Christ by a new song: *You are worthy to receive the book and open its seals, because you have been slain and have in your blood redeemed us for God from every tribe and language and people and nation* (Rv 5:9).

52. So too, in the Acts of the Apostles the apostle Peter said that the Lord Jesus was the source of life, when he rebuked the Jews because they had killed him. He said, *But you placed a burden on and rejected the holy and righteous one, and you asked that a murderer be allowed to live and be released to you, for you slew the source of life* (Acts 3:14-15). In another passage he says, *This is the stone rejected by you, the builders; it has become the cornerstone. For there is no other name under heaven given to human beings by which we can be*

saved. (Acts 4:11-12) Elsewhere he said, *The God of the fathers*[64] *has raised up Jesus whom you killed by hanging him on the cross. God has exalted him in his glory as prince and savior in order to grant to Israel repentance and the forgiveness of sins in him.* (Acts 5:30-31) Similarly, he says in another passage, *All the prophets bear witness to this man that everyone who believes in him receives the forgiveness of sins through his hand* (Acts 10:43). In the same book the apostle Paul says, *Let it be known to you, brothers, that the forgiveness of sins is proclaimed to you through this man. You were not able to be justified by all the prescriptions in the law of Moses, but everyone who believes in him is justified.* (Acts 13:38-39)

53. Whose pride and rebellion against God's truth would not be repressed by this great mass of testimonies? Many others can be found, but we must not overlook the need to bring this work to a close. I considered it superfluous to introduce numerous scriptural proofs in support of my position from the books of the Old Testament as well. For what is hidden there under the veil of apparently earthly promises is revealed in the preaching of the New Testament. The Lord himself briefly pointed out and described the usefulness of the old books, when he said that those things which were written about him in the Law and the Prophets and the Psalms had to be fulfilled, namely, that *it was necessary that Christ suffer and rise from the dead on the third day and that repentance and the forgiveness of sins be preached in his name to all nations, beginning from Jerusalem* (Lk 24:46-47). And Peter said, as I mentioned just before, that all the prophets bear witness to this man that everyone who believes in him receives the forgiveness of sins through his hand.

54. It is, nonetheless, more appropriate to introduce a few testimonies from the Old Testament which may serve to supplement or rather to top off what we already have. In speaking through the prophet, the Lord himself says in the psalm, *For the saints who dwell in the land, he has made all my wishes for them marvelous* (Ps 16:3), not their merits, but my wishes. For what did they have but what comes next? *Their weaknesses have been multiplied* (Ps 16:4), over and above the mere fact that they were weak. For this reason *the law entered in so that sin might abound* (Rom 5:20). But what does he add? *Afterward, they made haste* (Ps 16:4). When their weaknesses

---

64. The CSEL edition adds *nostrorum* (our). I have followed the ALG version.

were multiplied, that is, as sin abounded, they more eagerly sought
for a physician so that, where sin abounded, grace might be even
more abundant.[65] Then he says, *I will not gather their assemblies for
bloody sacrifices* (Ps 16:4), for, when they formerly gathered in the
tent or in the temple, the many bloody sacrifices proved them to be
sinners rather than purified them. *I will not now*, he says, *gather their
assemblies for bloody sacrifices*, for the one bloody sacrifice has
been offered for many so that they may be truly purified by it. Next
he says, *Nor will I remember their names upon my lips*, inasmuch as
they are purified and renewed. For their names were once children
of the flesh,[66] children of the world,[67] children of anger,[68] children of
the devil,[69] the unclean, sinners, the wicked. But afterward they were
children of God,[70] the new name for the new human beings singing
the new song in the New Testament. Let us not be ungrateful to the
grace of God, whether we are little ones or grown-ups, whether we
are young or old. The voice of the whole Church cries out, *I have
wandered off like a lost sheep* (Ps 119:176); the voice of all Christ's
members cries out, *We have all gone astray like sheep, and he was
handed over for our sins* (Is 53:6). This whole passage in Isaiah is
prophetic. When Philip explained it to him, the eunuch of Queen
Candace believed in Christ.[71] See how often it stresses this point
and teaches this to those who are proud and contentious. *He was a
wounded man*, it says, *and one who knew how to endure weaknesses;
for this reason his face is turned away, bearing injuries and not much
appreciated. He bears our infirmities, and he is amid sorrows on our
behalf. And we thought that he was suffering sorrows, wounds, and
punishment. But he was wounded on account of our sins, and he
became weak on account of our iniquities. In him we learned of our
peace; by his bruises we were healed. We all went astray like sheep,
and the Lord handed him over for our sins. And he did not open his
mouth because he was mistreated. He was led off like a sheep for
sacrifice, and like a lamb before his shearer, he made not a sound;
thus he did not open his mouth. His judgment was removed in humil-*

---

65. See Rom 5:20.
66. See Rom 9:8.
67. See Lk 20:34.
68. See Eph 2:3.
69. 1 Jn 3:10.
70. See Rom 9:8.
71. See Acts 8:27-29.

ity. Who will tell of his generation? For his life will be taken from the earth. He was brought to death by the iniquities of my people. I will repay the evil on account of his burial and the rich on account of his death, because he did no wrong and had no deceit upon his lips. The Lord wishes to cleanse him of his wound. If you have given your life on account of your sins, you will see offspring with a long life. The Lord wishes to remove his soul from sorrows, to show him the light and form his mind, to justify the righteous one who serves the many well, and he will bear their sins. For this reason he will have many heirs and share the spoils of the mighty, because his soul was handed over to death and he was reckoned as one of the wicked. And he bore the sins of many and was handed over on account of their iniquities. (Is 53:3-12) Note too the words of that same prophet which the Lord himself declared were fulfilled in his own person, when he held the office of reader in the synagogue, *The Spirit of the Lord is upon me; for this reason he has anointed me to bring the good news to the humble. He has sent me so that the broken-hearted might find comfort, to announce forgiveness to prisoners and sight to the blind.* (Is 61:1; Lk 4:18-19) Without any exception, then, let all of us who want to belong to his body, enter through him into his sheepfold, and share in the endless life and salvation which he promises to his people, recognize him—let us, I say, recognize the one *who committed no sin and bore our sins in his body on the cross, that we might be separated from sin and live with righteousness; by his wounds we have been healed,*[72] though we were weak, *like straying sheep* (1 Pt 2:22.24-25).

28, 55. Since this is so, sound faith and sound doctrine have held that no one of those who have come to Christ through baptism has ever been excluded from the grace of the forgiveness of sins and that no one can possess eternal salvation apart from his kingdom. For this eternal salvation was made ready *to be revealed in the last times* (1 Pt 1:5), that is, at the resurrection of the dead, who do not belong to the eternal death, which is called the second death,[73] but to the eternal life which God, who does not lie, has promised to his holy and faithful ones. All those who have a share in this life will be brought to life only in Christ, just as they have all died in Adam.[74] For, just as all

---

72. The Maurists suspect an omission in the text at this point.
73. See Rv 2:11; 20:6.14.
74. See 1 Cor 15:22.

who are born according to the will of the flesh[75] die only in Adam, *in whom all have sinned* (Rom 5:12), so from these persons all who are reborn according to the will of the Spirit are brought to life only in Christ in whom they are all made righteous. For, just as by one man all were brought to condemnation, so by one man all are brought to justification.[76] And there is no middle ground so that one who is not with Christ must be with the devil. Hence, the Lord himself wished to remove from the hearts of those whose faith was incorrect this middle ground which they try to assign to unbaptized little ones. They would have them to be in eternal life as if by the merit of their innocence, but not with Christ in his kingdom, since they were not baptized. To silence them the Lord uttered this decisive statement, when he said, *One who is not with me is against me* (Mt 12:30). Take any little ones then. If they are already with Christ, why are they baptized? But if— as the truth maintains—they are baptized so that they may be with Christ, those who are not baptized are certainly not with Christ. And since they are not with Christ, they are against him. For we must not and cannot undermine or change his statement, which is quite clear. Why, then, are they against Christ, if not because of sin? It is not, after all, because of their body and soul, each of which is God's creation. Moreover, if it is because of sin, what sin is found in that age but that original and ancient sin? There is in fact one sinful flesh in which all are born for condemnation, and there is one flesh in the likeness of sinful flesh,[77] through which all are set free from condemnation. It did not say "all" there, as if we are to understand that all those who are born in sinful flesh are purified through the flesh like sinful flesh. *For not all have faith* (2 Thes 3:2). Rather, we are to understand that all who share in the birth from a carnal union are born in sinful flesh, and all those who share in the birth from a spiritual union are purified only through the flesh like sinful flesh. That is, the former are born through Adam for condemnation; the latter through Christ for justification. It is as if we were to say, "There is one midwife in this city who assists at the birth of all," and "There is one teacher of literature who teaches all." In the first case we can understand only all who are born, and in the latter only all who learn. Yet not all who are born learn literature, but it is clear to anyone that it was correct to say in the former case,

---

75. See Jn 1:13.
76. See Rom 5:18.
77. See Rom 8:3.

"She assists at the birth of all," since no one is born without her help. And in the latter case it is correct to say, "He teaches all," because apart from his instruction no one learns.

56. Having considered all the divine testimonies which I mentioned, either discussing each one individually or combining many of them together, or other similar testimonies which I have not mentioned, I find nothing but what the universal Church maintains. She must remain vigilant against all profane novelties.[78] The Church holds that all human beings are separated from God unless they are reconciled to God through Christ, the mediator, and that one can be separated from God only by the barrier of sins. Hence, one can only be reconciled to God through the forgiveness of sins through the one grace of the most merciful savior,[79] through the one sacrifice of the true priest. Thus all the children of the woman who believed the serpent,[80] so that she was corrupted by lust, are set free from the body of this death[81] only through the son of the Virgin who believed the angel so that she gave birth without sinful lust.[82]

Concupiscence and the Goodness of Marriage

29, 57. The goodness of marriage, then, does not consist in the heat of concupiscence, but in the permissible and morally good way of using that ardor appropriate to the propagation of offspring, not to satisfying lust. It is this will, not that pleasure which belongs to marriage.[83] The fact, then, that the ardor of concupiscence stirs disobediently in the members of the body of this death,[84] that it tries to cast down and draw the whole mind to itself, that it does not arise when the mind wants and does not quiet down when the mind wants, is due to the evil of sin with which every human being is born. But when it is restrained from foul and illicit acts and is permitted only for bringing forth in an orderly manner new members of the human race, it is the good of marriage through which a human being is born in a well-

---

78. See 1 Tm 6:20.
79. See Ti 2:11.
80. See Gn 3:1-6.
81. See Rom 7:24.
82. See Lk 1:26-38.
83. The Maurists bracket this sentence, since it is omitted in a majority of the oldest manuscripts, but it is retained in the CSEL edition.
84. See Rom 7:24.

ordered society. No one is reborn in Christ's body unless he is first born in the body of sin.[85] But as it is evil to use something good in an evil way, so it is good to use something evil in a good way. There are, then, these two, good and evil, and there are another two, good use and evil use; combined together, they make four distinct groups. One makes good use of a good in dedicating one's continence to God; one makes evil use of a good in dedicating one's continence to an idol. One makes an evil use of an evil in giving concupiscence free rein for adultery; one makes a good use of an evil in confining concupiscence to marriage. Just as, then, it is better to make good use of a good than to make good use of an evil, although each of them is good, so too, one who gives his virgin to marriage does something good and one who does not give her to marriage does something better.[86] I have discussed this question to the extent that the Lord permitted me, given my weak abilities, much more extensively and satisfactorily in two other books, one, *The Excellence of Marriage*, the other, *Holy Virginity*. Those people, then, who exalt the flesh and blood of the transgressor in opposition to the flesh and blood of the redeemer, should not defend the evil of concupiscence by means of the excellence of marriage; they should not be bolstered in the pride of their strange error on account of the children, because the Lord offered us an example of humility drawn from their young age. He alone was born without sin whom the Virgin conceived without union with a man, not by the concupiscence of the flesh, but by the obedience of her mind. She alone was able to bear the medicine for our wound who did not bring forth her holy child from the wound of sin.

Jesus' Teaching on the Necessity of Baptism

30, 58. Let us now examine more carefully, to the extent that the Lord provides his help, the very chapter of the gospel where it says, *Unless one has been reborn of water and the Spirit, one will not enter the kingdom of heaven* (Jn 3:5). If these people were not moved by that statement, they would not think that little ones should be baptized at all. They argue, "It does not say, *Unless one has been reborn of water and the Spirit*, one will not have salvation or eternal

---

85. See Rom 6:6.
86. See 1 Cor 7:38.

life. It only says, *one will not enter the kingdom of heaven.* Hence, little ones are to be baptized precisely in order that they too might be with Christ in the kingdom of heaven, where they will not be, if they have not been baptized. And yet, even if little ones die without baptism, they will have salvation and eternal life, since they are not bound by any sin."[87] First of all, though they say this, these people never explain how it is just that the image of God, though sinless, can be separated from the kingdom of God. Second, let us see whether the Lord Jesus, the one and only good teacher,[88] has not indicated and shown in this gospel reading that it is only by means of the forgiveness of sins that the baptized attain the kingdom of God. And yet, for those who understand correctly, the statements, *Unless one has been born again, one cannot see the kingdom of God* (Jn 3:3) and *Unless one has been reborn of water and the Spirit, one cannot enter the kingdom of God*, ought to be sufficient. After all, why are we born again if we do not need to be made new? From what do we need to be made new but from our old state? From what old state but that in which our old human being is crucified along with Christ so that the body of sin might lose its power?[89] Or why does the image of God not enter the kingdom of God, unless the impediment of sin prevents this? Nonetheless, as we have proposed, let us attentively and carefully examine, as best we can, the whole context of this gospel reading which pertains to the topic of this discussion.

59. *There was a man*, it says, *among the Pharisees, by the name of Nicodemus, a leader of the Jews. This man came to him at night and said to him, Rabbi, we know that you have come from God as a teacher, for no one can produce these signs which you produce, if God is not with him. Jesus answered and said to him, Truly, truly I tell you, unless one has been born again, one cannot see the kingdom of God. Nicodemus said to him, How can one be born when one is old? Can one re-enter one's mother's womb and be born? Jesus answered, Truly, truly I tell you, unless one has been reborn of water and the Spirit, one cannot enter the kingdom of God. That which is born of the flesh is flesh, and that which is born of the Spirit is spirit. Do not be surprised that I said to you, You must be born again. The Spirit breathes where he wills, and you hear the sound he makes. But*

---

87. This is probably a quotation from the Pelagian work mentioned below in I, 34, 64.
88. See Mt 23:10.
89. See Rom 6:5-6.

*you do not know from where he comes or where he goes. So it is with
everyone who has been born of the Spirit. Nicodemus answered and
said to him, How can these things come about? Jesus answered him
and said, Are you a teacher in Israel and do not know this? Truly,
truly I tell you that we know what we speak and we bear witness to
what we see, but you do not accept our testimony. If I spoke to you
of earthly things and you have not believed, how are you going to
believe if I speak to you of heavenly things? No one ascends into
heaven but him who came down from heaven, the Son of Man, who
is in heaven. And as Moses raised up the serpent in the desert, so the
Son of Man must be raised up in order that everyone who believes in
him may not perish but have eternal life. For God so loved the world
that he gave his only-begotten Son so that everyone who believes in
him may not perish but have eternal life. For God did not send his
Son into the world in order that he might judge the world, but so that
the world might be saved through him. One who believes in him is
not judged, but one who does not believe has already been judged
because of not believing in the name of the only-begotten Son of God.
This is the judgment: the light has come into the world and people
loved the darkness more than the light, for their deeds were evil. For
all who do evil hate the light and do not come to the light so that
their deeds may not be made known. But those who act in accord
with the truth come to the light so that their deeds may be revealed,
for they were done in God.* (Jn 3:1-21) Up to this point the whole
conversation that has been developed is relevant to the topic we are
discussing; after this, the narrator takes a different tack.

31, 60. When Nicodemus failed to understand what had been said,
he asked the Lord how these things could come about. Let us see
what the Lord responds to this. Surely, if he agrees to answer the
question he was asked, namely, *How can these things come about?*
(Jn 3:9) he is going to say how human beings coming from a carnal
birth can attain a spiritual rebirth. Hence, he noted briefly the lack
of knowledge in one who considered himself superior to others because he was a teacher, and he rebuked the lack of faith of all such
people, because they did not accept the testimony given by the truth.
He also added that he spoke to them of earthly matters and that they
did not believe, and he asked and wondered how they would believe
heavenly matters. Nonetheless, he goes on, and to the question he
was asked, namely, how these things can come about, he answers

that others will believe, if they do not. He says, *No one ascends into heaven but him who came down from heaven, the Son of Man, who is in heaven* (Jn 3:13). He explains, "In this way, there will come about the spiritual birth that transforms earthly human beings into heavenly ones. Human beings could not attain this, unless they were made my members. Thus the same one ascends who came down, since no one ascends save the one who came down." Hence, all who need to be transformed and raised up must come together into the unity of Christ, so that the Christ who has come down may himself ascend. He does not regard his body, that is, his Church, as something distinct from himself. For, we quite correctly interpret, *They will be two in one flesh* (Gn 2:24), as referring to Christ and the Church, and he himself said of this flesh, *Therefore, they are no longer two, but one flesh* (Mt 19:6; Mk 10:8). But human beings were utterly unable to ascend, because *no one ascends into heaven but him who came down from heaven, the Son of Man, who is in heaven*. For, though he became the Son of Man on earth, he did not think it inappropriate to use the title, Son of Man, of his divinity, by which he remained in heaven, when he came down to earth. After all, he did not want us to understand two Christs, the one God and the other man, but one and the same Christ, both God and man: God, because *in the beginning was the Word, and the Word was God* (Jn 1:1), and man, because *the Word was made flesh and dwelled among us* (Jn 1:14). And thus, by reason of the distance between the divinity and human weakness, the Son of God remained in heaven, and the Son of Man lived on earth. But by reason of the unity of the person, by which the two substances are the one Christ, the Son of God lived on earth, and the Son of Man remained in heaven. Thus, from believing things that are more difficult to believe, one comes to believe things easier to believe. For the divine substance, which is far more remote and more lofty by reason of its incomparable superiority, was able on our account to take up a human substance so that there came to be one person, and thus the Son of Man, who was on earth on account of the weakness of the flesh, is himself in heaven by reason of the divinity in which the flesh shares. Hence, how much more believable it is that other holy human beings who believe in him become one Christ with the man Christ. Thus, when all ascend by reason of his grace and union with him, the one Christ who came down from heaven ascends into heaven. Thus the Apostle said, *As in one body we have many members, but all the members of the body, though they are many, are still one body, so it is with Christ* (1 Cor 12:12). He did not say, "And so it is with the Christs," that is, with the body of Christ and the members of Christ, but *so it is with Christ,* calling the head and body one Christ.

32, 61. This is a great and astounding honor. Because it cannot come about except by the forgiveness of sins, he goes on to say, *And as Moses raised up the serpent in the desert, so the Son of Man must be raised up in order that everyone who believes in him may not perish but have eternal life* (Jn 3:14-15). We know what happened in the desert back then.[90] Many were dying from snake bites. Then the people confessed their sins and prayed to the Lord through Moses so that this poison might be taken from them. And thus, at the command of the Lord, Moses raised up the bronze snake in the desert and told the people that whoever is bitten by a snake should look up at that bronze snake. As soon as they did this, they were cured. What is the raising of the snake but the death of Christ in that figure of speech in which the cause signifies the effect? Death, of course, came from the snake who persuaded the man to commit the sin as a result of which he merited to die. The Lord did not take into his flesh sin, which is like the venom of the snake, but he did take death. Thus the punishment of sin was present in the likeness of sinful flesh without guilt so that he might destroy in sinful flesh both the guilt and the punishment.[91] Just as, then, one who looked upon the snake that was raised up was both cured of the venom and freed from death, so now one who is conformed to the likeness of Christ's death through faith in him and his baptism is set free from sin by justification and from death by resurrection. This is, after all, what he says, *In order that everyone who believes in him may not perish but have eternal life.* What need, then, is there that a little one be conformed to the death of Christ through baptism, if he has in no way been poisoned by the bite of the snake.

33, 62. Moreover, if—as he goes on to say—*God so loved the world that he gave his only-begotten Son so that everyone who believes in him may not perish but have eternal life* (Jn 3:16), little ones were going to perish and were not going to have eternal life, if they did not believe in the only-begotten Son of God through the sacrament of baptism. He came for the time being, not so that he might judge the

---

90. See Nm 21:6-9.
91. See Rom 8:3.

world, but so that the world might be saved through him, especially since he goes on to say, *One who believes in him is not judged, but one who does not believe has already been judged because of not believing in the name of the only-begotten Son of God* (Jn 3:18). Where then do we locate the baptized little ones but among the believers, as the authority of the universal Church everywhere cries out? We locate them, then, among those who believe, for they receive this through the power of the sacrament and the responses of those who present them. And, accordingly, we rank those who have not been baptized among those who have not believed. Moreover, if those who have been baptized are not judged, these others are judged because they lack baptism. He adds, *This is the judgment: the light has come into the world and people loved the darkness more than the light* (Jn 3:19). Why did he say, *The light has come into the world*, unless he was speaking of his coming? Without the sacrament of his coming how can the little ones be in the light? Or how do those people in their love of darkness not hold this too? As they themselves do not believe, they suppose that their little ones need not be baptized, when they fear their bodily death. But he says that the works of those who come to the light are done in God, since they understand that their justification does not belong to their own merits but to the grace of God. *It is God, after all*, says the Apostle, *who produces in us the willing and the action in accord with good will* (Phil 2:13).[92] In this way there comes about the spiritual rebirth of all those who come to Christ from their birth in the flesh. Christ himself revealed this; he himself explained it, when he was asked how these things could come about; on this question he left to no one the freedom of human debate. Let the little ones not be kept from the grace of the forgiveness of sins; there is no other way to come to Christ. No one can be reconciled to God and come to God in any other way than through Christ.

The Very Form of Baptism Indicates Sins Are Forgiven

34, 63. What shall I say about the very form of the sacrament? I wish that some of those who think differently would bring a little

---

92. Here it is not clear whether the good will is that of God or of human beings. In the second book of this work, Augustine interprets the good will as that of human beings, though in his later *Correction and Grace* 9, 24, he clearly takes it as referring to God's will.

one to me for baptism. What does my exorcism do for the child, if it is not held in servitude to the devil? These persons would have to make the responses to me on behalf of the same little one whom they present, because the child could not make the responses on its own. How, then, are they going to say that the child renounces the devil, if the devil had no claim on the child? How are they going to say that the child is turning back to God, if the child had not been turned away? How are they going to say that, among other things, the child believes in the forgiveness of sins, if the child receives no forgiveness? If I thought that they held views contrary to these, I would not permit them to approach the sacraments with the little one. In this matter I fail to grasp their disposition before other human beings or their thoughts as they stand before God, and I do not want to say anything more harsh.

Some of them saw that a false and deceptive form of baptism is administered to little ones, when one seems to speak of and effect the forgiveness of sins, but none takes place, and they saw that nothing more damnable and detestable than that can be said or thought. Furthermore, with regard to the necessity of baptism for little ones, they grant that they need redemption, as is stated in the brief memo by one of them,[93] who was, nonetheless, unwilling to say anything clearer regarding the forgiveness of any sin. But as you have conveyed to me in your letter,[94] they admit, as you say, that baptism brings about the forgiveness of sins, even in the case of little ones. That is not surprising. After all, what else could they mean by redemption? But they say, "They began to have sin, not from their origin, but in their own life, after they were born."[95]

64. Hence, you see the wide range of opinions that exist among those people against whom I have already argued long and extensively in this work. I have read a book by one of them, and I have

---

93. The "brief memo" (*libellus brevissimus*) to which Augustine refers is the short work which Caelestius composed to defend himself before the episcopal tribunal in Carthage in 411. In Letter 175, 6, Augustine says, "Caelestius admitted in his memo in the Church of Carthage that even little ones receive redemption through the baptism of Christ." Augustine also refers to the memo in *The Grace of Christ and Original Sin* II, 18, 21.

94. Augustine refers to the letter of Marcellinus which occasioned the writing of this work; see above 1, 1.

95. This would seem to be a quotation from the Pelagian work mentioned in the following paragraph.

refuted its contents as best I could.[96] You see, then, the great difference of opinion that exists between those, as I began to say, who
maintain that little ones are completely pure and free from all sin,
both original and personal, and those who think that they have, after
having been born, contracted personal sins, from which they believe
that they need to be cleansed by baptism. Moreover, with an eye on
the scriptures and authority of the whole Church and the form of the
sacrament itself, the latter group correctly saw that baptism brings
about forgiveness of sins in little ones, but they either are unwilling to
say or cannot see that whatever sin they have stems from their origin.
The former group, however, looked to human nature, which is avail-
able for everyone's consideration, and correctly saw—as was easy to
do—that they could at that age have contracted no sin in their own
life. But to avoid admitting original sin, they claim that little ones
have no sin at all. On these points, then, let them first agree among
themselves about the individual truths they state, and the result will
be that they will in no way disagree with us. For if the former grant
to the latter that baptized little ones obtain the forgiveness of sins and
if the latter grant to the former that little ones have not yet contracted
any sin in their own life, as nature itself cries out in the silent infants,
then let both of them grant to us that in little ones there remains only
original sin that has to be removed by baptism.

Infants Have Committed No Sins in Their Own Lives

35, 65. Or do we need to investigate, discuss, and spend time on
this point too? That is, are we to prove and explain how infants, whom
everyone calls innocents for this very reason, have committed nothing
evil by means of their own will, without which there can be no sin
belonging to one's own life? Look at their great weakness of mind and
body, their ignorance of everything, their complete inability to obey
a command, their inability to understand or observe any law, whether
natural or written, and their lack of the use of reason for either side of
a question. Does not all this proclaim and demonstrate their freedom

---

96. Augustine never indicates who was the author of this Pelagian work, though he apparently quotes from it frequently in this and the next book. Some scholars have
suggested that the work is the *Liber fidei* by Rufinus the Syrian, the arguments of
which Augustine seems to have had in mind in Book One and which he even cited at
least once (see I, 18, 23).

from personal sin with a silence that bears stronger witness than any language of ours? Let the very obviousness of the matter speak for itself, for I am never so at a loss for words as when the matter under discussion is more obvious than anything one can say.

66. I would like whoever holds this opinion to tell me what sin he saw or suspected in an infant fresh from the womb, for whose redemption he admits that baptism is now necessary. Let him tell me what evil the infant committed in this its own life by its body or its mind. Perhaps it cries and bothers adults, but I would be surprised if this should be attributed to sinfulness and not rather to unhappiness. Is it that its crying is not stopped by any reasoning of its own or by the prohibition of someone else? But this is a mark of the profound ignorance in which it lies. As a result of this ignorance, when it becomes stronger after a while, it will, when angered, strike even its mother and often her breasts which it demands when it is hungry. These things are not merely tolerated, but even loved in little ones. With what sort of love do we love them but with the carnal love which finds pleasure in laughter and joking which are based on the apparent absurdity of even clever human beings? If their thoughts corresponded to what they said, we would not laugh at their wit, but at their folly. We even see that those foolish people, whom the common folk call "morons," are used for the amusement of the clever and are valued more highly than the clever in the estimate of the slave market. The carnal affection of those who are in no sense fools is able to take such delight over another's misfortune. For one person finds pleasure in the foolishness of another, though he would not himself want to be such a person.

Though a father looks forward with delight to such things and coaxes them from the baby talk of his little son, if he knew that his son would be a man of that sort when he grew up, he would surely not hesitate to mourn for him with greater sorrow than if he were dead. But as long as there is hope of development and one believes that the light of intelligence will dawn with the increase in years, children's verbal attacks, even against their parents, are not only not taken as harmful, but are even regarded as charming and pleasant. No prudent person would approve of children not merely not being restrained from words or deeds of this sort, once they can be held back, but even of their being provoked to do this, because some adults love laughter and silliness. For, in general, at an age at which they recognize their father and mother, they do not dare to speak ill of either of them, unless this sort of thing is either permitted or demanded by one or both of them. But these things are characteristic of those little ones who are already uttering words and can express the emotions of their mind by some spoken signs. Let us, rather, turn our eyes to the deep ignorance of the newly born, from which, as they develop, they come to this babbling but transient silliness, as if in growing up they were striving for knowledge and speech.

36, 67. Let us, I say, ponder the darkness of a mind that is, of course, rational; in that darkness they are even ignorant of God, and they resist his sacraments, even when they are baptized. I ask why and when they were plunged into this darkness. Did they acquire it here, and did they forget God through extreme negligence in this life of their own, though they lived prudently and religiously even in the wombs of their mothers? Let those who dare say such things; let those who wish listen to them; let those who are able believe such things. I myself am convinced that only those whose minds have been befogged by the stubbornness of defending their own views can hold this position.

Or is there no evil of ignorance and, hence, none to be removed? What then is the purpose of this plea, *Do not bear in mind the sins of my youth and of my ignorance* (Ps 25:7)? For, even if those sins deserve greater condemnation that are committed by persons with knowledge, still, if there were no sins of ignorance, we would not read the passage I cited, *Do not bear in mind the sins of my youth and of my ignorance*. Why or when or from where was the soul of a newly born infant thrust into that densest darkness of ignorance in which, though certainly a human soul, certainly a rational soul, it remains not only untaught, but unteachable? If it belongs to human nature to begin in this way and our nature is not now defective, why was Adam not created as such? Why was he able to obey a command and capable of naming his wife and all the animals? For he said of her, *She will be called woman* (Gn 2:23), and *Whatever Adam called a living soul, that is its name* (Gn 2:19). But this child does not know where it is, what it is, by whom it was created; it is already guilty of sin, though not yet capable of obeying a command; it is involved in and overwhelmed by so thick a fog of ignorance that it cannot be roused, as from sleep, so that it might at least become aware of these things, once they were pointed out. Rather, one must await the time when it has slept off this drunkenness of sorts, not during a single night, as usually happens even in the worst cases, but gradually over many months and years. Until this happens, we put up with so many things in little ones that we punish in adults that we cannot even count them. If little ones acquired this great evil of ignorance and weakness after they were born in this life, where, when, and how did they suddenly become wrapped in such darkness through the commission of some great act of godlessness?

37, 68. Someone will object, "If these things are not characteristics of a pure nature, but the beginnings of a defective nature, because Adam was not created in such a state, why did Christ, who was far more excellent and certainly born of the Virgin without any sin, come to us in the weakness of infancy?" We reply to this objection that Adam was not created in such a state, because he was not created in sinful flesh, since he had no parent who sinned before him. But we are born in this state, because we are born in sinful flesh, since Adam sinned before us. Christ, then, was born in this state, because he was born in the likeness of sinful flesh so that from sin he might condemn sin.[97] We are not, after all, dealing with the size of Adam's body, since he was not created as a little one, but had the full growth of his members. One can say that the animals were also created that way, and that it is, nonetheless, not the result of a sin of theirs that their young are born as little ones. But we are not presently investigating this question. Rather, we are dealing with the strength of his mind and his use of reason, so that he received with docility God's commandment and the law with its prescription and was able to obey it with ease, if he willed to do so. But now human beings are born so that they are utterly unable to do this on account of the terrible ignorance and weakness, not of the flesh, but of the mind, although we all admit that there is present in a little one a soul, not of another, but of the same substance as there was in the first human being, that is, a rational soul. And yet the great weakness of the flesh indicates, I believe, some penal condition. In any case I wonder whether, if those first human beings had not sinned, they would have had offspring of the sort that could not use their tongue or hands or feet. They would perhaps have had to be born as little ones on account of the size of the womb. And yet the rib which he made into the woman is a small

---

97. See Rom 8:3.

part of the body,[98] and God did not on that account make a little wife for the man. Hence, the omnipotence of the creator certainly could have made his children into adults immediately after they were born.

38, 69. But—to drop this point—he could certainly have given Adam's offspring what he has given even to many animals. Their young are little and do not develop mentally as their bodies grow, since they do not have a rational soul. But, even when they are at their smallest, they run about and recognize their mothers. They are not brought to suckle at the breasts by the care and help of another; rather, they themselves know how to find them with remarkable ease, though they are located in a hidden spot on the mother's body. A newly born human, on the other hand, does not have feet capable of walking or hands able even to scratch, and unless the nipple of the breast is inserted in its motionless lips by the help of a nurse, they do not see where they are and, despite their nearness to the breasts, they are better able to cry of hunger than to suck. Moreover, this weakness of the body corresponds perfectly to the weakness of the mind. The flesh of Christ would not have borne the likeness of sinful flesh, if this flesh were not the sinful flesh by the weight of which the rational soul is so weighed down,[99] regardless of whether the soul itself is derived from the parents or is created right there or breathed in from above. I put off for now any investigation of this topic.

Concupiscence Remains after Baptism

39, 70. In little ones the grace of God brings it about that sinful flesh loses its power[100] through the baptism of the one who came in the likeness of sinful flesh.[101] But it does not lose its power so that in the living flesh itself the concupiscence spread through and born into it is suddenly done away with and no longer exists; rather, it loses its power so that what was present at birth is not harmful at death. For, if one lives on after baptism and comes to an age capable of obeying a commandment, one has a means of fighting and, with God's help, of overcoming concupiscence, if one has not received his grace in vain and does not want to be rejected. After all, it is not granted even to

---

98. See Gn 2:22.
99. See Wis 9:15.
100. See Rom 6:6.
101. See Rom 8:3.

adults in baptism, unless perhaps by an ineffable miracle of the omnipotent creator, that the law of sin, which is present in the members,
struggling against the law of the mind,[102] is completely destroyed and
no longer exists. Rather, whatever evil one has thought, said, or done,
while enslaved through the mind's subjection to this concupiscence,
is completely destroyed and regarded as if it had not occurred. The
bond of guilt is broken by which the devil held the soul through that
concupiscence, and the wall is torn down by which he separated human beings from their creator. Yet, it continues on in the battle in
which we chastise our body and subject it to servitude.[103] It remains
either to be released for permissible and necessary purposes or to be
held in check by continence. But the Holy Spirit, who knows far better than we do everything past, present, and future about the human
race, has foreknown and predicted a human life of the sort that no living person is found righteous in the sight of God.[104] Hence, it happens
that through ignorance or weakness we do not exert all the powers
of our will against it, and we give in to it with regard to some things
which are not permitted. We give in more seriously and more often to
the degree that we are worse, and we give in less seriously and less
frequently to the degree that we are better. But this has to do with the
question whether there can be or is or will be a human being without
sin in this life, apart from the one who said, *Behold, the prince of
the world comes, and he will find nothing in me* (Jn 14:30). Since we
must discuss this question with somewhat greater care, let the present
volume end here so that we can investigate it from a fresh start.

---

102. See Rom 7:23.
103. See 1 Cor 9:27.
104. See Ps 143:2.

Book Two

The Question of Freedom from Sin in This Life

ı, 1. We have, I believe, my dear Marcellinus, sufficiently discussed the baptism of little ones in the previous book. We have
shown that they are baptized in order to attain not only the kingdom
of God, but also salvation and eternal life. No one can possess the
latter apart from the kingdom of God and without the community
with Christ the savior, for which he has redeemed us by his blood. In
the present book, however, I have undertaken to discuss and clarify,
with as much care and ability as God grants, the following question:
Is there anyone now living, or has anyone ever lived, or will anyone
ever live in this world without any sin whatever? I leave aside, of
course, the one mediator between God and human beings, the man
Christ Jesus *who gave himself up as redemption for all* (1 Tm 2:6).
But you should not be surprised, if the question of the sin and the
baptism of little ones repeatedly arises in this discussion because of
some need or on some given occasion, and we must not shirk the duty
of responding, as best we can, in those places to every question that
requires an answer from us.

The Lord's Prayer Indicates a Solution to the Question

2, 2. The solution of this question concerning human life free from
sin's stealthy attack or unexpected conquest is especially required on
account of our daily prayers. For there are some who rely so heavily
on the free choice of the human will that they suppose that we need no
help, even from God, in order to avoid sin, after our nature has once
and for all received the free choice of the will. From this it follows
that we need not pray so that we do not enter into temptation,[1] that
is, that we are not overcome by temptation, either when it deceives
and takes hold of us in our ignorance or when it pushes and pulls us
in our weakness. I do not have the words to explain how harmful to
our salvation in Christ, how destructive and contrary to the religion
which we have been taught, and how strongly opposed to the piety

---

1. See Mt 26:41.

with which we worship God it is that we do not beg the Lord to receive such a benefit or that we suppose that the words, *And bring*[2] *us not into temptation* (Mt 6:13), were inserted in the Lord's Prayer without any purpose.

Free Choice Alone Is Insufficient against Temptation

3, 3. They think that they say something clever—as if any of us were unaware of this—when they say that "if we do not will to, we do not sin, and God would not command human beings to do what would be impossible for the human will."[3] But they see less well that, in order to overcome temptation in the case of some things which we desire wrongfully or fear wrongfully, we at times need the great and full strength of the will. He who willed that the prophet truthfully say, *No living person will be found righteous in your sight* (Ps 143:2), foresaw that we will not in every case fully use this power. Knowing in advance that we were going to be such persons, the Lord gave us, even after baptism, certain salutary remedies against the guilt and the bonds of sin and willed that they be effective, namely, works of mercy.[4] For he said, *Forgive, and you will be forgiven; give, and they will give to you* (Lk 6:37-38). Who, after all, would leave this life with any hope of attaining eternal salvation, as long as the judgment stands, *Whoever has observed the whole law, but has offended on one point, has become guilty on every count* (Jas 2:10)? Yet there follows soon afterward, *Speak and act as if you are beginning to be judged by the law of freedom. For judgment will be without mercy for one who does not show mercy, but mercy triumphs over judgment!* (Jas 2:12-13)

4, 4. Concupiscence, then, remains in the members of the body of this death as the law of sin.[5] It is present in the little ones at birth, though its guilt is removed when little ones are baptized. It remains for the combat that is life, but it does not punish with damnation those

---

2. Augustine's Latin has *inferas* instead of the more usual *inducas*. In *The Lord's Sermon on the Mount* II, 9, 30, he says, "Some manuscripts have *And lead us not,* which I think amounts to the same thing. For the one Greek term can be translated in both ways."

3. Probably a quotation from the Pelagian work mentioned in I, 34, 64.

4. Augustine does not mention the sacrament of penance, because in the practice of the ancient Church there was only the public form of penance that was imposed for grave sins and only once in a person's life.

5. See Rom 7:23-24.

who die before engaging in that combat. It holds unbaptized little ones enmeshed in guilt and draws them to damnation, like children of anger,[6] even if they die as little ones. But in the case of baptized adults who have the use of reason, whenever the mind consents to that same concupiscence in order to sin, it is due to one's own will. After the destruction of all sins and after the removal of that guilt as well, by which it held them in bonds from their origin, it remains in the meanwhile for the combat that is life, until death shall be swallowed up by victory.[7] Then, when peace has been achieved, there will remain nothing more to be conquered. It will do no harm whatsoever to those who do not consent to it regarding what is forbidden. But it holds guilty those who consent to it regarding what is forbidden. And unless they are healed by the medicine of penance and works of mercy through the heavenly priest who makes intercession for us,[8] it brings them to the second death and to damnation.

For this reason, when the Lord was teaching us to pray, he advised us to say, among other things, *Forgive us our debts, as we also forgive our debtors. And bring us not into temptation, but deliver us from evil.* (Mt 6:12-13) For evil remains in our flesh, not by reason of the nature in which human beings were created by God, but by reason of the sinfulness into which they have fallen. Now, having lost their strength, they are not healed with the same ease of will with which they were wounded. The apostle says of this evil, *I know that the good does not dwell in my flesh* (Rom 7:18). He commands us not to obey this evil, when he says, *Let sin, then, not reign in your mortal body so that you obey its desires* (Rom 6:12). If, then, we consent to these desires stemming from the concupiscence of the flesh by an illicit turn of the will, we say in order to heal this wound, *Forgive us our debts.* And drawing a remedy from works of mercy, we add, *As we also forgive our debtors* (Mt 6:12). But so that we do not consent to it, we beg for help with the words, *And bring us not into temptation*—or as some manuscripts have it, *Lead us not into temptation.* It is not that God himself tempts someone with such a temptation. *For God is not a tempter toward evil; rather, he tempts no one* (Jas 1:13). But we pray that, if we should begin to be tempted by our concupiscence, we may not lack his help so that we may be

---

6. See Eph 2:3.
7. See 1 Cor 15:54.
8. See Heb 7:24-25.

victorious in him and not be enticed and carried off. Finally, we mention what will be accomplished in the end, when what is mortal will be swallowed up by life:[9] *But deliver us from evil* (Mt 6:13). At that time, after all, there will be no concupiscence of the sort that we are commanded to fight and to which we are commanded not to consent. We can, then, briefly ask for this whole cluster of three benefits as follows: "Forgive us those times in which we have been carried off by concupiscence; help us not to be carried off by concupiscence; take concupiscence away from us."

We Need God's Help if We Are to Act Righteously

5, 5. We are not, of course, helped by God to sin, but we cannot do what is right or carry out the commandment of righteousness in every respect, unless we are helped by God. The body's eye is not helped by light so that, closed and turned away, it may withdraw from the light; rather, it is helped by it to see, and it cannot do so at all unless the light helps it. In the same way, God, who is the light of the interior human being, helps the sight of our mind, so that we do something good, not according to our own righteousness, but according to his righteousness. But if we turn away from him, that is our fault; then we are wise according to the flesh; then we consent to the concupiscence of the flesh with respect to what is forbidden.[10] God, then, helps those who turn to him, but abandons those who turn away. But he also helps us to turn to him— something that this light certainly does not do for the eyes of the body. He commands us with the words, *Turn toward me, and I will turn toward you* (Zec 1:3), and we say to him, *Turn us to you, O God of our salvation* (Ps 85:5), and *God of power, turn us to you* (Ps 80:8). What else are we saying but "Grant what you command"?[11] He commands us with the words, *Be intelligent, you who are without understanding among the people* (Ps

---

9. See 2 Cor 5:4.
10. See Rom 8:5.
11. Augustine repeatedly claims that these texts of scripture say no more than "Grant what you command." In *Confessions* X, 29, 40, he had said, "Grant what you command, and command what you will," a formula which shocked Pelagius when he heard it quoted by a bishop. In *The Gift of Perseverance* 20, 53, Augustine says, "When at Rome these words of mine were quoted in the presence of Pelagius by a brother and fellow bishop of mine, he could not bear them; rather, he was quite upset and contradicted them, almost entering into a fight with the person who cited them."

94:8), and we say to him, *Give me understanding that I may learn your commandments* (Ps 119:73). What else are we saying but "Grant what you command"? He commands with the words, *You shall not go after your desires* (Sir 18:30), and we say, "We know that no one can be chaste unless God grants this."[12] What else are we saying but, "Grant what you command"? He commands with the words, *Act righteously* (Is 56:1), and he also says, *Blessed are those who hunger and thirst for righteousness, because they will be satisfied* (Mt 5:6). From whom ought we to ask the food and drink of righteousness but from him who promises those who hunger and thirst for it that they will be satisfied?

6. Let us then drive away from our hearing and from our minds those who say that, having received once and for all free choice of the will, we need not pray that God might help us not to sin. Not even the Pharisee of the gospel was blinded by such darkness. He was mistaken in thinking that his righteousness was perfect and in supposing that he had attained its fullness. But he still gave thanks to God, because he was not like other human beings, like the unjust, the thieves, and the adulterers, like the tax collector, since he fasted twice a week and gave away a tenth of all he possessed. He did not ask that his righteousness be increased, but by giving thanks to God for the things he had, he admitted that he had received everything from him. He nonetheless met with disapproval for two reasons: As though he had his fill, he asked to receive nothing to nourish his righteousness, and he acted in an insulting manner toward the tax collector, preferring himself to a man who hungered and thirsted for righteousness.[13] What, then, will befall those people who, even if they admit that they have no righteousness or that they do not have complete righteousness, presume that they must get it from themselves and need not ask for it from their creator, where its storehouse and source is found? Nor does it follow that we should rely on prayers alone in this matter and not bring to bear the strength of our will upon living a good life. After all, God is said to be our helper,[14] and we cannot be helped unless we try to do something ourselves, because God does not produce our salvation in us as if

---

12. See Wis 8:21.
13. See Lk 18:10-14.
14. See Ps 62:9.

we were mindless rocks or beings in whose nature he did not create reason and will. But why he helps one and not another, helps one to this extent and another to that, and helps one in this way and another in that, lies with him in the decision of his hidden justice and in his surpassing power.

The First Question: Can Human Beings Be Sinless in This Life?

6, 7. One need not, of course, with a rash incautiousness, immediately oppose those who say that there can be human beings in this life without sin. After all, if we say that it is impossible, we will be disparaging both the free choice of persons who use their will to strive for this as well as the power and mercy of God who brings it about by his help. But it is one question whether this is possible; it is quite another whether it is actually the case. It is still another question why it is not actually the case, if it is not so, though it is possible. And it is still another question not only whether there is someone who has never had any sin whatsoever, but whether there can or could ever be such a person. If someone asks me in accord with these four ways of posing the question whether a human being can be without sin in this life, I admit that one can be by the grace of God and free choice. I have no doubt that free choice itself belongs to the grace of God, that is, to God's gifts, not only insofar as it exists, but also insofar as it is good, that is, insofar as it turns to carrying out God's commandments. In that way God's grace not merely shows us what we are to do, but also helps us so that we are able to do what God has shown us. After all, what do we have that we have not received?[15] For this reason Jeremiah also says, *I know, Lord, that a man's path does not lie in his power and that it is not up to a man to walk and direct his steps* (Jer 10:23). For the same reason, when someone said to God in the Psalms, *You prescribed that your commandments be strictly observed* (Ps 119:4), he did not rely on himself to do it, but immediately expressed the hope, *May my paths be guided to observe your ordinances. Then I will not be put to shame, as I gaze upon all your commandments* (Ps 119:5-6). Does anyone hope for what so lies in his power that he needs no help to do it? He shows clearly enough in what follows from whom one should hope for this, since it does

---

15. See 1 Cor 4:7.

not come from chance or fate or anything else but God. He says, *Guide my journeys according to your word, and let not all sinfulness lord it over me* (Ps 119:133). From servitude to this damnable lordship those are set free whom the Lord Jesus gave the power to become children of God, when they welcomed him.[16] From this terrible dominion they needed to be set free, for he said to them, *If the Son sets you free, then you will truly be free* (Jn 8:36). Because of these and many other testimonies of this sort, I cannot doubt that God has not commanded human beings to do anything impossible and that nothing is impossible for God in terms of assisting and helping us to accomplish what he commands. Hence, human beings can, if they want, be without sin, if they are helped by God.

The Second Question: Is There Actually Someone without Sin?

7, 8. But if one asks the question I put in second place, namely, whether it is actually the case, I do not believe it is. For I prefer to believe the scripture which says, *Do not enter into judgment with your servant, because no living person will be found righteous in your sight* (Ps 143:2). There is, then, need of God's mercy which triumphs over judgment, and the person who does not show mercy will not have God's mercy.[17] When the prophet said, *I have said, Against myself I will declare my sin to the Lord, and you have forgiven the wickedness of my heart*, he immediately added, *Every holy person will pray to you for this at the proper time* (Ps 32:5-6). He said, *Every holy person*, not "every sinner." These are, after all, the words of holy persons: *If we say that we have no sin, we deceive ourselves, and the truth is not in us* (1 Jn 1:8). Hence, there are in the Revelation of the same apostle those one hundred and forty-four thousand holy men who did not defile themselves with women, for they remained virgins, and no lie was found on their lips, because they were beyond reproach.[18] They were, of course, beyond reproach, precisely because they truthfully reproached themselves. And no lie was found on their lips, precisely because, if they were to say that they had no sin, they would deceive themselves, and the truth would not be in them, and there would certainly be a lie where the truth was absent. For, the

---

16. See Jn 1:12.
17. See Jas 2:13.
18. See Rv 14:3-5.

righteous person certainly does not lie when he accuses himself as he begins to speak.[19]

Our Adoption as Children of God Remains Incomplete

9. Accordingly, because they consider the scriptures less than they should, they are greatly misled by the words of scripture, *Those who have been born of God do not sin and cannot sin, because his seed remains in them* (1 Jn 3:9), even if other passages say something of this sort. For they do not notice that people become children of God to the extent that they begin to exist in the newness of the Spirit[20] and begin to be renewed in the interior human being according to the image of him who created them.[21] All the old weakness is not done away with from the moment of one's baptism. Rather, the renewal begins with the forgiveness of all sins and is realized to the extent that one who is wise is wise about spiritual things.[22] But the other things are realized in hope, until they are brought about in reality as well, when the body itself will be renewed into the better state of immortality and incorruption with which we will be clothed at the resurrection of the dead. After all, the Lord called this a rebirth, not the sort that takes place in baptism, but a rebirth in the sense that what now has begun in the spirit will be completed in the body as well. He said, *In the rebirth when the Son of Man shall sit on his throne of majesty, you too will sit on twelve thrones, judging the twelve tribes of Israel* (Mt 19:28).

A total and complete forgiveness of sins is brought about in baptism. But suppose that there were immediately realized the total and complete change of the human being into a new and eternal state. I do not mean this in terms of the body which clearly is still tending toward its old corruption and death and must be renewed in the end when there will truly be a new condition. But apart from the body, if in the mind itself, which is the interior human being, a completely new condition were brought about in baptism, the Apostle would not say, *Though our exterior human being is being corrupted, the interior human being is being renewed from day to day* (2 Cor 4:16).

---

19. See Prv 18:17.
20. See Rom 7:6.
21. See Col 3:10.
22. See Rom 8:5.

Certainly those who are still being renewed from day to day have not been wholly renewed. And to the extent that they have not yet been renewed, to that extent they are in their old condition. Moreover, to the extent that they are still in their old condition, even though they have been baptized, to that extent they are still children of the world. But to the extent that they are in their new condition, that is, as a result of the full and complete forgiveness of sins and to the extent that they are wise in terms of the Spirit[23] and lead lives that correspond to this, they are children of God. For interiorly we put off the old human being and don the new one, because it is there that we set aside the lie and speak the truth, as well as the other things by which the Apostle explains what it means to put off the old human being and don the new one *who was created according to God in the righteousness and holiness of the truth* (Eph 4:22-24). He exhorts the baptized faithful to do this, but they would not still need this admonition, if it had already been completely accomplished in baptism. And yet it has been accomplished, just as we have been saved, for *he saved us through the bath of rebirth* (Ti 3:5). But in another passage he explains how this has been accomplished, *Not only they, but we too possess the first fruits of the Spirit, and we groan within ourselves, as we await our adoption, the redemption of our body. For we are saved in hope, but a hope that is seen is not hope. After all, why should one hope for what one already sees? But if we hope for what we do not see, we look forward to it with patience.* (Rom 8:23-25)

8, 10. Our adoption as God's children will become complete when our body is also redeemed. We now have the first fruits of the Spirit, and in that respect we have now really become children of God. In the other respects, however, as we have been saved and renewed in hope, so we are children of God in hope. But because our salvation has not yet become a reality, we are not yet fully renewed and are not yet children of God, but children of the world. We make progress, then, toward renewal and a righteous life inasmuch as we are children of God, and in that respect we cannot sin at all. We make progress until the whole of our being undergoes this transformation, even the respect in which we are still children of the world. In that respect, after all, we can still sin. Thus it is that, on the one hand, *Those who have been born of God do not sin* (1 Jn 3:9) and, on the other, *If we*

23. See Rom 8:5.

say that we have no sin, we deceive ourselves, and the truth is not in us (1 Jn 1:8). Our being children of the flesh and of this world, then, will be done away with, and our being children of God and persons reborn of the Spirit[24] will be brought to perfection. For this reason John also says, *Beloved, we are now children of God, and it has not yet been revealed what we shall be* (1 Jn 3:2). What do *we are* and *we shall be* mean, if not that we are in hope and we shall be in reality? For he goes on to say, *We know that, when he appears, we shall be like him, because we shall see him as he is* (1 Jn 3:2). Hence, we have now begun to be like him, because we have the first fruits of the Spirit, and we are still unlike him because of the remnants of our old condition. Hence, we are children of God because of our rebirth by the Spirit to the extent that we are like him, and we are children of the flesh and of the world to the extent that we are unlike him. As like him, then, we cannot sin, but as unlike him, *If we say that we have no sin, we deceive ourselves* (1 Jn 1:8). And this lasts until our adoption has become complete and the sinner is no more, so that, if you look in his place, you will not find him.[25]

Why the Righteous Do Not Give Birth to Righteous Children

9, 11. It was pointless, then, for some to have produced this argument and to have said, "If a sinner gave birth to a sinner so that a little one is freed from its guilt of original sin in the reception of baptism, [a righteous person] ought also to give birth to a righteous child."[26] The argument implies that one bears a child according to the flesh insofar as one is righteous and not rather insofar as the law of sin is stirred in one's members by concupiscence and is turned by the law of the mind to the purposes of propagation. Hence, one gives birth insofar as one still carries about the old condition among the children of the world, not insofar as one enters into the new condition among the children of God. *For the children of this world are born and beget children* (Lk 20:34). Hence, what is born is such as it is because what is born of the flesh is flesh. But only the children of God are righteous. Insofar, however, as they are children of God, they do not bear children according to the flesh, because they themselves

---

24. See Jn 3:5.
25. See Ps 37:10.
26. Probably another citation from the Pelagian work mentioned in I, 34, 64.

have been born of the Spirit, not of the flesh.[27] But those of them who give birth to children give birth as a result of this flesh, since they have not yet transformed completely all the remnants of their old condition into perfect newness. Hence, any children born as a result of that old and weak condition are necessarily themselves also old and weak. Thus they must themselves be renewed for another birth through the forgiveness of sins. But if they do not receive that rebirth, righteous parents will do them no good. Such parents are righteous in the Spirit, but they did not give them birth by the Spirit. But if they do receive that rebirth, even parents who are not righteous do them no harm. For in the latter case, the children have passed by spiritual grace into the hope of an eternal new condition; in the former case, they remain entirely in the old condition by reason of their carnal mind.

Noah and Daniel Were Righteous, but Not Sinless

10, 12. The testimony, then, which says, *Those who have been born of God do not sin* (1 Jn 3:9), does not contradict the testimony which says to those who have already been born of God, *If we say that we have no sin, we deceive ourselves, and the truth is not in us* (1 Jn 1:8). For as long as any human being, even though now wholly existing in hope and already partially renewed by spiritual rebirth, carries about *the body which is being corrupted and weighs down the soul* (Wis 9:15), one must distinguish, even in a single human being, to what part something belongs and on what grounds something is said. For, as I see things, scripture does not readily provide such great testimony to the righteousness of anyone as it does to the three servants of God, Noah, Daniel, and Job. The prophet Ezekiel said that they alone can be freed from the threat of God's anger;[28] he was, of course, using those three men as symbols for three kinds of human beings who were to be set free. He took Noah as the symbol of righteous leaders of peoples on account of his governance of the ark, which is like the Church; he took Daniel as the symbol of righteous celibates; he took Job as the symbol of righteous married people. If there should happen to be another interpretation, we need not discuss it now. It is, nonetheless, sufficiently clear from this testimony of the prophet and from other

---

27. See Jn 3:6.
28. See Ez 14:14.

divine testimonies how outstanding these men were in righteousness. And yet no sober person would say that drunkenness is not a sin, even though it befell such a great man. For Noah was, as we find in scripture, drunk,[29] though heaven forbid that he was a drunkard.

13. After the prayer which Daniel poured out to God, he said of himself, *I prayed and confessed to the Lord my God my sins and the sins of my people* (Dn 9:20). It was for that reason, unless I am mistaken, that Ezekiel, whom we mentioned above, said to a certain proud person, *Are you wiser than Daniel?* (Ez 28:3) Nor can one say in this case what some people argue in opposition to the Lord's Prayer. They say, "Although the apostles, who were holy and already perfect and who had absolutely no sin, said this prayer, it was on behalf of the imperfect and those still sinners that they said, *Forgive us our debts, as we also forgive our debtors* (Mt 6:12). Thus, by saying *our debts,* they showed that there existed in the one body both those who still had sins and they themselves who had absolutely no sin."[30] In Daniel's case one certainly cannot say this. He foresaw, I believe, as a prophet, that this presumptuousness would one day arise, since he often repeated in prayer, *We have sinned* (Dn 9:5.11.15). When he explained to us why he said this, we did not hear him say, "I prayed and confessed to the Lord my God the sins of my people."[31] Nor did he blur the distinction and say, "I confessed to the Lord my God our sins," so that it was uncertain whether he said that on account of their fellowship in one body. Rather, he spoke quite distinctly, as if stressing this distinction and strongly emphasizing it; he said, *My sins and the sins of my people.* Who is going to deny this evidence except persons who find more pleasure in defending what they think than in discovering what they should think?

Even Job Was Not Completely Sinless

14. But let us see what Job himself said after such a great testimony from God to his righteousness. He said, *In the truth I know that it is so. For how will one be righteous before the Lord? For if one wants to contend with him, he will not be able to obey him.* (Jb 9:2-3) And a little later he says, *Who will oppose his judgment? Even if I am*

29. See Gn 9:21.
30. Again apparently a quotation from the previously mentioned Pelagian work.
31. See Dn 9:20.

righteous, my mouth will speak wickedness. (Jb 9:19) Again much later he says, *I know that he will not let me go unpunished. Since I am wicked, why am I not dead? Even if I shall be purer than snow and have clean hands, you have sufficiently dipped me in filth.* (Jb 9:28-31) So too, he says in another discourse, *Because you have written down evils against me and wrapped me in the sins of my youth and set my foot in stocks, you have preserved all my deeds and you have examined the soles of my feet, which grow old like a bag or like a garment eaten by a moth. For a man born of a woman is short-lived and full of anger, and he passes like a flower when it blooms and fades; like a shadow he does not last. Have you not made concern for him enter into your judgment? For who will be clean from filth? No one, not even if one's life lasts only a single day.* (Jb 13:26—14:5) A little later he says, *You have counted all my deeds, and none of my sins has escaped your notice; you have sealed my sins in a bag, and you have noticed if I have done anything unwillingly* (Jb 14:16-17).

See, even Job confesses his sins and says that he knows in the truth that no one is righteous before the Lord. And he knows this in the truth, because, if we say that we have no sin, the truth is not in us.[32] Hence, in terms of human conduct, God offers this great testimony to his righteousness. But Job himself, measuring himself by that rule of righteousness which he sees in God, as best he can, knows in the truth that it is so and adds, *For how will one be righteous before the Lord? For if one wants to contend with him, he will not be able to obey him.* That is, if, in facing judgment, one wants to show that nothing worthy of condemnation can be found in him, he will not be able to obey God. After all, he also loses that obedience by which he could obey God who commands him to confess his sins. For this reason the Lord rebukes certain people with the words, *Why do you want to contend with me in judgment?* (Jer 2:29) To avoid this, the psalmist says, *Do not enter into judgment with your servant, because no living person will be found righteous in your sight* (Ps 143:2). Hence, Job also says, *Who will oppose his judgment? Even if I am righteous, my mouth will speak wickedness.* (Jb 9:19-20) That means: If I shall declare myself righteous contrary to his judgment in which that perfect rule of righteousness proves me unrighteous, my mouth will certainly speak wickedness, because it will speak against God's truth.

---

32. See 1 Jn 1:8.

15. He also showed the frailness or rather the damnation of the carnal generation stemming from the transgression of the original sin. When he dealt with his own sins, he said, as if he were stating their causes, that a man born of woman is short-lived and full of anger.[33] Of what anger? Surely of that anger as a result of which all, as the apostle said, were *by nature*, that is, from their origin, *children of anger* (Eph 2:3), because they are children of the concupiscence of the flesh and of the world. He goes on to show that human death is tied to this anger. For, when he said that a man is short-lived and full of anger, he also added, *And he passes like a flower when it blooms and fades; like a shadow, he does not last* (Jb 14:1-2). But when he added, *Have you not made concern for him enter into your judgment? For who will be clean from filth? No one, not even if one's life lasts only a single day* (Jb 14:3-4), he was, of course, really saying this: You have made concern for man with his short life enter into your judgment. For however brief his life might be, even if it were only a single day, he could not be clean from filth and, therefore, it is perfectly just that he comes into your judgment. He said, *You have counted all my needs, and none of my sins has escaped your notice; you have sealed my sins in a bag, and you have noticed if I have done anything unwillingly* (Jb 14:16-17). Did he not make it quite clear by this that one is justly held accountable even for those sins which are not committed out of the enticement of pleasure, but for the sake of avoiding some trouble, pain, or even death? For we say that these sins are committed out of some necessity, although they should all be overcome by love for and delight in righteousness. One can also view his words, *And you have noticed if I have done anything unwillingly* (Jb 14:17), as pertinent to the statement which says, *For I do not do what I want; rather, I do what I hate* (Rom 7:15).

16. Scripture, that is, the Spirit of the Lord, said that in all the things that happened to him Job did not sin with his lips before the Lord.[34] Why is it that the Lord, who gave such testimony to him, afterward rebuked him, when he spoke to him? Job himself bears witness to this, when he says, *Why, after having been admonished, do I still face judgment and hear the Lord's rebukes?* (Jb 39:33) But no one is justly rebuked unless there is something in that person that deserves a rebuke.

---

33. See Jb 14:1.
34. See Jb 1:22.

11. What sort of a rebuke is this? It is correctly understood as spoken in the person of Christ the Lord. He spells out for him the divine actions stemming from his power.[35] He rebukes him with the intention that it might be clear that he is saying: Can you do these great deeds which I can? What is the point but that Job should understand? After all, we believe that God inspired him so that he foreknew that Christ would come in order to suffer. Hence, the point was that he should understand how he ought to endure his sufferings with equanimity, if Christ did not refuse to be obedient in suffering, for Christ had absolutely no sin, though he became man on our account, and as God he had such great power. Job understood that with a purer intention of the heart and added to his response, *Before I heard you with the hearing of the ear, and now, behold, my eye sees you. Hence, I have reproached myself, wasted away, and regarded myself as dust and ashes.* (Jb 42:5-6) Why was he so displeased with himself in this great insight? After all, God's work which made him a man could not rightly displease him, since scripture also says to God, *Do not look down upon the works of your hands* (Ps 138:8). Rather, it was precisely in terms of that righteousness, by which he knew that he was righteous, that he reproached himself and wasted away and regarded himself as dust and ashes. For with his mind he saw the righteousness of Christ; there could not be any sin, not only not in his divinity, but also not in his soul and not in his flesh. In comparison to this righteousness which comes from God, the apostle Paul regarded his own righteousness, which was beyond reproach in terms of the righteousness which comes from the law, not only as loss, but even as rubbish.[36]

12, 17. Hence, that splendid testimony by which God praised Job does not stand in contradiction to the testimony which says, *No living person will be found righteous in your sight* (Ps 143:2). For it does not prove to us that there was absolutely nothing in him that he himself could truthfully or that God could correctly reprehend. And yet it was not falsely said of him that he was a righteous and true worshiper of God who refrained from every evil deed. These are, after all, God's words about him: *Have you noticed my servant, Job? For there is not a man like him upon the earth: without reproach,*

---

35. See Jb 38-39.
36. See Phil 3:6-8.

righteous, a true worshiper of God, refraining from every evil deed.
(Jb 1:8) By the first words, he is praised in comparison with human
beings who are on earth; in fact, he surpassed all who at that time
were able to be righteous on earth. But it does not follow that he was
absolutely without sin, merely because he went beyond the others
in his progress in righteousness. Then it adds *without reproach*: a
man about whose life no one justly complains; *righteous*: one who
has so developed in moral goodness that no one can equal him; *a
true worshiper of God*: one who truly and humbly confesses his sins;
refraining from every evil deed: it would be surprising if he refrained
as well from every evil word and thought.

We do not know how great Job was, but we know that he was
righteous. We also know that he was a great man who bore terrible
trials and afflictions; we know that he endured all those things, not on
account of his sins, but in order to reveal his righteousness. Nonetheless, these words by which the Lord praises him could also be said
of that man who finds pleasure in the law of God according to the
interior human being, but sees another law in his members resisting
the law of his mind,[37] especially when he says, *I do not do the good
that I want, but I do the evil that I hate. But if I do the evil that I hate,
then it is no longer I who do it, but the sin that dwells in me.* (Rom
7:19-20) Note that this man is free from every evil deed in terms of
the interior human being, because it is not he himself who does it, but
the evil that dwells in his flesh. And yet, since his finding pleasure in
the law of God[38] is something that he has only from the grace of God,
he still needs to be set free and cries out, *Wretched man that I am!
Who will set me free from the body of this death? The grace of God
through Jesus Christ, our Lord.* (Rom 7:24-25)

13, 18. There are, then, persons on earth who are righteous, great,
brave, prudent, chaste, patient, pious, merciful, and who endure all
temporal evils with equanimity for the sake of righteousness. But
granted that this is true, it is also true that *if we say that we have no
sin, we deceive ourselves* (1 Jn 1:8), and *no living person will be
found righteous in his sight* (Ps 143:2). Hence, those people are not
sinless, and none of them are so insanely arrogant as to think that
they have no need of the Lord's Prayer for some sins of their own.

---

37. See Rom 7:22-23.
38. See Rom 7:22.

Nor Were Zechariah and Elizabeth Completely Sinless

19. What shall we say about Zechariah and Elizabeth who are often raised as an objection to us in discussions of this question? Scripture, after all, bears witness that Zechariah was a man of outstanding righteousness among the high priests appointed to offer the sacrifices of the Old Testament.[39] But we read in the Letter to the Hebrews the testimony that I already quoted in the previous book,[40] that Christ alone was a high priest who, unlike those who were called high priests, had no need to offer sacrifice daily first for his own sins and then for the people. It says, *It was fitting, after all, that we have a high priest of this sort: righteous, without malice, undefiled, removed from sinners, raised above the heavens, who does not have the daily need, as the high priests did, to offer sacrifice first for his own sins* (Heb 7:26). To this series of priests there belonged Zechariah, Phinehas, and Aaron, who was the first in this order, as well as all the others who lived praiseworthy and righteous lives in that priesthood. Nonetheless, they needed to offer sacrifice first for their own sins, since Christ, whom they prefigured, was the only one who, as a spotless priest, did not need to do this.

20. What has been said in praise of Zechariah and Elizabeth that is not found in the Apostle's words about himself, before he believed in Christ? After all, he said that he was without reproach in terms of the righteousness that comes from the law.[41] We read this concerning them in these words: *But they were both righteous before God, walking in all the commandments and ordinances of the Lord without reproach* (Lk 1:6). Because whatever justice they had was not a matter of pretense before human beings, it said, *before God*. But the words of scripture about Zechariah and his wife, *in all the commandments and ordinances of the Lord*, were briefly summed up by Paul as *in the law* (Phil 3:6). For prior to the gospel they did not have one law and he another; rather, they all had one and the same law. It was the law which, as we read, was given through Moses to their forefathers and in accord with which Zechariah was a priest and offered sacrifice in his turn. And yet the Apostle who at that time possessed a similar righteousness goes on to say, *Those things which*

---

39. See Lk 1:6-7.
40. See above I, 27, 50.
41. See Phil 3:6.

had been my successes, I have come to regard as losses on account of Christ. And yet I consider everything to be a loss on account of the excellent knowledge of Christ Jesus, our Lord. On his account I have considered all things not only as disadvantages, but even as rubbish, in order that I might gain Christ and be found in him, not having my own righteousness derived from the law, but that which comes through faith in Christ, a righteousness that comes from God in faith. Thus I want to know him and the power of his resurrection and the sharing in his sufferings, as one who has been conformed to his death, in order that I may somehow attain the resurrection of the dead. (Phil 3:7-11)

We are, then, so far from believing on the basis of those earlier words that Zechariah and Elizabeth possessed perfect righteousness without any sin that we do not think that even the Apostle was perfect by the same lofty standard. I do not mean only in terms of that righteousness of the law which he, as well as they, possessed and which he ranked among losses and rubbish in comparison with the surpassing righteousness which lies in faith in Christ. I mean also in terms of the gospel itself, where he earned the high rank of being so great an Apostle. I would not dare to say this, if I did not consider it unthinkable not to believe him. For he goes on to say, *Not that I have already grasped the goal or have already become perfect. Rather, I struggle on in the hope that I may grasp it, as I have been grasped by Christ Jesus. Brothers, I do not think that I have already grasped it. But I do one thing: having forgotten the past and stretched out toward what lies ahead, I deliberately struggle on toward the reward of God's lofty calling in Christ Jesus.* (Phil 3:12-14) He himself admits that he has not yet grasped the goal, that he is not yet perfect in the full righteousness which he longs to attain in Christ, but that he still deliberately struggles on and, while forgetting the past, is stretched out to what lies ahead. He admits all this so that we may know that his words, *Though our exterior human being is being corrupted, the interior human being is being renewed from day to day* (2 Cor 4:6), hold true of him as well. For although he was a perfect wayfarer, he had not yet reached the end of the journey. Finally, he wants to take along with him the sort of companions whom he addresses, when he adds, *Let as many of us, then, as are perfect bear this in mind, and if you think differently, God will reveal this to you as well; nonetheless, let us walk in the knowledge we have already attained* (Phil 3:15-16).

This walking is not done by bodily feet but by the longings of the mind and the actions of one's life. In that way those who make progress on the straight road of faith by being renewed from day to day[42] become able to be perfect possessors of righteousness. They have already become perfect wayfarers toward that same righteousness.

14, 21. And so all those people whom the scriptures of God proclaimed to us because of their good will and acts of righteousness in this life and all the people of this sort who came after them, even though they were not proclaimed and praised by those testimonies, and those who exist even now or will exist hereafter are all great, all righteous, all truly praiseworthy, but they are not completely without sin. We believe, after all, the testimonies of the scriptures concerning the praises of these persons, and by those same testimonies we also believe that no living person is found righteous in the sight of God. For this reason, we pray that he may not enter into judgment with his servants,[43] and we believe that the Lord's Prayer, which he gave to his disciples, is necessary for all the faithful, not only in general, but even for each individual.

Why We Are Commanded to Be Perfect, if No One Is Sinless

15, 22. "But," they object, "the Lord said, *Be perfect, as your heavenly Father is perfect* (Mt 5:48). He would not command this, if he knew that he is commanding what is impossible."[44] At this point the question is not whether it is possible, if they take this perfection to mean that a person can be without sin, while living this life. For we have answered above that it is possible. Our present question is rather whether anyone has actually been sinless. We have long known that there is no one who exerts his will as much as the occasion demands, as the massive testimonies of the scriptures, which I mentioned, declare.

When scripture mentions the perfection of some individual, we must see in what respect scripture speaks of it. After all, I previously cited a testimony from the Apostle in which he admits that he is not yet perfect in terms of acquiring the righteousness he desires.[45] But

---

42. See 2 Cor 4:16.
43. See Ps 143:2.
44. Once again, probably a citation from the Pelagian work mentioned in I, 34, 64.
45. See Phil 3:12, which Augustine cited in II, 13, 20.

he immediately says, *Let as many of us, then, as are perfect bear this in mind* (Phil 3:15). He would not say both of these things, unless he were perfect in one respect and not so in another. Thus, suppose that someone is a perfect student of wisdom—something that those people were not to whom he said, *I gave you milk to drink, not solid food, for you were not yet able to take it, nor are you able even now* (1 Cor 3:2). He also said to them, *We speak wisdom among the perfect* (1 Cor 2:6), where he certainly meant us to understand "perfect students." It is possible, then, as I said, that one is already a perfect student of wisdom but is not also a perfect teacher of it. One can have perfect knowledge of righteousness and not yet practice it perfectly. One can be perfect to the point of loving one's enemies, but not yet perfect to the point of accepting suffering from them. And with regard to one who is perfect insofar as he loves all human beings, who has even attained a love for his enemies, the question still remains whether he is already perfect in that love. That is, does he love those he loves as much as the immutable standard of truth prescribes that they should be loved? When we read in scripture about the perfection of some person, we must carefully note in what respect the person is said to be perfect, since a person is not taken to be without sin merely on account of being called perfect in some respect. And yet one could say that a person is worthy of being called perfect, not because of having already arrived at the goal, but because of having advanced a good distance toward it. Accordingly, a person can be called perfect in the teaching of the law, even though he still lacks some knowledge. In that sense the Apostle called those people perfect to whom he said, *And if you think differently, God will reveal this to you as well; nonetheless, let us walk in the knowledge that we have already attained* (Phil 3:15).

16, 23. Nor ought we to deny that God commands that we should be so perfect in acting righteously that we have absolutely no sin. After all, whatever it is, it is not a sin, if God does not command that it should not be. "Why then," they ask, "does he command what he knows no human being is going to do?"[46] In the same way one can also ask why he commanded those first human beings, who were the only two, what he knew they would not do. Nor should we say that he gave the command precisely so that one of us would do it, if they

---

46. A citation from the same Pelagian source as above.

did not, for God gave to them alone the command that they should not take food from that tree.[47] Just as he knew the righteousness that they were not going to observe, so he knew the righteousness that he was going to produce from them. In that way, then, he commands all human beings not to commit any sin, although he foreknows that no one will fulfill the command. Thus he himself will produce what is right by damning all those who have wickedly and damnably held his commandments in contempt. So too, he will produce what is good by purifying all those who obediently and piously make progress in his commandments, even though they do not observe all he has commanded, and who forgive the sins of others, as they want to be forgiven themselves. How, after all, can persons be forgiven by God's mercy as they forgive, if there is no sin? Or if there is a sin, how can it not be forbidden by God's righteousness?

24. "But, look," they object, "the Apostle says, *I have fought the good fight; I have run the race; I have kept the faith. There remains for me the crown of righteousness* (2 Tm 4:7-8). He would not say this if he had any sin."[48] Quite the contrary, let them explain to me how he could say this, when there still remained for him so great a battle, so great a fight, in the suffering which he said still lay ahead for him. Had he all but finished the race, when he still had not reached the point at which he was going to face a fiercer and crueler enemy? With such words he may have expressed his joy with certitude and security, because he who had revealed that this suffering still lay ahead for him had made him certain and secure regarding his victory in the great fight to come. In that case, he said these things, not because of their full attainment, but because of his firm hope. Thus he spoke of what he was confident would be, as if it had already come about. If, then, he were to add to these words, "I now have no sin," we would understand that he said this too with regard to the perfection that lay in the future, not the perfection that already came about. For his being sinless—something that they think was already realized in him, because he said these things—belonged to the finishing of his race, just as his triumphing over his opponent belonged to the finishing of his race. But even these people must admit that this latter still had to be realized, when he said this.

---

47. See Gn 2:17.
48. A citation from the same Pelagian source as above.

We maintain, then, that all of this still had to be realized in him, when, trusting in God's promise, he stated all this as if it had already taken place. To finishing his race there belonged, of course, his forgiving his debtors their debts and his praying that his own debts be forgiven.[49] Because of the Lord's promise he was completely certain that he would have no sin at that final moment which, though still to come, he described as already realized because of his trust. For, to omit other matters, I wonder whether, when he said those words which led them to think that he was sinless, there had already been taken from him that thorn in his flesh. He had asked the Lord three times to take it away from him,[50] and he received the answer, *My grace is sufficient for you; virtue is made perfect in weakness* (2 Cor 12:9). It was necessary for the perfection of this great man that the angel of Satan not be taken from him. By that angel he was struck in the face so that he might not become proud on account of the greatness of his revelations.[51] Will, then, anyone dare to think or to say that a person subjected to the burden of this life is completely free of every sin?

25. Granted that there are outstanding human beings of such great righteousness that God spoke to them from out of the pillar of cloud.[52] *Moses and Aaron among his priests and Samuel among those who call upon his name* (Ps 99:6) were such men. Scripture which speaks the truth proclaims with great praise Samuel's piety and innocence from his early childhood, when his mother left him in the temple to fulfill her vow and offered him as a servant to the Lord. Scripture also says of such persons, *You were merciful to them and punished all their loves* (Ps 99:8). In anger he punishes the children of damnation, but with mercy he punishes the children of grace, since *he chastises the one whom he loves* (Prv 3:12) and *he scourges every son he acknowledges as his own* (Heb 12:6). But only sin deserves the punishment, correction, and scourge of God. I leave aside him who stood ready for the scourges,[53] so that he might experience all things like us apart from sin[54] and be the holy priest of a holy people, making intercession even for the holy.[55] Each of them truthfully says

---

49. See Mt 6:12.
50. See 2 Cor 12:7-8.
51. See 2 Cor 12:7-8.
52. See Ps 99:7.
53. See Ps 38:18.
54. See Heb 4:15.
55. See Heb 7:26-27.

of himself, *Forgive us our debts, as we also forgive our debtors* (Mt 6:12). Those people who argue against this are praiseworthy for their chaste life and morals, and they do not hesitate to follow the counsel that the Lord gave to the rich man who asked his advice about attaining eternal life. After he answered that he already observed all the commandments, the Lord told him that, if he wished to be perfect, he should sell all that he had and give it to the poor and transfer his treasure to heaven.[56] Yet none of these people dare to say that they are without sin. When they say this, we believe that they are speaking truthfully, but, if they are lying, they begin by that very fact to increase their sin or to be sinful.

The Third Question: Why No Human Being Lives a Sinless Life

17, 26. Let us now turn to the question I put in the third place. Since a human being can be without sin in this life, when God's grace helps the human will, I could easily and truthfully give as an answer to the question why no one is without sin: Because they do not will to be. But if someone asks me why they do not will to be, the question becomes a long one. I will, nonetheless, give a short answer to it, without precluding a more careful investigation. Human beings do not will to do what is right either because they do not know whether it is right or because they find no delight in it. For we will something with greater strength in proportion to the certainty of our knowledge of its goodness and the deep delight that we find in it. Ignorance and weakness, then, are defects which hinder the will from being moved to do a good deed or to refrain from an evil deed. But it is due to God's grace helping the human will that we come to know what is hidden and find pleasing what was not attractive. The reason why human beings are not helped by his grace lies in them, not in God. They were, after all, predestined either to be damned on account of their sinful pride or to face judgment and correction for their pride, if they are children of mercy. For this reason, when Jeremiah had said, *I know, Lord, that a man's path does not lie in his own power and it is not up to a man to walk and direct his steps*, he immediately added, *Rebuke me, Lord, but in your judgment, not in your anger* (Jer 10:23-24). It is as if he said, "I know that I deserve rebuke for receiving less help from you in order

---

56. See Mt 19:20-21.

that I might perfectly direct my steps. Nonetheless, do not deal with me as you would in your anger by which you have decided to damn the wicked, but as you would in your judgment by which you teach your own not to be proud." For this reason it says elsewhere, *And your judgments will help me* (Ps 119:175).

27. Consequently, do not attribute to God the cause of any human sin. The cause of all human failings is, after all, pride. It was to overcome and destroy this pride, that such a remedy came down from heaven; to human beings puffed up with pride, God came humbly out of mercy, revealing his grace with wondrous clarity in the man whom he assumed with such great love before his companions.[57] After all, he who was in that way united to the Word of God did not bring it about by any preceding merits of his will that the one Son of God also became the one Son of Man as a result of that union. It was necessary that there be just one. There would, however, have been two or three or more, if this were something that could be brought about, not by God's gift alone, but by the free choice of a human being. This point, therefore, is particularly emphasized; this point especially, as best I can judge, is what we teach and are taught from the treasures of wisdom and knowledge hidden in Christ.[58]

Hence, at one moment a person has the knowledge to undertake, perform, and complete a good deed; at another he does not. At one moment a person finds delight in this; at another he does not. In that way we can know that it is not due to our own ability but to the gift of God either that we have the knowledge or that we find such delight. And in that way we can be healed of our empty pride and know how truly scripture says, not about this earth, but in a spiritual sense, *The Lord will give it loveliness, and the earth will bear its fruit* (Ps 85:13). A good act is the more delightful in proportion to our love for God, the supreme and immutable good and author of all other goods. So that we may love God, *love is poured out in our hearts*, not by us, but *by the Holy Spirit who has been given to us* (Rom 5:5).

18, 28. We human beings strive to find in our will some good that is ours and that we do not have from God, but I do not know how one can find such a good. We have heard the words of the apostle, when he was speaking about human goods,[59] *For what do you have that you*

---

57. See Ps 45:8.
58. See Col 2:3.
59. See 1 Cor 4:1-3.

have not received? But if you have received, why do you boast as if you have not received? (1 Cor 4:7) But the path of reason, upon which such persons as we are can enter, presses each of us investigating this question not to defend grace in such a way that we seem to destroy free choice and not to stress free choice in such a way that we are judged ungrateful to the grace of God because of our wicked pride.

A False Solution to the Question Is Rejected

29. Some want to defend the words of the Apostle I mentioned by saying that we should attribute whatever good will we have to God, because it could not exist in us, if we human beings did not exist. Why should we not attribute to God as its author whatever good will we have, since we have it from God alone that we are anything at all and that we are human beings? For it would not exist unless we existed in whom it is found. But in that way one could also say that we should also attribute to God our bad will, because it could not exist in a human being unless the human being existed in whom it is found. God is the author of the existence of the human being. Thus, one would have to credit God with being the author of this bad will too, since it could not exist if it did not have a human being in which to exist. But it is utterly wrong to say that!

30. Hence, we must maintain not only that the choice of the will, which freely turns this way and that and which belongs to the natural goods which a bad person can misuse, but also that the good will, which already belongs to those goods which cannot be misused, can come to us only from God. Otherwise, I do not know how we are going to defend the words of scripture, *For what do you have that you have not received?* For, if we have from God a free will that can become either good or bad, while the good will comes from us, what comes from us is better than what comes from God. But if that is a ridiculous claim to make, we must admit that we obtain a good will from God. Moreover, I would be surprised if the will could stand in between so that it would be neither good nor bad. For, if we love righteousness, the will is good. And if we love it more, the will is better; if we love it less, the will is less good. But if we do not love it at all, the will is not good. Who is going to hesitate to say that a will that does not love righteousness at all is not only a bad will but the very worst will? If, then, the will is either good or bad and if we

certainly do not have a bad will from God, it remains that we have a good will from God. Otherwise, I do not know what other gift of his we ought to rejoice in, when we are made righteous by him. And for this reason, I believe, scripture says, *The will is prepared by the Lord* (Prv 8:35), and in the Psalms it says, *The Lord will guide a man's steps, and he will prosper his way* (Ps 37:23). The Apostle also says, *For it is God who produces in you the willing and the action in accord with good will* (Phil 2:13).

31. Our turning away from God is our own doing, and this turning is an evil will. But our turning toward God is something we cannot do unless he rouses us and helps us, and this turning is a good will. Hence, what do we have that we have not received? But if we have received, why do we boast as if we had not received?[60] And for this reason, *Let him who boasts boast in the Lord* (1 Cor 1:31; 2 Cor 10:17). For those to whom God wills to grant this, it is a sign of his mercy, not of their merits. But for those to whom God does not will to grant this, it is a sign of the truth. For sinners deserve just punishment, because *the Lord God loves mercy and truth* (Ps 84:12), and *mercy and truth have met* (Ps 85:11). So too, *All the ways of the Lord are mercy and truth* (Ps 25:10). Who can explain the frequency with which the divine scripture mentions these two together? At times the terms are changed so that "grace" is used in place of "mercy." Thus we have *And we have seen his glory, the glory as of the Only-Begotten from the Father, full of grace and truth* (Jn 1:14). At times "judgment" is used instead of "truth," for example, *I will sing to you, Lord, of mercy and judgment* (Ps 101:1).

32. But why he wills to turn these persons back to himself and to punish those for turning away stems from the plan of righteousness that lies more deeply hidden in him. No one, after all, is right to find fault with someone who mercifully grants a benefit, and no one is right to find fault with someone who truthfully exacts punishment. So, in the case of those workers in the gospel no one is right to blame the man who pays some the wage they agreed to and gives to others the same wage, though they had not agreed upon it.[61]

---

60. See 1 Cor 4:7.
61. See Mt 20:9-10.

Why God Withholds His Grace at Times

19. To the extent that God permits, let us bear in mind, and let us understand, if we can, that the good Lord God at times does not grant even to his holy people either the certain knowledge of or the victorious delight in some good deed, in order that they may know that they do not have from themselves but from him the light that enlightens their darkness[62] and the loveliness by which their earth brings forth fruit.[63]

33. But when we ask him for his help to do and accomplish what is right, what else do we ask for but that he disclose what was hidden and that he make attractive what was not pleasing? By his grace we have learned that we must ask him for this, though it was previously hidden, and we have by his grace come to love it, though we did not previously find it attractive. And thus one who boasts may boast not in himself but in the Lord. To be inflated with pride, of course, is due to the human being's own will, not to God's activity, for God neither compels nor helps one toward this. There first arises in the human will a desire for independence so that one becomes disobedient through pride. And if this desire did not exist, nothing would have been difficult, and one could have refused to be disobedient, when one wanted to. But there resulted from the punishment that was just and deserved such a defect that it was now difficult to be obedient to righteousness. And unless that defect is overcome with the help of grace, no one turns back to righteousness; unless it is healed as an effect of grace, no one enjoys the peace of righteousness. By whose grace is it overcome and healed but the grace of him to whom it was said, *Turn us to you, Lord of our salvation, and turn aside your anger from us* (Ps 85:5)? And if God does this, he does it out of mercy, so that we say, *He has not treated us according to our sins, nor has he repaid us according to our wickedness* (Ps 103:10). To those for whom he does not do this, he does not do so out of judgment. And who is going to say to him, "What have you done?" since in a spirit of piety the holy sing of his mercy and judgment.[64] For that reason he heals even his holy and faithful people more slowly of some of their defects. Thus in these cases the good attracts them less than suffices

---

62. See Lk 1:79.
63. See Ps 85:13.
64. See Ps 101:1.

for fully accomplishing what is right, whether it remains hidden from them or it is already clearly seen. As a result, in comparison with the integral rule of his truth, no living person is found righteous in his sight.[65] His purpose in all this is not that we become worthy of damnation, but that we become humble. He teaches us about his grace so that we do not suppose, because we have experienced an ease in all we do, that his gift is something that comes from us. For this error is very much opposed to religion and piety. On the other hand, we should not think that we ought to remain in those same defects. Rather, we should strive with vigilance, especially against pride, on account of which we are humbled by these defects, and we should ardently plead with him, always with the understanding that we have such striving and such prayer as his gift. Thus, in all things we will not have our gaze turned to ourselves, but our hearts raised up to the Lord our God, and we will give thanks and, when we boast, we will boast in him.[66]

The Fourth Question: Can or Could There Ever Be a Completely Sinless Human Being?

20, 34. The fourth question remains. When we have explained it to the extent that the Lord gives his help, this lengthy discussion will at last come to an end. The question is not only whether there has been someone among those human beings already born who never has had or never will have any sin, but also whether there ever could or can be such a person. It is absolutely certain that there is not, was not, and will not be anyone of that sort, except the one mediator between God and human beings, the man Christ Jesus.[67] For this reason we have already said a great deal about the baptism of little ones. For, if they have no sin, not only are there countless human beings without sin, but there also have been and will be. But if the answer we gave to our second question is correct, namely, that there is no one without sin, then little ones are certainly not without sin. It follows from this as something beyond any doubt that, even if there could be someone in this life so perfect in virtue as to attain complete righteousness and, consequently, be without any sin, that person was, nonetheless, previ-

---

65. See Ps 143:2.
66. See 1 Cor 1:31.
67. See 1 Tm 2:5.

ously a sinner and was transformed from that state into this newness of life. For we asked one question in the second place, and we have raised another question in this fourth spot. In that earlier question we asked whether anyone in this life did by God's grace and by effort of the will attain that perfect life which is completely without sin. In this fourth question we are asking whether among human offspring there was someone or there could have been or can be someone, not who has come to absolutely perfect righteousness from sin, but who has never been bound by any sin whatsoever. Hence, if those many statements we made about little ones are true, there is not and has not been and will not be any human being of that sort, apart from the one mediator between God and human beings. In him is found our atonement and justification,[68] by which the hostilities resulting from sin have been ended and we have been reconciled to God.[69] It is not, then, off the point to go over a few things concerning the beginning of the human race to the extent that seems sufficient for the present question, so that the reader's mind will be instructed by them against various arguments that could cause problems.

The Disobedience of Adam and Eve and Its Results

21, 35. Those first human beings, the one man, Adam, and his wife, Eve, who was formed from him, chose not to remain obedient, after they had received God's commandment; hence, they received the just punishment they deserved. For God had threatened that they would die on the day they ate the forbidden fruit.[70] Moreover, they had received the right to use every tree in paradise as food, and God had also planted there the tree of life. He had forbidden them only the tree which he called the tree of the knowledge of good and evil; that name was meant to signify the consequences they would experience, both the good they were going to discover if they kept the commandment and the evil they were going to discover if they violated it. We are, of course, correct in thinking that they refrained from the forbidden food before the devil maliciously persuaded them and that they made use of the foods that were permitted and, hence, of the other trees and especially of the tree of life. After all, what is

---

68. See Rom 3:25.
69. See Rom 5:10.
70. See Gn 2:17.

more absurd than to believe they took nourishment from the other trees, but not from that tree as well? It too was permitted them, and its principal benefit was that it did not allow their bodies, even though they were animal bodies, to be transformed through the corrupting influence of time and to grow old toward death. It gave this benefit to the human body from its own body, and it showed by its mystical signification what the rational soul derives from wisdom, of which it is the symbol. For, given life by its nourishment, the rational soul would in no sense turn to the corruption and death that is wickedness. For scripture correctly says of it, *It is the tree of life for those who embrace it* (Prv 3:18). As the former tree stands in the bodily paradise, so the latter stands in the spiritual paradise. The one provided vital strength to the senses of the exterior human being, the other to those of the interior human being, so that they did not change in the course of time into something inferior. They were, therefore, serving God with the piety of obedience that was so strictly enjoined upon them, for by it alone do we worship God. How great it is in itself and how it alone suffices to keep the rational creature subordinate to the creator could not be taught in a more excellent way than by their being forbidden a tree that was not bad. The creator of good things, after all, made all things, and *behold they are very good* (Gn 1:31). Heaven forbid that he planted something bad in the fertile soil of even that bodily paradise. Rather, in order to show to human beings, for whom it was most beneficial to serve under such a lord, the great goodness of obedience alone, he demanded only obedience from his servant. And yet, it would be profitable for a human being to obey him, not merely on account of his lordship, but also on account of the benefit that comes to one who serves him. They were forbidden that tree from which, if they had made use of it when they were not forbidden, they would have suffered no evil. Thus what they suffered when using it after it was forbidden is sufficient proof that it was not a deadly tree with poisonous fruit, but only the violation of obedience, that brought this upon them.

Adam and Eve before and after Their Disobedience

22, 36. Before they had gone against this obedience, they were pleasing to God, and God was pleased with them. And though they had an animal body, they felt nothing in that body stir against them in disobedience. The order of righteousness, of course, brought it about, that, because their soul had received the body as its servant, its body was obedient to it and offered a service appropriate to that life without any resistance, just as the soul was obedient to its Lord. Hence, they were naked and were not ashamed.[71] Now the rational soul feels shame out of a natural modesty, because by reason of a certain weakness it cannot bring about in the flesh, over which it received the power of a master over a servant, that its members are not aroused against its will and that they are aroused when it wills. On this account these members are correctly called shameful (*pudenda*), even in a chaste person, because they are aroused in opposition to their lord, the mind, as they want. It is as if they are in their own power and as if the reins of virtue have only sufficient control over them to prevent them from doing impure and forbidden actions. This disobedience of the flesh, which is now found in this stirring, even if it is not permitted to carry out the act, did not exist then in those first human beings, when they were naked and were not embarrassed. The rational soul, the lord over the flesh, had not yet emerged as disobedient to its Lord, so that it experienced the disobedience of its own servant, the flesh, with a certain sense of confusion and bother, and it certainly did not by its disobedience produce that feeling in God. After all, it is not something embarrassing or bothersome for God, if we do not obey him, for we are absolutely unable to diminish his sovereign power. But it is something embarrassing for us that the flesh does not obey our command, because this is the result of the weakness which we merited by sinning, and it is called the sin dwelling in our members.[72] It is, however, sin in the sense that it is the punishment of sin. After the transgression was committed and the disobedient soul had turned away from the law of its Lord, its servant, that is, its body, began to have the law of disobedience in opposition to it, and those human beings were ashamed of their nakedness, when they noticed the stirring which they had not previously felt. Their noticing this is what was meant by the opening of their eyes.[73] For they were certainly not wandering about in the midst of those trees with their eyes closed. It was in this sense that scripture said of Hagar, *Her eyes were opened, and she saw the well* (Gn 21:19). Then the human

---

71. See Gn 2:25.
72. See Rom 7:17.23.
73. See Gn 3:7.

beings covered their genitals;[74] God made those members, but they made them something to be ashamed of.

23, 37. From this law of sin there is born the sinful flesh that needs to be purified through the sacrament of the one who came in the likeness of sinful flesh,[75] so that the body of sin might be destroyed.[76] The Apostle also calls it the body of this death, and from it only the grace of God through Jesus Christ our Lord frees pitiful human beings.[77] For this law was passed from them to their descendants as the beginning of death, just as the burden of labor by which all human beings labor on the earth was passed on, just as the pains of birth were passed on to women.[78] For, when they were found guilty of sin, they merited these punishments from the sentence of God, which we see is carried out not in them alone but also in their descendants, in some more than in others, but in all of them. The initial righteousness of those first human beings consisted in their obeying God and not having this law of concupiscence in their members in opposition to the law of their mind.[79] Now, after their sin, since our sinful flesh is born from them, it is considered something great for those who obey God not to obey the desires of the same concupiscence, but to crucify in themselves the flesh along with its passions and concupiscence in order to belong to Jesus Christ.[80] He prefigured this on his cross, and he gave to them the power to become children of God by his grace. For he gave, not to all human beings, but to as many as welcomed him, that they who were born to this world in the flesh might be reborn for God by the Spirit. Thus scripture says of them, *But to as many as welcomed him, he gave the power to become children of God; they have been born, not from the flesh, not from the blood, not from the will of man, not from the will of the flesh, but from God* (Jn 1:12-13).

74. See Gn 3:7.
75. See Rom 8:3.
76. See Rom 6:6.
77. See Rom 7:24-25.
78. See Gn 3:17.16.
79. See Rom 7:23.
80. See Gal 5:24.

The Word Became Flesh That We Might Become Children of God

24, 38. He went on, however, to add, *And the Word was made flesh and dwelled among us* (Jn 1:14). He as much as said that something great was brought about in them: those who had first been born for the world from the flesh, even though they had been created by God, were to be born for God from God. But something far more wonderful has come about. It belonged to their nature to be born of the flesh, but it was a gift to be born of God. And in order that they might obtain this gift, he who was in his nature born from God deigned in his mercy to be born from the flesh. That is what it means that *the Word was made flesh and dwelled among us*. In this way, he says, God brought it about that we, who are born flesh from flesh, are afterward spirit by being born of the Spirit and dwell in God, because God, who was born from God, afterward also was made flesh by being born from flesh and dwelled among us. For the Word that was made flesh existed in the beginning and was God with God.[81] But his partaking of our lowliness so that we might partake of his loftiness had a certain middle point in the birth of the flesh, for we are born in sinful flesh, while he was born in the likeness of sinful flesh.[82] We are born not only from flesh and blood, but from the will of man and the will of the flesh;[83] he was born only from flesh and blood, not from the will of man or from the will of the flesh, but from God. And thus we face death on account of sin; he faced death on account of us without any sin. But just as the lowly condition by which he came down to us is not in every respect equal to the lowly condition in which he found us here, so too the loftier condition in which we rise up to him will not be equal to the loftier condition in which we shall find him there. For we were made children of God by his grace; he was always the Son of God by nature. Having at some point turned back to God, we will cling to him, though unequal to God; never having turned away, he remains equal to God. We *partake* of eternal life; he *is* eternal life. Therefore, he alone, having become man, while remaining God, never had any sin and did not assume sinful flesh, though he assumed flesh from the sinful flesh of his mother. Whatever of the flesh he took

---

81. See Jn 1:14.1.
82. See Rom 8:3.
83. See Jn 1:13.

from her, he either cleansed it to assume it or cleansed it by assuming it. And so he created his virgin mother; she did not conceive by the law of sinful flesh, that is, not by the stirring of carnal concupiscence; rather, by her pious faith she merited that the holy child come to be in her. He created her in order to choose her, from whom he chose to be created. How much more, then, does sinful flesh need to be baptized in order to escape judgment, if sinless flesh was baptized as an example to imitate.

Why Children of Baptized Parents Need to Be Baptized

25, 39. We replied above to those who say, "If a sinner gave birth to a sinner, a righteous person ought also to give birth to a righteous child."[84] We give the same answer to those who say that someone born of baptized parents ought to be regarded as having been baptized. They ask, "Why could they not, after all, be baptized in the loins of their father, if, according to the Letter to the Hebrews, Levi was able to receive tithes in the loins of Abraham?"[85] Those who say this should notice that Levi did not afterwards not receive tithes, because he had received tithes in the loins of Abraham. Rather, he received them because he was given the honor of the priesthood, so that he received tithes and did not give them. Otherwise, the rest of his brothers who gave tithes to him would not be given tithes, since they too had received tithes from Melchizedek in the loins of Abraham.[86]

40. No one should argue as follows: The sons of Abraham could rightly receive tithes, even though they had already received tithes in the loins of their father, because that tithing was something to be repeatedly performed in the case of each person. Accordingly, the Israelites used to offer to the Levites many tithes from all their crops every year, even for the whole of their lives. But baptism is a sacrament that is given once, and if one had already received it when he was in his father, he must be considered as having been baptized, since he was begotten from one who had been baptized. Let me be brief; one who argues that way should consider circumcision; it is performed once, but it is performed once on each individual. Just as during the time of that sacrament one begotten of a circumcised par-

---

84. See above II, 11, 11.
85. See Heb 7:9-10; another citation from the same Pelagian work mentioned in I, 34, 64.
86. See Heb 7:10.

ent had to be circumcised, so now one who is begotten of a baptized parent has to be baptized.

41. "The Apostle says, *Your children would be unclean, but now they are holy* (1 Cor 7:14). And so," they claim, "the children of believers do not now need to be baptized."[87] I am surprised that those people say this who deny that sin is derived from our origin from Adam. After all, if they interpret this statement of the Apostle so that they suppose that the children of believers are born in a state of holiness, why are they convinced that they must be baptized? Why do they, moreover, refuse to admit that some sin is derived from our origin from a sinful parent, if some holiness is derived from a holy parent? And, even if holy children are produced by believing parents, it is not contrary to our statement that, if they are not baptized, they face damnation. These people exclude them from the kingdom of heaven, although they claim that they have no sin, neither personal nor original. Or, if they think it wrong that holy persons are damned, how is it right that holy persons are separated from the kingdom of God? They would do better to consider why some sin is not derived from sinful parents, if some holiness is derived from holy parents and some uncleanness from unclean parents. After all, he who said, *Your children would be unclean, but now they are holy* (1 Cor 7:14), mentioned both of these. Let them also explain how it is just that both holy children born of believing parents and unclean children born of non-believing parents are equally prevented from entering the kingdom of God, if they have not been baptized. What benefit, then, do they get from that holiness? They might have said that unclean children born of non-believing parents are damned, but that the holy children of believing parents are still not damned, because they are holy, though they cannot enter the kingdom of heaven unless they have been baptized. Then there would be some sort of distinction. But they say that holy children born of holy parents and unclean children born of unclean parents equally escape damnation, because they have no sin, and are excluded from the kingdom of God, because they were not baptized. Who is going to believe that such fine minds fail to see this absurdity?

42. The Apostle said, *The one brought all to condemnation* and *the one brought all to righteousness of life* (Rom 5:16.18). Consider

---

87. Another citation from the Pelagian work cited above.

for a moment how it is not opposed to our view or, rather, to the Apostle's own view, that he says in another context, *Otherwise, your children would be unclean, but now they are holy* (1 Cor 7:14).

26. Sanctification is not all of one sort. I think, in fact, that even the catechumens are sanctified in their own way by the sign of Christ and prayer along with the imposition of hands. And though what they receive is not the body of Christ, it is, nonetheless, holy and more holy than the foods by which we are nourished, because it is a sacrament. But the same apostle said that those foods we use for the necessary sustenance of this life are sanctified by the word of God and the prayer we say,[88] when we are about to take refreshment for our bodies. The sanctification of those foods does not mean that what enters the mouth does not pass into the stomach and is not cast into the toilet because of the corruption that destroys all earthly things. It was for this reason that the Lord exhorted us to seek another food that does not corrupt. In the same way, if catechumens are not baptized, their sanctification is useless for entering the kingdom of heaven or for the forgiveness of sins. And for this reason, whatever sort of sanctification it is that the Apostle says is found in the children of believers, it has nothing at all to do with this question of baptism and of the origin and forgiveness of original sin. For he says in the same passage that non-believing spouses are sanctified by their believing spouses, when he says, *For a husband who does not believe is sanctified in his wife, and a wife who does not believe is sanctified in a brother; otherwise, your children would be unclean, but now they are holy* (1 Cor 7:14). None, I suspect, understand these words, however they interpret them, in so unbelieving a way that they think that a non-Christian husband does not need to be baptized because his wife is a Christian, and that he has attained the forgiveness of sins and will enter the kingdom of God because he was sanctified in his wife.

27, 43. If any are still disturbed over why children born of baptized parents are baptized, let them listen to this brief explanation. Just as the birth of sinful flesh through the one Adam brings to damnation all those who are born in that way, so the birth in the Spirit by grace through the one Jesus Christ leads to the justification of eternal life[89] all those who have been predestined and reborn in that way. The

---

88. See 1 Tm 4:5.
89. See Rom 5:18.

sacrament of baptism is, of course, the sacrament of rebirth. Hence, just as a human being who has not lived cannot die and one who has not died cannot rise, so one who has not been born cannot be reborn. From this it follows that no one who has not been born could be reborn in his parent. It is necessary, then, that everyone who has been born must be reborn, because *unless one has been born again, one cannot see the kingdom of God* (Jn 3:3). Even a little one, then, must be immersed in the sacrament of rebirth to avoid departing from this life without it in an evil state. And this is done only for the forgiveness of sins.[90] Christ also showed this in the same passage. When he was asked how this was possible, he recalled what Moses did when he raised up the serpent.[91] Since infants, then, are conformed to the death of Christ through the sacrament of baptism, we must confess that they are set free from the bite of the serpent, if we do not want to depart from the rule of Christian faith. Yet, they did not receive that bite in their own personal life, but in the one upon whom it was first inflicted.

Baptism Brings Forgiveness of All Sins, but Not Complete Renewal

44. The fact that parents' personal sins do them no harm after their conversion should not lead to misunderstanding. They claim, "For how much more do they not harm the child!"[92] Those who think this do not notice that, just as the personal sins of the parents do them no harm, because they have been reborn by the Spirit, so the sins derived from the parents will harm the child born of them, unless it is reborn in the Spirit. After all, the parents who have been renewed beget a child in the flesh, not from the first fruits of their new state, but from the remains of their old condition, and the children, though begotten entirely in the old sinful flesh as a result of the old condition of their parents, escape the damnation that was due to the old human being by the sacrament of spiritual rebirth and renewal. Here is something to which we ought to pay attention and which we ought to bear in mind, especially on account of the questions which have been and still can be raised on this subject: Baptism only brings about the full and complete forgiveness of sins, but it does not immediately trans-

---

90. See Acts 2:38.
91. See Jn 3:14.
92. Another quotation from the Pelagian work cited above.

form the whole condition of the human being. Rather, in those who are making good progress, as their renewal grows from day to day,[93] the first fruits of the Spirit transform into themselves what pertains to the old flesh, until the whole is so renewed that even the weakness of the animal body attains spiritual strength and incorruption.[94]

Concupiscence Remains, though the Guilt Is Forgiven

28, 45. The Apostle, however, also refers to this law of sin as "sin," when he says, *Let sin, then, not reign in your mortal body so that you obey its desires* (Rom 6:12). It does not remain in the members of those who have been reborn of water and the Spirit, as though it were not forgiven, once they received the full and complete forgiveness of sins and all the hostilities were destroyed, by which we were separated from God.[95] Rather, it remains in the old condition of the flesh as something overcome and destroyed, provided it does not to some extent revive through our consenting to what is wrong and it is not recalled into its own kingdom and dominion. But the Apostle sharply distinguished the life of the Spirit, in whose newness the baptized are reborn through the grace of God, from this old condition of the flesh in which this law of sin, or sin, has already been forgiven. It was not enough for him to say that such persons were not in sin; he also added that they were no longer in the flesh, even before they departed from this mortal life. He said, *But those who are in the flesh cannot please God; you, however, are not in the flesh, but in the Spirit, provided that the Spirit of God dwells in you* (Rom 8:8-9). And yet those who apply its members to good works make good use of this flesh, corruptible as it is, though they are not in this flesh, because they neither think nor live in accord with it. So too, those who with courage and patience offer their death for their brothers, for the faith, or for any true, holy, and just cause, make good use of death, which is the penalty of the first sin. In the same way, believing married couples make good use even of that law of sin which remains in the old condition of the flesh, though already forgiven, for, inasmuch as they are in the newness of Christ, they do not allow lust to rule over them. But inasmuch as they still bring with them the old condition

93. See 2 Cor 4:16.
94. See 1 Cor 15:44.
95. See Eph 2:16.

of Adam, they bear children subject to death who need to be reborn for immortality. And they have that sinful heritage which does not hold subject those who have been reborn and from which those who are born are released by being reborn. The law of concupiscence, then, remains in the members,[96] but, despite its remaining, its guilt is removed. It is removed in one who has received the sacrament of rebirth and has begun to be renewed. But one who is born from that old condition of concupiscence that remains needs to be reborn in order to be healed, because believing parents who have been born in the flesh and reborn in the Spirit have begotten children in the flesh. But how could children in any sense be reborn before they are born?

46. Do not be surprised that I said that, although the law of sin remains in concupiscence, its guilt is removed by the grace of the sacrament. For wicked thoughts, words, and deeds have passed away and no longer exist in terms of any movement of the mind and body they involved. But though they have now passed away and no longer exist, their guilt remains, unless it has been removed by the forgiveness of sins. So, conversely, this law of concupiscence has not passed away, but still remains, though its guilt is removed and no longer exists, when the full forgiveness of sins takes place in baptism. Moreover, if departure from this life immediately follows, there will be absolutely nothing to hold the one subject to guilt, since everything that held such a one has been removed. Just as, then, it is not surprising that the guilt of past thoughts, words, and deeds remains prior to the forgiveness of sins, so it ought, conversely, to come as no surprise that after the forgiveness of sins the guilt ceases, while the concupiscence remains.

No One Is Absolutely Sinless apart from the One Mediator

29, 47. Since this is the case, from the moment that *through one man sin entered the world, and through sin death, and thus it was passed on to all human beings* (Rom 5:12), until the end of this carnal generation and corruptible world, the children of which are born and beget children,[97] there is no human being present in this life whom one can truthfully call absolutely sinless, apart from the one

---

96. See Rom 7:23.
97. See Lk 20:34.

mediator, who reconciles us to our creator through the forgiveness of sins. This same Lord denies his saving medicine during no age of the human race prior to the last judgment, which is still to come, to those he predestined by his certain foreknowledge and just beneficence to reign with him for eternal life. After all, before the birth of his flesh, the weakness of his suffering, and the strength of his resurrection, he formed those who lived at that time by the faith in those events that were to come in order that they might inherit eternal life. By faith in those events when they were present, he formed those who were there when they took place and saw what had been foretold become reality. By faith in those events now in the past, he continues to form those who came later, as well as us and those who are still to come. Hence, there is one faith which saves all those who are saved from their birth in the flesh by being reborn spiritually; it is directed toward him who came to be judged and to die for us, the judge of the living and the dead. But the sacraments of this one faith have changed through the various ages in accord with the vantage point from which they expressed it.

48. There is, then, one and the same savior for little ones and adults. The angels said of him, *Today a savior has been born for you* (Lk 2:11). An angel also said of him to the Virgin Mary, *You shall call his name Jesus, for he will save his people from their sins* (Mt 1:21). There we have clear proof that he was given this name, "Jesus," by which he was called, on account of the salvation which he brought us. "Jesus," of course, means "savior" in Latin. Who, then, is going to dare to say that Christ, the Lord, is Jesus only for adults and not also for little ones? He came in the likeness of sinful flesh[98] in order to destroy the body of sin.[99] In that weak body of sin, with its infant members neither suited for nor capable of any use, the rational soul is weighed down by wretched ignorance. I certainly do not in any sense believe that this ignorance was present in that infant in whom the Word was made flesh in order to dwell among us,[100] nor do I think that there was in the little Christ that weakness of mind that we observe in little ones. For as a result of this weakness, when they are disturbed by irrational emotions, they are not brought under control by any reason, by any command, but by pain at times and by fear of

98. See Rom 8:3.
99. See Rom 6:6.
100. See Jn 1:14.

pain. There you can see the children of that disobedience which is aroused in the members, resisting the law of the mind,[101] and which does not quiet down, when reason wants. It is, rather, quieted either by bodily pain from, for example, a spanking or from fear or some such emotion, but it is not controlled by the will's command. But because there was in Christ the likeness of sinful flesh, he chose to undergo the changes in age, beginning from infancy, so that it seemed that his flesh could come to death by growing old, if he were not killed as a young man. But in the likeness of sinful flesh he willingly and obediently accepted that death which in sinful flesh is the just punishment of disobedience. As he was about to go to death and to suffer it, he said, *Behold, the prince of this world comes, and he will find nothing in me. But in order that all may know that I do the will of my Father, get up, let us leave here.* (Jn 14:30-31) After he said this, he went to the death which he did not deserve, *having become obedient even to death* (Phil 2:8).

Adam's Sin Brought About Death for All Human Beings

30, 49. These people say, "If the sin of the first man has caused us to die, Christ's coming should cause those who believe in him not to die," and they add, as if giving a reason, "For the transgression of the sinner did not do us more harm than the incarnation or redemption of the savior benefited us."[102] Why do they not instead pay attention to, listen to, believe without discussion what the Apostle has stated without any ambiguity: *Because death came through a man, the resurrection of the dead also comes through a man. For, just as all die in Adam, so too all will be brought to life in Christ.* (1 Cor 15:21-22) He was certainly not speaking of anything but the death of the body. He said, then, that one man brought about the death of all and promised that the one Christ would bring about the resurrection of everyone's body. How, then, did Adam do us more harm by sinning than Christ benefited us by redeeming us? After all, by the sin of the one we die in time, while by the redemption of the other we rise, not for a temporal life, but for an endless life. Our body, then, has died on account of sin, but Christ's body alone died without sin so that, by

---

101. See Rom 7:23.
102. Another citation from the Pelagian work cited above.

the shedding of his sinless blood, he might destroy the written record of all the sins,[103] by which those who believe in him were once held as debtors to the devil. Hence, he said, *This is my blood which will be shed on behalf of many for the forgiveness of sins* (Mt 26:28).

31, 50. He could also have granted to believers that they not experience the death of this body. But if he had done that, the flesh would have acquired a felicity of sorts, but faith would have decreased in strength. Human beings, after all, are so afraid of this death that they would declare Christians fortunate merely because they could not die. And for this reason no one would hasten to the grace of Christ with the courage to despise this death on account of that life which will be truly happy after death. Rather, with an eye to their own comfort, people would believe in Christ only for the sake of removing the pain of death. Hence, he offered more grace; he undoubtedly gave more to those who believe in him. After all, what would be so great about believing that one is not going to die, when one sees that those who believe do not die? How much greater, how much more courageous, how much more praiseworthy it is to believe so that we hope that we will live without end, though we are destined to die. Moreover, some will at the end receive the gift of not experiencing this death by reason of their sudden transformation; they will rather be snatched up in the clouds, along with those who will rise, to meet Christ in the air, and thus they will live forever with the Lord.[104] And it is right that they receive this gift, since they will not have any coming after them, who would believe not because they hope for what they do not see but because they love what they see. Such faith is weak and feeble, and we should not call it faith at all, since faith has been defined in this way: *Faith is the foundation of those who hope, the conviction of things which are not seen* (Heb 11:1). Hence, in the same Letter to the Hebrews where this is written, after he has gone on to enumerate those who pleased God by faith, he adds, *In accord with faith all these have died, though they had not received the promises. Rather, they saw them from afar and greeted them and confessed that they were strangers and pilgrims on earth.* (Heb 11:13) And shortly after this encomium of faith, he concludes in this way. He says, *And all who had accepted the testimony through faith did not have the promises,*

103. See Col 2:14.
104. See 1 Thes 4:16.

but they foresaw better things for us, so they should not attain full perfection without us (Heb 11:39). There would not be this encomium of faith, nor would there be faith at all, as I have already said, if human beings attained visible rewards for believing, that is, if in this world the reward of immortality were given to those who believed.

51. For this reason the Lord himself chose to die so that, as scripture says, *he might by death remove from power the one who had rule over death, that is, the devil, and might set free those who out of fear of death were through the whole of life subject to slavery* (Heb 2:14-15). This testimony shows clearly enough that this death of the body came about under the leadership and at the instigation of the devil, that is, as a result of the sin resulting from his persuasion. He would not, after all, truly be said to have the power of death for any other reason. Hence, he who died without any sin, whether original or personal, stated those words which I cited just before, *Behold, the prince of the world will come, that is, the devil who has the power of death, and he will find nothing in me,* that is, nothing of the sin by which he brought it about that human beings die. And as if someone asked him, "Why then are you going to die?" he said, *But in order that all may know that I do the will of my Father, get up, let us leave here,* that is, in order that I may die, though I do not have a cause for my death from sin under the power of the author of sin, but from the righteousness of obedience, *having become obedient even to death.* This testimony, then, has shown that the fact that believers conquer the fear of death belongs to the combat of faith, which would, of course, not occur if immortality immediately followed upon the act of faith.

32, 52. The Lord performed many visible miracles as a result of which the faith began to sprout up from its infancy and grow from its tender beginnings to full strength. But it is stronger to the extent that it no longer looks for such things. Thus he willed that we look forward, without seeing it, to the promised state we hope for so that the righteous might live from faith.[105] In fact, though he rose on the third day, he did not want to remain among human beings. Rather, after he had in his flesh provided an example of the resurrection for those whom he chose to have as witnesses of its reality, he ascended into heaven. Thus, he removed himself even from their sight and gave to the flesh of none of them anything like what he showed them in

---

105. See Rom 1:17; Gal 3:11.

his own flesh. Accordingly, they too could live from faith and could in the meanwhile look forward in patience to the reward of that righteousness by which one lives from faith—a reward which they did not then see, but which they would later see. We should, I believe, interpret in this sense his words concerning the Holy Spirit, *He cannot come, unless I leave* (Jn 16:7). For this amounts to saying, "You cannot live in righteousness from faith—which you will have from my gift, that is, from the Holy Spirit—unless I take from your sight what you are looking at so that your heart may develop spiritually by believing what you do not see." He again and again praises this righteousness based on faith[106] when he speaks of the Holy Spirit. He says, *He will convict the world regarding sin, righteousness, and judgment: regarding sin, because they did not believe in me; regarding righteousness, because I go to the Father and you will see me no more* (Jn 16:8-10). What does this righteousness on the basis of which they would not see him mean but that the righteous live from faith?[107] Thus, we do not look back to things that are seen, but to those which are not seen, and by the Spirit we look forward to the hope of righteousness based on faith.

33, 53. They say, "If this death of the body came from sin, we surely would not die after the forgiveness of sins which the redeemer has given us."[108] They do not understand that, though God has destroyed the guilt of those things so that they do us no harm after this life, he has allowed them to remain for the contest of faith so that we may learn from them and be exercised as we advance in the struggle for righteousness. After all, someone else who does not understand this point could say, "If on account of sin God said to the man, *In the sweat of your brow you will eat your bread, and the earth will bring forth thorns and thistles for you* (Gn 3:19.18), why does this toil continue even after the forgiveness of sins, and why does the earth bring forth these harsh and troublesome plants for believers? So too, if the woman was told on account of sin, *You will bear children with groaning* (Gn 3:16), why do believing women suffer those same pains in childbirth, even after the forgiveness of sins?" And yet it is certain that it was on account of the sin which they committed that those first human beings heard these words and deserved these punishments from God. No one rejects these

---

106. See Phil 3:9.
107. See Rom 1:17; Gal 3:11.
108. Another quotation from the previously mentioned Pelagian work.

words of God's book which I cited concerning the man's toil and the woman's childbirth except someone who is fully separated from the Catholic faith and is opposed to these same writings.

Once Punishments, Now Challenges for the Righteous

34, 54. But there are such people, and we answer them, once the question has been raised, by saying that before the forgiveness of sins those things were punishments, but after the forgiveness of sins they provide challenges and exercise for the righteous. And so we must say to the people who are similarly disturbed over the death of the body that we admit that it came about as a result of sin and that we do not deny that after the forgiveness of sins it was left as a challenge for us so that, as we grow in strength, we might conquer our great fear of it. If faith that works through love[109] demanded only a small amount of virtue, then it would not be so great a glory for the martyrs to conquer the fear of death, nor would the Lord say, *No one has greater love than that he gives his life for his friends* (Jn 15:13). In his Letter John puts it this way, *As he gave his life for us, so we too ought to give our life for our brothers* (1 Jn 3:16). We would never, then, have special praise for the suffering involved in enduring death or for making light of it for the sake of righteousness, if death did not entail very great and fierce pain. One who conquers the fear of it out of faith gains the great glory and just reward of that faith. Hence, we should not be surprised that death would not have been the lot of human beings if they had not committed a sin which entailed such a punishment, and that death is now the lot of believers so that their righteousness might be strengthened by conquering the fear of it.

55. The flesh that was originally created was not the sinful flesh in which human beings refused to remain in righteousness amid the delights of paradise. As a result God decreed that after their sin the sinful flesh that was propagated had to struggle in labors and difficulties to attain righteousness. For this reason too, after he was dismissed from paradise, Adam dwelled opposite Eden,[110] that is, opposite the place of delights. This was to signify that sinful flesh, which, before it was sinful flesh, did not observe obedience amid

---

109. See Gal 5:6.
110. See Gn 3:23.

delights, has to be taught obedience amid labors, which are opposite to delights. Those first human beings afterward lived righteously, and for that reason we are right to believe that they were set free from final punishment by the blood of the Lord. But they still did not in that life merit to be called back into paradise. In the same way, even if one lives righteously in it after receiving the forgiveness of sins, sinful flesh does not immediately merit not to suffer the death which it derived from the propagation of sin.

56. We are taught something of the sort in the Book of Kings with regard to the patriarch David. When the prophet was sent to him and threatened him that he would suffer disasters as a result of God's anger because of the sin he had committed, he merited pardon by confessing his sin, and the prophet told him that his outrageous crime was forgiven.[111] Nonetheless, those disasters which God had threatened took place so that he suffered humiliation from his son. Why do they not say with regard to this passage, "If God made that threat on account of the sin, why did he carry out what he threatened, once the sin was forgiven?" If they said that, would we not be perfectly correct in replying, "The sin was forgiven so that he would not be prevented from gaining eternal life, but the threat was carried out so that his piety could be tried and tested in that humiliation"? So too, God imposed upon human beings bodily death on account of sin, and after the forgiveness of sin he did not take bodily death away in order to test their righteousness.

The Middle Path of the Savior

35, 57. Let us, then, hold to the unwavering rule of faith. There is only one person who has been born without sin in the likeness of sinful flesh, who lived without sin in the midst of others' sins, and who died without sin on account of our sins. Let us turn neither to the right nor to the left.[112] For to turn to the right means to deceive oneself by claiming to be without sin, but to turn to the left means to surrender oneself to sins out of some perverse and depraved carefreeness, as if there were no punishment. *For the Lord knows the ways that are to the right; he alone is without sin and can destroy our sins. But those*

---

111. See 2 Sm 12:13.
112. See Prv 4:27.

to the left are perverse (Prv 4:27), namely, friendships with sin. In this way those twenty-year-old youths prefigured the new people; when they entered the promised land,[113] they turned, it is said, neither to the right nor to the left.[114] We should, of course, not compare the age of twenty to the innocence of little ones, but, unless I am mistaken, this number foreshadows and echoes something mystical. For the five books of Moses are preeminent in the Old Testament, while the authority of the four Gospels shines forth brilliantly in the New. These numbers multiplied by each other amount to twenty, for four times five or five times four are twenty. Such a people, as I said, instructed in the kingdom of heaven through the two Testaments, the Old and the New, will enter into the promised land, neither turning to the right in a proud claim to righteousness nor turning to the left in a carefree love of sin. There we will no longer pray for the forgiveness of our sins, nor will we have any fear of suffering their punishment in ourselves, once we have been set free by that redeemer who was not sold into slavery to sin[115] and has redeemed Israel from all her iniquities, whether those committed in the life of each individual or those derived from our origin.

36, 58. It was, after all, not a small concession that they made to the authority and truth of the scriptures of God, when they admitted that little ones needed redemption, even if they refused to state clearly in their writings that they needed the forgiveness of sins.[116] They used a different word, a word also drawn from Christian doctrine, but they said exactly the same thing. Those who read with faith, hear with faith, and embrace with faith the divine scripture should have no doubt about this point: The flesh first became sinful flesh by the will to sin, and then through succeeding generations sin and death were transferred to all. From that flesh only sinful flesh has been begotten with one exception: the likeness of sinful flesh, and that would not, of course, exist, if there were no sinful flesh.

59. With regard to the soul, one can ask whether it is propagated in the same way and is subject to the guilt which it needs to have forgiven. For we cannot claim that only a child's flesh, and not also

---

113. See Nm 14:29-31.
114. See Jos 23:6.
115. See Rom 7:14.
116. Augustine apparently is referring to the author of the "brief memo" which he mentioned in I, 34, 63.

its soul, needs the help of the savior and redeemer and that its soul
has nothing to do with the expression of thanksgiving we find in the
Psalms. We read there, *Bless the Lord, my soul, and do not forget
all his recompenses. He is forgiving toward all your sins; he heals
all your ills; he redeems your life from corruption.* (Ps 103:2-4) One
can also ask whether, if the soul is not propagated, it still needs the
forgiveness of the sin and redemption by reason of the fact that it is
weighed down and mingled with the flesh of sin, so that God judges
by his sovereign foreknowledge which little ones do not merit to be
absolved of that guilt, even though, when not yet born, they nowhere
did anything either good or bad in their own life.[117] And one could
ask how, if he does not produce souls by propagation, God is still not
the author of that guilt on account of which the soul of the little one
needs redemption through the sacrament. That is an immense question and requires another treatise, but one, as I see it, tempered by
such moderation that it would be praised for its careful investigation
rather than blamed for hasty assertions. After all, when one is debat-
ing about a very obscure matter without the help of certain and clear
proofs from the divine authorities, human presumption ought to hold
itself in check, doing nothing to favor one side or the other. For, even
if I am ignorant of how any one of these theories can be proved and
explained, I still believe that the authority of the words of God would
also be perfectly clear on this point, if human beings could not be
ignorant of it without loss of the salvation promised them.

---

117. See Rom 9:11.

Book Three

The Occasion for the Addition of the Third Book

Bishop Augustine, the servant of Christ and of Christ's servants, sends his greetings to his dear son, Marcellinus.

1, 1. I have already completed two long books on the questions you presented to me. It was especially on account of the baptism of little ones, which the universal Church administers in the manner of a loving mother, that you asked that I write a response for you against those people who claim that, even if he had not sinned, Adam would have died and that nothing passed to his descendants as a result of his sin by the process of generation. They also claim that in this life there are and have been and will be human beings who have absolutely no sin. In those books I did not think that I had dealt with all the ideas in everyone's mind on this topic. I do not know whether I or anyone could do that; in fact, I am convinced that no one could. But I thought that I had produced a work such that the defenders of the faith, which our predecessors have handed down on these matters, would not stand utterly defenseless against the innovations of those who hold other ideas. But only a few days later I read certain writings of Pelagius,[1] a holy man, as I hear, and a Christian of considerable religious development; they contained brief explanations of the letters of the apostle Paul.[2] I came to the passage where the Apostle says that through one man sin entered the world and, through sin, death, and thus it was passed on to all human beings.[3] There I found a new line of argument from those people who deny that little ones have original sin. I admit that I did not refute it in those long volumes of mine, because it never entered my mind that anyone could think or say such things. Accordingly, since I did not want to add anything to that work which I had brought to a definitive close, I thought that I should incorporate in this letter both that argument in the very words in which I read it and my own thoughts in opposition to it.

---

1. Augustine mentions Pelagius here by name for the first time; he speaks of him in a quite complimentary fashion, though he qualifies his praise with " as I hear."
2. The works in question are Pelagius' *Expositiones XIII epistularum Pauli*, ed. A. Souter (Cambridge 1926), reprinted in PLS I, 1110-1374.
3. See Rom 5:12.

The New Argument against the Transmission of Sin

2, 2. That argument is set forth as follows. He says, " But those who are opposed to the transmission of sin by generation try to attack it in this way. They say, 'If the sin of Adam did harm even to those who are not sinners, then the righteousness of Christ also benefits those who are not believers, because he says that human beings are saved through the one man in a similar way and in fact to a greater extent than they perished through the other.'"[4] As I said, I made no answer to this argument in those two books which I wrote for you, nor did I propose to refute it. Now then, take note of this, first of all. When they say, "If the sin of Adam harmed even those who were not sinners, then the righteousness of Christ also benefits those who are not believers,"[5] they take it to be obviously absurd and false that the righteousness of Christ also benefits those who are not believers. From this they think that they can infer that the sin of the first human being could not have done harm to little ones, just as the righteousness of Christ cannot benefit any who are not believers.

Let them tell us, then, what benefit the righteousness of Christ brings to baptized little ones; let them state whatever it is that they mean. After all, if they have not forgotten that they are Christians, they surely have no doubt that it brings them some benefit. Whatever benefit, then, it brings them, it cannot bring it to those who are not believers, as these people themselves state. Hence, they are forced to include baptized little ones in the number of believers and agree with the authority of the holy Church present throughout the world. The Church does not consider those unworthy to be called believers whom the righteousness of Christ, even according to the view of these people, could benefit, only if they were believers. Just as by the responses of those through whom they are reborn the Spirit of righteousness gives them a faith which they could not yet have by their own will, so the sinful flesh of those through whom they are born gives them a guilt which they have not yet contracted in their own life. And just as the Spirit of life gives them rebirth in Christ as believers, the body of death gave them birth in Adam as sinners. For the former birth is carnal; the latter is spiritual. The former produces children of the flesh; the latter children of the Spirit; the former

---

4. Pelagius, *Expositio in epistolam ad Romanos* 5, 15 (PLS I, 1137).
5. Ibid.

children destined to die, the latter children destined for resurrection. The former brings forth children of the world, the latter children of God; the former children of anger, the latter children of mercy. And, accordingly, the former brings forth children subject to original sin; the latter children set free from every bond of sin.

3. Finally, we are compelled by God's authority to assent to what we are unable to grasp even with the keenest of minds. As they admonish us to do, they correctly admit that the righteousness of Christ can benefit only believers and does in some way benefit the little ones. Hence, as we have said, they must without any equivocation include them in the number of believers after they have been baptized. It follows, then, that, if they are not baptized, they will be among those who do not believe. And, hence, they will not have life, but the anger of God remains over them. For *one who does not believe in the Son will not have life. Rather, the anger of God remains over him.* (Jn 3:36) Moreover, they have been judged, for *one who does not believe has already been judged* (Jn 3:18), and they will be condemned, for *those who believe and are baptized will be saved, but those who do not believe will be condemned* (Mk 16:16). Let them now consider with what sort of justice they attempt or try to claim that sinless human beings are destined, not for life, but for God's anger, and are judged and condemned by God, if they have no original sin, just as they have no personal sin.

4. In the other two books of my long work I have, I believe, already given a sufficient and clear answer to the other points which, as Pelagius tells us, are mentioned by those who argue against original sin. If some people find it either too short or obscure, I ask them to pardon this and to come to some agreement with those who perhaps find fault with it, not because it is too short, but because it is too long. And I ask those who still do not understand those points, which I think I stated quite clearly, given the nature of questions, not to criticize me unfairly for negligence or for my lack of ability. I ask them, rather, to beg God that they may receive understanding.

Other Arguments Reported by Pelagius

3, 5. We must, nonetheless, carefully note that this man—a fine and praiseworthy man, as those who know him say—did not introduce this argument against the transmission of sin in his own name.

Rather, he reported what those people say who do not accept the transmission of sin. This holds not only for the point I just stated and answered, but also for the other points which I recall having answered in those other books. For he said, "They say, 'If the sin of Adam harmed even those who were not sinners, then the righteousness of Christ also benefits those who are not believers.'"[6] From my response you see that he not merely does not attack what we say, but he even admonishes us as to what we should say. He goes on to add, "They say next, 'If baptism washes away that ancient transgression, those who have been born of two baptized parents ought to be free from this sin. For they could not pass on to their offspring what they themselves did not have.'" He adds, "They make the further point that, if the soul does not come by generation, but only the flesh, only the flesh has the transmitted sin, and it alone deserves punishment. They claim that it is unjust that a new-born soul that is not made from the mass of Adam should bear so ancient a sin of another. "They also say," he reports, "that there is no reason to grant that God who forgives personal sins holds one responsible for the sins of another."[7]

6. Do you see, then, I ask you, how Pelagius introduced all this into his writings, not in his own name, but in the name of others? He knew full well that this was some sort of innovation that had already begun to sound contrary to the ancient view of the Church. And as a result, he was either ashamed or afraid to make it his own. Perhaps he himself does not hold that human beings are born without sin, since he admits that they need baptism in which sins are forgiven. Perhaps he does not hold that sinless human beings are condemned, for we must count those who have not been baptized among non-believers, and the text of the gospel, which certainly cannot deceive us, states with utter clarity, *Those who do not believe will be condemned* (Mk 16:16). Finally, perhaps he does not hold that the sinless image of God is excluded from the kingdom of God, since *unless one has been reborn of water and the Spirit, one cannot enter the kingdom of God* (Jn 3:5). In that case, it would either be plunged into eternal death without sin, or—what is even more absurd—it would have eternal life outside the kingdom of God. For, when the Lord foretold that he would say to his own people in the end, *Come, blessed ones of my Father, receive*

6. Ibid.
7. Ibid.

the kingdom which has been prepared for you from the beginning of the world (Mt 25:34), he also made it clear what kingdom he was speaking about. He concluded, *As the others will enter eternal fire, the righteous will enter eternal life* (Mt 25:46). These opinions and others like them that go with this error are so perverse and opposed to the Christian truth that I do not believe that this exemplary Christian holds them.[8] It could be that he is so moved by the arguments of those opposed to the transmission of sin that he wants to hear or to know what one might say in reply to them. And for this reason he did not want to pass over in silence the claims of those opposed to the transmission of sin. In that way he could point out that the question needed to be discussed, while dissociating himself from it so that no one would think that he himself held these views.

We Must Cling to the Perfectly Clear Teaching of Scripture

4, 7. But even if I am not able to refute the arguments of these people, I see that we must, nonetheless, hold onto the points which are perfectly clear in the scriptures. Then, on the basis of these points one might clarify those which are obscure, or one might believe them without any hesitation, if the mind still cannot see them, once they have been pointed out, or cannot investigate them, if they remain hidden. What is more obvious than the many great testimonies from the words of God which make it perfectly clear that, apart from community with Christ, no one can attain eternal life and salvation and that no one can by God's judgment be unjustly condemned, that is, excluded from that life and salvation? Nothing else is accomplished by the baptism of little ones but that they are incorporated into the Church, that is, that they are joined to the body and members of Christ. Hence, it clearly follows that they would be subject to condemnation, if baptism were not conferred upon them. But they could not be condemned, if they had no sin whatsoever. Since at their age they could not contract any sin in their personal life, we are left to understand or, if we cannot yet understand it, at least to believe that little ones bring with them original sin.

---

8. Augustine continues to interpret Pelagius' views in the best light, though one senses that he is finding it difficult to do so.

8. And thus, if there is something ambiguous about the words of the Apostle where he says, *Through one man sin entered the world, and through sin death, and thus it was passed on to all human beings in whom all have sinned* (Rom 5:12), and if they can be interpreted and given another meaning, are these words also ambiguous: *Unless one has been reborn of water and the Spirit, he cannot enter the kingdom of God* (Jn 3:5)? Are these words also ambiguous: *You shall call his name Jesus, for he will save his people from their sins* (Mt 1:21)? Is it also ambiguous that *it is not those who are in good health who need a physician, but those who are sick* (Mt 9:12)? That is, it is not those who have no sin who need Jesus, but those who must be healed from sin. Is it also ambiguous that, unless human beings eat his flesh, that is, become partakers of his body, they will not have life?[9] These testimonies are brilliantly clear by the divine light and utterly certain by the divine authority. In them, as well as in others of the sort that I pass over at the moment, does not the truth proclaim without any ambiguity that unbaptized little ones not only cannot enter the kingdom of God, but cannot possess eternal life apart from the body of Christ and that, in order to be incorporated in this body, they are given the sacrament of baptism? Does not the truth bear witness beyond any doubt that they are carried in the arms of their believing sponsors to Jesus, that is, to the savior and to Christ the physician, for no other reason than that they may be healed by the medicine of the sacraments from the plague of sin? Why, then, do we hesitate to understand the words of the Apostle, about which we may have been in doubt, so that they agree with those testimonies about which we can have no doubt?

9. Nonetheless, in this whole passage in which the apostle speaks of the condemnation of many through the sin of one person and of the justification of many through the righteousness of one person,[10] I do not find anything ambiguous apart from his calling Adam the pattern of what is to come.[11] For, as a matter of fact, this not only fits the view in accord with which we understand that his offspring to come were born with sin after that same pattern, but these words can be interpreted in various other senses. After all, we ourselves have

---

9. See Jn 6:54. The force of this text depends upon the practice in the early Church of giving communion to the little ones at baptism.

10. See Rom 5:18.

11. See Rom 5:14.

interpreted it differently in the past,[12] and we will perhaps interpret it differently in the future.[13] Pelagius too has not explained it in just one way.[14] One must pay careful attention and consider the remaining things which are said there, as I certainly tried to do in the first of those two books. If one does so, even if they lead to a statement that is not completely clear by reason of the difficulty of the subject matter, they still could not have another sense than that which has caused the universal Church from its earliest days to maintain that believing little ones have received the forgiveness of original sin through Christ's baptism.

Two Witnesses from the Tradition of the Church

5, 10. Hence, blessed Cyprian has rightly made it quite clear how the Church has from the beginning preserved this in her faith and understanding. He stated that little ones fresh from the wombs of their mothers are already suited to receive Christ's baptism, when he was asked whether this might take place before the eighth day. He tried as best he could to show that they were ready, so that no one would think that they still had to be made ready over eight days, because infants were formerly circumcised on the eighth day.[15] But although he offered them the strong protection of his defense, he did not admit that they were free from original sin. For, if he denied this sin, he would have removed the reason for baptism itself, and it was

---

12. In his *Commentary on Some Statements in the Letter to the Romans* 29, Augustine offered the interpretation that Adam was the figure of Christ in the reverse sense that Christ benefited us more than Adam harmed us.

13. Augustine does, in fact, offer a wide variety of interpretations of this phrase. For example, Adam prefigured Christ, because as Eve was formed from the sleeping Adam's rib, so the Church was formed from the side of the crucified Christ (*Answer to Julian* I, 659). Or, as Adam left father and mother, so Christ left his Father in taking the form of the servant and left his mother, the synagogue, and clung to the Church (*Answer to Faustus, a Manichean* XIII, 8). Or Adam was the form of what was to come, since all the nations arose from him; indeed, in Greek the letters of his name are an anagram for the four directions (*Homilies on the Gospel of John* 9, 14). Or Adam was the form of the future, because he inflicted the form of death upon his posterity (Letter 157, 4).

14. See Pelagius, *Expositio in epistolam ad Romanos* 5, 14 (PLS I, 1137), where Pelagius says, "Either Adam was the pattern of Christ, because, just as Adam was created by God without intercourse, so Christ came forth from the Virgin by the working of Holy Spirit. Or he was, as some suppose, the pattern of Christ in a reverse sense, that is, as the former was the origin of sin, so the latter is the origin of righteousness."

15. See Cyprian, Letter 64.

for the sake of receiving it that he was defending them. You can read the letter of the aforementioned martyr on the baptism of little ones, if you wish, for there must be a copy in Carthage. But I believe that a few items should be also copied into this letter of ours to the extent that seems sufficient for the present question. Pay wise attention to this quotation: "Regarding infants," he said, "you claimed that they ought not to be baptized within a day or two after they have been born and that one should bear in mind the law regarding the circumcision of old. Thus you thought that the newborn should not be baptized and sanctified before the eighth day. Our episcopal council decided the matter in a far different way, for no one agreed with what you thought should be done. Rather, we all judged that no human child should be denied God's mercy and grace. Since, after all, the Lord says in his gospel, *The Son of Man did not come to destroy, but to save human souls* (Lk 9:56), insofar as it is up to us, no soul should be lost, if at all possible."[16] Do you see what he says? Do you see how he thinks that to depart from this life without that saving sacrament is deadly and lethal, not merely to the flesh, but also to the soul of the infant? Hence, if he said nothing more, we would have every right to conclude that a soul cannot be lost without sin. But notice what he says about them in all clarity, when he is defending the innocence of little ones a bit later. He says, "But if anything can prevent human beings from attaining grace, it is especially serious sins that can prevent adults, mature, and elderly persons. But even the most serious transgressors and those who formerly sinned much against God receive the forgiveness of sins, when they later believe, and we hold no one back from baptism and grace. How much the more, then, should we not hold back a newly born infant who has committed no sin apart from having contracted by the first birth the contagion of the ancient death by being born in the flesh as a child of Adam. The infant comes to receive the forgiveness of sins with greater ease by reason of the fact that it receives forgiveness not for its own sins but for those of another."[17]

11. You see with what immense confidence this great man speaks on the basis of the ancient and undoubted faith. He offered these most certain proofs so that he might bolster what was uncertain by means

---

16. Cyprian, Letter 64, 2.
17. Cyprian, Letter 64, 5.

of their strength. For the person to whom he is replying had consulted him about what was uncertain, and the council, as he mentions, drew up its decree, namely, that no one should hesitate to baptize an infant, even before the eighth day after its birth, if the infant is brought for baptism. After all, the council did not then establish as something new, or confirm as something under attack from some opponent, the teaching that infants are held subject to original sin. Rather, because of the law regarding circumcision of the flesh, the council raised and debated the question whether they might baptize children even before the eighth day. And none agreed with the person who said that one may not, because they already held it, not as a point for inquiry or discussion, but as something solid and certain, that a soul will be lost for eternal salvation, if it ends this life without the reception of that sacrament, even if little ones fresh from the womb are subject only to the guilt of original sin. For this reason, though it is much easier in their case, since it is the sins of others that are forgiven, they still need the forgiveness of sins. These certitudes resolved that uncertain question about the eighth day, and the council decided that one may provide help to human beings on any day after their birth so that they may not perish for eternity. The council also explained that the circumcision of the flesh foreshadowed what was to come, not in the sense that baptism should be administered on the eighth day after birth, but in the sense that we are spiritually circumcised in the resurrection of Christ. He rose from the dead on the third day after he suffered, but on the eighth day, that is, on the first day after the Sabbath in terms of the days of the week by which time passes.

Jerome's Testimony to the Presence of Original Sin

6, 12. And now, with the boldness typical of a new theory, some persons are trying to make us uncertain about principles that our predecessors appealed to as utterly certain in order to resolve points that people found uncertain. I do not know when this present discussion began, but I do know that even the saintly Jerome, a man who is presently occupied with ecclesiastical writings and enjoys an excellent reputation for his teaching, unhesitatingly used this most certain proof for resolving various questions in his books. In his commentary on the prophet Jonah, when he came to the passage where it mentions that even little ones were punished with fasting, he says, "Those who are older begin, but even the younger are included. For no one is without sin, even if his life has but a single day and the years of his life can be counted.[18] For if the stars are unclean in the sight of God, how much more are a worm and corruption[19] and those who are held subject to the sin of Adam the transgressor!"[20] If we could easily question this highly learned man, how many commentators on the divine scriptures in both languages and how many authors of Christian treatises could he mention who have held this same doctrine from the time Christ's Church was founded, who have received this same doctrine from their predecessors, and who have handed this same doctrine on to their successors! Though I have read far fewer works, I do not recall having heard any different teaching from Christians who accept both testaments, not only from those in the Catholic Church, but even from those in some heresy or schism. I do not recall that I have read any different doctrine in the authors I was able to read from among those who wrote on these topics and who followed the canonical scriptures or believed they did or wanted others to believe they did.

I do not know the source from which this problem has so suddenly come upon us. A short time ago when we were in Carthage, I heard in passing from certain persons, who were casually conversing, that little ones are not baptized in order to receive the forgiveness of sins, but in order to be sanctified in Christ. I was disturbed by this new idea, but since it was not the right moment for me to say something against it and since they were not the kind of persons about whose authority I was concerned, I readily considered the matter over and done with. And now look, it is being defended with burning zeal. See for yourself, it is being preserved in writing; see, the matter has reached a crisis so that we are asked about it by our brethren. See, we are being forced to argue and write against it.

7, 13. A few years ago in Rome there emerged a certain Jovinian[21] who is supposed to have persuaded nuns, even those of an advanced age, to marry. He did this not by seduction, because he wanted to take

18. See Jb 14:4-5.
19. See Jb 25:5-6.
20. Jerome, *Commentary on the Prophet Jonah* III, 5.
21. For Jovinian, see *Heresies* 82, where Augustine reports that the Jovianists also taught that all sins are equal, that one cannot sin after baptism, and that fasting and abstinence from certain foods was without benefit.

one of them as his wife, but by the argument that virgins with vows of virginity have no more merit before God than married believers. Yet the idea never entered his mind that he should try to maintain that human children are born without original sin. And certainly, if he had developed this argument, women would be much more readily inclined to marry, if they were going to bear children who were perfectly innocent. The brothers sent this man's writings to Jerome in order to be refuted, for he was so bold as to put his views in writing. Jerome not only did not find any argument of this sort in them, but for the refutation of certain of his foolish ideas he even asserted, among his many proofs, the following point as utterly certain. It concerned the original human sin, about which he believed that Jovinian also had no doubt. Here are Jerome's words. He said, *"Those who claim to abide in Christ ought themselves to live as he lived* (1 Jn 2:6). Let my opponent choose which of the two he prefers; we are giving him the option. Does he or does he not abide in Christ? If he abides in Christ, let him then live as Christ did. But if he finds it rash to promise to be like the Lord in the virtues, he does not abide in Christ, because he does not live as Christ. He *committed no sin, and no deception was found on his lips; when they spoke ill of him, he did not speak ill of them in return* (1 Pt 2:22-23). And like a lamb before the shearer, he did not open his mouth.[22] The prince of this world approached him and found nothing in him.[23] Though he committed no sin, God made him sin on our behalf.[24] But according to the Letter of James, *we all sin in many ways* (Jas 3:2), and *no one is clean from sin, even if one's life lasts only a single day* (Jb 14:4-5). *For who is going to boast of having a chaste heart? Or who is going to presume to be clean from sins* (Prv 20:9). We are held guilty in the likeness of Adam's transgression.[25] For this reason David too says, *See, I was conceived in iniquities, and my mother conceived me in transgressions* (Ps 51:7)."[26]

14. I have not quoted these words because we rely upon the views of certain writers as if they were a canonical authority. I did this, rather, so that it would be evident that, from the beginning up to the

---

22. See Is 53:7.
23. See Jn 14:30.
24. See 2 Cor 5:21.
25. See Rom 5:14.
26. Jerome, *Against Jovinian* II, 2.

present time when this new opinion arose, this teaching on original sin was preserved in the faith of the Church. And it was preserved with such great constancy that, in order to refute other false ideas, the commentators on God's words appealed to it as utterly certain rather than that anyone tried to refute it as false.

Moreover, the holy canonical books support this position with their perfectly clear and full authority. The apostle cries out, *Through one man sin entered the world, and through sin death, and thus it was passed on to all human beings in whom all have sinned* (Rom 5:12). Hence, one cannot simply say that Adam's sin did not harm those who did not sin, since scripture says, *in whom all have sinned.* And these sins are not called those of another, as if they did not belong to the little ones. For they all sinned then in Adam, when they were all still that one man in virtue of that power implanted in his nature by which he was able to beget them. They are, rather, called the sins of another, because the little ones themselves were not yet living their own lives, but the life of one human being contained whatever was in his future posterity.

Refutation of the Individual Arguments of the Pelagians

8, 15. They say, "There is no reason to grant that God, who forgives personal sins, holds one responsible for the sins of another."[27] He forgives sins, but for those reborn of the Spirit, not for those born of the flesh. Now he does not hold them responsible for the sins of another, but for their own. They were, of course, the sins of another, when these people did not yet exist who were going to have them through generation. But now they belong by reason of birth in the flesh to those who have not yet had them forgiven by spiritual rebirth.

16. They argue, "If baptism washes away that ancient transgression, those who have been born of two baptized parents ought to be free from this sin. For they could not pass on to their offspring what they themselves did not have."[28] Notice the source from which an error all too often draws its strength: people are capable of raising questions about matters which they are not capable of understanding. For to whom or with what words am I to explain this? Corrupt mortal

---

27. Pelagius, *Expositio in epistolam ad Romanos* 5, 15 (PLS I, 1137).
28. Ibid.

beginnings do no harm to those who have begun again from new immortal beginnings, and yet they harm the children whom those very persons, who are no longer harmed by them, have generated from those same corrupt beginnings. How are people to understand that, if prejudice in favor of their own view and the heavy chain of stubbornness further prevent their lazy mind? But suppose I had undertaken this argument against people who absolutely forbade infants to be baptized or maintained that there was no need to baptize them, claiming that the children born of believers necessarily receive the reward of their parents. In that case, I ought perhaps to have been roused to defeat this view with greater toil and effort. In that case, if on account of the obscure nature of the matter, I ran into difficulty with dense and stubborn persons in refuting what is false and in convincing them of what is true, I would perhaps have recourse to these examples that are in use and at hand. I would ask them this in turn: Since it bothers them that a sin which is washed away in baptism is present in those whom the baptized parents generate, how do they themselves explain that the foreskin that is removed by circumcision is present in those whom circumcised parents generate? How too is the chaff which is so carefully removed by human labor still found in grain which grows from wheat that has been threshed?

9, 17. By these and similar examples I would try somehow or other to persuade the people who believe that it is not necessary to administer the sacraments of cleansing to the children of those who have been cleansed that to baptize the children of baptized parents is the correct thing to do. I would try to show them how it is possible that persons reborn through the Spirit, who have both the seed of death in the flesh and the seed of immortality in the spirit, are not harmed by what harms their child born in the flesh. I would try to persuade them that in them forgiveness has washed away what in the child needs to be washed away by a similar forgiveness, just as in the case of circumcision or of threshing and winnowing. But since we are now dealing with those who admit that the children of baptized parents must be baptized, we do much better to say to them: You claim that the children of parents who have been cleansed from the stain of sin ought to have been born without sin. Why do you fail to notice that one can by the same argument say to you that the children of Christian parents ought to have been born Christian? Why, then, do you think they must become Christian? Did their parents lack Christian bodies, even though scripture said of them, *Do you not know that your bodies are members of Christ?* (1 Cor 6:15)

Or was the body born from Christian parents perhaps Christian, but it did not receive a Christian soul? This would be much more surprising. For you may hold one of these two views regarding the soul. After all, you certainly believe with the apostle that, before it was born, the soul had done nothing good or bad.[29] Hence, the soul either came to be through generation, and then, just as a body of Christian parents would be Christian, so the soul ought also to be Christian. Or, as created by Christ, either in a Christian body or for the sake of a Christian body, it ought to have been created or sent as Christian.

Perhaps you are going to say that Christian parents could beget a Christian body and that Christ himself could not create a Christian soul. And so, yield to the truth and see this: As you yourselves admit, a non-Christian can be born of Christians, and one who is not a member of Christ can be born of members of Christ. And to include as well all those who belong to any religion, even if a false one, one not initiated can be born to initiated parents. In the same way, one not cleansed can be born from parents who have been cleansed. How are you going to explain why a non-Christian is born of Christians, unless it is not birth, but rebirth that produces Christians? Give yourselves the same explanation, because in the same way no one is cleansed from sins by being born, but all are cleansed by being reborn. And so, a human being born from human beings who have been cleansed, because they have been reborn, must be reborn in order to be cleansed. The parents were able to pass on to their offspring what they themselves did not have, not only as grain passes on chaff and a circumcised person passes on a foreskin, but also as—a point you yourselves admit—believers pass on to their offspring unbelief. This defect no longer belongs to those who have been reborn through the Spirit; it belongs, rather, to the mortal seed from which they were generated in the flesh. For you certainly do not deny that those little ones, who in your judgment need to be made into believers through the sacrament of believers, were born non-believers from believing parents.

---

29. See Rom 9:11.

Pelagius and the Difficult Question of the Soul

10, 18. They also hold this: "If it is not the soul but only the flesh that comes by generation, only the flesh has the transmitted sin, and it alone deserves punishment. They claim that it is unjust that a newly born soul that is not made from the mass of Adam bears so ancient a sin of another."[30] I have copied those words which I just cited from Pelagius' book. I beg you, please pay attention to how, as a man of circumspection, he is well aware that he is in the midst of the difficult question of the soul. After all, he does not say that the soul does not come from generation, but "if it is not the soul that comes from generation." He is indeed right to speak with hesitation rather than with confidence regarding a matter so obscure, about which we cannot find, or can find only with difficulty, any certain and clear testimonies in the holy scriptures.

Hence, I too will reply to the present question with a statement that is equally cautious: If the soul does not come from generation, then what sort of justice is it that a soul recently created, certainly free from every transgression, and completely pure from all contamination with sin, is forced in little ones to undergo the sufferings and various torments of the flesh and—what is worse—the attacks of demons? For the flesh does not suffer any of these without the living and sentient soul suffering these penalties even more. For if one shows that this is just, then one can also show by what sort of justice the soul is subject in sinful flesh to original sin, which must be washed away by the sacrament of baptism and the mercy of grace. But if one cannot show the former, I do not think that we can show the latter either. Let us, then, put up with the fact that both of these are hidden from us and remember that we are human beings, or, if it seems necessary, let us at some other time undertake another work on the soul in which we discuss the matter with sobriety and caution.

Conclusion and Summary of the Work

11, 19. The Apostle said, *Through one man sin entered the world, and through sin death, and thus it was passed on to all human beings in whom all have sinned.* Let us now interpret those words so that we are not judged to contradict, with great folly and to our own

---

30. Pelagius, *loc. cit.*

misfortune, so many great and clear testimonies of the divine scriptures. They teach us that no one can attain eternal life and salvation apart from the community with Christ, which we have in him and with him, when we receive his sacraments and are made members of his body. For he did not say to the Romans, *Through one man sin entered the world, and through sin death, and thus it was passed on to all human beings* in any other sense than he said to the Corinthians, *Death came through a man, and the resurrection of the dead came through a man. For, just as all die in Adam, so too all will be brought to life in Christ* (1 Cor 15:21-22). No one, of course, can fail to see that these last words refer to the death of the body, since the question of the resurrection of the body was the focus of the Apostle's attention. And so we see that he made no mention of sin there, since the question did not concern righteousness. But in writing to the Romans, he mentioned both of them and taught at great length about both of these: sin in Adam along with righteousness in Christ, and death in Adam along with life in Christ. I examined and explained, as I said, all these words of the Apostle to the extent of my ability and to the extent that seemed sufficient in the first of the previous two books.[31]

20. And yet, even in the Letter to the Corinthians, at the end he concluded the passage that we have discussed at length concerning the resurrection in such a way that he left us no doubt that the death of the body came about as a punishment for sin. For he said, *The corruptible body must put on incorruptibility, and this mortal body must put on immortality. But when this corruptible body has put on incorruptibility and this mortal body has put on immortality, then the words of scripture will be fulfilled: Death has been swallowed up in victory. Where, O death, is your victory? Where, O death, is your sting?* Then he added, *But the sting of death is sin, and the power of sin is the law.* (1 Cor 15:53-56) As the clear words of the Apostle reveal, death will be swallowed up in victory when this corruptible and mortal body will put on incorruptibility and immortality, that is, when God will bring to life even our mortal bodies on account of his Spirit dwelling in us.[32] Hence, it is clear that sin is the sting of even this death of the body, which is the opposite of the resurrection

31. See I, 8, 8-9,10.
32. See Rom 8:11.

of the body. It is the sting by which death came to be, not the sting which death has caused. For we die as a result of sin; we do not sin as a result of death. Therefore, scripture spoke of *the sting of death* in the way it spoke of *the tree of life* (Gn 2:9); it was not the tree which human life made, but the tree from which human life might come to be. It also spoke of it in the way it spoke of *the tree of knowledge* (Gn 2:9); it was the tree which would produce human knowledge, not a tree which human beings might produce by their knowledge.[33] And so, it is *the sting of death* by which death came to be, not the sting which death made. After all, we call a cup of death one from which someone has died or could die, not one that a dead or dying person has made. Sin, then, is the sting of death; pierced by sin, the human race has been put to death.

Why do we still ask whether it is the death of the soul or of the body? Or whether it is the first death by which we all now die or the second by which the wicked will die later?[34] There is no reason to raise the question; there is no room for escape. The words of the Apostle, where he deals with this, give the answer. He says, *When this mortal body has put on immortality, then the words of scripture will be fulfilled: Death has been swallowed up in victory. Where, O death, is your victory? Where, O death, is your sting?* (1 Cor 15:54-56) He was referring to the resurrection of the body, because death will be swallowed up in victory, when this mortal body has put on immortality. Then we will laugh in the face of death, which will be swallowed up in victory by the resurrection of the body. Then we will say to it, *Where, O death, is your victory? Where, O death, is your sting?* We will say this to the death of the body. For victorious immortality will swallow this up, when this mortal body will have put on immortality. Then, we will say to the death of the body, *Where, O death, is your victory?* by which you conquered all human beings so that even the Son of God did battle with you and overcame you, not by avoiding you, but by taking you on. You have conquered in those who die; you have been conquered in those who rise. Your victory, by which you swallowed up the bodies of the dying, was temporal; our victory, by which you are swallowed up in the bodies of those who rise, will last eternally.

---

33. See Gn 2:9.
34. See Rv 2:11; 20:6.14.

Where is your sting? that is, the sin by which we were pierced and poisoned so that you came to be even in our bodies and owned them for so long a time. *But the sting of death is sin, and the power of sin is the law.* We all sinned in the one man, so that we all died in the one man; we received the law, not so that we might bring sin to an end by our becoming better, but so that we might increase it by our transgression. *But the law entered in so that sin might abound* (Rom 5:20) and *scripture has enclosed all things under sin* (Gal 3:22). *But thanks be to God who has given us the victory through our Lord, Jesus Christ* (1 Cor 15:57). And so, where sin was abundant, grace might be even more abundant,[35] and *on the basis of faith in Jesus Christ the promise might be given to those who believe* (Gal 3:22). Thus we might also conquer death through deathless resurrection, and conquer sin, its sting, through the free gift of justification.

12, 21. Let no one, then, be mistaken about this matter and mislead others. This clear meaning of the holy scripture banishes and removes all ambiguity. Just as death in the body of this death comes from our origin,[36] so too sin in this sinful flesh has come from our origin. To heal this sinfulness contracted by birth and increased by our will and to raise up this flesh, the physician came in the likeness of sinful flesh. It is not those who are in good health who need him, but those who are sick,[37] and he did not come to call the righteous, but sinners.[38] Moreover, when the apostle advised the faithful not to separate from unbelieving spouses, he said, *For a husband who does not believe is sanctified in his wife, and a wife who does not believe is sanctified in a brother; otherwise, your children would be unclean, but now they are holy* (1 Cor 7:14). We must either interpret these words as we have explained them elsewhere[39] or as Pelagius explained them when he was commenting on this same letter to the Corinthians.[40] The explanation is that there had already been examples of husbands who won their wives and of wives who won their husbands for Christ, as well as examples of little ones in whose case the Christian desire of the one parent prevailed to make them

---

35. See Rom 5:20.
36. See Rom 7:24.
37. See Mt 9:12.
38. See Mk 2:17; Lk 5:32.
39. *The Lord's Sermon on the Mount* I, 16, 45.
40. Pelagius, *Expositio in epistolam primam ad Corinthios* 7, 14 (PLS I, 1201).

Christians. Or perhaps, as the words of the Apostle seem rather to suggest and in some sense even to demand, we should understand in this passage some other sanctification by which a non-believing husband or a wife is sanctified through the spouse who believes or by which the children of believers are born holy. Perhaps they refrained from intercourse at the time of the wife's period, because either the husband or the wife read this in the law. Ezekiel, after all, lists this among the commandments which are not to be interpreted figuratively.[41] Or it may have been on account of some other conferral of sanctity that is not clearly stated, coming from the union of spouses and their children. But, whatever that sanctification may be, we must hold it as beyond any doubt that it is unable to make them Christians and to forgive sins, unless they become believers by the teaching and sacraments of Christ and the Church. For, no matter how holy and righteous their spouses are, non-believers are not cleansed from the sinfulness which compels those who have been excluded from the kingdom of God to enter into condemnation. And no matter how holy and righteous the parents are who begot them, little ones are released from the guilt of original sin only if they have been baptized in Christ. For these we must speak the more unstintingly, the more they are unable to speak for themselves.

13, 22. The point of that discussion, after all, was that some people think that infants have no need to be baptized, and we must oppose that novel idea with the ancient truth. They do not state this point in plain words for fear that the well-established and salutary custom of the Church would be unable to tolerate those who violate it. If we are commanded to help orphans, how much more ought we to labor for these children who, even with their parents, will remain more destitute and more wretched than orphans, if they are denied the grace of Christ for which they themselves are unable to ask.

23. These people claim, however, that some human beings, who already have the use of their own reason, will live, have lived, or are now living without any sin. We should hope that this will be the case; we should strive to make it so; we should pray that it will be so. We should not, however, presume that it is already the case. After all, for those who hope for and strive after and pray for this

---

41. See Ez 18:6.

with suitable prayers, whatever is left of their sins is daily removed by the words we truthfully say in the prayer, *Forgive us our debts, as we also forgive our debtors* (Mt 6:12). Whoever claims that this prayer is not necessary in this life for anyone, even for a holy person who knows and does God's will, except for the Holy of Holies,[42] is greatly mistaken and is utterly unable to please the very one whom he praises. If persons believe that they are such, they deceive themselves, and the truth is not in them,[43] for no other reason than that they believe what is false. That physician, then, whom those in good health do not need, though the sick do,[44] knows full well how, by his healing, to bring us to perfection for eternal salvation. Although it was imposed as a punishment for sin, he does not in this age take death itself away from those whose sins he forgives so that, through having to overcome the fear of death, they might take up the struggle out of pure faith. And in certain cases he does not help even his righteous ones to bring their righteousness to perfection, because they can still become proud. Thus, as long as no living person is found righteous in his sight,[45] we will always owe a debt of gratitude to his mercy, and by holy humility we will be healed from that first cause of all sins, that is, from the swelling of pride. Though my intent here was to produce a short letter, I have given birth to a long book. I wish it had not merely at last come to an end, but had attained as well a comparable completeness.

---

42. See Dn 9:24.
43. See 1 Jn 1:8.
44. See Mt 9:12.
45. See Ps 143:2.

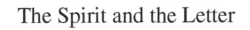

The Spirit and the Letter

Introduction

The Spirit and the Letter is Augustine's second major work in the
Pelagian controversy.[1] It was written in the last months of 412, or at
latest in the spring of 413, and was occasioned by a letter from Augustine's friend, the tribune Marcellinus, for whom he had recently
written *The Punishment and Forgiveness of Sins and the Baptism
of Little Ones* (section 1). In the second book of the previous work
Augustine had maintained two theses which Marcellinus found contradictory: that human beings could be sinless in this life by God's
grace and their free choice, and that, apart from the one mediator,
there never has been or will be such a human being. To Marcellinus
it seemed absurd to maintain that something is possible and yet never
has occurred and never will occur. Augustine appeals to a series of
examples from scripture for events which are certainly possible for
God, though we have no example of their occurring, for example, a
camel passing through the eye of a needle, the protection of Christ
at his Passion by angels, and the immediate rather than the gradual
destruction of the nations occupying the land promised to Israel.[2]

One might, of course, dismiss such scripturally guaranteed possibilities as irrelevant on the grounds that such events are ones that are
up to God to do or not to do, while righteousness is the work or function—indeed, the finest work or function—of a human being. To this
Augustine replies that, though becoming righteous is the task of a human being, it is also God's gift and God's work (section 2). Augustine
at this point finds no difficulty with those people who claim that,
as a matter of fact, there are, have been, or will be some sinless hu-

---

1. Shortly after *The Punishment and Forgiveness of Sins and the Baptism of Little Ones*,
probably early in 412, Augustine also wrote Letter 140, which is also known as *The
Grace of the New Testament*. In it he answered five quite diverse questions from
scripture proposed to him by his friend Honoratus; the questions dealt with Christ's
words from Psalm 21 spoken on the cross, the meaning of a passage in Paul, the
identity of the wise and foolish virgins and of the outer darkness, and the meaning of
the Word's becoming flesh. Then, with a view to "the new heresy opposed to God's
grace," he added, he tells us in the *Revisions* II, 62 (36), a sixth question on the grace
of the New Testament.
2. To maintain that only those things are possible which are actual at some time in the
past, present, or future would limit God's power to the actual course of events so
that God could not be said to be able to do anything other than what he has done, is
doing, and will do.

man beings, though he is personally convinced by the testimonies of scripture that no mere human being ever has been or will be perfectly sinless (section 3).[3]

What Augustine does find wholly unacceptable is the idea that the power of the human will is able by itself, without the help of God, to attain righteousness or to make progress in it. However, the unnamed people who are the cause of Augustine's concern do not simply deny the need for God's help; rather, they locate his help in the free choice with which human beings are created and the instruction provided them through the commandments (section 4). Against this view Augustine insists that we also need to receive the Holy Spirit who pours out the love of God in our hearts so that we may find delight in and love the good (section 5).

Having set forth the issue, Augustine proceeds to the body of the work. It has four main parts; of these the first two present his principal theses and the latter two answer objections that they are likely to evoke. In the first part (sections 6-20), he explains the Pauline doctrine that *the letter kills, but the Spirit gives life* (2 Cor 3:6). Without the presence of the life-giving Spirit, the instruction received from the commandments is the letter that kills. Augustine admits that 2 Cor 3:6 can be legitimately taken in the sense that a literal interpretation of a figurative passage of scripture can be fatal, for example, if one takes the Song of Songs as speaking of carnal love. It was, in fact, Ambrose's preaching that led Augustine to interpret spiritually passages of scripture that had proved deadly to him during his Manichean years.[4] He insists, however, that

---

3. Despite the clear statements of scripture regarding universal human sinfulness, Augustine remained open for a time to the view that some human beings led sinless lives with, of course, the help of God's grace. *In Nature and Grace* 60, 70, he referred to the position that some persons led a sinless life on earth as "a legitimate question among true and pious believers." On this point, see also *The Spirit and the Letter* 36, 66; *Nature and Grace* 42, 49; 44, 51; 68, 82. In his notes to the present work in ALG I, 654, A. Zumkeller claims that the reason for Augustine's tolerant attitude toward this position was Ambrose's statement in his *Commentary on the Gospel of Luke* I, 17-18 that Zechariah and Elizabeth led sinless lives. See also *Nature and Grace* 36, 42 for Augustine's refusal to discuss any sin on Mary's part. As late as 417 Augustine regarded the question as matter for discussion among Catholics rather than between Catholics and heretics; see *The Deeds of Pelagius* 30, 55. Nonetheless, the Council of Carthage in 418 declared the universality of human sinfulness a matter of Christian faith; see DS 228-230. Thus in 419 Augustine rejected as against the faith the view that human beings could, even with the help of grace, be without sin; see his *Answer to the Two Letters of the Pelagians* IV, 10, 27.
4. See *Confessions* V, 14, 24; VI, 4, 6.

in its literal interpretation the text, *The letter kills*, refers to the law that commands *You shall not desire* (Ex 20:17), and he claims with St. Paul that without that law he would not have known desire and that sin killed him through the commandment. The law is itself good, but unless the Holy Spirit provides help, "substituting good desire for evil desire, that is, pouring out love in our hearts" (section 6), the law increases evil desire by its prohibition, just as an obstacle in a stream increases the force of the water that flows around it. "Somehow or other, the very object of desire," Augustine observes, "grows more attractive when it is forbidden."

Turning to a detailed examination of the context of 2 Cor 3:6, Augustine sets out to show that the letter that kills is the law forbidding evil. He claims that, when he has made this point, it will be clear that living a good life is a gift of God, not merely because God has given human beings free choice and the commandments teaching them how to live, but because he has poured out love in their hearts through the Holy Spirit. Once these points have been established, Augustine is confident that Marcellinus will see that the attainment of human righteousness "must be attributed to God, though it is not attained without the human will" (section 7). Hence, human righteousness is possible in this life, since all things are possible for God, even though there is no example of anyone's having attained such perfect righteousness in this life.

Augustine appeals to the Letter to the Romans to show that the law that teaches that we should not sin kills without the presence of the life-giving Spirit; without the Spirit it leads us to know sin rather than avoid it, increases it rather than lessens it (section 8). Though, according to Rom 5:20, the law entered in so that sin might abound, and though where sin abounded, there grace was even more abundant, it is wrong, Augustine warns, to suppose that one ought to sin so that grace may abound. People needed, rather, to be shown that the holy and good commandments were of no use against the disease of sin and merely increased their sinfulness. Thus they would come to realize that they needed God, not merely as a teacher, but as a helper, and would have recourse to his mercy (section 9).

Augustine appeals to Rom 6:3-11 to show that the medicine by which human beings could be healed was revealed in the suffering and resurrection of Christ. The abolition of sinfulness and the renewal of righteousness began not from the letter of the law but from faith in Jesus Christ (section 10). This realization preserves people from the pride of attributing to themselves what belongs to God. Though they themselves do the works of righteousness, they do them only to the extent they draw from the fountain of life and share in the true light (section 11). Paul, whose very name means "little," vigorously opposed the proud in his defense of the grace of God. His own life and his letters stress God's grace; his Letter to the Romans almost wearies his readers with this question of grace (section 12). There is, for example, Rom 2:17-29, in which Paul accuses the Jews of boasting over their own righteousness. Augustine draws the comparison between them and those who would have God praised insofar as they are human beings, "but want themselves to be praised because they are righteous" (section 13).

These unnamed persons "praise God as the source of our justification inasmuch as he gave the law so that, by considering it, we would know how we ought to live" (section 14). Against them Augustine insists with Paul that no human being is justified before God on the basis of the law; rather, knowledge of sin came through the law. And Paul meant here by the law the commandment, *You shall not desire,*[5] which Augustine takes as the summary prohibition of all sin. At this point Augustine suggests that his unnamed opponents might argue that one is not justified on the basis of the law, which only provides knowledge of what is to be done, but on the basis of free choice by which one observes the law. In reply Augustine points to Rom 3:21, where Paul stresses that it is not our righteousness but the righteousness of God that has been revealed through faith in Jesus Christ. All boasting in our own righteousness is ruled out by the fact that we have been *gratuitously justified by his grace* (Rom 3:24). Though our justification does not come about without our will, "the law shows that our will is weak so that grace may heal our will and so that a healthy will may fulfill the law, without being subject to the law or in need of the law" (section 15).

Augustine turns to 1 Tm 1:8-9, which presents the paradox of claiming that the law is good, if used rightly, though it was not established for the righteous. He argues that, though the law is good and leads to grace like a schoolmaster, we are justified gratuitously

---

5. See Rom 3:20 and 7:7.

by grace, not because we have done good works, but so that we may do them. The unrighteous use the law correctly insofar as it leads them to grace by revealing their helplessness; the righteous use the law correctly by fulfilling it with the help of grace, and the righteous one, namely, God, uses the law correctly by imposing it upon the unrighteous to terrify them and bring them to grace (section 16). Hence, all proud boasting is excluded, though boasting in the Lord need not be excluded (section 17). Augustine points out that these thoughts lead to true piety, the worship of God, whose chief purpose is thanksgiving. "For this reason, in the truest and only sacrifice we are admonished to give thanks to the Lord, our God" (section 18). But the soul that attributes to itself what it has from God is filled with pride, as if it were wise. By pride even "great men"—he surely means the greatest of the Neoplatonists—fell into idolatry. Paul, for his part, declared his readiness to preach the gospel to both wise and foolish, Jew and Greek, for *it is the power of God for salvation for everyone who believes* and *the righteousness of God is revealed in it* (Rom 1:16.17). This is the salvation by which God saves us and the righteousness by which he makes us righteous. Hence, in section 19, Augustine turns to what Paul says of the punishment of those great minds who searched for him and found him, but in their pride did not glorify God or give him thanks.[6] The application to the Pelagians is clear: knowledge of God and of his law is simply not enough. With this Augustine draws the first part of the work to a close, having shown from Romans that God helps us to act with righteousness, not through the law with its holy and good commandments, but by helping our will, without which we can do nothing good, and by raising it up through the gift of his grace. Without such help the teaching of the law is simply the letter that kills (section 20).

The second major part of the work (sections 21-42) spells out the distinction between the law of works and the law of faith. Augustine immediately mentions that to say that the law of works is found in Judaism and the law of faith in Christianity is simply mistaken. Though confident that Marcellinus is sharp enough to have seen this point, Augustine returns to the texts from Paul in an endeavor to make it clear to others. He points out that it is the law of works which commands, *You shall not desire* (Ex 20:17; Rom 7:7), but insists that the

---

6. See Rom 1:18-23.

law of faith has the same commandment. If, then, the law of faith has the same commandment, why is it not the law of works? Once again, the works of the law in question are not the rites of the Old Testament, such as circumcision, but the observance of the Ten Commandments, which are summed up in Ex 20:17. Again, since the law of faith has the same commandment that brought death, why is it not the law of works? In section 22 Augustine answers, "What the law of works commands by its threats the law of faith obtains by its faith." Or, to put it another way which echoes Augustine's famous words in his *Confessions*, by the law of works God says, "Do what I command," while by the law of faith we say, "Give what you command."

Augustine acknowledges that in Rom 2:25-29 Paul did refer to circumcision and other Jewish observances as the law. He explains that Christians do not now observe such prescriptions which, as symbols, foreshadowed the reality of the New Testament. Nonetheless, when Paul spoke of the works of the law by which no one is justified, he meant the observance of the Ten Commandments, all of which—with the exception of the observance of the Sabbath—Christians are obliged to keep (section 23). Paul makes this point even more clearly in 2 Cor 3:3-9 (section 24), and Augustine finds it further confirmed in Rom 7:6-25 (section 25). Hence, without the new condition brought about by the Spirit, the letter of the law makes people guilty insofar as it makes the commandment known without helping them to fulfill it. If one observes the commandment servilely out of fear of punishment, not out of a love of righteousness, one does not really observe it. Only faith which works through love enables one " to find delight in the law of God in the interior human being" (section 26), and such delight is a gift of the Spirit, which increases as the interior human being is renewed from day to day, as one is being set free *from the body of this death by the grace of God through Jesus Christ, our Lord* (Rom 7:24).

The grace unveiled in the New Testament remained veiled in the Old. To that hiddenness belonged the commandment about the Sabbath observance, which the Jews observed carnally; it was the only one of the ten to be concealed in a symbol. Augustine sees the abstinence from servile work it commands as signifying the avoidance of sin, noting that God made the seventh day holy and that holiness lies in not sinning (section 27). Those who have the Spirit of freedom observe the Sabbath spiritually, finding delight in not sinning because of the love that is poured out in their hearts. Augustine points out the remarkable agreement between the two testaments insofar as the commandments were written by the finger of God and the finger of God is the Holy Spirit, and insofar as there were fifty days between the celebration of the first Passover and the reception of the Mosaic law, just as there were fifty days between Christ's death and resurrection and the reception of the Holy Spirit on Pentecost (section 28).

Despite such striking similarities, Augustine points to their differences, especially to the fact that the finger of God formerly wrote on stone tablets but now writes the law on human hearts by pouring out in our hearts the love of God which is the fulfillment of the law (section 29). Hence, the works of love, when they are written on stone tablets to strike fear, are the law of works and the letter that kills. But when love is poured out in the hearts of believers, those works are the law of faith and of the Spirit. And this accords perfectly with 2 Cor 3:3, Augustine points out (section 30). The old law was written outside human beings to strike fear from the outside; the new law is written within to justify them within. So too, *the law was given for the sake of transgression* (Gal 3:19) and is called the ministry of death and of condemnation, while the law of the New Testament is the ministry of the Spirit and of righteousness,[7] because through the gift of the Spirit we do the works of righteousness and are set free from the condemnation owing to the transgression (section 31).

Augustine applies all this to his unnamed Pelagian opponents (section 32). He notes that they may shrink from the intolerable claim that we become righteous without the grace of God, but warns that they should also not equate the grace of God with the law, with teaching, or with the commandments, for these are the letter that kills, if the Spirit is not present, making us " love the very same thing, now written within, which the law made us fear, when it was written exteriorly" (section 32). In the following sections (33-40) Augustine uses Jeremiah's prophecy of the New Testament as a confirmation of his distinction between the Old and the New Testaments. Jer 31:31-34 is, he points out, the sole text in the Old Testament that refers to the new by name (section 33). His explanation of Jeremiah's prophecy in the light of Paul's teaching as partially fulfilled in the present age

---

7. See 2 Cor 3:7-9.

and as still to be fulfilled in the kingdom of heaven to come is better read than summarized.

The third part of the work (sections 43-51) takes up a possible objection to Augustine's position. Having used the text of Jer 31:31-34 to confirm the distinction between the Old and the New Testaments, Augustine must confront the difficulty posed by Rom 2:14-15, in which Paul says that the Gentiles have the law written in their hearts. He offers two solutions. First, in sections 44-46, he presents the easiest solution, though not one that fits best the context in the Letter to the Romans. It identifies these Gentiles as believing Christians from the non-Jewish world; as believers they belong to the New Testament and, consequently, have the law written in their hearts. But since Paul says that they do by nature what the law commands, he is faced with a further difficulty. Hence, in section 47 Augustine explains how these believers from the Gentile world do by nature what the law commands, appealing to his doctrine that the image of God in human nature was not completely destroyed by sin and is being restored in believers through the Holy Spirit.

In sections 48-49 Augustine offers a second interpretation which accords better with the context. On this view the Gentiles Paul mentions are neither Jews nor Christians but non-believers who fulfill some of the prescriptions of the law, since the image of God in which they were created has not been completely effaced by sin. He notes, however, that though their external actions may be beyond reproach, their motive is seldom found to be praiseworthy. In any case, without the grace of God a few good works can no more bring an unbeliever to eternal life than a few venial sins can keep a righteous person from eternal life. But however we understand those who do by nature what pertains to the law, it is certain that Jeremiah promised the grace of God to the people of the New Testament so that God's laws are written in their hearts and so that they all know him through the gift of the Holy Spirit poured out in their hearts (section 49). Hence, we should not boast as if we have not received, and what we have received is more than the letter of the law set before our eyes. In sections 50-51 Augustine again summarizes his position that no one is justified by reason of the works of the law but through faith by the grace of God, which pours out the Holy Spirit in our hearts so that we observe the law not out of fear but with delight.

In the fourth part of the work (sections 52-60), Augustine turns to a second possible objection to his doctrine of grace, namely, that it destroys free choice. He draws an analogy: As faith does not do away with the law, so grace does not do away with free choice. In fact, instead of doing away with free choice, grace strengthens the will, heals its wounds, restores its health, so that we love righteousness and fulfill the law (section 52). Augustine examines whether faith itself lies in our power; for this purpose he distinguishes having the power (*posse*) from willing (*velle*), and he concludes that we are said to have in our power what we do if we will it and what we do not do if we do not will it (section 53). Hence, Augustine concludes that faith is surely in our power, since faith is an act of assent, and we assent willingly when we assent to something. Furthermore, our power is from God, since Rom 13:1 maintains that there is no power except from God; on the other hand, the gift of the power does not impose necessity (section 54).

The faith which the Apostle commends is not just any faith, but the faith by which we believe God (section 55). Those under the law, however, believe God in the sense that they try to achieve their own righteousness out of a servile fear of punishment, while those who are children of God—both Jew and Greek—live from faith, a faith that works through love. That love is poured out in their hearts by the gift of the Holy Spirit and excludes on their part all boasting, as if they had not received it as a gift (section 56). Though not every act of the will comes from God, as all power does, the will to believe is itself a gift of God. We cannot say to God that in the will to believe we have something we have not received; yet, Augustine immediately adds that those who do not believe are not thereby excused (section 57).

Why, then, does everyone not have this will to believe, since the same God created every nature and, according to 1 Tm 2:4, wills that all be saved? Augustine proposes as a somewhat tentative answer that the free choice we have received from the creator is a neutral power that can turn either to believing or not believing at God's call. God wills that all be saved, but not so that he deprives anyone of free choice. Whether one believes or refuses to believe, the will of God remains undefeated, since unbelievers do not escape God's just punishment (section 58). At this point in the development of his thinking on grace, Augustine seems to take God's universal salvific will as found in 1 Tm 2:4 without any restriction and to situate the will to believe or not to believe in the free choice of the individual, given God's call. In section 59 Augustine uses Psalm 102 as an illustration and confirmation of the way God transforms by his grace our old deformity so that we may live from the faith that works through love.

Augustine warns that we should not think that sin which is committed by free choice is to be attributed to God, even though we attribute to God as his gift the will by which we believe, because it arises from the free choice with which we are created. The will to believe is to be attributed to God not only because it arises from the free choice which is part of our nature, "but also because God brings it about by the enticements of our perceptions that we will and that we believe" (section 60). In order to believe by free choice, the soul needs God's enticement or invitation, which he produces either externally through exhortations and commandments or internally through acting upon the mind. Hence, God "certainly produces in human beings the will to believe. . . . But to assent to God's invitation or dissent from it is . . . in the power of one's will" (section 60). To the further question of why one person is stirred to the point of believing and another is not, Augustine can only offer in reply Paul's cry, *O the depth!* or his question, *Is there injustice in God?* (Rom 11:33; 9:14)

Augustine then turns to the conclusion of the work, pointing out that the unnamed Pelagians stand in opposition not merely to Augustine's views but also to those of Paul and even to those of him who spoke through his apostles (section 61). Returning to Marcellinus' specific problem with how something can be possible, though it never has and never will occur, Augustine sums up his answer and confirms it with an appeal to Christ's words that, with faith like a grain of mustard seed, one can command that a mountain be thrown into the sea and it will happen, though it never has (sections 62-63). We fail to attain complete righteousness in this life, because our knowledge and love of God is incomplete compared to the knowledge and love we shall have when we see him face to face (section 64). Augustine nonetheless allows for an incomplete righteousness in this life that is compatible with the need of the righteous to pray for the forgiveness of their sins. In any case, whatever righteousness they have, they have received (section 65). Finally, Augustine challenges his unnamed opponents to find someone who does not have any sin needing God's pardon. He insists that, if there are such persons, they are helped by God's grace, which consists not in the teaching of the law but in the Spirit of grace poured out in their hearts. He is convinced that scripture precludes their finding any such sinless persons, though he cannot deny that God has the power to bring about in this life the perfection of righteousness that he will bring about in his saints in the next life (section 66).

The Text and Translations

The text translated is that edited by C. F. Urba and J. Zycha in CSEL LX (Vienna 1913) 155-229. I have also profited on occasion from variant readings adopted by the editors of the ALG text. The work has been translated many times. Apart from the English translations, only the most recent are noted. It has been translated into English by P. Holmes in NPNF I/5 (New York 1887; repr. 1971) 83-114; his translation is also found in *Basic Writings of Saint Augustine* (New York 1948) I, 459-518. The work has likewise been translated into English by J. Burnaby in LCC VIII (Philadelphia 1955). In the twentieth century it has been translated into French by J. D. Burger (Neuchâtel 1951); into Spanish by E. López in BAC L (Madrid 1956) 686-810; into German by S. Kopp in ALG I (Würzburg 1971) 301-434; and into Italian by I. Volpi in NBA XVII/1 (Rome 1981) 253-363.

Revisions II, 63 (37)

I had written for Marcellinus three books with the title *The Pun-ishment and Forgiveness of Sins*, in which I carefully discussed the baptism of little ones. He wrote back to me that he was disturbed because I said that it was possible that human beings might be with-out sin if their will does not lack God's assistance as a help, although no one has had or has or will have such perfect righteousness in this life. He asked how I could say that it is possible if there is no example of it. On account of this question of his, I wrote the book whose title is *The Spirit and the Letter*. In it I examined the state-ment of the Apostle where he says, *The letter kills, but the Spirit gives life* (2 Cor 3:6). In that book I fiercely argued, to the extent of God's help, against the enemies of the grace of God by which the sinner is justified. When I dealt with the observances of the Jews who abstain from certain foods in accord with the old law, I spoke of "the ceremonies regarding certain foods" (21, 36), a term which is not used in the sacred writings. It seemed, nonetheless, appropriate to me, because I had it in mind that ceremonies took their name from "lacking" (*carendo*), as if the word were *carimoniae*, since those who follow this observance lack those things from which they abstain. But if this word, which is foreign to the true religion, has another origin, I did not speak in accord with it but in accord with the one I mentioned above. This book begins: "You have read the works, my dear son Marcellinus, that I have recently composed for you."

The Spirit and the Letter

The Occasion of the Work: Marcellinus' Question

1, 1. You have read the works, my dear son Marcellinus, that I recently composed for you concerning the baptism of little ones and the perfection of human righteousness.[1] In this life it seems that no one either has attained or will attain that perfection, except for the one mediator, who endured the human condition in the likeness of sinful flesh without any sin whatsoever. You wrote back that you were disturbed by my statement in the second of the two books. I had said that it was possible for a human being to be sinless,[2] if with the aid of God's power the will is not lacking, but that, apart from the one in whom all are brought to life,[3] there has been no one and will be no one in whom this perfection is to be found while in this life. It strikes you as absurd to say that something is possible when we have no example of it. And yet, I suspect, you are certain that a camel has never passed through the eye of a needle, though the Lord said that this was possible for God.[4] You can also read that twelve thousand legions of angels could have fought for Christ to prevent his suffering,[5] and yet it did not happen. You can read in scripture that the nations could all have been wiped out at one time from the land which God gave to the children of Israel,[6] but that God willed that this take place gradually.[7] A thousand other things come to mind which we admit either could have taken place or can take place, though we cannot offer examples of their having taken place. Consequently, we ought not to deny that a human being can be without sin, on the grounds that we can produce no human being in whom this has been realized, apart from the one who was not only a human being but also God by nature.

---

1. Augustine refers to *The Punishment and Forgiveness of Sins and the Baptism of Little Ones*.
2. See *The Punishment and Forgiveness of Sins* II, 6, 7; 20, 34; the letter of Marcellinus referred to is not extant.
3. See 1 Cor 15:22.
4. See Mt 19:24.26.
5. See Mt 26:53. The word "thousand" is not found in Matthew, though it is found in other citations of the passage by Augustine and other Fathers.
6. See Dt 31:3.
7. See Jgs 2:3.

Human Sinlessness Is Possible with God's Help,
Even though Christ Is the Only Example

2, 2. You might reply as follows: These events, which I said did not occur, but were possible, are works of God, but being a sinless human being is the work of a human being. Indeed, you might say that it is the finest work of a human being to realize a righteousness that is full and perfect and absolute in every respect. And hence, one should not suppose that there was not and is not and will not be anyone in this life who accomplishes this work, if it can be accomplished by a human being. But you ought to bear in mind that, though it pertains to a human being to do this, it is also the gift of God and, hence, you ought not to doubt that it is a work of God. *For it is God who produces in you*, says the Apostle, *both the willing and the action in accord with good will* (Phil 2:13).

3. Hence, those people who claim that a human being is living or has lived on earth without any sin at all pose no great problem, and we should insist with them that they show, if they can, that it is really so. For the testimonies of the scriptures have, I think, determined that no human being living in this life, despite the use of free choice, is found without sin. For example, we find, *Do not enter into judgment with your servant, because no living person will be found righteous in your sight* (Ps 143:2), as well as other such passages. If anyone can show that they should be interpreted otherwise than they sound and proves that someone has or some people have lived here without any sin whatsoever, we should not merely not be opposed but be deeply grateful. Otherwise, we would seem to be motivated by no small amount of jealousy. I personally tend to believe that there neither has been nor is nor will be anyone of such perfect purity. But even if one claims that there has been or is or will be, that is no great error in my judgment, nor is it harmful when one is misled because of such good will, provided that people who think this do not think that they themselves are such, unless they really and clearly see that they are.

God's Help Is Not Just Free Choice and the Commandments

4. But we must fiercely and strongly oppose those who think that the power of the human will can by itself, without the help of God, either attain righteousness or make progress in tending toward it. When these people begin to be pressed as to how they presume to

claim that this is possible without God's help, they hold themselves in check and do not dare to make this claim, because they see that it is godless and intolerable. Rather, they say that these things are not done without God's help, because God created human beings with free choice and, by giving the commandments, he teaches them how they should live. Moreover, they say that he certainly helps them, insofar as by his teaching he removes ignorance so that people know what they should avoid and what they should pursue in their actions. Thus, by following the path he pointed out to them, they may, by the free choice implanted in their nature, live chaste, righteous, and pious lives and merit to attain to the blessed and eternal life.

3, 5. We, on the other hand, say that the human will is helped to achieve righteousness in this way: Besides the fact that human beings are created with free choice of the will[8] and besides the teaching by which they are commanded how they ought to live, they receive the Holy Spirit, so that there arises in their minds a delight in and a love for that highest and immutable good that is God, even now while they walk by faith, not yet by vision.[9] By this [love] given to them like the pledge of a gratuitous gift, they are set afire with the desire to cling to the creator and burn to come to a participation in that true light,[10] so that they may have their well-being from him from whom they have their being. For free choice is capable only of sinning, if the way of truth remains hidden. And when what we should do and the goal we should strive for begins to be clear, unless we find delight in it and love it, we do not act, do not begin, do not live good lives. But so that we may love it, *the love of God* is poured out *in our hearts*, not by free choice which comes from ourselves, but *by the Holy Spirit who has been given to us* (Rom 5:5).

Without the Spirit's Presence the Law Is the Letter That Kills

4, 6. That teaching from which we receive the commandment to live in continence and rectitude is the letter that kills, unless the life-giving Spirit is present. We read in scripture, *The letter kills, but the Spirit gives life* (2 Cor 3:6). We ought not to understand this merely in this sense: that we should not interpret literally something that

---

8. Following some of the oldest manuscripts, the CSEL edition omits "of the will."
9. See 2 Cor 5:7.
10. See Jn 1:9.

scripture expresses figuratively, when its proper sense is absurd, and that we should consider what else it signifies and nourish the interior human being with its spiritual interpretation. After all, *to be wise according to the flesh is death, but to be wise according to the Spirit is life and peace* (Rom 8:6). For example, someone might interpret in a carnal sense many of the things which are said in the Song of Songs, not as referring to the fruit of bright love, but to the longing of lustful desire. We should not, then, interpret in this sense alone the Apostle's words, *The letter kills, but the Spirit gives life*; rather, we should interpret them in the sense—and especially in the sense—that he expresses in another passage with perfect clarity: *I would not have known desire, if the law had not said, You shall not desire* (Rom 7:7). And a little later he said, *Having seized the opportunity, sin deceived me by the commandment and killed me through it* (Rom 7:11). See what *the letter kills* means! And the commandment, *You shall not desire*, is certainly not some figurative expression that is to be interpreted otherwise than in the literal sense. It is, rather, a perfectly clear commandment highly useful toward salvation. Whoever observes it will be completely without sin. After all, the Apostle chose this general, all-inclusive expression[11] as if it were the voice of the law forbidding every sin, precisely because it says, *You shall not desire* (Ex 20:17). For no sin is committed without desire. Hence, the law that commands this is good and praiseworthy. But if the Holy Spirit does not provide help, substituting good desire for evil desire, that is, pouring out love in our hearts,[12] though the law is good, it increases the evil desire by its prohibition. In the same way, if a stream of water does not stop flowing in that direction, when an obstacle is placed in its path, it becomes stronger. And when it surmounts the obstacle, rushing on in greater quantity, it flows with more force on its downward path. Somehow or other, the very object of desire grows more attractive when it is forbidden. And this is what it means that sin misleads by the commandment and by it brings death,[13] when transgression is added, which does not exist where there is no law.[14]

---

11. See Rom 7:7.
12. See Rom 5:5.
13. See Rom 7:11.
14. See Rom 4:15.

A Detailed Examination of Paul's Teaching

5, 7. But let us consider the whole passage from the letter of the Apostle, if it is all right with you, and let us study it as God gives us his help. I want, if I can, to show that the statement of the Apostle, *The letter kills, but the Spirit gives life,* was not speaking of figurative expressions, though it can be taken in that sense as well. Rather, in plain language it referred to the law that forbids what is evil. When I have made that point, it will of course be more obviously apparent that to live a good life is a gift of God. This is the case, not merely because God gave human beings free choice, without which one lives neither a good life nor a bad life, and not merely because he gave the commandment by which he teaches them how they should live, but because by the Holy Spirit he has poured out love in their hearts.[15] He foreknew them in order that he might predestine them; he predestined them in order that he might call them; he called them in order that he might justify them, and he justified them in order that he might glorify them.[16] When this has been made clear, you will see, I believe, that it is wrong to say that only the things that God does are possible if there is no example. We have, for instance, mentioned the camel's passing through the eye of a needle and other such things that are impossible for us, but easy for God. You will see, then, that it is wrong to say that human righteousness ought not to be included among these, since it ought not to be counted as a work of God, but as the work of human beings. After all, one might argue that, if the perfection of righteousness is possible in this life, there is no reason why one should believe that there is no example of it. It will become quite clear that it is wrong to say this, when it has been shown that human righteousness itself must be attributed to the action of God, though it is not attained without the human will. Hence, we cannot deny that the perfection of righteousness is possible even in this life, since all things are possible for God.[17] This holds for those things he does by his will alone and for those which he has determined can be done by him with the cooperation of the will of his creature. And so, any of those things that he does not do remain without an example in the works he has done, but with God they have a cause both in his power, by which they can be done,

15. See Rom 5:5.
16. See Rom 8:29-30.
17. See Mt 19:26.

and in his wisdom, as to why they have not been done. Although this cause is not known to human beings, they should not forget that they are human and should not, for that reason, think God foolish because they cannot fully grasp his wisdom.

8. Pay attention then to the Apostle as he explains to the Romans his words to the Corinthians, *The letter kills, but the Spirit gives life* (2 Cor 3:6). He shows clearly enough that one should rather interpret it as we said above, namely, that the letter of the law, which teaches that we should not sin, kills if the life-giving Spirit is not present. For it leads us to know sin rather than to avoid it and increases sin rather than lessens it, because the transgression of the law is added to the evil desire.

6, 9. The Apostle, then, wanted to praise the grace which came to all peoples through Jesus Christ, so that the Jews would not consider themselves better than other peoples because they had received the law. He said that sin and death entered the human race through one man and through one man there came righteousness and eternal life,[18] indicating with perfect clarity that the former was Adam, the latter Christ. Then he said, *The law entered in so that sin might abound, but where sin abounded, there grace was even more abundant, so that, as the reign of sin led to death, so the reign of grace might through righteousness lead to eternal life through Jesus Christ, our Lord* (Rom 5:20-21) Then he posed a question for himself and asked, *What then shall we say? Shall we remain in sin so that grace might abound? Heaven forbid!* (Rom 6:1-2) For he saw that perverted people could perversely interpret his statement that *the law entered in so that sin might abound, but where sin abounded, there grace was even more abundant* (Rom 5:20), as if he said that it was good to sin so that grace might abound. To dispose of this idea, he said, *Heaven forbid!* and added, *How shall we who have died to sin continue to live in it?* (Rom 6:2) That is, since grace has given us the gift of dying to sin, what else will we be doing, if we continue to live in sin, but be ungrateful for grace? After all, one who praises the benefit of a medicine does not say that it is good to have the diseases and wounds which it cures. Rather, the greater the praises one heaps upon a medicine, the more one criticizes and fears the wounds and diseases from which the highly praised medicine sets one free. Thus the praise and

---

18. See Rom 5:12.21.

proclamation of grace is the censure and condemnation of sins. For human beings had to be shown the foulness of their disease; against their sinfulness the holy and good commandment was of no use. It increased sinfulness rather than lessened it when the law entered in so that sin might abound. Then, when they had in that way been found guilty and were put to shame, people would see that they needed God not only as a teacher but as a helper who would direct their journeys so that all sinfulness might not lord it over them.[19] And then, by having recourse to the help of his mercy, they would be healed, and thus, where sin abounded, there grace might be even more abundant, not because of the merit of the sinners, but because of the assistance of their rescuer.

10. In what follows, the Apostle pointed out that the same medicine was mystically revealed in the suffering and resurrection of Christ. He said, *Do you not know that those of us who have been baptized in Christ Jesus were baptized into his death? We were, then, buried with him through baptism into death so that, as Christ has risen from the dead by the glory of the Father, so we might also walk in the newness of life. For, if we have been united to the likeness of his death, we will also be united to the likeness of his resurrection. We know that our old human self was crucified with him so that the body of sin might be destroyed, and we might no longer be enslaved to sin. For one who has died is justified from sin. But if we have died with Christ, we believe that we will live together with him. We know that Christ rising from the dead dies no more and death no longer has dominion over him. The death he died to sin he died once, but the life he lives he lives for God. And so you too must consider yourselves dead to sin, but living for God in Christ Jesus.* (Rom 6:3-11) It is quite clear that the mystery of the Lord's death and resurrection symbolized the end of our old life and the beginning of our new life and has revealed the abolition of sinfulness and the renewal of righteousness. And so, did such a great benefit come to human beings through the letter of the law? No, it came through faith in Jesus Christ.

7, 11. This holy thought guards human beings under the protection of God's wings. They hope to be inebriated by the richness of his house and to drink at the torrent of his pleasure. For with him is the source of life, and in his light we shall see the light. He extends his

---

19. See Ps 119:133.

mercy to those who know him and his righteousness to those who are upright of heart.[20] For he extends his mercy not because they do know him but in order that they may know him, and he extends his righteousness, by which he justifies the sinner,[21] not because they are upright of heart but in order that they may be upright of heart. This thought does not lead to pride, a vice which arises when we rely on ourselves and make ourselves our own source of life. Through that stirring of pride one withdraws from the fountain of life from which alone one can draw and drink righteousness, namely, the good life. One also withdraws from that unchangeable light by participation in which the rational soul is in a sense set alight so that it is itself a light that has been made and created. In that sense John was *a lamp burning and bright* (Jn 5:35). Yet he acknowledged the source of his brightness and said, *We have received from his fullness* (Jn 1:16).[22] Whose fullness was this but the fullness of him in comparison to whom John was not the light? After all, that *was the true light that enlightens every human being that comes into this world* (Jn 1:9). Hence, after the psalmist had said in the same psalm, *Extend your mercy to those who know you and your righteousness to those who are upright of heart*, he added, *Let not the foot of pride come near me or the hands of sinners move me. There have fallen all whose works are wicked; they are cast out and cannot stand up.* (Ps 36:11-13) By this godlessness people attribute to themselves what belongs to God, and by it they are driven into their own darkness, namely, the works of sin. For they themselves clearly do these works, and they are themselves capable of carrying them out. But they only do the works of righteousness to the extent that they draw from that fountain and share in that light. Their life lacks nothing, and there is found no variation or shadow of change.[23]

12. The apostle Paul, who was previously called Saul,[24] had no other reason, it seems to me, for choosing this name but to point out his own smallness as the least of the apostles.[25] Hence, in order to praise

20. See Ps 35:8-11.
21. See Rom 4:5.
22. Augustine takes Jn 1:16 with the preceding verse so that it is part of the testimony given by John the Baptist, though most modern translations take it as a statement of the evangelist.
23. See Jas 1:17.
24. See Acts 13:9.
25. See 1 Cor 15:9. The Latin word *paulus* means "small" or "little."

this grace of God, he frequently fought courageously and vigorously against the proud and the arrogant and those who relied on their own works. For the grace of God was really seen more clearly and more obviously in him. Although in persecuting the Church of God he did the sort of deeds for which he deserved to be punished most severely, he received mercy instead of condemnation and obtained grace instead of punishment. For good reason he cries out and struggles more than others in its defense and does not heed the hatred of those who in this profound and mysterious matter do not understand and who twist his sound statements to a distorted meaning. Despite that, he preaches the gift of God which alone brings salvation to the children of the promise, the children of God's beneficence, the children of grace and mercy, the children of the New Testament. Evidence of this is, first, that each of his letters begins as follows: *Grace and peace to you from God the Father and the Lord Jesus Christ* (Rom 1:7). Then, in the Letter to the Romans he examines this question almost exclusively and with such persistence and in so many ways that he wearies the attention of the reader. It is, nonetheless, a weariness that is useful and salutary, for he provides exercise to the members of the interior person rather than exhausts them.

8, 13. Among these are the passages I cited above; among them is his complaint against the Jews. He says that they call themselves Jews, but do not fulfill what they profess. He says, *If you call yourself a Jew and rely upon the law and boast of God and know his will and approve what is excellent, because you are instructed in the law, if you are confident that you are a guide for the blind, a light for those who are in darkness, an educator of those who are foolish, a teacher of infants, one who has the standard of knowledge and truth in the law, you then who teach others, do you not teach yourself? You who preach that one should not steal, do you steal? You who say that one should not commit adultery, do you commit adultery? You who abhor idols, do you commit sacrilege? You who boast of the law, do you dishonor God by transgressing the law? As scripture says, The name of God suffers blasphemy among the Gentiles because of you.*[26] *Circumcision is valuable, if you observe the law, but if you are a transgressor of the law, your circumcision has become the lack of circumcision. If then the uncircumcised observe the precepts of the law, will not the lack*

---

26. See Is 52:5.

of circumcision be counted as circumcision? And those who physi-
cally lack circumcision, but fulfill the law, will condemn you who are
a transgressor of the law because of the letter of the law and circumci-
sion. For one who is a Jew only externally is not a real Jew, and the
circumcision that is only external in the flesh is not real circumcision.
The real Jew is one who is a Jew interiorly and by the circumcision
of the heart, spiritually, not literally. Such a person's praise comes
from God, not from human beings. (Rom 2:17-29) Here he showed the
sense in which he said, *You boast of God* (Rom 2:17). For if Jews who
were truly Jews boasted of God in the way demanded by grace which
is given gratuitously, not on account of meritorious works, they would
have praise from God, not from human beings.[27] But they boasted of
God as if they alone had merited to receive his law, in accord with
the words of the psalm in which it says, *He did not do this for any*
other nation, and he did not reveal his judgments to them (Ps 148:20).
Nonetheless, they thought that they fulfilled this law of God by their
own righteousness, though they were rather transgressors of it. For
this reason it brought God's anger upon them,[28] and sin, which was
being committed by people with knowledge, became more abundant,
because those who did what the law commanded without the help
of the Spirit of grace did so out of a fear of punishment, not out of a
love of righteousness. And for this reason God did not see in their will
what human beings saw in their action; rather, they were held guilty
as a result of what God knew that they preferred to do, if only they
could have done so with impunity. He calls circumcision of the heart
a will that is free from every forbidden desire. This is not the result
of the teaching and threat of the letter, but of the help and healing of
the Spirit. For this reason the praise of such persons comes not from
human beings but from God, who by his grace gives them the basis on
which they are praised. Scripture says of him, *In the Lord will my soul*
be praised (Ps 34:3), and says to him, *With you is my praise* (Ps 22:26).
These people are not like those who want God to be praised because
they themselves are human beings, but want themselves to be praised
because they are righteous.

---

27. See Rom 2:29.
28. See Rom 4:15.

Further Pelagian Attempts to Circumvent the Scriptures

14. They say, "But we also praise God as the source of our justification inasmuch as he gave the law so that, by considering it, we would know how we ought to live."[29] They do not listen to the words of scripture, *No flesh will be justified before God on the basis of the law* (Rom 3:20). It is, after all, possible [to be justified] before human beings, but not before him who sees the heart itself and the inner act of the will.[30] There he sees what one would prefer to do, if it were permitted, even if one who fears the law does something else. And no one should imagine that the Apostle said that no one was justified on the basis of that law, which contains many symbolic commandments among the old sacraments, including the circumcision of the flesh, which the law commanded that little ones receive on the eighth day.[31] For, he immediately indicated the law he meant and said, *The knowledge of sin came through the law* (Rom 3:20). That is the law of which he later says, *I knew sin only through the law, for I would not have known desire, if the law had not said, You shall not desire* (Rom 7:7)? For what else does this mean but *The knowledge of sin came through the law.*

9, 15. At this point the human presumption that does not know the righteousness of God and wants to establish its own[32] might say that the Apostle was correct in saying that *no one will be justified on the basis of the law.* After all, the law only revealed what one should do or what one should avoid so that what the law revealed the will might carry out. And in that way one is not justified through the command of the law, but through free choice. But notice, people, what follows; he said, *But now the righteousness of God has been revealed apart from the law, though the law and the prophets have borne witness to it* (Rom 3:21). Is that not loud enough for deaf ears? He says, *The righteousness of God has been revealed.* This is the righteousness that those who want to establish their own do not know; this is the righteousness to which they refuse to be subject.[33] He said, *The righteousness of God has been revealed.* He did not say, "The righteous-

---

29. A Pelagian statement for which Augustine gives no source.
30. See Prv 24:12.
31. See Lv 12:3.
32. See Rom 10:3.
33. See Rom 10:3.

ness of human beings or of our own will." He said, *The righteousness of God*, not that by which God is righteous, but that with which he clothes a human being when he justifies a sinner. This is testified to by the law and the prophets; to this the law and the prophets bear witness. The law bears witness, because by commanding and threatening and yet justifying no one it indicates clearly enough that human beings are justified by the gift of God through the assistance of the Holy Spirit. The prophets bear witness, because the coming of Christ has fulfilled what they foretold. He goes on from this point and adds, *But the righteousness of God through the faith of Jesus Christ* (Rom 3:22), that is, through the faith by which we believe in Christ. Just as this faith mentioned is not the faith of Christ by which Christ believes, so that righteousness of God was not the righteousness by which God is righteous. Each of these, after all, is ours, but they are said to be God's and Christ's, because they are given to us by God's generosity. The righteousness of God, then, is apart from the law but was not revealed apart from the law. For how did the law bear witness to it, if it was revealed apart from the law? But the righteousness of God is apart from the law, and God bestows this righteousness upon the believer through the Spirit of grace without the help of the law. That is, the believer is not helped by the law, since God shows human beings their weakness through the law in order that they might take refuge in his mercy through faith and be healed. Scripture said of his wisdom that it bears on its tongue the law and mercy,[34] the law, that is, by which he makes the proud guilty, but mercy by which he justifies those who have been humbled. *The righteousness of God, then, through the faith of Jesus Christ for all who believe; for there is no distinction. For all have sinned and lack the glory of God* (Rom 3:22-23), not their own glory. For what do they have that they have not received? But if they have received, why do they boast, as if they have not received?[35] They lack, then, the glory of God. And note what comes next: *They have been gratuitously justified by his grace* (Rom 3:24). They were not, then, justified by the law; they were not justified by their own will, but *gratuitously justified by his grace*. It is not that this comes about without our will; rather, the law shows that our will is weak so that grace may heal our will and so that a healthy will may fulfill the law, without being subject to the law or in need of the law.

---

34. See Prv 3:16.
35. See 1 Cor 4:7.

The Resolution of a Pauline Paradox

10, 16. *For the law was not established for the righteous; yet it is good, if one uses it correctly* (1 Tm 1:9.8). When the Apostle joins these two apparently contradictory ideas together, he warns and stirs the reader to look into and solve the question. After all, how can it be true that *the law is good, if one uses it correctly*, if what follows is also true, *We know that the law was not established for the righteous* (1 Tm 1:8-9)? For who but the righteous use the law correctly? Yet it was not established for such persons, but for the unrighteous. Or ought the unrighteous to use the law correctly in order to be justified, that is, in order to become righteous, since the law like a schoolmaster leads them to grace,[36] and by grace alone they can fulfill what the law commands? By grace they are, of course, justified gratuitously, that is, without any preceding merits from their own works. *Otherwise, grace is no longer grace* (Rom 11:6). It is given not because we have done good works but so that we might be able to do them, that is, not because we have fulfilled the law but in order that we might be able to fulfill the law. For, he said, *I have come not to destroy the law, but to fulfill it* (Mt 5:17). Scripture said of him, *We have seen his glory, the glory as of the Only-Begotten from the Father, full of grace and truth* (Jn 1:14). This is the glory of which scripture said, *For all have sinned and lack the glory of God*, and this is the grace of which it immediately adds, *They have been gratuitously justified by his grace.* The unrighteous, then, correctly use the law in order to become righteous, but once they have become righteous, they no longer use it as a vehicle, since they have arrived, or—to use instead the comparison just mentioned—they no longer use it as a schoolmaster, since they have already been educated.[37] How then can it be that the law was not established for the righteous? For the righteous also need it, not in the way it brings the unrighteous to justifying grace, but certainly in the way those who are already righteous use it correctly.[38] Does not the righteous one perhaps—no, not perhaps—rather does not the righteous one certainly use the law correctly, when he imposes it upon the unrighteous to terrify them? As a result, when the disease of concupiscence that has taken root in them begins to grow because

---

36. See Gal 3:24.
37. See Gal 3:24.
38. See 1 Tm 1:8.

of the stimulus of the commandment and the increase of transgression, they may take flight through faith to justifying grace. There, delighted by the sweetness of righteousness through the gift of the Spirit, they may escape the punishment that the letter threatens. In that way the two statements will not be contradictory, nor will there be a conflict between them. Rather, the righteous use the good law correctly, and yet the law was not established for the righteous. After all, they were not justified as a result of it, but as a result of the law of faith; by that faith they believed that only God's grace could help their weakness to fulfill what the law of works commands.

17. Therefore, he says, *Where is your boasting? It has been excluded. By what law? By the law of works? No, but by the law of faith.* (Rom 3:27) Perhaps he meant the praiseworthy boasting which one does in the Lord and that it is excluded, that is, not beaten so that it departs, but hammered so that it stands out. In that sense artisans who work with silver are called smiths.[39] Hence, we have in the Psalms, *That those who have been tested may be excluded like silver* (Ps 68:31), that is, that those who have been tested may stand out like the word of God. For elsewhere scripture says, *The words of the Lord are pure words, silver tested by the fire* (Ps 12:7). Perhaps he wanted to mention the wrongful boasting that comes from pride, the boasting of those who, when in their own eyes they live righteously, boast as if they had not received this.[40] Then he meant that it was excluded not by the law of works but by the law of faith, that is, cast out and thrown away, because by the law of faith people know that, if they live a good life, they have this from the grace of God and that they will attain perfection in the love of righteousness from no other source.

11, 18. Such thoughts make them pious, because piety is true wisdom. I mean the piety which the Greeks call *theosebeia*. The words we read in the Book of Job commend it to us, *See, piety is wisdom* (Jb 28:28). Moreover, if it is translated into Latin according to its etymology, it can be called the worship of God, which was principally established so that the soul might not be ungrateful to God. For this reason, in the truest and only sacrifice we are admonished to give thanks to the Lord, our God.[41] But the soul will be ungrateful, if it

---

39. The Latin *exclusores* can mean smiths, those who hammer silver.
40. See 1 Cor 4:7.
41. Augustine alludes to the introduction to the Preface of the Mass.

attributes to itself what it has from God, especially its righteousness. Then the soul is filled with pride over works of righteousness as if they were its own and as if it produced them for itself by itself. That soul is not filled with pride, as is commonly the case, over wealth or bodily beauty or eloquence or other external [or internal] [42] goods of either the body or the soul, which even bad persons have. Rather, it is filled with pride, as if it were wise, over these goods which are in the true sense the goods of good people. By this vice even great men were driven back from the unchangeableness of the divine substance and fell into the disgrace of idolatry. Hence, the same Apostle in the same letter in which he vigorously defended grace said that he was under obligation to both Greeks and barbarians, to both the wise and the foolish, and that, therefore, for his part, he was ready to preach the gospel even to those who were in Rome.[43] He adds, *For I am not ashamed of the gospel; it is the power of God for salvation for everyone who believes, for the Jew first and then for the Greek. For the righteousness of God is revealed in it from faith to faith, as scripture says, The righteous live from faith* (Rom 1:16-17; Hb 2:4). This is the righteousness of God which, though veiled in the Old Testament, is revealed in the New. It is called the righteousness of God, because by bestowing it God makes us righteous. So too, *With the Lord there is salvation* (Ps 3:9), the salvation by which he makes us saved. And this is the faith from which and to which it is revealed, namely, from the faith of those foretelling it to the faith of those who accept it. By that faith of Jesus Christ, that is, which he bestowed upon us, we believe that we now have from God and will have more fully from him the righteous life we live. Hence, we offer him our thanks with the piety by which he alone is to be worshiped.

The Punishment of Pride and Ingratitude

12, 19. With good reason the Apostle turned from this section to mentioning with horror those who by that vice I mentioned above became empty and puffed up and who were raised up by their own efforts as if through the empty air. They did not come to rest there, but were broken and plunged downward, falling upon the statues of

---

42. The Maurist adds *sive internis*, which seems required, though it has no basis in the manuscripts.
43. See Rom 1:14.

idols as upon rocks. For, since he was praising the piety of the faith for which we ought to be thankful to God, since we are gratuitously justified by it, he introduced its opposite at which we should be horrified. He said, *God's anger is being revealed from heaven upon all godlessness and unrighteousness of people who suppress the truth in their wickedness. For what can be known of God is obvious to them, because God has shown it to them. From the creation of the world his invisible reality, namely, his everlasting power and divinity, is seen and understood through the things that have been made. Hence, they are without excuse, because, though they knew God, they did not glorify him as God or give thanks. Rather, they became vain in their thoughts. And their foolish heart was darkened. Though they said they were wise, they became fools and exchanged the glory of the incorruptible God for the likeness of the image of a corruptible human being and birds and animals and reptiles.* (Rom 1:18-23) See how he said that they were not ignorant of the truth, but that they suppressed the truth in their wickedness. And it occurred to him that someone might ask the source from which they could have this knowledge of the truth, since God had not given them the law. Hence, he stated the source from which they could have it. For he said that through the visible things of creation they came to an understanding of the invisible reality of the creator. For great minds truly persisted in the search, and they were able to find him. Where then is their godlessness? It is, of course, that, *though they knew God, they did not glorify him as God or give thanks. Rather, they became vain in their thoughts.* (Rom 1:21) Their vanity is really a disease; they mislead themselves, when they suppose they are something, though they are nothing.[44] Then they cast a shadow over themselves by this swelling of pride. The holy psalmist prays that pride's foot may not come to him;[45] he said, *In your light we will see light* (Ps 36:10). They are turned away from the light of the immutable truth, *and their foolish heart was darkened* (Rom 1:21). Though they had known God, their heart was not wise, but rather foolish, because they did not glorify him as God or give thanks. *For he said to man, See, piety is wisdom.* And, for this reason, *though they said they were wise,* which is not to be understood in any other sense than that they attributed this to themselves, *they became fools* (Rom 1:22).

---

44. See Gal 6:3.
45. See Ps 36:12.

20. What need is there to mention the following paragraphs of this letter? God resists the proud,[46] and the depths to which those people have fallen through this godlessness and in which they lie submerged—I mean those people who were able to know the creator through the creature—teach us better than the remainder of this letter which we are citing here.[47] Nor have we undertaken a commentary on this letter in this work; rather, we are striving, as best we can, to show, especially by testimony from it, that we are helped by God to act with righteousness, not insofar as God gave us a law full of good and holy commandments, but insofar as our own will, without which we can do nothing good, is helped and raised up through the gift of the Spirit of grace. Without this help that teaching is the letter that kills, because it holds persons guilty of transgression rather than justifies the sinner. Those who knew the creator through his creation received from that knowledge no benefit toward salvation, *because, though they knew God, they did not glorify him as God or give thanks, though they said they were wise* (Rom 1:21.22). In the same way, those who know through the law of God how they should live are not justified by that knowledge, because, *wanting to establish their own righteousness, they were not subject to the righteousness of God* (Rom 10:3).

The Distinction between the Law of Works and the Law of Faith

13, 21. It is worth the effort to consider how the law of actions, that is, of works, which does not exclude that boasting, and the law of faith, which does exclude it, differ from each other, if only we can grasp the distinction. For one might say right off that the law of works is found in Judaism and the law of faith in Christianity, because circumcision and other such works belong to the law and Christian practice does not observe them anymore. But we have for a long time been trying to show how mistaken that distinction is. We may have already shown this to sharper minds and especially to you and others like you. But since the point is important, it is not inappropriate for us to return to the testimonies again and again in making it clear to

---

46. See Jas 4:6; 1 Pt 5:5.
47. See Rom 1:26-27.

more people. For he said that no one is justified by the law and that the law entered in so that sin might abound,[48] but he defended the law so that no uneducated person would blame it and no sacrilegious person would attack it on that account. He said, *What then shall we say? That the law is sin? Heaven forbid! But I knew sin only through the law, for I would not have known desire if the law had not said, You shall not desire. And so, having seized the opportunity, sin produced in me through the commandment every desire* (Rom 7:7-8). He also says, *The law is indeed holy and the commandment holy, righteous, and good. But in order that sin might be seen as sin, it produced death for me through what is good.* (Rom 7:12-13) It is, then, the letter that kills which says, *You shall not desire.* He likewise says of it the words I cited just before, *For knowledge of sin came through the law. But now the righteousness of God has been revealed apart from the law, though the law and the prophets have borne witness to it. The righteousness of God through the faith of Jesus Christ for all who believe; for there is no distinction. For all have sinned and lack the glory of God, but they have been gratuitously justified by his grace through the redemption in Christ Jesus. For God has made him the sacrifice of atonement in his blood through faith. This was to reveal his righteousness in overlooking past sins in the time of God's patience in order to reveal his righteousness in the present time that he is righteous and justifies those who have faith in Jesus.* Then he added the passage we are now discussing, *Where is your boasting? It has been excluded. By what law? By the law of works? No, but by the law of faith.* (Rom 3:20-27) It is, then, this law of actions which says, *You shall not desire,* because the knowledge of sin comes through it. I want to know, then, if anyone would dare to ask me whether the law of faith does not say, *You shall not desire.* After all, if it does not say that, what reason is there why we who live under it do not sin without a care and with impunity? For those people thought that the Apostle said this, and he said of them, *And some people whose judgment is not right claim that we say, Let us do evil that good may come of it* (Rom 3:8). But if it also says, *You shall not desire,* as so many commandments from the gospel and the apostle unceasingly cry out their testimony, why is it also not called the law of works? The fact that it does not have the works of the old sacraments, namely, circumcision

---

48. See Rom 5:20.

and the rest, does not mean that there are no works which it has in its own sacraments that are appropriate to its own time. But was there any question of the works of such sacraments when the Apostle said of the law that knowledge of sin came through it and, for that reason, no one is justified by it?[49] Why then is boasting not excluded by it, but by the law of faith,[50] from which the righteous live?[51] Does not knowledge of sin come through this law of faith, since it also says, *You shall not desire?*

22. What then is the difference? I will explain it briefly. What the law of works commands by its threats the law of faith obtains by its faith. The former says, *You shall not desire*; the latter says, *Since I knew that no one can be continent unless God grants this and to know from whom this gift comes was itself the mark of wisdom, I went to the Lord and pleaded with him* (Wis 8:21). This is the wisdom that is called piety; by it one worships the Father of lights from whom there comes *every best gift and every perfect gift* (Jas 1:17). He is worshiped by the sacrifice of praise and thanksgiving so that those who worship him do not boast in themselves, but in him.[52] Accordingly, by the law of works God says, Do what I command! By the law of faith we say to God, Give what you command! After all, the law commands in order to remind us of what faith should do. It commands, that is, so that, if those to whom the command is given are not as yet able to observe it, they may know what to ask for. But if they are immediately able to do what is commanded and do it in obedience, they ought to know by whose gift they are able to do it. *For we have not received the spirit of this world,* said that same steadfast preacher of grace, *but the Spirit that comes from God so that we may know what God has given us* (1 Cor 2:12). What is the spirit of this world but the spirit of pride which darkened the foolish heart of those people, who, though they knew God, did not glorify him as God by giving thanks?[53] It is the same spirit who deceives those who, *not knowing the righteousness of God and wanting to establish their own righteousness, were not subject to the righteousness of God* (Rom 10:3). Hence, they seem to me to be more children of faith

49. See Rom 3:20.
50. See Rom 3:27.
51. See Rom 1:17.
52. See 2 Cor 10:17.
53. See Rom 1:21.

who know from whom they should hope for what they do not yet
have than those who give themselves credit for what they have. And
yet we ought to prefer to both these kinds of people, those who both
have these gifts and know from whom they have them, provided that
they do not believe that they already are what they are not yet. Otherwise, they would fall into the sin of the Pharisee; though he thanked
God for the gifts he had, he did not ask to receive anything, as if he
had no need to increase and perfect his righteousness.[54] Having then
weighed and considered these points in accord with the ability that
God is pleased to give us, we conclude that human beings are not
justified by the commandments that teach us to live well, but only
through faith in Jesus Christ, that is, not by the law of works, but by
the law of faith, not by the letter, but by the Spirit, not by the merits
of actions, but gratuitously by grace.

The Letter That Kills Is the Ten Commandments

14, 23. The Apostle seems to rebuke and correct those who were
persuaded to receive circumcision in that by the term "law" he refers
to circumcision and other such observances of the law.[55] Christians
do not now observe them, since they were foreshadowings of what
was to come.[56] And they now actually possess what was promised
symbolically through those foreshadowings. The Apostle nonetheless wanted us to understand that the law, by which he says that no
one is justified, is found not only in those sacraments which they
had as symbols of what was promised, but also in those works which
amount to a righteous life for whoever does them. Among them we
also find the commandment, *You shall not desire*. And so that what
we are saying may be made more clear, let us look at the Ten Commandments. For on the mountain Moses certainly received the law
that was to be given to the people written on stone tablets by the finger of God.[57] This law is limited to the Ten Commandments in which
there is no commandment about circumcision and nothing about the
animal victims which Christians do not now offer in sacrifice. Apart
from the observance of the Sabbath, what is there in those Ten Com-

54. See Lk 18:11-12.
55. See Rom 2:25-29.
56. See Col 2:17.
57. See Ex 31:18.

mandments that a Christian is not to observe, whether about not making and not worshiping idols and other gods besides the one true God or about not taking the name of God in vain or about honoring parents or about avoiding fornication, murder, theft, false witness, adultery, and desiring another's possessions?[58] Which of these has anyone claimed that a Christian need not observe? Was it perhaps not this law written on those two tablets that the Apostle called the letter that kills, but that law about circumcision and the other sacred rites that have now been abolished? But how are we to think that, when we find in it *You shall not desire*? By that commandment, though it was holy and righteous and good,[59] *sin deceived me and killed me through it* (Rom 7:11). What else does that mean but that *the letter kills*?

24. It is even clearer in the same passage to the Corinthians, where he says, *The letter kills, but the Spirit gives life*, that he wants us to understand the letter as the Ten Commandments written on those two tablets. For he speaks as follows: *You are a letter from Christ delivered by us, written not with ink, but by the Spirit of the living God, not on stone tablets, but on tablets of flesh, your hearts. Such confidence do we have through Christ before God, not that we are sufficient to have a single thought as our own, but our sufficiency comes from God. He has made us able ministers of the New Testament, not of the letter, but of the Spirit, for the letter kills, but the Spirit gives life. But if the ministry of death carved in letters of stone was inaugurated in glory so that the people of Israel could not look upon the face of Moses on account of the glory of his face, though it was a passing glory, will not the ministry of the Spirit be in greater glory? For if the ministry of condemnation was glorious, the ministry of righteousness will abound much more in glory.* (2 Cor 3:3-9) One could say a great deal about these words, but perhaps there will be a better occasion later. For the moment note what he calls the letter that kills, to which he contrasts as its opposite the Spirit that gives life. It is certainly the ministry of death carved in stone letters and the ministry of condemnation,[60] because *the law entered in so that sin might abound* (Rom 5:20). But the commandments

---

58. See Ex 20:2-17.
59. See Rom 7:12.
60. See 2 Cor 3:7.9.

themselves are for one who observes them so useful and conducive to salvation that one can possess life only by observing them. Or are the Ten Commandments called the letter that kills on account of the one commandment it contains concerning the Sabbath? For anyone who up to the present observes that day in the literal sense of the commandment is wise according to the flesh, but *to be wise according to the flesh is death* (Rom 8:6). And are we to suppose that those nine commandments which it is right to observe in their literal sense do not pertain to the law of works by which no one is justified[61] but to the law of faith by which the righteous live?[62] Who would be so foolish as to think that it was called the ministry of death carved in letters of stone not on account of all ten commandments, but on account of that one commandment that has to do with the Sabbath? What then are we to do with the words, *The law produced anger, for where there is no law, there is no transgression* (Rom 4:15)? Or with the words, *Before the law there was sin in the world, but sin was not imputed, when the law did not exist* (Rom 5:13)? Or with these words, which we have mentioned so many times, *Knowledge of sin came through the law* (Rom 3:20)? Or especially with this statement in which he quite clearly expresses the point at issue, *I would not have known desire, if the law had not said, You shall not desire?*

25. Consider the whole passage and see whether he says anything on account of circumcision or the Sabbath or any other foreshadowing sacred rite and does not rather say everything for the following reason. The letter forbidding sin does not give life to human beings, but rather kills them by increasing desire and augmenting sinfulness because of transgression, unless through the law of faith in Christ Jesus grace sets them free, when love is poured out in our hearts through the Holy Spirit who has been given to us.[63] For when he said, *That we may serve in the new condition of the Spirit and not under the old condition of the letter* (Rom 7:6), he said, *What then shall we say? That the law is sin? Heaven forbid! But I knew sin only through the law, for I would not have known desire if the law had not said, You shall not desire. But having seized the opportunity, sin produced in me through the commandment every*

---

61. See Rom 3:20.
62. See Rom 1:17; Gal 3:11.
63. See Rom 5:5.

desire. For without the law sin lay dead. I was once living without the law, but with the arrival of the commandment sin came back to life. I died, and the commandment which was meant for life was found in my case to spell death. For, having seized the opportunity, sin deceived me by the commandment and killed me through it. Hence, the law is indeed holy and the commandment holy and righteous and good. Did what was good become death for me? Heaven forbid! But in order that sin might be seen as sin, it produced death in me through what is good, so that through the commandment sin might become sinful beyond measure. For we know that the law is spiritual, but I am carnal, sold under the power of sin. I do not know what I do, for I do not do what I want; rather, I do what I hate. But if I do what I do not want, I agree that the law is good. Now it is not I who do that, but the sin that dwells in me. For I know that the good does not dwell in me, that is, in my flesh. I can will the good, but I cannot do it. I do not do the good that I want, but I do the evil that I do not want. But if I do what I do not want, it is no longer I who do it, but the sin that dwells in me. I find, therefore, a law that, when I want to do good, evil lies at hand for me. For I delight in the law of God in the interior human being, but I see another law in my members that resists the law of my mind and holds me captive in the law of sin which lies in my members. Wretched man that I am! Who will set me free from the body of this death? The grace of God through Jesus Christ, our Lord. Therefore, I serve the law of God with my mind, but the law of sin with my flesh. (Rom 7:7-25)

Delight in the Law of the Lord Is a Gift of the Spirit

26. It is clear, then, that, if the new condition of the Spirit is lacking, the old condition of the letter makes people guilty by reason of the knowledge of sin rather than sets them free from sin. For this reason scripture says elsewhere, *One who adds knowledge adds pain* (Eccl 1:18), not because the law itself is evil, but because the good of the commandment lies in the letter that makes it known, not in the Spirit who helps to fulfill it. If that commandment is observed out of fear of punishment, not out of the love of righteousness, it is observed in the manner of a slave, not in the manner of someone free, and for that reason it is not observed. For there

is lacking the good fruit that springs up from the root of love. But if *faith that works through love* (Gal 5:6) is present, one begins to find delight in the law of God in the interior human being. This delight is a gift, not of the letter, but of the Spirit, even if another law in one's members resists the law of the mind,[64] until the whole old condition has passed over into the new condition. This new condition is being increased in the interior human being from day to day,[65] as we are set free *from the body of this death by the grace of God through Jesus Christ, our Lord* (Rom 7:24).

15, 27. This grace remained veiled in the Old Testament; it has been unveiled in the gospel of Christ in accord with the perfect temporal order of providence, for God knows how to arrange all things. And perhaps it is a part of that hiddenness that in the Ten Commandments given on Mount Sinai only what pertains to the Sabbath was concealed in a symbolic commandment. The Sabbath is the day of sanctification. And there is good reason that among all the works which God made, sanctification is first mentioned at the point where he rested from all his works;[66] this is not the place to discuss that point. Nonetheless, I think that it suffices for the matter we are dealing with that there was a reason that the people received the commandment to abstain from all servile work on that day.[67] Servile work signified sin, for not to sin pertains to sanctification, that is, to the gift of God through the Holy Spirit. In the law written on the two tablets of stone this commandment alone among the others was expressed in the shadow of a symbol. The Jews observe the Sabbath in that shadow. This very fact signifies that it was then the time for concealing the grace which was to be unveiled in the New Testament through Christ's passion, as if by the tearing of the temple veil.[68] He says, *When you have gone over to Christ, the veil will be removed* (2 Cor 3:16).

16, 28. *The Lord is the Spirit, but where the Spirit of the Lord is, there is freedom* (2 Cor 3:17). This is the Spirit of God by whose gift we are justified; by his gift there comes to be in us a delight in not sinning so that we have freedom. So too, without

---

64. See Rom 7:22.
65. See 2 Cor 4:16.
66. See Ex 20:11.
67. See Ex 20:10.
68. See Mt 27:51.

this Spirit we find delight in sinning so that we are enslaved. We must abstain from the works of such slavery; that is, we must observe the Sabbath in a spiritual way. This is the Holy Spirit by whom love is poured out in our hearts,[69] and love is the fulfillment of the law.[70] In the gospel this Holy Spirit is also called the finger of God.[71] Those tablets were written by the finger of God,[72] and the finger of God is the Spirit of God by whom we are sanctified so that we live from faith and do good works through love.[73] Who can fail to be struck by the agreement as well as the difference? Through Moses God commanded that the Passover be observed with the killing of a lamb as a symbol,[74] in order to signify the future passion of the Lord. And we count fifty days from the celebration of Passover up to the day on which Moses received the law that the finger of God had written on those tablets. So too, when fifty days had passed from the killing and rising of him who *was led off like a sheep for sacrifice* (Is 53:7), the finger of God, that is, the Holy Spirit, filled the faithful who were gathered in one place.[75]

The Law of Faith Is the Love Poured Out in Our Hearts

17, 29. Despite this remarkable agreement there surely remains a very great difference. In the former case the people were prevented by terrifying fear[76] from approaching the place where the law was given, but in the latter case the Holy Spirit came over those who were gathered together in one place and were waiting for him.[77] In the former case the finger of God wrote on stone tablets; in the latter upon human hearts. In the former case, then, the law by which the unrighteous were terrified was given outwardly; in the latter case the law by which they are justified was given inwardly. *For You shall not commit adultery, You shall not kill, You shall not desire, and*

---

69. See Rom 5:5.
70. See Rom 13:10.
71. See Lk 11:20.
72. See Dt 9:10.
73. See Gal 5:6.
74. See Ex 12:3-10.
75. See Acts 2:1-4.
76. See Ex 19:12-13.19.
77. See Acts 2:1.

any other commandment there is—that has been written in those
tablets—*has been,* he said, *summed up in these words: You shall
love your neighbor as yourself. Love of the neighbor does no evil.
Rather, love is the fulfillment of the law.* (Rom 13:9-10) This love is
not written on stone tablets, but *has been poured out in our hearts
by the Holy Spirit who has been given to us* (Rom 5:5). The law of
God, then, is love. To this love *the wisdom of the flesh is not subject,
and it cannot be* (Rom 8:7). When the works of love are written on
tablets in order to strike fear in this wisdom of the flesh, it is the law
of works and the letter that kills their transgressor. But when love
itself is poured out in the hearts of those who believe,[78] it is the law
of faith and the Spirit who gives life to their lovers.

30. Consider now how this distinction agrees with the words of
the Apostle which I mentioned a little earlier for another reason,
though I postponed until later a more careful examination of them.
He says, *You have shown that you are a letter from Christ delivered
by us, written not by ink, but by the Spirit of the living God, not
on stone tablets, but on tablets of flesh, your hearts* (2 Cor 3:3).
See how he shows that the former law was written outside human
beings in order to strike fear into them from the outside, while the
latter law is written in the human beings so that it justifies them
within. By *tablets of flesh, your hearts,* he did not mean tablets of
the wisdom of the flesh; rather, he meant tablets that were alive and
had minds in comparison with stone which has no mind. And a little
later he says that the people of Israel were not able to gaze upon the
face of Moses and so he spoke to them through a veil.[79] This means
that the letter of the law justifies no one, but a veil has been drawn
in their reading of the Old Testament, until they pass over to Christ
and the veil is removed,[80] that is, until they pass over to grace and
understand that our justification, by which we do what he commands, comes from him. He gives us the commandments precisely
so that, when we ourselves fail, we may take refuge in him. And so
he said with the utmost carefulness, *Such confidence do we have
through Christ before God,* and so that we would not attribute this
to ourselves, he immediately instructed us on the point at issue. He

---

78. See Rom 5:5.
79. See 2 Cor 3:7.13.
80. See 2 Cor 3:16.

said, *Not that we are sufficient to have a single thought as our own, but our sufficiency comes from God. He has made us able ministers of the New Testament, not of the letter, but of the Spirit. For the letter kills, but the Spirit gives life.* (2 Cor 3:4-6)

18, 31. Elsewhere he said, *The law,* that is, this letter written outside human beings, *was given for the sake of transgression* (Gal 3:19). Hence, he also called it the ministry of death and the ministry of condemnation. But this law, that is, the law of the New Testament, he calls the ministry of the Spirit and the ministry of righteousness,[81] because through the gift of the Spirit we do the works of righteousness and we are set free from the condemnation owing to transgression. And so, the former is being done away with, while the latter continues, since the schoolmaster who strikes terror is done away with,[82] as love takes the place of fear, *for where the Spirit of the Lord is, there is freedom.* He says that this ministry does not come from our merits, but from his mercy: *Therefore, since we have this ministry because we have obtained mercy, let us not grow weak; rather, let us cast aside hidden shameful practices, not walking in cunningness or mixing the word of God with deceit* (2 Cor 4:1-2). He means for us to understand by this cunningness and deceit the hypocrisy by which the proud want to be seen as righteous. Hence, in that psalm which the same Apostle mentioned as testimony to this very grace, it says, *Blessed are they to whom God has not imputed sin and on whose lips there is no deceit* (Ps 32:2).[83] This is the confession of those who are humble and holy, not of those who boast of being what they are not. A little later he adds, *For it is not ourselves that we preach, but Jesus Christ as Lord and ourselves as servants through Jesus, because God, who commanded that light shine forth from the darkness, has shone in our hearts to illumine the knowledge of his glory upon the face of Christ* (2 Cor 4:5-6). This is the knowledge of his glory by which we know that he is the light which enlightens our darkness. Pay attention to how he teaches this. He says, *We have this treasure in vessels of clay to show that the transcendent power belongs to God and does not come from us* (2 Cor 4:7). And a little later he praised this same grace even more extensively and came to that cloak of righteousness, that is, to faith. Clothed with it, we will

81. See 2 Cor 3:7-9.
82. See Gal 3:24.
83. See Rom 4:8.

not be found naked, and for this reason we groan, weighed down by our mortality, while we long to put on our heavenly dwelling, so that what is mortal may be swallowed up by life.[84] Notice what he adds, *But the one who has brought this about in us is God who has given us the pledge of the Spirit* (2 Cor 5:5). And after this he added, *So that in him we might be the righteousness of God* (2 Cor 5:21). This is not the righteousness of God by which he himself is righteous, but that by which he makes us righteous.

19, 32. Let no Christian then depart from this faith, for it alone is the Christian faith. Some may be ashamed to claim that we become righteous by ourselves without the grace of God producing this in us, for they see that the pious faithful cannot tolerate such a statement. But they should not resort to saying that the reason we cannot be righteous without the grace of God is that he gave us the law, that he provided us with teaching, that he imposed the good commandments. For all that is undoubtedly the letter that kills, if the Spirit does not provide help. But when the life-giving Spirit is present, he makes us love the very same thing, now written within, which the law made us fear, when it was written exteriorly.

Jeremiah Foretold the Coming of the New Testament

33. Examine this teaching for a little while in the testimony which the prophet stated with perfect clarity on this point: *Behold, the days will come, says the Lord, and I will complete a new testament with the house of Israel and with the house of Judah, not like the testament I made with their fathers on the day on which I took their hand in order to bring them out of the land of Egypt. For they had not kept to my testament and I did not trouble myself over them, says the Lord. This is the testament that I will make with the house of Israel: After those days, says the Lord, I will put my laws in their heart and I will write them upon their minds, and I will be their God and they will be my people. And individuals will no longer teach their fellow citizens or kinfolk, saying, Know the Lord, because they will all know me from the littlest to the greatest of them, for I will forgive their wickedness and I will no longer remember their sins.* (Jer 31:31-34) What shall we say to that? Apart from this passage in

---

84. See 2 Cor 5:2-4.

the prophet we find no mention at all of the New Testament in the old books, or only with difficulty do we find in them any mention of it where it is called by this very name. There are many passages that refer to it and foretell its coming, but not so that we also find its name expressed. Consider, then, with care the difference between these two testaments, that is, the Old and the New, to which God has borne witness.

34. When he said, *Not like the testament I made with their fathers on the day on which I took their hand in order to bring them out of the land of Egypt*, see what he added: *for they had not kept to my testament* (Jer 31:32). He attributes it to their sins that they did not keep to his testament so that they would not think that the law which they then received deserved the blame. It is, after all, the law which Christ came not to destroy but to fulfill,[85] and yet the wicked are not justified by that same law, but by grace. The life-giving Spirit, without whom the letter kills, does this. *For, if a law had been given which could give life, righteousness would, of course, come from the law. But scripture has enclosed all things under sin so that on the basis of faith in Jesus Christ the promise might be given to those who believe.* (Gal 3:21-22) Because of this promise, that is, because of this gift of God, the law is being fulfilled; without that promise the law produces transgressors. At times it even leads to doing evil actions, if the flame of concupiscence leaps over the restraints of fear. At times it remains in the will alone, if the fear of punishment conquers the sweetness of lust. The words, *Scripture has enclosed all things under sin so that on the basis of faith in Jesus Christ the promise might be given to those who believe* (Gal 3:22), express the usefulness of this act of enclosing. After all, for what purpose did scripture do this enclosing, if not for the purpose it goes on to state: *Before faith came, we were guarded and enclosed under the law for the faith that was later revealed* (Gal 3:23)? The law, then, was given in order that we would seek after grace; grace was given so that we might fulfill the law. For it is not because of some failure of its own that the law is not fulfilled, but because of the failure of the wisdom of the flesh. That failure had to be revealed by the law, but it had to be healed by grace. *For what the law could not do inasmuch*

---

85. See Mt 5:17.

as it was weakened by the flesh God has done; he sent his own Son in the likeness of sinful flesh, and by sin he condemned sin in the flesh so that the righteousness of the law might be fulfilled in us who walk not according to the flesh but according to the Spirit (Rom 8:3-4). Hence, in that testimony of the prophet it says, *I will complete a new testament with the house of Israel and with the house of Judah.* What does *I will complete* mean but I will fulfill it, but *like the testament I made with their fathers on the day on which I took their hand to bring them out of the land of Egypt* (Jer 31:31-32)?[86]

20, 35. The former, then, was old, because the latter was new. But why was the former old and the latter new, though the same law is fulfilled by the New Testament which in the Old commanded, *You shall not desire*? He says, *For they had not kept to my testament and I did not trouble myself over them, says the Lord* (Jer 31:32). Therefore, the former is called the Old Testament on account of the human injury which is not healed by the command and threat of the letter; the latter is called the New Testament on account of the new condition of the Spirit which heals the new human being from the wound of the old condition. Then notice what follows and see how brilliantly clear it makes the point which those who trust in themselves refuse to see. He says, *This is the testament that I will make with the house of Israel: After those days, says the Lord, I will put my laws in their heart and I will write them upon their minds* (Jer 31:33). There you have the reason why the Apostle says what I quoted above, *not on stone tablets, but on the tablets of your hearts*, because it is written *not by ink, but by the Spirit of the living God* (2 Cor 3:3). In that letter he said, *He has made us able ministers of the New Testament, not of the letter, but of the Spirit* (2 Cor 3:6). I do not think the Apostle had any other reason to mention the New Testament in that passage, except that he had that prophecy in mind, when he said, *not on stone tablets, but on tablets of flesh, your hearts* (2 Cor 3:3). For that prophecy, in which the New Testament was promised by name, said, *I will write them in their hearts* (Jer 31:33).

---

86. The Maurists and the ALG editors punctuate the previous sentence somewhat differently; I have followed the CSEL edition.

The Laws of God in Our Hearts Are the
Presence of the Spirit

21, 36. What then are the laws of God that are written by God himself on our hearts but the very presence of the Holy Spirit? He is the finger of God;[87] by his presence love is poured out in our hearts,[88] the love which is the fulfillment of the law and the goal of the commandment.[89] For the promises of the Old Testament were earthly. I leave aside the sacraments' rites which were foreshadowings of what was to come,[90] such as circumcision, the Sabbath, the other feast days, the ceremonies regarding certain foods, and the many rites of the sacred sacrifices, which were all appropriate to the old condition with its carnal law and servile yoke. Yet the Old Testament contained the sort of commandments of righteousness that we are even now commanded to obey; these were, above all, those found on those two tablets and were not wrapped in the shadows of some symbolic expression. For example, *You shall not commit adultery; you shall not kill; you shall not desire; and any other commandment there is has been summed up in these words: You shall love your neighbor as yourself* (Rom 13:9). And yet the Old Testament lists earthly and temporal promises which are goods of this corruptible flesh, even though they symbolize everlasting and heavenly goods which, of course, pertain to the New Testament. Now we are promised the good of the heart, the good of the mind, the good of the Spirit, that is, the intelligible good, when it says, *Putting my laws in their minds, I will also write them in their hearts* (Jer 31:33). By this he signified that they would not fear the law that strikes terror from the outside, but that they would love the righteousness of the law that dwells within.

22, 37. Then he added the reward, *And I will be their God, and they shall be my people* (Jer 31:33). This is what the psalmist said to God, *It is good for me to cling to God* (Ps 73:28). He said, *I will be their God, and they shall be my people.* What could be better than this good, what could be happier than this happiness of living for God,[91]

---

87. See Lk 11:20.
88. See Rom 5:5.
89. See Rom 13:10; 1 Tm 1:5.
90. See 2 Cor 2:17.
91. See Rom 6:11.

and of living from God? For with him there is the source of light and in his light we shall see the light.[92] Of this life the Lord said, *This is eternal life, that they know you, the one true God and him whom you sent, Jesus Christ* (Jn 17:3), that is, you and Jesus Christ whom you have sent, the one true God. This is what he promises to those who love him; he says, *Those who love me keep my commandments, and those who love me are loved by my Father. I too will love them, and I will show myself to them* (Jn 14:21). He will, that is, show himself to them in the form of God in which he is equal to the Father, not in the form of the servant in which he showed himself even to sinners.[93] Then there will be fulfilled the words of scripture, *The godless will be taken away so that they do not see the glory of the Lord* (Is 26:10), when those on the left will enter eternal fire, but the righteous will enter eternal life.[94] This eternal life, as I mentioned, has been declared to consist in their knowing the one true God.[95] For this reason John too says, *Beloved, we are now children of God, and it has not yet been revealed what we shall be. We know that, when he appears, we shall be like him, because we shall see him as he is.* (1 Jn 3:2) This likeness to him is now beginning to be formed again as human beings are interiorly renewed from day to day[96] *according to the image of him who created them* (Col 3:10).

23, 38. But in comparison to the perfection of that excellent state that will then exist, what does this present state amount to? Using an example drawn from familiar things to speak of those ineffable ones, the Apostle used a comparison with childhood and adulthood. He said, *When I was a child, I spoke like a child, I thought like a child, I reasoned like a child, but when I became a man, I set aside what belonged to the child.* He went on to show why he said this with the words, *We see now through a mirror dimly, but then we shall see face to face. Now I know in part, but then I shall know as I am known.* (1 Cor 13:11-12)

24, 39. Moreover, this prophet whose testimony we are examining also made the point that the reward, the goal, the perfect state of happiness, the pinnacle of the blessed and eternal life, is found

---

92. See Ps 36:10.
93. See Phil 2:6-7.
94. See Mt 25:46.
95. See Jn 17:3.
96. See 2 Cor 4:16.

in God. For when he said, *And I will be their God, and they shall be my people,* he immediately added, *and individuals will no longer teach their fellow citizens and their kinfolk, saying, Know the Lord, because they will all know me from the littlest to the greatest of them* (Jer 31:34). Now is certainly the time of the New Testament which the prophet promised by these words that we have quoted. Why then do individuals still say to their fellow citizens and kinfolk, *Know the Lord?* They do say this, don't they, when the gospel is preached, and doesn't its being preached mean precisely that this is said everywhere? After all, why did the Apostle say that he was the teacher of the Gentiles,[97] except that his words were being fulfilled: *How will they call upon him in whom they have not believed? Or how will they believe in him of whom they have not heard? But how will they hear of him without someone to preach?* (Rom 10:14) Now, since this preaching is spreading everywhere, how can it be the time of the New Testament? For the prophet said of the New Testament, *And individuals will no longer teach their fellow citizens and their kinfolk, saying, Know the Lord, because they will all know me from the littlest to the greatest of them.* It can only be that he included in his promise the eternal reward of the same New Testament, that is, the fully blessed contemplation of God himself.

40. What do the words, *all from the littlest to the greatest of them,* mean but all who spiritually belong to the house of Israel and the house of Judah, that is, to the children of Isaac, to the offspring of Abraham? For this is the promise made to him, *Your offspring will be named after Isaac. For it is not the children of the flesh that are children of God, but the children of the promise are counted as offspring. This is the wording of the promise: I will return at this season, and Sarah will have a son. Not only this, but Rebecca too bore children from having relations once with our father, Isaac. They were not yet born and had done nothing either good or bad, but in order that God's plan might remain in accord with his choice, scripture said, The older will serve the younger, not because of any works, but because of the one who calls.* (Rom 9:7-13) It is the house of Israel or the house of Judah on account of Christ who came from the house of Judah. It is the house of the children of the promise, that is, children

---

97. See 1 Tm 2:7.

not because of their own works, but because of God's kindness. God
promises only what he himself does; after all, it is not he who makes
the promise while someone else carries it out. That would not be
promising, but predicting. Hence, it says, *Not because of works, but
because of the one who calls* (Rom 9:12), so that the attainment is
not due to them, but to God, so that the reward is not regarded as
something owed them, but as grace.[98] Otherwise, grace would no
longer be grace.[99] Its vigorous defender and preacher is the least of
the apostles, who worked harder than all of them, though it was not
he himself, but the grace of God that worked with him.[100] It says, *All
will know me* (Jer 31:34), that is, all of the house of Israel and of the
house of Judah. For it is not all who are from Israel who are Israel,
but those to whom the psalm says, *To welcome the morning,* that is,
the new light coming from, of course, the New Testament, *all you
offspring of Jacob, glorify him; let every offspring of Israel fear him*
(Ps 22:1.24-25). Absolutely all the offspring, that is, all the offspring
that received the promise and were called, but those who were called
by his choice.[101] *But those whom he predestined he also called, and
those whom he called he also justified, and those whom he justified
he also glorified* (Rom 8:30). *Therefore, it was on the basis of faith so
that the promise might be assured as grace for all the offspring, not
merely to the offspring which comes from the law,* that is, the offspring
that comes from the Old Testament to the New, *but also to that which
comes from faith,* not because the law was promised them, *but from
the faith of Abraham.* I mean those who imitate the faith of Abraham,
*who is the father of us all. As scripture says, I will make you the father
of the nations* (Rom 4:16-17). All these, then, who have been predestined, called, justified, and glorified know God by the grace of the
New Testament from the littlest to the greatest of them.

The Difference between the Old and
New Testaments Summed Up

41. The law of works written on stone tablets and its reward, that
promised land which the carnal house of Israel received when it was

98. See Rom 4:4.
99. See Rom 11:6.
100. See 1 Cor 15:9-10.
101. See Rom 8:28.

set free from Egypt, pertains to the Old Testament. So too, the law of faith written in our hearts and its reward, the beauty of contemplation which the spiritual house of Israel will perceive once it has been set free from this world, pertains to the New Testament. Then the words of the Apostle will be fulfilled: *Prophecies will be done away with; tongues will cease; knowledge will be done away with* (1 Cor 13:8). He means that knowledge of little ones with which we live in this life; it is partial, in a mirror, and dim.[102] After all, prophecy is necessary for this life, in which the future still takes the place of the past. For this life tongues are necessary, that is, the multiplicity of meanings; in it we receive now this, now that admonition from different persons, since we do not as yet contemplate the eternal light of the clear truth with a mind that has been fully purified. *But when that which is perfect has come* (1 Cor 13:10), and all this which is partial shall have been done away with, then the Word who was revealed to flesh, because he assumed flesh, will disclose himself to those who love him; then there will be the eternal life in which we will know the one true God.[103] Then *we shall be like him* (1 Jn 3:2), because then we shall know him as we are known.[104] Then *individuals will not teach their fellow citizens or kinfolk, saying, Know the Lord; for all will know him from the littlest to the greatest of them*. This can be interpreted in many ways. For example, it can mean that even there each of the saints will differ in glory as one star differs from another.[105] It makes no difference whether one says, *from the littlest to the greatest of them*, as scripture has it, or "from the greatest to the littlest of them." So too, it makes no difference if we understand the little ones to be those who can only believe and the greatest to be those who can also understand the incorporeal and immutable light, to the extent that is possible in this life. Or he may have intended us to take the littlest as those who came later in time and the greatest as those who came earlier, for all will receive at one time the promised contemplation of God. Those who came earlier foresaw better things for us in such a way that they did not attain perfection without us.[106] And, therefore, the littlest ones are found to be like those who came earlier, since

102. See 1 Cor 13:12.
103. See Jn 17:3.
104. See 1 Cor 13:12.
105. See 1 Cor 15:41.
106. See Heb 11:40.

they waited less. It is just as we find in the parable about the day's wage in the gospel. Those who came to the vineyard later received their pay first.[107] There may be still another way of interpreting the littlest and the greatest, but it escapes me at present.

25, 42. Pay as careful attention as you can to the point that I am making such a great effort to elaborate. When the prophet promised the New Testament, he did not do so in accord with the testament that was earlier made with the people of Israel, when they were set free from Egypt. He said nothing about changing the sacrifices or any sacred rites, although that change was undoubtedly going to come, as we see that it has come. The same prophetic scripture bears witness to this in many other passages. But the prophet instructed us about only this difference, namely, that God would place his laws in the minds of those who belonged to this testament and would write it in their hearts. From this idea the Apostle drew his words, *not by ink, but by the Spirit of the living God, not upon stone tablets, but upon tablets of flesh, your hearts* (2 Cor 3:3). And as the eternal reward of this justification he promised not the land from which were driven the Amorites and the Hittites and the other nations, which are mentioned there,[108] but God himself. It is good to cling to him,[109] since the goodness of God that they love is the very God whom they love. Only sins separate God and human beings, and sins are removed only by the same grace. Hence, after he had said, *For all will know me from the littlest to the greatest of them*, he immediately added, *because I will forgive their sinfulness and I will not remember their sins any more* (Jer 31:34). By the law of works, then, the Lord says, *You shall not desire*; by the law of faith the Lord says, *Without me you can do nothing* (Jn 15:5). He was, after all, speaking about good works, that is, about the fruits of the branches.[110] The difference, then, between the Old and the New Testament is seen to be this: in the former the law is written on tablets, in the latter upon hearts, so that what in the former struck fear from without might in the latter produce delight within. In the former one became a transgressor because of the letter that kills; in the latter one becomes a lover be-

---

107. See Mt 20:8-12.
108. See Jos 12:2.8.
109. See Ps 73:28.
110. See Jn 15:1-5.

cause of the Spirit that gives life. Hence, we should not say that God helps us to do works of righteousness and produces in us *both the willing and the action in accord with good will* (Phil 2:13), because he externally produces sounds in our ears with the commandments of righteousness, but because he internally gives the increase,[111] by pouring out love *in our hearts by the Holy Spirit who has been given to us* (Rom 5:5).

How the Gentiles Have the Law Written in Their Hearts

26, 43. We must see what the Apostle meant when he said, *When the Gentiles, who do not have the law, by nature do what belongs to the law, these people, who do not have the law, are themselves the law for themselves. They reveal the work of the law written in their hearts.* (Rom 2:14-15) Otherwise, it might seem that the distinctiveness of the New Testament disappears, since the Lord promised to write his laws in the hearts of his people, but the Gentiles possessed this as part of their nature. We must, therefore, examine this question of no minor import which has arisen. After all, someone will say: If God distinguishes the New from the Old Testament inasmuch as in the Old Testament he wrote his law upon tablets, while in the New he wrote it upon hearts, how are the faithful of the New Testament distinguished from the Gentiles? For the latter have the work of the law written in their hearts as a result of which they do by nature what belongs to the law. They seem to be better off than the old people of God who received the law on tablets, and they seem to have anticipated the new people who received through the New Testament what nature gave to them.

44. Did the Apostle perhaps mean to say that those Gentiles who belong to the New Testament have the law written in their hearts? We must see how he came to this point in the letter. First, he said in praise of the gospel, *It is the power of God for salvation for everyone who believes, for the Jew first and then for the Greek. For the righteousness of God is revealed in it from faith to faith, as scripture says, The righteous live from faith.* (Rom 1:16-17; Hb 2:4) Next he speaks of those godless people whom even the knowledge of God did not benefit because of their pride, since *they did not glorify him*

---

111. See 1 Cor 3:7.

as God or give thanks (Rom 1:21). Then he turns to those who judge others, while doing the sort of things they condemn.[112] He says this especially on account of the Jews who boasted over the law of God, although he still does not mention them by name. On this point he says, *Anger and indignation, tribulation and distress for every human soul that does evil, Jew first and then Greek, but glory and honor and peace for everyone who does good, Jew first and then Greek. For there is no partiality on God's part. Those who have sinned without the law will perish without the law, and those who have sinned under the law will be judged by the law. For it is not the hearers of the law who are righteous before God; rather, those who observe the law will be justified.* (Rom 2:8-14) He immediately adds to these words the statement in question and says, *When the Gentiles, who do not have the law, by nature do what belongs to the law* (Rom 2:14) and the rest which I cited above. Hence, he seems here to use the term "Gentiles" to refer to those whom he called Greeks above, where he said, *Jew first and then Greek.* Moreover, the gospel *is the power of God for salvation for everyone who believes, for the Jew first and then for the Greek* (Rom 1:16), and *anger and indignation, tribulation and distress for every human soul that does evil, Jew first and then Greek, but glory and honor and peace for everyone who does good, Jew first and then Greek* (Rom 2:8-10). Paul referred to these Greeks as the Gentiles who do by nature what pertains to the law and who have the work of the law written in their hearts. The Gentiles who have the law written in their hearts surely belong to the gospel; for these people who believe, it is the power of God for salvation. But to which Gentiles, despite their good actions, would he promise glory, honor, and peace, if they stood apart from the grace of the gospel? After all, there is no partiality on God's part, and it is not those who hear the law but those who observe it who are justified.[113] Therefore, whether it is a Jew or a Greek, that is, a believing Gentile, they will equally obtain salvation in the gospel; *for there is no distinction.* So too, he later says, *For all have sinned and lack the glory of God, but they have been gratuitously justified by his grace* (Rom 3:22-24). How then could Paul have said that the Greek, who observes the law, is justified without the grace of the Savior?

---

112. See Rom 2:3.
113. See Rom 2:11-13.

45. After all, he would not contradict himself with the words, *Those who observe the law will be justified* (Rom 2:13), as if people were justified by works and not by grace. For he says that it is *gratuitously* that *human beings are justified by faith without the works of the law* (Rom 3:24.28). He meant nothing else to be understood by his term *gratuitously* but that works do not precede justification. Elsewhere he says plainly, *If it is by grace, it is not on the basis of works; otherwise, grace is no longer grace* (Rom 11:6). We must rather understand *Those who observe the law will be justified* (Rom 2:13) so that we realize that they fulfilled the law only because they are justified. Thus justification does not follow upon the observance of the law; rather, justification precedes the observance of the law. For what else does *justified* mean but made righteous by the one, of course, *who justifies sinners* (Rom 4:5), so that from sinners they become righteous? After all, if we were to express ourselves with the words, "Human beings will be set free," one would understand by this that freedom is given to those who were already human beings. But if we were to say, "Human beings will be created," one would certainly not understand that those who already were human beings are created, but that they became human beings by being created. So too, if it were said, "Those who observe the law will be honored," we would correctly interpret it only in the sense that honor is given to those who were already observing the law. But when it said, *Those who observe the law will be justified*, what else did it say but that the righteous will be made such? After all, those who observe the law are certainly righteous. Accordingly, it is the same as if one were to say, "Those who observe the law will be created," not because they already existed, but so that they might exist. Then the Jews, who were hearers of the law, would understand that they need the grace of the God who justifies so that they could be observers of the law. Or it is certainly true that they *will be justified* in the sense that they will be regarded as righteous, that they will be counted as righteous. In that sense scripture says of a certain man, *But he, wanting to justify himself* (Lk 10:29), that is, wanting to be regarded and counted as righteous. For this reason we say in one sense that God sanctifies his holy ones, and we say in another sense, *May your name be sanctified* (Mt 6:9). We use the former expression because he sanctifies those who were not holy, but we use the latter so that what is always holy in itself might be regarded as holy by human beings, that is, that they might have a holy fear of it.

46. In mentioning the Gentiles, then, who do by nature what pertains to the law and have the work of the law written in their hearts,[114] he wanted us to understand those who believe in Christ. They do not come to the faith, as the Jews do, by having the law given to them. Hence, there is no reason why we should try to distinguish them from those to whom the Lord promised the New Testament through the prophet, when he said that he would write his laws in their hearts.[115] For through the wild olive tree's having received the gift of being grafted on, as he says,[116] they belong to the same natural olive tree, that is, to the same people of God. Moreover, the testimony of the Apostle is in better agreement with the statement of the prophet that belonging to the New Testament means that they have the law of God written not on tablets but in their hearts, that is, that they embrace the righteousness of the law with an interior love. There faith works through love,[117] because God justifies the nations on the basis of faith. Scripture foresaw this and foretold it to Abraham with the words, *All nations will be blessed in your offspring* (Gn 22:18).[118] By the grace of this promise the wild olive tree was grafted onto the natural olive tree, and the nations who believed became children of Abraham in the offspring of Abraham, that is, in Christ,[119] through imitating Abraham's faith. Although he had not received the law on the tablets and did not yet have even circumcision, *he believed God and it was credited to him as righteousness* (Gn 15:6).[120] And so what the Apostle said about Gentiles of this sort, namely, that they have the law written in their hearts,[121] will be much the same as what he said to the Corinthians, *Not upon tablets of stone, but in tablets of flesh, your hearts* (2 Cor 3:3). After all, in that way they become members of the house of Israel, since their foreskin is counted as circumcision, because they do not reveal the righteousness of the law by a cutting away of the flesh, but guard it by the love of their heart. For, *if the uncircumcised observe the precepts of the law*, he says, *will not the lack of circumcision be counted as circumcision?* (Rom 2:26) And, for this reason, in the house of the true Israel, *in whom there is no*

114. See Rom 2:14-15.
115. See Jer 31:33.
116. See Rom 11:24.
117. See Gal 5:6.
118. See Gal 3:8.
119. See Gal 3:16.
120. See Rom 4:3.
121. See Rom 2:15.

guile (Jn 1:47), they share in the New Testament, because God puts the laws into their minds and writes them on their hearts[122] by his finger, the Holy Spirit, who pours out in their hearts the love[123] which is the fulfillment of the law.[124]

27, 47. Do not be concerned that he said that they do what pertains to the law by nature, not by the Spirit of God, not by faith, not by grace. After all, the Spirit of grace acts to restore in us the image of God, the image in which we were created in terms of our nature. An injury that grace heals is surely against nature; because of this grace we say to God, *Have mercy on me; heal my soul, for I have sinned against you* (Ps 41:5). Hence, people naturally observe what pertains to the law; those who do not do this fail to do it as a result of their woundedness. By that woundedness the law of God has been removed from their hearts, and so, once that wound has been healed, the law is written there, and they naturally do what pertains to the law. This does not mean that grace has been denied through nature, but rather that nature has been repaired through grace. *Through one human being sin entered the world, and through sin death, and thus it was passed on to all human beings in whom all have sinned* (Rom 5:12). And for that reason there is no distinction; they lack the glory of God, though they have been gratuitously justified by his grace.[125] By that grace there is written in the renewed interior human being the righteousness that sin had removed, and this mercy came upon the human race through Jesus Christ our Lord. *For God is one; one too is the mediator between God and human beings, the man Christ Jesus* (1 Tm 2:5).

A Second Interpretation of What Paul Meant

48. But these who by nature do what pertains to the law are not immediately to be considered as belonging to the number of those whom the grace of Christ justifies. They may even belong to the number of those who are unbelievers and who do not worship the true God in truth and righteousness. We may read or come to know or hear of some actions of theirs which we not only cannot blame by the standard of righteousness, but which we rightly and deservedly praise.

---

122. See Jer 31:33 and Heb 10:16.
123. See Rom 5:5.
124. See Rom 13:10.
125. See Rom 3:23-24.

And yet, if we carefully examine the motive out of which they are done, we seldom find any that deserve the praise and defense that belongs to righteousness.

28. Nonetheless, the image of God has not been removed from the human soul by the stain of earthly loves to such a point that not even the faintest outlines of it remain. Hence, the soul can be correctly said to observe or know some elements of the law even amid the godlessness of its life. Perhaps this is what the Apostle meant when he said that the Gentiles who do not have the law do by nature what pertains to the law and that such people are themselves a law for themselves and have the work of the law written in their hearts.[126] That is, what was impressed upon the soul by the image of God, when it was created, has not been entirely removed. In this way too, the distinction is preserved by which the New Testament differs from the Old. That is, the law of God, which through the Old Testament was written on tablets, is written on the hearts of the faithful through the New. For by their renewal there is written in those hearts what was not entirely destroyed by their old condition. The very image of God, which godlessness had not completely wiped out, is renewed in the mind of those who believe through the New Testament—for it had remained true that the soul of a human being could not exist without being rational. In the same way the law of God, which unrighteousness had not entirely wiped out, is surely written in the soul, when it is renewed by grace. The law written on tablets could not bring about for the Jews this writing of the law upon hearts, which is justification, but could only bring about transgression. For they were human beings, and that power of nature was present in them by which a rational animal both knows and observes some part of the law. But the piety which brings us to another life that is happy and eternal has a spotless law that transforms souls.[127] They are renewed by that light, and there is fulfilled in them the words, *The light of your countenance has shone upon us, O Lord* (Ps 4:7). They turned away from it and merited to grow old, but they cannot be renewed except by Christ's grace, that is, except by the intercession of the mediator. *For God is one; one too is the mediator between God and human beings, the man Christ Jesus, who gave himself up as redemption for all* (1 Tm 2:5-6). If those about whom we are speaking, namely, those who by nature do what pertains

---

126. See Rom 2:14-15.
127. See Ps 19:8.

to the law,[128] in the manner we amply discussed above, are separated from this grace, what benefit will they derive from thoughts that excuse them *on the day on which God will judge the secrets of human beings* (Rom 2:16), except that they may receive a milder punishment? Just as a few venial sins, without which no one lives this life, do not keep a righteous person from eternal life, so too a few good works, which are almost always to be found even in the lives of the worst human beings, are of no value to an unbeliever for eternal salvation. Nonetheless, as in the kingdom of God the saints differ in glory as one star from another,[129] so in the condemnation to eternal punishment it will be easier for Sodom than for some other city,[130] and some will be twice as much the children of hell as certain others.[131] So too, God's judgment will not overlook the fact that one person has sinned more or less than another in this godlessness that merits condemnation.

49. In order to restrain the boastfulness of the Jews, the Apostle said, *It is not the hearers of the law who are righteous before God; rather, those who observe the law will be justified* (Rom 2:13). He immediately went on to speak of those who, though they do not have the law, do by nature what pertains to the law.[132] What then did the Apostle have in mind? Are we supposed to understand by those people not ones who have a share in the grace of the mediator, but rather those who, though they do not worship the true God with true piety, do nonetheless have some good deeds in their godless life? Did he perhaps think that this was supposed to prove his previous statement that *there is no partiality on God's part* (Rom 2:11) as well as his later claim that he is not the God of the Jews only but of the Gentiles as well.[133] For even the least works of the law would not be found implanted by nature in those who have not received the law, if it were not for the remains of the image of God. And God does not hold that image in contempt, when they believe in him who shows no partiality.[134] But whichever of these views one accepts, it is certain that the grace of God was promised to the New Testament even by the prophet and that the same grace was described as follows: The

128. See Rom 2:14.
129. See 1 Cor 15:41.
130. See Lk 10:12.
131. See Mt 23:15.
132. See Rom 2:14.
133. See Rom 3:29.
134. See Rom 2:11.

laws of God will be written in human hearts,[135] and they will come
to that knowledge of God in which *individuals will no longer teach
their fellow citizens or kinfolk, saying, Know the Lord, because they
will all know him from the littlest to the greatest of them.* This is the
gift of the Holy Spirit by which love is poured out in our hearts,[136]
not just any love but *the love of God from a pure heart, a good conscience, and sincere faith* (1 Tm 1:5). From that faith the righteous
live during this pilgrimage, and they are also brought from it to vision
after this state in which we see through a mirror, dimly, and only in
part. Then they will know him face to face, as they are also known
by him.[137] For they ask but one thing from the Lord and plead for it,
namely, that they may dwell in the house of the Lord all the days of
their lives so that they may contemplate the delights of the Lord.[138]

29, 50. People should, then, not boast because of what they supposedly have, as if they had not received it.[139] And they should not suppose
that they have received it because the letter of the law is externally set
before their eyes to be read or is recited to be heard. *For if righteousness
comes through the law, then Christ has died in vain* (Gal 2:21). But if he
has not died in vain, *he has ascended on high, taken captivity captive,
and given gifts to human beings* (Eph 4:8).[140] Whoever has anything
has received it from him, but any who claim that they have not received
what they have from him either have nothing or will have what they
have taken from them.[141] *For there is one God who justifies the circumcised from faith and the uncircumcised through faith* (Rom 3:30). It
was not said this way to indicate a difference, as if *from faith* meant
one thing and *through faith* another, but simply to vary the expression.
In another passage when he was speaking about the Gentiles, that is,
about the uncircumcised, he said, *Scripture foresaw that God justifies
the Gentiles from faith* (Gal 3:8). So too, in speaking of the circumcised
to which he himself belonged, he says, *We are Jews by birth, not sinners
from the Gentiles. We know that people are not justified from the works
of the law, but through faith in Jesus Christ, and we believe in Christ*

135. See Jer 31:33.
136. See Rom 5:5.
137. See 1 Cor 13;12.
138. See Ps 27:4.
139. See 1 Cor 4:7.
140. See Ps 67:19.
141. See Lk 8:18; 19:26.

Jesus. (Gal 2:15-16) See, he said that the uncircumcised are justified from faith and the circumcised through faith, if only the circumcised hold onto the righteousness of faith. For in that way *the Gentiles who were not pursuing righteousness have obtained righteousness, but a righteousness that comes from faith.* They have received it from God; they have not presumed to have it from themselves. *But Israel, though pursuing the law of righteousness, did not arrive at the law. Why is that? Because it was pursuing it not from faith, but as if from works.* (Rom 9:30-32) That is, they were pursuing it as though they were producing it by themselves, not believing that God produced it in them. *For it is God who produces in* us *the willing and the action in accord with good will* (Phil 2:13). And for this reason *they have tripped over the stumbling block* (Rom 9:32). For he explained his words, *Because* [Israel] *was pursuing it not from faith, but as if from works* (Rom 9:32), when he said, *For not knowing the righteousness of God and wanting to establish their own righteousness, they were not subject to the righteousness of God. For the end of the law is Christ for righteousness for everyone who believes.* (Rom 10:3-4) Are we still in doubt about which are the works of the law which do not justify human beings, if they believe them to be their own without the help and gift of God that comes from faith in Jesus Christ? Do we have in mind circumcision and other works of that sort, because in other passages we read some statements like this about these sacraments as well? But in this passage they certainly did not want to establish circumcision as their own righteousness, for God had by his command established it. Nor can this statement be understood in reference to those works of which the Lord says to them, *You set aside the commandment of God in order to uphold your traditions* (Mt 7:9). For Paul said, *Israel, though pursuing the law of righteousness, did not arrive at the law* (Rom 9:31); he did not say, "Pursuing, that is, following their own traditions." Here is the only difference: they themselves took credit for the commandment, *You shall not desire*, and the other holy and righteous commandments.[142] In order that human beings may be able to observe them, God works in people through faith in Jesus Christ, who is the end [of the law] for righteousness for everyone who believes.[143] That is, when they have been incorporated in him through the Spirit and have become his members, they can, because he gives the

---

142. See Rom 7:12.
143. See Rom 10:4.

increase interiorly,[144] do the works of righteousness. Of these works the Lord himself said, *Without me you can do nothing* (Jn 15:5).

51. Therefore, the righteousness of the law is set before them, because those who observe it will have life in it.[145] When they recognize their own weakness, they attain righteousness, not by their own strength or through the letter of the law—that is not possible. Rather, by winning favor through faith with the one who justifies, they attain righteousness, observe it, and live in it. For a work that brings life to the one who does it is only done by a person who has been justified. But justification is obtained through faith; scripture says of it, *Do you say in your heart, Who will go up to heaven? That is, to bring Christ down. Or Who will go down to the depth? That is, to bring Christ back from the dead. But what does it say? The word is near to you, on your lips and in your heart.* (Dt 30:12-14) *This is the word of faith that we preach. For, if you confess with your lips that Jesus is Lord and believe in your heart that God has raised him from the dead, you will be saved* (Rom 10:6-9). We are righteous to the extent that we are saved. After all, through this faith we believe that God will also raise us from the dead, for the time being, in the spirit so that in the newness of his grace *we may live with* temperance, *righteousness, and piety in this world* (Ti 2:12), but afterward our flesh will rise for immortality. The spirit earns this for the flesh, because it preceded it in a resurrection suited to it, namely, in justification. *For we were buried with Christ through baptism into death so that, as Christ has risen from the dead by the glory of the Father, so we might also walk in the newness of life* (Rom 6:4). By faith, then, in Jesus Christ we obtain salvation both to the slight extent that its reality has begun for us and to the extent that we await its perfection with hope. *For everyone who calls upon the name of the Lord will be saved* (Jl 2:32; Rom 10:13). The psalm says, *How great is your sweetness, Lord, which you have hidden from those who fear you, but have made perfect for those who hope in you* (Ps 31:20). Because of the law we fear God; because of faith we hope in God. But for those who fear punishment grace remains hidden. The soul struggles under that fear when it does not conquer evil desire, and that fear, like a stern guard, does not go away. Let the soul take refuge through faith in the mercy of God so that he may give what he commands. By the inspiration of

144. See 1 Cor 3:7.
145. See Lv 18:5; Rom 10:5.

the sweetness of grace through the Holy Spirit, he will make what he commands more delightful than the delight of what he forbids. Thus the great abundance of his sweetness, that is, the law of faith, his love written and poured out in hearts, is made perfect in those who hope in him, so that the soul, healed not by the fear of punishment, but by the love of righteousness, may perform good works.

Grace Does Not Destroy Free Choice, but Strengthens It

30, 52. Are we then doing away with free choice through grace? Heaven forbid! Rather, we make free choice stronger. After all, as the law is not done away with through faith, so free choice is not done away with but strengthened by grace.[146] For the law is not fulfilled without free choice. But *knowledge of sin came through the law* (Rom 3:20); through faith we obtain grace to struggle against sin; through grace the soul is healed from the wound of sin; through the good health of the soul we have freedom of choice; through free choice we have the love of righteousness; through the love of righteousness we fulfill the law. The law is not done away with but strengthened by faith, because faith obtains the grace by which we fulfill the law. In the same way, free choice is not done away with by grace but strengthened, because grace heals the will by which we freely love righteousness. All these items which I linked together like a chain have their own expression in scripture. The law says, *You shall not desire*; faith says, *Heal my soul, for I have sinned against you* (Ps 41:5); grace says, *See, you have been healed; now sin no more so that nothing worse happens to you* (Jn 5:14); good health says, *Lord, my God, I have cried out to you, and you have healed me* (Ps 30:3); free choice says, *I will willingly offer you sacrifice* (Ps 54:8); the love of righteousness says, *Sinners described pleasures to me, but none like your law, Lord* (Ps 119:85). Why then do wretched human beings dare to be proud of their free choice, before they are set free, or of their own powers, if they have already been set free? They do not notice that in the very name for free choice we hear freedom; *but where the Spirit of the Lord is, there is freedom* (2 Cor 3:17). If then they are slaves of sin, why do they boast of free choice? *For one has become a slave to that by which one has been defeated* (2 Pt 2:19). But if they have been set free, why do

---

146. See Rom 3:31.

they glory as if it were their own doing and boast as if they had not received?[147] Or are they so free that they do not want to have as their Lord even him who says to them, *Without me you can do nothing* (Jn 15:5), and *If the Son sets you free, then you will truly be free* (Jn 8:36)?

Faith Lies in Our Power

31, 53. Someone will ask whether faith itself, which seems to be the beginning of salvation or of this chain leading to salvation, which I mentioned, lies in our power. We will see this more easily, if we first examine somewhat more carefully what power is. For there are two things: willing and being able. As a result, one who wills is not immediately able, nor does one who is able immediately will. After all, just as at times we will what we cannot do, so also at times we can do what we do not will to do. It is quite clear, and the sound of the words indicates that will (*voluntas*) takes its name from willing (*velle*), and power (*potestas*) from being able (*posse*). Hence, as one who wills has the will, so one who is able has the power. But in order that something be done by one's power, the will must be there. After all, people are not usually said to have done something with their power, if they did it unwillingly. And yet, if we pay more careful attention, even what people are forced to do against their will, they do with their will, if they do it. But because they would prefer to do something else, they are said to do it against their will, that is, unwillingly. They are compelled by some evil to do it; willing to avoid this evil or to remove it from themselves, they do what they are forced to do. After all, if, the will is so great that they prefer not to do this rather than to suffer the alternative, they undoubtedly resist the compulsion and do not do the deed. And so, if they do it, they do not do it with a complete and free will, and yet they only do it with the will. And since the result follows upon this will, we cannot say that the power was lacking to the agent. After all, if, yielding to the compulsion, they were willing to do it and could not, we would say that the will was there, though coerced, but that the power was lacking. But when they did not do it, because they were unwilling, there was certainly the power, but the will was lacking, as long as they did not do it out of resistance to the compulsion. For this reason, those who use force or

---

147. See 1 Cor 4:7.

persuasion often say, "Since you have it in your power, why do you not free yourself from this evil?" And those who simply cannot do something they are being forced to do, because they are believed to be able to do it, often reply by excusing themselves and say, "I would do it, if it were in my power." What more then are we looking for? We call it power when the will has the ability to act. Hence, people are said to have in their power what they do, if they will, and what they do not do, if they do not will.

54. Turn your attention to the point which we set out to discuss, namely, whether faith lies in our power. We are now speaking of this faith which we use when we believe something, not of the faith which we pledge when we make a promise, for this latter is also called *fides*.[148] In the one sense we say, "He had no faith in me"; in the other sense we say, "He did not keep faith with me." The first means: He did not believe what I said; the latter means: He did not do what he said. In accord with this faith by which we believe, we are faithful to God; in accord with the faith by which one does what one promises, God himself is faithful toward us. The Apostle, after all, says this, *God is faithful; he does not allow you to be tempted beyond your ability* (1 Cor 10:13). We are asking whether that faith by which we believe God or believe in God is in our power. On this point scripture says, *Abraham believed God and it was credited to him as righteousness* (Gn 15:6; Rom 4:3), and *For one who believes in him who justifies the sinner his faith is counted as righteousness* (Rom 4:5). Look now! Do people believe if they are unwilling to or do they fail to believe if they will to believe? Isn't that absurd? For what is it to believe but to assent that what is said is true? Assent is certainly an act of someone who wills. Hence, faith is surely in our power. But, as the Apostle says, *There is no power except from God* (Rom 13:1). What reason is there why scripture should not say to us about this power as well, *For what do you have that you have not received?* (1 Cor 4:7) That we believe is God's gift. But we never read in the holy scriptures: There is no will except from God. And it is right that scripture does not say that, because it is not true. Otherwise, if there were no will except from God, God would be—heaven forbid!—the author even of sins. For an evil will by itself is already

---

148. The Latin *fides* has various meanings: faith or belief, a pledge, a sign of good faith, a downpayment, or bail.

a sin, even if the execution is lacking, that is, if the will lacks the power. Moreover, when an evil will receives the power to carry out its intention, it comes from the judgment of God with whom there is no injustice.[149] For he punishes in this way, and he does not do so unjustly, because he punishes in a hidden way. Sinners only realize that they are being punished when through an obvious punishment they unwillingly perceive the greatness of the evil that they have willingly committed. This is the point that the apostle makes with regard to some of them: *God handed them over to the desires of their heart so that they would do what is improper* (Rom 1:24.28). And for this reason the Lord said to Pilate, *You would not have power over me, if it were not given to you from above* (Jn 19:11). But when the power is given, necessity is certainly not imposed. Hence, when David received the power to kill Saul, he preferred to spare him rather than strike him.[150] Hence, we understand that evil persons receive power leading to the condemnation of their evil will, but that good persons receive power for the purpose of proving their good will.

The Faith That the Apostle Praises

32, 55. Faith, then, is in our power, because we believe when we will, and, when we believe, we believe willingly. Next we must investigate or rather recall what sort of faith it is that the Apostle recommends with such great emphasis. After all, it is not good to believe just anything, for there is the passage: *Brothers, do not believe every spirit, but test whether the spirit is from God* (1 Jn 4:1). Nor should we interpret the words spoken in praise of love, *It believes everything* (1 Cor 13:7), in the sense that we discredit anyone's love, if the person does not immediately believe what he or she hears. Does not the same love admonish us that we should not readily believe something bad about a brother or sister? And, when something of the sort is said, does this love not judge that its duty is not to believe it? Finally, the love which believes everything does not believe every spirit, and thus it believes everything, but believes God. Scripture did not say: It believes everyone. Therefore, no one has any doubt that the faith which the Apostle commends is the faith by which we believe God.

---

149. See Rom 9:14.
150. See 1 S 24:5-6.

56. But we still need to make another distinction. For those people who are under the law try to achieve their own righteousness out of fear of punishment and do not, for this reason, achieve the righteousness of God. Only love does that, love which only finds pleasing what is permitted, not fear which is forced to do what is permitted, while it has something else in its will by which it would prefer, if it were possible, that what is not permitted be permitted. These people, then, believe God, for if they did not believe at all, they would surely not fear the punishment of the law. But this is not the faith that the Apostle commends when he says, *For you have not received the spirit of servitude so as to live in fear again; rather, you have received the Spirit of adoption as children. In it we cry out, Abba, Father.* (Rom 8:15) That fear is servile and, though one believes the Lord in it, one does not love righteousness, but fears condemnation. But the children cry out, *Abba, Father*; of these two words the one comes from the circumcised, the other from the uncircumcised, *Jew first and then Greek* (Rom 2:9), because *there is one God who justifies the circumcised from faith and the uncircumcised through faith* (Rom 3:30). But when they cry out, they ask for something, and what do they ask for but that for which they hunger and thirst? And what is this but what scripture says of them, *Blessed are those who hunger for righteousness, because they will be satisfied* (Mt 5:6)? Let those who are under the law, then, pass over to this side so that from servants they may become children, but not so that they cease to be servants. Rather, let them serve their Lord and Father freely as children, because they have received this too. After all, that only Son gave the power *to become children of God to those who believe in his name* (Jn 1:12). And he admonished them to seek, to ask, to knock so that they might receive and find and have the door opened for them.[151] He adds a rebuke and says, *If you, though you are evil, know how to give good gifts to your children, how much more will your Father, who is in heaven, give good things to those who ask him!* (Mt 7:11) Therefore, the power of sin, the law, kindled the sting of death[152] so that sin seized the opportunity and roused every desire through the commandment.[153] From whom, then, ought one to ask for continence but from him who knows how to give good gifts to

---

151. See Mt 7:7.
152. See 1 Cor 15:56.
153. See Rom 7:8.

his children?[154] Are foolish persons perhaps unaware that no one can be continent without God's gift?[155] In order to know this, then, such persons need wisdom. And so, why do they not listen to the Spirit of their Father speaking through the apostle of Christ or Christ himself who says in his gospel, *Ask and you will receive* (Mt 7:7; Lk 11:9)? He also speaks through the lips of his apostle, *If any of you lack wisdom, let them ask it from God who gives to all abundantly without rebuking them, and it will be given to them, but let them ask with faith, without any hesitation* (Jas 1:5-6). This is the faith from which the righteous live;[156] this is the faith by which we believe in him who justifies the sinner;[157] this is the faith that excludes boasting,[158] whether in the sense that our proud boasting is removed, or in the sense that our boasting in the Lord is emphasized.[159] *For by the Spirit we await the hope of righteousness from faith* (Gal 5:5). Here we can still ask whether by *the hope of righteousness* he meant that which righteousness hopes for or the righteousness by which one has hope, since the righteous who live from faith[160] certainly hope for eternal life. And the same faith which hungers and thirsts for righteousness makes progress in it by the renewal of the interior human being from day to day[161] and hopes to be satisfied with it in eternal life when there will be realized what the psalm says about God, *He satisfies your desire with good things* (Ps 103:5). This is the faith by which they are saved to whom it is said, *You have been saved by grace through faith. This does not come from you; rather, it is God's gift. It is not the result of works so that no one may be filled with pride. For we are his workmanship, created in Christ Jesus for the good works which God prepared so that we might live our lives in them.* (Eph 2:8-10) Finally, this is the faith which works through love,[162] not through fear, not fearing punishment, but loving righteousness. What is the source of this love, that is, of this charity, through which faith

---

154. See Mt 7:11.
155. See Wis 8:21.
156. See Rom 1:17.
157. See Rom 4:5.
158. See Rom 4:5.
159. See above, 10. 17, where Augustine explains the two senses of *excluditur*. It can mean that its subject is removed or is brought into relief as when silver is hammered by a smith.
160. See Rom 1:17.
161. See 2 Cor 4:16.
162. See Gal 5:6.

works,[163] if not the source from which faith obtained it? For it would not be in us, however much there is in us, if it were not poured out in our hearts by the Holy Spirit who has been given to us.[164] The love of God said to be poured out in our hearts is not that by which he loves us, but that by which he makes us love him. In the same way, the righteousness of God is that by which we are made righteous by his gift and the salvation of God is that by which he makes us saved, and the faith of Jesus Christ is that by which he makes us believers. This is the righteousness of God which he not only teaches through the commandment of the law, but also gives through the gift of the Spirit.

The Very Will to Believe Is God's Gift

33, 57. It follows that we should investigate a little whether the will by which we believe is itself a gift of God or arises from the free choice belonging to our nature. After all, if we say that it is not a gift of God, we must fear that we think that we have found an answer we can make to the Apostle when he chides us and says, *For what do you have that you have not received?* We could say: Look, we have the will to believe which we have not received; look, there is the reason for our boasting that we have not received. But if we say that even this sort of will is only the gift of God, we have once again to be afraid that unbelievers and sinners may not unreasonably think that they have a just excuse for not having believed, because God refused to give them this will. Scripture says, *For it is God who produces in us the willing and the action in accord with good will.* It is already a sign of the grace which faith obtains that human beings can perform good works. Faith performs them through the love[165] which is poured out in the heart by the Holy Spirit who has been given to us.[166] But we believe in order that we may obtain this grace, and we certainly believe with the will. The question concerns the source from which we get this will. If we get it from nature, why does everyone not have it, since the same God is the creator of all? If we get it as God's gift, again why does everyone not have it, since he wills that all human beings be saved and come to the knowledge of the truth?[167]

---

163. See Gal 5:6.
164. See Rom 5:5.
165. See Gal 5:6.
166. See Rom 5:5.
167. See 1 Tm 2:4.

58. Let us, then, first set forth this idea and see whether it provides a satisfactory answer to our question. The free choice which the creator has given to the rational soul as part of its nature is a neutral power that can either turn to faith or fall into unbelief. Therefore, human beings cannot be said to have this will by which they believe God unless they have received it, when at God's call it arises from the free choice which they received as part of their nature when they were created. God wills that all human beings be saved and come to the knowledge of the truth,[168] but not so that he deprives them of free choice, since they will be judged with perfect justice according to their good or bad use of it. Consequently, unbelievers act against the will of God when they do not believe his gospel, but they do not on that account defeat his will. Rather, they deprive themselves of the great and supreme good and plunge themselves into evils which are punishments. They are destined to experience in punishment the power of the God whose mercy they held in contempt in his gifts. Thus the will of God is never defeated, but it would be defeated, if it could not find something to do with those who hold him in contempt or if they could somehow escape what he has appointed for them. He says, for example, I will that all these servants of mine work in the vineyard and that, after their labor, they rest and feast. But if any of them refuse to do this, they will forever grind grain at the millstone. Any who held him in contempt would seem to act against the will of their lord, but they would defeat it if they took flight from the millstone out of contempt—something that could never happen under God's power. Hence, scripture said, *God has spoken once*, that is, immutably—though one could also understand this with regard to the only Word. Then, adding what he spoke immutably, it says, *These two things have I heard: that power belongs to God and to you, Lord, belongs mercy; you repay all according to their works* (Ps 62:12-13). Therefore, they will be liable to condemnation under his power who, with regard to believing, have held his mercy in contempt. But those who believe and entrust themselves to God to be forgiven all their sins and to be healed from all their wounds and to be enkindled and enlightened by warmth and light will have good works as a result of his grace. By them they will be redeemed from the corruption of bodily death; they will be crowned and satisfied with goods—not temporal ones, but eternal ones, beyond what we ask for and understand.[169]

---

168. See 1 Tm 2:4.
169. See Eph 3:20.

59. The psalm follows this order where it says, *Bless the Lord, my soul, and do not forget all his recompenses; he is forgiving toward all your sins; he heals all your ills; he redeems your life from corruption; he crowns you with kindness and mercy; he satisfies your desire with good things.* And so that the deformity of our old condition, that is, of our mortality, might not despair of these great goods, he says, *Your youth will be renewed like an eagle's* (Ps 103:2-5), as if to say, "These things you heard belong to the new human being and to the New Testament."

Recall these with me for a bit, I beg you, and gaze with delight upon the praise of mercy, that is, of the grace of God. It says, *Bless the Lord, my soul, and do not forget all his recompenses.* It does not say gifts, but recompenses,[170] because he repays evil with good. *He is forgiving toward all your sins*; he does this in the sacrament of baptism. *He heals all your ills*; he does this in the life of one who believes. For the flesh lusts against the spirit and the spirit against the flesh so that we do not do what we will,[171] and another law in the members resists the law of the mind. We can will the good, but cannot carry it out.[172] If we make progress with a steady intention, these ills of our old condition are healed, as our new condition increases from day to day by the faith that works through love.[173] *He redeems your life from corruption*; he does this in the final resurrection of the dead. *He crowns you with kindness and mercy*; he does this in the judgment, when the righteous judge will sit upon his throne and repay all according to their works. Who will then boast of having a pure heart? Or who will boast of being free of sin?[174] It was, then, necessary to mention the gentleness and mercy of the Lord in that passage where it could seem that debts are being called in and wages are being paid in such a way that there seemed no room for mercy. He crowns us, then, with gentleness and mercy, but he also does so according to our works.[175] For they will be placed on his right to whom he says, *I was hungry and you gave me to eat* (Mt 25:35), for *judgment will be without mercy for one who does not show mercy* (Jas 2:13). *But blessed are the merciful, for they will be shown mercy*

170. The Latin has: *non attributiones, sed retributiones.*
171. See Gal 5:17.
172. See Rom 7:23.18.
173. See Gal 5:6.
174. See Prv 20:8-9; Mt 16:27.
175. See Ps 62:13.

(Mt 5:7). When those on the left enter into eternal fire, the righteous will enter eternal life,[176] for *this*, he said, *is eternal life, that they know you, the one true God and him whom you sent, Jesus Christ* (Jn 17:3). By that knowledge, by that vision, by that contemplation, the desire of their soul will be filled with good things.[177] For this alone is enough for them; they have nothing beyond this to desire, to long for, or to seek. That man was ablaze with the desire for this fullness who said to the Lord, *Show us the Father, and it is enough for us* (Jn 14:8). He received the answer, *One who has seen me has seen the Father* (Jn 14:9), because *this is eternal life, that they know the one true God and him whom you sent, Jesus Christ* (Jn 17:3). But if one who has seen the Son has also seen the Father, certainly one who sees the Father and the Son also sees the Holy Spirit of the Father and the Son. And so we do not destroy free choice, and our soul blesses the Lord, not forgetting all his recompenses,[178] and it does not want to establish its own righteousness in ignorance of God's righteousness,[179] but believes in him who justifies the sinner.[180] And so the soul lives from faith,[181] until it is brought to vision; it lives, of course, from that faith which works through love.[182] This love is being poured out in our hearts neither by the sufficiency of our own will nor by the letter of the law, but by the Holy Spirit who has been given to us.[183]

34, 60. If this discussion is enough to resolve the question, let it suffice. But someone might answer that we must be careful that no one thinks that sin which is committed by free choice is to be attributed to God. For one might think that, if the words of scripture, *What do you have that you have not received?* attribute the will by which we believe to the gift of God, because it arises from the free choice that we received when we were created. Let that person pay attention and see that this will is to be attributed to God's gift, not only because it arises from the free choice which is created in us as part of our nature, but also because God brings it about by the enticements of our perceptions that we will and that we believe. He does

---

176. See Mt 25:46.
177. See Ps 103:5.
178. See Ps 103:2.
179. See Rom 10:3.
180. See Rom 4:5.
181. See Rom 1:17.
182. See Gal 5:6.
183. See Rom 5:5.

this either externally through the exhortations of the gospel, where the commandments of the law also have a role to play. For they can remind people of their weakness, so that by believing they may take refuge in justifying grace. Or he does this internally where none have control over what comes into their minds, though to assent or dissent is in the power of their will. God, then, works in these ways with the rational soul so that it believes him. For it cannot so much as believe anything by free choice, if there is no enticement or invitation which it can believe. God, then, certainly produces in people the will to believe, and his mercy anticipates us in every respect.[184] But to assent to God's invitation or to dissent from it is, as I said, in the power of one's will. This fact not only does not weaken the words, *What do you have that you have not received?* but rather confirms them. The soul can, of course, receive and have the gifts about which it hears this only by assenting. Accordingly, what it has and what it receives come from God, but the receiving and the having certainly come from the one who receives and has them. Now if someone should press us to examine the profound question of why one person is stirred to the point of being convinced, while another is not, there occur to me at the moment only two answers that I would want to make, *O the depth of the riches!* (Rom 11:33) and *Is there injustice in God?* (Rom 9:14) Those who are displeased with this reply should look for people who are more learned, but they should beware that they do not find someone more presumptuous.

Summary and Conclusion of the Work

35, 61. Let us, then, at last bring the book to a close; I do not know whether we have accomplished anything with all its length. I do not mean in your regard, for I know your faith, but with the minds of those on account of whom you wanted me to write. They are not doing battle against our views, but they are certainly doing battle against views that the great apostle Paul stated more than once and against his vigorous, intense, and watchful efforts. I am using gentler language and do not say that they are doing battle against the view of him who has spoken in his apostles. They prefer to defend their own views rather than to listen to Paul entreating them by God's mercy

---

184. See Ps 59:11.

and saying by the grace of God which has been given to him,[185] *Not to be more wise than one ought to be, but to be wise in moderation, as God has given to each one the measure of faith* (Rom 12:3).

62. Turn your attention to the question you proposed for me and to the results of this long discussion. You were, of course, concerned about my having said that it is possible that human beings be without sin, if with God's help the will was not lacking, even though no one had or has or will have such perfect righteousness in this life. For in those books which I earlier wrote for you, I made this point as follows: "If someone asks me," I said, "whether a human being can be without sin in this life, I admit that one can be by the grace of God and free choice. I have no doubt that free choice itself belongs to the grace of God, that is, to God's gifts, not only insofar as it exists, but insofar as it is good, that is, insofar as it turns to carrying out God's commandments. In that way God's grace not merely shows us what we are to do, but also helps us so that we are able to do what God has shown us."[186] You thought it absurd that something that is possible should be without an example. That gave rise to the topic of this book, and it was, accordingly, our task to show that something is possible, even though it is without an example. For this reason we quoted certain passages at the beginning of this book from the law and from the gospel, such as the passing of a camel through the eye of a needle,[187] the twelve thousand legions of angels who could have fought for Christ, if he had willed,[188] and those peoples whom God says he could at one time have wiped out before his people.[189] None of these things happened. To these could be added the things we read about in the Book of Wisdom: the many unheard-of torments God could inflict upon sinners, since creation stands ready to serve at his least indication, and yet he did not inflict them.[190] One could also mention that mountain which faith could move into the sea,[191] though we have never read or heard that this occurred. If any persons say that one of these things is impossible for God, you see how foolish they are and how they contradict the reliability of his scripture.

---

185. See Rom 12:1.3.
186. See *The Punishment and Forgiveness of Sins* II, 6, 7.
187. See Mt 19:24.
188. See Mt 26:53.
189. See Dt 31:3; Jgs 2:3.
190. See Wis 16:24.
191. See Mk 11:23.

Many other things of this sort can occur to one who reads or thinks of them, and we cannot deny that they are possible for God, though we have no example of them.

63. Those things can be said to be God's works, while to live righteously belongs among our works. Hence, I undertook to show that this too is God's work, and I did this in this book with perhaps more words than were needed. But against the enemies of God's grace I have, as I see it, said too little. And I find pleasure in speaking at such length only where his scripture is very much on my side and where the goal is that one *who boasts should boast in the Lord* (2 Cor 10:17) and that in all things we give thanks to the Lord, our God, lifting our hearts on high, from where every best gift and every perfect gift is given by the Father of lights.[192] For, if it is not the work of God, because it is done by us or because we do it with his gift, then it is not God's work that the mountain is moved into the sea, because the Lord said that it was possible through the faith of human beings. He attributed this to their work, when he said, *If you have in yourselves faith like a grain of mustard seed, you shall say to this mountain, Be lifted up and thrown into the sea, and it will happen, and nothing will be impossible for you* (Mt 17:19; Mk 11:23). It is certain that he said *for you*, not "for me" or "for the Father," and yet a human being certainly does not do this unless God grants it and does it. There you see how perfect righteousness can be without an example in human beings and yet not be impossible. For it would come to be, if as much will were brought to bear as was sufficient for something that great. But our will would be that great, if none of those things which have to do with righteousness were unknown to us and if they so delighted our mind that the delight would overcome whatever other pleasure or pain might interfere. The fact that it is not the case is due not to its impossibility but to God's judgment. After all, who is unaware that what human beings know is not in their power? And yet it does not follow that they pursue what they know they should pursue, unless it delights them to the point that they cannot but love it? But that is the mark of a soul in good health.

36, 64. Someone might suppose that we lack nothing with regard to the knowledge of righteousness, since the Lord summed up and shortened his word upon the earth[193] and said that the whole law and

---

192. See Jas 1:17.
193. See Rom 9:28.

the prophets depended on two commandments. He did not fail to state
them and did so in plain language. He said, *You shall love the Lord
your God with your whole heart and your whole soul and your whole
mind* and *you shall love your neighbor as yourself* (Mt 22:37.39).
What could be truer than that, when we have fulfilled these, we have
fulfilled all righteousness? And yet one who hears this should also
bear in mind the passage about how we all sin in many ways,[194] while
we think that what we do pleases or at least does not displease the
God whom we love. And then afterward, having been admonished
by his scripture or by clear and certain reason, we learn that it did not
please him, and we repent and pray for his forgiveness. Human life
is full of such examples. But why do we fail to know what pleases
him? Is it not that we do not know God himself well enough? *For we
see now through a mirror dimly, but then we shall see face to face*
(1 Cor 13:12). But who will dare to think that, when we have reached
that point of which scripture says, *Then I shall know, as I am known*
(1 Cor 13:12), those who contemplate God will have only as much
love of God as his faithful now have or that this present love should be
in any sense almost equated with that love of theirs? Moreover, if our
love will be greater in proportion to the greatness of our knowledge,
we must believe that we now lack perfect righteousness in proportion
to our lack of love. After all, we can know or believe something and
not love it, but we cannot love what we neither know nor believe.
Through believing, the saints were able to attain so great a love that
the Lord himself bore witness that there could not be a greater love
in this life than they had, for they laid down their lives for the faith
or for their brothers.[195] But when from this wayfaring in which we
now walk by faith we have come to the vision[196] which we do not yet
see but hope for and await in patience,[197] this love will undoubtedly
be not only greater than what we now have, but far greater than what
we now ask for and understand.[198] And yet it cannot be greater than
with the whole heart, the whole soul, and the whole mind.[199] After
all, there remains nothing in us that could be added to the whole,

194. See Jas 3:2.
195. See Jn 15:13.
196. See 2 Cor 5:6-7.
197. See Rom 8:25.
198. See Eph 3:20.
199. See Mt 22:37.

because, if anything will remain, the former state will not be whole. Hence, the first commandment of righteousness by which we are ordered to love God with the whole heart and the whole soul and the whole mind,[200] upon which there follows the second about loving the neighbor, we will fulfill in that life, when we shall see face to face.[201] But this commandment has been given to us now in order to admonish us about what we ought to ask for in faith, about where we ought to place our hope, and about how we ought to forget what lies behind and stretch ourselves out toward what lies ahead.[202] Accordingly, so far as I can judge, they who know how far they are from the perfection of righteousness, despite their progress, have made much progress in the righteousness which still needs to be made perfect.

65. One can speak of a lesser righteousness appropriate to this life in which the righteous live from faith.[203] Although they are on a journey away from the Lord and, therefore, walk by faith, not yet by vision,[204] it is not incorrect to say that this righteousness entails that the righteous do not sin. After all, even if the love of God cannot yet be as great as that full and perfect knowledge deserves, it should not be counted as sin. For it is one thing not yet to attain total love; it is another not to go after one's lust. Hence, though people love God far less than they can love him when he is seen, they ought to pursue nothing forbidden. Similarly, in these objects present to the senses of the body the eye cannot find pleasure in darkness; on the other hand, it cannot be fixed upon brilliant light. But look, this is the way we should picture the human soul in this corruptible body. Though it has not yet swallowed up and destroyed all those stirrings of earthly lust by that supereminent perfection of love, still it does not in this lesser righteousness assent to the same lust out of any inclination to do something forbidden. Hence, the commandment, *You shall love the Lord your God with your whole heart and with your whole soul and with your whole strength* (Mt 22:37), pertains to that immortal life, but *Let sin not reign in your mortal body so that you obey its desires* (Rom 6:12) pertains to this life. *You shall not desire* pertains to that life, but *you shall not go after your desires* (Sir 18:30) pertains to this life. To seek nothing more than to remain in that perfection pertains

200. See Mt 22:37.
201. See 1 Cor 13:12.
202. See Phil 3:13.
203. See Rom 1:17; Gal 3:11.
204. See 2 Cor 5:6-7.

to that immortal life; it pertains to this life to do one's task and to hope for the perfection of that life as a reward. In that life the righteous will live forever in the vision which they desired in this life, but the righteous live from faith in this life,[205] in which they desire that life as their certain goal. Under these circumstances, it will be a sin for someone living from faith to consent at times to some forbidden pleasure, not merely in perpetrating terrible crimes and outrages, but even in those slight offenses, such as listening to some word that one should not listen to, or uttering something that one should not say, or thinking something in the heart, so that one wishes that something were permissible that gives evil pleasure, though it is known to be forbidden by a commandment. And one would have given consent to the sin, if the punishment did not cause fear.[206] Do such righteous persons living from faith have no need to say, *Forgive us our debts, as we also forgive our debtors* (Mt 6:12)? Do they prove false the words of scripture, *No living person will be found righteous in your sight* (Ps 143:2)? Or the words, *If we say that we have no sin, we deceive ourselves, and the truth is not in us* (1 Jn 1:8)? Or the words, *There is not a human being who will not sin* (1 K 8:46)? Or the words, *There is not a righteous person on earth who will do good and will not sin* (Eccl 7:21)? These last two passages offer testimony not about the past, so that they say "sinned," but about the future, so that they say "will sin." Do such righteous persons prove false any other statements that holy scripture mentions in this vein? Since these statements cannot be false, I see that it follows that, no matter what kind or how great may be the righteousness we decide is found in this life, there is no human being in this life who has absolutely no sin. Moreover, it is necessary for every human being to give in order to receive and to forgive in order to be forgiven.[207] And if people have some righteousness, they must not presume to have it from themselves but from the grace of God who justifies, and they must still hunger and thirst for righteousness from him[208] who is *the bread of life* (Jn 6:51) and with whom is *the fountain of life* (Ps 36:10). He produces justification in his saints as they labor amid the temptations of this life. But in this

---

205. See Rom 1:17; Gal 3:11.
206. The Maurists regard the text at this point as corrupt and believe that the preceding two sentences should follow "fixed upon the brilliant light" (on the previous page). I have followed the reading in CSEL.
207. See Lk 6:38.37.
208. See Mt 5:6.

life there remains something for him to add with generosity as they ask and to forgive with mercy as they make confession.

66. But let these people find, if they can, somebody living under the burden of this corruption who does not now have anything for God to pardon. Unless they admit that such a person was helped to be such, not by the teaching given in the law, but by the pouring out of the Spirit of grace, they incur the guilt of not just any sin, but of godlessness. If they interpret those divine testimonies in a proper manner, they cannot, of course, find someone of that sort; on the other hand, one should not say that God lacks the power to help the human will to bring to full perfection in a human being not only that righteousness which comes from faith[209] but even that righteousness with which we are later to live for eternity in the contemplation of him. God could will that this corruptibility should now in some individual don incorruptibility,[210] and he could command that person, who would not be destined to die, to live here among human beings who are going to die. Then, with the old condition completely destroyed, no law in the members would resist the law of the mind,[211] and that person would know the omnipresent God as the saints will know him hereafter. Who would be insane enough to say that God cannot do this? But people ask why God does not do this, and those who ask this do not bear in mind their own humanity. I know that with God there is no injustice,[212] just as there is nothing impossible, and I know that he *resists the proud, but gives grace to the humble* (Jas 4:6). I also know that the Apostle who was given a thorn in the flesh, an angel of Satan who would strike him so that he would not become filled with pride, prayed once, twice, three times and was told, *My grace is sufficient for you, for virtue is made perfect in weakness* (2 Cor 12:9). Hence, there always remains something in the hidden depths of God's judgments so that the mouths of everyone, even of the righteous, are closed for their own praise[213] and are only opened for the praise of God. But who is able to examine this, who is able to search it out, who is able to come to know it? So

---

209. See Rom 10:6.
210. See 1 Cor 15:53.
211. See Rom 7:23.
212. See Rom 9:14.
213. See Rom 3:19.

inscrutable are his judgments, and unsearchable his ways! Who has known the mind of the Lord? Or who has been his counselor? Who first gave something to him so that he will be repaid? For all things are from him and through him and in him. To him be glory forever and ever. Amen. (Rom 11:33-36)

Nature and Grace

Introduction

The Date and Place of Composition

At the Synod of Jerusalem at the end of July 415, Orosius reported to the assembled clergy that "blessed Augustine was in the process of writing a full answer to a book of Pelagius, which the disciples of Pelagius handed over to him with the request for a response."[1] The book which Pelagius' disciples handed over to Augustine can only be Pelagius' *Nature*, and the response to it was Augustine's *Nature and Grace*. The latter work, then, was not completed by the time of Orosius' departure from Africa for Palestine, though it was under way. The fact that Orosius did produce at the synod Augustine's Letter 157, but did not produce either Pelagius' *Nature* or Augustine's *Nature and Grace*, confirms the view that Augustine had not completed the latter by the time of Orosius' departure from Hippo in late winter or spring of 415.[2] Unfortunately, it is not possible to pinpoint Orosius' date of departure more closely than "between January and April 415, with the possibility of going back as far as December and coming down to May 415."[3] In any case, by 416, when Augustine wrote *The Deeds of Pelagius*, he had completed the work, sent it to Pelagius' former disciples, Timasius and James, and received their letter of gratitude in return.[4]

Of more importance for our knowledge of the development of Pelagius' thought is the date of the composition of his *Nature*. Two dates and places of composition have been traditionally suggested. A smaller number of scholars has claimed that it was written in Sicily in 410-411, while the majority opinion has maintained that the work was written in Palestine in 413 or 414.[5] Recently Y.-M. Duval has

---

1. Orosius, *Defense against the Pelagians* 3:3-4.
2. For the dating of Augustine's work and for Pelagius' *Nature*, I rely on the conclusions of Yves-Marie Duval's article, "La date du 'De natura' de Pélage. Les premières étapes de la controverse sur la nature de la grâce," REA 36 (1990) 257-283, here 258-259.
3. Duval 259; the translation here and elsewhere from this article is my own.
4. See *The Deeds of Pelagius* 24, 48, where Augustine quotes the whole of Letter 168, the letter of Timasius and James.
5. Duval 261. For the earlier dating and Sicilian place of composition, Duval gives, among the moderns, E. Amann and R. Hedde (DTC XII, 680), and G. de Plinval (BA XXI, 224); for the later dating and Palestinian place of composition, he gives A. Zumkeller (ALG I, 45-46). B. R. Rees implies a date for *Nature* subsequent to the Synod of Diospolis! See B. R. Rees, *Pelagius: A Reluctant Heretic* (Woodbridge 1988) 2.

argued that the work was written in Rome "not only prior to 411, but
... between 406 and 410, closer, as I see it, to the first date than the
second...."[6] Hence, he links the work to the controversy that arose
in Rome shortly after 400.[7] Such an early dating of Pelagius' *Nature*
rests, as Duval admits, on a "bundle of probabilities."[8] It is, however,
a bundle of probabilities that I find quite convincing. If his argument
is sound, a number of important consequences follow for our understanding of the Pelagian controversy. As Duval himself points out,
"First of all, far from having to wait until 413 or 414 to present a co-
herent defense of his system, Pelagius was brought to state his ideas
with precision between 405 and 410, and did this at Rome and to
the scandal of the Romans in his regard."[9] Such an early date for the
composition of *Nature* would also confirm the already well accepted
position that Augustine was not the origin of the doctrine of original
sin. After all, Pelagius' denial that all sinned in Adam "on account of
a sin contracted by reason of their origin through being born, but on
account of the imitation of Adam's sin,"[10] presupposes that the transmission of sin by generation was being taught, and taught in Rome.[11]

The earlier dating of this work also helps to account for the fact
that the heresy came to be called Pelagianism rather than Caelestian-
ism. Rees, who gives the date of the composition of *Nature* as 414 or
415,[12] claims that Pelagius became, *faute de mieux*, the eponymous

6. Duval 274.
7. Ibid.
8. Ibid. 278.
9. Ibid. 278.
10. *Nature and Grace* 9, 10, citing Pelagius' *Nature*.
11. F. Refoulé's article, "Datation du premier concile de Carthage contre les Pélagiens
et du *Libellus fidei* de Rufin," REA 9 (1963) 41-49, showed that Rufinus' work was
written prior to Augustine's *The Punishment and Forgiveness of Sins and the Baptism
of Little Ones*. The fact that Rufinus' work was a source of Augustine's "nous oblige
à penser que la conception dite augustinienne du péché originel et du sort des petits
enfants morts sans baptême constituait une 'theologoumenon', non seulement en
Afrique, mais aussi en Italie (puisque Rufin dut écrire son traité à Rome, où il résida
de 399 jusqu' à au moins 410) avant même les débuts de la crise pélagienne en 411"
(p. 49). So too, in "Les origines africaines de la doctrine augustinienne sur la chute
et le péché originel," *Augustinus* 12 (1967) 97-116, G. Bonner has pointed out, "La
première attaque sur le Pélagianisme en Afrique fut déclenché par le diacre milanais
Paulin, le biographe de saint Ambroise . . ." (p. 100) and says, "il reste significatif que
le premier adversaire du Pélagianisme en Afrique était un milanais, comme plus tard
les dénonciateurs de Pélage même en Palestine étaient un prêtre espagnol, Orose, et
deux anciens évêques provençaux, Héros d'Arles et Lazare d'Aix" (p. 102).
12. See Rees 140, where he dates it circa 414, and 2, where he implies that it was written
in response to his acquittal by the Synod of Diospolis.

founder of a heresy for which he was both then and for ever after to be held responsible. Once he had written his two treatises *Free Will* and *Nature* the die was cast: it was only a matter of time before the mills of the Church would grind him out of existence.[13]

Though the earlier dating of *Nature* does not mean that Augustine or Jerome, who first attacked the Pelagians, knew the work before it came into Augustine's hands in 414 or 415, it does explain how rumors could have spread concerning Pelagius' opposition to the grace of Christ. Augustine reports, for example, in *The Deeds of Pelagius* 22, 46, "I first heard people mention the name of Pelagius with great praise, when he was far off and residing in Rome. Later, I began to hear by rumor that he was arguing against the grace of God." If Pelagius had written a systematic defense of his position while still at Rome, as Duval's thesis maintains, then it becomes understandable that Augustine could already hear rumors of him as an enemy of grace and that he was, nonetheless, hesitant to attack him by name in the absence of hard evidence in the form of a work that he could be certain was that of Pelagius.[14]

The Disciples of Pelagius

Any hesitation Augustine had regarding the orthodoxy of Pelagius was removed when he received from Timasius and James a copy of *Nature* and examined it with care. "Then it became clear to me beyond any doubt how dangerous the poison of that perverse error was to salvation in Christ."[15] Augustine describes Timasius and James as "servants of God, ... good and honest men."[16] In his Letter 179 to John of Jerusalem, he says that these disciples of Pelagius, "young men of excellent birth and trained in liberal pursuits, at his [that is, Pelagius'] exhortation abandoned their worldly hopes and dedicated themselves to the service of God."[17] As Duval has pointed out this letter distinguishes several stages. Augustine tells John that "they

13. Ibid. 90.
14. Caelestius' inability or perhaps refusal at the Council of Carthage to name anyone besides Rufinus who denied the transmission of sin by generation is perhaps explicable by the fact that Rufinus was probably already dead, while Pelagius was not; see *The Grace of Christ and Original Sin* II, 3, 3.
15. *The Deeds of Pelagius* 23, 47.
16. Ibid. In 411 Timasius was part of the entourage of Pinianus, one of the recipients of Augustine's *The Grace of Christ and Original Sin*; see Duval 265 for the evidence.
17. Letter 179, 2.

were found to be arguing against the grace of God on account of
which we are Christians and in which by the Spirit we look for the
hope of righteousness from faith." Augustine goes on to say that,
"when they began to be corrected by our admonitions, they gave me
the book which they said was that of this same Pelagius, asking that
I reply rather to him." When Augustine came to see that he should
answer Pelagius, "so that the wicked error might be more completely
removed from their hearts," he read and answered it.[18]

Duval has argued that the two disciples were not in Palestine, as
is commonly supposed. A careful reading of Augustine's account
of how he came to have Pelagius' book in his possession seems to
imply their presence in Africa, where they were admonished by him,
perhaps orally, perhaps in writing, and where they gave him the book
of their former master. These points are confirmed by Letter 168, the
letter of gratitude sent by Timasius and James to Augustine. The pair
distinguish their earlier abandonment of the errors of Pelagius under
Augustine's instruction from the effect of their reading Augustine's
Nature and Grace. "As for ourselves, we earlier cast off our subjection
to this error, after having been instructed by the spirit of love which is
present in you. We now also give thanks that we have learned to teach
to others what we have come to believe, since the rich explanation
of Your Holiness makes the path more easy." With regard to their
reading of the book Augustine sent them, they say, "We find that Your
Holiness has opened up the text of that small book with such care
that we are stunned by the answers given to the individual points,
whether in those matters which a Christian should refute and detest
and flee from, or in those in which Pelagius is not clearly shown to
have been in error, although by some form of craftiness he believed
that he should eliminate the grace of God in them as well." They have
one regret, " that this splendid gift of the grace of God has shone forth
somewhat late. For, as it is, there are no longer present certain people
whose blindness needed to be illumined by the brilliance of this pure
truth." These persons who have come to be absent and cannot benefit
from Augustine's book include, as Augustine tells us, Pelagius. "For
they had him especially in mind, when they said that they regretted
that I had written that book so late."[19] They do not, however, "give up
hope that this same grace will, by God's goodness, reach them, even

---

18. Ibid.
19. *The Deeds of Pelagius* 25, 49.

if it is somewhat later, for *he wills all human beings to be saved and come to the knowledge of the truth* (1 Tm 2:4)." As Duval has pointed out, the letter implies that Pelagius has become absent from the place in which his two former disciples are now present. Since Pelagius left Africa for Palestine, it would seem obvious that Timasius and James remained in Africa. Furthermore, it would seem that they received a copy of *Nature* from Pelagius before he left Africa, hence, before 411.

The handing over of Pelagius' book by the two young men to Augustine has been characterized as "a betrayal."[20] The case for calling it treason is, of course, strengthened if one thinks of the pair as having been summoned to Palestine by Pelagius, who made known to them and other disciples "the more secret mysteries of the heresy."[21] If, on the other hand, one holds that they remained in Africa when Pelagius left and that, after teaching Pelagius' doctrine for a time, they were corrected by the admonitions of Augustine and that they then gave him the copy of *Nature* in order that Pelagius might benefit from Augustine's response to it as they had benefited by his admonitions, the picture is quite changed. They regretted that Pelagius who had so strong an influence for good upon their lives had left Africa too soon, and they wanted him to share in the benefit that they had received from Augustine.

The Contents of the Work

Nature and Grace is a pivotal work in terms of Augustine's attitude toward Pelagius. In a letter he tells Paulinus of Nola that his love for Pelagius changed as a result of reading it.[22] Having loved him as someone who held the true faith, Augustine came to love him, as a result of reading *Nature*, as one who needed to be freed from views hostile to the grace of God. Augustine nonetheless never mentions Pelagius by name in the work—much less the Pelagians—in the hope that Pelagius will be corrected rather than offended.[23]

The work is divisible into an introduction (sections 1-7), five parts dealing with different kinds of objections from Pelagius' work, and a conclusion. The first part (sections 8-20) focuses upon Pelagius' claim

---

20. Duval 265-266, where he cites O. Wermelinger, *Rom und Pelagius* (Stuttgart 1975) 39.
21. The phrase is that of H. de Noris in *Historia pelagiana et dissertatio de Synodo V oecomenica* (Louvain 1702), I, 6, p. 26 (cited from Duval 262).
22. See Letter 186, 1.
23. See *The Deeds of Pelagius* 23, 47. Following Augustine, I have avoided using Pelagius' name in the translation, though I have used "Pelagius" and "Pelagians" in the introduction.

that human beings can be without sin. The second part (sections 21-36) answers the claim of Pelagius that human nature has not suffered any weakening or change due to sin, especially due to the sin of Adam. The third part (sections 37-51) returns to Pelagius' doctrine of human sinlessness. The fourth part (sections 52-70) confronts Pelagius' claim that human nature received from its creator the inamissible ability not to sin. The fifth part (sections 71-81) takes up Pelagius' appeal to various ecclesiastical writers in support of his position. Finally, the work ends with a summary and conclusion (sections 82-84).

In the opening section Augustine tells Timasius and James that in reading the book they sent him, he found a man burning with zeal against those who blame their sins on human nature rather than on their own will. Though Pelagius is filled with zeal, he is one of those who do not know the righteousness of God and desire to establish their own.[24] Those who understand that righteousness does not come from the law, but from the grace of Christ, understand why they are Christians. After all, if there are some people who have no sin, they certainly have no need to become Christians.

Human nature born from Adam's flesh cannot fulfill the law or attain righteousness on its own (section 2). Augustine introduces a long quotation from Pelagius' *Nature* that indicates Pelagius' concern for the salvation of those who have not been able to hear the preaching of the gospel, either because they lived before Christ or because they are now living in some remote part of the world where the gospel has not yet been proclaimed. The passage clearly indicates that he believes that such people can attain salvation by believing in God the creator of heaven and earth and by fulfilling his will through living good lives, even without any faith in the suffering and resurrection of Christ. To this Augustine replies that, if that is possible, *Christ has died in vain* (Gal 2:21). If Paul was correct in saying this with regard to the mosaic law, then it is correct to say, "If righteousness comes about through nature, then Christ has died in vain!"

Though human nature was originally created blameless and without defect, the human nature in which we are now born is not in good health and needs a physician (section 3). Its intellectual darkness and moral weakness came from the original sin committed by free choice so that we were born as children of anger, even if we have now been

---

24. See Rom 10:2-3.

brought to life with Christ by whose grace we have been saved.[25] This grace without which neither infants nor adults can be saved is not the recompense of our merits but a free gift (section 4). Those who are not set free by that grace—no matter what the reason—are rightly condemned. The whole mass of humanity owes a debt of punishment such that, if all suffered damnation, the penalty would be just (section 5). Hence, those who are set free are not called vessels of their own merits, but vessels of mercy[26]—of the mercy of Christ. If one holds this position in accord with the scriptures, one is not forced to argue against the grace of Christ, claiming that human nature in little ones is healthy and in no need of a physician and that in adults it is self-sufficient for attaining righteousness. Such claims are the wordy wisdom that does away with the cross of Christ.[27]

As he draws the introduction to a close, Augustine insists that, as Pelagius burned with zeal against those who blamed the weakness of human nature for their sins, we ought to burn with greater zeal that the cross of Christ is not done away with. For it is being done away with by those who maintain that righteousness and eternal life can be attained in any other way than "by the sacrament of Christ" (section 7). Augustine is willing to admit that Pelagius does not realize what he is doing, though he presents a great danger because of his persuasive power.

The first of set of arguments from Pelagius to which Augustine replies rests upon the distinction between what is (*esse*) and what is possible (*posse*). Pelagius concedes that the scriptures say that no one has been or is sinless, but points out that they do not address the question of whether one can be sinless. He argues that, if persons could not avoid sin, they would not be blameworthy (section 8). In reply Augustine says (section 9) that little ones who die unbaptized, because they were born in a place where they could not receive baptism, could not be without sin. And he challenges the Pelagians to declare them innocent and admit them to the kingdom of heaven, contrary to the words of the Lord in Jn 3:5. Nor did the Apostle declare them innocent, Augustine adds, citing Rom 5:12.

The Pelagians admit that all sinned in Adam, not "on account of a sin contracted by reason of their origin through being born, but on account of the imitation of Adam's sin" (section 10). But if Adam

---

25. See Eph 2:3-5.
26. See Rom 9:23.
27. See 1 Cor 1:17.

were the source of all subsequent sinners for that reason, then Abel rather than Christ should be called the head of all the righteous. Augustine sets aside the question of infants and asks whether or not people living where they could not hear the name of Christ could become righteous by nature and free choice. If they can, *then Christ has died in vain* (Gal 2:21). To an objector who says that one can be righteous, but by the grace of God, Pelagius had replied that one who says this not merely concedes that one can be righteous, but goes on to show how one can be. The objector still complains that, in not mentioning the grace of God, Pelagius seems to deny it. Augustine insists that Pelagius must admit that "without God's help human beings cannot be without sin, for it is wicked and godless to deny this" (section 11). Pelagius maintained that, in admitting the actuality of righteousness, he surely admits any means or helps necessary to its attainment. Though Augustine's initial reaction to reading this was joy that Pelagius did not deny the grace of God, he soon became suspicious (section 12), since the examples he used to illustrate the sort of helps he meant were all elements of nature as it was created rather than means toward its healing.

To the claim that certain venial sins cannot be avoided because they overwhelm people by reason of their great number, Pelagius had maintained that, if such sins are unavoidable, they should not receive the slightest correction (section 13). Pelagius has failed to understand, Augustine replies, the purpose of the law, namely, to accuse one of wrongdoing and to lead one, like a schoolmaster, to take refuge in the grace of the merciful Lord. Some ask the Pelagians whether they are themselves without sin; Pelagius dismisses the question as irrelevant and admits that it is due to his negligence, if he is not without sin (section 14). Here Augustine adds that he should also ask for the help of the Lord and not merely rely on his own efforts to attain righteousness.

Although scripture never explicitly says that people can be without sin, as some objectors pointed out, Pelagius insists that the precise words are not important (section 15). Augustine suggests that the precise words may not be insignificant, since, though some people, for example, Job, Zechariah, and Elizabeth, are said to be without reproach, only Christ is said to have been without sin.[28] John's state-

---

28. See 2 Cor 5:21; Heb 4:15.

ment that *those who have been born of God do not sin and cannot sin* (1 Jn 3:9) needs to be interpreted in the light of 1 Jn 1:8, and Augustine refers the reader to his interpretation on these passages in *The Punishment and Forgiveness of Sins*, while accepting another interpretation, possibly from Pelagius.

Pelagius had interpreted Jas 3:8 not as a statement but as a question and a reprimand: Can then no human beings tame their tongues? Augustine argues that the context shows that James was not saying that it was easy to tame the tongue; rather, he said this so that we would beg the help of divine grace to tame the tongue (section 16). In fact, James emphasizes the great evil of the tongue (section 17), and he shows that it is the wisdom that comes from above that can tame it, adding that, if one lacks such wisdom, one should ask for it from God.[29] Augustine also points out that no one should use as an objection to the Pelagians Paul's words, *But those who are in the flesh cannot please God* (Rom 8:8). What he wants to hear from them is: Do those who live according to the Spirit and are in that sense not in the flesh live according to the Spirit by the grace of God? Or do they do this by the ability of nature and by their own will that they received when they were created? (section 18). Pelagius warns that we should be on guard against culpable ignorance, but he does not warn that we should ask for wisdom from God (section 19). According to Pelagius, we must pray to God for the forgiveness of sins, since only the power of God can "make undone what has been done" (section 20).[30] But Pelagius is silent about the need to pray for help not to sin, though the Lord's Prayer clearly teaches otherwise.

In section 21, as he begins the second part of the work, Augustine accuses the author of *Nature* of portraying human nature as if it were completely free from any defect and of indulging in the wordy wisdom that does away with the cross of Christ. In fact, Augustine states, the cross of Christ will prevail, and he prays that Pelagius may repent of what he has said. In order to show that human nature has not been weakened and changed by sin, Pelagius had argued that sin is not a substance or a thing, but an act of wrongdoing and that, as lacking substance, sin could not harm our nature. Augustine points to the psalmist's prayer, *Heal my soul, for I have sinned against you* (Ps 40:5),

---

29. See Jas 3:17; 1:5-6.
30. Pelagius' expression seems to indicate that, in pardoning sins, God makes the past action of sinning such that it never occurred! Given this view, it is easy to see why he would reject any consequences of a sin remaining after the forgiveness of the sin.

and suggests that the wounded sinner would send Pelagius to continue his debate with the one who came to call not those in good health but the sick, not the righteous but sinners.[31] Augustine claims that Pelagius' aim is that we think that the words, *You shall call his name, Jesus, for he will save his people from their sins* (Mt 1:21), were uttered with absolutely no point (section 22). He admonishes Pelagius that it would be enough to believe, but Pelagius wants to argue. First believe the scriptures that human nature can be harmed by sin, Augustine advises; then investigate how this is possible. To show how it is possible, Augustine points out that the act of abstaining from food can harm the substance of the body; so too, the soul's withdrawing from God, "the only true food of the rational creature," can injure it. Despite the clear words of scripture that *Christ Jesus came into the world to save sinners* (1 Tm 1:15), Pelagius argues that sins should not have caused any illness; "otherwise, this punishment would lead to more sins being committed" (section 23). As Augustine reads him, Pelagius would not have Adam condemned to death for his sin and would not have Adam's descendants born any weaker than Adam himself was at his creation, though he can see, Augustine notes, the actual helpless state of newborn infants. Pelagius even declares these infants to be in good health and in no need of Christ the physician.[32]

Pelagius finds that punishment is the source of sin, if the sinner is weakened to the point of sinning more (section 24). On the contrary, Augustine argues that it is only just that the light of truth abandon sinners so that they fall, injure themselves, and cannot get up. He appeals to Rom 1:21-31 to show how sins led to the darkening of the hearts of sinners so that they fell into worse sins as a penalty for their wickedness. Pelagius may correctly claim that God does not force them to commit these sins, when he abandons sinners (section 25). But Augustine maintains that, deprived of the light of righteousness, sinners have become darkness and bring forth the works of darkness, until they obey the command, *Get up, you sleeper, rise from the dead, and Christ will enlighten you* (Eph 4:14). While the truth declares sinners dead, Pelagius claims that they cannot be injured or harmed

31. See Mt 9:12-13.
32. If Pelagius' *Nature* was written while he was still in Rome, as Duval has argued, and if Augustine is reporting what Pelagius said in that work, then it would seem that Pelagius had taught at Rome several of the propositions of Caelestius that were condemned in Carthage in 411 or 412.

by sin, since sin is not a substance. He not merely "says nothing at all about this grace and help and mercy without which we cannot live a good life. In fact he even speaks quite openly against the grace of Christ by which we are justified, when he defends nature as if it were sufficient unto itself for righteousness."

Pelagius points out that the Lord was able to die, though he was without sin, obviously aiming to show that death is not the result of sin (section 26). Augustine replies that Christ's birth also reveals the power of his mercy rather than the condition of his nature and that his death redeemed us from death—precisely the point that the Pelagians try to deny in their defense of human nature. Christ died not by the necessity of nature but by reason of the will to obey.

Another argument of Pelagius rests on the premise that no evil is the cause of any good. Yet Augustine notes that, though punishment is not a good, many people have by the mercy of God been corrected by punishments; hence, there are evils that do lead to good (section 27). Augustine uses Ps 29:7-8 to illustrate this point, though he concedes in section 28 that proud hearts do not understand it. Hence, we would do better to pray for them, as we do for ourselves, than to debate them. Pelagius claims that sin was necessary in order for God to have reason to show mercy, which Augustine denies. Yet he does admit that the wickedness of the first sin was greater insofar as it was more easily avoided. As a result of that sin of disobedience to God, human beings to some extent lost the obedience of their own bodies so that they are now born with the law of sin in their members resisting the law of the mind.[33] Pelagius grants that God's mercy helps human beings after sin, but does not admit that his mercy is needed so that we do not sin (section 29). The heavenly physician, Augustine insists, not merely heals the wounds of our nature so that they no longer exist, but helps us to live righteously afterward. Unlike a human physician, God does not heal the sinner and then abandon him, but continues to provide the means of avoiding sin.

The objection was made to the Pelagians that it was necessary that human beings not be sinless in order to remove the occasion for pride and boasting. Pelagius had declared it absurd that one should think that sin had to exist in order that sin might not exist (section 30). Augustine says that at times pain is necessary to relieve pain, for example, when a boil is lanced. Though God can heal everything, he

---

33. See Rom 7:23.

acts as he knows best and does not allow the sick person to prescribe the cure (section 31). Paul prayed repeatedly for God to remove the thorn in his flesh, but God left it there so Paul would not be filled with pride. While the other vices are found only in wrong actions, pride is found even in good actions and serves to warn us not to attribute our good actions to our own power. We need to work out our salvation with fear and trembling on account of our will, which so easily succumbs to pride. Hence, though it is not necessary to sin to avoid sin, God does at times abandon a person in something over which he is proud so that we may learn not to be proud (section 32).

Pelagius tries to show that every sin is a sin of pride, presumably to eliminate sins of ignorance and weakness (section 33). Augustine, on the other hand, admits that many sins are committed out of pride, but "not every wrong action is done with pride. Many are done by the ignorant, by the weak, and often by persons weeping and groaning." But he also maintains that there is a distinct sin of pride of the sort by which the devil fell and by which Adam fell.

Pelagius asks, "How could persons be responsible to God for the guilt of that sin which they do not recognize as their own?... Or, if it is theirs, then it is voluntary, and if it is voluntary, it can be avoided" (section 34). Augustine, though somewhat puzzled over what Pelagius meant, replies that the sin is theirs and that their injured and as yet unhealed nature led them to commit it. The Pelagians should pray for God's healing grace and not suppose that they can be healed by the same power by which they were injured. Augustine warns in section 35 that pride lies in ambush to attack the human spirit even in good actions, leading us to suppose that we make ourselves righteous by our own power. Though we do not make ourselves righteous, we do something along with God whose mercy goes before us to heal us and comes after us to strengthen us further.[34] God's words strike fear even in those who walk in his way so that they do not become proud (section 36). Hence, Paul tells Christians to work out their salvation with fear and trembling,[35] and the psalmist warns us to serve the Lord in fear so that we do not perish from the righteous way.[36]

---

34. See Pss 59:11; 23:6.
35. See Phil 2:12.
36. See Ps 2:11-13.

In sections 37-51, Augustine turns to a series of objections raised against Pelagius which Pelagius reports and answers in his book. Some, for example, have argued that, if human beings were sinless, they would be equal to God.[37] Augustine insists that the creature will not be equal to the creator, even if the creature has attained the highest degree of righteousness. Though some suppose that human beings can make such progress in righteousness that they will be changed into the divine substance, Augustine remains unconvinced (sections 37). Others object to Pelagius that his claim that human beings can be sinless is pride; Augustine agrees with Pelagius' reply that it is wrong to link the truth with pride and humility with falsity (section 38). John, after all, spoke the truth, not something false, when he said, *If we say that we have no sin, we deceive ourselves, and the truth is not in us* (1 Jn 1:8). Pelagius, however, defends human nature in such a way that he rejects the mercy and healing of the physician, which he locates only in the pardon of past sins, not in the help to avoid future ones (section 39). Thus, he praises the creator, Augustine argues, to the point of making the savior unnecessary.

Again Augustine concedes that Pelagius is correct in holding that scriptural examples of holy and righteous persons who sinned are not meant to make us despair of avoiding sin so that, convinced of our damnation, we give ourselves to sin without a worry; they are meant, rather, to bring us to repent humbly and not to give up hope, even amid our failures (section 40). Pelagius poses a question regarding the death of these holy persons, asking whether they left this life with sin or without sin. If one holds that they died with sin, their damnation would seem to follow; if one holds that they died without sin, then one has to admit that some human beings were sinless in this life, at least toward death. Augustine argues in section 41 that Pelagius overlooks the Christian's daily prayer for forgiveness which obtains pardon so that one is able to die without sin, even if one cannot live without sin.[38]

Pelagius adds a long list of biblical women and men who, he claims, did not sin and lived righteously. Of Mary, Pelagius says,

---

37. See the note on the translation at this point. If Duval's dating of *Nature* is correct, the objection cannot be drawn from Jerome's Letter 133 to Ctesiphon, as some have suggested. See Duval 262-263.
38. Pelagius seems to have held the view that all sins are serious in the sense that they lead to damnation.

"Piety demands that we admit that she had no sin." Augustine does not concede that Mary was sinless, though he refuses to discuss her in the context of sin "on account of the honor due to the Lord" (section 42). He adds, "After all, how do we know what wealth of grace was given to her in order to conquer sin completely, since she merited to conceive and bear the one who obviously had no sin?"[39] Of all the other righteous people Pelagius mentioned, Augustine asks whether or not they would have cried out with John, *If we say that we have no sin, we deceive ourselves, and the truth is not in us*, arguing that, if the truth is in them, they would have had sin and admitted it.

Another objection to Pelagius claims that scripture could not mention the sins of everyone, a point which Augustine takes to be true. Pelagius, however, presents the rather feeble argument that, while the objection might hold for those about whom scripture reports neither good nor bad actions, it does not hold for those whose righteousness is mentioned. In response, Augustine asks Pelagius whether in the crowd of people who welcomed Jesus with great faith on his entry into Jerusalem there was no one who had any sin whatsoever, just because scripture does not mention any sin (section 43). Pelagius perhaps saw this line of reply, since he went on to exclude cases in which scripture dealt with large numbers, but he tries to maintain the truth of his principle with regard to the beginnings of the race, inferring that, if Abel had sinned, scripture would have mentioned it (section 44). Augustine replies that Pelagius has overlooked the large number of venial sins committed even by a single human being. He notes, moreover, that, unless one admits that there are many facts that scripture does not mention, even in the beginning, one would be obliged to infer that Cain had intercourse with his mother. Hence, scripture had no need to recount all the venial sins of Abel—the sort of sins against which we all must fight a daily battle (section 45).

Pelagius had appealed to the fundamentalist hermeneutical principle that one should believe what one reads and add nothing to what one reads.[40] In section 46, Augustine first notes that we should not believe everything we read and that we can surely add what we

---

39. The passage obviously is an important one for the question of what Augustine held regarding Mary's freedom from original and actual sin. Unfortunately, it would seem that it at most does not deny Mary's sinlessness and leaves the question open.
40. See *Nature and Grace* 37, 44, for the principle. See *Answer to Maximinus* for an Arian appeal to the same principle and Augustine's reply to it.

have ourselves experienced, even if we have not found it in writing. Even if the principle is limited to what we read in scripture, what we should not add is something contrary to what we read there, not merely something other than what we read there. Augustine also points out that Pelagius should believe what he reads, for example, in Rom 5:12. He adds, "How I wish that, as a Christian, he would read that apart from Jesus Christ there is no name under heaven in which we can be saved."[41] Perhaps, Augustine suggests, Pelagius thinks that we need the name of Christ in order to learn from his gospel how we ought to live, but not in order to be helped by his grace to live as we ought (section 47). If so, Pelagius ought at least to admit the great darkness of the human mind that knows how to tame wild animals, but does not know how it ought to live. If Pelagius means that free choice and the natural law suffice, this is, Augustine cries, "the wordy wisdom that does away with the cross of Christ."[42]

Another objection which Pelagius' opponents raise is that the Apostle said, *For all have sinned* (Rom 3:23), with regard to people in the past. Somewhat puzzled over why Pelagius mentioned this objection, Augustine points out that Rom 5:12 includes all people, those in the past and those in more recent times (section 48). Pelagius also uses Rom 5:18 in support of his taking "all" in a less than all-inclusive sense, since the righteousness of Christ did not justify everyone. Augustine replies that Paul used "all" in the sense that no one is justified "without believing in him and being washed by his baptism." Pelagius retreats even further, conceding that scripture does say that all were sinners, but insists that his thesis concerns not what human beings have been or are, but what they can be (section 49). At this point, Augustine notes that Pelagius does admit that no one is righteous in God's sight,[43] and with regard to the possibility of not sinning, Augustine adds that he is not very concerned about whether or not some people have attained or will attain a perfect love of God in this life, provided one admits that the human will is healed and helped by God's grace. Augustine warns that Pelagius would do better to acknowledge both the creator and the savior rather than to destroy the help of the savior in defending the creature.

41. See Acts 4:12.
42. See 1 Cor 1:17.
43. See Ps 143:2.

Pelagius is correct that God made human beings such that they could be free from sin, if they wanted to be (section 50). We are now, however, "dealing with that man whom robbers left half-dead on the road," Augustine notes, alluding to his interpretation of the man who went down from Jerusalem to Jericho as the human race and the Good Samaritan as Christ. God does not command the impossible; rather, by his commandment he warns us to do what we can and to ask for what we cannot. While Pelagius maintained, "Natural ability does not depend on the will," Augustine claimed that, given the woundedness of our nature, "one will be able to be as a result of medication what one cannot be because of one's injury." Hence, Augustine brings this part to a close by insisting "on the sole or almost the sole point of contention we have with these people" (section 51). That point is not whether there have been or are sinless people or whether there can be people without sin, but whether there are people without sin who have not been justified *by the grace of God through Jesus Christ, our Lord* (Rom 7:25).

Pelagius himself raises the crucial issue as an objection to himself, "You maintain that a human being can be free from sin without the grace of God" (section 52). Augustine agrees that this is the intolerable point. Pelagius responds with outrage at the ignorance that supposes that he defends without the grace of God what must be attributed to God alone. Thus far Augustine is in perfect agreement. But Pelagius contends that the ability to be without sin does not come from human choice but from nature and, in that sense, from the author of nature (section 53). That is, Pelagius locates the ability for an action in the necessity of one's God-given nature, but he locates the action itself in human choice. For example, that I can speak is part of my nature, while the fact that I do speak is due to my choice. Augustine points out that we can in fact lose an ability through an injury inflicted upon ourselves and in other ways. Pelagius goes on to imply that natural necessity is incompatible with the will, and Augustine says that our willing to be happy belongs to the will, despite our inability to will to be unhappy, and that an inability to will to sin does not imply that God does not will to be righteous (section 54).

Pelagius claims that actions lie in our power, but that the ability to do the actions does not lie in our power but in a natural necessity (section 55). In opposition to that, Augustine insists that the ability to see does lie in our power, since we have it in our power to blind ourselves, that is, we have it in our power to deprive ourselves of the ability to see. Furthermore, when we are in the dark, it is not in our power to see, and we often see and hear things we could not avoid seeing or hearing. Augustine notes that Pelagius' comparisons do not hold up to scrutiny and that the point he used to make them fails as well. Pelagius claimed that "not sinning is up to us, but the ability not to sin is not up to us" (section 56). Augustine points out that, even if our nature were whole and healthy, we would still need God's help not to sin. But since the question concerns our nature as it is at present, Augustine is astonished at the claims that "not sinning is up to us, even without the help of our savior . . . [and] the ability not to sin comes from our nature." Pelagius held that, "because not sinning is up to us, we can both sin and not sin" (section 57). Augustine says that not willing unhappiness is up to us, but that it does not follow that we can will it as well as not will it. Moreover, not sinning lies in God's power, and it does not follow that he can sin. Pelagius is, of course, trying to show that we cannot lose the natural ability not to sin. As Augustine rephrases it, Pelagius maintains that, "whether we will it or not, we have the ability not to sin . . . and this is implanted in our nature." Augustine concedes that this might hold of a nature that was not wounded, just as human beings with healthy feet have the ability to walk, whether they will to or not. But our present nature is wounded and needs a physician and savior. We are like someone with a broken foot who first needs to be healed before he can walk again. Against Pelagius' claim that "no will can remove something inseparably implanted in nature" (section 58), Augustine appeals to Paul's complaint that he does not do the good that he wants, but does the evil that he hates.[44] He asks, "Where is the ability that is found to be inseparably implanted in nature?"

In order to avoid the hostility of Christians, Augustine notes, Pelagius locates the ability not to sin in the necessity of nature rather than in the power of choice and adds the claim that whatever lies in the necessity of nature surely pertains to the author of nature (section 59). He then asks how one can suppose "that what is shown to pertain to God as his very own is said to exist apart from God's grace." That is, Pelagius has identified the grace of God with the God-given nature with its inseparable ability not to sin. He has ruled out any weakness of the will such that human beings can will the good, but cannot do the good they

---

44. See Rom 7:9.

will, despite Paul's statement to the contrary in Rom 7:18. Augustine again concedes that Pelagius' claim would be somewhat acceptable, if he were speaking of an innocent and healthy nature, though even that nature did not have an ability not to sin that could not be lost.

Pelagius then turns to objections which he raises against his own position (section 60). For example, he mentions Paul's statement that the flesh is opposed to us.[45] In reply, he claims that the flesh is not opposed to one who has been baptized, since the baptized are not in the flesh, according to Rom 8:9. Here Augustine notes that Pelagius implies that human nature is injured and wounded in those who are not baptized. Citing once more the parable of the Good Samaritan, he says, "He surely grants that at least in them nature was injured, if that wounded man, now among the baptized, emerged from the inn in good health or is in good health in the inn where the merciful Samaritan brought him to be cared for." Augustine argues that human flesh and spirit are God's creation and are good because he is good; hence, the injury to human nature, as a result of which all need the help of the savior, must have been inflicted by the human will.

Paul, however, said that the flesh is opposed to the spirit and the spirit to the flesh in the baptized as well as in the unbaptized (section 61). Even the baptized do not have the ability not to sin, which Pelagius claimed was inseparably implanted in human nature. It is not the nature of the flesh, but the defects of the flesh which are opposed to the spirit. In any case, the flesh is opposed to the spirit, even in the baptized, so that they do not do the good that they want.

The grace we need in order to avoid sin, Augustine argues, is not "the grace by which human beings were created, but the grace by which they are saved through Jesus Christ, our Lord" (section 62). The petition, *Bring us not into temptation, but deliver us from evil* (Mt 6:13), asks for the latter grace. We do not ask to be freed from the substance of the flesh, but from its defects. Our nature "is wounded, injured, beaten, ruined; it is in need of a true confession, not of a false defense." Pelagius declares the grace by which we are healed, restored, and saved unnecessary, when he does not mention it.

Pelagius then shows by many citations from St. Paul that he uses "flesh" to refer to the works of the flesh, not the substance of the flesh. He also argues that the flesh and the spirit, along with the God who

45. See Gal 5:17.

created them both, are good and infers that flesh and spirit cannot, therefore, be opposed to each other (section 63). Augustine counters that hot and cold are also created by God and are surely opposed to each other; though hot and cold are qualities, not substances, substances are only opposed by reason of their qualities. But the flesh's being opposed to the spirit so that we do not do what we want is not our nature, but a defect from which we need to be healed. Moreover, having admitted that the flesh and the spirit are opposed to each other in the unbaptized, Pelagius has to explain how this can be, since their flesh and spirit were made by the same good creator (section 64). If Pelagius takes back what he implied about the unbaptized, he cannot take Paul's question, *Who will set me free from the body of this death?* (Rom 7:24) as words placed in the mouth of someone unbaptized. But if he grants that nature is injured at least in the unbaptized, he should grant that it needs Christ the physician.

Paul asked to be set free from the just punishment of sin and could not set himself free. Wherever freedom was lost, the ability Pelagius assigned to nature was surely separated from it (section 65). If Pelagius would only cry out with Paul's words, he would realize that he needed not only baptism for the forgiveness of past sins but help and strength not to sin in the future. Paul saw another law in his members, not merely resisting him, but holding him captive. Pelagius would prevent him from demanding the help and the mercy of Christ the physician. If the Pelagians would allow at least the unbaptized to implore the help of the savior, we would have won no small victory (section 66), but they should also see that the opposition between the flesh and the spirit is present in the baptized. Augustine points to Gal 5:17 as proof that even in the baptized there is the opposition between the flesh and the spirit (section 67); he notes that Paul added, *If you are led by the Spirit, you are no longer under the law* (Gal 5:18), for those led by the Spirit have the love of God poured out in their hearts. Our present condition is mixed: insofar as we are led by the Spirit, we find delight in the law of God; insofar as we find another law in our members, we stand under the law in fear like slaves.

As we ought to be grateful for the past healing we have received, so we ought to pray for continued healing so that we may be brought to full health (section 68). Pelagius, on the other hand, Augustine claims, attributes such power to the will that he would even have us resist the devil without praying for God's help. Augustine grants that Pelagius

Saint Augustine — Pelagians

correctly infers from the fact that many want to be without sin that it is possible to be without sin, but points out that he overlooks the grace of God which makes this possible (section 69). Pelagius does not want us to pray for help not to sin. In his defense of the nature with which we are created, he refuses to acknowledge that our nature was injured so that it needs healing or is not self-sufficient so that it needs help.

Augustine concedes that it is a "legitimate question among true and pious Christians" whether anyone has attained or will attain a righteous life completely free from sin (section 70). Though he finds such passages as Ps 142:2 to be convincing proofs that no one has attained or will attain such perfect righteousness in this life, he is well aware that Ambrose of Milan had clearly attributed such righteousness to Zechariah and Elizabeth.[46] There are, however, many more persons who know that they need to pray daily for the forgiveness of their sins, and no Christian can claim to make progress in true righteousness in any other way than by the grace of Christ crucified and by the gift of the Spirit.

In *Nature* Pelagius had appealed to a number of ecclesiastical writers as supportive of his views on human sinlessness. In section 71 Augustine turns to the statements of these men whom Pelagius had cited and claims that these texts are neutral, neither against Pelagius' view nor against his own. Pelagius did not mention the name of the first author he cited, and Augustine was unable to identify him. The author is Lactantius, and Augustine merely cautions Pelagius about the need to understand correctly the sense in which Christ conquered sin and overcame the desires of the flesh, since he had in himself no sin to conquer and no concupiscence of the flesh. In sections 72-73, Augustine points out that the citations from Hilary of Poitiers do not support Pelagius' claim that some human beings, such as Job, have attained perfect righteousness in this world, and he cites another passage from Hilary to show that he held that there is no one without sin.

Turning to Ambrose of Milan, Augustine concedes that "Saint Ambrose is really opposed to those who say that human beings cannot be without sin in this life" (section 74). But though Ambrose appealed to Zechariah and Elizabeth as examples of such sinlessness, he certainly did not deny, Augustine argues, that they attained

---

46. See Ambrose, *Commentary on the Gospel of Luke* I, 17.

such sinlessness by the grace of God. Augustine, moreover, quotes another passage from Ambrose's *Commentary on the Gospel of Luke* in which the bishop of Milan cited Prv 8:35, *The will of human beings is prepared by God*, and he points out that Pelagius omitted a line from Ambrose's work in which the bishop had said that it was not possible for the Church to be spotless from the beginning (section 75).

Pelagius had cited John Chrysostom, though the citation has not been found in his works, as saying that sin is not a substance but an action and that it is not natural but arises from free choice. Augustine concedes both points as harmless, if properly understood, but points out that Pelagius defends nature and free choice as if they were sufficient to avoid sin without the aid of grace (section 76).

Pelagius attributed to Xystus II, a third-century bishop of Rome, three quotations that, according to Jerome, stemmed from Sextus the Pythagorean philosopher. At the time of writing *Nature and Grace*, Augustine did not question the attribution of the quotations to Pope Xystus, though he adopted Jerome's view of their authorship by the time he wrote his *Revisions*.[47] Hence, in section 77, he takes the texts from Sextus in a Christian sense; in doing so, he notes that the question about the attainment of sinlessness in this life is one properly raised among pious people.

Jerome was the source of two statements that Pelagius had cited in support of his position (sections 78-79). In neither of them does Augustine find anything with which to disagree, though he admits "there is a certain necessity of sinning due to the defects of nature, not to the way nature was created," so that we need to pray, *Deliver me from my necessities* (Ps 24:17), until grace brings us full freedom.

Pelagius had also cited a passage from Augustine's *Free Choice*, parts of which—most of the first two books—were written soon after his conversion, while much of the third book was completed almost ten years later. In the passage in question Augustine had stated that

47. See Henry Chadwick, *The Sentences of Sextus. A Contribution to the History of Early Christian Ethics* (Cambridge: Cambridge University Press, 1957), for the Greek text along with Rufinus of Aquileia's Latin translation. Through a careful examination of the external and internal evidence, Chadwick concludes that the sentences are the work of a Christian; he does not rule out the possibility that they are the work of Xystus II. He regards Jerome's ascription of the sentence to a Pythagorean author as simply another attempt on Jerome's part to discredit his former friend Rufinus.

sin was avoidable; here he acknowledges the statement as his own, insisting that sin can be avoided by the help of grace (section 80). Then, in section 81 Augustine points out that, if Pelagius had attended to the words immediately following those he quoted, he would have seen that Augustine had gone on to speak of the ignorance and weakness resulting from sin and to claim that the free will to do what is right belonged to the nature with which human beings were created, not to the nature with which we are now born. Augustine adds, " The whole dispute with these people turns on this point: that we do not render meaningless the grace of God, which is found in Christ Jesus, our Lord, by a misguided defense of nature."

Twelve years later, in his *Revisions*,[48] Augustine reviewed a long series of statements he made in *Free Choice* that might seem to favor the Pelagian position. He again insisted that he had in his earlier work stated the need for grace, though in a work directed against the Manicheans, such as *Free Choice*, he was not engaged in a defense of God's grace. He did, on the other hand, admit the absence in the earlier work of any discussion of the grace of predestination: "There was no discussion in those books of the grace of God by which he has predestined his elect so that he prepares the wills of those who use their free choice, since the question was raised on account of the latter. But when the occasion allowed the mention of grace, it was mentioned in passing. It is, after all, one thing to investigate the origin of evil, and it is something quite different to investigate how one returns to the original good or attains a greater good."[49] There was, as Augustine himself acknowledged in *The Predestination of the Saints*, a marked change in his thought on grace that dated from the time of his writing the second book of his *Miscellany of Questions in Response to Simplician* in 396.[50]

In drawing the work to a close, Augustine agrees with Pelagius' exhorting "cold and sluggish minds to live good lives," but adds that one should first exhort them to faith or, if they already have the faith, one should use the fear of punishment and praise of the rewards of a good life, without forgetting to exhort them to prayer. Once people have begun to live good lives, they will be thankful for being able to

---

48. See *Revisions* I, 8 (9), 3-6.

49. *Revisions* I, 8 (9), 2.

50. See *The Predestination of the Saints* 4, 8, where Augustine corrects his own earlier interpretation of various statements in the Letter to the Romans.

do so without difficulty or, if they find difficulty, they will pray to be able to act with ease. Again, Augustine leaves open the question of when people will attain the perfection of righteousness, probably out of respect for the position of Ambrose. But whenever perfection is attained, it is attained only by the grace of God (section 82). While Pelagius had maintained that it was possible to avoid sin, Augustine in a sense goes beyond this, claiming that it is not merely possible but easy to do what God commands. "Everything is, of course, easy for love; for love alone Christ's burden is light" (section 83). Thus, Augustine sums up his position, "the beginning of love is the beginning of righteousness; progress in love is progress in righteousness; great love is great righteousness; perfect love is perfect righteousness" (section 84). On the other hand, Augustine himself holds that such perfect love is probably not attained in this life. In any case, such love is poured out in our hearts by the Holy Spirit.

The Text and Translations

The text translated is that of the CSEL edition by C. F. Urba and J. Zycha (Vienna 1913) 233-299. I have adopted some modifications and suggestions from the texts in the ALG and BA editions. The work has been translated into English by P. Holmes in NPNF I/5 (New York 1887; repr. 1971); his translation has been reprinted in *Basic Writings of Saint Augustine* (New York 1948) I, 519-579. The work has also been more recently translated by J. Mourant and W. Collinge in FC LXXXVI (Washington 1992) 22-90. In the present century it has also been translated into Spanish by V. Capanaga in BAC L (Madrid 1956) 245-423; into French by J. de La Tullaye in BA XXI (Paris 1966) 245-412; into German by A. Maxsein in ALG I (Würzburg 1971) 519-579; and into Italian by I. Volpi in NBA XVII/1 (Rome 1981) 379-487.

Revisions II, 68 (42)

There also came into my hands at that time a book of Pelagius in which he defended human nature, with as much argumentation as he could, in opposition to the grace of God by which the sinner is justified and by which we are Christians. I therefore called the book by which I answered him *Nature and Grace*. In it I did not defend grace in opposition to nature, but the grace by which nature is set free and ruled. In it I defended some words which Pelagius cited as those of Xyxtus, the Roman bishop and martyr, as if they really were the words of that Xyxtus. But I later read that they were the words of Sextus the philosopher, not of Xystus the Christian. This book begins: " ... the book you sent me."

Nature and Grace

Pelagius' Basic Teaching on Human Nature

1, 1. My dear sons, Timasius and James, I left aside for the moment other work in progress, and I rapidly but with considerable attention read through the book you sent me.[1] I found in it a man aflame with ardent zeal against those people who ought to lay the blame for their sins upon the human will, but try to excuse themselves by laying the blame on human nature instead. He is far too incensed at this evil, which authors of worldly literature have also strongly denounced, crying out, "The human race unfairly complains about its nature."[2] This author has certainly stressed this idea with all the powers of mind that he could muster. But I am afraid that he sides with those *who have zeal for God, but not in accord with knowledge. For, not knowing the righteousness of God and wanting to establish their own, they were not subject to the righteousness of God.* (Rom 10:2-3) The Apostle goes on to explain the meaning of the righteousness of God, of which he is speaking, when he adds, *For the end of the law is Christ for righteousness for everyone who believes* (Rom 10:4). Therefore, this righteousness is not to be found in the fearsome commandment of the law, but in the help of Christ's grace. The fear produced by the law, like a schoolmaster, is useful only in leading one to his grace.[3] Those who understand this understand why they are Christians. *For if righteousness comes through the law, then Christ has died in vain* (Gal 2:21). But if he did not die in vain, the sinner is justified only in him, and *for one who believes in him who justifies the sinner faith is counted as righteousness* (Rom 4:5). *For all have sinned and lack the glory of God, but they have been gratuitously justified by his blood* (Rom 3:23-24).[4] If we suppose that there are some who do not belong among all those who have sinned and lack the glory of God, they certainly have no need to become Christians. After all, it is not those who are in good

---

1. The book is Pelagius' *Nature* (*De natura*), which has been lost, except for various citations. In PL 48, 599-606, J. Garnier offers a reconstruction of the work.
2. Sallust, *The War against Jugurtha* (*Bellum Iugurthinum*) I, 1.
3. See Gal 3:24.
4. Both the Greek and the Vulgate have "grace" where Augustine's translation has "blood."

health who need a physician, but those who are ill. This is the reason he did not come to call the righteous, but sinners.[5]

2, 2. And so, if this nature of the human race born from the flesh of that one transgressor can be capable by itself of fulfilling the law and attaining perfect righteousness, it ought to be sure of its reward, that is, of eternal life, "even if among a certain people, or in an earlier time, faith in the blood of Christ remained hidden. For God is not unjust so that he cheats the righteous out of the reward of their righteousness, if the mystery of the divinity and humanity of Christ, that was revealed in the flesh,[6] has not been preached to them. For how were they to believe what they had not heard? Or how were they to hear without someone to preach to them?[7] For, as scripture says, *faith comes from hearing, but hearing comes from the word of Christ. I ask,* Paul says, *Have they not heard? Their voice has gone forth to the whole earth, and their words have reached the ends of the earth.* (Rom 10:17-18) But what about before this began to happen, and before this preaching finally reaches to the ends of the whole earth? After all, there are still remote peoples, though very few, it is said, to whom the word has not yet been preached. What is human nature to do, or what did it do? For it either previously had not heard that this event would take place or has still not found out that it has taken place. What is human nature to do but believe in the God who made heaven and earth, the God whom it naturally perceives as its maker, and, by living correctly, fulfills his will, though it has not received any instruction in the faith concerning the suffering and resurrection of Christ?"[8] But if that was possible or is possible, then I too say what the Apostle said with regard to the law, *Christ has died in vain* (Gal 2:21). After all, if that man said this with regard to the law received by a single people, the Jews, it is by far more just to say with regard to the law of nature received by the whole human race, "If righteousness comes about through nature, then Christ has died in vain!" But if Christ has not died in vain, then the whole of human nature can be justified and redeemed from the perfectly just anger of God, that is, from punishment, in no other way than by faith and the mystery of Christ's blood.

---

5. See Mt 9:12-13.
6. See 1 Tm 3:16.
7. See Rom 10:14.
8. G. de Plinval has convincingly argued that this long section is a quotation from Pelagius' lost work, *Nature*; see BA XXI, 600.

Augustine's Basic Teachings on Nature and Grace

3, 3. Human nature was in the beginning created blameless and without any defect. But that human nature, in which each of us is born of Adam, now needs a physician, because it is not in good health. All the goods which it has in its constitution—life, the senses, and the mind—it has from the sovereign God, its creator and maker. But the defect which darkens and weakens those natural goods, so that there is need for enlightenment and healing, did not come from its blameless maker. It came from the original sin which was committed by free choice. And thus a nature subject to punishment is part of a punishment that is completely just. After all, if we are now a new creature in Christ,[9] *we were*, nonetheless, *by nature children of anger, just as the others. But God who is rich in mercy, on account of the great love with which he loved us, even when we were dead by sins, brought us to life with Christ, by whose grace we have been saved.* (Eph 2:3-5)

4, 4. This grace of Christ without which neither infants nor adults can be saved is not a recompense for our merits, but a free gift. This is the reason it is called grace. Paul says that they *have been gratuitously justified by his blood* (Rom 3:24). Hence, those who are not set free by it are rightly condemned. It makes no difference whether it is due to the fact that they are still unwilling to hear the word or that they are unwilling to obey or even that, though they could not hear the word by reason of their age, they did not receive the bath of regeneration which they could receive and by which they might be saved.[10] They are rightly condemned because they are not free from sin, either that which they contracted from their origin or that which they have added to it by their evil lives. *For all have sinned*—whether in Adam or in their own persons—*and lack the glory of God* (Rom 3:23).

5, 5. The whole mass of humanity owes a debt of punishment, and if all suffered the penalty of damnation they deserved, they certainly would not be paying an unjust penalty. Those then who are set free from it by grace are not called vessels of their own merits, but vessels of mercy.[11] Of whose mercy, if not the mercy of him who sent Christ

9. See 2 Cor 5:17.
10. See Ti 3:5.
11. See Rom 9:23.

Jesus into this world to save the sinners?[12] He foreknew, predestined, called, justified, and glorified them.[13] Who then is going to be so wildly insane as not to offer inexpressible thanks to the mercy of God, if he sets free those whom he wills, since one could in no way find fault with his justice, if he condemned absolutely everyone?

6, 6. If we hold this in accord with the scriptures, we are not forced to argue against the grace of Christ and to say things by which we try to prove that in little ones human nature has no need of a physician, because it is healthy, and that in adults it is able to be self-sufficient for righteousness, if it wants. These claims have the semblance of cleverness, but they are spoken with that wordy wisdom that does away with the cross of Christ.[14] *Such wisdom does not come down from above* (Jas 3:15). I do not want to mention what follows[15] for fear of being thought to do an injustice to our friends,[16] for we want their vigorous and quick minds to move in the right direction, not in the wrong one.

The Point-by-Point Refutation of Pelagius' Book

7, 7. The author of this book which you sent me was burning with great zeal against those who look for an excuse for their sins in the weakness of human nature. We ought to be afire with a much more ardent zeal that the cross of Christ not be done away with.[17] But it is done away with, if one says that it is possible to attain righteousness and eternal life in some other way than by the sacrament of Christ. I do not want to say that what he does in this book[18] he does knowingly, because I want to avoid the judgment that its author should not be regarded even as a Christian.[19] Rather, I believe that he does this without knowledge, but with great strength. But I want that strength to be healthy, not the sort often found in lunatics.

12. See 1 Tm 1:15.
13. See Rom 8:29-30.
14. See 1 Cor 1:17.
15. James adds that this wisdom is earthly, animal, diabolical.
16. To whom is Augustine referring? To Timasius and James who were earlier loyal disciples of Pelagius? Or perhaps to others who still remained followers of Pelagius in Africa.
17. See 1 Cor 1:17.
18. The book is Pelagius' *Nature.*
19. R. B. Rees has given the subtitle *A Reluctant Heretic* to his book on Pelagius; again and again Augustine indicates that he was a reluctant anti-Pelagian.

Against the View that Human Beings Can Be Sinless in This Life

8. Now he first makes this distinction: "It is one thing to ask whether something can be—this pertains only to its possibility; it is something else to ask whether it is."[20] No one has any doubt about the correctness of this distinction. After all, it follows that what is can be, but it does not follow that what can be also is. Since the Lord raised up Lazarus,[21] he was undoubtedly able to do this, but because he did not raise up Judas, are we to say that he could not? He could, then, but he did not will to. For, if he had willed to, he would have done this with the same power, since *the Son also gives life to those he wills* (Jn 5:21). But notice where he is going and what he is trying to accomplish with this correct and clear distinction. He says, "We are speaking about the possibility alone. For unless something is established as certain in its regard, we consider it a very serious disorder to go on to something else."[22] He turns this idea around in many ways and with a long discussion in order that no one would think that he is asking about anything but the possibility of not sinning. As a result, among the many points he makes, he also says this: "I repeat the same thing again: I say that a person is able to be without sin. What do you say? That a person is unable to be without sin. I do not say," he declares, "that there is a human being without sin, and you do not say that there is no human being without sin. We are arguing about what is possible and what is not possible, not about what is and what is not."[23]

Next, he mentions that some of those passages from the scriptures which are often cited against them are not relevant to the question of whether people can or cannot be without sin. He cites: *For no one is clean from filth* (Jb 14:4), and *There is not a human being who does not sin* (1 K 8:46), and *There is not a righteous person on the earth* (Eccl 7:21), and *There is not a single person who does good* (Ps 14:1.3). "And other passages like these," he says, "reveal what is not the case, not what cannot be. Examples of this sort show the kind of human beings there once were; they do not show that they could not be anything else. Accordingly, they

20. Pelagius, *Nature*.
21. See Jn 11:43-44.
22. Pelagius, *Nature*.
23. Ibid.

were rightly found to be blameworthy. After all, if they were such persons, because they could not be anything else, they would not have any guilt."[24]

8, 9. You see what he said. I say, on the other hand, that little ones who are born in a place where they could not be helped by Christ's baptism and are overtaken by death are in that situation, that is, of having died without the bath of regeneration, because they could not be anything else. Let this fellow, then, declare them innocent, and let him open to them the kingdom of heaven contrary to the decision of the Lord.[25] But the Apostle did not declare them innocent; he says, *Through one man sin entered the world, and through sin death, and thus it was passed on to all human beings in whom all have sinned* (Rom 5:12). It is right, then, that they are not admitted into the kingdom of heaven because of that condemnation that pervades the whole mass of humanity, even though they neither were nor could be Christian.

9, 10. But these people say, "They are not condemned, because the statement that all have sinned in Adam was not uttered on account of a sin contracted by reason of their origin through being born, but on account of the imitation of Adam's sin."[26] If then Adam is called the source of all the sinners who came after him, because he was the first sinner in the human race, why is not Abel rather than Christ declared the head of all the righteous, since he was the first righteous man in the human race? I will leave aside the case of infants. Young or old persons have died in regions where they could not hear the name of Christ. Could they become righteous by nature and free choice or could they not? If these people say that they could, then you see what it means to do away with the cross of Christ;[27] it is to maintain that without the cross of Christ a person can become righteous by the natural law and the choice of the will. Here too we should say, *Then Christ has died in vain* (Gal 2:21). For all human beings could be righteous, even if he had not died. And if they were unrighteous, they were such because they wanted to be, not because they could not be righteous. But if they absolutely could not be justified without the grace of Christ, let this man, if he dares, also declare such persons innocent in accord with

---

24. Ibid.
25. See Jn 3:5.
26. Pelagius, *Nature*.
27. See 1 Cor 1:17.

his words, for "if they were such persons, because they could not be anything else, they would not have any guilt."[28]

10, 11. He raises an objection for himself as if someone else had stated it and says, "You will say, 'One can [be righteous], but by the grace of God.' " Then, as if he were replying, he adds, "I thank you for your kindness. You had long attacked my statement, but now you are not satisfied merely with not attacking or with[29] admitting my statement, but you even go on to give it your approval. For what else does saying, 'One can, but by this means or that,' amount to but that one not only agrees that one can, but also shows how and in what sense one can? No one grants the possibility of something more than the person who also admits a condition of the thing, because a condition cannot exist without the thing."[30]

Having said this, he again raises an objection for himself, "But since you do not mention the grace of God in that passage, you seem to deny it." Then he answers, "Is it I who deny it, for in admitting the reality, it is necessary that I also admit the means by which it can be attained, or is it you, for in denying the reality you undoubtedly deny whatever it is by which it is brought about?"[31] He has already forgotten that he is replying to one who does not deny the reality. He had a little before stated the objection of that person who said, "One can, but by the grace of God." How does one deny that possibility for which this man has struggled so much by saying to him, "One can, but by the grace of God"? Nonetheless, having dismissed the one who already admitted the reality, he moves against those who deny that it is possible that a human being be without sin. How does this concern us? Let him attack whom he will, provided that he admits that without God's grace human beings cannot be without sin, for it is wicked and godless to deny this. Therefore, he says, "Whether it is by grace or by a help or by mercy or whatever it is by which a human being can be without sin, whoever admits the reality also admits the means to it as well."[32]

---

28. Pelagius, *Nature*; see above 7, 8.
29. On the basis of some of the oldest manuscripts, the CSEL edition has a "not" (*non*) here too. Along with the BA and ALG editions, I have followed the Maurists in omitting it.
30. Pelagius, *Nature*.
31. Ibid.
32. Ibid.

11, 12. I admit to you, my friends, that, when I read those words, I was suddenly flooded with joy, because he did not deny the grace of God which is the only means by which a human being can be justified. After all, that is what I especially detest and abhor in the discussions of these people. But as I went on to read the rest, I first began to have suspicions on the basis of the comparisons he used. For he says, "Now, if I say that a human being can argue, a bird can fly, a rabbit can run and if I do not mention as well the means by which these actions can be done, that is, the tongue, wings, feet, have I who have admitted the activities themselves denied the conditions of these activities?"[33] He seems, in any case, to have mentioned things that nature can do, for these members, namely, the tongue, wings, and feet, were created for natures of this sort. He has not said the sort of thing that we want to be understood in the case of the grace without which a human being cannot be justified, where there is a question of healing, not of creating natures. Already uneasy for this reason, I began to read the rest, and I found that my suspicions were not mistaken.

Pelagius' Doctrine of Sinlessness Ignores Prayer and Grace

12, 13. Before I come to point this out, look at what he said. When he was treating the question of differences among sins, he raised for himself the objection that some people claim that certain venial sins cannot all be avoided by reason of their very multitude, for they often overwhelm people. He denied that such sins should receive even a slight correction, if they are entirely unavoidable.[34] He failed to note the passages of the New Testament where we have learned what the purpose of the law is: It makes accusations so that on account of the wrong things that are done one might take refuge in the grace of the merciful Lord, for the law like a schoolmaster encloses us in the same faith which was later revealed.[35] In that faith wrong actions are both forgiven and, by the help of grace, avoided. This is the path of those who are making progress, and those who are making good progress are called perfect travelers. But the highest perfection is that to which nothing can be added, when we have begun to possess the goal toward which we are moving.

33. Ibid.
34. A less than literal citation from Pelagius' *Nature*.
35. Gal 3:24.23.

13, 14. The question which is addressed to them, "Are you yourself without sin?"[36] is not really relevant to the matter of our investigation. He says that it should rather be attributed to his negligence that he is not without sin, and he is correct. But he should for that reason be willing to ask the Lord that this sinful negligence not dominate him. We ask this of the Lord, when we say, *Guide my journeys according to your word, and let not sinfulness dominate me* (Ps 119:133). He should ask this of the Lord for fear that, in relying upon his own diligence as if upon his own resources, he may fail to attain true righteousness either in this life or in the life to come, where we should undoubtedly desire and hope for its perfection.

Pelagius' Appeal to Scripture and Augustine's Reply

14, 15. He easily refutes the objection which certain people raise against them that scripture nowhere says in these very words that a person can be without sin. He says, "The question at issue does not concern the words by which a view is expressed."[37] The objection is, nonetheless, perhaps not without grounds, since we find that the scriptures several times say that human beings are beyond reproach.[38] But we find no one who is said to be without sin except that one person alone of whom scripture clearly says, *Him who did not know sin* (2 Cor 5:21). And in the passage dealing with the holy priests, it says, *He has, in fact, experienced everything, just like us, apart from sin* (Heb 4:15), that is, in that flesh which was like sinful flesh, though it was not sinful flesh.[39] He would not bear this likeness if the other flesh of every human being were not sinful flesh. Now then, how are we to interpret the words, *All those who have been born of God do not sin and cannot sin, because his seed remains in them* (1 Jn 3:9)? After all, as if he were not born of God or as if he were speaking to those who were not born of God, the same apostle John clearly stated, *If we say that we have no sin, we deceive ourselves, and the truth is not in us* (1 Jn 1:8). In the books I wrote on this topic for Marcellinus, I was careful to explain this point as

---

36. Pelagius, *Nature.*
37. Ibid.
38. See Jb 1:8; Lk 1:6.
39. See Rom 8:3.

best I could.[40] That the words *cannot sin* were said in the sense that one ought not to sin[41] seems to me to be a claim of this man of which we should not disapprove. After all, who would be insane enough to say that sin should be committed, when something is a sin precisely because it should not be committed?

15, 16. But I certainly do not think that the words of the apostle James, *No human beings can tame their tongues* (Jas 3:8), should be interpreted as he wanted to explain them, "as if they were words of reproach, as much as to say, 'Can then no human beings tame their tongues?' It amounts then to a reprimand: 'You can tame wild animals; can you not tame your tongue?'"[42] I do not think that this is the meaning of that passage. After all, if James meant us to think that it was easy to tame our tongue, the rest of the passage would continue the comparison with animals. But it goes on, *It is a restless evil; it is full of deadly venom* (Jas 3:8), certainly more harmful than that of animals and snakes. For that venom kills the flesh, but this kills the soul. For *the mouth that lies kills the soul* (Wis 1:11). Therefore, Saint James did not make that statement in the sense that it was easier than taming animals, nor did he want it to be interpreted in that sense. Rather, he wanted to show that the human tongue is so great an evil that it cannot be tamed by any human being, though even wild animals are tamed by humans. Nor did he say this so that we would allow this evil to continue to dominate us because of our negligence, but so that we would beg the help of divine grace to tame the tongue. He did not say that no one can tame the tongue, but that no human beings can do so. Hence, when it is tamed, we would admit that this is done by God's mercy, by God's help, by God's grace. The soul should, then, try to tame the tongue and, while it tries, it should beg for help. Let the tongue pray that the tongue may be tamed by the gift of him who said to his own disciples, *It is not you who speak; rather, it is the Spirit of your Father who speaks in you* (Mt 10:20). Hence, the command reminds us to do something for which we should beg God's help, since, despite our trying, our own strength is not sufficient.

16, 17. James emphasized the great evil of the tongue, saying among other things, *These things should not be done, my brothers*

40. See *The Punishment and Forgiveness of Sins* II, 6, 9–8, 10.
41. Perhaps a citation from Pelagius' *Nature.*
42. Pelagius, *Nature.*

(Jas 3:10). Then he immediately pointed out, as soon as he finished what he was saying on that topic, the help by which we might avoid those things which he said should not be done. *Are there then any who are wise and disciplined among you? Let them display their action through their good manner of living in the gentleness of wisdom. But if you have bitter jealousy and quarrels in your hearts, do not be boastful and do not speak lies against the truth. Such wisdom does not come down from above; rather, it is earthly, animal, diabolical. For where there is jealousy and quarreling, there is disorder and every evil deed. But the wisdom that comes from above is, first of all, pure, then peaceful, modest, open to persuasion, full of mercy and good works, impartial, and without pretense.* (Jas 3:13-17) This is the wisdom that tames the tongue; it comes down from above and does not arise from the human heart. Or will someone dare to remove it too from God's grace and in pride and vanity locate it in the power of a human being? Why then do people pray that they may receive it, if having it depends upon them? Is someone going to oppose this prayer to avoid harm to free choice, because it is sufficient unto itself by its natural ability to observe all the commandments pertaining to righteousness? Let them oppose the apostle James himself, who warns with the words, *If any of you lack wisdom, let them ask it from God who gives to all abundantly without rebuking them, and it will be given to them, but let them ask with faith, without any hesitation* (Jas 1:5-6). This is the faith to which the commandments drive us so that the law commands and faith obtains what we ask. By the tongue, which no human being can tame, but the wisdom coming down from above can tame, *we all offend in many ways* (Jas 3:2). For this apostle did not state this in any other sense than his words, *No human beings can tame their tongues* (Jas 3:8).

17, 18. Nor should anyone raise the following text as an objection to them in order to show the impossibility of not sinning: *The wisdom of the flesh is an enemy of God, for it is not subject to the law and it cannot be. But those who are in the flesh cannot please God.* (Rom 8:7-8) The Apostle was speaking of the wisdom of the flesh, not the wisdom that comes down from above.[43] It is clear that he did not mean by those who are in the flesh people who had not yet left

---

43. See Jas 3:15.

the body, but those who lived according to the flesh.[44] But that is not the question with which we are dealing. What I am waiting to hear from him, if I can, is this: Do those who live according to the Spirit and are, for this reason, in a sense not in the flesh, even though they are still living here, live according to the Spirit by the grace of God? Or are they able to do this by themselves by the ability of nature and by their own will which they received when they were created? For the fulfillment of the law is nothing but love,[45] and *love is poured out in our hearts*, not by us, but *by the Holy Spirit who has been given to us* (Rom 5:5).

19. This fellow also discusses sins of ignorance and says that we should be on guard to avoid ignorance, and that ignorance is blameworthy, because through our negligence we do not know something that we should have known if we had taken care. Meanwhile, he argues every point rather than praying with the words, *Give me understanding, and I will learn your commandments* (Ps 119:73). After all, it is one thing not to care to know, and we see that such sins of negligence were expiated even by certain sacrifices of the law.[46] It is something quite different to want to understand, without being able to, and to act against the law by not understanding what it wants us to do. For this reason we are warned to ask for wisdom from God, *who gives to all abundantly* (Jas 1:5), at least to all those who ask as one should and as much as one should for something so important.

18, 20. He admits, nonetheless, that the sins we have committed must be wiped away by God and that we must pray to God over them, that is, in order to earn pardon, because that power of nature, which he has praised so much, and the will of a human being cannot, by his own admission, make undone what has been done.[47] Hence, one is left with this necessity of praying for pardon. But that one should pray so as to be helped not to sin—that is something he never said, something I have not found here. His silence on this point is utterly astounding, since the Lord's Prayer teaches that we should ask for both of these: that our debts be forgiven and that we not be led into temptation,[48] the former so that past sins be wiped away, the latter so

---

44. See Rom 8:12.
45. See Rom 13:10.
46. See Lv 4:2-3.
47. A less than literal citation from Pelagius' *Nature*.
48. See Mt 6:12-13.

that future sins be avoided. Although this does not happen without our willing it, the will alone is not enough to accomplish it. Hence, the prayer offered to the Lord for this purpose is neither superfluous nor shameless. After all, what is more foolish than to pray that you may do what lies in your power to do?

Against Pelagius' Doctrine that Human Nature Suffered No Weakening or Injury from Adam's Sin

19, 21. Consider now a point quite pertinent to our topic, namely, how he tries to portray human nature as if it were completely free of any defect and how, in opposition to perfectly clear passages of scripture, he takes delight in a wordy wisdom which does away with the cross of Christ.[49] It will, of course, not do away with the cross; rather, such wisdom will be overthrown. For, when we have explained this point, God's mercy will perhaps intervene so that even this man repents of having said these things. "First of all," he says, "we must debate the claim that nature is said to be weakened and changed by sin. For this reason, I think we must investigate before all else," he says, "what sin is. Is it a substance, or is it a word completely lacking substance which expresses not some thing, not an existence, not some body, but an act of wrongdoing?" Then he adds, "I believe that it is the latter. And if it is, how can that which lacks substance weaken or change human nature?"[50]

Consider, please, how in his ignorance he strives to destroy the highly salutary words of those scriptures meant for our healing: *I said, Lord, have mercy on me; heal my soul, for I have sinned against you* (Ps 41:5). What is there to heal, if nothing is wounded, nothing injured, nothing weakened and harmed? On the other hand, if there is something to heal, what harmed it? You hear the psalmist's admission; why do you desire someone to debate? He says, *Heal my soul.* Ask him what harmed that which he asked to be healed, and listen to what comes next: *for I have sinned against you.* Let this fellow question the psalmist; let him ask him what he thinks we should ask for. Let him say, "You who cry out, *Heal my soul, for I have sinned against you*, what is sin? A substance, or a word completely lacking

---

49. See 1 Cor 1:17.
50. Pelagius, *Nature.*

substance which expresses not a thing, not an existence, not some
body, but an act of wrongdoing?" The psalmist answers, "You are
right; sin is not some substance; rather, this word expresses an act of
wrongdoing." This fellow then objects, "Why then do you cry out,
Heal my soul, for I have sinned against you? How could what lacks
substance harm your soul?" Consumed with grief over his wound,
would that man not reply very briefly in order not to be distracted from
prayer by an argument, saying, "Leave me alone, please"? Would he
not say, "Rather debate, if you can, with him who says, *It is not those
who are in good health who need a physician, but those who are sick.
I came not to call the righteous, but sinners*" (Mt 9:12-13)? For in that
passage he referred to the righteous as those in good health and to the
sinners as those who are ill.

20, 22. Do you see where his argument is headed and what it is
after? Its aim is that we think that these words were uttered with
absolutely no point: *You shall call his name Jesus, for he will save
his people from their sins* (Mt 1:21). How will he save them if there is
no illness? The sins from which the gospel says the people of Christ
must be saved are, of course, not substances and cannot, in this man's
opinion, do any harm.

My brother, it is good to bear in mind that you are a Christian. To
believe these points would perhaps be enough, but you want to argue.
There is nothing against that; in fact, it can even be of benefit, if solid
faith comes first and we do not suppose that human nature cannot be
harmed by sin. Rather, believing the divine scriptures that it can be
harmed by sin, let us investigate how this could have happened. We
have already said that sin is not a substance. Is it not obvious—to
omit other examples—that not eating is also not a substance? One
abstains, of course, from a substance, since food is a substance. But
abstaining from food is not a substance. And yet, if one completely
abstains from food, the substance of the body wastes away; it is
destroyed by an imbalance in health, is drained of strength, and is
weakened and broken by exhaustion to the point that, even if one
somehow continues to live, he can scarcely be enticed back to food,
though by abstaining from it his health was injured. So too, sin is not
a substance, but God is a substance and the highest substance and
the only true food of a rational creature. Listen to what the creature
says, because it has withdrawn from this food by disobedience and is
unable to take, by reason of weakness, what it ought to have enjoyed,

My heart has been beaten and dried out like hay, because I have forgotten to eat my bread (Ps 102:5).

21, 23. Notice, however, how he continues to push himself into a corner with specious arguments against the truth of holy scripture. The Lord Jesus was called Jesus precisely because he saved his people from their sins, and the Lord Jesus stated, *It is not those who are in good health who need a physician, but those who are sick. I came not to call the righteous, but sinners.* For this reason the Apostle too says, *It is a reliable message worthy of complete acceptance that Christ Jesus came into the world to save sinners* (1 Tm 1:15). And against this reliable message worthy of complete acceptance, this fellow says that this illness ought not to have been contracted from sins; otherwise, this punishment of sin would lead to more sins being committed.[51]

We seek such a great physician to help even the little ones, and this fellow says, "What are you seeking? Those for whom you are seeking a physician are in good health. Even the first human being was not on this account condemned to death, for afterward he did not sin."[52] He says this, as if he later heard something concerning the perfection of his righteousness besides what the Church teaches, namely, that he too was set free by the mercy of Christ the Lord. This fellow says that Adam's descendants were also not only not weaker than he, but even observed many commandments, while he had neglected to observe one. He sees that Adam's descendants are born in a way in which Adam certainly was not created. For they are not only incapable of obeying a commandment which they cannot be aware of at all, but are barely capable of finding a breast when they are hungry. When he who saves his people from their sins wants to save these infants from their sins in the bosom of their mother, the Church, people oppose this and with their unhealthy words pronounce them to be in good health, as if they knew better than he how to examine the creature he made.

22, 24. He says that punishment is the source of sin, if the sinner was weakened to the point that he sinned more.[53] He does not consider how fitting it is that the light of the truth abandons the transgressor. Deprived of that light and therefore blind, he will necessarily

---

51. A less than literal citation from Pelagius' *Nature.*
52. Pelagius, *Nature.*
53. A less than literal citation from Pelagius' *Nature.*

stumble more, and in falling, he will be injured, and once injured, he will not get up. And so, for that reason alone he hears the word of the law by which he is admonished to implore the grace of the savior. Or is that no punishment for those people? The Apostle says of them, *Though they knew God, they did not glorify him as God or give thanks. Rather, they became vain in their thoughts. And their foolish heart was darkened.* (Rom 1:21) Certainly, this darkening of their heart was punishment and penalty, and yet through this penalty, that is, through the blindness of their heart, which is caused by the light of wisdom abandoning them, they fell into many serious sins. *Though they said they were wise, they become fools* (Rom 1:22). This penalty is severe, if one understands it. And see where they go as a result of this penalty. *They exchanged,* Paul says, *the glory of the incorruptible God for the likeness of the image of a corruptible human being and birds and animals and reptiles* (Rom 1:23). They did these things as the result of the penalty of sin by which *their foolish heart was darkened.* On account of these sins—for they were sins, though they were part of the penalty—he went on to say, *God handed them over to the desires of their heart, to impurity* (Rom 1:24). Observe how God punished them more severely in handing them over to the desires of their heart, to impurity. See what they do as a result of this punishment, he says, *so that among themselves they treat their own bodies shamefully* (Rom 1:24). And he teaches more clearly that this is the penalty of wickedness, though it is itself wickedness, when he says, *They transformed God's truth into a lie and worshiped and served a creature rather than the creator, who is blessed forever. Amen. For this reason*, he says, *God handed them over to shameful passions.* (Rom 1:25-26) See how many times God inflicts punishment, and from the same punishment many more serious sins arise. *For their women exchanged natural intercourse for that which is against nature. Likewise, the men too abandoned natural relations with women and burned with desire for one another, men committing perversities upon men.* (Rom 1:26-27) And to show that these are sins, though they are also penalties for sins, he added to these words, *They received in themselves the mutual recompense of their error, as they deserved* (Rom 1:27). See how often he punishes, and he punishes with the same punishment that brings forth and breeds sins. Notice further; he says, *And as they did not judge it good to bear God in their mind, God handed them over to an evil mind so that they*

would do what is improper, filled with every wickedness, with trick-
ery, malice, greed, full of envy, murder, strife, deceit, evil; grumblers,
slanderers, enemies of God, shameless, proud, puffed up, plotters of
evil, disobedient to their parents, foolish, disorderly, without love
and mercy (Rom 1:28-31). At this point let this fellow now say, "Sin
should not have been punished in such a way that the sinner commits
more sins by reason of the punishment."[54]

The Consequences of Adam's Sin

23, 25. He might perhaps reply that God does not force them to
these sins, but merely abandons persons who deserve to be abandoned. If he says this, he speaks the truth. They are bereft, as I said,
of the light of righteousness and, for this reason, have become darkness. What else are they going to bring forth but all these works of
darkness which I have mentioned, until someone says to them, if
only they would obey the command, *Get up, you sleeper, rise from*
the dead, and Christ will enlighten you (Eph 5:14)? The truth declares them dead; in the same sense another passage says, *Let the*
dead bury their dead (Mt 8:22; Lk 9:60). The truth, then, declares
those people dead whom this fellow claims cannot be injured and
harmed by sin, because he has, it seems, learned that sin is not a
substance. No one says that human beings were made so that they
could pass from righteousness to sin, but could not return from sin to
righteousness. But in order to pass to sin, the free choice by which
they harmed themselves is sufficient. To return to righteousness,
however, they need a physician because they are not well; they need
someone to bring them to life, because they are dead. This fellow
says nothing at all about grace, as if they could heal themselves by
their own wills alone, because they were able to harm themselves by
the will alone. We are not telling him that the death of the body leads
to sin, since it is merely punishment. After all, no one sins by dying
the death of the body. But death of the soul leads to sin, since its life,
that is, its God, abandons it, and it necessarily produces dead works
until the grace of Christ brings it back to life. Heaven forbid that
we should say that hunger and thirst and the other bodily afflictions
entail the necessity of sinning. The life of the righteous shines forth

---

54. Pelagius, *Nature*; see the beginning of 22, 24.

more gloriously when it is tried by such afflictions, and by overcoming them through patience it stores up for itself a greater glory. But it does so helped by the grace of God, helped by the Spirit of God, helped by the mercy of God, not raising itself up by its proud will, but earning strength by its humble confession. It knew, after all, how to say to God, *You are my patience* (Ps 71:5). I do not know why this fellow says nothing at all about this grace and help and mercy without which we cannot live a good life. In fact, he even speaks quite openly against the grace of Christ by which we are justified, when he defends nature as if it were sufficient unto itself for righteousness, if only the will is there. I have already explained as best I could, in those books to Marcellinus of blessed memory, why, even though bodily death came from sin, it still remains to test our faith, after the guilt of sin has been removed by grace.

24, 26. He says that the Lord was able to die, though he was without sin.[55] But that he was born also reveals the power of his mercy, not the condition of his nature. So too, he died by that power, and that is our price by which he redeemed us from death. And this is what the argument of these people strives to do away with, when they defend human nature in such a way that free choice has no need of this price in order to bring them from the power of darkness and of the prince of death into the kingdom of Christ. And yet when the Lord came to his Passion, he said, *Behold, the prince of this world will come, and he will find nothing in me* (Jn 14:30). He will certainly find no sin, on the basis of which the prince of death might exercise his right to kill him. *But in order that all may know*, he continues, *that I do the will of my Father, get up, let us leave this place* (Jn 14:31). That is, I do not die by reason of the necessity of sin, but by reason of the will to obey.

Further Arguments of Pelagius against the Woundedness of Human Nature

27. He says that no evil is the cause of any good.[56] He implies that punishment is something good. And yet, many have been corrected by it. There are, then, evils which, by the marvelous mercy of God, lead to good. Did the psalmist suffer something good when

---

55. A less than literal citation from Pelagius' *Nature*.
56. A less than literal citation from Pelagius' *Nature*.

he said, *You turned your face away from me, and I became confused* (Ps 30:8)? Certainly not! And yet this confusion was in some sense a remedy against his pride. He had, after all, said in his prosperity, *I will never be shaken* (Ps 30:7) and attributed to himself what he had from the Lord. For what did he have that he had not received?[57] Hence, he had to be shown the source of what he had so that he might receive in humility what he had lost through pride. Thus he says, *Lord, in your good will you have given strength to my glory* (Ps 30:8). And by reason of that strength I said amid my prosperity, *I will never be shaken*, though I had this from you, not from myself. Thereupon, *you turned your face away from me, and I became confused* (Ps 30:8).

25, 28. A proud heart[58] completely fails to grasp this, but the Lord is great, and he can convince one of this, as he himself knows how. For we are more inclined to look for answers to make to the objections raised against our error than to keep before our mind how salutary they are in keeping us from error. As a result, we should not so much carry on debates with these people as pray for them as we do for ourselves. After all, we do not say to them what this man said to himself as an objection: Sin was necessary so that there would be a reason for God's mercy.[59] How I wish that such misery did not exist so that this mercy would not be necessary![60] Rather, we say that the wickedness of sin was greater to the extent that human beings could more easily avoid sin, since they were as yet not prevented by any weakness. There followed a perfectly just punishment so that they received in themselves the fitting recompense for their sin, since to some extent they lost the obedience of their own bodies that had been placed under them. It was, after all, obedience under their Lord for which in particular they showed their contempt. And since we are now born with that law of sin which in our members resists the law of the mind,[61] we ought not to grumble against God or argue against an evident fact, but seek and implore his mercy with regard to our punishment.

---

57. See 1 Cor 4:7.
58. The CSEL edition has *amicus* (friend) on the basis of 72, 73, where Augustine refers to Pelagius as *huic amico nostro* (this friend of ours). Yet the majority of the manuscripts and the Maurists have *animus* (mind or heart). I have followed the BA and ALG editions which have given the preference to the Maurist reading. See also G. de Plinval in REA 11 (1965) 295.
59. A less than literal citation from Pelagius' *Nature*.
60. Augustine plays upon *miseria* (misery) and *misericordia* (mercy).
61. See Rom 7:23.

26, 29. Consider carefully the meaning of his words: "God shows his mercy on this side too, if it is ever necessary, for it is necessary to help human beings in this way after sin, not because God wanted the cause of this necessity."[62] Do you see how he does not say that the mercy of God is necessary so that we do not sin, but because we have sinned? Then he adds, "A physician ought to be prepared to cure someone already wounded, but he ought not to want someone in good health to be wounded."[63] If this comparison fits the matter under discussion, human nature, after all, cannot be wounded by sin, because sin is not a substance![64] Just as, for example, someone limping due to a wound is treated so that, once the past injury is healed, the person walks correctly in the future, so the heavenly physician heals our injuries not only so that they no longer exist, but so that we can thereafter walk correctly— something we could not do, even in good health, without his help. After all, when a human physician heals someone, he entrusts the person to God to be sustained thereafter by bodily elements and nourishment; in that way the person's health becomes strong by suitable help and continues. For God provides such things to persons living in the flesh, and those things which the physician employed in healing also come from God. A physician certainly does not heal anyone by means of things he has created, but from the riches of the one who creates everything necessary for those who are in good health and those who are sick. But God himself spiritually heals the sick and restores the dead to life, that is, justifies the sinner, through the mediator between God and human beings, the man Jesus Christ.[65] And he brings them to perfect health, that is, to perfect life and righteousness; unless they abandon him, he does not abandon them, so that they may always live piously and righteously. For, just as the eye of the body, even if fully healthy, cannot see unless it is helped by the brightness of light, so even if human beings have been fully justified, they cannot live correctly unless they are divinely helped by the eternal light of righteousness. God, then, heals us not only to destroy the sins we have committed, but also to provide us with the means of not sinning.

---

62. Pelagius, *Nature*.
63. Ibid.
64. This sentence, it seems to me, could well be taken as a continuation of Pelagius' statement, though I have followed the recent German, French and Italian translations, all of which treat it as Augustine's ironic comment on the preceding statement of Pelagius.
65. See 1 Tm 2:5.

27, 30. The author cleverly examines and turns this way and that the objection made to them; in his own opinion he refutes and rebuts this objection, namely, that, in order to remove the occasion of pride and boasting, it was necessary that human beings be unable to be without sin. He believes that it is utterly absurd and foolish that sin should exist in order that sin might not exist, since pride itself is also certainly a sin.[66] He says this as if it were not true that a boil is painful and that lancing it produces pain so that the pain is removed by pain. If we had not experienced this and heard of it in some areas where such things have never been done, we would undoubtedly use this man's words and say with mockery that it is completely absurd that pain was necessary in order that the pain of the boil might not exist.

31. "But God," these people say, "can heal everything."[67] He certainly acts with the aim of healing everything, but he acts according to his own judgment and does not take from the sick person the prescription for the cure. He undoubtedly wanted to make that man the strongest of apostles to whom he said, *Virtue is made perfect in weakness* (2 Cor 12:9), and despite his frequent prayers, he did not remove from him the thorn in his flesh— whatever that was. He says that it was given him, so that he would not become filled with pride amid the greatness of his revelations.[68] The other vices, after all, are found only in wrong actions, but pride must be avoided even in actions that are right. By it people are warned so that they do not boast and attribute God's gifts to their own power and perish in a worse manner than if they did nothing good. They are told, *With fear and trembling work out your own salvation; for it is God who produces in you the willing and the action in accord with good will* (Phil 2:12-13).[69] Why should we act with fear and trembling instead of with calm security, if God does this, unless it is on account of our will? Without it we cannot do what is right, and so the idea can easily enter the human mind that our good actions are ours alone. And thus we might say in the midst of prosperity, *I will never be shaken.* And so, he who in his good will gives strength to our glory turns his face

---

66. A less than literal citation from Pelagius' *Nature*.
67. Pelagius, *Nature*.
68. See 2 Cor 12:8.7.
69. Here Augustine seems clearly to understand the good will as God's, since he links Phil 2:13 with Ps 30:8.

slightly away so that the one who said this might become confused,[70] for this is the swelling that must be healed by pain.

28, 32. Hence, people are not told, "It is necessary to sin so that you do not sin." Rather, they are told, "God at times abandons you in the matter over which you are proud so that you may know that it does not come from you but from him and you may learn not to be proud." Consider what the words of the Apostle mean! Are they not so amazing that they would not[71] be credible if it were not for the fact that we dare not contradict the one who says them, because he speaks the truth? After all, who of the faithful does not know that the first enticement to sin came from Satan[72] and that he is the first author of all sins? And nonetheless certain persons are handed over to Satan so that they may learn not to blaspheme.[73] How then does the work of Satan exclude the work of Satan? Let him look at these passages and others like them so that he does not regard as overly paradoxical those passages which sound paradoxical, but which do not turn out to be such, once they have been examined. Why is it that he uses comparisons which actually present us with the replies we should make to him? "What more shall I say," he says, "but that one can believe that fires are put out by fires, if one can believe that sins are healed by sins?"[74] What difference does it make, if no one can put out fires with fires? But pains can, as I have shown, be healed by pains. Poisons too can, if one is willing to investigate and learn, be expelled by poisons. Moreover, if he also takes note that the heat of fevers is at times broken by the warmth of certain medicines, he will perhaps also grant that fires are put out by fires.

Not Every Sin Is a Sin of Pride

29, 33. "How," he asks, "are we going to distinguish pride itself from sin?"[75] Now, why does he press this point, since it is obvious that pride is itself a sin? He says, "As to sin is to be proud, so to be proud is to sin. Examine what any sin involves and see whether you

---

70. See Ps 30:8.
71. The editors of the CSEL edition omit the negative; following the BA and ALG editions and the majority of the older manuscripts, I have retained it.
72. See Gn 3:1-6.
73. See 1 Tm 1:20.
74. Pelagius, *Nature*.
75. Ibid.

find any sin that cannot be called pride."[76] But he follows up this idea and tries to prove it in this way: "Unless I am mistaken," he says, "every sin is contempt for God, and all contempt for God is pride. After all, what is so proud as to have contempt for God? Sin then is precisely pride, as scripture also says, *The beginning of all sin is pride*" (Sir 10:15). Let him investigate carefully, and he will find that the sin of pride was sharply distinguished in the law from other sins. Many sins are, after all, committed out of pride, but not every wrong action is done with pride. Many wrong actions are done by the ignorant, by the weak, and often by persons weeping and groaning. There is also a certain pride, which is itself a great sin and exists by itself without other sins. With swiftness and stealth, it quite often overtakes one, as I said, not in one's sins but in one's good actions. Though this man understood it in a different way, scripture said with perfect truth, *The beginning of all sin is pride*, for it cast down the devil with whom sin originated, and by his subsequent envy he brought down the man who stood in the place from which the devil had fallen. For that serpent certainly sought a doorway for pride by which he might enter, when he said, *You will be like gods* (Gn 3:5). For this reason scripture said, *The beginning of all sin is pride*, and *The beginning of pride in a person is to withdraw from God* (Sir 10:14).

30, 34. But what does he mean when he says, "Moreover, how could persons be responsible to God for the guilt of that sin which they do not recognize as their own? For it is not theirs," he says, "if it is necessary. Or, if it is theirs, then it is voluntary, and if it is voluntary, it can be avoided."[77] We reply: It is certainly theirs, but the injury that leads them to commit it has not been completely healed. Its increase has come from an abuse of their healthy state. Now, as a result of this injury, they are in poor shape and commit many sins either out of weakness or out of blindness. Hence, they should pray that they may be healed and live thereafter in continuous good health. They should not be filled with pride, as though human beings could be healed by the same power by which they are injured.

31, 35. I want to say this; I admit that I do not know God's higher judgment, the reason why he does not also immediately heal pride itself which lies in ambush for the human spirit, even in good actions.

---

76. Ibid.
77. Ibid.

For its healing, pious souls entreat him with tears and mighty groans to stretch forth his right hand to those who are trying to overcome it and in a sense to trample it under foot and destroy it. For at the moment a person rejoices to have also overcome pride in some good work, pride raises its head as a result of this joy and says, "See, I am still alive. Why are you triumphant? And I am alive precisely because you are triumphant." It is perhaps premature to take delight in triumphing over pride as if it were defeated, since its last shadow will, I believe, be blotted out by that noonday brightness of which scripture speaks. It says, *He will bring forth your righteousness like a light and your judgment like the noon* (Ps 37:6). It promises this noonday brightness, if one does what the psalm previously said, *Reveal to the Lord your way; hope in him, and he will do it* (Ps 37:5); it is not, as some suppose, that they themselves will do it. For the psalmist seems to have had in mind, when he said, *And he will do it*, precisely those who say, "It is we who do it," that is, it is we who make ourselves righteous. We too, of course, do something, but we do something along with God who also does it, because his mercy goes before us.[78] But it goes before so that we might be healed, because it also comes after so that, once we are healed, we might also grow strong. It goes before so that we might be called; it comes after so that we might be glorified. It goes before so that we might live in piety; it comes after so that we might live with him forever, since we can do nothing without him.[79] After all, scripture says both of these, *My God will go before me with his mercy* (Ps 59:11), and *Your mercy will come after me all the days of my life* (Ps 23:6). Let us, then, reveal to him our way[80] in confession rather than praise it in self-defense. For, if the way is not his, but ours, it is certainly not the right one. Let us reveal it by confessing, since it is not hidden from him, even if we try to hide it. However, *It is good to confess to the Lord* (Ps 92:2).

32, 36. Then he will give us what pleases him, if we too are displeased with what displeases him in us. As scripture says, he will turn our paths from his way,[81] and he will make his way ours, for to those who believe in him and hope in him it is granted that he will do it

78. See Ps 59:11.
79. See Jn 15:5.
80. See Ps 37:5.
81. See Ps 44:19.

himself.[82] This is, after all, the righteous way which they do not know *who have zeal for God, but not in accord with knowledge, and wanting to establish their own, they were not subject to the righteousness of God. For the end of the law is Christ for righteousness for everyone who believes.* (Rom 10:2-4) He said, *I am the way* (Jn 14:6). God's word fills with fear even those who walk in this way so that they do not become proud, as if they walked by their own powers. For this reason the Apostle says to them, *With fear and trembling work out your own salvation; for it is God who produces in you the willing and the action in accord with good will* (Phil 2:12-13). For this same reason the psalm also says to them, *Serve the Lord in fear, and rejoice with trembling. Learn discipline for fear that the Lord one day may become angry and you may perish from the righteous way, when his wrath suddenly blazes forth upon you.* (Ps 2:11-13)

It does not say, "*for fear that the Lord one day may become angry* and not show you the righteous way or not lead you to the righteous way." Rather, it meant to frighten those who were already walking on it, and so it said, *For fear that you may perish from the righteous way* (Ps 2:12). Why is that, if not that pride—as I have said so often and as it should often be said—must be avoided even in good actions, that is, in the righteous way? Otherwise, when people take credit for what comes from God, they lose what comes from God and wind up with what is their own. Hence, let us act in accord with what the psalm says at the end, *Blessed are all who trust in him* (Ps 2:13), who trust that he will do it. Let us trust that he will show his way, since we say to him, *Show us, Lord, your mercy* (Ps 85:8). Let us trust that he will give us good health so that we can walk, for we say to him, *Give us, Lord, your salvation* (Ps 85:8). Let us trust that he will lead us along the same way, for we say to him, *Lead me, Lord, along your way, and I will walk in your truth* (Ps 86:11). Let us trust that he will guide us to those promises to which the way leads, for we say to him, *Your hand will guide me, and your right hand lead me there* (Ps 139:10). Let us trust that he will feed those who recline there with Abraham, Isaac, and Jacob, since scripture said of him, *He will make them recline and will come and serve them* (Lk 12:37). After all, when we say such things, we do not take away the choice of the will, but we proclaim the grace of God. Who benefit from all these things, unless

82. See Ps 37:5.

they are willing? But they must be willing with humility and not raise themselves up with pride over the powers of the will, as if it alone were sufficient for the perfection of righteousness.

Pelagius Fields a Series of Objections to Sinlessness

33, 37. Heaven forbid that we should say to him what he says some have raised as an objection to him, namely, that human beings are placed on a par with God, if they are said to be without sin.[83] That would imply that an angel who is without sin is on a par with God. For my part I hold that, even when we shall have such great righteousness that absolutely no addition could be made to it, the creature will not be equal to the creator. But if some suppose that our progress will be so great that we will be changed into the divine substance and become exactly what he is, let them see how they may support their view. I confess that I myself am not convinced of it.

34, 38. Now I do, of course, side with the author of this book in his response to those people who say, "What you claim seems to be reasonable, but it is proud to say that human beings can be without sin." He replies that one should absolutely not say that it is proud, if it is true. For he says with both cleverness and truth, "On what side, then, are we to place humility? Certainly, on the side of falsity, if we agree that pride is on the side of truth."[84] And for this reason he holds, and he is correct to hold, that humility should rather be placed on the side of truth, not on the side of falsity. From this it follows that we should not have the least doubt that the apostle spoke the truth when he said, *If we say that we have no sin, we deceive ourselves, and the truth is not in us* (1 Jn 1:8). We should not think that he said something false out of humility. This was the reason he added, *And the truth is not in us*. It would probably have been sufficient to say, *We deceive ourselves*, if he had not seen that some might suppose that

---

83. Pelagius, *Nature*. Both the BA and the NBA editions give a reference to Jerome, Letter 133, 8, for this objection. If it was Pelagius' source, he has certainly given it a different spin. In arguing that God does not command what is impossible, Jerome says, "Did God command me to be what God is so that there would be nothing between me and the Lord, the creator …?" He clearly expected the answer: No, God did not command something impossible. Jerome goes on to add, "Scripture said of him as something proper to him: *He committed no sin, and no deception was found on his lips* (1 Pt 2:22). If I had this in common with Christ, what will he have as proper to him?" See Duval 262-263 for discussion of whether Pelagius cited Jerome's letter here.

84. Pelagius, *Nature*.

he said, *We deceive ourselves,* because people who praise themselves even for a true good are filled with pride. Therefore, by adding, *and the truth is not in us,* he clearly showed, as our author has decided in complete correctness, that it is not at all true, *if we say that we have no sin.* Otherwise, if humility were placed on the side of falsity, it should lose the reward of truth.

39. Moreover, though he thinks that he is pleading God's case in defending nature, he fails to notice that, in declaring this same nature healthy, he rejects the mercy of the physician. The God who is his creator is also his savior. Hence, we should not praise the creator so that we are forced to say, indeed so that we are found guilty of saying, that the savior is unnecessary. We should, then, honor human nature with the praises it deserves, and we should refer those praises to the glory of the creator. But we should be grateful that he created us in such a way that we are not ungrateful that he heals us. We should attribute our defects which he heals not to God's work but to the human will and his just punishment. As we admit that it was within our power that they not occur, so we should admit that it lies in his mercy rather than in own power that they be healed. Our author locates this mercy and healing help of the savior in this alone, "that he pardons sins committed in the past, not that he helps to avoid future ones."[85] Here he is under the influence of a very dangerous error. Here, though without realizing it, he holds us back from watching and praying so that we do not enter into temptation,[86] since he insists that it lies in our power alone that this does not happen to us.

35, 40. This man is correct on the following point. He says that the examples of certain persons who sinned, as we read in scripture, have not been recorded in order to make us despair of avoiding sin and to think that we may in some sense sin without a worry. Rather, they were recorded so that we might learn either to be humbly repentant or not to give up hope of salvation, even in the midst of such failures.[87] For certain people, who have fallen into sin, perish more by reason of despair; they not only neglect the remedy of penance but become the slaves of passions and wicked inclinations in order to carry out their shameful and sinful desires. They act as if they suffer a loss, if they fail to do what lust prompts them to do, since certain

---

85. Ibid.
86. See Mk 14:38.
87. A less than literal citation from Pelagius' *Nature.*

damnation already awaits them. Against this highly dangerous and deadly disease, it helps to recall the sins into which even holy and righteous people have fallen.

41. Our author seems to ask a clever question: How we are to believe those holy persons departed from this life? With sin or without sin? For, if one answers that they departed with sin, their damnation is supposed to follow, and that is wrong to believe. But if one says that they left this life without sin, one admits that some human beings were without sin in this life, at least at the approach of death. Here, though he is very clever, he does not sufficiently note that even the righteous pray, *Forgive us our debts, as we also forgive our debtors* (Mt 6:12), and that, when Christ the Lord taught and explained this prayer, he added, *For if you forgive others their sins, your Father will forgive you your sins* (Mt 6:14). We offer this daily prayer like spiritual incense before God on the altar of our heart, which we are taught to lift up to the Lord.[88] By means of it we are able to die without sin, even if we cannot live this life without sin, since pardon immediately wipes away the sins we repeatedly commit out of ignorance or weakness.

The Righteous Persons in Scripture Were Not Sinless

36, 42. Next our author mentions those "who, as scripture reports, not only did not sin, but lived righteously: Abel, Henoch, Melchizedek, Abraham, Isaac, Jacob, Joseph, Joshua the son of Nun, Phinehas, Samuel, Nathan, Elijah, Elisha, Micah, Daniel, Hananiah, Azariah, Mishael, Ezekiel, Mordecai, Simeon, Joseph, to whom the Virgin Mary was betrothed, and John." He also includes women: "Deborah, Anna the mother of Samuel, Judith, Esther, another Anna the daughter of Phanuel, Elizabeth, and also the mother of our Lord and savior. Piety demands, he says, that we admit that she was without sin."[89] Let us then leave aside the holy Virgin Mary; on account of the honor due to the Lord, I do not want to raise here any question about her when we are dealing with sins. After all, how do we know what wealth of grace was given to her in order to conquer sin completely, since she merited to conceive and bear the one who certainly had no sin? Apart then from this virgin, if we could gather together all

---

88. Augustine alludes to the introduction to the Preface at Mass, which already at his time included "Lift up your hearts" (*Sursum corda*).

89. Pelagius, *Nature.*

those holy men and women when they were living this life and could ask whether they were without sin, what are we to suppose that they would have answered? Would they answer what this fellow says or what the apostle John says? No matter how great was the excellence of their holiness when they lived in this body, if we could have asked them this question, they would have all cried out together, *If we say that we have no sin, we deceive ourselves, and the truth is not in us.* Would they give this answer out of humility rather than out of the truth? But he holds, and he is correct to hold, that one should not locate praise for humility on the side of falsity.[90] Hence, if they spoke the truth, they would have sin, and because they confessed this with humility, the truth would be in them. But if they lied about this, they would still have sin, because the truth would not be in them.

37, 43. "Some will perhaps say," this man remarks, "scripture could not recount the sins of all, could it?"[91] And those who say this speak the truth to them. I do not see that this man has made a valid response to this point, although I see that he did not want to remain silent. Please, notice what he said. He says, "This can be correctly said with regard to those of whom scripture records neither good nor bad actions. But with regard to those whose righteousness it recalls, it would also undoubtedly have recalled their sins, if it was aware that they sinned in any way."[92] Let him, then, claim that the great faith of those people had nothing to do with righteousness, who in large numbers accompanied the Lord's donkey; they cried out, *Hosanna, Son of David, blessed is he who comes in the name of the Lord* (Mt 21:9), even in the midst of those who were furious because they did this. Let him dare to say, if he can, that there was no one in that multitude who had any sin at all. But if it is absurd to say this, why did scripture not mention any of their sins, though it was careful to mention the great goodness of their faith?

44. Yet this fellow may have seen this himself and, therefore, went on to say, "Granted, in other times, because of the large number of people, scripture refrained from mentioning the sins of all. But right at the very beginning of the world, when there were only four human beings, how are we going to explain," he asks, "why scripture refused to mention the sins of everyone? Was it on account of the

---

90. See above 34, 38.
91. Pelagius, *Nature.*
92. Ibid.

very numerous population? It did not yet exist. Or was it because it remembered only those who had committed sins, but could not remember the one who had committed none."[93] He goes on to add more words to support this view more fully and clearly. "Certainly," he says, "in the first age scripture tells us of only four human beings: Adam and Eve and their sons, Cain and Abel. Eve sinned. Scripture tells us that. Adam also fell. The same scripture does not omit that fact. Moreover, scripture has likewise testified that Cain sinned. It not merely indicates the sins, but also the nature of these sins.[94] If Abel had sinned, scripture would certainly have said so, but it did not. Hence, he did not sin; indeed scripture even describes him as a righteous person. Let us then believe what we read, and let us believe that it is wrong to add what we do not read."[95]

38, 45. In saying this, he has not paid sufficient attention to the statement he had made a bit earlier that, once a great multitude of human beings were born, because of the large number of people, scripture could have refrained from recounting the sins of all.[96] For, if he had paid sufficient attention to this point, he would have seen that scripture could not mention the great crowd or multitude of venial sins even in a single human being. Or, if it could, it should not mention them. A limit had to be set for those sins which were recorded, and by a few examples the reader was to be instructed on many necessary points. For example, scripture declined to mention how many human beings there were at that time, even though they were few, or to give their names, that is, how many sons and daughters Adam and Eve brought forth and the names they gave them. Hence, some people, who fail to consider how many facts scripture passes over with no mention, have thought that Cain had intercourse with his mother and from her fathered the child which scripture mentioned.[97] They supposed that Adam's sons did not have sisters, because scripture did not mention them at that point, though later by way of summary it brings in what it had omitted, namely, that Adam had fathered sons and daughters,[98] though it does not give the time of their birth, their num-

---

93. Ibid.
94. See Gn 3:6; 4:8.
95. Pelagius, *Nature*.
96. See above 37, 44.
97. See Gn 4:17.
98. See Gn 5:4.

ber, or their names. Thus there was no need for scripture to mention
it, if Abel, though he was deservedly called righteous,[99] at some time
laughed or joked too much in a moment of relaxation or if he looked
upon something with desire or picked some fruit a bit intemperately
or slightly overindulged in food or if he thought of something else,
while he was praying, so that his attention was drawn to that other
topic. How often such things and many others like them must have
crept up on him! Or are they perhaps not sins, even though we are
warned in a general manner by the Apostle's commandment to avoid
them or refrain from them? He says, *Let sin, then, not reign in your
mortal body so that you obey its desires* (Rom 6:12). Certainly, we
have to wage a daily and constant battle so that we do not obey these
desires with regard to things which are wrong or less proper. For as
the result of this defect our eye turns or is allowed to turn where it
should not. If this defect grows strong and assumes control, it leads
to the commission of adultery even with the body. But adultery is
committed with greater quickness with the heart inasmuch as thought
is faster and permits no obstacle to delay it. Some have to a large
extent held in check this sin, that is, this inclination toward sinful
love, so that they do not obey its desires and do not offer to it their
members as the weapons of sin.[100] They too have merited to be called
righteous, and this is due to the help of God's grace. But because sin
often sneaks up upon people in slight matters and occasionally in
unforeseen ones, they were both righteous and yet not without sin.
Finally, if the love of God by which alone a righteous person is truly
righteous was present in the righteous Abel, it was still such that it
could and ought to grow, for whatever was lacking in it stemmed
from a defect. And whose love is not lacking, until one attains that
degree of love in which all human weakness is swallowed up?

*Pelagius Should Heed His Own Admonition
and Listen to the Scriptures*

39, 46. Our author concludes this passage with an obviously important idea, when he says, "Let us then believe what we read, and
let us believe that it is wrong to add what we do not read, and let it

---

99. See Mt 23:35; Heb 11:4.
100. See Rom 6:12-13.

suffice to have said this on all topics."[101] On the contrary, I say that we ought not to believe everything we read because of the Apostle's words, *Read everything; hold onto what is good* (1 Thes 5:21), and I also say that it is not wrong to add something which we do not read. After all, we can, as reliable witnesses, add something that we have experienced, even if we may not have read it. He may reply to this, "When I said this, I was speaking of the holy scriptures." How I wish that he would add nothing—I will not say: other than he reads in these writings, but contrary to what he reads there! Let him with faith and obedience listen to what scripture says, *Through one man sin entered the world, and through sin death, and thus it was passed on to all human beings in whom all have sinned* (Rom 5:12). Let him not weaken the grace of such a great physician by refusing to admit that human nature was corrupted! How I wish that, as a Christian, he would read that, apart from Jesus Christ, there is no name under heaven in which we can be saved[102] and that he would not defend the ability of human nature so that human beings believe that they can be saved through free choice even without that name.

40, 47. Perhaps he thinks that the name of Christ is needed so that we may learn through his gospel how we ought to live, but not so that we may also be helped by his grace to live a good life. On such grounds he should at least admit that there is a terrible darkness in the human mind that knows how to tame a lion, but does not know how it ought to live. Or does free choice and the natural law suffice for one to know this as well? This is the worldly wisdom that does away with the cross of Christ.[103] But the Apostle said, *I will destroy the wisdom of the wise* (1 Cor 1:19), because this cross cannot be done away with. This wisdom is, of course, overthrown by the foolishness of the preaching which brings salvation to those who believe.[104] After all, if one's natural ability through free choice is sufficient for knowing how one ought to live and for living a good life, *then Christ has died in vain* (Gal 2:21); *then the scandal of the cross has been done away with* (Gal 5:11). Why should I too not cry out? Indeed, I will cry out and scold these people because of the pain I feel as a Christian, *You have been removed from Christ; you who are justified* by nature *have fallen away from grace* (Gal 5:4). For

---

101. Pelagius, *Nature*; see also above 37, 44.
102. See Acts 4:12.
103. See 1 Cor 1:17.
104. See 1 Cor 1:21.

not knowing the righteousness of God and wanting to establish your own, you are not subject to the righteousness of God.[105] For, just as Christ is the end of the law, so he is the savior of corrupt human nature for righteousness for everyone who believes.[106]

41, 48. But why did he raise the objection for himself that his opponents say, "The Apostle obviously made the statement, *For all have sinned*, with regard to the people of that time, that is, about the Jews and the Gentiles."[107] But the statement I quoted, *Through one man sin entered the world, and through sin death, and thus it was passed on to all human beings in whom all have sinned*, clearly includes under that formula both persons of old and more recent ones, both us and those who will come after us. He also cites another text to prove that, when it says "all," it is not necessary to understand absolutely everyone with no exception. He says, "*Just as the sin of one led to condemnation of all human beings, so the righteousness of one led to the justification of life for all human beings* (Rom 5:18). But there is no doubt," he adds, "that Christ's righteousness did not sanctify all, but only those who were willing to obey him and were cleansed by the bath of his baptism."[108] He clearly does not prove what he wants by that text. For, as scripture said, *Just as the sin of one led to the condemnation of all human beings*, without omitting anyone, so in the words, *the righteousness of one led to the justification of life for all human beings*, no one is omitted. It does not mean that all believe in him and are washed by his baptism, but that no one is justified without believing in him and being washed by his baptism. It says, "all," then, so that we do not believe that anyone can be saved in some other way apart from him. For example, when there is a single teacher of literature appointed in a city, we correctly say, "This person teaches literature to everyone here." We do not mean that all the citizens learn literature, but that none learn it unless he teaches them. In the same way, none are justified unless Christ makes them righteous.

42, 49. "All right," he says, "I will agree that scripture testifies that all were sinners. After all, it states what people were, not that they could not be different. Hence, even if it could be proved that all human beings are sinners, that would present no problem for our

---

105. See Rom 10:3.
106. See Rom 10:4.
107. Pelagius, *Nature*.
108. Ibid.

thesis, since we are defending not so much what human beings are but what they can be."[109] Here he is right in finally agreeing that no living person will be found righteous in God's sight.[110] He maintains that the question does not concern that point, but the very possibility of not sinning, and there is no need for us to to oppose him on that point either. For I am not terribly concerned about whether in this life there were or are or can be some people who had or have or will have so perfect a love of God that nothing could be added to it. For that love is the truest, most complete, most perfect righteousness. For, since I admit and maintain that it is possible, if the human will is helped by God's grace, I do not need to argue too much about when or where or in whom it is realized. Nor am I opposed to the very possibility. For, once the human will has been healed and helped, the possibility emerges at the same time as the actuality in those who are holy, provided that *the love of God is poured out in our hearts by the Holy Spirit who has been given to us* (Rom 5:5) to the fullest extent that our nature, now healed and cleansed, can receive it. And so, one pleads God's case—the case which this fellow claims to plead in defending nature—better when one acknowledges both the creator and the savior than when one destroys the help of the savior by defending the creature, as if it were healthy and at full strength.

43, 50. His statement, however, is true that God, who is both good and righteous, made human beings such that they were able to be without the evil of sin, at least if they had wanted to be.[111] After all, who does not know that they were created healthy and innocent and endowed with free choice and the free ability to live righteously? But we are now dealing with that man whom robbers left half-dead on the road.[112] Injured and seriously wounded, he cannot rise up to the peak of righteousness as he was able to come down from there, and if he is already in the inn, he is still undergoing treatment. God, then, does not command what is impossible; rather, by his commandment, he warns you to do what you can and to ask for what you cannot. Let us now examine the reason why one has the ability and the reason why one does not. This man says, "Natural ability does not depend

109. Ibid.
110. See Ps 143:2.
111. A less than literal citation from Pelagius' *Nature.*
112. See Lk 10:30-34.

upon the will."[113] I say, "A human being certainly is not righteous as a result of the will, if one can be by nature, but one will be able to be as a result of medication what one cannot be because of one's injury."

44, 51. What need is there, then, to delay over many points? Let us come to the heart of the matter which in this question is the sole or almost the sole point of contention we have with these people. After all, he says that it is not relevant to the point under discussion that we ask whether there were or are some human beings in this life without sin, but whether there could be or can be.[114] And even if I agree that there have been or are such human beings, I still in no sense maintain that there have been or are such human beings unless they have been justified by *the grace of God through Jesus Christ, our Lord* (Rom 7:25), *and him crucified* (1 Cor 2:3). That faith, of course, healed the righteous people of old, and it now heals us, that is, faith in *the mediator between God and human beings, the man Jesus Christ,* faith in his blood, faith in his cross, faith in his death and resurrection. *Having, then, the same spirit of faith, we too believe, and for this reason we speak out* (2 Cor 4:13).

Pelagius' Basic Error That Every Christian Must Oppose: The Ability to Avoid Sin Is Inseparable from Our Nature

52. Let us pay attention to his response, when he raises for himself the issue on which the hearts of Christians find him truly intolerable. For he says, "But this is, you say, the point that upsets many people: you maintain that a human being can be free from sin without the grace of God."[115] This is, of course, the point that upsets many people; this is what we object to. He states the very point; this is what we endure with deepest displeasure. Because of the love we have for others and for these people, we do not tolerate the discussion of such things by Christians. Let us then listen to how he frees himself from the objection on this issue. He says, "O the blindness of ignorance! O the sluggishness of the uncultivated mind, that thinks that I defend without the grace of God what he hears must be attributed to God alone!"[116] If we did not know what follows, we would think, from

---

113. Pelagius, *Nature.*
114. A less than literal citation from Pelagius' *Nature.*
115. Pelagius, *Nature.*
116. Ibid.

hearing just these words, that we had believed false reports about these people. Rumor spreads them about, and certain of our brothers, who are suitable witnesses, have borne witness to them. After all, what could be said with greater brevity and greater truth than that the possibility of not sinning, to whatever extent it exists or will exist in human beings, ought to be attributed to God alone? We too say this; let us shake hands on it.

45, 53. Or must we listen to the other points? Clearly we must listen, and we must certainly correct or at least avoid them. He goes on, "For one says that this ability does not come from human choice, but from nature, from the author of nature, namely, from God. Is it, then, possible that what is regarded as properly pertaining to God can be understood to exist without God's grace?"[117] What he means already begins to be obvious, but he explains it more extensively and clearly so that we cannot be mistaken. He adds, "But to make this clearer, we must discuss it a little more at length. For we say that the ability for anything lies not so much in the power of human choice as in the necessity of nature."[118] He illustrates what he means by examples or comparisons. "For example," he says, "I can speak. That I can speak is not up to me. But that I do speak is up to me, that is, it is due to my own will. And since that I do speak is up to me, I can both speak and not speak. But since that I can speak is not up to me, that is, is not due to my choice and will, it is necessary that I always be able to speak. And even if I will not to be able to speak, I cannot be unable to speak, unless I should perhaps remove the member by which I can carry out the function of speaking."[119] We could, of course, mention many ways in which a person could, if one wanted to, remove the ability to speak, without removing the member by which we speak. For example, if something happens which destroys the voice itself, one could not speak, even though the members remain intact. For the voice is not a member of a human being, and this can, of course, happen if some inner organ is injured, though not removed. But I do not want to appear to put too much weight on a word and have someone stubbornly reply, "To injure is the same as to remove." We can achieve the same result if the mouth is closed and sealed by some clamps so that we cannot open it even slightly. Then, though it was in our power to close

117. Ibid.
118. Ibid.
119. Ibid.

it, it will not be in our power to open it, despite the fact that the members remain whole and healthy.

46, 54. But how does this concern us? Let us see what he makes of this point. He says, "Whatever is bound by natural necessity, after all, lacks the choice of the will and deliberation."[120] There is a problem here. For it is utterly absurd for us to claim that our willing to be happy does not pertain to the will, on the grounds that we absolutely cannot not will it, because of some constraint of nature, and a good constraint at that.[121] Nor do we dare to say that God does not have the will but the necessity to be righteous, on the grounds that he cannot will to sin.

47, 55. Notice also what comes next. He adds, "This same point can also be seen in the case of hearing, smell, or sight, since to hear or to smell or to see lies in our power, but to be able to hear or to smell or to see does not lie in our power, but in a natural necessity."[122] Either I do not understand what he is saying, or he doesn't. After all, how do we not have in our power the ability to see, if we have in our power the necessity of not seeing? For we have blindness in our power, and we can by it deprive ourselves of the ability to see, if we want. But how do we have it in our power to see, if we want, when we cannot see, if we want, either at night when the outdoor sources of light are not present or when someone locks us in a dark place, even though the nature of our bodily eyes is sound and unimpaired? So too, if our ability to hear or inability to hear lies not in our power but in the constraint of nature, while that we do hear or do not hear lies in our own will, why does he not notice how many things we hear against our will? Many sounds penetrate our awareness, even when our ears are plugged, such as the nearby screeching of a saw or the squealing of pigs? The plugging of our ears shows that it is not in our power not to hear when our ears are open, and yet a plugging of our ears that destroys our sense itself also proves that not being able to hear is also in our power. As for what he says about smell, he pays insufficient attention to his statement that the ability to smell or the inability to smell is not in our power, but it is in our power, that is, in our free will, to smell or not to smell.[123]

---

120. Ibid.
121. The editors of the ALG edition place a major punctuation here, though the CSEL editors link this sentence with the following.
122. Pelagius, *Nature.*
123. A less than literal citation from Pelagius' *Nature.*

Suppose that we were placed in the midst of strong and foul odors and that someone put us there with our hands tied, though our members were whole and healthy; we would want not to smell those odors, but would be unable not to. For, when we are forced to take a breath, we at the same time draw in the odor that we do not want.

Pelagius Presupposes that Our Nature Has Suffered No Injury

48, 56. Just as these comparisons are false, so the point for which he wanted to use them is also false. For he goes on to say, "In a like manner, then, with regard to the possibility of not sinning, we must understand that not sinning is up to us, but that the ability not to sin is not up to us."[124] Even if he were speaking about a whole and healthy human nature, he would not be correct. But that is not the sort of nature we have at present, *For we are saved in hope, but a hope for what is seen is not hope. But if we hope for what we do not see, we look forward to it with patience.* (Rom 8:24.25) He would not be correct in saying that not sinning depends only upon us, even though sinning would depend upon us. For even then there would be God's help, and it would offer[125] itself to those who want it, like a light to help healthy eyes to see. But we are discussing the present life in which *the body which is being corrupted weighs down the soul, and the earthly dwelling presses down the mind that thinks many thoughts* (Wis 9:15). And so I am astonished at the disposition of his heart that allows him to think that not sinning is up to us, even without the help of the medicine of our savior, and to maintain that the ability not to sin comes from our nature. And yet it is so obvious that our nature has been corrupted that the failure to see this is a mark of a still greater corruption.

49, 57. "Because not sinning is up to us," he says, "we can both sin and not sin."[126] What will he say if someone else says, "Because not willing unhappiness is up to us, we can both will it and not will it?" And yet we absolutely cannot will it. After all, who could in any sense will to be unhappy, even if one wills something else that leads to one's unhappiness against one's will. Moreover, since not

---

124. Pelagius, *Nature.*
125. The CSEL edition has *praebere* which the ALG editors has changed to *praeberet*; see de Plinval, REA XI (1965) 292.
126. Pelagius, *Nature.*

sinning lies in God's power far more than in ours, are we going to dare to say that he can both sin and not sin? Heaven forbid that we should say that God can sin! It is not true, after all, that he will not be omnipotent, as some foolish people suppose, because he cannot die and *cannot deny himself* (2 Tm 2:13). What, then, is it that he is saying, and by what rules of logic is he trying to convince us of what he refuses to consider with care? He goes on to say, "But since the ability not to sin does not come from us, even if we will not to be able not to sin, we cannot fail to have the ability not to sin."[127] He stated this in a convoluted manner and, for that reason, it is somewhat obscure. But it could be stated more clearly as follows: "Because the ability not to sin does not come from us, we have the ability not to sin, whether we will to or not." For he does not say, "We do not sin, whether we will to or not." For we undoubtedly do sin, if we will to. Nonetheless, he maintains that, whether we will it or not, we have the ability not to sin, and he says this is implanted in our nature. But one can without any problem say of human beings with healthy feet: whether they will to or not, they have the ability to walk. But if their feet are broken, they do not have that ability, even if they will to walk. That nature has been injured of which scripture says, *Why are earth and ashes filled with pride?* (Sir 10:9) It has been injured; it begs the physician; it cries out, *Save me, Lord* (Ps 12:2); it cries out, *Heal my soul* (Ps 41:5). Why does he cut off these cries so that, in defending the allegedly present ability, he prevents future good health?

50, 58. See what he adds to this as what he takes to be a confirmation of it. He says, "For no will can remove something that is proved to be inseparably implanted in nature."[128] What is the reason, then, for that cry, *So that you do not do those things which you will* (Gal 5:17)? What is the reason for this one as well, *For I do not do the good that I want, but I do the evil that I hate* (Rom 7:19)? Where is the ability that is found to be inseparably implanted in nature? You see, human beings do not do the things that they want. And the Apostle was talking about not sinning, not about flying, since they were human beings, not birds. You see, human beings do not do the good that they want, but they do the evil that they do not want. Willing the good is in their power, but doing it is not.[129] Where is the ability that is found

127. Ibid.
128. Ibid.
129. See Rom 7:18.

to be inseparably implanted in nature? For in whosesever's name the Apostle is speaking, if he is not saying these things about himself, he is certainly speaking in the name of a human being.[130] But this man maintains that human nature itself has the inseparable ability not to sin. This is expressed with these words by one who speaks without knowledge, but it is not expressed without the knowledge of the one who suggests these statements to people who are not on guard, though they fear God. And thus the grace of Christ is done away with, as though human nature sufficed for its own righteousness.

For Pelagius Grace Amounts to the Nature Given by the Creator

51, 59. He wants to avoid the hostility of Christians who cry out on behalf of their salvation and say, "Why do you say that human beings are able not to sin without the help of God's grace?" And so he says, "The ability not to sin lies not so much in the power of choice as in the necessity of nature. Whatever lies in the necessity of nature undoubtedly pertains to the author of nature, namely, God. How, then, can one suppose," he asks, "that what is shown to pertain to God as his very own is said to exist apart from God's grace?"[131] The idea which was hidden has been expressed; there is no way that it can be concealed. He has attributed the ability not to sin to God's grace, precisely because God is the author of the nature in which he claims that the ability not to sin is inseparably implanted. When human beings will to, they do the action;[132] because they do not will it, they do not do it. After all, if they have an inseparable ability, they cannot have a weakness of will, or rather the presence of the will along with the lack of its accomplishment. If, then, that is the case, why do we have the words, *I can will the good, but I cannot do it* (Rom 7:18). For if the author of this book was speaking of that human nature which was in the beginning created innocent and healthy, his statement would be in some sense acceptable. And yet that nature should not have been said to have an inseparable ability, that is, one that cannot be lost. After all, it could be injured and need to seek a physician who would heal its eyes and restore its ability to see which

---

130. See 2 Cor 11:13-15.
131. Pelagius, *Nature.*
132. I follow Migne and the text in BA rather than CSEL which has *faciat* instead of *facit.*

was lost through blindness. For I think that a blind person wants to see but cannot. But if one wants to and cannot, the will is present, but the ability has been lost.

52, 60. Also look at the obstacles which he tries to overcome, if he can, to advance his idea. For he raises an objection to himself with these words, "But you must admit that the flesh is opposed to us, as the Apostle says."[133] Then he asks, "How is it possible that the flesh is opposed to anyone who has been baptized, since, following the same Apostle, we understand that such a person is not in the flesh? After all, he says, *But you are not in the flesh* (Rom 8:9)."[134] Well, then, he says that the flesh cannot be opposed to those who have been baptized; later we will see whether this is true. But now, since he could not completely forget that he is a Christian, but remembered it, though only slightly, he pulled back from his defense of nature. Where, then, is this inseparable ability? Are those who are not yet baptized not included in human nature? It is on this point, right on this point, that he could have been alert and, if he pays attention, he still can be. He says, "How is it possible that the flesh is opposed to anyone who has been baptized?"[135] The flesh can, then, be opposed to those who have not been baptized. Let him explain how this is possible, since these people also have that nature he has defended so much. He surely grants that at least in them nature was injured, if that wounded man, now among the baptized, emerged from the inn in good health or is in good health in the inn where the merciful Samaritan brought him to be cared for.[136] Now, if he grants that the flesh is opposed at least to these, let him state what has happened. After all, each of them, that is, both the flesh and the spirit, is the creation of one and the same creator, and undoubtedly good, because he is good. It must be that this is an injury which was inflicted by their own will. And precisely so that this injury in their nature might be healed, there is need of the savior who, as its creator, established the nature. If we admit that the small and the great, that is, wailing infants and old grey heads, need this savior and that medicine of his, namely, that the Word be-

---

133. See Gal 5:17.
134. Pelagius, *Nature.*
135. Ibid.
136. See Lk 10:30-35.

come flesh in order to dwell among us,[137] the entire question under dispute between us has been resolved.

Paul Saw the Opposition of the Flesh Even in the Baptized

53, 61. Let us now see whether scripture says that the flesh is opposed to the baptized as well. Where and to whom did the Apostle speak these words? *The flesh lusts against the spirit, and the spirit against the flesh, for these are opposed to each other so that you do not do those things which you will* (Gal 5:17). He wrote them to the Galatians, I believe, the same people to whom he said, *Did he who gave you the Spirit and worked miracles among you do this because of the works of the law or because of the acceptance of the faith?* (Gal 3:5) From these passages it is clear that he is speaking to Christians and to people to whom God has given the Spirit; he is speaking, then, to those who have been baptized. See, we have discovered that the flesh is opposed even to the baptized and they do not have that ability which he says is inseparably implanted in nature. What has happened to his question, "How is it possible that the flesh is opposed to anyone who has been baptized?"[138] The term "flesh" in this passage, in fact, refers not to the nature of the flesh, which is good, but to its defects. But no matter how he might understand "flesh," notice that the flesh is, nonetheless, opposed even to the baptized. How is it opposed? So that they do not do what they will. See, the will is present in a person; where is that ability of nature? Let us admit that grace is necessary; let us cry out, *Wretched man that I am! Who will set me free from the body of this death?* And our answer is: *The grace of God through Jesus Christ, our Lord.* (Rom 7:24-25)

62. After all, when one asks these people, as it is perfectly correct to do, "Why do you claim that apart from the help of God's grace a human being can be without sin?" the question does not have to do with the grace by which human beings were created, but with the grace by which they are saved through Jesus Christ, our Lord. Moreover, in prayer the faithful say, *Bring us not into temptation, but deliver us from evil* (Mt 6:13). If they have the ability, why do they make this prayer? Or from what evil do they ask to be set free if not especially

---

137. See Jn 1:14.
138. Pelagius, *Natura*; see above 52, 60.

from the body of this death, from which they are set free only by *the grace of God through Jesus Christ, our Lord*. They do not ask to be set free from the substance of the flesh which is good, but from the defects of the flesh from which human beings are not set free without the grace of the savior, not even when they leave the body through the body's death. In order to make this point, what did the Apostle previously say? *I see another law in my members that resists the law of my mind and holds me captive in the law of sin which lies in my members* (Rom 7:23). See the injury which the will's disobedience has inflicted upon human nature. Let him pray to be healed! Why does he expect so much from the ability of nature? It is wounded, injured, beaten, ruined; it is in need of a true confession, not of a false defense. Let it ask, then, for the grace of God, not that by which it is created, but that by which it is restored. This grace alone is what this man declares unnecessary when he does not mention it. If he said nothing at all about God's grace and if, in order to avoid hostility toward himself on this point, he did not bring up and try to solve this question, one could have thought that he held the truth, but did not state it. After all, one does not have to say everything all the time. But he brought up the question about grace, and he answered with what he had in his heart. The question has been clarified; it was not a question of our choosing, but one in which we were in doubt about what he held.

54, 63. Next he tries to show by many citations from the Apostle a point about which there is no dispute, namely, that he calls the flesh by that name with the intention that we understand not the substance, but the works of the flesh.[139] How is this relevant? The injuries of the flesh are opposed to the human will. It is not nature that is accused; rather, a physician is sought for its injuries. Why does he ask, "Who made for human beings their spirit?" And he answers, "It was certainly God." So too, he asks, "Who created the flesh?" Again he answers, "The same God, I believe." Thirdly, he asks, "Is the God who created both of them good?" He answers, "No one doubts this." Again he asks, "Is each of those things which God created good?" To this he answers, "We must admit this." Finally, he concludes, "If then both the spirit is good and the flesh is good, since they were created by the good creator, how is it possible that two good things be opposed to each other?"[140]

---

139. A less than literal citation from Pelagius' *Nature*.
140. Pelagius, *Nature*.

I am not going to mention the fact that this whole argument would be destroyed if someone asked him, "Who created heat and cold?" He would undoubtedly answer, "God." I am not going to ask many questions. He can himself decide whether these elements can be said not to be good or whether they are not clearly opposed to each other. He might say, "These are qualities of substances, not substances." So they are; that is true. But they are natural qualities, and they undoubtedly belong to God's creation. In any case, substances are said to be opposed to one another, not by reason of themselves, but by reason of their qualities. What if flesh and spirit are like that? We are not claiming that they are; rather, we said this to show that his argument did not arrive at its conclusion by a necessary inference. After all, there can also be opposing elements that struggle against one another, but are balanced by each other and produce good health. For example, bodily health consists in the balancing of dryness and moistness, cold and warmth in the body. But the fact that the flesh is opposed to the spirit so that we do not do what we want is a defect, not nature. Let us ask for healing grace, and let us bring the dispute to an end.

64. How then can these two goods created by the good God be opposed to each other in those who have not been baptized, contrary to this man's argument? Or is he also going to regret having made that statement he uttered with a touch of Christian faith? After all, when he said, "How is it possible that the flesh is opposed to anyone who has already been baptized?"[141] he implied that the flesh can be opposed to those who have not been baptized. For why did he add, "who has already been baptized," when he could have said, without that addition, "How is it possible that the flesh is opposed to anyone?" And he could have used that argument of his to prove this point, for each of them is a good created by the good God and, therefore, they cannot be opposed to each other. If the unbaptized, then, to whom he certainly admits the flesh is opposed, press him with his questions and ask, "Who made the human spirit?" he will answer, "God." Likewise, they will ask, "Who created the flesh?" And he will answer, "The same God, I believe." Thirdly, they will ask, "Is the God who created them both good?" And he will reply, "No one doubts this." And they will ask him the remaining question, "And are

141. See above 54, 63.

both of these things which the good creator made good?" And he will admit that they are. Then they will slay him with his own sword by drawing his conclusion and saying, "If then the spirit is good and the flesh is good inasmuch as they were created by the good creator, how is it possible that two good elements can be opposed to each other?" At this point he may answer, "Pardon me; I should not have said that the flesh cannot be opposed to anyone who has been baptized so that I implied that it is opposed in this way to you who have not been baptized. I should, rather, have said that the flesh is opposed to no one without any exception." See what a corner he has got himself into. See what this man says who does not want to cry out with the Apostle, *Who will set me free from the body of this death? The grace of God through Jesus Christ, our Lord.* "But why," he asks, "should I cry out in this way, since I have already been baptized in Christ? Let those cry out like that who have not yet received this benefit. It is the words of those people which the Apostle makes his own, if they do in fact say such a thing."[142] But this defense of nature does not allow even those people to utter this cry. After all, it is not true that nature is found in the baptized but is not found in the unbaptized. Or if one grants that nature is injured at least in the unbaptized so that they cry out, *Wretched man that I am! Who will set me free from the body of this death?* and that they find help in the next verse, *The grace of God through Jesus Christ, our Lord,* one should at long last grant that human nature needs Christ as a physician.

55, 65. I ask, however, where nature lost this freedom which it longs to receive when it says, *Who will set me free?* After all, the Apostle does not blame the substance of the flesh, when he says that he desires to be set free *from the body of this death,* since the nature of the body as well as that of the soul should be attributed to God, the good creator. Rather, he is surely speaking about the body's defects. For the death of the body separates one from the body, but there cling to one the defects contracted from it. To them the just punishment is due, as that rich man found out in hell.[143] From this punishment the man who said, *Who will set me free from the body of this death?* could, of course, not set himself free. But wherever he may have lost

---

142. The translators of the ALG edition regard this as a citation from Pelagius' *Nature.* I take it rather as words Augustine put in the mouth of Pelagius like the previous sentences in quotation marks which are introduced with: "At this point he may (*forte*) answer."
143. See Lk 16:22-26.

this freedom, that ability of nature is certainly inseparable; he has the ability as a natural help; he has the will from free choice. Why does he seek the sacrament of baptism? Is it on account of sins committed in the past so that only those sins are forgiven whose occurrence cannot be undone? Leave the man alone; let him cry out what the Apostle was crying out. For he does not desire merely that through forgiveness he may not be punished for past sins, but also that he may be strong and robust so as not to sin in the future. After all, he finds delight in the law of God in the interior human being, but he sees another law in his members resisting the law of his mind. He sees that it is so; he is not recalling that it had been the case. He is under pressure at the present; he is not recalling the past. He sees that it is not merely resisting him, but holding him captive to the law of sin.[144] That law is now in his members; it is not merely something in the past. This is the reason that he cries out, *Wretched man that I am! Who will set me free from the body of this death?* Allow him to pray; allow him to demand the help of a most powerful physician. Why oppose him? Why shout him down? Why prevent the wretch from seeking the mercy of Christ? At least, why should Christians do this? There were, after all, companions of Christ who tried to prevent the blind man from crying out and begging to see the light, but even amid the uproar of those who were stopping him, Christ heard his cry.[145] Hence, this Apostle heard the answer, *The grace of God through Jesus Christ, our Lord.*

66. If we get these people to grant that those who have not yet been baptized should implore the help of the grace of the savior, this is no small victory against that false defense of nature and the power of free choice, on the grounds that they are self-sufficient. After all, he was not self-sufficient who said, *Wretched man that I am! Who will set me free from the body of this death?* Or are we to say that one has full freedom while still begging to be set free?

56. Nonetheless, let us also see whether those who have been baptized do the good actions they will to do without any opposition from the concupiscence of the flesh. This fellow reminds us what we should say on this point where he brings this passage to a conclusion. He states, "As we have said, we should understand the passage containing *The flesh lusts against the spirit* not with reference to the

---

144. See Rom 7:23.
145. See Mk 10:47-49.

substance of the flesh, but with reference to its works."[146] We too say that the passage refers not to the substance of the flesh but to its works, which arise from concupiscence of the flesh, namely, from the sin about which the Apostle commands that it not reign in our mortal body so that we obey its desires.[147]

57, 67. But this fellow should also note that scripture said to those who had already been baptized, *The flesh lusts against the spirit, and the spirit against the flesh, so that you do not do those things which you will.* And so that he does not make us give up the fight and is not thought to open the door to sinning through this statement, he adds, *But if you are led by the Spirit, you are no longer under the law* (Gal 5:18). After all, they are under the law who see that they hold back from sinful actions out of a fear of the punishment which the law threatens, not out of a love of righteousness. Such persons are not yet free from nor strangers to the will to sin. They are blameworthy by the very will by which they would prefer, if it were possible, that there would not be what they fear so that they could freely do what they secretly desire. Hence, he says, *If you are led by the Spirit, you are no longer under the law*, that is, under the law which strikes fear, not that which bestows love. For *the love of God is poured out in our hearts*, not by the letter of the law, but *by the Holy Spirit who has been given to us* (Rom 5:5). This is the law of freedom, not of servitude, because it is the law of love, not of fear. Of it the apostle James said, *One who looks into the perfect law of freedom* (Jas 1:25). Hence, the apostle Paul is not now terrified by the law of God like a slave, but finds delight in it in the interior human being.[148] Nonetheless, he sees another law in his members resisting the law of his mind.[149] So too, he says, *But if you are led by the Spirit, you are no longer under the law.* Insofar as one is led by the Spirit, one is not under the law, because insofar as one finds delight in the law of God, one is not under fear of the law, because fear produces pain, not delight.

58, 68. Hence, if we are thinking correctly, just as we ought to give thanks for the healing our members have received, we ought to pray for the future healing of our members so that we may enjoy an absolute good health to which nothing can be added, the perfect sweetness

146. Pelagius, *Nature.*
147. See Rom 6:12.
148. See Rom 7:22.
149. See Rom 7:23.

of God, and complete freedom. After all, we do not deny that human
nature can be without sin, nor ought we in any sense to deny that it
can be made perfect, as we do not deny that it is making progress,
provided it is by *the grace of God through Jesus Christ, our Lord.*
We say that it is being justified and blessed by the help of him who
created it so that it exists. It is easy, then, to refute the statement this
fellow claims some people raise as an objection to him, "The devil is
our adversary."[150] We, of course, answer this objection with the same
words which he uses, "Let us resist him, and he will flee. The blessed
apostle says, *Resist the devil, and he will flee from you* (Jas 4:7). Here
we should mark well the sort of harm he can do to people from whom
he flees, and we should understand the amount of power he has who
can prevail only against those who do not resist."[151] These are my
words as well; it cannot be stated more correctly.

But there is this difference between these people and us. We
not merely do not deny, but even proclaim that we should demand
God's help, even when we resist the devil. These people, however,
attribute such power to the will that they remove prayer from a life
of piety. For, precisely in order that we may resist the devil and that
he may flee from us, we say in prayer, *Bring us not into temptation.*
Precisely for this reason we have been warned, like soldiers, by our
commander who exhorts us with the words, *Watch and pray so that
you do not enter into temptation* (Mk 14:38).

59, 69. He makes a point in arguing against those who say, "And
who would not want to be without sin, if this lay in the power of
a human being?" He argues correctly that they admit that it is not
impossible by the very fact that many or all people want this.[152] If he
would also admit what makes this possible, there would be peace. It is,
after all, *the grace of God through Jesus Christ, our Lord*; this fellow
never wanted to admit that we are helped by it, when we pray that we
may not sin. If he perhaps holds this in secret, he must pardon us for
suspecting otherwise. For he is the one responsible for the fact that,
though he meets with so much hostility over this question, he chooses
to hold this view, but refuses openly to admit or profess it. Why was
it so difficult for him to say this, especially since he undertook to discuss and explain this point as an objection raised against him by some

150. Pelagius, *Nature.*
151. Ibid.
152. A less than literal citation from Pelagius' *Nature.*

opponents? Why did he want at that point to defend nature alone? He claimed that human beings were created so that they were able not to sin, if they did not will to sin. He declared that, by the very fact that they were created in that way, this ability pertained to the grace of God, that is, the ability by which they do not sin, if they do not will to. But he was unwilling to say anything about the fact that nature itself is either healed, because it was injured, or helped, because it is not self-sufficient, by *the grace of God through Jesus Christ, our Lord?*

Augustine Is Willing to Admit the Fact of Sinlessness, Provided the Grace of God Is Not Denied

60, 70. After all, whether there has been or is or can be someone who lives so righteously in this world that he has no sin at all is a legitimate question among true and pious Christians. Anyone who doubts that people can be such after this life is certainly foolish. But I do not want to argue even about this life. I do not think that the passage, *No living person will be found righteous in your sight* (Ps 143:2), and others of the sort, should be interpreted in any other sense. Yet I wish that one could show that these passages can be better interpreted in another sense or that perfect and complete righteousness, to which no addition whatsoever can be made, was found in some persons in the past, while they lived in this body, or that it is present there now or will be in the future. There are, in any case, many more persons who have no doubt that it is necessary for them to say in all truth right up to the last day of this life, *Forgive us our debts, as we also forgive our debtors,* while they trust that their hope in Christ and his promises is true, certain, and solid. But if someone claims that any can attain to complete perfection or that anyone can make some progress in true and godly righteousness in any other way than by the help of the grace of the savior, Christ crucified, and by the gift of his Spirit, I do not know whether such a person can correctly be counted among Christians of any sort whatever.

Arguments Drawn from Various Christian Writers: From Lactantius

61, 71. For this reason the passages he cited are neutral, neither against our view nor against his. He cited them not from the canonical scriptures but from some writings of Catholic commentators, in order to answer those who said that he was the only one who held these views. He chose also to include some statements from my books among these, with the idea that I was also someone who seemed worthy of being mentioned with them. Hence, I ought not to be ungrateful, and out of a feeling of friendship I do not want the man who paid me this honor to be in error.

I did not find there the name of the author of the first passage he cited, either because he did not mention it or because the manuscript which you sent me lacked it due to some faultiness. Hence, why should we discuss it, especially since I am not bound by the writings of any mere human beings? For I owe assent without any reserve only to the canonical scriptures. But something bothers me in what he quoted from the writings of that man whose name I did not find. He stated, "The master and teacher of virtue had to become so like human beings that, by conquering sin, he might teach human beings to conquer sin."[153] The author of this opinion should consider how he might explain the sense of that statement, for we have absolutely no doubt that Christ had in himself no sin to conquer.[154] He was born in the likeness of sinful flesh,[155] not in sinful flesh.

Our author cited another passage from the same man, "Again 'that by overcoming the desires of the flesh he might teach that sinning does not stem from necessity, but from choice and will.'"[156] Provided that the desires mentioned here are not those of illicit concupiscences, I accept the desires of the flesh, such as hunger, thirst, the need for rest when tired, and things like that. For, even though they are not blameworthy, some people fall into sins through these desires. This was not the case with the savior, although we see, according to the testimony of the gospel, that these desires were found in him because of the likeness of sinful flesh.

From Hilary of Poitiers

62, 72. He cited the following words from blessed Hilary, "For only when we have been made perfect in the Spirit and transformed by

153. Firmianus Lactantius, *The Divine Institutes* IV, 24.
154. See 2 Cor 5:21.
155. See Rom 8:3.
156. Firmianus Lactantius, *The Divine Institutes* IV, 25.

immortality will we see what is immortal in God, something which is prepared for the clean of heart alone."[157] I do not see how what he said is in opposition to what we said or how it helps this fellow, except that it bears witness that there can be a human being with a clean heart. But who is going to deny that point, provided that it is brought about by *the grace of God through Jesus Christ, our Lord* and not by the freedom of choice alone? So too, he mentions that Hilary asked, "What books had Job read that he refrained from everything evil?[158] For he reveres God with the mind alone that is free from vices, but to worship God is the proper function of righteousness."[159] Hilary mentions what Job did; he does not say that he attained perfection in this world or that he acted well or attained perfection without the grace of the savior whom he foretold. After all, even persons who have sin but do not allow it to reign over them refrain from everything evil, and if a bad thought takes them by surprise, they do not allow it to lead to action. In any case, it is one thing not to have sin and quite another not to obey its desires. It is one thing to fulfill the commandment, *You shall not desire* (Ex 20:17), and it is quite another, by an effort at self-control, at least to do what we also find in scripture: *You shall not go after your desires* (Sir 18:30). It is still another to know that one can do neither of these as one should without the grace of the savior. Hence, to act with righteousness means to fight an interior battle with the interior evil of concupiscence in the true worship of God, but to have attained perfect righteousness means having no opponent at all. For one who is fighting is still at risk and at times is wounded, even if not laid low. But one who has no opponent enjoys perfect peace. And that person is said in complete truth to be without sin in whom no sin dwells, not the one who, by refraining from the evil action, says, *It is no longer I who do it, but the sin that dwells in me* (Rom 7:20).

73. Job himself is not silent about his own sins, and our friend is certainly correct that humility should in no sense be placed on the side of falsehood.[160] Hence, what Job confesses, since he is a true worshiper of God,[161] he undoubtedly confesses truthfully. And when explaining the passage of the psalm where it says, *You have rejected*

---

157. Hilary, *Commentary on Matthew* IV, 7.
158. See Jb 1:1.
159. Hilary, *Commentary on Job*, fragment 2.
160. A reference to the words of Pelagius; see above 34, 38.
161. See Jb 1:1.

all those who depart from your decrees (Ps 119:118), Hilary himself says, "After all, if God were to reject sinners, he would, of course, reject all human beings, because there is no one without sin. But he rejects those departing from him, whom he calls apostates."[162] You see how he did not say that there was no one without sin, as if he were speaking about the past, but said that there is no one without sin. As I said, I am not arguing about this point; after all, if one does not yield to the apostle John who said, *If we say that we have no sin* (1 Jn 1:8)—not that we had no sin—how is the person going to yield to bishop Hilary? I cry out on behalf of the grace of Christ; no one is justified without it, as if the free choice of our nature were sufficient. Indeed Christ himself cries out on its behalf; let us yield to him as he says, *Without me you can do nothing* (Jn 15:5).

From Ambrose of Milan

63, 74. In the passage which this man cites, Saint Ambrose is really opposed to those who say that human beings cannot be without sin in this life.[163] In order to make this point, he chose the examples of Zechariah and Elizabeth, since the gospel mentions that they walked in all the decrees of the law without reproach.[164] But does he deny that they did this by *the grace of God through Jesus Christ, our Lord*? There is no doubt that, even before his Passion, the righteous lived by faith in him who gives the Holy Spirit through whom that love is poured out in our hearts.[165] That love alone justifies all those who are righteous. The aforementioned bishop advises us to beg for this Spirit with prayers in his hymn where he says,

> He grants to constant prayers
> That one merits the Holy Spirit.[166]

So convinced is he that without God's aid the will is not enough!

---

162. Hilary, *Commentary on the Psalms, On Psalm 118*, XV, 10. See Jb 34:18.
163. Ambrose, *Commentary on the Gospel of Luke* I, 17. After citing Lk 1:6, Ambrose says, "What reply do those people make to this who, in looking for solace in their sins, think that human beings cannot be without frequent sins and use the verse found in Job, *No one is clean from filth, not even if this life last but a single day* (Jb 14:4)? One must answer them that they must first define what it means to be without sin: does it mean that they never sinned at all or that they ceased sinning? For if they think that to be without sin means to have ceased sinning, I myself agree."
164. See Lk 1:6.
165. See Rom 5:5.
166. Ambrose, *Hymn* III, 7-8.

75. I too will mention a passage from this same work of Saint
Ambrose from which he cited the passage he thought worth citing.
He says, *"It seemed good to me* (Lk 1:3). That which he says seemed
good to him cannot have seemed good to him alone. After all, it
did not seem good to him on the basis of the human will. Rather,
it seemed good to him *who speaks in me, Christ* (2 Cor 13:3), for
he brings it about that what is good can also seem good to us. For
he also calls those on whom he has mercy. And for this reason one
who follows Christ can answer, when asked why he wanted to be
a Christian, *It seemed good to me.* When he says this, he does not
deny that it seemed good to God. After all, *the will of human beings
is prepared by God* (Prv 8:35 LXX), for it is due to God's grace that
God is honored by the saint."[167] See what our author should think, if
the words of Ambrose please him; he holds that *the will of human
beings is prepared by God*, and there is little or no dispute about
who will attain perfection or when, provided there is no doubt that
this cannot be achieved without the grace of Christ. Moreover, how
important it would have been for him to pay attention to one verse
from the words of Ambrose which he cited. For when he said, "Since
the Church has been gathered together from the Gentiles, that is,
from sinners, how could she become spotless from members who
were not spotless, unless she was first cleansed from sin by the grace
of Christ and, second, refrained from sins by reason of the ability not
to sin?"[168] Then Ambrose added a line, and it is clear why this man
refused to add it. For Ambrose says, "Nor was the Church spotless
from the beginning—this is impossible for human nature. Rather, by
God's grace and by its own condition, since it does not now sin, it is
being transformed so that it may be seen as spotless."[169] Who can fail
to see why this man does not add these words? This transformation
is, of course, now being carried out in this world in order that the holy
Church may attain that spotless purity, which all the saints desire, so
that it may in the world to come live an absolutely pure life in God's
eternity without any evil persons mixed in with it and without any
law of sin in it resisting the law of the mind.[170] Let this man, nonetheless, note what bishop Ambrose said in accord with the scriptures,

167. Ambrose, *Commentary on the Gospel of Luke* I, 10.
168. Ibid. I, 17.
169. Ibid.
170. See Rom 7:23.

"Nor was the Church spotless from the beginning—this is impossible for human nature."[171] He means, of course, the beginning in which we are born of Adam. For Adam himself was undoubtedly created spotless, but in those people who are by nature children of anger,[172] who derive from him what was corrupted in him, he declared that it was impossible for human nature that they be spotless.

From John of Constantinople

64, 76. He also cites the position of John, the bishop of Constantinople, who says that sin is not a substance, but an evil action. Who would deny this? He also says that it is not natural—and thus a law was established against it—and that it stems from the freedom of choice.[173] Who would deny this either? But our question is not about human nature as it is found in this life; our question is rather about God's grace by which it is healed through Christ the physician, whom it would not need if it were healthy. And yet this man defends nature as if it were healthy and as if the choice of the will were self-sufficient for being able not to sin.

From Xystus

77. So too, what Christian does not know the statement of blessed Xystus, the bishop of the church of Rome and martyr of the Lord, which he mentions, namely, that "God entrusted to human beings the freedom of their choice in order that, by living purely and without sin, they might become like God."[174] But it pertains to choice to listen to and to believe him who calls and to beg from him in whom one believes the help not to sin. He says "that they might become like God," and they will, of course, be like God through the love of God. That love has been poured out in our hearts, not by the

---

171. Ambrose, *Commentary on the Gospel of Luke* I, 10.
172. See Eph 2:3.
173. The John who is referred to is John Chrysostom. His words are otherwise unknown.
174. Pelagius, following Rufinus of Aquileia, attributed this and the next two quotations to Pope Xystus II (d. 258). In his *Revisions* II, 68 (42), Augustine says that he later learned, probably from Jerome, that these were the words of Sextus the Pythagorean philosopher. See H. Chadwick, *The Sentences of Sextus* (Cambridge 1959) 16-17. Chadwick rejects Jerome's view and defends the Christian character of the maxims, not ruling out the possibility that Xystus II was their author.

ability of nature or by the free choice we have, but by the Holy Spirit who has been given to us.[175]

The same martyr said, " A pure mind is a holy temple for God, and a pure and sinless heart is for him the best altar."[176] Who does not know that a pure heart must be brought to that perfection, as the interior human being is renewed from day to day,[177] but not without *the grace of God through Jesus Christ, our Lord.* He also says, "A chaste and sinless human being has received from God the power to be a child of God."[178] He of course mentioned this for fear that, when one has become so chaste and sinless—and there is some question about where and when this will be accomplished, for this question is properly raised among pious people; they are, nonetheless, agreed that it is possible and that it is only possible with the mediator of God and human beings, the man Jesus Christ.[179] Nonetheless, as I began to say, Xystus wisely mentioned this for fear that, when persons have become such and have, for this reason, been rightly numbered among the children of God, they might suppose that this power which they received from God through grace came from themselves. They did not, after all, have it in their nature that had already been corrupted and destroyed. Thus we read in the gospel, *But to as many as welcomed him, he gave the power to become children of God* (Jn 1:12). They certainly were not such by nature nor would they be such in any sense, unless by welcoming him they received such a power through his grace. This is the power that the strength of love claims as its own, a love that is present in us only *by the Holy Spirit who has been given to us* (Rom 5:5).

From Jerome, the Priest

65, 78. And what was it that the venerable priest Jerome said in the passage which this man cites? He was explaining the passage, *Blessed are the pure of heart, because they shall see God* (Mt 5:8). He said, "No awareness of sin makes accusation against them," and he adds, "The pure [God] is seen by a pure heart; the temple of God

---

175. See Rom 5:5.
176. Chadwick 16-17.
177. See 2 Cor 4:16.
178. Chadwick 18-19.
179. See 1 Tm 2:5.

cannot be defiled."[180] It is surely being brought about in us by our efforts, labor, prayers, and pleas that by his grace we are being brought through Jesus Christ, our Lord, to that perfection in which we can see God with a pure heart. Similarly, he states that the aforementioned priest said, "God created us with free choice, and we are drawn neither to virtue nor to vice by necessity. Otherwise, if necessity holds sway, there is no crown of victory."[181] Who would not accept this? Who would not welcome it with their whole heart? Who would deny it [and claim] that human nature was created in some other way? But there is no chain of necessity when we act correctly, precisely because there is the freedom of love.

66, 79. Return then to the statement of the Apostle: *The love of God is poured out in our hearts by the Holy Spirit who has been given to us.* Who has given the Spirit but him who *has ascended on high, taken captivity captive, and given gifts to human beings* (Eph 4:8). But let human beings hear that there is a certain necessity of sinning due to the defects of nature, not to the way nature was created, and let them learn to say to God, in order to escape that same necessity, *Deliver me from my necessities* (Ps 25:17). For in this sort of prayer one does battle against the tempter who fights against us out of this necessity. In that way, with the help of grace through our Lord, Jesus Christ,[182] the evil necessity will be removed, and full freedom will be given us.

From Augustine's Own Work, Free Choice

67, 80. Let us turn to ourselves. He says, "So too, bishop Augustine says in his books on *Free Choice*, 'Whatever this cause of the will is, if one cannot resist it, one yields to it without sin. But if one can resist it, let one not yield to it, and one will not sin. Does it perhaps deceive those who are not careful? Let them be careful then so that they are not deceived. Or is the deception so great that it cannot be avoided at all? Then there are no sins. For who sins in a matter that can in no way be avoided? But sin is committed; hence, it can be avoided.'"[183] I acknowledge them; they are my words. But let him now be so kind as to acknowledge everything which I have said above. We are, after all,

180. Jerome, *Commentary on the Gospel of Matthew* I, v, 8.
181. Jerome, *Against Jovinian* II, 3.
182. See Rom 7:25.
183. *Free Choice* III, 18, 50.

dealing with the grace of God which comes to our help as medicine through the mediator; we are not dealing with the impossibility of righteousness. One can then resist that cause [of the will], whatever it is; one clearly can. For we beg help for this when we say, *Bring us not into temptation.* We would not demand this help, if we believed that we could not resist. Sin can be avoided, but it is avoided with the help of him who cannot be deceived. If we truthfully say, *Forgive us our debts, as we also forgive our debtors,* this too is helpful for avoiding sin. Even in the body there are two ways of avoiding the evil of disease: both by preventing its occurrence and, if it has occurred, by quickly healing it. Let us avoid the occurrence of sin by saying, *Bring us not into temptation*; let us avoid sin through its quick healing by saying, *Forgive us our debts, as we also forgive our debtors.* Whether sin threatens or is already present, it can, then, be avoided.

81. But I want my views on this matter to be sufficiently clear not only to this man but also to the others. These others may not read those books of mine on *Free Choice* which he read, and they may read this man without having read my books. Hence, I must mention some passages from these books. If he were to hold such views and put them in his writings, there would remain no dispute between us. Immediately after those words of mine which he cited, I myself added what could have presented a problem and commented on it as best I could, saying, "And yet certain things, even though done out of ignorance, are blamed and judged to be in need of correction, as we read in the authoritative scriptures of God."[184] Then, using examples, I also spoke of weakness, saying, "There are some things done with necessity that should be blamed, in a case where a person wills to do the right action and cannot. Otherwise, what do these words mean: *I do not do the good that I want, but I do the evil that I hate* (Rom 7:19)?"[185] Then, after mentioning other passages from the words of God in support of this idea, I said, "But all of these are words of human beings who come from that condemnation to death. For, if this is not a punishment of human beings, but their nature, these are not sins."[186] A little later I said, "There remains, then, that this just punishment comes from the condemnation of human beings. And we should not be surprised at

---

184. Ibid. III, 18, 51.
185. Ibid.
186. Ibid.

it. For either, because of ignorance, they do not have free choice of the will to choose the right thing to do or, because of the resistance of carnal habit, which has grown almost into a nature through the power of mortal propagation, they see what is the right thing to do and will to do it, but cannot carry it out. For it is a perfectly just punishment of sin that people lose what they refused to use well, though they could have done so without any difficulty, if they willed to. But that means that those who knowingly do not do the right thing lose the knowledge of what is right, and those who refuse to do the right thing, though they could, lose the ability to do it, though they will to do it. Every[187] soul that sins really has as its punishment these two things: ignorance and difficulty. As a result of ignorance it suffers the shame of error; as a result of difficulty it is afflicted with pain. But to take what is false for what is true so that one errs against one's will, and not to be able refrain from acts of passion, because of the resistance and the biting pain of the flesh's chain, is not the nature of human beings as they were created, but their punishment after they were condemned. When we speak of the free will to do what is right, we are, of course, speaking about the free will with which human beings were created."[188] Since some people raise a complaint in the name of justice over the defects of this ignorance and difficulty that have been passed on and transmitted to the offspring of the first human beings, we reply as follows: "Our answer to them is brief. They should quiet down and stop muttering against God. They might have a just complaint if there were no human conqueror of error and desire. But he is present everywhere; in many ways through the creation that serves him as Lord, he calls those who are turned away; he teaches those who believe, consoles those who hope, exhorts those who love, helps those who try, hears those who pray. Hence, it is not counted against you as sin that you lack knowledge against your will, but that you neglect to seek out what you do not know. Nor is it counted against you that you do not bandage your wounded members, but that you hold in contempt the one who wants to heal you."[189] And so I both exhorted them, as much as I could, to live good

---

187. The CSEL edition has *omnia* instead of *omni*, which is found in the Maurist edition. The latter reading seems clearly preferable. See G. de Plinval, "Corrections au De natura et gratia," REA XI (1965) 292.
188. *Free Choice* III, 18, 51.
189. Ibid.

lives, and I did not destroy the grace of God without which human nature cannot be enlightened and healed, once it has been plunged into darkness and injured. The whole dispute with these people turns on this point: that we do not render meaningless the grace of God, which is found in Christ Jesus, our Lord, by a misguided defense of nature. I said of this nature a little later, "We understand this nature in one sense when we are speaking properly of the human nature in which human beings were first created blameless in their kind; we understand it in another sense in that nature in which we are born condemned and mortal,[190] ignorant and subject to the flesh, as the result of the punishment of those first human beings. In accord with this sense, the Apostle says, *We were by nature children of anger, just as the others*" (Eph 2:3).[191]

Summation and Conclusion: Righteousness Is the Love Poured Out in Our Hearts, Not by the Choice of the Will, but by the Holy Spirit

68, 82. If, then, we want "by Christian exhortations to arouse and set afire cold and sluggish minds to live good lives,"[192] let us first of all exhort them to the faith by which they might become Christians and be subject to the name of him without whom they cannot be saved. But if they are already Christians and are neglecting to live properly, we should beat them down with the fear of punishment and raise them up by praise for the rewards. We should remember to exhort them not only to good actions but also to pious prayers and to instruct them with this sound doctrine. Thus, once they have begun to live good lives, they will be thankful for having done something without difficulty, and when they do experience some difficulty, they will persist in asking the Lord with faith-filled and persevering prayers and with eager works of mercy that they may act with ease.

As for those who are making progress in this way, I am not very concerned about where and when they will attain the perfection of complete righteousness; whenever and wherever they will become perfect, I insist that they cannot become perfect except *by the grace*

---

190. The CSEL edition of this work omits *et mortales*, which is found in the edition of the Maurists and in Green's edition of *De libero arbitrio* in CSEL LXXIV, 134.
191. *Free Choice* III, xix, 54.
192. Probably a citation from Pelagius' *Nature*.

of God through Jesus Christ, our Lord. In any case, when they clearly see that they have no sin, they will not say that they have sin, lest the truth not be in them, just as the truth is not in those who say they have no sin, when they do.[193]

69, 83. Certainly, "the commandments are good," if we use them as the law prescribes.[194] By our firm belief that "the good and just God could not command what is impossible,"[195] we are taught both what we should do in easy cases and what we should ask for in difficult ones. Everything is, of course, easy for love; for love alone Christ's burden is light, or rather it alone is the burden which is itself light.[196] In this sense scripture says, *And his commandments are not burdensome* (1 Jn 5:3). Hence, people who find them burdensome should consider that God could only say that they are not burdensome, because there can be a disposition of the heart for which they are not a burden, and such persons should beg for what they lack so that they may fulfill what is commanded. If the words addressed to Israel in Deuteronomy are understood in a pious, a holy, and a spiritual sense, they mean the same thing. For, the Apostle recalled the passage, *The word is near to you on your lips and in your heart* (Dt 30:14; Rom 10:8), and Deuteronomy has here *in your hands* (Dt 30:14 LXX), for the heart has spiritual hands.[197] The Apostle adds, *This is the word of faith that we preach* (Rom 10:8). Whoever then have turned to the Lord their God, as they are commanded in that passage, with their whole heart and their whole soul will not find God's commandment heavy. After all, how can it be heavy when it commands love? For either one does not love, and then it is heavy, or one loves, and it cannot be heavy. But people love if, as Israel was instructed in that passage, they turn to the Lord their God with their whole heart and their whole soul. He says, *I give you a new commandment, that you love one another* (Jn 13:34), and *One who loves the neighbor has fulfilled the law* (Rom 13:8), and *Love is the fulfillment of the law* (Rom 13:10). In this sense scripture also said, *If they walked the paths of goodness, they would surely have found the paths of righteousness easy* (Prv 2:20). How then could scripture say, *On account of the words of your lips I*

---

193. See 1 Jn 1:8.
194. See 1 Tm 1:8.
195. Probably a citation from Pelagius' *Nature*.
196. See Mt 11:30.
197. Augustine's Old Latin version follows the Septuagint at Dt 30:14. See his *Observations on the Heptateuch* V, 54, where the text reads: *Prope est verbum hoc valde in ore tuo et in corde tuo et in manibus tuis facere illud.* As Augustine indicates there, he knew that the addition was lacking in the Hebrew.

have kept your difficult ways (Ps 17:4), unless both are true? They are difficult for fear, but easy for love.

70, 84. Hence, the beginning of love is the beginning of righteousness; progress in love is progress in righteousness; great love is great righteousness; perfect love is perfect righteousness. But it is *love from a pure heart, a good conscience, and sincere faith* (1 Tm 1:5), and it is at its greatest in this life when for its sake one holds this life in contempt.[198] I would be surprised if it did not have room to grow, when one has departed from this mortal life. But wherever or whenever it is so complete that no addition to it is possible, it is, nonetheless, not *poured out in our hearts* by the powers of nature or of the will which are found in us, but *by the Holy Spirit who has been given to us*. He comes to the aid of our weakness and along with us restores our good health. For this love is *the grace of God through Jesus Christ, our Lord*, who with the Father and the Holy Spirit has eternity and goodness forever and ever. Amen.

---

198. See Jn 15:13.

The Predestination of the Saints
and
The Gift of Perseverance

Introduction

Problems in Provence

The last two works in this volume, *The Predestination of the Saints* and *The Gift of Perseverance*, are really two parts of one work which seems to have originally borne the title, *The Predestination of the Saints*, though from at least the ninth century they have been treated as separate works.[1] They were written in response to letters from Prosper of Aquitaine and Hilary. The first was a well-known layman and author who was born in Aquitaine and moved to Marseilles where he was at the time when the monks in the city and environs protested against certain points in Augustine's teaching on the beginning of faith, predestination, and perseverance.[2] Hilary was an otherwise unknown layman and an ardent supporter of Augustine. Both Prosper and Hilary, it seems, wrote other letters to Augustine on the problems which had arisen among the monks of Provence, but they are not extant.[3] In the past scholars gave the date of the two extant letters as 429, though at present more and more scholars date the letters from as early as 427.[4] The earlier date has the advantage of allowing more time for the composition of the two works at a very busy period of Augustine's life during which he was writing his *Unfinished Work in Answer to Julian* as well as his *Heresies* and *Revisions*. Moreover, it allows for more time before the Vandal invasion of Africa cut off communication between Africa and Gaul at some point before Augustine's death in 430.

The reaction against Augustine's doctrine emerged in the city of Marseilles and other areas of Gaul, including Arles and Lérins, now

---

1. The second work seems to have been originally called *The Good of Perseverance—De bono perseverantiae* rather than *De dono perseverantiae*.
2. For a brief overview of Prosper's life and works, consult *Patrology* IV. *The Golden Age of Latin Patristic Literature from the Council of Nicea to the Council of Chalcedon*, ed. Angelo di Berardino, tr. Placid Solari (Westminster, MD 1991) 551-558.
3. See Letters 225, 2 and 226, 9 for indications of other letters to Augustine from these men.
4. The traditional dating of the letters as written in 429 rests upon Hilary's reference in Letter 226, 9 to the recent installation of Hilary of Arles as bishop of Arles. Owen Chadwick, in "Euladius of Arles," *The Journal of Theological Studies* 46 (1945) 200-205, and others have convincingly argued on the basis of one manuscript which has *Elladium* in place of *Hilarium* that Letter 226 refers to Euladius who was bishop of Arles in 426-427. See William Collinge's introduction to *St. Augustine: Four Anti-Pelagian Writings*, Fathers of the Church LXXXVI,186-187. Collinge favors the reading of Euladius. On the other hand, the "note complémentaire" in BA 24 by M. J. Chéné simply reports the evidence for "Euladius," while retaining "Hilary."

the island of Saint Honorat, off the coast of Cannes. Though the only person mentioned by name in the letters of Prosper and Hilary is Euladius of Arles—or Hilary of Arles, if one accepts the more traditional view—the main personage behind the protest is John Cassian, who founded the monastery of Saint Victor in 415 or 416 in Marseilles.[5] Cassian introduced into southern Gaul the monastic spirituality which he had absorbed during a stay of more than fifteen years in Egypt and during a briefer stay in Constantinople with John Chrysostom. His *Conferences* emphasized Christian asceticism as a preparation for grace. The monastery of Saint Honoratus on the isle of Lérins was second only to Marseilles as a center of the anti-Augustinian movement in Gaul. Lérins had a series of distinguished abbots including Vincent of Lérins and produced many of the bishops of southern Gaul, such as Maximus, the successor of Honoratus as abbot and later bishop of Riez; Lupus, who became bishop of Troyes; Eucherius, who held the see of Lyons; Hilary, who became bishop of Arles; and Faustus, who became bishop of Riez.

The Views of the Monks of Provence

The letters of Prosper and Hilary are the principal sources for the views of the monks who objected to certain parts of Augustine's teaching on grace and predestination. In his letter Prosper indicates that many of the servants of God in Marseilles found Augustine's teaching on "the calling of the elect according to God's plan" to be in opposition to the teaching of the Fathers and the mind of the Church. Prosper points out that Augustine's book, *Rebuke and Grace*, did not settle the problem for a good number of them (section 2). Though the monks accepted the doctrine of original sin and the need for rebirth through the grace of God, they held, "All human beings without exception have, nonetheless, been offered the reconciliation which is present in the mystery of the blood of Christ so that whoever chooses to come to the faith and to baptism can be saved." They also held that God foreknew those who were going to believe and to persevere in faith with the help of grace and that he predestined those whom he foreknew (section 3).

---

5. For a brief overview of Cassian's life and works, see *Patrology* IV, 512-523. For a more detailed study, see Owen Chadwick, *John Cassian*, 2nd ed. (Cambridge: Cambridge University Press, 1968).

They objected that, if the plan of God's calling is thought to have divided the vessels of honor from the vessels of dishonor before the creation of the world, sinners lose any motive to rise up from their sins and the saints find an occasion for tepidity. The monks claimed that under the term "predestination" Augustine introduced fatalism and made it seem that God created two different natures of human beings. The monks of Provence, moreover, contended that Augustine's interpretation of Saint Paul was unprecedented in the Church and presented an obstacle to the edification of those who hear it (section 3).

Prosper added that some of the monks came close to Pelagianism in wanting the grace of Christ to pertain to the nature of each human being as each was created by God with free choice and rationality. Thus, by making good use of this initial grace, a person attains the grace of salvation. For these monks God's plan of salvation amounted to no more than God's having determined to require baptism for admission to his kingdom. They held that all human beings are called to salvation and that those who will to become children of God do become children of God. The monks produced testimonies from scripture filled with exhortation and claimed that people are sinners or saints in accord with what they will to be (section 4).

When confronted with the deaths of little ones, the monks claimed that "such infants are lost or saved in accord with how the divine foreknowledge foresees they would have been in their later years" (section 5). The monks insisted that Christ died for the whole human race and that the sacrament of mercy belongs to all human beings. For his part God has prepared eternal life for all, but it is attained only by those who have freely believed in God and received the help of grace. The principal motive for the monks' teaching was that they did not want to admit that God created some human beings for an honorable purpose and others for a dishonorable purpose. Nor did they accept the view that the number of the predestined can be neither increased nor decreased. For they believed that such a view left no room for exhortation. Each person is called to correct his life, and in those who have the use of reason human obedience to the word of God comes before the grace of salvation (section 6).

The Letter of Hilary presents a similar perspective on the reaction in Gaul to Augustine's teaching on grace. According to Hilary the monks claimed that Augustine's view of God's plan in accord with which some are chosen and given the will to believe, while others are not, undermines the effectiveness of preaching since there remains nothing in a human being which can respond to preaching. They held that the sinner's will to be healed should not be considered a work for which grace is required. Our believing, the monks held, is something we offer to God from the ability which God gave to our nature. One who begins to believe receives the help of grace, but a will able to believe is given to all human beings, and by it they can reject or obey God's call (section 2).

The monks held that the gospel is not preached to some people because God foreknows that they will not believe if the gospel is preached to them. In fact, the monks appealed to Augustine's earlier works in support of this view, and Hilary supplies the texts to which they appealed (section 3).

God's foreknowledge, predestination, or plan means only that he foreknew those who would believe. Moreover, the monks insisted that, regarding this faith, one could not ask the question, *What do you have that you have not received?* (1 Cor 4:7) since the ability to believe lies in human nature. The monks accepted Augustine's claim that no one perseveres unless he has been given the power to persevere, but they attributed the power to persevere to the will, which is free to will or not to will to accept any remedy. They did not, however, want this perseverance to be preached as something which one can neither merit by prayer nor lose by rebellion. The monks also rejected as non-canonical the Book of Wisdom, from which Augustine cited the text about one who *was carried off so that evil would not change his mind* (Wis 4:11), and they rejected the idea that anyone is given perseverance in such a way that he is not permitted to abandon it (section 4).

The monks maintained that the practice of exhortation is rendered useless if people are predestined to salvation or damnation. Exhortation can, rather, arouse in the sinner a sorrow over his infirmity, a sorrow which provides a reason why he is accepted and another rejected (section 5). The monks also disliked Augustine's distinction between the grace of Adam and the grace of other human beings. For, on Augustine's view, Adam had a grace without which he could not persevere with free choice, but now the saints predestined to the kingdom of God receive the gift of perseverance by which "they cannot fail to persevere."[6] The view that "the saints now receive such a help that they cannot fall away from righteousness" renders useless any exhortation or threats. The monks also claimed that the nature of all other human beings differs from that of Adam and that the predestined can lose any gift they have received (section 6).

Hence, they insisted that the number of the predestined is not fixed and that God wills that all human beings be saved. The monks rejected as inappropriate the testimonies Augustine cited regarding the attainment of kingship by Saul and David (section 7). They also refused to take the situation of the little ones as a model for the gratuity of grace in the case of adults, and they pointed to Augustine's early position in his work, *Free Will*, where he left the question of the lot of infants who die without baptism undetermined (section 8).

The monks of Provence, then, clearly differed from Augustine not merely on the beginning of faith but also on their understanding of predestination, on the efficacy of the grace of Christ, on the determinateness of the number of the predestined, and on the universality of God's salvific will.

The Structure and Content of The Predestination of the Saints

The monks of Provence maintained that our beginning to believe (*initium fidei*) is simply the free response of a human being to the word of God, though they conceded that the increase of faith (*augmentum fidei*) requires God's grace. That grace, however, turns out to be a recompense for the beginning of faith so that the initiative for one's salvation and even one's perseverance in grace up to the end of this life rests with each person rather than with God. In *The Predestination of the Saints* Augustine defends the thesis that the beginning of faith is a totally gratuitous gift of God—a teaching which was later declared a matter of faith for the Catholic Church—but he also maintains that the grace to believe is not offered to all human beings and that grace not merely enables one to believe but even makes one believe. Neither of the latter views has been accepted as official Church teaching.

In the introduction Augustine assures Prosper and Hilary that their letters have not been a bother to him (section 1) and encourages

---

6. *Rebuke and Grace* 12, 34.

them to be confident that the monks of Provence will come to the full truth. For they already believe with the Church that every human being is born subject to original sin and can be set free from it only by Christ, that the grace of God comes before human willing, and that no one can begin or carry out any good work by himself (section 2).

Augustine first undertakes to show that the faith which makes us Christians is a gift of God. He claims that the view of the monks of Provence, that we offer to God the beginning of our faith and that he in return gives us an increase in faith, is very close to the Pelagian position that grace is given in accord with our merits (section 3). In response to this position Augustine cites a series of scripture texts to the contrary to which he adds a few comments (section 4), but then focuses upon Paul's words that we are not *sufficient to have a single thought as if from ourselves* (2 Cor 3:5). He argues that thinking must come before believing and defines the act of believing as "thinking with assent." Hence, if we cannot have a single thought from ourselves, we cannot have the beginning of faith from ourselves (section 5). Similarly, God promised to Abraham the faith of the nations, and Abraham believed that God could do what he promised.46[7] Hence, God produces in us both the beginning of faith and its increase (section 6).

Augustine admits that he had earlier held a position similar to that of the monks of Provence and did not believe that faith was preceded by the grace of God. He points to some of his works written before he became a bishop and quotes at length from his *Revisions* on his *Commentary on Some Statements in the Letter to the Romans* (section 7). His own "conversion" occurred, he tells us, while he was writing his *Miscellany of Questions in Response to Simplician,* when God revealed to him, as he commented on God's choice of Jacob over Esau, that we have nothing which we have not received[8] and that no one can say that he has faith which he has not received (section 8). To the objection that faith has remained a part of our fallen nature, Augustine replies by citing from Saint Paul the texts which show that no human being has any grounds to boast before God[9] (section 9). Augustine admits that there are natural gifts or

---

7. See Rom 4:20-21.
8. See 1 Cor 4:7.
9. See 1 Cor 1:30-31; 1 Cor 4:6-7.

graces which we have as rational beings which set us apart from others, such as beauty or intelligence, but insists that to believe or not to believe does not lie in the choice of the human will (section 10). To the objection that those who do not believe do not will to believe, Augustine replies that the objectors are correct in what they say, but overlook the fact that the will of some is prepared by the Lord,49[10] while the will of others is not. For God's ways by which he shows mercy to some and justice to others are unsearchable (section 11). Another objection claims that Saint Paul distinguished faith from works, so that grace does not come from works but from faith. Augustine observes that Jesus himself called believing in him the work of God[11] (section 12).

Augustine now turns to the Bread of Life discourse in the Gospel of John, where he singles out the words, *Everyone who has heard my Father and learned comes to me* (Jn 6:46). He argues that this school in which the Father is heard and teaches is far removed from the senses of the flesh and is the grace by which he produces the children of the promise and the vessels of mercy[12] (section 13). Yet the Father does not teach all human beings to come to Christ; rather, he teaches those whom he teaches out of mercy and does not teach the others out of judgment. The Father can be said to teach all human beings only in the sense that no one comes to Christ unless the Father teaches him (section 14). Hearing the Father and learning from him is nothing else but receiving from the Father the gift of believing in Christ (section 15). Hence, both the beginning of faith and its increase are God's gifts (section 16).

Augustine had written in Letter 102 a reply to Deogratias on the question of the philosopher Porphyry as to why Christ came only after so many centuries. His reply, which he cites extensively, was basically that God foreknew when and where human beings would believe and revealed himself to those who, as he foreknew, would believe (section 17). Augustine defends himself, pointing out that his answer in Letter 102 had deliberately skirted the more difficult question of God's hidden plan of salvation and had spoken only of foreknowledge, which provided a sufficient answer in the context (section 18). In the same

---

10. See Prv 8:35 LXX.
11. See Jn 6:29.
12. See Rom 9:23.

letter Augustine had stated that the salvation of the Christian religion was "never lacking to anyone who was worthy"—another statement seeming to favor the view of the monks of Provence. He explains that one must ask why one person is worthy and another is not. His answer is that one's worthiness is due to God's grace or predestination. He distinguishes predestination from grace: "predestination is the preparation for grace, while grace is its actual bestowal." By predestination God foreknew what he himself was going to do; by foreknowledge he also knows what others will do (section 19). Thus, in promising to Abraham the faith of the nations, God foreknew what he himself was going to produce. If God promised only the good works of the nations, not their faith, then it will be in the power of human beings whether or not God keeps his promise, since the works of righteousness come from faith (section 20). To someone who fears the incertitude of God's will in his own regard, Augustine insists that it is safer to place one's trust in the Lord than in oneself (section 21).

The monks of Provence objected that, where scripture says, *If you believe, you will be saved* (Rom 10:9), faith is required of us and therefore lies in our power. Augustine replies that both our faith and our salvation are God's gifts, for we pray that he will increase our own faith and will grant faith to those who do not yet believe. God commands that we have faith, but he gives what he commands (section 22). Despite the clarity of the scriptural testimonies to the gratuity of grace, the argument that grace is not given according to our merits might meet with some difficulty in the case of adults, but in the case of little ones and in that of the mediator himself every claim to prior human merits collapses (section 23).

When the Apostle said that each of us will *receive recompense for what we have done in the body* (2 Cor 5:10), he did not add, "Or what we were going to do." Little ones who die before they have any actions of their own are not going to be judged in accord with the merits they would have had if they had lived longer but only in terms of original sin or of their deliverance from its guilt through the bath of rebirth (section 24). The objection that some infants do not receive baptism because God foreknew that they would not do penance if they lived, but that others receive baptism because he foreknew that they would do penance, implicitly denies original sin, since each infant would be judged only according to the personal sins he would have committed or good actions he would have done (section 25).

Cyprian pointed out the benefit of death insofar as it removed one from the possibility of sinning and appealed to the words of the Book of Wisdom, *He was carried off so that evil would not change his mind*. The monks of Gaul rejected the text as coming from a non-canonical book. Augustine first insists that the text teaches the truth, namely that, if a righteous person is taken by an early death, he is in a place of rest and free from any fear of committing sin (section 26). But he also defends the authority of the Book of Wisdom and declares it unnecessary to provide any defense of the statement from previous Catholic commentators on the scriptures (section 27). The Book of Wisdom, after all, has greater authority than any commentator on it. Augustine points out that Cyprian, who cited the text, argued that death rescues us from the fear of temptations and falling into sin (section 28). The gratuity of grace is most evident in little ones, some of whom die after being baptized, while others die without baptism, thus revealing God's mercy and his judgment. Hence, the monks of Gaul who are opposed to the Pelagian error ought not to reject the words of the Book of Wisdom and ought not to uphold the absurd idea that anyone of the dead is judged by what he would have done if he lived longer (section 29).

Jesus Christ himself as man provides a clear example of predestination and grace. For the man Jesus Christ in no way merited to be assumed into the unity of the person of the Son of the Father, but was Son of God from the first moment of his existence (section 30). From the beginning of our faith each of us becomes a Christian by the same grace by which that man became Christ from his beginning. Each of us is reborn by the same Spirit by whom he was born, and each of us received forgiveness of sins through the same Spirit who made him to be without any sin. God foreknew and foresaw that he would do all this; hence, the predestination of the saints is seen most clearly in Christ. Paul says that God *predestined him to be the Son of God in power* (Rom 1:4). As Christ had no preceding merits for being born as the Son of God, so we have no preceding merits for being reborn as his members (section 31).

Augustine distinguishes the calling by which God calls his predestined to the faith from that calling by which those people were called who, when invited, refused to come to the wedding[13] (section 32).

---

13. See Lk 14:16-20.

He struggles with the passage in Romans where Paul spoke of the Jews as enemies in relation to the gospel, but as beloved on account of their forefathers in terms of the election.[14] Again in this case he distinguishes those who have been chosen, those who have been taught by God and called irrevocably from those who have been blinded and who belong among the many who are called, but not among the few who are chosen (section 33). Though the apostles were chosen from the world by Jesus when he lived here, they were chosen before the creation of the world by the predestination by which God foreknew what he was going to do. So God chooses believers in order that they might be believers, not because they already were believers (section 34).

Augustine uses the beginning of the Letter to the Ephesians to confirm the doctrine of predestination, the predestination by which God chose us in Christ *before the creation of the world* and *predestined us to be his children by adoption through Jesus Christ in accord with the purpose of his will* (Eph 1:4-5). He asks who could hear these words of the Apostle and have any doubt about the truth of the predestination he himself is defending (section 35). A Pelagian might say that God foreknew those who were going to be holy and spotless and, for that reason, chose them, but Augustine insists that Paul teaches that God chose us in order that we might be holy and spotless, not because we were going to be such (section 36). God predestined us according to his plan—his plan, not ours, the plan from which there comes the calling proper to the chosen (section 37). The monks of Provence would admit that the Pelagians are refuted by Paul's words, but these brothers say that God foreknew only the beginning of our faith and, for that reason, chose us before the creation of the world. Against this view Augustine insists that God chose us, not because he foreknew that we would believe, but in order that we might believe (section 38).

Finally, Augustine appeals to a series of scripture texts which indicate that the beginning of faith is a gift of God. Saint Paul, for example, thanks God for the recent faith of the Ephesians and of the Thessalonians[15] (section 39). Similarly, Augustine interprets Paul's prayer that God may open for him a door for God's word as proof that the acceptance of the preached word is a gift of God[16] (section

14. See Rom 11:28-29.
15. See Eph 1:16; 1 Thes 2:13.
16. See Col 4:2-4.

40). Augustine likewise points to God's opening the mind of Lydia so that she paid attention to what Paul said as evidence of the gift of faith[17] (section 41). The monks of Provence had rejected Augustine's use of the scripture texts concerning Saul and David in *Rebuke and Grace* as inapplicable; hence, he presents a list of other texts to show how God acts in human hearts (section 42). In conclusion Augustine repeats that the beginning of faith is a gift of God (section 43).

The Structure and Content of The Gift of Perseverance

The second book of the reply to Prosper and Hilary can be divided into two principal parts. The first part teaches that final perseverance is a gift and a gratuitous gift of God (sections 1 to 33); the second part explains the proper way in which one should teach the doctrine of predestination (sections 34 to 65), followed by a conclusion (sections 66 to 68).

Augustine begins with a statement of the principal thesis of this book, namely, that perseverance up to the end of this life is a gift of God (section 1). He appeals to Paul's words, *To you it has been given on behalf of Christ, not only that you believe in him, but also that you suffer for him* (Phil 1:29), words in which he finds that the beginning of faith and death in the faith as a martyr are both said to be given by God. As the beginning of faith is God's gift, so perseverance in the faith up to the end is a gift of God (section 2). The prayer of Christians, especially the Lord's Prayer, shows that perseverance is a gift of God (section 3). With support from Cyprian's work, *The Lord's Prayer*, Augustine then proceeds to show that in each of the individual petitions of the prayer—with the exception of the fifth—Christians pray for the gift of perseverance (sections 4 to 9).

The monks of Provence objected that one should not preach that perseverance cannot be merited by prayer or lost by rebellion. Augustine points out that he is speaking of perseverance up to the end of this life and that one who has it cannot not have it. Perseverance can, he admits, be merited by prayer, but cannot be lost by rebellion (section 10). If the objectors persist and claim that perseverance can be lost before it is attained, Augustine replies that God commanded us to pray for perseverance and is able to give what he commanded us to

---

17. See Acts 16:14.

ask for and that, if God hears our prayer, we cannot lose perseverance (section 11). He concedes that a person abandons God by his will, but claims that God so works in our will that we do not abandon God if he hears our prayer that we may not be brought into temptation (section 12). Were there no other testimonies, the Lord's Prayer alone would be sufficient proof that our perseverance is God's gift (section 13). Augustine again appeals to the beginning of the Letter to the Ephesians as clear proof of God's predestining us in Christ (sections 14-15).

Final perseverance is not given in accord with merits, and it is not given to all. In his mercy God sets many free from the perdition all deserve, and he would not be unjust if he set no one free (section 16). The gratuity of final perseverance is most clear in little ones. To account for their different treatment, Augustine appeals to the parable of the workers in the vineyard. Those who worked all day and received the same recompense as those who worked for only an hour were told by the owner of the vineyard, "This is what I will." His generosity toward some did not mean that he was unjust to the others (section 17). If pressed as to why God sets one free from condemnation rather than another, Augustine has nothing to say but that God's judgments are inscrutable[18] (section 18).

Turning to perseverance in the case of adults, Augustine faces the objection that there are two different natures of human beings. Augustine points out that, if such were the case, there would be no grace, since deliverance would be a recompense owed to the nature of those who persevere. Moreover, God has judged it better to allow some who will not persevere to be mingled with the elect so that no one can feel assured of his salvation (section 19). Augustine appeals to Ambrose's claim that no one can flee from this world without God's help, for we do not have in our own power our heart and our thoughts (section 20). Of two persons one is called so that he perseveres up to the end, and the other is either not called or not called in that way. The reason for the difference lies in God's inscrutable judgments, but it is certain that the former is one of the predestined, called according to God's plan, and chosen in Christ before the creation of the world[19] (section 21).

Augustine again insists that no one is judged by what God foreknew that the person would have done if he had lived longer.

---

18. See Rom 11:33.
19. See Rom 8:28; Eph 1:4.
.

Otherwise, Tyre and Sidon would not be condemned for, if the Lord had performed miracles in them, they would have done penance[20] (section 22). If we are asked why the Lord produced such great miracles among a people who were not going to believe and did not produce them among the people of Tyre and Sidon who would have believed, we certainly cannot say, as Augustine said in his Letter to Deogratias, that God foreknew that they would not believe in his miracles. The Lord said that Tyre and Sidon will be punished on the day of judgment, though less than the cities in which Jesus preached, but if the people of Tyre and Sidon are judged according to what they were going to do if Jesus produced his miracles among them, they would not be punished at all, but would attain salvation on the basis of the penance they would have done (section 23).

An unidentified exegete proposed that Jesus did not work miracles in Tyre and Sidon because he foreknew that they would later abandon the faith after having believed and that out of mercy he did not produce miracles in them. Augustine points out that this interpretation does not claim that these peoples were judged according to what they would have done. In any case one ought, as Augustine states, to be ashamed even to refute the opinion that the dead are punished for sins they would have committed if they had lived longer (section 24). In little ones the gratuity of grace is clear, for they can have no preceding merits, and the same gratuity of grace holds for adults. Grace is given to no one according to his merits, nor is anyone punished except for his merits (section 25).

The monks of Provence objected to Augustine's taking the situation of the little ones as a model for adults and appealed to his book, *Free Will*,[21] in which, against the Manicheans, he had presented four hypothetical solutions to explain why human beings are born with ignorance and difficulty and showed that on any of the hypotheses God is not to be blamed (section 26). Augustine cites his own comments on his earlier work from his *Revisions* and argues that his whole intention in *Free Will* was to refute the Manicheans. He admits that in *Free Will* he discussed the little ones in such a way that, even if the Pelagians were correct in denying original sin, the Manichean doctrine of the two natures of good and evil would be defeated (sec-

---

20. See Mt 11:21.
21. *Free Will* III, 23, 66-70.

tion 27). The grace of God, then, is not given in accord with merits. In giving to some the grace they did not merit God shows his mercy; in not giving grace to everyone he shows what all merited (section 28). The gratuity of grace is defended even if little ones do not have original sin, as the Pelagians hold, for in no case do little ones have any merits of their own by which they are admitted to the kingdom of heaven. Just as Augustine here defends the gratuity of grace whether or not there is original sin, so in *Free Will* he defeated the Manicheans whether ignorance and difficulty are natural conditions or the punishment of sin (section 29). Augustine protests that *Free Will* was written against the Manicheans and does not preclude his demonstrating that grace is not given according to our merits. Moreover, he points out that, if he began those books when he was still a layman and was still in doubt about the condemnation of the little ones, these monks should not forbid him to make progress in his thinking (section 30).

In trying to avoid the Pelagian view that grace is given in accord with our merits, the monks of Provence adopted the monstrous view that little ones who have died are judged in accord with the actions they would have done if they had lived. If one rejects both these views, as one should, one is left with that of the Catholic Church, namely, that grace is not given in accord with merits (section 31). Hence, given the facts that some little ones are taken from this life without having been baptized, while others are taken from this life after having been baptized and that some baptized adults are left in this life until they fall into sin, while others are taken from this life before they sin, the monks have no reason to maintain that grace is given in accord with our merits if they reject Pelagianism and the absurd view that the dead are judged according to what they would have done (section 32). The grace of God both for the beginning of faith and for perseverance up to the end are not given in accord with our merits but in accord with his hidden but just, wise, and beneficent will (section 33).

The second part of the book concerns the teaching of the doctrine of predestination. The monks of Provence held that the Augustinian doctrine posed an obstacle to the usefulness of preaching. Augustine argues that the same scripture which teaches the doctrine of predestination contains preaching, commands, exhortations, and rebukes. Hence, the doctrine of predestination cannot be such an obstacle (section 34). Augustine argues that God foreknew those to whom he was going to grant faith and perseverance so that none of them would be lost. "The predestination of the saints is nothing other than the foreknowledge and the preparation of the benefits of God by which he most certainly sets free whoever are set free." The others are left in the mass of perdition where God left the people of Tyre and Sidon who were not blinded as the Jews were, for the people of Tyre and Sidon would have believed if the Lord worked his miracles among them (section 35). Cyprian showed that the preaching of obedience is not incompatible with the preaching of perseverance (section 36). Though obedience is a gift of God, we exhort people to obedience; those who hear obediently our exhortation already have the gift of obedience (section 37). The same objections can be raised on the basis of God's foreknowledge as the monks of Provence raised on the basis of predestination, and yet no one dares to doubt divine foreknowledge (section 38). There are likewise some people who do not pray because of the words of the Lord, namely, that God knows what we need before we ask him[22] (section 39).

Though some truths need not be stated, other truths, including the truth of predestination, entail too great a danger if they are left unstated (section 40). The only alternative to preaching predestination as it is contained in the scriptures, according to which God's gifts and calling are irrevocable,[23] is to admit that the Pelagians are correct in holding that grace is given in accord with our merits. As grace comes before faith and before all obedience, so it comes before perseverance up to the end. Though chastity is a gift of God, a chaste person does not cease to strive to be chaste, because he hears that he will be what he will be by God's gift (section 41). As chastity is God's gift, so are the other virtues, as the monks concede, and yet they are not afraid that the doctrine of predestination poses an obstacle to exhorting people to the virtues. They should likewise have no fear that the doctrine of predestination poses an obstacle to exhortations to faith or perseverance (section 42).

Though the monks agreed that wisdom and continence are gifts of God, they claimed that the beginning of faith and remaining in it up to the end is not due to God but to us. If the monks preach that wisdom and continence are gifts of God without any fear that such preaching

---

22. See Mt 6:8.
23. See Rom 11:29.

may cause despair, they ought to preach that the beginning of faith and perseverance up to the end are gifts of God without any such fear (section 43). The apostle James clearly taught that wisdom is a gift of God and at the same time rebukes the restless and quarrelsome. In the same way we should rebuke non-believers and those who do not persevere in the faith, while we preach that faith and perseverance are God's gifts (section 44). The monks of Provence admitted that the other virtues are gifts of God and exhorted people to the practice of them; hence, they ought to have had no problem in admitting that faith and perseverance are God's gifts, while exhorting people to them (section 45). Their objection that a person abandons the faith by his own will does not mean that faith is not a gift of God (section 46).

God's foreknows all these gifts which he gives to those whom he has chosen, but these gifts are only foreknown if there is the sort of predestination Augustine is defending. Scripture at times uses the term "foreknowledge" in place of "predestination." For example, Saint Paul says that *God has not rejected his people whom he foreknew* (Rom 11:2), where one correctly understands "whom he predestined" (section 47). Augustine argues that the doctrine of predestination has always been taught in the Church and appeals to texts he has already cited from Cyprian and Ambrose (section 48). He adds two further passages from Ambrose's *Commentary on the Gospel of Luke* and one from a sermon of Gregory of Nazianzen (section 49). Augustine argues that, if these men admitted that conversion to God and remaining in Christ are God's gifts and did not deny God's foreknowledge that he would give these gifts, they knew the predestination which Augustine is defending, and yet they preached obedience and exhorted the people to it (section 50).

The monks of Provence objected that, even if the doctrine of predestination is true, it should not be preached to the people. Augustine argues that, just as we must preach piety, chastity, and love so that people live in accord with these virtues, so we must preach predestination so that no one boasts in himself (section 51). These brothers claimed that the Catholic faith had long been defended without the doctrine of predestination and pointed to some books of Augustine as proof of this. Augustine acknowledges that he came to a fuller knowledge of the truth in writing his *Miscellany of Questions for Simplician* (section 52). He also points to the passage in his *Confessions* in which he prayed to God, "Give what you command,

and command what you will,"[24] the very passage which Pelagius found terribly upsetting when he first heard it. And he emphasizes the story of his own conversion as evidence of God's grace, while admitting that it was not necessary to defend the predestination of the saints before the Pelagians came along (section 53).

Augustine insists that predestination must be preached in order to present an insurmountable defense of the genuine grace of God, that is, of grace which is not given in accord with merits (section 54). He admits that in *Rebuke and Grace* he stated that to persevere up to the end is a gift of God and that he had never or hardly ever previously stated this point so explicitly. He insists, however, that Cyprian taught that we should pray for perseverance and that he himself implicitly taught that final perseverance is a gift of God in his work for Simplician and in other writings (section 55). Hence, one who does not want to be ungrateful to God should confess his gratuitous grace not merely in the virtues of Christian life, but also in the beginning of faith and in final perseverance (section 56).

Predestination should not be preached in such a way that our preaching seems to the uneducated to be an attack on it (section 57). We should not speak of predestination to a group of believers so that we imply that some of them have not come to the faith (section 58), nor should we say that some of them are still dallying in their sins because grace has not raised them up (section 59). Neither should we say to a congregation of believers that some of them who are predestined, but have not yet been called, will be chosen (section 60). Much less should we say to such a group that, if some of them are predestined to be rejected, they will be rejected (section 61).

Someone preaching predestination ought to encourage his listeners to hope that they will persevere and to pray for perseverance (section 62). The prayers of the Church for the conversion of non-believers and for perseverance in faith on the part of believers should be a guide for the uneducated people who cannot understand the scriptures or their explanations (section 63). After all, even our prayer is a gift of God (section 64), and in his predestination God has given to those whom he called all these gifts which the Church prays for (section 65).

In conclusion, Augustine prays that the brothers of Provence may understand and confess the genuine grace of God which is not given

---

24. *Confessions* X, 31, 45; 37, 60.

in accord with any preceding merits (section 66). He again appeals to the man Jesus Christ as a model of our own predestination (section 67). Finally, he prays that his readers may understand this work and that he may receive correction and instruction from the teachers of the Church (section 68).

The Text and Translations

For *The Predestination of the Saints* I have translated the text found in PL XLIV, 959-992, and for *The Gift of Perseverance* I have used the text in PL XLV, 933-1034. These works have been translated many times in several languages, most notably in English by Peter Holmes and Robert E. Wallis in the Nicene and Post-Nicene Fathers I/5 and by John A. Mourant and William J. Collinge in The Fathers of the Church LXXXVI.

Background Correspondence
Note

The two letters that follow, one by Prosper of Aquitaine and the other by a certain Hilary, served as the occasion for the writing of and provide background to *The Predestination of the Saints* and *The Gift of Perseverance*. Each letter, moreover, is referred to in both works. Prosper, who died sometime after 455, was himself a theologian of note and an untiring defender of Augustine. But Hilary, a layman like Prosper, is otherwise unknown.

A Letter of Prosper of Aquitaine to Augustine[1]

To Augustine, my lord, most blessed bishop, and most excellent patron, who is ineffably admirable and worthy of incomparable honor, Prosper sends his greetings.

1. Though I am unknown to you by my appearance, I am, if you recall, known to you by my thoughts and words. For I sent to you a letter and received one back from you by hands of my holy brother, the deacon Leontius.[2] I now, however, venture to write to Your Beatitude not merely out of a desire to greet you, as I did then, but out of a love for the faith which is the life of the Church. For, since you keep watch for all the members of the body of Christ with your most vigilant efforts and fight against the plots of heretical teachings with the power of the truth, I thought that I need have absolutely no fear of being a burden or bother to you in a matter which concerns the salvation of many persons and, for this reason, Your Piety.[3] For I would otherwise consider myself guilty if I did not report to a special protector of the faith those matters which I understand to be extremely dangerous.

2. In the writings of Your Holiness, which you produced against the Pelagian heretics, many of the servants of Christ who dwell in the city of Marseilles think that whatever you discussed in them concerning the calling of the elect according to God's plan is opposed to the opinion of the Fathers and to the mind of the Church. And though they preferred for some time to blame their own slowness rather than to find fault with what they did not understand, some of them wanted to ask for a clearer and a simpler explanation of your writings on this point. God's mercy so arranged things that, when similar problems disturbed certain persons in Africa,[4] you published the book, *Rebuke and Grace*, which is filled with divine authority. When it was brought to our attention by an unexpected opportunity, we thought that all the complaints of the opposition would be put to rest. For on all the questions about which Your Holiness was about to be consulted, you had

---

1. Prosper's Letter is Letter 225 among the letters of Augustine. The Latin text can be found in CSEL LVII, 454-468.
2. The letter to which Prosper refers is not extant.
3. Augustine alludes to Prosper's concern about being a bother to Augustine in the first paragraph of *The Predestination of the Saints*.
4. Prosper refers to the monks of Hadrumetum for whom Augustine wrote *Grace and Free Choice* and *Rebuke and Grace*.

there replied as fully and completely as if you were especially concerned to settle those issues which were stirred up among us. After examining this book of Your Beatitude, those who were previously following the holy and apostolic authority of your teaching acquired much greater understanding and instruction, but those who were handicapped by the darkness of their own conviction went off more unfavorably disposed than they had been. There is reason to fear their abrupt disagreement first on their own account, lest the spirit of the Pelagian impiety should mislead such men who are so renowned and so outstanding in the pursuit of all the virtues. And, there is reason to fear, secondly, that certain more simple people who have a great reverence for these men from having observed their goodness may judge that what they hear these men maintain, whose authority they follow without discretion, is perfectly safe for themselves.

3. For the following is what they state and profess: Every human being certainly sinned when Adam sinned, and no one can be saved by his own works, but only by rebirth through the grace of God. All human beings without exception have nonetheless been offered the reconciliation which is present in the mystery of the blood of Christ so that whoever chooses to come to the faith and to baptism can be saved. But God foreknew prior to the creation of the world those who are going to believe or who are going to continue in that faith which after its reception needs the help of grace, and he predestined for his kingdom those whom he foresaw would, after having been gratuitously called, be worthy of election and would leave this life by a good death. And, therefore, every human being is admonished by the teaching of God to believe and to act in order that no one may despair of attaining eternal life, since a reward has been prepared for a person's willing devotion.

This plan of God's calling, however, which is said to have separated those who would be chosen and those who would be rejected, either before the beginning of the world or at the creation of the human race, so that in accord with the decision of the creator some were created as vessels of honor and others as vessels of dishonor, both removes from those who have fallen any concern to rise up and offers to the saints an occasion for tepidity. For in both cases toil is useless if one who has been rejected cannot enter the kingdom by any effort and if one who has been chosen cannot fall away by any negligence. For, however they act, nothing else can happen in their regard than what God has determined, and when hope is uncertain, one cannot hold to a consistent course because, if the choice of God who predestines one is different, the intention of the person who makes an effort is meaningless. And, therefore, all effort is removed, and all the virtues are destroyed if God's decision comes before human willing. Under this term "predestination" a necessity due to fate is introduced, and God is said to be the creator of different natures, if no one can be other than he was created.[5]

In order to explain more briefly and fully what they hold, everything which, in accord with the mind of your opponents, Your Holiness mentioned as objections for yourself in this book or whatever you refuted with great power in the books, *Answer to Julian*,[6] which Julian raised as objections on this question—all this these holy men proclaim with great intensity that they accept.

And when we produce in answer to them the writings of Your Beatitude which you filled with countless and very strong testimonies of the divine scriptures and when we ourselves construct an argument to trap them on the model of your treatises, they defend their stubbornness by invoking tradition and maintain that the passages from the Letter of Paul the apostle, writing to the Romans, which are produced to show that grace comes before the merits of the elect had never been interpreted by anyone in the Church in the sense in which they are now being interpreted. And when we ask that they interpret them in accord with the meaning of those commentators they prefer, they claim that they have found nothing with which they are satisfied and insist that one should remain silent on those issues whose depth no one can plumb. Ultimately, their whole obstinacy comes down their declaring that our belief is something opposed to the edification of those who hear it, and so, even if it is true, it should not be brought into the open. For it is dangerous to hand on teachings which should not be accepted, and it involves no danger to pass over in silence ideas which cannot be understood.

4. Certain of them, however, do not wander very far from the paths of the Pelagians. For, when they are forced to acknowledge the grace of Christ which anticipates all human merits—otherwise, if it is repayment for merits, it is called "grace" to no point at all—they

5. See *The Gift of Perseverance* 8, 19, where Augustine answers the charges that there are different natures of human beings.
6. Prosper alludes to the six books of Augustine's *Answer to Julian*, specifically to IV, 8.

want this grace to pertain to the creation of every human being; by their creation the grace of the creator has established each of them with free choice and rationality, but without any prior merits, since none of them previously existed. And thus a person could direct his will through the discernment of good and evil to knowing God and to obeying his commandments and could come to that grace by which we are reborn in Christ, that is, through one's natural ability, by asking, seeking, and knocking, in order to receive, to find, and to enter.[7] For, having made good use of the good of nature, one will merit by the help of this initial grace to arrive at the grace of salvation.

They locate the plan of the grace of vocation entirely in the point that God has determined to receive no one into his kingdom except through the sacrament of rebirth and that all human beings are universally called to this gift of salvation, either by the natural law or by the written law or by the preaching of the gospel. Thus those become children of God who will to, and those are without excuse who refuse to believe. The justice of God, after all, consists in the fact that those who have not believed perish, but his goodness is evident in the fact that he excludes no one from life but wills that all persons without any distinction among them *be saved and come to the knowledge of the truth* (1 Tm 2:4).

Here they produce testimonies from the divine scriptures in which exhortation rouses to obedience the wills of people who with free choice either do or neglect to do what they are commanded. And they think that it follows that, because a transgressor is said not to have obeyed because he did not will to, a believer is also without a doubt said to have been devout because he willed to be. And each person has as great a power for good as he has for evil, and his mind directs itself with equal force either to vices or to virtues. And the grace of God cherishes one who seeks the good, while just condemnation follows upon one who pursues evil.

5. Among these points there is raised for them the objection of the countless number of little ones who have as yet no wills, no actions of their own. They are set apart in the judgment of God, nonetheless, only by reason of original sin, because of which all human beings are likewise born under the condemnation of the first human being. And yet, of those who will be taken from the enjoyment of this life be-

---

7. See Mt 7:7.

fore the discernment of good and evil, some will be adopted through rebirth as heirs of the kingdom of heaven, while others will pass without baptism into the company of those meriting eternal death. They say that such infants are lost or saved in accord with how the divine knowledge foresees that they would be in their later years, if they attained the age at which they could act. They do not consider that they subject the grace of God which they want to accompany, not to precede, human merits, to those wills which they think that they do not deny are anticipated by grace. But they subject God's election to any pretended merits whatever to the extent that, because there are no past merits, they imagine future merits which will not exist, and, by their new kind of absurdity, actions which will not be done are foreknown and those actions which are foreknown are not done.

Of course they think that they can more reasonably defend this foreknowledge of God regarding human merits, in accord with which the grace of God who calls us works, when they turn to the consideration of those nations which in past ages were left to follow their own ways[8] or are also now still lost in the impiety of their old ignorance, nor has any light from either the law or the gospel shone upon them. Yet insofar as a door has been opened and a path cleared for its preachers, the people of the nations who sat in the darkness and in the shadow of death have seen a great light,[9] and those who were once not a people are now the people of God, and to those to whom he once did not show mercy he has now shown mercy.[10] They say that the Lord foresaw that these people would believe and that each nation received at the proper times the services of teachers when there was going to arise the faith of those with good wills. And that assertion, that *God wills all persons to be saved and come to the knowledge of the truth*, remains unshaken. They are in fact without excuse who could be led to the worship of the one true God by their natural intelligence and who have not heard the gospel because they would not have accepted it.

6. Our Lord Jesus Christ has, however, died for the whole human race, and no one is exempt from the redemption of his blood, even if one passes the whole of this life with his mind completely estranged from him. For the sacrament of divine mercy belongs to all human

---

8. See Acts 14:15.
9. See Mt 4:16; Is 9:2.
10. See Hos 2:2; Rom 9:25.

beings. And very many are not renewed by it because God foreknows that they do not have the will to be renewed by it. And so, insofar as it pertains to God, eternal life is prepared for all, but insofar as it pertains to the freedom of choice, eternal life is attained by those who have freely believed in God and have received the help of grace by the merit of their belief.

The principal reason which led these people, whose opposition makes us upset, to preach such grace, though they previously had a better view, is this: If they admitted that grace comes before all good merits and that grace grants the possibility that good merits exist, they would necessarily have to concede that, according to his plan and the counsel of his will, by his hidden judgment but evident action, God creates one vessel for an honorable purpose and another for a dishonorable purpose.[11] For no one is made righteous except by grace, and no one is born except in sin. But they refuse to admit this, and they fear to ascribe to the work of God the merits of the saints.

Nor do they accept the view that the predestined number of the elect can be neither increased nor decreased for fear that the stings of exhortations would have no place in the lives of those who do not believe or who are negligent, and that the imposition of activity or of labor would be useless for one whose striving is going to be frustrated because he is not among the elect. Finally, each person can be called to correct his life and to make progress if he knows that he can be good by his own effort and that his freedom will be assisted by the help of God for the reason that he has chosen to do what God commands. And so, since in these people who have reached the age of free will there are two factors which produce human salvation, namely, the grace of God and the obedience of the human being, they want the obedience to come before grace, so that one believes that the beginning of salvation depends on the one who is saved and not on the one who saves, and that it is the will of a human being which brings forth the help of divine grace for itself, not grace which subjects to itself the human will.

7. And since we have come to know through the merciful revelation of God and the instruction of Your Beatitude that this view of theirs is most perverse, we can indeed stand firm against believing this, but we are not equal to the authority of those who hold such

11. See Rom 9:21.

views. For they surpass us greatly by the merits of their life, and some of them are our superiors by having recently attained the honor of the highest priesthood,[12] nor has anyone readily dared to contradict the words of such high-ranking persons, except a few fearless lovers of perfect grace. As a result the danger has increased along with their dignities, not only for these people who hear them, but also for those very persons to whom the people listen, since reverence for them has either held many back in an unprofitable silence or has led them on to a careless agreement. And they regard it as most salutary that this view meets with reproach from almost no opponent.

Hence, if the heart of this not mediocre virulence is fostered in these remnants of the Pelagian depravity; if the beginning of salvation is wrongly located in a human being; if the human will is impiously preferred to the will of God, so that a person is helped because he has willed to be and not so that he wills to because he is helped; if one who is evil from his origin is wrongly believed to initiate the reception of the good not from the highest good but from himself; and if God is only pleased by what he himself has given, then grant us on this issue, most blessed bishop and best father, to the extent that you can with the help of the Lord, the concern of Your Piety. Deign to open up, by explanations which are as clear as possible, those issues which in these questions are rather obscure and quite difficult to grasp.

8. And, first of all, since many do not think that the Christian faith is violated by this disagreement, disclose the great danger which lies in their conviction. Then, explain how free choice is not impeded by this grace which is at work before free choice and at work along with free choice. Also, explain whether the foreknowledge of God remains in accord with God's plan, so that those things which he has planned should be accepted as foreknown or whether these vary in accord with the kinds of situations and categories of persons, that is, because the calls to salvation are different. In the little ones who are saved, though they are not going to do any action, it seems as if God's plan alone is involved, but in people who are going to do some good actions, God's plan can follow upon his foreknowledge. Or is the situation the same in both cases, so that foreknowledge is subject to God's plan in some order, though one cannot by a temporal

---

12. According to the editors of BA 24, Prosper probably refers to Hilary of Lérins, who had recently been elected bishop of Arles, and possibly to Lupus, who became bishop of Troyes in 426 or 427.

distinction divide foreknowledge from God's plan? And just as there is no action of whatever sort it may be which divine knowledge does not anticipate, so there is nothing good which has not flowed down from God, its source, into our partaking of it. Finally, explain how this preaching of God's plan, by which those who have been predestined for eternal life become believers, is not an obstacle for any of those who need to be exhorted, and how people have no excuse for negligence if they have despaired of having been predestined.

We also ask you to show us, while you patiently put up with our foolishness, how this question may be resolved, namely, that, when one examines the opinions of earlier teachers on this point,[13] one finds one and the same view in the case of nearly all of them, that is, that they have accepted the plan and predestination of God as based on foreknowledge, so that God made some into vessels of honor and others into vessels of dishonor precisely because he foresaw the end of each person and knew in advance his future willing and action even under the help of grace.

9. When you have untangled all these questions and have also examined many others which with your more penetrating gaze you can see pertain to this issue, we believe and hope not only that our weakness will be strengthened by the support of your arguments, but also that those men renowned for their merits and high function over whom the darkness of this opinion has cast its shadow will accept the purest light of grace. For Your Beatitude should know that one of them, a man of great authority and of spiritual interests, the saintly Hilary, the bishop of Arles,[14] is an admirer and follower of your teaching in all other points, and that on this one point which he raises as a complaint he has long since wanted to present his views to Your

---

13. Prosper gives no clue as to the identity of these earlier teachers. The editors of BA 24 suggest in a note some possibilities, namely, Origen and John Chrysostom among the Eastern Fathers and Hilary of Poitiers and Ambrose of Milan among the Latin Fathers. For example, in commenting on Mt 22:23, Ambrose says in *Faith* V, 6, 83: "And then referring to the Father, [Jesus] added, *For whom it has been prepared*, to show that even the Father is not swayed by prayers, but by merits, for God has no favoritism regarding persons. Hence, the Apostle also says, *And he also predestined those whom he foreknew*. For he did not predestine them before he had foreknowledge of them; rather, he predestined the rewards of those whose merits he foreknew."
14. Recent scholars have argued on the basis of the reading in one manuscript that Prosper referred not to Hilary, who became bishop of Arles in 429, but to Euladius, or Helladius, who was bishop of Arles from 426 to 427. See the note in BA 24, 808, "Sur la mention d'Hilaire, évêque d'Arles, dans la lettre de Prosper," for the details of the argument. The BA editors simply recount the arguments without accepting the conjecture of Euladius.

Holiness in writing. But since it is uncertain whether he is going to do this or to what purpose he is going to do this, and since the weariness of us all revives in the vigor of your love and knowledge, since the grace of God provides this comfort for the present age, instruct the humble and reprove the proud. It is necessary and beneficial to put into writing even what has already been written so that no one thinks that a point which is not often discussed is trifling. For they suppose that what does not hurt is healthy, nor do they feel a wound covered over by skin. But let them realize that a wound which has a persistent swelling will have to be lanced.

May the grace of God and the peace of our Lord Jesus Christ give you a crown for all time and for eternity glorify you who progress from virtue to virtue, my lord, most blessed bishop, and most excellent patron, who are ineffably admirable and worthy of incomparable honor.

A Letter of Hilary to Augustine[15]

To Augustine, my most blessed lord and father worthy of being loved with all my heart and to be warmly embraced in Christ, Hilary sends his greetings.

1. When the questions of our opponents cease, we generally find pleasing the inquiries of those who desire to know in order that they may learn even those things which go unknown without any danger. Hence, I think that you will find quite pleasing the attention to detail in our report. For, when it points out certain teachings opposed to the truth according to the presentations of certain people, it aims, not so much for its own sake as for the sake of those people who are upset and who upset others, to remedy this situation through the counsel of Your Holiness, my most blessed lord and father worthy of being loved with all my heart and to be warmly embraced in Christ.

2. These are the ideas, then, which are being discussed at Marseilles as well as in some other places in Gaul, namely, that it is a new idea and one opposed to the usefulness of preaching that it is said that some people will be chosen according to God's plan in such a way that they can neither acquire this election nor hold onto it unless they have been given the will to believe. They think that all

---

15. This is Letter 226 among the letters of Augustine; the Latin text is found in CSEL LVII, 468-481.

the effectiveness of preaching is excluded if one says that nothing has remained in human beings which preaching can rouse. They agree that every human being perished in Adam and that no one can be set free from this perdition by one's own choice. But they claim that the following view is in conformity with the truth and suitable for preaching, namely, that, when one proclaims to people who lie prostrate and will never rise up by their own powers the chance to obtain salvation, they attain, by the merit of willing and believing that they can be healed of their disease, both an increase of this faith and the result of their complete health. Yet they agree that no one can be sufficient by himself to begin, not to mention to complete, any good work, for they do not think that one must attribute it to some work involved in their healing that every sick person wills to be healed with a fearful and suppliant will.

For they maintain that the words of scripture, *Believe, and you will be saved* (Rom 10:9), demand one of these and offer the other. That is, we are given what we are offered on account of what is demanded of us, if we have done it. Hence, they think that it follows that someone offers his faith to God because the will of the creator has given this ability to that person's nature, and they think that no nature has been so corrupted or destroyed that one should not or cannot will to be healed. On this account a person either is healed of his disease or, if he is unwilling, is punished along with it. And they claim that grace is not denied if such a will which seeks so great a physician, though it is itself unable to do anything, is said to precede grace. For they want to interpret the testimonies, such as this one, *as he has given to each a measure of faith* (Rom 12:3), and others like it, in the sense that one who has begun to will is helped, but not in the sense that one's willing is also a gift and that others are excluded from this gift who are equally guilty and who could be set free in a similar way, if that will to believe, which is given to those equally unworthy, were likewise given to them. If, however, a person holds, they say, that there has remained in all human beings at least such a will by which one is able either to reject or to obey God's call, they think that one can essentially account for those who have been chosen and for those who have been rejected insofar as each person receives the merit of his own will.

3. But when we ask them why the gospel is preached or not preached to some people and in some places and why the gospel is

now preached to almost all peoples, though it was previously not, just as it is now not preached to some people, they say that it pertains to the foreknowledge of God that the truth has been preached or is preached to those people at the time and in the place when and where he foreknew that it would be believed. And they claim that they prove this not only by the testimonies of some Catholics but also by the somewhat older study of Your Holiness where you, in fact, taught the same grace with just as much clarity of the truth. For example, Your Holiness said the following against Porphyry in the question, "On the Time of the Christian Religion": "Christ willed to appear to human beings and willed that his teaching be preached when he knew and where he knew that there would be people who would believe in him."[16] Or there is the passage from the book on the Letter to the Romans, *"Therefore, you say to me, Why does he still complain? For who resists his will?"* (Rom 9:19) You say, of course, that he replied to this question in order that we might understand that, for men who are spiritual and do not live in accord with their earthly self, there are accessible the first merits of faith and of unbelief, insofar as by his foreknowledge God chooses those who will believe and condemns those who will not believe, though he does not choose the former on the basis of works and does not condemn the latter on the basis of works. Rather, he gives to the faith of the former their doing good works and hardens the disbelief of the latter by abandoning them so that they do evil works."[17]

And again in the same work you say a little earlier, "Prior to merit all are equal, and one cannot speak of a choice in things which are completely equal. But since the Holy Spirit is given only to those who believe, God does not choose the works which he himself gives, when he gives the Holy Spirit in order that we may act out of love, but he still chooses faith, because, unless one believes and persists in the will to receive the gift of God, one does not receive that gift, that is, the Holy Spirit, through whom, once love has been poured out, we can do what is good. He does not, therefore, in his foreknowledge choose the works of anyone which he himself is going to give, but he chooses in his foreknowledge faith, so that he chooses one whom he foreknows will believe, to whom he gives the Holy Spirit in order that

---

16. Letter 102, II, 14.
17. *Commentary on Some Statements in the Letter to the Romans* [Rom 9:15-21] 62.

by doing good works he may also attain eternal life. For the Apostle says, *The same God does all things in all people* (1 Cor 12:6). But scripture never says that God believes all things in all people. For the fact that we believe is up to us, while the fact that we do good works is due to him."[18] And there are in the same work other passages which they claim that they accept and approve of, as conformed to the truth of the gospel.

4. But they insist that God's foreknowledge, predestination, or plan means only that God foreknew, predestined, or planned to choose those who were going to believe and that one cannot say with regard to this faith, *What do you have that you have not received?* (1 Cor 4:7) since the ability to believe has remained in the same nature, though damaged, which was originally given as healthy and whole. They accept the words of Your Holiness, namely, that no one perseveres unless he has received the power to persevere, with the qualification that in those to whom this power is given, it is attributed, nonetheless, to their own prior though ineffective choice, and they say that it is free only to will or not to will to accept any remedy. But they also claim that they detest and condemn it if anyone thinks that any strength has remained in someone by which he can attain healing.

But they do not want this perseverance to be preached in the sense that it can be neither merited by prayer nor lost by rebellion. Nor do they want to be referred to the incertitude of God's will since, as they suppose, they clearly have the beginning of their will, however weak it may be, for gaining or losing[19] it. That testimony which you cited, namely, *He was carried off so that evil would not change his mind* (Wis 4:11), they declare should be omitted as non-canonical. Hence, they accept that foreknowledge in the sense that persons are to be understood as foreknown on account of the faith they will have, and they hold that no one is given such perseverance that he is not permitted to abandon it, but such perseverance by which he can by his will fall away and grow weak.

5. They maintain that the practice of exhortation is useless if one says that there has remained nothing in a person which a rebuke can rouse, and they admit that they say that something is present in our

---

18. Ibid. [Rom 9:11-13] 60.
19. I have followed the reading in PL of *amittendum* in place of *admittendum* which is found in CSEL.

nature such that it will be drawn to the benefit of the present grace by the very fact that the truth is preached to someone who does not know it. For, if people are predestined, they say, to each side so that no one can move from the one side to the other, what good does such great insistence upon rebukes from someone else do, if there does not arise from the person if not an integral faith, at least a sorrow over his painful infirmity, or if he is not terrified at the danger of the death he has been shown? For, if a person cannot fear the source of his terror except by a will which he receives, he should not be blamed because he does not now have that will. Rather, he should be blamed in the one and with the one who long ago did not will this and merited to incur that damnation along with all his descendants, so that he never willed to desire what is right but always willed to desire what is wrong. If, however, there is any sorrow which arises at the exhortation of one who gives a rebuke, they say that this is the reason why one is rejected and another is accepted, and that there is no need to set up two groups to which nothing can be added or subtracted.

6. Next, they dislike the distinction between the grace which was given to the first man and that which is now given to all human beings, that is, that Adam received for perseverance "not the help which made him persevere but the help without which he could not persevere by free choice. But now the saints who have been predestined to the kingdom of God by grace are not given such a help toward perseverance, but a help by which they receive perseverance itself, not only so that they cannot persevere without this gift but also so that by this gift they cannot fail to persevere."[20]

They are so upset by these words of Your Holiness that they say that these words give human beings grounds for despair. For, according to you, they say, Adam received a help so that he could remain standing in righteousness or fall away from righteousness, while the saints now receive such a help that they cannot fall away from righteousness. For they either have received such a perseverance in willing that they cannot will anything else, or some are abandoned to the point that they either do not attain righteousness or fall away from it if they have attained it. Hence, the usefulness of exhortation or threats, they say, was applicable to Adam's will, which possessed the free power either to remain righteous or to fall away, but not to our

---

20. *Rebuke and Grace* 12, 34.

will, which involves the rejection of righteousness with an inevitable necessity. The only exception is those people who, though they were created along with these who were condemned with the entire mass, were picked to be set free by grace.

Hence, these men want the nature of all human beings to differ from that of the first man only insofar as grace, without which he could not have persevered, helped him who willed with the unimpaired strength of his will, while grace not merely raises up the rest who lie prostrate, with their strength lost and destroyed, but also supports them as they walk, provided that they have faith. Moreover, they contend that whatever has been given to the predestined can be lost or retained by each person's own will, and this would be false if they thought it was true that certain people received that perseverance in such a way that they could not fail to persevere.

7. From this there also comes this idea which they equally do not admit, that is, they reject the claim that the number of those who will be chosen and of those who will be condemned is fixed, and they do not accept as an explanation of this view what you set forth; rather, they hold that God wills that all people be saved, and not just those who pertain to the number of the saints, but absolutely all people without any exception. Nor should one worry that some are said to perish against his will. Rather, they say, just as he does not will that anyone sin or abandon righteousness, and yet people continually abandon it against his will and commit sins, so he wills that all people should be saved, and yet not all people are saved.

They think that the testimonies of scripture concerning Saul or David[21] which you quoted do not have to do with the question concerned with exhortation, but they introduce other testimonies which they interpret as commending that grace by which each person is helped subsequent to his will or toward that calling which is offered to those who are unworthy. They claim that they prove this from passages of your works and from those of others whom it would take a long time to mention.

8. They will not, however, permit us to introduce the situation of the little ones as a model for adults, and they say that even Your Holiness had touched upon this issue only to the extent that you wanted

---

21. See *Rebuke and Grace* 14, 45, where Augustine appeals to 1 Sm 10:25-27 and 1 Chr 12:18 concerning the choices of Saul and of David for kingship.

that the question be left undecided and rather preferred to remain in doubt about their punishments. You remember that you stated this in the third book of *Free Will*, where you provided them an occasion for this objection.[22] They do the same thing with regard to the books of others who have some authority in the Church, something which Your Holiness sees offers no small help to these attackers unless we produce greater proofs or at least ones that are not inferior. For in your wise piety you are well aware of how many there are in the Church who hold a position or move from one position to another on the basis of the authority of certain names.

Finally, when we are all weary, their attack or rather complaint turns, with the agreement even of those who do not dare to disapprove of this position, to ask, "What need was there that the hearts of so many simple people be disturbed by the uncertainty of such an argument? For the Catholic faith has been defended no less effectively for so many years without this doctrine," they say, "both against other heretics and especially against the Pelagians, by so many previous books of yours and of others."

9. To confess my deepest desires, I would, my father, have preferred to present to you in person these points and an endless number of other ones or, since I have not merited this, at least to gather up over a longer period of time and send on to you all the points by which these people are upset in order that I might hear to what extent one ought to refute their objections or to tolerate them if one can no longer refute them. But since neither of them came about in accord with my desire, I preferred to send to you these points which I have grasped as best I could rather than to be completely silent about the great opposition of certain people.

Some of them are persons of such rank that lay persons must pay them the highest reverence in accord with the custom of the Church. We have in fact taken care to preserve this practice with the help of God in such a way that, when it was necessary, we did not pass over in silence what the little talents we have suggested for the statement of this question. But now, as if to alert you, I have raised these points in summary to the extent that the haste of the courier has permitted. It is up to Your Holy Prudence to see what action is needed to overcome or to control the intensity of such good and important men. For this

---

22. See *Free Will* III, 23, 66-68, where Augustine seems to incline toward the view that little ones who die without baptism receive neither reward nor punishment in the next life.

purpose I think that it will do little good at this point for you to give an explanation unless you also add your authority which their tirelessly contentious hearts cannot go against. But I clearly ought not to pass over in silence the fact that they claim to be admirers of Your Holiness in all your words and actions with this one exception. You will have to decide how one ought to put up with their opposition on this point. Do not be surprised that I have expressed some other things otherwise in this letter and added other things than those I wrote in my previous letter, for this is their position at present, apart from those points which I have perhaps passed over out of haste or of forgetfulness.

10. When the books which you are preparing concerning all your works have been published, may we please merit to receive a copy,[23] especially in order that the authority of these books may allow us not to have any fear to hold those passages separate from the reverence due to your name, if there are any passages in your books of which you do not approve. We also do not have your book, *Grace and Free Choice*; it remains that we may merit to receive it because we are confident that it is useful for this question.

I do not, however, want Your Holiness to think that I am writing these things as if I am in doubt about the teaching in those books which you have just published.[24] Let it suffice for me as a punishment that, exiled from the delights of your presence, where I drew nourishment from your salutary heart, I am tormented not only by your absence but also by the stubbornness of certain persons who not only reject what is evident but also find fault with what they do not understand. But I am free of this idea to the extent that I rather consider my weakness blameworthy whereby I tolerate such people with too little patience.

I leave it, however, to your wisdom, as I said, how you judge that you should deal with these matters. For I believed that, in virtue of the love which I owe to Christ and to you, it was my duty not to pass over in silence those issues which come into question. Given that grace which we, both little ones as well as the great, admire in you, we shall most gratefully welcome whatever you choose or are able to say as a matter settled by an authority most beloved and revered by us.

---

23. Hilary refers to Augustine's *Revisions*, which he was writing at the same time as he wrote the works for the monks of Hadrumetum and Provence.
24. Hilary probably refers to *Grace and Free Choice* and to *Rebuke and Grace*.

Since, under pressure from the courier, I was afraid that I would either not be able to write everything or would write these things in a less worthy manner, conscious as I am of my abilities, I persuaded a man renowned for his morals, his eloquence, and his zeal to convey to you by his letter all the information he could gather, and I have taken care to send you his letter along with mine. For he is a man of such a caliber that, apart from this necessity, he should be judged worthy of your knowledge.

The holy deacon, Leontius, one of your admirers, sends you ample greetings along with my parents. May Christ the Lord grant Your Paternity to his Church for many years, and may you be mindful of me, my lord and father.

I would like Your Holiness to know that my brother, because of whom especially we left there, has vowed perfect continence to God along with his wife, by her agreement. Hence, we ask Your Holiness to be so kind as to pray that the Lord may deign to confirm and preserve this vow in them.[25]

---

25. The Latin text indicates that the last paragraph was added somewhat like a postscript.

The Predestination of the Saints

A Book for Prosper and Hilary

1, 1. We know, of course, that the Apostle said in the Letter to the Philippians, *To write the same things to you is no bother for me, but it is safe for you* (Phil 3:1). In writing to the Galatians, when the same Apostle saw that he had sufficiently done among them through the ministry of his word what he knew was necessary for them, he nonetheless said, *For the rest let no one cause me trouble* (Gal 6:17), or as we read in many manuscripts, *Let no one be a bother to me*. But I admit that I find it bothersome that people do not yield to so many and such clear words of God by which the grace of God is proclaimed—the grace which does not exist at all if it is given in accord with our merits. Yet, my very dear Prosper and Hilary, I am so greatly pleased by your zeal and fraternal love that I cannot express it, for it makes one wish that such people not be in error, and I am inexpressibly pleased that you desire that I write still more on this topic after so many books or letters of mine on this subject. And yet I do not dare to say that I am pleased as much as I ought to be. Hence, see, I write to you again, and though I am not now dealing with you, I am still dealing through you with an issue that I believed I had sufficiently dealt with.

2. You have a pious worry that those brothers hold the view of the poet which says, "Let each be his own hope,"[1] and fall under that statement which was not said by a poet but by a prophet, *Cursed be everyone who places his hope in a human being* (Jer 17:5). Having considered your letters, it seems to me that these brothers should be treated in the way the Apostle treated those to whom he said, *And if on some point your thoughts differ, God will also reveal this to you* (Phil 3:15). For they are, of course, still in the dark on the question concerning the predestination of the saints, but they have that on the basis of which, if on some point their thoughts differ, God may also reveal this to them, if they continue to walk in the path to which they have come. On this account, after the Apostle had said, *If on some point your thoughts differ, God will also reveal this to you*, he said, *yet let us continue in the same path to which we have come* (Phil 3:16).

---

1. Virgil, *Aeneid* XI, 309.

419

These brothers of ours over whom your pious love is concerned have, however, come to believe with the Church of Christ that the human race is born subject to the sin of the first man and that no one is set free from this evil except by the righteousness of the second man. They have also come to admit that the wills of human beings are anticipated by the grace of God and agree that no one is by himself sufficient for either beginning or carrying out any good work. The retention of these convictions to which they have come, therefore, separates them very much from the error of the Pelagians. Hence, if they continue in these convictions and pray to him who gives understanding, God will also reveal this to them, if on some point their thoughts differ concerning predestination. Let us, nonetheless, show them the affection of love and the ministry of the word, as he whom we have asked grants to us that we may say in this letter those things which are suited to and beneficial for them. For how do we know that God may not perhaps will to produce that benefit through this service of ours by which we serve them in the free love of Christ.

Even the Beginning of Faith Is a Gift of God

2, 3. We must, therefore, first show that the faith by which we are Christians is a gift of God, at least if we can do this with greater care than we have already done in so many and such large volumes. But I now see that I must reply to those who say that the divine testimonies which we have used on this topic indicate that we have faith from ourselves, but that its increase comes from God, as if faith were not given us by him but is only increased in us by him because of that merit by which it was begun by us. This idea does not, therefore, diverge from that statement which Pelagius himself was compelled to condemn in the episcopal court in Palestine,[2] as the same proceedings testify,[3] namely, that "the grace of God is given in accord with our merit," if our beginning to believe is not due to the grace of God, but only what we receive in addition in order that we may believe more fully and more perfectly, and if, for this reason, we first give to God the beginning of our faith in order to receive in return an increase in it, as well as anything else we ask for in faith.

---

2. Augustine refers to the Synod of Diospolis held in Palestine at the end of 415; Pelagius was acquitted but only because he condemned a number of propositions which he denied that he held.
3. See *The Deeds of Pelagius* 33, 57-58; 35, 65.

The First Testimonies from Scripture

4. But against these ideas why do we not instead listen to these words, *Who has first given to him so that he will be repaid in return? For all things are from him and through him and in him.* (Rom 11:35-36) From whom, then, does the very beginning of our faith come but from him? For it is not the case that other things come from him with the exception of this; rather, *all things are from him and through him and in him.* But who would say that a person who has already begun to believe merits nothing from him in whom he has believed? Hence it is that the other things are said to be given in addition by divine repayment to one who merits them, and on this account grace is said to be given in accord with our merits. When this was raised as an objection for Pelagius, he himself condemned it in order that he himself would not be condemned. Whoever, then, wills completely to avoid this view worthy of condemnation should understand that the words of the Apostle were spoken with truth, *It has been given to you for the sake of Christ not only that you believe in him but that you suffer for his sake* (Phil 1:29). He showed that both are gifts of God because he said that both were given. He did not say, That you believe in him more fully and more perfectly, but, *That you believe in him.* Nor did he say that he obtained mercy that he might be more a believer, but in order that he might be a believer, for he knew that he did not first give to God the beginning of his faith and receive from God in return its increase, but that God who also made him an apostle made him a believer. For the beginnings of his faith were also recorded in scripture and are very well known because they are frequently read in the Church. When he was turned away from the faith which he was persecuting and was strongly opposed to it, he was suddenly converted to it by a more powerful grace. He was converted by him to whom the prophet said, as he was about to do this, *You will convert us and give us life* (Ps 85:7). He not only became someone willing to believe from someone who was unwilling, but from a persecutor he became someone who suffered persecution in the defense of that faith which he was persecuting. It was given to him by Christ not only that he believe in him, but also that he suffer for him.

5. And so, in commending this grace which is not given in accord with some merits, but which produces all good merits, he said, *Not that we are sufficient to have a single thought as if from ourselves, but our sufficiency comes from God* (2 Cor 3:5). Let those who think

that the beginning of faith comes from us and that the increase of faith comes from God pay attention here and weigh these words. After all, who does not see that thinking comes before believing? No one, of course, believes anything unless he first thought that it should be believed. For, although certain thoughts fly quickly, even most swiftly, before the will to believe, and the will follows so soon afterward that it accompanies it as if it were united to it, it is nonetheless necessary that thought precede everything which we believe. In fact, the very act of believing is nothing other than to think with assent. Not everyone, after all, who thinks believes, for many think in order not to believe. But everyone who believes thinks, and a believer thinks when believing and, in thinking, believes. Insofar, therefore, as it pertains to religion and piety (for the Apostle was speaking of this), if we are not *sufficient to have a single thought as if from ourselves, but our sufficiency comes from God*, we are certainly not sufficient to believe something as if by ourselves, something we cannot do without thinking, *but our sufficiency* by which we begin to believe *comes from God.* Hence, just as no one is sufficient to begin or to complete any good work, which these brothers already agree is true, as your letters indicate, so no one is sufficient by himself either to begin to have faith or to bring it to completion, *but our sufficiency comes from God.* For, without thinking, there is no faith at all, and we are not *sufficient to have a single thought as if from ourselves, but our sufficiency comes from God.*

6. One must avoid, my brothers whom God loves, that a human being should become filled with pride before God when he says that he does what God promises. Was not the faith of the nations promised to Abraham, and did he not, in giving glory to God, most fully believe that *he is also able to do what he promised* (Rom 4:20-21)? God, therefore, who is able to do what he promised, produces the faith of the nations. But, if God produces our faith, working in a marvelous manner in our hearts in order that we believe, need we fear that he cannot do the entire work? And does a human being, for this reason, claim for himself its first parts in order that he might merit to receive the last parts from God? See whether one achieves anything else in this way but that the grace of God is somehow or other given in accord with our merits and that in that way *grace is no longer grace* (Rom 11:6). For in this way it is paid back as something owed, not given gratuitously. It is, after all, owed to one who believes that

his very faith be increased by the Lord and that the increase in faith should be the reward of the faith already begun. Nor does one see that, when one says this, this reward is credited to believers, not as grace, but as something owed. But I completely fail to see why the whole work should not be ascribed to a human being, that is, that one who is able to begin for himself what he did not have should himself increase what he began, unless it is impossible to resist the utterly clear testimonies of God which show that faith from which piety takes its beginning is also a gift of God. Take for example the passage, *God has given to each the measure of faith* (Rom 12:3), or this passage, *Peace to the brothers and love along with faith from God the Father and the Lord Jesus Christ* (Eph 6:23), and others of the sort. Not wanting, then, to resist these very clear testimonies and yet wanting to have his believing from himself, a person makes a deal, as it were, with God and claims for himself a part of his faith and leaves a part for God. And what is more presumptuous, he claims the first part for himself and gives the second part to God, and in that work which he says belongs to both, he puts himself first and God second.

Augustine's Earlier Errors regarding Faith

3, 7. That pious and humble teacher did not think that way; I am speaking of the most blessed Cyprian, who said, "We must boast over nothing since we have nothing of our own."[4] In order to prove this, he used as a witness the Apostle who said, *But what do you have that you have not received? If, however, you have received, why do you boast as if you have not received?* (1 Cor 4:7) I myself was convinced principally by that testimony since I was similarly mistaken, thinking that the faith by which we believe in God is not a gift of God, but that we have it from ourselves and that by it we obtain the gifts of God by which *we live temperately, justly, and piously in this world* (Ti 2:12). For I did not think that faith was preceded by the grace of God in order that through faith we might be given what we asked for in a profitable manner, except in the sense that we could not believe unless the truth were first preached to us. But I thought that it was our very own and something we had from ourselves that we assented to the gospel which was preached to us.

---

4. Cyprian, *Three Books of Testimonies for Quirinus* III, 4.

Some of my smaller works written before I became a bishop clearly reveal this error of mine. Among these works is found that one which you cited in your letter,[5] and they include my *Commentary on Some Statements in the Letter to the Romans.*[6] Also, I was reviewing all my works and carrying out that revision in writing, and I had already completed two books of that work before I had received your more lengthy letters.[7] When I came to review this book in the first volume, I expressed myself as follows.[8]

"Likewise, I was discussing what it was that God chose in the as yet unborn child whom he said that the older brother would serve and what it was that he rejected in the same older brother who was also as yet unborn. Paul mentioned these brothers on account of the testimony of the prophet, although it was uttered long afterward, *I loved Jacob, but I hated Esau* (Mal 1:3; Rom 9:13). I brought the argumentation to the point that I said, 'God, therefore, did not in his foreknowledge choose the works of anyone, works which he himself was going to give. Rather, he chose in his foreknowledge faith, that is, he chose the one whom he foreknew would believe and to whom he would give the Holy Spirit in order that by doing good works he would also gain eternal life.'[9] I had not yet investigated carefully enough, and I had not yet discovered the nature of the gratuitous election of which the same Apostle said, *The rest were saved through the election of grace* (Rom 11:5). It is, of course, not grace if any merits come before it, for what is given, not as grace, but as something due, is a repayment for merits rather than a gift. Then, as I immediately said, 'For the same Apostle says, *It is the same God who produces all things in all* (1 Cor 12:6), but scripture never says, God believes all things in all.'[10] And I immediately added, 'That we believe, then, comes from us, but that we do good comes from him who gives the Holy Spirit to those who believe.'[11] I certainly would not have said this if I already knew that faith itself also belongs among the

---

5. See the Letter of Hilary 3.
6. Augustine wrote this work on the Letter to the Romans in 394 shortly before his *Miscellany of Questions in Answer to Simplician,* a work which was written in 396 and marked a turning point in Augustine's position on grace.
7. Augustine was at the time working on his *Revisions* in which the last work to be mentioned is *Rebuke and Grace.*
8. The following is a long quotation from *Revisions* I, 23, 2-4, in which Augustine quotes again and again from his *Commentary on Some Statements in the Letter to the Romans.*
9. *Commentary on Some Statements in the Letter to the Romans* 52.
10. Ibid.
11. Ibid.

gifts of God which are given in the same Spirit.[12] Both of these, then, are ours on account of the choice of the will, and yet both are given through the Spirit of faith and of love. For it is not love alone, but, as scripture says, *Love along with faith from God the Father and the Lord Jesus Christ* (Eph 6:23). And a little later I said, 'For it is up to us to believe and to will, but it is up to him to give to those who believe and who will the ability to act well through the Holy Spirit through whom love is poured out in our hearts.'[13] This is true, of course, but according to the same rule. Both are due to him because he prepares the will,[14] and both are due to us because they are not done unless we are willing. And in this way I also said later, 'Because we are unable to will unless we are called, and when we will after being called, our will and our running are not sufficient unless God offers strength to those who run and brings them to where he calls.'[15]

"And then I added, 'It is evident, then, that our acting well is not due to the one who wills or who runs, but to God who shows mercy,'[16] and this is perfectly true. But I said too little about the calling which takes place in accord with God's plan.[17] For not all those who are called, but only the chosen, are called in that way. Therefore, what I said a little later, 'For, just as in these whom God chose, it is not works but faith which begins merit so that it is by a gift of God that they act well, so too in those he condemns, unbelief and impiety begin the merit of punishment so that they also act wrongly on account of this very punishment.'[18] I stated this with complete truth, but I neither thought that I should ask myself whether the merit of faith was also the gift of God, nor did I say that it was.

"And in another place I said, 'He makes the one toward whom he shows mercy to act well, and he leaves the one whose heart he hardens to act wrongly. But that mercy is due to the preceding merit of faith, while this hardening is due to the preceding sinfulness.'[19]

12. See 1 Cor 12:9.
13. *Commentary on Some Statements in the Letter to the Romans* 53; also see Rom 5:5
14. Prv 8:35 LXX.
15. *Commentary on Some Statements in the Letter to the Romans* 54; *The Predestination of the Saints* has *bene operamur*, while *The Commentary on Some Statements in the Letter to the Romans* has *bonum operamur*.
16. Ibid.; see also Rom 9:16.
17. See Rom 8:28.
18. *Commentary on Some Statements in the Letter to the Romans* 54.
19. Ibid. 54; *The Predestination of the Saints* has *iniquitati* where the *Commentary on Some Statements in the Letter to the Romans* and the *Revisions* has *impietati*.

This is in fact true, but one still needs to examine whether the merit of faith also comes from the mercy of God, that is, whether God shows this mercy to a human being only because he is a believer or whether he also shows it to him in order that he might be a believer. For we read in the words of the Apostle, *I have obtained mercy in order that I might be a believer* (1 Cor 7:25). He did not say, Because I was a believer. God, then, shows mercy to a believer, but he also shows mercy in order that one might be a believer. In another place in the same book I said with complete correctness, 'Because, if we are called to believe, not because of works, but because of the mercy of God and if, as believers, we are given our ability to do good actions, this mercy should not be grudgingly held back from the nations,'[20] although I dealt there less carefully regarding that calling which takes place through the plan of God."[21]

The Revelation of the Truth

4, 8. You certainly see what I then held concerning faith and works, though I was working hard to commend the grace of God, and I see that these brothers of ours still hold that view, because they have not taken care to make progress with me as they read my books, as they have taken care to read them. For, if they had taken such care, they would have found that this question was resolved in accord with the truth of the divine scriptures in the first book of the two which I wrote at the very beginning of my episcopacy for Simplician of blessed memory, the bishop of the church of Milan and the successor of Saint Ambrose.[22] But perhaps they did not know those books; if that is the case, make them familiar with them. Concerning this first book of those two I spoke at the beginning of the second book of the *Revisions*, and these are my words, "Of the books which I composed as bishop, the first two dealt with various questions for Simplician, the bishop of the church of Milan, who succeeded the most blessed Ambrose. In the first book I took two of these questions from the Letter of Paul the apostle to the Romans. The first of these concerns the words of scripture, *What, then, shall we say? Is the law sin? Heaven*

---

20. Ibid., 56.
21. *Revisions* I, 23, 2-4.
22. Augustine refers to his *Miscellany of Questions in Response to Simplician* which he wrote for Simplician in 396.

forbid! up to where he says, *Who will set me free from the body of this death? The grace of God through Jesus Christ our Lord.* (Rom 7:7-25) In this passage I explained the words of the Apostle, *The law is spiritual, but I am carnal* (Rom 7:14), and the remaining words by which he showed that the flesh is in conflict with the spirit; I explained them as if they were describing a human being still under the law, not yet situated under grace. For long afterward I learned that these words could also be those of a spiritual person—and this is more probable.

The second question in this book begins from the passage where it says, *And not only this, but when Rebecca conceived by a single act of intercourse with Isaac our father* up to where it says, *If the Lord of hosts had not left us children, we would have become like Sodom and we would have been like Gomorrah.* (Rom 9:10-29) In resolving this question I worked hard in defense of the free choice of the human will, but the grace of God conquered. The inevitable result was that we must understand that the Apostle stated with the clearest truth, *For who has set you apart? But what do you have that you have not received? If, however, you have received, why do you boast as if you have not received?* (1 Cor 4:7) When the martyr Cyprian wanted to prove this point, he put this whole issue under the title, "We must boast over nothing since we have nothing of our own."[23] See why I said above that I myself was convinced principally by this testimony when I had other thoughts on this topic.[24] God revealed this to me when, as I said, I was writing to bishop Simplician on the resolution of this question. This testimony, then, of the Apostle where he said in order to repress the pride of human beings, *For what do you have that you have not received?* does not permit any of the faithful to say, I have faith which I have not received. These apostolic words, then, repress the whole pride of this reply. But one cannot say even this, Though I do not have perfect faith as my own, I still have as my own its beginning by which I originally believed in Christ. For here too the reply is given, *But what do you have that you have not received? If, however, you have received, why do you boast as if you have not received?*

---

23. Cyprian, *Three Books of Testimonies for Quirinus* III, 4.
24. See above 3, 7.

Grace Is Not a Grace in the Way Our Nature Is

5, 9. But these brothers suppose that "it cannot be said of this faith, *For what do you have that you have not received?* because faith has remained in the same nature, though damaged, which was previously given us as healthy and perfect."[25] But one can understand that this statement has no value for their purposes, if one thinks of why the Apostle said this. He was, after all, working to avoid that anyone should boast in a human being, because dissensions had arisen among the Christians of Corinth. Thus one of them said, *I belong to Paul, but another, I belong to Apollos,* and still another, *I am a follower of Cephas,* and from this he came to the point where he said, *God chose the foolish things of the world to confound the wise, and God chose the weak things of the world to confound the strong, and God chose the lowly and despicable things of the world, even those which do not exist as if they were something, in order that he might do away with those which are something, so that no flesh might boast before God* (1 Cor 1:27-29). Here the intention of the Apostle is certainly quite clearly opposed to human pride, so that no one may boast in a human being and, for this reason, may boast in himself.

Again, when he had said, *So that no flesh might boast before God,* he immediately added, in order to show in whom a human being ought to boast, *But because of him you are in Christ Jesus whom God made our wisdom, righteousness, sanctification, and redemption, in order that, as scripture says, one who boasts may boast in the Lord* (1 Cor 1:30-31). From this his intention brought him to the point of saying afterwards as a rebuke, *You are, after all, still carnal. For, when there is jealously and strife among you, are you not still carnal, and do you not live in a merely human fashion? For, when someone says, I am Paul's, and another says, I belong to Apollos, are you not merely human? What, then, is Apollos? What is Paul? Ministers through whom you came to believe, as the Lord granted to each. I planted; Apollos watered, but God gave the increase. Therefore, neither the one who plants nor the one who waters is anything, but only God who gives the increase.* (1 Cor 3:2-7) Do you see that the Apostle is striving for nothing else than that a human being may be humbled and that God alone may be exalted? For, in the case of those who are planted and watered, he

---

25. The Letter of Hilary 4.

says that the one who plants and the one who waters are nothing, but only God who gives the increase, even though he attributes not to them but to God the very fact that the one plants and the other waters when he says, *As the Lord granted to each. I planted; Apollos watered.*

Continuing, then, in the same intention, he came from here to where he said, *Let no one, then, boast in a human being* (1 Cor 3:21). For he had already said, *That one who boasts may boast in the Lord* (1 Cor 1:31). After these points and some others which are connected to them, his intention brought him to where he said, *But I have, my brothers, applied this to myself and to Apollos on your account in order that from us you may learn, in accord with what scripture says,*[26] *not to be puffed up with pride, one against another. For who has set you apart? But what do you have that you have not received? If, however, you have received, why do you boast as if you have not received?* (1 Cor 4:6-7)

Paul Was Not Speaking of Natural Gifts

10. In this perfectly clear intention of the Apostle, by which he speaks against human pride so that no one may boast in a human being but in the Lord, it is utterly absurd, as I see it, to think of the natural gifts of God, whether the whole and perfect nature as it was given in the original creation or the remnants, such as they are, in our damaged nature. After all, are human beings distinguished from other human beings by these gifts which are common to all human beings? But the Apostle first said, *For who has set you apart?* and then he added, *But what do you have that you have not received?* A person puffed up with pride against another could, of course, say, My faith, my righteousness, or something else sets me apart.

Countering such thoughts the good teacher says, *But what do you have that you have not received?* From whom but from him who sets you apart from another to whom he has not given what he gave to you? *If, however, you have received,* he says, *why do you boast as if you have not received?* Does he aim at anything else but that *one who boasts may boast in the Lord*? Nothing, however, is so contrary to this idea as that anyone should boast of his own merits as if he himself,

---

26. The clause is difficult; it literally says, "not beyond what is written."

not the grace of God, produced these merits for him. But the grace which sets the good apart from the evil is not common to the good and the evil.

Granted, then, there is a grace ascribed to nature by which we are rational animals and are set apart from the other animals. Granted, then, there is also a grace ascribed to nature by which among human beings the handsome are set apart from the ugly and the talented are set apart from the slow, and any other differences of this sort. But the person whom the apostle was restraining was not puffed up with pride over against an animal or over against another human being in terms of some natural gift which could be present even in the very worst human being. Rather, that person was puffed up with pride, attributing to himself, not to God, some good which pertains to the good life. Hence, he deserved to hear, *For who has set you apart? But what do you have that you have not received?*

For, though to be able to have faith belongs to our nature, does it also belong to our nature to have faith? *For not all have faith* (2 Thes 3:2), though all are able to have faith. But the Apostle did not say, But what can you have that you have not received the ability to have? Rather, he said, *But what do you have that you have not received?* Hence, to be able to have faith, just as to be able to have love, belongs to the nature of human beings, but to have faith, just as to have love, belongs to the grace of the faithful.

That nature, therefore, in which we were given the possibility of having faith, does not set one human being apart from another. But faith itself sets a believer apart from one who does not believe. And for this reason where it says, *For who has set you apart? But what do you have that you have not received?* whoever dares to say, "I have faith from myself; I have not, then, received it," certainly contradicts this most evident truth. It is not that to believe or not to believe does not lie within the choice of the human will, but that in those who have been chosen the will is prepared by the Lord.[27] Hence, the words, *For who has set you apart? But what do you have that you have not received?* also apply to the faith which is found in the will.

---

27. See Prv 8:35 LXX.

Though a Gift of God, Faith Is Voluntary

6, 11. [The objection is raised:] "Many hear the word of the truth, but some believe and others reject it. The first, therefore, will to believe, but the latter do not." Who does not know this? Who would deny it? But since for some the will is prepared by the Lord and for others it is not prepared, we must, of course, distinguish what comes from God's mercy and what comes from his judgment. The Apostle says, *Israel did not obtain what it was seeking. The chosen, however, have obtained it, but the rest have been blinded, as scripture says, God gave to them a spirit of stupor, eyes so that they do not see and ears so that they do not hear, up to the present day. And David says, Let their table become a snare, a retribution and a stumbling block. Let their eyes be dimmed so that they do not see, and bend their back forever.* (Rom 11:7-10)

There you see mercy and judgment: mercy toward the chosen who have obtained the righteousness of God, but judgment for the rest who have been blinded. And yet the one group believed because they willed to, and the other did not believe because they did not will to. Mercy and judgment, then, were produced in their very wills. Their being chosen is, of course, due to grace, certainly not to their merits. For he had said before, *So too, then, a remnant has also been saved in the present time through the election of grace. But if it is by grace, it is no longer because of works; otherwise, grace is no longer grace.* (Rom 11:5-6) What the chosen have obtained, therefore, they have obtained gratuitously. They did not already have something of their own which they might first give to him in order that they might be repaid. He saved them in return for nothing. But the rest who were blinded, as the Apostle did not fail to mention there, received this blindness as a repayment. *All the ways of the Lord are mercy and truth* (Ps 25:10). But *his ways* are *unsearchable* (Rom 11:33). Unsearchable, then, are both the mercy by which he gratuitously sets some free and the judgment by which he justly judges others.

The Distinction between Faith and Works

7, 12. They may perhaps say, "The Apostle distinguishes faith from works. He says that grace does not come from works, but he does not say that it does not come from faith." That is true, but Jesus says that faith itself is also a work of God and commands that we do this work. For the Jews said to him, *What shall we do in order to do the work of God? Jesus replied and said to them, This is the work of God, that you believe in him whom he sent.* (Jn 6:28-29) The Apostle, therefore, distinguishes faith from works, just as in the two kingdoms of the Hebrews Judah is distinguished from Israel, though Judah is Israel. But he says that a human being is made righteous because of faith, not because of works, for faith is given first. And by it one obtains the other things by which one lives righteously, and these are called works in the proper sense. For he also says, *You have been saved by faith, and this does not come from you, but is a gift of God,* that is, what I said is "by faith" does not come from you. Rather, faith is also a gift of God. He adds, *Not because of works so that no one may be filled with pride.* (Eph 2:8-9)

For it is often said that someone merited to believe because he was a good man even before he believed. This could be said of Cornelius whose alms were accepted and whose prayers were heard before he believed in Christ.[28] Nor did he give alms and pray without some faith. For how could he call upon him in whom he did not believe?[29] But if he could have been saved without faith in Christ, the apostle Peter would not have been sent like an architect to build him up, and yet *unless the Lord builds the house, those who build it labor in vain* (Ps 127:1). And they say to us, "Faith comes from us; the other things which pertain to the works of righteousness come from the Lord," as if faith does not pertain to the building—as if, I say, the foundation does not pertain to the building. But if it pertains to it first of all and most of all, he labors in vain, building up the faith by preaching, unless the Lord builds it up interiorly by showing mercy. Whatever good works, then, Cornelius did before he believed in Christ and when he believed and after he believed, must all be attributed to God, so that no one might be filled with pride.

Proof from the Words of the Lord Jesus

8, 13. Hence, after the one Teacher and Lord himself had said, as I mentioned above, *This is the work of God, that you believe in him*

28. See Acts 10:4.
29. See Rom 10:14.

whom he sent (Jn 6:29), he said a little later in his same discourse, *I said to you that you have seen me and have not believed. Everything which the Father gives me will come to me.* (Jn 6:36.37) What does *will come to me* mean but will believe in me? But it is a gift of God that this takes place. So too, he says a little later, *Do not murmur among yourselves. No one can come to me unless the Father who sent me draws him, and I shall raise him up on the last day. And it was written in the prophets, And they will all be taught by God. Everyone who has heard my Father and has learned comes to me.* (Jn 6:43-46)

What does *Everyone who has heard my Father and has learned comes to me* mean but that there is no one who has heard my Father and has learned who does not come to me? If everyone who has heard my Father and has learned comes, then everyone who does not come has not heard my Father or has not learned. For, if one had heard and had learned, he would come. For no one has heard and learned and has not come, but *everyone*, as the Truth said, *who has heard my Father and has learned comes.*

This school in which the Father is heard and teaches in order that one might come to the Son is far removed from the senses of the flesh. The Son himself is also there, because he is the Father's Word by which he teaches in this way, nor does he do this with the ear of the flesh but with the ear of the heart. The Spirit of the Father and of the Son is also there with them, for he too teaches and he does not teach separately. We, of course, say that the works of the Trinity are inseparable. And he is certainly the Holy Spirit of whom the Apostle says, *Having, however, the same Spirit of faith* (2 Cor 4:13). But this is attributed to the Father most of all because from him the Only-Begotten is born and from him the Holy Spirit proceeds. It would take a long time to discuss this more precisely, and I think that our work in fifteen books of *The Trinity*, which is God, has already come into your hands.[30]

This school, I repeat, in which God is heard and teaches, is far removed from the senses of the flesh. We see that many come to the Son because we see that many believe in Christ, but we do not see where and how they heard this from the Father and learned it. This

---

30. Augustine's *Trinity* was so popular a work that the first twelve books were stolen from the author and published without his permission. The work was completed by Augustine in 420 or later.

grace has been too well hidden, but who has any doubt that it is grace? This grace, therefore, which the divine generosity gives in a hidden manner to human hearts is not rejected by any hard heart. It is, in fact, given precisely in order that hardness of heart may first of all be removed. When, therefore, the Father is heard interiorly and teaches so that one comes to the Son, he removes the heart of stone and gives a heart of flesh, as he promised by the preaching of the prophet.[31] In that way he makes the children of the promise and the vessels of mercy which he prepared for glory.[32]

Why the Father Does Not Teach Everyone

14. Why, then, does he not teach all people in order that they may come to Christ, unless it is that he teaches out of mercy all those whom he teaches but out of judgment does not teach those whom he does not teach? For *he shows mercy to whom he wills and he hardens whom he wills* (Rom 9:18), but he shows mercy by giving them good gifts and hardens by repaying them with the punishments they deserved. Or, as some prefer to distinguish them, these words are those of the person to whom the Apostle says, *You, then, say to me.* In that case this person is taken to have said, *Therefore, he shows mercy to whom he wills and he hardens whom he wills,* as well as those which follow, that is, *Why does he still find fault? For who can resist his will?* (Rom 9:19) But did the Apostle reply to this, "What you, a human being, have said is false"? No! He rather replied, *Who are you, a human being, to answer back to God? Does the pot say to its maker, Why have you made me so? Does the potter not have power to make from the same lump of clay*, and the rest which you know very well?

And yet, in a certain way the Father teaches all people to come to the Son. For it was not written pointlessly in the prophets, *And all will be taught by God* (Is 54:13). After he had set forth that testimony, he then added, *Everyone who has heard my Father and has learned comes to me* (Jn 6:45). Just as, then, we speak correctly when we say of some teacher of literature who is the only one in a city, "This person teaches literature to everyone here," not because everyone learns, but because no one of those who learn literature learns

31. See Ez 11:19.
32. See Rom 9:23.

it except from him, so we say correctly, "God teaches everyone to come to Christ," not because everyone comes to him, but because no one comes to him in any other way. But the Apostle discloses, to the extent he judged it should be disclosed, why he does not teach everyone, namely, *Wanting to manifest his anger and to demonstrate his power, he endured with much patience the vessels of anger which were made for destruction in order also to make known the riches of his glory toward the vessels of mercy which he prepared for glory* (Rom 9:22-23).

It is for this reason that *the word of the cross is folly for those who are perishing, but the power of God for those who are being saved* (1 Cor 1:18). God teaches all these latter to come to Christ, for he *wills that all* these *be saved and come to the knowledge of the truth* (1 Tm 2:4). For, if he had willed to teach those others to come to Christ for whom the word of the cross is folly, they too would undoubtedly come. After all, he neither deceives nor is deceived who said, *Everyone who has heard my Father and has learned comes to me*. Heaven forbid, then, that anyone does not come who has heard the Father and has learned.

15. "Why," they ask, "does he not teach everyone?" If we say that those whom he does not teach do not want to learn, we will receive the reply, "And what has happened to those words we say to him, *O God, you will convert us and give us life*" (Ps 85:7)? Or, if God does not make persons willing from unwilling, why does the Church pray for her persecutors in accord with the Lord's command?[33] For Saint Cyprian also wanted us to understand in that sense the words we say, *May your will also be done on earth as it is in heaven* (Mt 6:10),[34] that is, just as your will is done in those who have already believed and are like heaven, so may it also be done in those who do not believe and are, for this reason, like earth.

Why, then, do we pray for those who do not will to believe if not in order that God might also produce the will in them?[35] The Apostle certainly says of the Jews: *Brothers, the good will of my heart and prayer to God is certainly for them, that they may be saved* (Rom 10:1). What does he ask for on behalf of those who do not believe but that they may believe? For they do not obtain salva-

---

33. See Mt 5:44.
34. See Cyprian, *The Lord's Prayer* 17.
35. See Phil 2:13.

tion in any other way. If, then, the faith of those who pray anticipates the grace of God, does the faith of those for whom they pray that they may believe anticipate the grace of God? After all, our prayer for them is that faith itself may be given to those who do not believe, that is, to those who do not have the faith.

When, therefore, the gospel is preached, some believe, and some do not believe, but those who believe when the preacher speaks externally hear the Father internally and learn. Those, however, who do not believe hear him externally but do not hear him internally and do not learn. That is, the former receive the gift of faith; the latter do not. For *no one*, he says, *comes to me unless the Father draws him* (Jn 6:44). Later he says this more clearly. For after a while, when he was speaking about eating his flesh and drinking his blood and some of his disciples also said, *This is a hard saying; who can hear it? Jesus, knowing in himself that his disciples were murmuring about this, said to them, Does this scandalize you?* (Jn 6:60-61) And a little later he said, *The words which I have spoken to you are spirit and life, but there are some among you who do not believe* (Jn 6:64-65). And after that the evangelist said, *For Jesus knew from the beginning who were going to believe and who was going to betray him, and he said, This was the reason I said to you: No one can come to me unless it has been given to him by my Father* (Jn 6:65-66). Therefore, being drawn to Christ by the Father and hearing the Father and learning from him to come to Christ is nothing else than to receive from the Father the gift of believing in Christ. For he who said, *No one comes to me unless it has been given to him by my Father*, was distinguishing not those who hear the gospel from those who do not hear it but those who believe from those who do not believe.

In Both Its Beginning and Its Completion Faith Is a Gift

·   16. Faith, then, both in its beginning and in its completion, is a gift of God, and let absolutely no one who does not want to be opposed to the perfectly clear sacred writings deny that this gift is given to some and not given to others. But why it is not given to all ought not to disturb a believer who believes that because of the one all have entered into condemnation,[36] which is undoubtedly most just, and

---

36. See Rom 5:18.

that there would be no just grounds for blaming God even if no one were set free from it. From this we are shown that it is a great grace that very many are set free and recognize what they deserved in those who are not set free, so that *one who boasts may boast* not in his own merits which he sees are equal to those of the condemned but *in the Lord*. But as to why he sets free this person rather than that one, *his judgments are inscrutable, and his ways unsearchable* (Rom 11:33). After all, it is better in this case too that we hear or say, *Who are you, a man, to answer back to God?* (Rom 9:20) rather than dare to say, as if we had knowledge of it, what he willed to be hidden who could not, nonetheless, will anything unjust.

Augustine's Answer to Porphyry

9, 17. You call to mind what I said in a certain book of mine against Porphyry under the title, "The Time of the Christian Religion."[37] I said that so that I might pass over a more careful and toilsome discussion of grace, without, of course, omitting its meaning, since I did not want to explain in that place that doctrine which could be explained elsewhere or by others. For, in replying to the question raised for me, namely, why Christ came after so long a time, I said, among other things, the following: "Hence," I wrote, "they do not object to Christ that all do not follow his teaching. For even they realize that this objection can by no means be justifiably raised either against the wisdom of the philosophers or even against the divinity of their gods. Let us leave aside the depth of the wisdom and the knowledge of God[38] in which there perhaps lies hidden far more deeply another divine plan, and let us also leave without prejudice other reasons which could be sought by the wise. What reply will they make to us, if in the discussion of this question we say this merely for the sake of brevity, namely, that Christ then willed to reveal himself to human beings and willed that his teaching be preached among them when he knew and where he knew there were those people who would believe in him? For he foreknew that in these times and these places in which

---

37. See the Letter of Hilary 3, where Hilary calls to mind what Augustine had written in Letter 102 to the priest, Deogratias, who had asked Augustine to reply to six questions with regard to the pagans. The second question is entitled "The Time of the Christian Religion."

38. See Rom 11:33.

his gospel was not preached they would all react to the preaching of the gospel just as many, but not all, reacted to his bodily presence, that is, those who refused to believe in him even when he raised the dead. Even now, when the predictions of the prophets concerning him have been fulfilled with such great evidence, we see that many such people still refuse to believe. They prefer to resist with human cleverness rather than to yield to the authority of God, which is so clear and evident, so lofty and loftily spread throughout the world. They refuse to believe as long as the tiny and weak intellect of a human being is unable to attain the divine truth. Why, then, is it surprising, if Christ knew that the world was full of such non-believers during the previous ages, that he rightly did not will to reveal himself or be preached to those whom he foreknew would not believe either his words or his miracles? For it is not unbelievable that at that time they were all the same sort of people as, much to our surprise, we see that so many of them are from his coming up to this time.

"And yet, from the beginning of the human race, occasionally in a more hidden way, occasionally in a more evident way, as God saw that it was appropriate to the times, he did not cease to speak in prophecies, and there were not lacking those who believed in him, both from Adam up to Moses and in the people of Israel, which was by a particular mystery a nation of prophets, as well as in other nations before Christ came in the flesh. For some are already mentioned in the holy books of the Hebrews from the time of Abraham, people not his descendants according to the flesh, nor members of the people of Israel, nor those who joined the people of Israel from another society; they were, nonetheless, sharers in this mystery. Why, then, should we not believe that there were also others now and then at other times and in other peoples, even though we do not find that they were mentioned in the same authorities? In that way the salvation brought by this religion, the only true religion by which true salvation is also truly promised, was never lacking to anyone who was worthy of it, and one to whom it was lacking was unworthy of it. And from the beginning of the propagation of the human race up to the end, this salvation is preached to some for their reward, to others for their judgment. And for this reason, God foreknew that those to whom it was not preached at all were not going to believe, and yet those who were not going to believe, though salvation was proclaimed to them, were revealed as an example to those others. But these people who were going to believe when salvation is proclaimed are being prepared for the kingdom of heaven and the company of the holy angels."[39]

18. Do you see that I wanted to say about the foreknowledge of Christ, without prejudice to the hidden plan of God and other causes, what seemed sufficient to refute the unbelief of the pagans who raised this question as an objection? For what is more true than that Christ knew in advance who would believe in him and when and where they would? But I did not think it was necessary at that point to investigate and to discuss whether they were going to have faith by themselves, when Christ was preached to them, or whether they were going to receive it as a gift from God, that is, whether God only foreknew them or also predestined them.

Hence, my words, "At that time Christ willed to reveal himself to human beings and willed that his teaching be preached among them when he knew and where he knew there were those who would believe in him,"[40] can also be rephrased as follows: At that time Christ willed to reveal himself to human beings and willed that this teaching be preached among them when he knew and where he knew that there were those who were chosen in him before the creation of the world.[41] But since, if I stated it that way, it would turn the reader's attention to those questions which it is now necessary to discuss more completely and more laboriously because of the warning from the Pelagian error, it seemed to me that I should say briefly what was enough at that time, leaving aside, as I said, the depth of the wisdom and knowledge of God[42] and without any prejudice to other causes about which I thought that I would speak more appropriately, not then, but at another time.

The Difference between Predestination and Foreknowledge

10, 19. Likewise I said, "The salvation brought by this religion was never lacking to anyone who was worthy, and one to whom it was lacking was unworthy."[43] If one examines and asks why anyone is worthy, there are not lacking those who say that this is due to the

---

39. Letter 102, 14-15.
40. Ibid. 14.
41. See Eph 1:4.
42. See Rom 11:33.
43. Letter 102, 15.

human will. But we say that it is due to God's grace or predestination. Between grace and predestination, however, there is only this difference, namely, that predestination is the preparation for grace, while grace is its actual bestowal. And so, the Apostle's words, *Not on the basis of works, lest anyone might perhaps be filled with pride, for we are his work, created in Christ Jesus for good works,* are grace, but what follows, *which God prepared in order that we might walk in them* (Eph 2:9-10), is predestination. Predestination cannot exist without foreknowledge, but foreknowledge can exist without predestination. By predestination, of course, God foreknew those things which he himself was going to do; for this reason it was said, *He produced those things which will be* (Is 45:11 LXX). But he is able to foreknow even those things which he himself does not produce, such as sins of any sort. For there are some sins which are sins in such a way that they are also punishments of sins, for which reason scripture says, *God handed them over to an evil frame of mind so that they would do actions which are not right* (Rom 1:28). There you find not God's sin but his judgment. Hence, the predestination of God which is for the good is, as I said, the preparation for grace, but grace is the result of predestination.

God therefore promised to Abraham in his offspring the faith of the nations when he said, *I have made you the father of many nations* (Gn 17:4-5). Because of this the Apostle says, *Therefore, on the basis of faith in order that the promise according to grace may be firm for every descendant* (Rom 4:16). God made this promise not on the basis of the power of our will but on the basis of his predestination. For he promised what he himself was going to do, not what human beings were going to do. For, though human beings do good actions which pertain to worshiping God, he himself brings it about that they do what he commands; they do not bring it about that he does what he promised. Otherwise, it would lie not in God's power but in the power of human beings that God's promises are kept, and human beings themselves would give to Abraham what God promised. But Abraham did not believe in that way; rather, *giving glory to God,* he believed *that he is also able to do what he promised* (Rom 4:20-21). He does not say, To foretell; he does not say, To foreknow. For he can also foretell and foreknow what others do. Rather, he says, *He is also able to do*—and, for this reason, to do, not what others do, but what he himself does.

God Promised Abraham the Faith,
Not the Works of the Nations

20. Or did God perhaps promise to Abraham the good works of the nations in his descendant, that is, did he promise what he himself does, but did not promise the faith of the nations which human beings produce for themselves? Rather, God foreknew that human beings would have faith, while he promised what he himself does. Certainly the Apostle does not speak that way; God, of course, promised children to Abraham who would follow in the footsteps of his faith, and he says this most clearly.

But if he promised the works of the nations and not their faith, then, since good works only come from faith—after all, *The righteous live from faith* (Hb 2:4; Rom 1:17), and, *Everything which does not come from faith is sin* (Rom 14:23), and, *Without faith it is not possible to please God* (Heb 11:6)—it is nonetheless in the power of human beings that God fulfills what he promised. For, unless a person does what pertains to a person apart from God's gift, God himself will not produce what he gives. That is, unless a person has faith from himself, God does not fulfill what he promised, namely, that God gives the works of righteousness. And, for this reason, it is not in the power of God, but in the power of the person, that God can fulfill his promises. If truth and piety forbid that we believe this, let us believe along with Abraham that God is also able to do what he promised.[44] But God promised children to Abraham, and they could not be children unless they had faith. Therefore, he also gives faith.

It Is Better to Trust God's Promise Than Oneself

11, 21. Since the Apostle says, *Therefore, on the basis of faith in order that the promise according to grace may be firm,* I am truly amazed that human beings prefer to entrust themselves to their own weakness rather than to the firmness of God's promise. "But," someone says, "I am uncertain about God's will for me." What then? Are you certain about your own will for yourself? And do you not fear these words, *Let one who thinks he stands watch out that he does not fall* (1 Cor 10:12)? Since each of these, therefore, is uncertain, why

---

44. See Rom 4:21.

does a person not entrust his faith, hope, and love to the more firm rather than the less firm?

An Answer to an Objection from Scripture

22. They assert, "But when scripture says, *If you believe, you will be saved* (Rom 10:9), one of these is demanded, the other offered. What is demanded is in the power of a human being; what is offered is in the power of God."[45] Why are both of them, what he commands and what he offers, not in the power of God? For we ask that he may give what he commands;[46] believers ask that their faith may be increased; they ask for non-believers that faith may be granted to them. But both in its increments and in its beginnings faith is a gift of God. Scripture, however, says, *If you believe, you will be saved*, in the same sense as it says, *If by the spirit you put to death the deeds of the flesh, you will live* (Rom 8:13). For in this case too one of these two is demanded and the other offered. *If by the spirit*, it says, *you put to death the deeds of the flesh, you will live*; hence, it is demanded that by the spirit we put to death the deeds of the flesh, but it is offered us that we live.

Do you, then, want us to say that to put to death the deeds of the flesh is not a gift of God and to profess that it is not a gift of God, because we hear that it is required of us, while the reward of life is offered us, if we do this? Heaven forbid that those who partake of grace and defend it should be pleased with this! This is the damnable error of the Pelagians, whose mouths the Apostle soon closed when he added, *For, as many as are driven by the Spirit of God, these are the children of God* (Rom 8:14), so that we would not believe that we put to death the deeds of the flesh not by the Spirit of God but by our own spirit. He also said there of this Spirit of God, *But one and the same Spirit does all these works, apportioning to each one as he wills* (1 Cor 12:11). Among all these works he also mentioned faith, as you know. Though it is a gift of God to put to death the deeds of the flesh, it is nonetheless demanded of us, and we are offered the reward of life in return. In the same way, then, faith is also a gift of God, though it is

---

45. See the Letter of Hilary 2.
46. An allusion to Augustine's prayer in *Confessions* X, 29, the words which triggered a violent reaction from Pelagius when he first heard them. See *The Gift of Perseverance* 20, 53, where Augustine recounts this incident.

demanded of us, and we are offered the reward of salvation in return, when scripture says, *If you believe, you will be saved.* For we are commanded to do these actions, and they are shown to be gifts of God in order that we might understand both that we do them and that God makes us do them, as he says most clearly through the prophet Ezekiel. For what could be clearer than where he says, *I shall make you do it* (Ez 36:27)? Pay attention to this passage of scripture, and you will see that God promises that he will make them do what he commands them to do. He is, of course, not silent there about their merits, but they are evil merits.[47] He shows by them that he gives good merits in return for evil ones by the fact that he makes them henceforth have good works when he makes them observe the divine commandments.

Two Examples of Gratuitous Predestination

12, 23. But this whole argument by which we are maintaining that the grace of God through Jesus Christ our Lord is truly grace, that is, that it is not given in accord with our merits, is stated with the greatest clarity by the testimonies of the words of God. Yet it encounters some difficulty, with respect to the age of adults who already have the use of the choice of the will, among people who suppose that they are being held back from every pursuit of piety unless they ascribe something to themselves which they may first give to God in order to be repaid in turn. But when we come to the little ones and to the very mediator between God and human beings, the man Jesus Christ,[48] every claim to human merits preceding the grace of God collapses. For those little ones are not set apart from the rest by any good merits, so they belong to the deliverer of human beings, nor was he made the deliverer of human beings by any preceding human merits, since he too was a man.

The Predestination of the Little Ones

24. For who would listen to the idea that at their infant age little ones leave this life after being baptized in return for their future merits and that others at the same age die without baptism because their future merits, though evil ones, were also foreseen? Thus God would

---

47. See Ez 36:31.
48. See 1 Tm 2:5.

not reward or condemn them for living a good or a bad life, but for not having lived at all.[49] The Apostle, in fact, set a limit beyond which the imprudent conjecture—to put it mildly—of a human being ought not to go. For he says, *We shall all stand before the judgment seat of Christ in order that each of us may receive recompense for what we have done in the body, either good or evil* (2 Cor 5:10). He says, *have done*; he did not add, or was going to do. But I do not know how it entered the minds of such people that God is going to reward or punish future merits of little ones which are not going to be.

But why was it said that a human being will be judged in accord with what he did in the body, since many things are done by the mind alone, not through the body or through any member of the body? And often such thoughts are so grave that they deserve a most just punishment, for example, to pass over other examples, the fact that *the fool said in his heart, There is no God* (Ps 14:1). What, then, does *for what we have done in the body* mean but, For what we have done during the time we were in the body, so that we understand *in the body* to mean, During the time we are in the body? After leaving the body, however, no one will be in the body except at the final resurrection, not to earn any merits, but to receive rewards for good merits and punishments for evil merits. But during this intervening time between setting aside the body and receiving it back, souls are either tormented or at rest in return for what they did during their time in the body. To this time in the body there also pertains original sin, which the Pelagians deny but the Church of Christ confesses. And when infants die, with that sin either removed by the grace of God or not removed by the judgment of God, they either pass by the merit of rebirth from evil to good or pass by the merit of their origin from evil to evil. The Catholic faith knows this; some heretics also agree to this without any opposition. But, though in wonder and amazement, I cannot fathom how men whose talents, as your letters reveal, do not deserve contempt could think that anyone is judged not in accord with the merits he had while he was in the body but in accord with the merits he would have had if he had lived longer in the body. Nor would I dare to believe this unless I did not dare not to believe you.

But I hope that God will provide help in order that, once they have been admonished, they may quickly see that, if those sins

---

49. See the Letter of Prosper 5.

which according to them would have been committed can rightfully be punished by the judgment of God in the case of the non-baptized, they can also be forgiven by the grace of God in the case of the baptized. For whoever says that future sins can only be punished by God's judgment, but cannot be forgiven by God's mercy, ought to consider how great an injury he does to God and to his grace, as if God could foreknow a future sin, but could not also pardon it.[50] But if this is absurd, he ought even more to have rescued by the bath which washes sins away the infants who die at a tender age, but who would have become sinners if they lived longer.

An Idea That Tends to Do Away with Original Sin

13, 25. But they may perhaps say that sins are forgiven those who do penance and that these infants who die at a tender age are not baptized because God foreknew that they would not do penance if they had lived, whereas God foreknew that those who are baptized and leave the body as little ones would have done penance if they had lived. Let them, then, pay attention and see that, if this is the case, original sins are no longer punished in little ones who die without baptism, but the sins of each one which would have been committed if he lived. Let them also pay attention and see that original sins are not forgiven the baptized, but their sins which would have been committed if they lived, since they could only sin at a later age. But God foresaw that some would do penance and that others would not, and for this reason some left this life after being baptized and others without baptism.

If the Pelagians dared to maintain this, they would no longer struggle, when they deny original sin, to find for the little ones a place of some sort of happiness outside the kingdom of God, especially when they are convinced that they cannot have eternal life because they have not eaten the flesh or drunk the blood of Christ.[51] Moreover, in the case of those who have absolutely no sin, baptism which is conferred for the forgiveness of sins is a fraud.

For the Pelagians would, of course, say that there is no original sin, but that those infants who are released from their bodies are either

---

50. Augustine plays on the Latin *praenosci possit, nec possit ignosci.*
51. See Jn 6:54.

baptized or not baptized in accord with the merits they would have if they lived and that in accord with their future merits they either receive or do not receive the body and blood of Christ without which they cannot, of course, have life. And they would say that they are baptized for the genuine forgiveness of sins, though they contracted no sin from Adam, because they are forgiven the sins for which God foreknew that they would do penance. In that way they would easily press and win their case, by which they deny that there is original sin and maintain that the grace of God is only given in accord with our merits. But because the future merits of human beings which will not exist are undoubtedly no merits—and it is quite easy to see this—not even the Pelagians could, therefore, have said this, and for even better reasons these brothers ought not to have said this. I cannot express how annoying I find it that these men have not seen what the Pelagians saw was utterly false and absurd, though these men condemn along with us the error of those heretics by the Catholic authority.

The Testimony of Cyprian and of the Book of Wisdom

14, 26. Cyprian wrote a book called *Mortality*, which is highly praised by many and nearly all who are fond of ecclesiastical writing. In it he says that death is not only not without benefit for the faithful but is even found to be beneficial for them, precisely because it removes human beings from the dangers of sinning and places them in the security of not sinning.[52] But what good does it do if even future sins which are not committed are punished? Cyprian nonetheless shows quite amply and very well that the dangers of sinning are not lacking in this life and do not continue after it. He also cited there the testimony from the Book of Wisdom: *He was carried off so that evil would not change his mind* (Wis 4:11).[53]

I too cited that passage, and you said that those brothers rejected it on the grounds that it was not drawn from a canonical book, as if without the testimony of this book the matter which we wanted to teach by it is itself not clear. For what Christian would dare to deny that, if a righteous man is taken by an early death, he is in a place of rest?[54] What person of sound faith will suppose that anyone who said

---

52. Cyprian, *Mortality* 15.
53. Ibid. 23.
54. See Wis 4:7.

this must be resisted? The same thing is true if he says that, if a righteous person abandons his righteousness in which he lived for a long time and dies in that impiety in which he lived—I do not say "for one year," but "for one day"—he will go from here into the punishments owed to the wicked, and his past righteousness will profit him nothing. Who among the faithful would contradict this obvious truth? But if we are asked whether, if he had died when he was righteous, he would have met with punishments or rest, would we hesitate to reply that he would have found rest?

This is the whole reason why it was said by whomever it was said, *He was carried off so that evil would not change his mind.* For this was said in terms of the dangers of this life, not in terms of the foreknowledge of God, who foreknew what was going to be, not what was not going to be; that is, he foreknew that he was going to grant him an early death in order to remove him from the uncertainty of temptations, but he did not foreknow that this man was going to sin who was not going to remain in temptation. We read about this life, of course, in the Book of Job, *Is not human life on the earth a temptation?* (Jb 7:1 LXX) But as to why it is granted to some that they are taken from the dangers of this life while they are righteous, but other righteous persons are kept in the same dangers by a more prolonged life until they fall from righteousness, *who has known the mind of the Lord?* (Rom 11:34) And yet we are allowed to understand from this that even those righteous people who preserve good and pious morals up to the ripeness of old age and to the last day of this life ought not to boast in their own merits, but in the Lord. For he who carried off the righteous man by the shortness of his life *so that evil would not change his mind* guards a righteous man in a life of however great a length so that evil may not change his mind. But as to why he kept here a righteous person who was going to fall and whom he could have taken from here before he fell, his judgments are absolutely most just, but inscrutable.

The Authority of the Book of Wisdom

27. Since this is so, the statement from the Book of Wisdom ought not to have been rejected, for that book has merited to be proclaimed by the order of lectors in the Church of Christ for so many years and merited to be heard by all Christians, from bishops to the least of

the lay believers, penitents, and catechumens, with veneration for the authority of God. For, if from the commentators on the divine scriptures who preceded us I should bring forth a defense of this statement, which we are forced to defend with greater care and more extensively than usual against the new error of the Pelagians, that is, that the grace of God is not given in accord with our merits and is given gratuitously to whomever it is given, because it does not depend on the one who wills or on the one who runs, but on God who shows mercy,[55] but that by his just judgment it is not given to one to whom it is not given, because there is no injustice in God[56]—if I should bring forth a defense of this statement from the Catholic commentators on the words of God who came before us, these brothers for whom we are now writing this would certainly yield. For you indicated this in your letter.[57]

But what need is there for us to examine the books of those who, before this heresy arose, had no compelling reason to be concerned over this difficult question in order to resolve it? They would undoubtedly have done this if they were forced to reply to such people. The result of this is that they touched briefly and in passing in certain passages of their writings on what they thought concerning the grace of God. But they spent more time on those questions which they were defending against the enemies of the Church and on the exhortations to certain virtues by which one serves the living and true God in order to acquire eternal life and true happiness. But their frequent prayers showed in a simple way the power which the grace of God has. For they would not have asked of God that they might do what he commanded unless it was God who gave them the accomplishment of what he commanded.

28. But those who want to be instructed by the statements of commentators must rank this Book of Wisdom where we read, *He was carried off so that evil would not change his mind*, before all commentators, because outstanding commentators very close to the times of the apostles ranked it before themselves. For, when they used it as a witness, they believed that they were using nothing but the testimony of God. And it is surely clear that, in order to teach the benefit of an earlier death, blessed Cyprian argued that those who end this life in which one can sin are rescued from the dangers

---

55. See Rom 9:16.
56. See Rom 9:14.
57. The Letter of Hilary 9.

of sinning. In the same book he says among other things, "Why do you, a person destined to be with Christ and secure because of the promise of Christ, not welcome the fact that you are called to Christ and rejoice that you are free of the devil?"[58] And in another passage he says, "Children escape the danger of a perilous age."[59] So too, in another passage he says, "Why do we not make haste and run in order that we may be able to see our fatherland and to greet our parents? A great number of persons dear to us await us there, parents, brothers, sisters, and children. A numerous and large crowd, already secure about their own safety, but still concerned about our salvation, also longs for us."[60]

By these and similar statements that teacher testifies sufficiently and clearly in the brilliant light of the Catholic faith that up to the point when we set aside this body we must fear the dangers and temptations of sinning, but that afterward no one will suffer anything of the sort. But even if he did not give this testimony, when would any Christian whatsoever have any doubt about this? How, then, would it not have benefited a person who has fallen and ends this life wretchedly in that same fallen state and who is entering into the punishments owed to such people, how, I say, would it not have benefited this person very much and to the highest degree if he was carried off by death from this place of temptation before he fell?

29. And for this reason, if we are not faced with an excessively mindless stubbornness, this whole question is at an end regarding that person *who was carried off so that evil would not change his mind.* Nor should the Book of Wisdom, which has merited to be read in the Church of Christ for so great a number of years and in which we read these words, suffer any injury because it opposes those who are led astray in defense of the merits of human beings so that they attack the perfectly clear grace of God. This grace is most evident in little ones; since some of them come to the end of this life after being baptized and others without having been baptized, they sufficiently reveal mercy and judgment, mercy that is, of course, gratuitous and judgment that is deserved. For, if people were judged according to the merits of their life which they did not have because they were prevented by death, but which they would have had if they lived, it

---

58. Cyprian, *Mortality* 3.
59. Ibid. 15.
60. Ibid. 26.

would not have profited that man at all who *was carried off so that evil would not change his mind*; it would not have profited in any way those who die after having fallen if they had died before their fall—something that no Christian will dare to say.

Hence, our brothers who along with us attack the danger of the Pelagian error in defense of the Catholic faith ought not so highly to favor this Pelagian view, whereby they think that the grace of God is given in accord with our merits. In that way they try to destroy the true and fully Christian statement stemming from antiquity, *He was carried off so that evil would not change his mind*, something the Pelagians themselves do not dare to do, and they try to uphold an idea which we would not think anyone would I will not say believe but dream of, namely, that any of the dead are judged in accord with those actions they would have done if they had lived for a longer time. In that way, of course, it is clear that our claim remains undefeated, namely, that the grace of God is not given in accord with our merits, so that intelligent human beings who are opposed to this truth are forced to express these ideas which must be banished from the ears and the thoughts of all.

The Predestination of Christ the Man

15, 30. There is also the most brilliant beacon of predestination and of grace, the savior himself, the very mediator between God and human beings, the man Jesus Christ.[61] By what preceding merits of his, either of works or of faith, did the human nature which is in him obtain such a dignity? Please reply! How did he merit to be assumed by the Word coeternal with the Father into the unity of his person and to be the only-begotten Son of God? What good on his part or what sort of good came first? What did he do beforehand, what did he believe, what did he ask for that he attained this ineffable excellence? Did this man not begin to be the only Son of God from the moment he began to be because the Word created and assumed him? Did not that woman who was full of grace conceive the only Son of God? Was not the only Son of God born of the Holy Spirit and the Virgin Mary, not through the desire of the flesh, but through a singular gift of God? Was there any need to fear that, as he grew up, that man

---

61. See 1 Tm 2:5.

would sin by free choice? Or did he for this reason lack free will? And did he not rather have it to a greater degree to the extent that he was more unable to be a slave to sin? In him human nature, that is, our nature, received in a singular manner, without any preceding merits on its part, all these singularly admirable gifts as well as any others which can most truly be said to be his own. Let this man reply to God, if he dares, and say, "Why do I too not have the same?" And if he hears, *Who are you, a human being, to answer back to God?* (Rom 9:20) let him not hold himself in check, but let him increase his impudence and say, "How is it that I hear, *Who are you, a human being?* If I am what I hear I am, that is, a human being, the same as that one about whom I am speaking, why should I not be what he is? But he, after all, is so good and great by the grace of God. Why is the grace different where the nature is the same? Surely *there is no favoritism before God*" (Gn 3:25). Who would say this—I do not mean a Christian, but even a madman?

31. In our head, then, let this fountain of grace be seen, from which grace is poured out through all his members according to the measure of each. Each person becomes a Christian from the beginning of his faith by the same grace by which that man became Christ from his beginning. Each person is reborn by the Spirit by whom he was born. The same Spirit who brought it about that he had no sin produced in us the forgiveness of sins. God certainly foreknew that he was going to do these things. God certainly foresaw that he would do these things. This, then, is the predestination of the saints which was seen most clearly in the Holy One of all holy ones,[62] and who of those who understand correctly the words of the truth can deny this? For we have learned that the very Lord of glory was predestined insofar as he became man. The teacher of the nations cries out in the beginning of his letters: *Paul, a servant of Jesus Christ, called to be an apostle, set apart for the gospel of God which he had previously promised through his prophets in the holy scriptures concerning his Son, who was born for him according to the flesh of the offspring of David, who was predestined to be the Son of God in power according to the Spirit of holiness by resurrection from the dead* (Rom 1:1-4).

Jesus, therefore, was predestined so that he who was going to be the son of David according to the flesh would, nonetheless, be the

---

62. See Dn 9:24.

Son of God in power according to the Spirit of holiness, because he was born of the Holy Spirit and the Virgin Mary. This is that assumption by God the Word of the man which was ineffably brought about so that he would be truly and properly called at the same time Son of God and Son of Man, Son of Man on account of the man who was assumed, and Son of God on account of the only-begotten God who assumed the man. Otherwise, we would have to believe in a quaternity, not a trinity. That elevation of human nature was predestined, an elevation so great and so lofty and supreme, that it had no higher point to which it might be raised, just as the divinity itself had no point to which it might descend lower for us than the assumed nature of man along with the weakness of the flesh up to the death of the cross. Just as, then, that one was predestined to be our head, so we many have been predestined to be his members.

Let human merits which perished through Adam here fall silent, and let the grace of God reign, which reigns through Jesus Christ our Lord, the only Son of God, the one Lord. Let whoever finds in our head preceding merits for that singular birth look for preceding merits for the multiple rebirth in us who are his members. For that birth was not given to Christ in recompense, but simply given, so that, free from every bond of sin, he was born of the Spirit and the Virgin. In the same way it was not given to us in recompense for some merit, but was gratuitously given to us, so that we would be reborn of water and the Spirit. And if faith brought us to the bath of rebirth, we ought not for this reason to think that we first gave something to God so that we would receive in recompense the saving rebirth. He certainly made us believe in Christ who made for us the Christ in whom we believe. He produces in human beings the beginning of faith and its perfection in Jesus, who made the man *Jesus the author and perfecter of faith* (Heb 12:2), for he is referred to in that way, as you know, in the Letter to the Hebrews.

The Twofold Call to the Faith

16, 32. For God calls his many predestined children in order to make them members of his predestined only Son, not by that calling by which they too were called who refused to come to the wedding.[63] By that calling, of course, the Jews were also called for whom Christ

---

63. See Lk 14:16-20.

crucified is a scandal, as well as the nations for whom Christ crucified is folly.[64] But he calls the predestined by that calling which the Apostle specified when he said that he preached to those who were called, both Jews and Greeks, *Christ, the power of God and the wisdom of God* (1 Cor 1:24). For he said, *But to those who have been called* (1 Cor 1:24), in order to show that those others were not called. He knew, after all, that there is a special calling which is certain for those who have been called according to God's plan, *whom he foreknew and predestined to be conformed to the image of his Son* (Rom 8:28-29). Referring to that calling, he said, *Not on the basis of works, but because of the one who calls, it was said to him, The older will serve the younger* (Rom 9:12.13). Did he say, "Not on the basis of works, but because of the one who believes"? To be sure, he took this too away from human beings in order that he might ascribe everything to God. He therefore said, *But because of the one who calls*, not by just any calling, but by that calling by which one becomes a believer.

33. He also had this calling in mind when he said, *The gifts and calling of God are irrevocable* (Rom 11:29). Pay attention for a little while to what he was doing there. For, after he had said, *For I do not want you, brothers, to be ignorant of this mystery, for fear that you may be wise in yourselves. For blindness has been produced in a part of Israel until the fullness of the nations has entered, and in that way all of Israel will be saved. As it is written, A deliverer will come from Zion, and he will turn impiety away from Jacob, and this will be my testament to them when I take away their sins* (Rom 11:25-27), he immediately added something that needs to be carefully understood, *In terms of the gospel they are certainly enemies for your sake, but in terms of the election they are beloved on account of their fathers* (Rom 11:28-29). What does *in terms of the gospel they are certainly enemies on your account* mean except that their hostility, because of which they killed Christ, undoubtedly benefited the gospel, as we see? And he showed that this came from God's plan of salvation, for he knew how to make good use even of the evil, not in order that the vessels of anger might benefit him, but in order that, in his making good use of them, they might benefit the vessels of mercy. For what could have been said more clearly than the words of the Apostle, *In terms of the gospel they were certainly enemies for your sake*?

---

64. See 1 Cor 1:23.

It is, then, in the power of the evil to sin, but it is not in their power, but in the power of God who divides the darkness and orders it to his ends, that, by sinning in their malice, they bring about this or that effect. And in that way only the will of God is accomplished even by that which they do against the will of God. We read in the Acts of the Apostles that, when the apostles came to their own brothers after having been released by the Jews and indicated to them what the priests and elders had said to them, they all raised their voice in one accord to the Lord and said, *Lord, it is you who made heaven and the earth and the sea and all the things which are in them; it is you who said through the lips of our father, David, your holy servant, Why have the nations raged and peoples devised vain plans? The kings of the earth arose, and the princes gathered together against the Lord and against his Christ. For Herod and Pilate and the people of Israel truly gathered together in this city against your holy servant, Jesus, whom you anointed, to order that they might do everything which your hand and plan predestined to take place.* (Acts 4:24-28)

There you see what was meant by *in terms of the gospel they were certainly enemies for your sake.* The hand of God and his plan certainly predestined that the Jews, his enemies, would do for our sake everything which was necessary for the gospel. But what do the next words mean, *But in terms of the election they were beloved on account of their fathers?* Were those enemies of God who perished in their enmities, as well as those from this people who are opposed to Christ and are still perishing, those chosen and beloved by God? Heaven forbid! Who would say this, even if he was an utter fool? But though these two are contrary to each other, that is, to be enemies and to be beloved, even if they do not apply to the same human beings, they nonetheless apply to the same people of the Jews and to the same carnal offspring of Israel, since some of them belong to the limping, and others to the blessing of Israel.[65] For he explained this idea more clearly above where he said, *Israel did not attain what it was seeking, but the chosen have attained it. The rest, however, were blinded.* (Rom 11:7) The same Israel is nonetheless in both groups. Therefore, when we hear, *Israel did not attain,* or *The rest were blinded,* we should understand there, *enemies for our sake,* but where we hear, *But the chosen have attained it,* there we should understand,

---

65. See Gn 32:25-32. When Jacob, or Israel, wrestled with God, God put his thigh out of joint so that he limped and then blessed him.

beloved on account of their fathers, those fathers, that is, to whom the promises were made. *The promises were* certainly *made to Abraham and his offspring* (Gal 3:16).

For this reason the wild olive tree of the nations is grafted onto this domesticated olive tree.[66] Surely the election of which he speaks ought already to come to mind, because it is according to grace, not according to what is owed, for *the remnant was saved by the election of grace* (Rom 11:5). These chosen ones have obtained what they sought, while the rest have been blinded. In accord with this election the people of Israel are beloved on account of their fathers. For they were not called by that calling of which it was said, *Many are called* (Mt 20:16), but by that by which the elect are called. For this reason, here too, after he had said, *But in terms of the election they were beloved on account of their fathers*, he immediately added the words with which we are dealing, *For the gifts and calling of God are irrevocable* (Rom 11:29), that is, they have been determined steadfastly and immutably.

All those who are taught by God belong to this calling, nor can any of them say, "I believed in order that I might be called in this way." The mercy of God, of course, anticipated him, for he was called so that he would believe. For all who are taught by God come to the Son because they heard the Father and learned from him through the Son, who says with utter clarity, *Everyone who has heard the Father and has learned from him comes to me* (Jn 6:45). But none of these perishes, because nothing which the Father has given him will perish.[67] Whoever, then, belongs to that number will absolutely not perish. On this account it was said, *They went forth from us, but they did not belong to us; if they had belonged to us, they would certainly have remained with us* (1 Jn 2:19).

The Apostles Were Chosen before the Creation of the World

17, 34. Let us, then, understand the calling by which they become the chosen, not those who are chosen because they believed, but those who are chosen in order that they may believe. *You have not chosen me, but I have chosen you* (Jn 15:16). For, if they were chosen because they believed, they would of course have first chosen him by believing in him in order that they might merit to be chosen. But he

---

66. See Rom 11:17.
67. See Jn 6:39.

absolutely removes this idea who says, *You have not chosen me, but I have chosen you.* And they of course undoubtedly chose him when they believed in him. Hence, he says, *You have not chosen me, but I have chosen you,* for no other reason than that they did not choose him in order that he might choose them, but he chose them in order that they might choose him, for his mercy anticipated them as grace, not as something owed. And so he chose them from the world when he lived here in the flesh, but they had already been chosen in him before the creation of the world. This is the unchangeable truth of predestination and grace. For what do the words of the Apostle mean, *Just as he chose us in him before the creation of the world* (Eph 1:4)? If he said this because God foreknew that they would believe, not because he was himself going to make them believers, the Son denies this foreknowledge when he says, *You have not chosen me, but I have chosen you.* For, according to that foreknowledge, God would rather have foreknown that they were going to choose him in order that they might merit to be chosen by him.

The apostles were, therefore, chosen before the creation of the world by that predestination in which God foreknew his own future actions, but they were chosen from the world by that calling by which God carried out what he foreknew. For *those whom he predestined he also called,* that is, by that calling according to his plan. Not others, then, but those whom he predestined, he also called; not others, but *those whom he called* in this way, *he also made righteous*; not others, but *those whom* he predestined, called and *made righteous, he also glorified* (Rom 8:30). And of course he did that with that end which has no end.

God, therefore, chose believers, but in order that they might be believers, not because they already were. The apostle James says, *Has God not chosen the poor in this world to be rich in faith and heirs of the kingdom which God promised to those who love him?* (Jas 2:5) By choosing them, then, he made them rich in faith as well as heirs of the kingdom. He is, of course, correctly said to choose in them this faith, since he chose them in order to bring it about in them. I ask, who is there who hears the Lord say, *You have not chosen me, but I have chosen you,* and dares to say that human beings believe in order that they may be chosen? They are rather chosen in order that they may believe. Otherwise, those to whom Christ says, *You have not chosen me, but I have chosen you,* might be found to have chosen Christ contrary to the statement of the Truth.

A Proof from the Letter to the Ephesians

18, 35. Who would hear the Apostle saying, *Blessed be the God and Father of our Lord, Jesus Christ, who blessed us in Christ with every spiritual blessing in the things of heaven, just as he chose us in him before the creation of the world, that we might be holy and spotless before him in love. He predestined us to be his children by adoption through Jesus Christ in accord with the purpose of his will,*[68] *by which he bestowed his grace upon us in his beloved Son. In him we have redemption through his blood, the forgiveness of sins, according to the riches of his grace which abounded for us in all wisdom and insight in order that he might reveal to us the mystery of his will in accord with his good will, which he set forth in Christ as a plan for the fullness of time, to restore in Christ all things which are in heaven and on earth. In him we have also obtained our lot, predestined according to the plan of him who accomplishes all things according to the counsel of his will that we may live for the praise of his glory* (Eph 1:3-12)? Who, I repeat, would with care and intelligence hear the Apostle saying this and would dare to have doubts about this very clear truth which we are defending? Before the creation of the world God chose in Christ his members, and how would he choose those who did not as yet exist except by predestining them? He therefore chose them by predestining them. Would he choose the impious and unclean? For, if the question is raised whether he should choose these or rather the holy and spotless, who would hesitate about what he should answer and not immediately cast his vote in favor of the holy and spotless?

Ephesians Condemns the Pelagian View of Predestination

36. The Pelagian says, "Therefore, he foreknew who were going to be holy and spotless through the choice of their free will, and for this reason, before the creation of the world, he chose in his foreknowledge those whom he foreknew would be such people. Before they existed, therefore, he chose his predestined children whom he foreknew would be holy and spotless; of course he did not make them to be such, nor did he foresee that he would make them such, but he foresaw that they would be such."

---

68. Augustine omits here the words, *to the praise of the glory of his grace*, which he includes when he cites the same passage in *The Gift of Perseverance* 7, 15.

Let us, then, look at the words of the Apostle and see whether God chose us before the creation of the world because we were going to be holy and spotless or in order that we might be such. Paul says, *Blessed be the God and Father of our Lord, Jesus Christ, who blessed us in Christ Jesus with every spiritual blessing in the things of heaven, just as he chose us in him before the creation of the world, that we might be holy and spotless* (Eph 1:3-4). He chose us, therefore, not because we were going to be, but in order that we might be holy and spotless. Of course it is certain; of course it is clear; we were going to be such precisely because he chose us, predestining us to be such by his grace. For this reason, then, he *blessed us in Christ Jesus with a spiritual blessing in the things of heaven, just as he chose us in him before the creation of the world, that we might be holy and spotless before him in love. He predestined us to be his children by adoption through Jesus Christ.* (Eph 1:3-5) Pay attention to what he adds next; he says, *In accord with the purpose of his will,* so that we would not boast in the purpose of our own will over so great a benefit of grace. He says, *By which he bestowed his grace on us in his beloved Son* (Eph 1:5-6); in his will, then, he made us graced. "Made graced" (*gratificavit*) is derived from "grace" (*gratia*), in the same way that "made just" (*justificavit*) is derived from "justice" (*justitia*).

The Apostle says, *In him we have redemption through his blood, the forgiveness of sins, according to the riches of his grace which abounded for us in all wisdom and insight in order that he might reveal to us the mystery of his will in accord with his good will* (Eph 1:7-9). In this mystery of his will God located the riches of his grace in accord with his good will, not in accord with our good will which could not be good unless, in accord with his good will, he came to our help in order to make our will good. But after he said, *In accord with his good will,* he added, *which he set forth in Christ as a plan for the fullness of time, to restore in Christ all things which are in heaven and on earth. In him we have also obtained our lot, predestined according to the plan of him who accomplishes all things according to the counsel of his will that we may live for the praise of his glory.* (Eph 1:9-12)

37. It would take too long to discuss the individual expressions. But you undoubtedly see the great clarity with which this grace is defended by the words of the Apostle. Against this grace human merits are filled with pride, as if a human being first gives something to God in order that he may receive recompense. *God,* therefore, *chose us* in Christ *before the creation of the world; he predestined us to be his children*

by adoption, not because he knew that we were going to be holy and spotless; rather, but he chose us and predestined us in order that we might be such. But he did this *in accord with the purpose of his will* in order that no one might boast of his own will, but of the will of God toward him; he did this *according to the riches of his grace, in accord with his good will* which he set forth in his beloved Son in whom *we have obtained our lot, predestined according to the plan*, not according to a plan of ours, but *of him who accomplishes all things*, to the degree that he himself produces in us even the willing.[69] He works, however, *according to the counsel of his will in order that we may live for the praise of his glory*. This is the reason why we cry out, *That no one may boast in a human being* (1 Cor 3:21) and, for this reason, not in oneself either, but *he who boasts should boast in the Lord* (1 Cor 2:31), *in order that we may live for the praise of his glory*, certainly as holy and spotless. For this reason, he called us and predestined us before the creation of the world. From this plan of his there comes that calling proper to the chosen along with whom he *makes all things work for the good*, because *they were called according to his plan* (Rom 8:28), and *the gifts and calling of God are irrevocable* (Rom 11:29).

Predestination Does Not Rest Upon God's Foreknowledge

19, 38. But these brothers of ours, with whom and about whom we are now concerned, perhaps say that the Pelagians are refuted by this testimony of the Apostle, where he says that we were chosen in Christ and predestined before the creation of the world in order that we might be holy and spotless before him in love. For they think that, "after we have received the commandments, we now by ourselves become by the choice of our free will holy and spotless before him in love. Because God foreknew that this would be the case, he chose us before the creation of the world and predestined us in Christ."

The Apostle did not say, "Because he foreknew that we would be such," but said, "In order that we might be such through the election *of his grace, by which he bestowed his grace upon us in his beloved Son*." Therefore, when he predestined us, he foreknew his own work by which he makes us holy and spotless. Hence, the Pelagian error is rightly refuted by this testimony; they, however, say, "But we say that

---

69. See Phil 2:13.

God foreknew only our faith by which we begin to believe and for this reason chose us before the creation of the world and predestined us that we might be holy and spotless by his grace and work." But let them also listen to this testimony, where it says, *We have obtained our lot, predestined according to the plan of him who accomplishes all things.* He, then, *who accomplishes all things* brings it about that we begin to believe. This faith did not, of course, precede that calling of which it was said, *For the gifts and calling of God are irrevocable,* and of which it was said, *Not because of works, but because of him who calls* (Rom 9:12), since he could have said, "But because of him who believes." Nor did this faith precede the election to which the Lord referred when he said, *You have not chosen me, but I have chosen you.* For he chose us not because we believed but in order that we might believe, so that we would not be said to have first chosen him and so that—heaven forbid!—these words would be false, *You have not chosen me, but I have chosen you.* We are called not because we have believed but in order that we might believe, and that calling which involves no repentance works and brings it about that we believe. And it is not necessary to repeat on this point all the many things we have said.

The Scriptural Texts on the Beginning of Faith

39. Finally, in the verses which follow this testimony, the Apostle gives thanks to God regarding these people who came to believe, not, of course, because the gospel was preached to them, but because they came to believe. For he says, *In him you also heard the word of truth, the good news of your salvation; in him you have believed and have been sealed by the Holy Spirit who was promised and who is the pledge of our inheritance until we acquire redemption to the praise of his glory. For this reason, having heard of your faith in Christ Jesus and [your love][70] for all the saints, I too do not cease to offer thanks for you.* (Eph 1:13-16) Their faith was new and fresh since the gospel was just preached to them, and because he heard of that faith, the Apostle offers thanks to God on their behalf. If he offered thanks to a human being for what he either thought or knew that he had not done, it would more truly be called flattery or mockery than thanksgiving.

---

70. Augustine, as well as other ancient sources, omits the words in brackets. I have supplied them since they seem requisite to the sense of the passage.

Make no mistake: God will not be mocked (Gal 6:7), for the faith, even in its beginning, is also his gift; otherwise, the Apostle's giving thanks would be rightly judged false or deceitful.

What then shall we say? Is not the beginning of the faith on the part of the Thessalonians clear? Yet the same Apostle offers thanks to God for it when he says, *On this account we also offer thanks to God without ceasing, for, when you received from us the word of God's message, you received it not as the word of human beings but as the word of God, as it truly is, because he in whom you have believed is at work in you* (1 Thes 2:13). Why is it that he gives thanks to God for this? It is, of course, vain and pointless if God to whom he gives thanks did not himself do this. But because this is not vain and pointless, God himself, to whom he gives thanks for this action, did this so that, when they had received from the Apostle the word of God's message, they received it not as the word of human beings but as the word of God, as it truly is. By that calling, then, which is according to his plan and of which we have said a great deal, God is at work in the hearts of human beings in order that they may not hear the gospel to no avail, but that, having heard it, they may be converted and believe, receiving it not as the word of human beings but as the word of God, as it truly is.

God Opens Human Hearts to Hear His Word

20, 40. The Apostle reminds us that even that beginning of faith is a gift of God, for he teaches this when he says in the Letter to the Colossians, *Be persistent in prayer; be vigilant in that thanksgiving, praying at the same time for us as well, that God may open for us a door for his word, to speak the mystery of Christ, on account of which I am also bound in chains in order that I may make it known in the way I ought to speak it* (Col 4:2-4). How is a door for the word opened except when the mind of the hearer is opened in order that he may believe and, after the beginning of faith has been produced, may accept those things which are preached and discussed in order to build up sound teaching? Otherwise, with his heart closed through unbelief, he might disapprove and reject what is said. Hence, he says to the Corinthians, *But I shall remain at Ephesus until Pentecost, for a great and prominent door has been opened for me, and there are many enemies* (1 Cor 16:8.9). What else can be understood here but that, after the gospel was first preached there by him, many believed and many opponents of the same faith arose in accord with the words of the Lord, *No one comes to me unless it has been given to him by my Father* (Jn 6:66), and, *To you it has been given to know the mystery of the kingdom of the heavens, but to them it has not been given* (Mt 13:11)? A door, then, was opened in those to whom it was given, but there were many enemies among those to whom it was not given.

41. Likewise, the Apostle says to the same people in his second Letter, *After I had come to Troas for the gospel of Christ and a door had been opened for me in the Lord, I did not have rest for my spirit because I did not find Titus, my brother, but saying goodbye to them, I departed for Macedonia* (2 Cor 2:12-13). To whom did he say goodbye but those who had believed, that is, those in whose hearts a door was opened for the preacher of the gospel? But notice what he adds; he says, *But I thank God who always makes us triumph in Christ and reveals the fragrance of his knowledge through us in every place, because we are for God the good odor of Christ in those who are being saved and in those who are perishing, but for some the odor of death leading to death, and for others the odor of life leading to life* (2 Cor 2:14-16). See why the fiercest soldier and most unconquerable defender of grace gives thanks; see why he gives thanks: because the apostles are for God the good odor of Christ both in those who are being saved by his grace and in those who are perishing by his judgment. But in order that those who understand too little may be less disturbed at this, he warns when he adds and says, *And who is sufficient for these things?* (2 Cor 2:16)

But let us return to the opening of the door by which the Apostle indicated the beginning of faith in his hearers. For what is *praying at the same time also for you that God may open for us a door for his word* (Col 4:3) but a most clear proof that even the beginning of faith is a gift of God? For he would not ask it of him in prayer if he did not believe that God gives it.

This gift of heavenly grace had come down upon that seller of purple, for whom, as scripture says in the Acts of the Apostles, *God opened her mind, and she paid attention to what Paul was saying* (Acts 16:14). For she was called in such a way that she believed. God of course does what he wills in the hearts of human beings, whether by helping or by judging, in order to accomplish through them what his hand and his counsel have been predestined to accomplish.[71]

---

71. See Acts 4:28.

42. In vain, therefore, have they claimed that what we proved by the testimony of scripture from Kings and Chronicles does not pertain to the issue with which we are dealing, namely, that, when God wills the accomplishment of something which only willing human beings can do, their hearts are inclined to will this, that is, he inclines their hearts who produces in us in a marvelous and ineffable way the willing as well. What else does their saying nothing amount to but contradicting this? Or have they perhaps given you some reason why they had this idea which you preferred to pass over in silence in your letters?[72] But I do not know what that reason could be. Or, because we showed that God acted in the hearts of human beings and brought the wills of those whom he chose to the point that they made Saul or David king, do they perhaps think that these examples do not suit this issue, because to reign in this world for a time is not the same thing as to reign with God for eternity? And do they for this reason think that God inclines wills to establish earthly kingdoms, but that God does not incline the will of those he chooses to obtain the heavenly kingdom?

But I think that these next words were said on account of the kingdom of heaven, not on account of an earthly kingdom, *Incline my heart toward your testimonies* (Ps 119:36), or, *The steps of human beings are directed by the Lord, and they will chose his path* (Ps 37:23), or, *The will of a person is prepared by the Lord* (Prv 8:35 LXX), or, *May our Lord be with us, as he was with our fathers; let him not abandon us nor turn us away from him; let him incline our hearts toward him in order that we may walk in all his ways* (1 K 8:57-58), or, *I shall give them a heart for knowing me and ears to hear* (Bar 2:31). Let them also hear these words, *I shall put my spirit in you, and I shall make you to walk in my ordinances and observe and carry out my judgments* (Ez 36:27). Let them hear, *The steps of human beings are directed by the Lord, but how will mortals understand his ways?* (Prv 20:24) Let them hear, *Every man seems righteous to himself, but the Lord directs his heart* (Prv 21:2). Let them hear, *As many as were destined for eternal life believed* (Acts 13:48). Let them hear these words and any others which I have not mentioned by which it is shown that God prepares the wills of human beings and turns them even toward the kingdom of heaven and to eternal life. But think of what an absurdity it is that we should believe that God produces the

---

72. See the Letter of Hilary 7, where Hilary mentions the texts on the choice of Saul and of David which Augustine cited in *Rebuke and Grace* 14, 45.

wills of human beings to establish earthly kingdoms, but that human beings produce their own wills to attain the kingdom of heaven.

The Conclusion: The Beginning of Faith Is a Gift

21, 43. We have said much, and perhaps we have long since been successful in persuading the brothers of what we intend, and we still continue to speak to such fine minds as if they were dull, the sort of minds for which even what is too much is not enough. But may they pardon us, for a new question has driven us to this. For, though in our previous works we have shown with testimonies which were quite sufficient that even faith is a gift of God, some people found the objection that those testimonies were sufficient to show that an increase of faith is a gift of God, while the beginning of faith by which one first believes in Christ comes from human beings themselves and is not a gift of God. Rather, they claim, God demands this beginning of faith so that, once we have it, the other things which are gifts of God follow as if because of its merit, and none of these gifts are given gratuitously, though among these gifts they preach the grace of God, which is only gratuitous. You see how absurd this is; on this account we undertook, to the extent that we could, to demonstrate that the beginning of faith is also a gift of God. Even if we have done this at more length than these men on whose account we did this would want, we are ready to accept their rebuke for this, provided, nonetheless, they admit that, even if at much greater length than they wanted, even if to the distaste and boredom of those with understanding, we did what we did, namely, that we taught that even the beginning of faith is a gift of God, just as self-control, patience, justice, piety, and the other things are gifts, about which there is no argument with these men. Let this, then, be the end of this volume lest the excessive length of a single book cause offense.

The Gift of Perseverance

A Second Book for Prosper and Hilary

1, 1. We must now discuss perseverance with greater care. For, when in the previous book we dealt with the beginning of faith, we also said some things about it. We state, therefore, that the perseverance by which one perseveres in Christ up to the end is a gift of God. But I mean the end at which this life, in which alone there is danger that one might fall, comes to an end. And so, it is uncertain whether anyone has received this gift as long as he is living this life. For, if he falls before he dies, he is of course said and most truly said not to have persevered. How, then, is someone who has not persevered said to have received or to have had perseverance? For, if someone has chastity and falls away from it and becomes unchaste—and the same things hold for justice, patience, and faith itself—he is correctly said to have had it and no longer to have it. He was chaste or was just, patient, or believing as long as he was, but when he stopped being such, he was no longer what he was. But how was someone persevering who has not persevered, since by persevering each person shows himself to be persevering, something this person did not do?

And so that no one will fight back and say, "If from the time anyone became a believer, he has lived, for example, for ten years and in the middle of that time he fell away from the faith, did he not persevere for five years?" I am not going to argue over words if someone thinks that we should also call that perseverance as if lasting for its own time. One who has not persevered up to the end is certainly not to be said to have this perseverance which we are now discussing, the perseverance by which one perseveres in Christ up to the end. A believer of one year, and for any shorter a period one can think of, had this perseverance if he lived as a believer until he died, rather than a believer of many years if he fell away from his stability in the faith for a short time before death.

Perseverance up to the End Is God's Gift

2, 2. With that settled, let us see whether this perseverance of which it was said, W*hoever perseveres up to the end will be saved* (Mt 10:22), is a gift of God. If it is not, how is what the Apostle says

465

true, *To you it has been given on behalf of Christ, not only that you believe in him, but also that you suffer for him* (Phil 1:29)? The one of these, of course, pertains to the beginning; the other to the end.[1] Each of them, nonetheless, is a gift of God because each was said to have been given, as we have already said above.[2] After all, what is a truer beginning for a Christian than to believe in Christ? What is a better end than to suffer for Christ? But with regard to what pertains to believing in Christ, some have discovered some way of opposing this, so that they said that it was not the beginning but the increase of faith which is a gift of God, and with the help of God we have replied to that opinion more than enough.

But how can one explain why perseverance in Christ up to the end is not given to one to whom it has been given to suffer for Christ or, to speak more plainly, to whom it has been given to die for Christ? For even the apostle Peter shows that this is a gift of God when he says, *If that is God's will, it is better to suffer for doing good than for doing evil* (1 Pt 3:17). When he says, *If that is God's will,* he shows that God grants, though not to all the saints, that they suffer for Christ. For those for whom it is not the will of God that they attain the experience and glory of such suffering do nonetheless attain the kingdom of God if they persevere in Christ up to the end. But who would say that God does not give this perseverance to people who die in Christ because of an illness of the body or from any accident, though he gives a far more difficult perseverance to those who also face death itself for Christ? It is much more difficult to persevere when one's persecutor does this precisely so that one may not persevere and so that one suffers even death in order to persevere. Hence, it is more difficult to have this latter perseverance and easier to have the former. But for him for whom nothing is difficult it is easy to give each of them. For God promised this when he said, *I shall put fear of me in their hearts in order that they may not withdraw from me* (Jer 32:40). What else does this mean but that the fear of me which I shall put in their hearts will be of such a kind and so great that they will cling to me with perseverance?

---

1. That is, they pertain to the beginning and the end of Christian life in this world.
2. See *The Predestination of the Saints* 2, 4.

A Proof from the Prayer of Christians

3. But why do we ask for this perseverance from God if God does not give it? Or is this petition also a mockery when we ask from him what we know he does not give, but what lies in the power of a human being without God's giving it? In the same way that thanksgiving is also a mockery if we give thanks to God because of what he did not give us or do. But what I said there,[3] I say here as well, *Do not make a mistake*, the Apostle says, *God will not be mocked* (Gal 6:7). O man, God is witness not only of your words but also of your thoughts; if you truthfully and faithfully ask something from one so rich, believe that you receive what you ask from him from whom you ask it. Do not honor him with your lips and in pride raise yourself above him in your heart, believing that you have from yourself what you pretend to pray for from him. Or do we perhaps not ask him for this perseverance? One who says this does not now need to be refuted by my arguments, but to be overwhelmed by the prayers of the saints. Or is there any of them who does not ask from God for himself that he may persevere in him? For, when the saints pray the very prayer which is called the Lord's, because the Lord taught it to them, they realize that they ask for almost nothing but perseverance.

The First Petition of the Lord's Prayer

4. Read somewhat more carefully the explanation of this prayer in the book which the blessed martyr Cyprian composed on it, which has the title *The Lord's Prayer*, and see what an antidote he prepared so many years before against these Pelagian poisons which were still to come. For there are three points, as you know, which the Catholic Church especially defends against them. One of them is that the grace of God is not given according to our merits, because all the merits of the righteous are also the gifts of God and conferred by the grace of God. The second is that no one can live in this corruptible body without some sins, no matter how great one's righteousness is. The third is that a human being is born subject to the sin of the first man and bound by the chain of condemnation unless the guilt which is contracted by birth is removed by rebirth. Of these three, only that one which I put in the last place is not discussed in the book

---

3. See *The Predestination of the Saints* 19, 39.

of the glorious martyr which I mentioned above. But with regard to the other two his discussion in that book is so clear that we find the aforementioned heretics, the new enemies of the grace of Christ, to have been refuted long before they were born. Among these merits of the saints, therefore, which are nothing but the gifts of God, he includes perseverance, which he says is also a gift of God.

Cyprian says, "We say, *May your name be made holy* (Mt 6:9), not because we wish God to be made holy by our prayers, but because we ask of God that his name may be made holy in us. Besides, by whom is God made holy, for it is he who makes holy? But because he said, *Be holy, because I also am holy* (Lv 19:2), we pray and ask that we who have been made holy in baptism may persevere in what we have begun to be."[4] And a little later, while still discussing this same point and teaching us to ask for perseverance from the Lord, something he would not correctly and truthfully do unless this too was his gift, he says, "We pray that this holiness may remain in us, and, because our Lord and judge sternly warns those whom he has healed and brought to life not to sin lest something worse happen to them, we make this prayer with continuous petitions; we ask day and night that the holiness and restoration to life which we received from the grace of God may be preserved by his protection."[5]

This teacher, therefore, understands that we ask of God perseverance in holiness, that is, that we may persevere in holiness when we say, *May your name be made holy.* What else does it mean to ask for what we have received but that we may also be given the gift of not ceasing to have it? In the same way, then, when a holy person asks that he may be holy, he of course asks that he may continue to be holy; so too, when a chaste person asks to be chaste, when a continent person asks to be continent, when a righteous persons asks to be righteous, a pious person asks to be pious, and the other virtues which we maintain against the Pelagians to be gifts of God, they undoubtedly ask that they may continue in these goods which they know they have received. If they accept this teaching, they certainly accept that perseverance itself is also a great gift of God by which the other gifts of God are preserved.

---

4. Cyprian, *The Lord's Prayer* 12.
5. Ibid. 12.

The Second Petition of the Lord's Prayer

5. What then does it mean when we say, *May your kingdom come* (Mt 6:10)? Do we ask for anything else but that there may come to us that which we do not doubt will come to all the saints? And so, here too what do those who are already holy pray for except that they may persevere in that holiness which has been given to them? For otherwise the kingdom of God will not come to them, for it is certain that the kingdom of God will come not to others but to these persons who persevere up to the end.

The Third Petition of the Lord's Prayer

3, 6. The third petition is, *May your will be done in heaven and on earth* (Mt 6:10), or as we read in many manuscripts and is more frequently used by those who pray, *On earth as it is in heaven*, which many understand in this way: May we also do your will as the holy angels do. But that teacher and martyr wants us to understand by "heaven and earth" the spirit and the flesh and wants us to pray that we may do the will of God with each of these in harmony with the other.[6] He also saw in these words another meaning which is in harmony with the soundest faith; we have already spoken about it above,[7] namely, that the faithful, who, having put on the heavenly man, are not without reason called heaven, are understood to pray for non-believers who are still earth, bearing only the earthly man from their first birth.[8] There he clearly showed that the beginning of faith is a gift of God since the holy Church prays not only for believers that their faith may be increased or persevere, but also for non-believers that they may begin to have that faith which they did not have at all and to which their hearts are opposed.

But now we are not discussing the beginning of faith about which we have already said much in the previous book; we are, rather discussing that perseverance which one must have up to the end. Holy people who do God's will certainly ask for this when they say in prayer, *May your will be done*. For, since his will has already been done in them, why do they still ask that it be done, if not that they

---

6. See Cyprian, *The Lord's Prayer* 16.
7. See *The Predestination of the Saints* 8, 15.
8. See Cyprian, *The Lord's Prayer* 17.

may persevere in what they have begun to be? And yet one could say
here that holy persons do not ask that the will of God may be done
in heaven, but that it may be done on earth as in heaven, namely, that
earth may imitate heaven, that is, that a human being may imitate an
angel or a non-believer a believer. And for this reason holy persons
ask that what is not yet may come to be, not that what already is
may continue. For with however much holiness human beings are
endowed, they are not yet equal to the angels of God;[9] therefore, the
will of God is not yet done on earth as it is in heaven. If that is so, in
the case when we desire that human beings may become believers
from non-believers, it is clear that we pray not for their perseverance
but for their beginning. But in the case when we desire that human beings may be equal to the angels in doing the will of God, holy persons
clearly pray for perseverance when they make this prayer. For no one
attains that highest happiness which is found in the kingdom unless
he perseveres to the end in that holiness which he acquired on earth.

The Fourth Petition of the Lord's Prayer

4, 7. The fourth petition is *Give us today our daily bread* (Mt 6:11).
Here blessed Cyprian shows how it is understood in this case too that
we ask for perseverance. He says, in fact, among other things, "But
we ask that this bread be given to us daily so that those of us who are
in Christ and daily receive the Eucharist as food for our salvation may
not be separated from the body of Christ, if some more serious sin has
been committed so that we are forced to abstain and not partake of
the heavenly bread."[10] These words of the holy man of God show that
the saints certainly ask for perseverance from the Lord when they say,
Give us today our daily bread, with the intention that they may not
be separated from the body of Christ but may remain in that holiness
in which they commit no grave sin by which they would merit to be
separated from him.

The Fifth Petition of the Lord's Prayer

5, 8. In the fifth petition of the prayer we say, *Forgive us our
debts as we also forgive our debtors* (Mt 6:12). In this petition alone

9. See Lk 20:36.
10. Cyprian, *The Lord's Prayer* 18.

there is found no prayer for perseverance. For the sins which we pray may be forgiven us are past, but perseverance, which brings us to salvation for eternity, is not necessary for the period of this life which is already past, but for the time which remains up to the end. It is worthwhile, nonetheless, to observe for a moment how even in this petition the heretics who would arise long afterwards were back then run through by the tongue of Cyprian, as if by an invincible sword of the truth. For the Pelagians even dare to say that a righteous person can in this life have absolutely no sin and that in such human beings there already exists in the present time the Church which has neither spot nor wrinkle nor anything of the sort,[11] the Church which is the one and only spouse of Christ, as if that Church were not his spouse, which says throughout the whole earth what it learned from him, *Forgive us our debts as we also forgive our debtors.*

But notice how the most glorious Cyprian does them in. For, when he explained this passage of the Lord's Prayer, he said among other things, "How necessary it is, how providential and salutary, that we are warned that we are sinners who are forced to pray because of our sins. Thus, when we ask pardon of God, our mind recalls its own guilty conscience. Lest anyone be pleased with himself as if he were innocent and lest, by being filled with pride, he perish even more, we are instructed and taught that we sin daily when we are commanded to pray daily because of our sins. Finally, John too put this in his Letter when he said, *If we say that we have no sin, we deceive ourselves, and the truth is not in us* (1 Jn 1:8),"[12] and the rest which it would take too long to include here.

The Sixth Petition of the Lord's Prayer

9. But when holy persons say, *Bring us not into temptation, but deliver us from evil* (Mt 6:13), what else do they pray for but that they may persevere in holiness? For, after this gift of God has been granted to them, which is quite clearly shown to be a gift of God when they ask for it from him, after, I repeat, this gift of God has been granted to them so that they are not brought into temptation, none of the saints lacks perseverance in holiness up to the end. For no one ceases to

---

11. See Eph 5:27.
12. Cyprian, *The Lord's Prayer* 22.

persevere in the Christian way of life unless he is first brought into temptation. If, therefore, one receives what he prays for, namely, that he not be brought into temptation, he of course continues by a gift of God in the holiness which he received as a gift of God.

Objections from the Brothers in Provence

6, 10. But, as you write, these brothers "do not want this perseverance to be preached in the sense that it can neither be merited by prayer nor lost by rebellion."[13] Here they pay too little attention to what they are saying. For we are speaking of that perseverance by which one perseveres up to the end; if that perseverance has been given, one has persevered up to the end, but if one has not persevered up to the end, it has not been given, as we have explained more than enough above.[14] And so, let people not say that perseverance up to the end has been given to anyone unless he to whom it has been given is found to have persevered up to the end, when the end itself has come.

We of course say that someone is chaste who we know is chaste, whether or not he is going to remain in that chastity. And if he has some other gift of God which can be kept or lost, we say that he has it as long as he has it, and if he has lost it, we say that he used to have it. But since no one has perseverance up to the end unless he perseveres up to the end, many can have it, but no one can lose it. For there is no reason to fear that, when someone has persevered up to the end, an evil will might perhaps arise in him so that he does not persevere up to the end. This gift of God, then, can be merited by prayer, but, once it has been given, it cannot be lost by rebellion. For, when someone has persevered up to the end, he cannot lose either this gift or any others which he could have lost before the end. How, then, can one lose that which prevents one from losing even what one could lose?

11. But someone might say that perseverance up to the end can by no means be lost once it has been given, that is, when one has persevered up to the end, but that it can be lost at the point when a person acts rebelliously so that he cannot attain it. In the same way we say that a person who has not persevered up to the end has lost eternal life or the kingdom of God, not something he had already received

---

13. The Letter of Hilary 3.
14. See above 1, 1.

and possessed, but something he would receive and possess if he had persevered. Let us remove any controversies over words, and let us say that some things which we do not possess, but which we hope to possess, can also be lost. Let anyone who dares tell me that God is unable to give what he commanded that we ask of him. Certainly anyone who thinks this I would not call merely foolish but insane. God, however, commanded that his saints say to him in prayer, *Bring us not into temptation.* Whoever, then, is heard when he asks for this is not brought into temptation to rebellion, by which he could lose or deserves to lose perseverance in holiness.

12. But, after all, "each person abandons God by his own will so that he is deservedly abandoned by God."[15] Who would deny this? But we ask that we not be brought into temptation precisely so that this does not happen. And if we are heard, of course it does not happen, because God does not permit it to happen. For nothing happens except what he himself does or what he himself permits to happen. He is, therefore, able to turn wills from evil to good and to turn back to him wills likely to fall away and to direct them into a path pleasing to him. We do not say to him in vain, *O God, you convert us and give us life* (Ps 85:7); we do not say to him in vain, *Do not allow my foot to be moved* (Ps 66:9); we do not say to him in vain, *Do not hand me over to the sinner in accord with my desire* (Ps 140:9). Finally, in order not to mention too many, since more passages perhaps come to your mind, we do not say in vain, *Bring us not into temptation.* For whoever is not brought into temptation is certainly not brought into temptation coming from his own evil will, and whoever is not brought into temptation coming from his own evil will is certainly brought into no temptation. For *each person*, as it is written, *is tempted, drawn and enticed by his own concupiscence. But God tempts no one* (Jas 1:14.13), that is, by a harmful temptation. For there is also a useful temptation by which we are neither misled nor overwhelmed, but tested, in accord with the words of scripture, *Test me, Lord, and try me* (Ps 26:2). By that harmful temptation, then, which the Apostle referred to when he said, *Lest the tempter has perhaps tempted you, and our labor may be in vain* (1 Thes 3:5), God, as I said, tempts no one, that is, brings or leads no one into temptation. For to be tempted without being brought into temptation is not evil; in fact, it is even

---

15. Though this is clearly an objection, it is not taken from the Letters of Prosper and Hilary.

good, for it is good to be tested. By our words, therefore, to God, *Bring us not into temptation*, what do we say but "Do not allow us to be brought into temptation"? For this reason some people phrase their prayer this way, and we read this formula in many manuscripts, and most blessed Cyprian cited it this way, *Do not allow us to be led into temptation*. In the gospel in Greek, nonetheless, I found only *Bring us not into temptation*.

And so we live more safely if we ascribe everything to God, and do not attribute to him a part and to us a part, as this venerable martyr saw. For, when he explained the same passage of the prayer, he said after the other things, "But when we ask that we may not come into temptation, we are warned of our weakness and infirmity, provided that we ask in such a way that no one insolently becomes filled with pride lest he claim something for himself with pride and arrogance, lest he consider it his own glory to have confessed the faith or suffered for it. For, the Lord himself said, teaching humility, *Watch and pray in order that you may not enter into temptation; the spirit is indeed ready, but the flesh is weak* (Mt 26:41). In that way, when a humble and submissive confession comes first and everything is attributed to God, whatever one asks for in prayer and with fear of God is given by his piety."[16]

The Lord's Prayer Alone Is Sufficient Proof

7, 13. If, then, there were not other testimonies, this prayer of the Lord would alone be enough for us for the cause of grace which we are defending, for it leaves nothing to us in which we might boast as if in something of our own. For it shows that we should attribute only to God even the fact that we do not separate ourselves from God. For one who is not brought into temptation does not separate himself from God. That we do not separate ourselves from God does not fall by any means within the powers of free choice such as they are at present; Adam had such a choice before he fell. What this freedom of the will was capable of in the excellence of its first creation is seen in the angels; when the devil fell along with his followers, they remained standing in the truth and merited to attain the perpetual assurance that they would not fall, the state in which we are most certain that they now are. But after the

---

16. Cyprian, *The Lord's Prayer* 26.

fall of Adam, God willed that it should be only by his grace that a human being would come to him, and he willed that it should be only by his grace that a human being would not abandon him.

14. He located this grace in him *in whom we have obtained our lot, predestined according to the plan of him who accomplishes all things* (Eph 1:11). And on this account, as he is at work in order that we may draw near, so he is at work in order that we may not withdraw from him. On this account the prophet said to him, *Let your hand be upon the man of your right hand and upon the son of man whom you have confirmed for yourself, and we will not depart from you* (Ps 80:18.19). This man is certainly not the first Adam in whom we departed from him, but the second Adam upon whom God's hand is placed in order that we may not depart from him. For Christ is the whole Christ along with his members, on account of the Church, which is his body, his fullness.[17] When, therefore, the hand of God is placed upon him so that we do not depart from God, the work of God of course comes to us, for this is the hand of God. The work of God causes us to remain in Christ and not to depart from God, as we did in Adam. For in Christ *we have obtained our lot, predestined according to the plan of him who accomplishes all things*. It is therefore due to the hand of God, not to our hand, that we do not depart from God. It is, I say, due to the hand of him who said, *I shall put fear of me in their heart in order that they may not withdraw from me* (Jer 32:40).

15. This is the reason he willed that we also ask of him that we not be brought into temptation, for, if we are not brought into temptation, we will in no way depart from him. He could give this to us, even if we did not pray for it, but he wanted us to be reminded by our prayer that we receive these benefits from him. After all, from whom do we receive them if not from him by whom we were commanded to ask for them? In this matter the Church does not, of course, await laborious arguments but pays attention to its daily prayers.

She prays that the non-believers may believe; God therefore converts them to the faith. She prays that believers may persevere; God therefore gives them perseverance up to the end. God foreknew that he would do this; this is the predestination of the saints whom *he chose* in Christ *before the creation of the world that* they *might be holy and spotless before him in love. He predestined* them *to be his children by*

---

17. See Eph 1:23.

adoption through Jesus Christ in accord with the purpose of his will to the praise of the glory of his grace[18] by which he bestowed his grace upon them *in his beloved Son. In him* they have *redemption through his blood, the forgiveness of sins, according to the riches of his grace, which abounded for* them *in all wisdom and insight, in order that he might reveal* to them *the mystery of his will in accord with his good will, which he set forth in Christ as a plan for the fullness of time, to restore in Christ all things which are in heaven and on earth, in him in whom we have also obtained our lot, predestined according to the plan of him who accomplishes all things.* (Eph 1:4-11) In opposition to such a clear trumpet blast of the truth, what man of sober and vigilant faith would listen to any human words?

Perseverance to the End Is an Utterly Gratuitous Gift

8, 16. But "why," he asks, "is the grace of God not given in accord with human merits?" I answer, Because God is merciful. "Why, then," he asks, "is it not given to all?" And here I answer, Because God is judge. And for this reason he gives his grace gratuitously, and his just judgment toward others shows what grace confers on those to whom it is given. We are not, therefore, ungrateful because, *according to the plan of his will to the praise of the glory of his grace,* God in his mercy sets so many free from the perdition which they deserved so fully that he would not be unjust if he set no one free from it. Because of the one all have, of course, been condemned to enter into a condemnation which is not unjust but just. Let one, then, who is set free hold grace dear, and let one who is not set free acknowledge what he deserves. If one recognizes goodness in remitting a debt and equity in exacting it, one will never find injustice in God.

The Gratuity of Perseverance in the Case of Infants

17. "But why," he asks, "is God's judgment so different, when the situation not only of little ones but of twins is identical?" Is there not a similar question as to why God's judgment is the same when the situation is different? Let us, then, recall those workers in the

---

18. In citing this passage in *The Predestination of the Saints* 17, 35, Augustine omitted the words *to the praise of the glory of his grace,* so that *by which he bestowed* seemed to modify *his will.* Here it seems to modify *his grace.*

vineyard who labored the whole day and those others who labored only one hour. The situation was, of course, different in terms of the labor expended, and yet the judgment is the same in the allotment of a reward. Did those who complained even in this case receive any other reply from the head of the house but: This is what I will? His generosity toward some certainly did not mean that he was unjust toward the others. And both these groups of workers were certainly included among good people; nonetheless, with respect to justice and grace, God can also rightly say of the guilty person who is set free what he says to the guilty person who is condemned, *Take what is yours, and go. But to this one I will to give* what is not owed to him. *Or am I not permitted to do what I will? Is your eye evil because I am good?* (Mt 20:14-15) Here, if someone says, "Why not give it to me too?" he will deservedly hear, *"Who are you, a human being, to answer back to God?* (Rom 9:20) You surely see that God is a most generous benefactor toward one of you, but that in your case he most justly exacts punishment, by no means unjustly. For, since he is just, even if he punished both, the one who is set free has reason for giving thanks, but the one who is condemned has no reason to complain."

18. "But," he says, "if it was necessary that God show what all deserved by condemning some, and that he commend his grace as more gratuitous to the vessels of mercy, why will he in the same situation punish me rather than that fellow or set free that fellow rather than me?" I have nothing to say; if you ask me why, I admit that the reason is that I do not find anything to say. And if you again ask why, I reply that the reason is that, just as in this area his anger is just, just as his mercy is great, so his judgments are inscrutable.[19]

The Gratuity of Perseverance in Adults

19. Let him go on and say, "Why to some who worshiped him with good faith did he not give perseverance up to the end?" Why do you think if it was not that he does not lie who says, *They went forth from us, but they did not belong to us; if they had belonged to us, they would certainly have remained with us* (1 Jn 2:19)? Are there, then, two different natures of human beings? Heaven forbid! If there were two different natures, there would be no grace. For deliverance

---

19. See Rom 11:33.

would be given to neither of them as gratuitous if it were repaid to nature as something owed. But in the eyes of human beings it seems that all who are seen to be good believers ought to have received perseverance up to the end. God, however, has judged that it is better that some who will not persevere be mingled with the certain number of his saints in order that those people for whom it is not useful to be assured of their salvation amid the temptation of this life cannot be assured of their salvation.

Many, after all, are held back from ruinous pride by the words of the Apostle, *Hence, let one who thinks he stands watch out that he does not fall* (1 Cor 10:12). One, however, who falls falls by his own will, but one who stands stands by the will of God. *For God is able to hold him upright* (Rom 14:4); therefore, it is not he who makes himself stand, but God. It is, nonetheless, good not to think proud thoughts, but to be fearful.[20]

But each person either falls or stands by his own thought. As the Apostle said, however, in the words which I recalled in the previous book, We are not *sufficient to have a single thought as if from ourselves, but our sufficiency comes from God* (2 Cor 3:5). Following him, blessed Ambrose too dares to say, "For our hearts and our thoughts are not in our power."[21] And everyone who is humbly and truly pious realizes that this is most true.

Our Hearts and Thoughts Are Not in Our Own Power

20. But when he said this, Ambrose was speaking in that book he wrote, namely, *Flight from the World*. He was teaching that we must flee this world not by the body but by the heart, and he stated that this could only be done by the help of God. For he said, "We frequently speak of fleeing from this world, and would that our desire were as cautious and careful as our words are facile. But what is worse, the snare of earthly desires frequently creeps in, and a cloud of vanities fills the mind, so that you ponder and turn about in your mind what you desire to avoid. For a human being this is difficult to avoid, but impossible to remove completely. Finally, the prophet testifies that this is more a matter of desire than of actual attainment when he says, *Incline my heart toward*

20. See Rom 11:20.
21. Ambrose, *Flight from the World* 1, 1.

your testimonies and not toward greed (Ps 119:36). For our heart and our thoughts are not in our power. When they pour in unexpectedly, they confuse the mind and spirit and drag it elsewhere than you intended to go. They call us back to worldly things, introduce earthly ideas, inflict desires for pleasure, and weave snares, and at the very moment when we prepare to raise up the mind, we are filled with empty thoughts and are often cast down to things of earth."[22]

It is not, therefore, in the power of human beings, but in the power of God, that human beings have *the power to become children of God* (Jn 1:12). They of course receive it from him who gives to the human heart pious thoughts by which it may have the faith that works through love.[23] In order to receive and hold onto this good and to make progress in it with perseverance up to the end, we are not *sufficient to have a single thought as if from ourselves, but our sufficiency comes from God* (2 Cor 3:5), in whose power are our hearts and our thoughts.

9, 21. From two little ones equally bound by original sin, why is the one adopted, but the other left? And from two non-believers who are already adults, why is this one called so that he follows the one who calls him, but that one is either not called or not called in that way? These are God's inscrutable judgments. But from two believers, why is perseverance up to the end given to this one and not given to that one? These are judgments of God that are even more inscrutable. Yet this ought to be absolutely certain for the faithful, namely, that the former person belongs among the predestined, while the latter does not. *For, if they had belonged to us*, as one of the predestined said who had drunk this secret at the Lord's heart, *they would certainly have remained with us*. What does this mean, I ask you: *They did not belong to us, for if they had, they would certainly have remained with us*? Were not both groups created by God; were not both born of Adam; were not both made from the earth; and did they not receive souls of one and the same nature from him who said, *I have created every breath* (Is 57:16)? Finally, were not both groups called and did they not follow the one who called them? Were not both groups made righteous from wicked and both renewed by the bath of rebirth?

But if he who undoubtedly knew what he was saying heard these words, he could reply and say, All this is true; in all these respects

---

22. Ibid.
23. See Gal 5:6.

they belonged to us. Nonetheless, in terms of another criterion they did not belong to us; for, *if they had belonged to us, they would certainly have remained with us.* But[24] what is this criterion? The books of God lie open; let us not turn away our gaze. The divine scripture cries out; let us listen. They did not belong to them, because they were not *called according to the plan* (Rom 8:28); they were not *chosen in Christ before the creation of the world* (Eph 1:4); they had not in him *obtained their lot*; they were not *predestined according to the plan of him who accomplishes all things* (Eph 1:11). For, if they had been, they would have belonged to them, and they would undoubtedly have remained with them.

No One Is Judged by What He Would Have Done but Did Not Do

22. I do not want to repeat how it is possible for God to convert to faith in him the wills of human beings that are turned away from and opposed to it, and how he works in their hearts so that they yield to no adversities and do not withdraw from him after having been overcome by some temptation. For he can also do what the Apostle said, namely, not allow them to be tempted beyond their ability.[25] To avoid repeating this, therefore, certainly God who foreknew that they would fall could have taken them from this life before that happened.

Or are we going to return to the point of further discussing the great absurdity with which it is said that, after having died, human beings are also judged by these sins which God foreknew that they would have committed if they lived?[26] But that is so foreign to Christian or even to human ways of thinking that I am ashamed to refute it. Why, after all, should one not say that it is in vain that the gospel was preached or is still preached with such great labor and sufferings of the saints if human beings could have been judged, even without having heard the gospel, in accord with the rebellion or obedience which God foreknew that they would have if they had heard it? Nor would Tyre and Sidon be condemned, even though less severely than those cities in which the Lord worked miraculous signs for non-believers, because, if those signs were produced in them, they would have done penance in ashes and

---

24. I have followed the reading *tamen* found in all the manuscripts in place of *tandem*.
25. See 1 Cor 10:13.
26. See *The Predestination of the Saints* 10, 13, where Augustine already discussed this point.

sackcloth.[27] These are the words of the truth in which the Lord Jesus revealed to us with greater profundity the mystery of predestination.

23. For, if we are asked why such great miracles were produced among those who were not going to believe when they saw them and were not produced among those who would believe if they saw them, what shall we reply? Are we going to say what I said in that book in which I replied to a certain six questions of the pagans,[28] though without wanting to exclude other reasons which the wise could investigate? As you know, when I was asked why Christ came after so long a time, I said this, "In these times and in these places in which his gospel was not preached, he foreknew that all of them would react to the preaching of him in the same way as many reacted to his bodily presence when they refused to believe in him even after he raised the dead."[29] Likewise, a little later in the same book and on the same question, I said,"Why is it surprising if Christ knew that in earlier ages the world was so full of non-believers that he rightly did not want to be preached to those people who he foreknew would believe neither his words nor his miracles?"[30] We certainly cannot say this of Tyre and Sidon, and in their case we know that these divine judgments pertain to those reasons for predestination, those hidden reasons which I then said that I did not want to exclude by my reply.

It is certainly easy to blame the disbelief of the Jews, stemming from free will, for they refused to believe despite the great miracles which were produced among them. Even the Lord reproached and blamed this when he said, *Woe to you, Chorazin and Bethsaida! For, if the miracles which were produced in you were produced in Tyre and Sidon, they would long since have done penance in ashes and sackcloth.* (Mt 11:21) But we cannot say, can we, that even the people of Tyre and Sidon would have refused to believe or would not have believed if such miracles had been worked among them? For the Lord himself testifies that they would do penance in great humility if those signs of God's power were worked among them. And yet on the day of judgment they will be punished, though by a lesser punishment than those cities which

---

27. See Mt 11:21.
28. See Letter 102, a letter which Augustine wrote for the deacon Deogratias in which he dealt with six questions, the second of which treated with the question of the philosopher Porphyry about the late emergence of the Christian religion.
29. Letter 102, 14, with a slight omission.
30. Ibid.

refused to believe in the miracles which were worked among them. For the Lord went on and said, *I tell you, nonetheless: on the day of judgment it will be easier for Tyre and Sidon than for you* (Mt 11:22). These latter cities, then, will be punished more severely, and those others less severely, but they will nonetheless be punished.

But, if the dead were going to be judged according to the actions they were going to do if they lived, then, since these people were going to be believers if the gospel was preached to them with such great miracles, they are surely not going to be punished. But they will be punished. Therefore, it is false that the dead are also judged according to what they would have done if the gospel reached them when they were living. And if this is false, there is no reason why it should be said of infants, who die without baptism and perish, that this happens to them because of that merit, namely, that God foresaw that, if they lived and the gospel had been preached to them, they would have heard it without believing.

It remains, then, that they are held guilty by original sin alone, and on account of it alone they enter into condemnation. We see that others who are found in the same situation receive rebirth only through the gratuitous grace of God, and that by his judgment which is hidden but still just, because there is no injustice in God,[31] certain others will perish by living badly even after baptism. And yet they are kept in this life until they perish, though they would not perish if bodily death came before their fall and rescued them. Otherwise the people of Tyre and Sidon would not suffer punishments in accord with what they did, but they would instead attain salvation through great penance and through faith in Christ in accord with what they would have done, if those gospel miracles had been worked in their midst.

Another Interpretation of the Words about Tyre and Sidon

10, 24. A certain Catholic exegete of some renown[32] explained this passage as follows. He said that the Lord foreknew that the people of Tyre and Sidon would have later abandoned the faith after they had believed because of the miracles worked among them. Hence, out of mercy he did not work these miracles there. For they would have been

---

31. See 2 Chr 19:7; Rom 9:14.
32. The identity of this exegete remains unknown.

subject to more serious punishment if they abandoned the faith which they had embraced than if they never embraced it. Why does it now fall to me to say what points still need to be investigated in the view of this learned and also very clever man, since it too supports us in what we are doing? For, if out of mercy the Lord did not work among these peoples the miracles by which they could have become believers, so that they would not be punished more severely when they later became non-believers, as he foreknew that they were going to be, it is shown quite clearly that after death no one is judged by those sins which God foresaw that a person would have committed if he, in fact, somehow received the help of grace so that he did not commit them. In the same way, if that view is correct, Christ is said to have helped the people of Tyre and Sidon when he preferred that they not come to the faith rather than that they abandon the faith by a much graver sin, a sin which he foresaw that they were going to commit if they came to the faith.

And yet, if someone should say, "Why were they not instead brought to believe, and why were they not given the gift of departing from this life before they abandoned the faith?" I do not know what reply can be made. For one who says that those who were going to abandon the faith had received as a benefit their not beginning to have what they would have abandoned by a graver impiety indicates well enough that a person is not judged on the basis of the evil which God foreknows he would have done, if he is helped by any sort of benefit so that he does not do it. That person, therefore, was also helped who *was carried off so that evil would not change his mind* (Wis 4:11). But as to why the people of Tyre and Sidon were not helped in this way, so that they believed and were carried off in order that evil would not change their mind, one who wants to solve this question in this way might perhaps reply, "But with regard to what I do, I see that it is enough that according to this view human beings are also shown not to be judged by the things which they did not do, even if God foresaw that they were going to do them." And yet, as I said, one ought even to be ashamed to refute this opinion, by which it is thought that the dying or the dead are punished for sins which God foreknew that they would commit if they lived; otherwise, it might seem that we considered it to be of some importance because we chose to refute it by arguments rather than to pass it over in silence.

God's Judgment Is in Accord with Mercy and Truth

11, 25. Hence, as the Apostle says, *It does not depend on the one who wills or the one who runs but on God who shows mercy* (Rom 9:16), for he also helps the little ones whom he wills to help, even they do not will or run. He chose them in Christ before the creation of the world[33] in order to give them grace gratuitously, that is, without any preceding merits of theirs coming from faith or works. And he does not help adults whom he does not will to help, even those he foresaw would believe because of his miracles if they were worked among them. In his predestination he decided otherwise about them in a hidden but just way. For there is no injustice in God,[34] but *his judgments are inscrutable, and his ways are unsearchable* (Rom 11:33), and *all the ways of the Lord are mercy and truth* (Ps 25:10). His mercy, therefore, is unsearchable by which he shows mercy to whom he wills without any preceding merits on the part of that person, and his truth is unsearchable by which he hardens the heart of whom he wills, with preceding evil merits on the part of that person, but generally evil merits in common with the one to whom he shows mercy.

For example, the outcome is different for two twins, of which the one is taken and the other left, but they have their merits in common. And yet one of them is set free by the great goodness of God, while the other is condemned with no injustice on his part. For is there injustice in God? Heaven forbid! But his ways are unsearchable. Therefore, without any doubt we believe in his mercy in the case of those who are set free and in his truth in the case of those who are punished, and we do not try to examine what is inscrutable or to search out what is unsearchable. He of course prepares his praise from the mouth of infants and sucklings,[35] so that we do not hesitate in the least to accept as happening also in adults what we see in these little ones whose deliverance is preceded by no good merits of theirs, and in these little ones whose condemnation is preceded only by those original merits common to both. That is, we do not suppose either that grace is given to anyone according to his merits or that anyone is punished except because of his merits, whether those who are set free and are punished have equal or unequal guilt. For that

---

33. See Eph 1:4.
34. See 2 Chr 19:7; Rom 9:14.
35. See Ps 9:3.

reason, *let one who thinks he stands watch out that he does not fall* (1 Cor 10:12), and *let one who boasts boast in the Lord* (1 Cor 1:31), not in himself.

An Objection Drawn from Augustine's Free Will

26. Contrary to the Pelagians, these brothers do not doubt that there is original sin which entered the world through one man,[36] and that as a result of that one sin all entered into condemnation.[37] But why, as you write, do they "not permit us to introduce the situation of the little ones as a model for adults"?[38] The Manicheans also do not accept this sin, for they not only reject all the scriptures of the old dispensation as not having any authority but also accept those scriptures which pertain to the New Testament, while relying on their privilege—or rather sacrilege[39]—to accept what they want and to reject what they do not want. I opposed them in the books of *Free Will*, the work from which these brothers think that they must dictate to us.[40] In fact, I did not want to resolve completely the very troublesome questions which arise, for fear that the work would be too long. For in it the authority of the divine testimonies gave me no help against such misguided people. And I was able to conclude, as I did, by a certain argument that whichever of these solutions that I set forth as hypotheses was true, God is to be praised in all things without any need to believe that two coeternal substances of good and evil have been mixed together, as they claim.

27. Again, in the book *Revisions*, a work of mine which you have not yet read, when I came to review the same books, that is, *Free Will*, I spoke as follows, "In these books many things were discussed in such a way that some questions which arise, and which I either could not resolve or which required a long discussion at that moment, were postponed. And so, after consideration of both sides or all the sides of the same questions, in which it was not apparent which of them better conformed to the truth, our reasoning nonetheless concluded that, whichever of them were true, we should believe, or it has even been proven, that God is to be praised. That discussion was, of course, undertaken on

---

36. See Rom 5:12.
37. See Rom 5:18.
38. See the Letter of Hilary 8.
39. Augustine plays upon the words *privilegio* and *sacrilegio*.
40. See *Free Will* III, 23, 66-70.

account of those who deny that the origin of evil stems from the free choice of the will and who claim that in that case God, the creator of all natures, must be blamed. In that way they want to introduce in accord with the error of their impiety—for they are Manicheans—a certain immutable nature of evil that is coeternal with God."[41]

Likewise, after a while I said in another place, "Next we spoke of that misery which was inflicted upon sinners with full justice and from which the grace of God sets us free. For Adam could fall willingly, that is, by free choice, but could not also rise up, and this misery of just condemnation includes the ignorance and difficulty which every human being suffers from the first moments of his birth, and no one is set free from this evil except by the grace of God. The Pelagians do not want this misery to come from just condemnation, since they deny original sin. And yet, even if ignorance and difficulty belong to the original and natural conditions of a human being, God is not, even in that case, to be blamed, but to be praised, as we argued in the same third book.[42] We had to use this argument against the Manicheans who do not accept the holy scriptures of the old dispensation, in which there is found the account of the original sin, and they claim with a detestable impudence that any element of that teaching found in the letters of the apostles was inserted there by people who corrupted the scriptures, as if the apostles did not say this. But against the Pelagians we must defend what each part of the scriptures teaches, since they claim that they accept both parts."[43]

I said these things in the first book of the *Revisions* when I reviewed the books of *Free Will*. But I certainly did not say there only these things about those books, but many other things as well, which I thought it would take too long to insert for you in this work and which I thought unnecessary. And I suspect that you will also make the same judgment when you have read them all. And so, though I discussed the little ones in the third book of *Free Will* in such a way that, even if the Pelagian claim were true, that the ignorance and difficulty without which no human being is born are the original condition of our nature, not its punishment, the Manicheans would be defeated who want there to be two coeternal natures, namely, of good and evil. Is then the faith which the Catholic Church defends

41. *Revisions* I, 9, 2.
42. See *Free Will* III, 22, 64-65.
43. *Revisions* I, 9, 2.

against the Pelagians to be called into doubt or abandoned, because the Church maintains that there is original sin, whose guilt is contracted by birth and must be removed by rebirth? But if even these brothers admit this along with us in order that on this issue we may together destroy the error of the Pelagians, why do they think that one should doubt that God rescues even the little ones, to whom he gives his grace through the sacrament of baptism, from the power of darkness and transfers them into the kingdom of his beloved Son?[44] Given the fact, then, that he gives this grace to some and not to others, why do they refuse to sing to the Lord of mercy and judgment?[45] But as to why this grace is given to these rather than to those, *who has known the mind of the Lord?* (Rom 11:34) Who is able to examine his inscrutable judgments? Who is able to search out his unsearchable ways?

The Grace of God Is Given with Mercy and Justice

12, 28. It is established, therefore, that the grace of God is not given in accord with the merits of those who receive it, but in accord with the choice of his will, to the praise and glory of his grace,[46] so that *he who boasts may boast* in no way in himself, but *in the Lord.* For the Lord gives his grace to human beings to whom he wills to give it because he is merciful, and if he does not give it, he is just. And he does not give his grace to those to whom he does not will to give it *in order that he might make known the riches of his glory toward the vessels of mercy* (Rom 9:23). For, by giving to certain people what they do not merit, he of course willed his grace to be gratuitous and, for this reason, to be grace. By not giving it to everyone, he showed what all merited. He is good in the benefit he gives to certain persons, and he is just in the punishment of the rest. He is good toward all because it is good when a debt is paid, and he is just toward all because it is just when something not owed is given without depriving anyone of what is owed.

The Gratuity of Grace Was Defended in Either Case

29. But the grace of God, that is, true grace, is defended without any merits, even if, as the Pelagians hold, baptized little ones are not rescued

---

44. See Col 1:13.
45. See Ps 101:1.
46. See Eph 1:5-6.

from the power of darkness, because they are not held subject to any sin, as the Pelagians suppose, but are only transferred into the kingdom of the Lord.[47] For, even in that case, the kingdom of heaven is given without any good merits to those to whom it is given, and without any evil merits it is not given to those to whom it is not given. We frequently say this against the same Pelagians when they object to us that we attribute the grace of God to fate when we say that it is not given in accord with our merits.[48] For it is rather they themselves who attribute the grace of God to fate in the case of little ones, when they say that fate prevails where there is no merit. Even according to those Pelagians, certainly no merits can be found in little ones, because of which some are admitted into the kingdom, while others are kept apart from it.

Now, in order to show that the grace of God is not given in accord with our merits, I have preferred to defend this point in accord with both views, that is, both in accord with the position of us who say that little ones are bound by original sin and in accord with the position of the Pelagians who deny that there is original sin. But I do not think that anyone needs to doubt that little ones have what he, who saves his people from their sins,[49] forgives them. In the same way, in the third book of *Free Will*, I resisted the Manicheans in accord with both views, namely, whether ignorance and difficulty were punishments or whether they were the first natural conditions without which no human being is born. And yet I hold one of these, and that was expressed by me there clearly enough, namely, that this is not the nature of man as created, but the punishment of man as condemned.[50]

The Books on Free Will Were Written against the Manicheans

30. In vain, then, do they forbid me on the basis of that old book of mine to pursue the case of little ones, as I ought to, and to demonstrate from it by the light of the plain truth that the grace of God is not given according to the merits of human beings. For if, though I finished the books concerning free will as a priest, I began them as a layman, when I was still in doubt about the condemnation of unbaptized infants and about the deliverance of those who are reborn, no

---

47. See Col 1:13.
48. See *Answer to the Two Letters of the Pelagians* II, 5-6, 9-12, and *Answer to Julian* IV, 8, 46, for such accusations against Augustine.
49. See Mt 1:21.
50. See *Free Will* III, 20, 23.

one, I think, would be so unjust and envious that he would forbid me to make progress and would decide that I had to remain in this state of doubt. But one could be more correct and understand that there is no need to believe that I was in doubt about this issue because I thought that I should refute those opponents against whom my efforts were directed in such a way that, whether there was the punishment of original sin in little ones, as is the truth, or whether there was not, as some misguided people suppose, no one would in any case believe that there is a mixture of two natures, namely, of good and of evil, which the Manichean error introduces. Heaven forbid that we should abandon the cause of little ones and say that we are uncertain whether those reborn in Christ enter into eternal salvation if they die as little ones and whether those not reborn enter into eternal death.

For the words of scripture, *Through one man sin entered the world, and through sin death, and in that way it was passed on to all human beings* (Rom 5:12), cannot be correctly interpreted in any other way. Nor does anyone but him who, without any original or personal sin of his own, died for the sake of forgiving both our original and personal sins set any child or adult free from the everlasting death which is the most just recompense for sin. But why does he set these free rather than those? Again and again we say, nor does it bother us to do so, *Who are you, a human being, to answer back to God?* (Rom 9:20) *Inscrutable are his judgments and unsearchable his ways* (Rom 11:33). And let us add, *Do not search out things too high for you, and do not examine things which surpass you* (Sir 3:22).

No One Will Be Judged by What He Would Have Done

31. For you see, my dear brothers, how absurd it is and how foreign to the soundness of the faith and the purity of the truth to say that little ones who have died are judged in accord with those actions which God foreknew they would do if they lived. But these people were compelled to adopt this view at which every human mind, with however slight a reason it is endowed, but especially every Christian mind, stands in horror. For they wanted to be free from the error of the Pelagians in such a way that they would still think that one ought to believe and also to defend by arguments that the grace of God through Jesus Christ our Lord was given according to our merits, the grace which alone helps us after the fall of the first man in whom we

all fell. Before his judges, the Eastern bishops, Pelagius himself condemned this view out of fear that he himself would be condemned. But if one does not say this about the works of the dead, that is, about both the good works and the evil ones which they would have done if they lived and which, for this reason, will not exist even in the foreknowledge of God; if, then, one does not say this—and you see the great error with which it would be said—what remains except that, with all contention set aside, we admit that the grace of God is not given according to our merits, the position which the Catholic Church defends against the Pelagian heresy, and that we see this most of all in little ones because the truth is there more obvious?

For God is not forced by fate to go to the aid of those infants, but not to go to the aid of the others, since both groups have in common the same situation. Nor do we suppose that human affairs in the case of the little ones are not governed by divine providence but by fortuitous chances, since the little ones are rational souls either to be condemned or to be set free. After all, not even a sparrow falls to the ground without the will of our Father who is in heaven.[51] Nor should one attribute it to neglect on the part of the parents that little ones die without baptism, so that God's judgments play no role there, as if those little ones who in that way die in sin chose by their own will parents neglectful of them from whom they would be born.

What shall I say when a little one at times expires before it can be helped by the ministry of someone baptizing it? For often, though the parents are making haste and the ministers are ready to give baptism to the little one, baptism is nonetheless not given because God does not will it, who did not keep the little one in this life a little longer in order that it might be given. Also, what shall I say when at times little children of non-believers were able to be helped by baptism so that they did not enter into perdition, but the children of believers were not able to be helped? There we certainly see that there is no favoritism in God.[52] Otherwise, he would set free the children of his worshipers rather than of his enemies.

The Mystery of God's Gift of Perseverance

13, 32. But now, since we are at present discussing the gift of perseverance, why is it that someone not baptized is helped in order that

---

51. See Mt 10:29.
52. See Rom 2:11; Col 3:25.

he might not die without baptism and someone baptized who is going to fall is not helped in order that he might die before falling? Or are we still perhaps going to listen to that absurdity which claims that it does not benefit anyone to die before he falls, because he is going to be judged according to those actions which God foreknew that he was going to do if he lived? Who would listen with patience to this perversity so strongly opposed to the soundness of the faith? Who would put up with this? And yet those who refuse to say that the grace of God is not given in accord with our merits are pressured to say this. But for those who refuse to say that each of the dead is judged according to those actions which God foreknew that he would do if he lived, since they see the obvious falsity and great absurdity of saying this, there remains no reason why they should say what the Church condemned in the Pelagians and made Pelagius himself condemn, namely, that the grace of God is given according to our merits. For they see that some little ones who have not been reborn are taken from this life for eternal death, while others who have been reborn are taken from this life for eternal life, and that, of those who have been reborn, some leave this life having persevered up to the end, while others are kept in this life until they fall, though they would surely not have fallen if they had left this life before they fell. Again, some who have fallen do not leave this life until they return, though they would surely have perished if they left this life before they returned.

33. Hence, it is quite evident that the grace of God both for beginning and for persevering up to the end is not given according to our merits, but is given according to his most hidden and at the same time most just, most wise, and most beneficent will. For *those whom he predestined he also called* (Rom 8:30) by that calling of which it was said, *The gifts and the calling of God are irrevocable* (Rom 11:29). People should not say with a claim to certitude that any person shares in this calling except when he has departed from this world. But in this human life, which is a temptation upon the earth,[53] *Let one who thinks he stands watch out that he does not fall.* For this reason, of course, as we have already said above,[54] the most provident will of God mingles together those who are not going to persevere with those who are going to persevere in order that we may learn *not to*

---

53. See Job 7:1.
54. See above 8, 9.

think lofty thoughts, but to agree with the lowly (Rom 12:16) and to work out our salvation with fear and trembling. *For it is God who produces* in us *both the willing and the action in accord with good will* (Phil 2:12.13).

We will, therefore, but God also produces in us the willing; we therefore, work, but God also produces in us the action in accord with good will. It is useful for us both to believe and to say this; it is pious; it is true. Let our confession be humble and submissive and let everything be ascribed to God. While thinking we believe; while thinking we speak; while thinking we do whatever we do, but with regard to the path of piety and the true worship of God we are not *sufficient to have a single thought as if from ourselves, but our sufficiency comes from God* (2 Cor 3:5). "For our hearts and our thoughts are not in our own power."[55] Hence, the same person who says this, Ambrose, likewise says, "But who is so happy as one who always rises up in his heart? But how can he do this without divine help? In no way, of course. Also," he adds, "the same scripture says above,[56] *Blessed is the man whose help comes from you, Lord, a man who rises up in his heart*"[57] (Ps 84:6). Ambrose, of course, said this not only because he read it in the sacred writings but also because he felt it in his own heart, as we should undoubtedly believe of that man.

The action, then, which is mentioned in the sacraments of the faithful, namely, that we should lift up our hearts to the Lord, is a gift of the Lord; after these words which say this, the faithful are admonished by the priest to give thanks to the Lord our God for this gift, and they reply that it is right and just.[58] For, since our heart is not in our own power, but is lifted up by the help of God, so that it may rise upward and taste *not the things which are on earth, but the things which are above, where Christ is seated at the right hand of God* (Col 3:2.1), to whom ought we to give thanks for this great benefit if not to the Lord our God, its author, for, in setting us free from the depth of this world by so great a benefit, he chose us and predestined us before the creation of the world.

---

55. Ambrose, *Flight from the World* 1, 1.
56. Ambrose previously cited Ps 119:36.
57. Ambrose, *Flight from the World* 1, 2.
58. Augustine alludes to the dialogue between the priest and the congregation at the beginning of the Preface in the Mass.

Predestination Can and Ought to Be Taught

14, 34. But they say that the doctrine of predestination is an obstacle to the usefulness of preaching.[59] As if it were an obstacle to the preaching of the Apostle! Did not that teacher who taught the nations in the faith and the truth very often teach predestination without ceasing from preaching the word of God? He said, *It is God who produces in you both the willing and the action in accord with good will.* Did he himself, therefore, not exhort us to will and to do what is pleasing to God? And he said, *He who began the good work in you will bring it to completion on the day of Christ Jesus* (Phil 1:6). Did he himself, therefore, not urge human beings to begin and to persevere up to the end? The Lord himself in fact commanded that human beings believe and said, *Believe in God and believe in me* (Jn 14:1). And yet his idea is not false, nor is his statement meaningless where he says, *No one comes to me*, that is, no one believes in me, *unless it has been given him by my Father* (Jn 6:66). And again, it does not follow that, because this statement is true, his command is meaningless. Why, then, do we think that for preaching, for giving commands, for exhorting, and for rebuking, all of which are frequently found in scripture, the doctrine of predestination is useless, though the same divine scripture teaches it?

A Definition of the Predestination of the Saints

35. Or will anyone dare to say that God did not foreknow to whom he was going to grant that they would believe in his Son, or whom he was going to give to his Son in order that he would not lose any one of them? If he in fact foreknew these things, he certainly foreknew the benefits of his by which he deigns to set us free. This predestination of the saints is nothing other than the foreknowledge and the preparation of the benefits of God by which he most certainly sets free whoever are set free. But where are the rest left by the most just judgment of God save in the mass of perdition?

In that mass God left Tyre and Sidon, which could also have believed if they had seen those miraculous signs of Christ. But because it was not given to them that they should believe, there was also denied to them the means by which they might believe. From this we

---

59. See the Letter of Hilary 2 and the Letter of Prosper 3. 6.

see that some people naturally have in their native ability a divine gift of intelligence by which they may be moved to the faith if they hear words or see signs which are suited to their minds, and yet if by the more profound judgment of God they are not set apart from the mass of perdition by the predestination of grace, they are not presented with those divine words or deeds by which they could have believed if they heard or saw such things.

The Jews who were not able to believe in the great and obvious miracles that were performed before their eyes were also left in that same mass of perdition. For the gospel did not pass over in silence the reason why they could not believe; it said, *Though he worked such great signs before them, they did not believe in him in order that the words which the prophet Isaiah spoke might be fulfilled, Lord, who has believed our message? And to whom has the arm of the Lord been revealed? And, therefore, they could not believe, for Isaiah again said, He blinded their eyes and hardened their heart in order that they might not see with their eyes and might not understand with their heart and be converted so that I might heal them.* (Jn 12:37-40)

The eyes of the people of Tyre and Sidon, then, were not blinded in that way, nor was their heart hardened in that way, for they would have believed if they had seen such signs as these people saw. But it did not do them any good that they were able to believe, because they were not predestined by him whose judgments are inscrutable and whose ways are unsearchable,[60] nor would it have been an obstacle to them that they were not able to believe if it had been predestined that God would enlighten them in their blindness and would will to take away a stony heart from those whose hearts were hardened.

But what the Lord said about Tyre and Sidon can perhaps be interpreted in some other way; yet one who hears the divine message, not with deaf ears of the heart but by the ears of the flesh, undoubtedly confesses that no one comes to Christ unless it has been given him, and that it is given to those who were chosen in him before the creation of the world. And yet this predestination, which is also quite clearly expressed by the words of the gospel, did not prevent the Lord from saying with reference to our beginning the words I mentioned a little before, *Believe in God, and believe in me,* and from saying with reference to our persevering, *It is necessary to pray always and not*

---

60. See Rom 11:33.

to give up (Lk 18:1). For those to whom it has been given hear and do this, but those to whom it has not been given do not do this, whether they hear it or do not hear it. *For to you*, he said, *it has been given to know the mystery of the kingdom of heaven, but to those it has not been given* (Mt 13:11). Of these two one pertains to the mercy and the other to the judgment of him to whom our soul says, *I shall sing to you, Lord, of mercy and judgment* (Ps 101:1).

Cyprian Taught Perseverance and Exhorted His Flock

36. Nor ought the preaching of the faith which perseveres and makes progress to be impeded by the preaching of predestination. For those who have been given the gift of obedience need to hear what is necessary. For *how will they hear without someone to preach?* (Rom 10:14). Again, the preaching of the faith which makes progress and remains up to the end should not impede the preaching of pre-destination. For one who lives with faith and obedience must not be filled with pride over this obedience as if over his own good, which he did not receive, but *one who boasts should boast in the Lord.* For "we must boast over nothing since we have nothing of our own."[61]

This is what Cyprian saw with complete faith and declared with full confidence, and by it he certainly proclaimed predestination to be most certain. For, if "we must boast over nothing, we have nothing of our own," we must not, then, boast over our obedience either, no matter how persevering it is, nor should we call it ours as if it were not given to us from above. And it is therefore a gift of God which he foreknew, as every Christian admits, that he would give to those he called by that calling of which it was said, *The gifts and calling of God are irrevocable.*

This is, then, the predestination which we preach with faith and humility. And yet the same man who both taught and put his teaching into action, who both believed in Christ and lived most perseveringly in holy obedience up to the point of suffering for Christ, did not stop preaching the gospel and exhorting people to faith, pious conduct, and perseverance up to the end, because he said, "We must boast over nothing since we have nothing of our own." And by this he taught without any ambiguity the true grace of God, that is, the grace which is not given in accord with our merits. And since God foreknew that

---

61. Cyprian, *Three Books of Testimonies for Quirinus* III, 4.

he would give this grace, these words of Cyprian undoubtedly preach predestination, and if these words did not keep Cyprian from preaching obedience, they certainly ought not to keep us from that either.

37. Therefore, though we say that obedience is a gift of God, we exhort people to obedience. But to those who hear obediently the exhortation of the truth, the gift of God has itself already been given, namely, that they hear it obediently, but it has not been given to those who do not hear it in that way. For it is not just anyone, but Christ who said, *No one comes to me unless it has been given him by my Father* (Jn 6:66), and, *To you it has been given to know the mystery of the kingdom of heaven, but to those it has not been given* (Mt 13:11). And with regard to celibacy he said, *Not all accept this word, but those to whom it has been given* (Mt 19:11). And when the Apostle was exhorting spouses to marital chastity, he said, *I would like all people to be as I myself am, but each has his own gift from God, one this gift, the other that* (1 Cor 7:7). There he showed well enough that not only celibacy but also the chastity of married people is a gift of God.

Though this is the case, we still exhort people to these virtues to the extent that each of us has been given the ability to do so, because this too is the gift of him who holds in his hand both us and our words.[62] For this reason the Apostle says, *According to the grace which was given to me, I laid the foundations like a wise builder* (1 Cor 3:10). And in another place he said, *To each as the Lord gave, I planted; Apollo watered, but God gave the increase. And so neither the one who plants nor the one who waters is anything, but only God who gives the increase.* (1 Cor 3:5-7) And for this reason, just as one exhorts and preaches correctly, but only if he has received this gift, so he who has received this gift certainly hears obediently one who exhorts and preaches correctly.

For this reason, though the Lord was speaking to those who had their ears of flesh open, he still said, *Let those who have ears hear* (Lk 8:8), for he undoubtedly knew that all did not have ears to hear. But the Lord showed from whom whoever have these ears have them when he said, *I shall give them a heart for knowing me and ears to hear* (Bar 2:31). Ears to hear, therefore, are the gift of obeying, so that those who have it might come to him to whom no one comes unless it has been given to him by his Father.

---

62. See Wis 7:16.

And so we exhort and preach, but those who have ears to hear hear us obediently, while in those who do not have such ears there comes about what scripture says, *That, though hearing, they may not hear* (Mt 13:13), that is, though hearing with the sense of the body, they may not hear with the assent of the heart. But as for why those have ears to hear and these others do not, that is, why it was given to the former by the Father that they may come to the Son, but was not given to the rest, *Who has known the mind of the Lord or who has been his counselor?* (Rom 11:34) or, *Who are you, a human being, to answer back to God?* (Rom 9:20) Should one, therefore, deny what is obvious because one cannot comprehend what lies hidden? Are we, I ask, going to say that something which we see in a certain way is not that way, because we cannot see why it is that way?

Foreknowledge Faces the Same Objections as Predestination

15, 38. But, as you write, they say, "No one can be roused by the stings of rebuke if it is said in the assembly of the church in the hearing of many: The definitive judgment of the will of God regarding predestination is such that some of you came to the faith from unbelief after receiving the will to obey or that you remain in the faith after receiving perseverance, but the rest of you who dally in the delight of sins have not yet risen up because the help of merciful grace has not yet raised you up. Yet if any of you have not yet been called, but he has predestined you by his grace to be chosen, you will receive the same grace by which you are going to will this and be chosen. And if any of you are now obedient, but are predestined to be rejected, the power to obey will be withdrawn, and you will stop obeying."[63]

When they say these things, they should not keep us from confessing the true grace of God, that is, the grace which is not given according to our merits, and from confessing the predestination of the saints in accord with that grace, just as we are not kept from confessing the foreknowledge of God if someone from that people should speak in this way and say, "Whether you now live correctly or do not live correctly, you will be hereafter such as God has foreknown that you will be, either good if he foreknew that you would be good or evil if he foreknew that you would be evil." For, if after hearing this, some

---

63. The Letter of Hilary 5.

people fall into laziness and apathy and, giving up the struggle and following desire, go after their concupiscences,[64] are we to regard as false what was said of the foreknowledge of God? If God foreknows that they will be good, will they not be good, no matter how much evil they are involved in at present, but if he foreknows that they will be evil, will they not be evil, no matter how much evil they are now seen to be involved in?

There was a certain man in our monastery who, when the brothers rebuked him because he did various actions which ought not to be done and because he did not do others which ought to be done, replied, "Whatever sort of man I now am, I will be the sort of man that God foreknew that I will be." He certainly spoke the truth and, because of this truth, failed to make progress in goodness, but he made progress in evil to the point that, after having abandoned the monastic community, he became a dog which returns to its vomit,[65] and yet it is still uncertain what sort of man he will be. Are we, then, on account of these souls, to say that those true things which are said about God's foreknowledge ought to be either denied or passed over in silence, precisely, that is, when, if they are not said, other errors are incurred?

16, 39. There are also people who either do not pray or pray without fervor because they learned from the words of the Lord that God knows what we need before we ask it from him.[66] Are we to suppose that on account of such people we ought to abandon the truth of this view or delete it from the gospel? On the contrary, it is clear that God has prepared some things to be given even to those who do not pray, such as the beginning of faith, and other things to be given only to those who pray, such as perseverance up to the end. Hence, one who thinks that he has this perseverance from himself certainly does not pray to have it. We must therefore be careful not to extinguish prayer and to kindle pride out of a fear that exhortation may become too heated.

The Need to Speak the Truth about Perseverance

40. Let the truth be stated, then, especially when some question demands that it be stated, and let those grasp it who are able to grasp it. Otherwise, when one keeps silent on account of those who cannot grasp

64. See Sir 18:30.
65. See Prv 26:11; 2 Pt 2:22.
66. See Mt 6:8.

it, those who can grasp the truth by which they may avoid error will not only be deprived of the truth but also trapped in error. For it is easy and even useful to pass over in silence some truth on account of those who are not capable of it. This, after all, is the reason for the Lord's words, *I still have many things to tell you, but you cannot at present bear them* (Jn 16:12), and those words of the Apostle, *I could not speak to you as to spiritual persons, but as to ones still carnal. I gave to you as to little ones in Christ milk to drink, not solid food. For you were not yet capable of it, but you are still not capable.* (1 Cor 3:1-2)

And yet in a certain way of speaking it is possible that what is said may be both milk for the little ones and solid food for the adults. For example, *In the beginning was the Word, and the Word was with God, and the Word was God* (Jn 1:1). Can any Christian pass this over in silence? Can anyone grasp it? Or can anything more sublime be found in sound teaching? That teaching which is not passed over in silence for little ones or for adults is nonetheless not hidden from the little ones by the adults.

But a reason for keeping silence about the truth is one thing, while the need for speaking the truth is another. It would take a long time to search out and list all the reasons for keeping silence about the truth. Yet one of these is to avoid making those who do not understand worse when we want to make those who do understand more learned. For, if we are silent about something, these people will surely not become more learned, but they will also not become worse.

But when the truth is such that, when we state it, a person who cannot grasp it becomes worse, whereas, if we remain silent, one who can understand it becomes worse, what do we think we should do? Should we not state the truth in order that one who can grasp it may grasp it rather than keep silence so that both not only do not grasp it, but that the one who is more intelligent is also worse? For, if he heard and grasped it, many would also learn it through him. After all, to the extent that one is more capable of learning, one is more suited for teaching others. The enemy of grace persists and urges in every way that we believe that grace is given in accord with our merits, and in that way grace would no longer be grace.[67] And are we unwilling to say what we can say with scripture as our witness? Are we, after all, afraid, for example, that someone who cannot grasp the truth may be offended when we speak, and are we not afraid that someone who can grasp the truth may be trapped in error because we are silent?

---

67. See Rom 11:6.

Silence about Predestination Betrays the Gratuity of Grace

41. For either predestination should be preached in the way in which the holy scripture clearly states it, namely, that in the predestined the gifts and calling of God are irrevocable,[68] or one should admit that the grace of God is given according to our merits, as the Pelagians think, though this statement, as we have already often said, is found to have been condemned even by the lips of Pelagius himself in the trial before the Eastern bishops.[69] But these men on whose account we are dealing with these issues are far removed from the heretical perversity of the Pelagians. For, though they do not want to admit that those who by the grace of God become obedient and remain obedient are predestined, still they do admit that this grace comes before the will of those who receive it. Grace comes first, of course, so that we believe that grace is given gratuitously, as the truth says, and not according to the merits of a will which comes first, as the Pelagian error states in opposition to the truth. Grace, therefore, also comes before faith; otherwise, if faith came before grace, the will also came before grace, since faith cannot exist without the will. But if grace comes before faith because it comes before the will, it certainly comes before all obedience; it also comes before the love by which alone we truly obey God with delight. And grace produces all these things in those to whom it is given, and it comes before all these things in them.

Perseverance up to the End Is God's Gift

17. There remains in these goods that perseverance up to the end which we daily ask for from the Lord to no purpose, if the Lord does not produce it through his grace in one whose prayers he hears. See now how foreign to the truth it is to deny that perseverance up to the end of this life is a gift of God. For he himself brings this life to an end when he wills, and if he brings it to an end before an imminent fall, he makes the person persevere up to the end. But the generosity of God's goodness is more amazing and more evident to believers because this grace is given even to little ones who cannot at that age be given obedience.

---

68. See Rom 11:29.
69. See above 12, 31 and *The Deeds of Pelagius* 14, 30-37.

God undoubtedly foreknew, then, that he was going to give these gifts of his to whomever he gives them, and he prepared them in his foreknowledge. Therefore, *those whom he predestined, he also called* with that calling which it does not bother me to mention so often. Of that calling it was said, *The gifts and calling of God are irrevocable.* For to arrange his own future works in his foreknowledge, which cannot be deceived or changed, is nothing other than to predestine them. But just as a person who God foreknew would be chaste strives to be chaste, though he himself is not certain about this, so a person whom God predestined to be chaste does not cease to strive to be chaste because he hears that he will be what he will be because of God's gift, though he himself is not certain about this. In fact, his love even rejoices over this but is not puffed up with pride, as if he had not received it.[70] He is therefore not only not kept from this work by the preaching of predestination, but he is even helped to the point that, when he boasts, he may boast in the Lord.[71]

42. But what I said about chastity can be said with complete truth about faith, about piety, about love, about perseverance, and—not to continue with every one of them—about the obedience by which one obeys God. But these people place in our own power only the beginning of faith and perseverance up to the end, supposing that they are not gifts of God and that God does not produce our thoughts and willing in order to have and retain them, but they concede that God gives the other things when we ask for them from him with the faith of a believer. Why are they not afraid that the doctrine of predestination may be an obstacle to the exhortation to these other things and the preaching of them? Or do they perhaps say that these are also not predestined? They are, then, either not given by God, or he did not know that he was going to give them. But if they are given by God and he knew that he was going to give them, he certainly predestined them.

These people, then, also exhort others to chastity, love, piety, and the other virtues which they admit are God's gifts, and they cannot deny that they were foreknown by him and, for this reason, predestined. Nor do they say that the preaching of God's predestination, that is, the preaching of God's foreknowledge concerning these future gifts of his, is an obstacle to their exhortations. In the same way,

---

70. See 1 Cor 13:4; 1 Cor 4:6.
71. See 1 Cor 1:31.

let them see that the preaching of predestination is not an obstacle to their exhortations either to faith or to perseverance, if they too are said to be gifts of God, as is true, and to be foreknown, that is, predestined to be given. Rather, this preaching of predestination is an obstacle to and overthrows only that most destructive error which says that the grace of God is given according to our merits, so that one who boasts may boast not in the Lord but in himself.

Wisdom Is a Gift, but We Exhort People to It

43. To explain this more clearly for the sake of those who are a little slow, let those to whom the talent has been given to fly ahead bear with my dallying. The apostle James says, *If any one of you needs wisdom, let him ask it from God, who gives to all generously and without reproach, and it will be given to him* (Jas 1:5). It is also written in the Proverbs of Solomon, *For God gives wisdom* (Prv 2:6). And in the Book of Wisdom, whose authority has been relied on by many great and learned men who commented on the words of God long before us, we read regarding continence, *For I knew that no one can be continent unless God grants it, and this too was a mark of wisdom, to know whose gift this was* (Wis 8:21). These, then, are God's gifts, that is, wisdom and continence—not to mention the others. And these brothers agreed, for they are not Pelagians, so that they fight against this clear truth with stubborn and heretical perversity.

"But," they say, "faith which begins with us obtains that these things are given to us by God," and they claim that to begin to have faith and to remain in it up to the end is due to us, as if we do not receive this from the Lord. Here they undoubtedly contradict the Apostle, who says, *What do you have that you have not received?* (1 Cor 4:7) They also contradict the martyr Cyprian, who says, "We must boast over nothing since we have nothing of our own."[72] We have said these things and many others which it is a bother to repeat, and we have shown that both the beginning of faith and perseverance up to the end are gifts of God, and that God could not fail to foreknow any of his future gifts, both those gifts which he was going to give and those to whom he was going to give them. And we have shown that, for this reason, those whom he sets free and crowns were predestined by him. But they think that

---

72. Cyprian, *Three Books of Testimonies for Quirinus* III, 4.

they should reply that the doctrine of predestination is an obstacle to the usefulness of preaching because, once this doctrine is heard, no one could be roused by the stings of a rebuke.[73]

When they say these things, they do not want it to be preached to people that their coming to the faith and remaining in the faith are gifts of God, for fear that this might seem to bring despair rather than encouragement when those who hear it think that it is uncertain for human ignorance to whom God gives and to whom God does not give these gifts.[74] Why, then, do they too preach along with us that wisdom and continence are gifts of God? But if, when these are preached as gifts of God, the exhortation by which we exhort people to be wise and continent is not impeded, what reason is there, then, to think that the exhortation is impeded by which we exhort people to come to the faith and to persevere in it up to the end, if these are said to be gifts of God, as is proved by the testimony of the scriptures?

44. Look, to say nothing of continence and to discuss only wisdom here, the apostle James whom we mentioned above says, *The wisdom which comes from above is, first of all, pure, then peaceful, modest, open to reason, full of mercy and good fruits, without calculation, without pretense* (Jas 3:17) Do you see, I ask, how it comes down from the Father of lights, filled with many and great goods? *Every best gift*, as the same apostle says, *and every perfect gift is from above, coming down from the Father of lights* (Jas 1:17). Why, then, to omit other things, do we rebuke the impure and the quarrelsome to whom we nonetheless preach that pure and peaceful wisdom is a gift of God, and why are we not afraid that, disturbed by the uncertainty of the divine will, they might find in this preaching more despair than encouragement and be roused by the stings of rebuke not against themselves but rather against us, because we rebuke them for not having these things which we say are not produced by the human will but given by the divine generosity?

Why, finally, did the preaching of this grace not deter the apostle James himself from rebuking the restless and saying, *If you have bitter jealousy and quarrels in your hearts, do not boast and be liars against the truth; this is not the wisdom that comes down from above, but earthly, animal, diabolical wisdom. For where there is*

---

73. See the Letter of Prosper 6 and the Letter of Hilary 2. 5, as well as above 15, 38.
74. See the Letter of Hilary 6.

jealousy and quarrels, there is also incontinence and every evil work (Jas 3:14-16)? The restless, then, are to be rebuked both on the basis of the testimony of scripture and on the basis of the rules which these people hold in common with us, nor is this rebuke impeded by the fact that we preach that the peaceful spirit by which the quarrelsome are corrected and healed is a gift of God. In the same way, non-believers or those who do not persevere in the faith are to be rebuked, without the preaching of the grace of God being impeded, which teaches that this faith and our persevering in it are also God's gifts.

For, even if wisdom is obtained on the basis of faith, after having said, *If any of you needs wisdom, let him ask God who gives to all generously and without reproach, and it will be given to him*, the apostle James immediately added, *But let him ask in faith without hesitation* (Jas 1:5-6). And yet, even if faith is given before the one who receives it asks for it, we should not say that for that reason faith is not a gift of God but comes from ourselves, because we have received it even without asking for it. For the Apostle states most clearly, *To the brothers peace and love along with faith from God the Father and the Lord Jesus Christ* (Eph 6:23). From the one from whom peace and love come, there also comes faith, and for this reason we ask not only that faith be increased for those who have it, but also that it be given to those who do not have it.

These Monks Exhort People to the Other Gifts of God

45. Nor do these brothers for whose sake we are saying these things, these men who shout that the preaching of predestination and grace is an obstacle to exhortation, exhort people only to those gifts which they maintain are not given by God but come from ourselves, such as the beginning of faith and perseverance in it up to the end. They certainly ought to do this so that they exhort only non-believers to believe and only believers to continue to believe. But with regard to those virtues which along with us they do not deny are gifts of God, in order that along with us they may destroy the Pelagian error—I mean such virtues as modesty, continence, patience, and the other virtues by which we live righteously and which we obtain from God on the basis of faith—they ought to have shown that we are to pray for them and that we ought only to pray for them either for ourselves or for others, but not exhort anyone to acquire them or

retain them. But, since they exhort people to these virtues to the extent they can and admit that people should be exhorted to them, they certainly indicate well enough that such preaching is not an obstacle to exhortations to faith or to perseverance in the faith up to the end, for we preach that these are gifts of God and are not given by anyone to himself, but by God.

46. But they object, "Each one abandons the faith by his own fault when he yields and consents to the temptation by which he is brought to abandon the faith." Who would deny this? But perseverance in the faith is not for this reason to be said not to be a gift of God. For one who says, *Bring us not into temptation*, daily asks for this, and if he is heard, he receives this. And for this reason, when he asks each day that he may persevere, he certainly places the hope of his perseverance not in himself but in God. I do not want to exaggerate with my words, however, but I leave it instead for those men to ponder so that they may see the sort of position of which they have convinced themselves, namely, that "the preaching of predestination brings despair rather than encouragement." For this is to say: A human being despairs of his own salvation when he has learned to place his hope not in himself but in God, though the prophet cries out, *Cursed be everyone who puts his hope in a human being* (Jer 17:5).

The Doctrine of Predestination Is Found in Scripture

47. These, then, are gifts of God which are given to those who have been chosen, to those who have been called according to God's plan; included in these gifts are both beginning to believe and persevering in faith up to the end of this life, as we have proved by such great evidence from reason and from authorities. These gifts of God, I insist, are only foreknown by God if there is the predestination which we are defending. But they are foreknown. There is, then, the predestination which we are defending.

18. For this reason the same predestination is at times also signified by the term "foreknowledge," as the Apostle says, *God has not rejected his people whom he foreknew* (Rom 11:2). Here the expression, *he foreknew*, is only correctly understood as "he predestined". For he was speaking of the remnant of Israel which was saved, while the others were perishing. After all, he had said previously that the prophet said to Israel, *All day long I have stretched out my hands to a people that*

does not believe and rebels (Rom 10:21). And as if someone replied to him, "Where, then, are the promises which God made to Israel?" he immediately added, *Therefore, I say, Has God rejected his people? Heaven forbid! For I too am an Israelite, of the race of Abraham, of the tribe of Benjamin* (Rom 11:1), as if to say, "For I belong to this people."

Then he added the expression which we are now discussing: *God has not rejected his people whom he foreknew.* And to show that a remnant was left by the grace of God, not by the merits of their works, he went on to say, *Or do you not know what scripture said of Elijah, how he pleaded with God against Israel?* (Rom 11:2), and the rest. *But what,* he asks, *did the divine response say to him? I left for myself seven thousand men who have not bent their knee before Baal.* (Rom 11:4) He did not, after all, say, "They were left for me," or, "They left themselves for me," but, *I left for myself.* He adds, *Thus, even in the present time a remnant was produced by the election of grace. But if by grace, then not by works; otherwise, grace is no longer grace.* (Rom 11:5-6)

And connecting together those things which I already quoted above, he asked, *What then?* and replying to this question, he said, *Israel did not attain this, but those who were chosen attained it, while the rest were blinded* (Rom 11:7). In this election, then, and in this remnant which was produced by the election of grace, he wanted us to understand the people whom God did not reject because he foreknew them. This is that election by which he chose those whom he willed to choose in Christ *before the creation of the world* in order that they might be *holy and spotless before him in love,* predestining them *for adoption as his children* (Eph 1:4-5). No one who understands this, then, is permitted to deny or to doubt that, where the apostle says, *God has not rejected his people whom he foreknew,* he wanted to signify predestination. For he foreknew the remnant which he himself was going to produce according to the election of grace. He therefore predestined this; for he undoubtedly foreknew it if he predestined it, but to have predestined is to have foreknown what he himself was going to do.

Predestination Has Always Been Taught in the Church

19, 48. What prevents us, then, from understanding the same predestination, when in some commentators on the word of God we read of the foreknowledge of God, where they are discussing the calling of the elect? For on this topic they perhaps preferred to use this term, which is more easily understood and does not conflict with the truth, but is, rather, in harmony with the truth which is preached concerning the predestination of grace. This I know: no one could have argued against this predestination which we defend in accord with the holy scriptures without being in error. Yet I think that those holy men who are praised everywhere for their faith and teaching, Cyprian and Ambrose, whose clear testimonies we have already cited, ought to be enough for those who demand the views of the commentators on this topic. And I think that they ought to be enough for both points, that is, that they believe in every way and preach in every way that the grace of God is gratuitous, as it must be believed and preached, and that they do not think that the same preaching is opposed to the preaching by which we exhort the sluggish or rebuke the evil.

For, when these men preached the grace of God, one of them said, "We must boast over nothing since we have nothing of our own,"[75] and the other said, "Our heart and our thoughts are not in our power."[76] Yet they did not cease from exhorting and rebuking in order that the commandments might be observed. Nor did they fear that some people would say to them, "Why are you exhorting us? Why are you rebuking us, if it is not up to us to have anything good and if our heart is not in our power?" By no means could those holy men fear that these objections would be made to them, for in their mind they understood that it was given to very few that they should receive the doctrine of salvation through God himself or through the angels of heaven, without any human being preaching to them, but that it was given to many that they would believe in God through human beings. In whatever way the word of God is spoken to a person, it is undoubtedly a gift of God by which he hears in such a way that he obeys God.

The Teaching of Cyprian and Ambrose on Predestination

49. Hence, the most excellent commentators on the words of God whom we mentioned above both preached the true grace of God as it should be preached, that is, the grace which no human merits precede, and constantly exhorted people to carry out God's commandments so

75. Cyprian, *Three Books of Testimonies for Quirinus* III, 4.
76. Ambrose, *Flight from the World* 1, 1.

that those who had the gift of obedience would hear the commandments which they must obey. For, if any merits of ours come before grace, it is of course the merit of some action or some words or some thought in which the good will itself is also understood. But he very briefly summed up all the kinds of merits when he said, "We must boast over nothing since we have nothing of our own."[77] But the man who said, "Our heart and our thoughts are not in our own power,"[78] did not pass over actions and words. For there is no action or word of a human being which does not come from the heart and thought. But what more could the most glorious martyr and most brilliant teacher, Cyprian, have done on this topic than to warn us that it is necessary to pray in the Lord's Prayer even for enemies of the Christian faith? There he showed what he thought about the beginning of faith which is also a gift of God, and he showed that the Church of Christ also prays daily for perseverance up to the end, because only God gives it to those who persevere up to the end.

And when Blessed Ambrose was explaining the words of the evangelist Luke, *It seemed good to me as well* (Lk 1:3), he said, "It is possible that what he said seemed good to him did not seem good to him alone. For it did not seem good only by reason of the human will, but as it was pleasing to Christ who speaks in me.[79] For he is at work so that what is good may also seem good to us; for he calls one to whom he shows mercy. And for this reason one who follows Christ can, when asked why he chose to be a Christian, reply, *It seemed good to me as well*. And when he says this, he does not deny that it seemed good to God, for the will of human beings is prepared by God.[80] For the fact that a holy person gives honor to God is the grace of God."[81]

Likewise, in the same work, that is, in the commentary on the same gospel, when he came to the place where the Samaritans refused to welcome the Lord as he was making his way to Jerusalem, he said, "Learn at the same time that he did not want to be welcomed by those who were not sincerely converted. For, if he had wanted this, he would have changed them into people devoted to him from people lacking such devotion. But the evangelist himself mentioned

77. Cyprian, *Three Books of Testimonies for Quirinus* III, 4.
78. Ambrose, *Flight from the World* 1, 2.
79. See 2 Cor 13:3.
80. See Prv 8:35 LXX.
81. Ambrose, *Commentary on the Gospel of Luke* I, 10.

why they did not welcome him, when he said, *Because his face was set in the direction of one going to Jerusalem* (Lk 9:53). His disciples, however, desired to be welcomed into Samaria. But God calls those whom he pleases and he makes religious whom he wills."[82]

What do we seek from the commentators on the word of God that is more obvious and more clear, if one wants also to hear from these men what is clear in the scriptures? But to these men who ought to have been enough, we also add Saint Gregory as a third, who testifies that both our believing in God and our confessing what we believe are gifts of God. He says, "Confess, I beg you, the Trinity of the one deity or, if you want to put it otherwise, say, 'of one nature,' and we will pray to God that the Holy Spirit will give a voice," that is, we will ask God that he permit that you be given a voice by which you may be able to confess what you believe. "For he will give it, I am certain: he who has given what is first will also give what is second."[83] He who has given our belief will also give our confession of it.

50. These illustrious teachers say that there is nothing which God has not given over which we may boast as if it were our own. They say that our heart and our thoughts are also not in our power. They attribute everything to God and confess that we receive from him that we are converted to him, destined to remain with him, so that what is good also seems good to us and so that we will that good in order to honor God and to receive Christ who turns us into devout and religious people from those lacking devotion. And thus we believe in the Trinity and also confess with our voice what we believe. They of course attribute all these to the grace of God; they recognize the gifts of God and testify that we have them from him, not from ourselves.

But are any going to say that they confessed the grace of God in such a way that they dared to deny his foreknowledge, which not only the learned but also the unlearned confess? But if they knew that God gives these things and also knew that he foreknew that he would give them and could not fail to know to whom he would give them, they undoubtedly knew the predestination which against the new heretics, we vigorously and diligently defend as it was preached by

---

82. Ibid. VII, 27.
83. See Gregory Nazianzen, Sermon 41, 8. Augustine used the Latin translation of Rufinus with some changes and adaptations which are difficult to explain. For Rufinus' translation, see "On Pentecost" 8. In both Gregory's words and Rufinus' translation the homilist prays that those who do not believe in the divinity of the Holy Spirit may be given the word "God" to speak of him.

the apostles. And yet, when they preached obedience and fervently exhorted people to it as each of them was able to do, it would nonetheless not in any way be correct to say to them, "If you do not want the obedience for which you are setting us afire to grow cold in our heart, do not preach to us this grace of God by which you admit that God gives those things which you exhort us to do."

Predestination Must Be Preached to the Faithful

20, 51. Hence, if the apostles and the teachers of the Church who have come after them and have imitated them did both of these, that is, truly preached the grace of God which is not given in accord with our merits and taught pious obedience by salutary commandments, why it is that these brothers of ours, though trapped by the invincible force of the truth, think that they are correct to say, "Even if what is said about the predestination of the divine benefits is true, it should not be preached to the people"[84]? It certainly must be preached in order that *one who has ears may hear* (Lk 8:8). But who has such ears if he has not received them from him who says, *I shall give them a heart for knowing me and ears to hear* (Bar 3:31). Certainly let one who has not received these ears reject the word, provided that one who receives it takes and drinks, drinks and lives. For, just as piety must be preached in order that God may be correctly worshiped by one who has ears for hearing, chastity must be preached in order that one who has ears for hearing may do nothing with his sex organs that is forbidden. Love must be preached in order that one who has ears for hearing may love God and neighbor. And in the same way the predestination of the benefits of God must be preached in order that one who has ears for hearing may not boast in himself but in God.

Augustine's Early Teaching on Predestination

52. When they say that there was no need "that so many hearts of simple people be disturbed by the uncertainty of such an argument. For the Catholic faith has been defended no less effectively for so many years without this doctrine of predestination, both against other heretics and especially against the Pelagians, by so many previous books of other

---

84. See the Letter of Prosper 3 and the Letter of Hilary 2.

Catholics and of your own,"[85] I am greatly surprised that they say this. I am greatly surprised that they do not notice those books of ours (not to mention others) which were written and published before the Pelagians began to appear. And I am greatly surprised that they do not see the many passages in them by which we cut down the future Pelagian heresy, without knowing it, when we preached the grace by which God sets us free from our sinful errors and conduct, not because of any preceding good merits of ours but doing so according to his gratuitous mercy. I began to have a fuller knowledge of this truth in that treatise which I wrote for Simplician of happy memory, the bishop of Milan, at the beginning of my episcopacy, when I realized and stated that the beginning of faith is also the gift of God.[86]

53. But which of my works could have been more widely known and more favorably received than the books of my *Confessions*? Though I published them also before the Pelagian heresy emerged, I certainly said in them to our God and often said, "Give what you command, and command what you will."[87] When these words of mine were cited at Rome by some brother and fellow bishop of mine in Pelagius' presence, he could not tolerate them and, attacking them somewhat emotionally, he almost came to blows with the one who had cited them. But what does God command first of all and most of all but that we believe in him? And he himself, then, gives us this faith if it is right to say to him, "Give what you command."

And in those same books I recounted my conversion, as God converted me to the faith, which I was attacking by my most wretched and most insane wordiness. Do you not remember that I recounted all that in order to show that God granted to the faithful and daily tears of my mother that I should not perish?[88] There, of course, I taught that God by his grace converts to the faith the wills of people which are not only turned away from the correct faith but are also opposed to that faith. But you both know and can check again when you want to know how I beseeched God concerning my growth and perseverance. Who,

---

85. Ibid. 8. The Latin has "of our own" because it treats the sentence as indirect discourse. Since I treated it as a direct quotation, I changed "our" to "your."
86. See *The Predestination of the Saints* 4, 8, where Augustine recounts his insight into the absolute gratuity of grace which he received while he was writing his *Miscellany of Questions for Simplician*, a work written before Simplician became bishop of Milan in 397.
87. *Confessions* X, 31, 45; 37, 60.
88. Ibid. III, 11, 19-12, 21; IX, 8, 17.

therefore, would dare I will not say to deny but even to doubt that God foreknew that he would give all the gifts of God which I either prayed for or praised in that work and that he could never have failed to know to whom he would give them? This is the clear and certain predestination of the saints which necessity forced me later to defend with greater care and effort when we were arguing against the Pelagians. For we know that individual heresies have introduced into the Church their particular questions against which the divine scripture had to be defended more carefully than if no such necessity forced this. What, however, forced us to defend at greater length and more precisely by this labor of ours those passages of scripture which teach predestination but the fact that the Pelagians say that the grace of God is given according to our merits? What else is that but the complete denial of grace?

Neither Faith Nor Perseverance Comes from Us

21, 54. Therefore, to destroy this view, which is ungrateful to God and inimical to the gratuitous benefits of God by which we are set free, we have in accord with the scriptures, from which we have already quoted extensively, defended the truth that both the beginning of faith and perseverance in it up to the end are gifts of God. For, if we say that the beginning of faith comes from ourselves in order that we may by it merit to receive the other gifts of God, the Pelagians conclude that the grace of God is given according to our merits. The Catholic faith stands in such horror of this that Pelagius himself condemned it out of fear that he would be condemned.[89] Likewise, if we say that our perseverance comes from ourselves, not from the Lord, they answer that we have the beginning of faith from ourselves, just as we have its end. They argue that for even better reasons we have from ourselves that beginning, if we have from ourselves our persevering up to the end, since to bring something to the end is greater than to begin it. And so they draw the same conclusion, namely, that the grace of God is given according to our merits. But if each of them is a gift of God and if God foreknew that he would give these gifts of his—and who would deny this?—predestination must be preached in order that the genuine grace of God, that is, grace which is not given according to our merits, can be defended by an insurmountable bulwark.

---

89. Augustine again alludes to the Council of Diospolis held in late 415; see *The Deeds of Pelagius* 14, 30-37.

Augustine's Recent Teaching Contains Nothing New

55. And in that book entitled *Rebuke and Grace*, of which there were not enough copies for all those who love us, I think that I stated that it is also a gift of God to persevere up to the end.[90] And, unless my memory deceives me, I either never or hardly ever previously wrote this so explicitly and so clearly. But I have not now said this in such a way that no one has said it before me. Blessed Cyprian, as we have already shown, explained our petitions in the Lord's Prayer; he said that we ask for perseverance in the first petition, claiming that we pray for it when we say, *May your name be made holy*, namely, that we may persevere in what we have begun to be, since we were already made holy in baptism.[91]

Let those brothers, then, to whom I ought not to be ungrateful since they love me, who profess, as you write, that they embrace all my views apart from this point which has come into question—let those men, I repeat, see whether in the latter parts of the first book of those two which I wrote for Simplician of Milan at the beginning of my episcopacy before the Pelagian heresy emerged, there remains anything by which one might call into doubt the view that the grace of God is not given according to our merits.[92] Let them see whether I did not there amply show that even the beginning of faith is a gift of God and whether from what I said the result does not clearly emerge, even if it is not expressly stated, that perseverance up to the end is also given only by him who predestined us for his kingdom and glory.

Furthermore, did I not publish years ago the letter which I wrote for Saint Paulinus, the bishop, against the Pelagians, though they have just now begun to attack it?[93] Let them also look at the letter which I sent to Sixtus, a priest of the Church of Rome,[94] when we were engaged in the fiercest battle against the Pelagians, and they will find that letter contains the same doctrine as the one to Paulinus. Hence, let them recall that these teachings, which strangely enough

---

90. *Rebuke and Grace* 10, 26.

91. See Cyprian, *The Lord's Prayer* 12.

92. Augustine refers to his *Miscellany of Questions in Response to Simplician*, which he wrote in 396 and which is generally regarded as a turning point in his views on grace.

93. See Letter 186 among the letters of Augustine, a letter which Augustine and Alypius wrote in 417 for Paulinus of Nola, in which they explained the dangers of Pelagianism.

94. See Letter 194 among the letters of Augustine, a letter which Augustine wrote for the future Pope Sixtus, the very letter which Florus found in Alypius' monastery at Uzalis, copied, and sent back to his monastery at Hadrumetum.

are now displeasing to these men, were already stated and written some years ago against the Pelagian heresy.

And yet I would not want anyone to embrace all my views in order to be my follower, but only those points on which he sees that I am not mistaken. For I am now writing the books in which I have undertaken to review my works in order to show that I have not always held the same views;[95] rather, I think that, as I wrote, I made progress by the mercy of God, but not that I started off with perfection. For I speak with more arrogance than truth if I say that I have now at this age come to perfection without any error in my writing. But it makes a difference how much and on what issues one is in error and how easily one is corrected or with what stubbornness one tries to defend his error. We can, of course, have good hope for someone if the last day of this life finds him making progress so that he receives in addition what was lacking to him as he made progress, and we may judge him worthy of perfection rather than of punishment.

56. Hence, if I do not want to be ungrateful to those men who have loved me because some benefit from my labor reached them before they loved me, how much more do I not want to be ungrateful to God, whom we would not love if he had not first loved us and made us lovers of him. For love comes from him,[96] as they said whom he made not merely his great lovers but also his great preachers. But what is more ungrateful than to deny the very grace of God by saying that it is given according to our merits? The Catholic faith stands in horror of this position which it hurled against Pelagius himself as a capital charge and which he condemned, not out of a love for the truth, but out of fear for his own condemnation.[97]

But let whoever, as a Catholic believer, stands in horror at saying that the grace of God is given according to our merits not subtract from the grace of God faith itself by which he has obtained mercy in order to become a believer.[98] And for this reason let him also attribute perseverance up to the end to the grace of God, by which he obtains the mercy he daily asks for so that he is not brought into temptation.[99]

---

95. Augustine alludes to his *Revisions,* in which he reviewed his books, at times admitting his mistakes and at other times defending what he said or amending it.
96. See 1 Jn 4:7.
97. Augustine again alludes to the Council of Diospolis where Pelagius condemned the proposition that grace is given in accord with our merits.
98. See 1 Cor 7:25.
99. See Mt 6:13.

Between the extremes of the beginning of faith and the perfection of perseverance there are those in-between virtues by which we live correctly, and these brothers also agree that they are given to us by God because faith wins them. But God foreknew that he would give to those he called all these gifts of his, namely, the beginning of faith and all the other gifts up to the end. Hence, it is a mark of excessive contentiousness to speak against predestination or to have doubts about it.

The Proper Way to Teach Predestination

22, 57. Predestination ought nonetheless not to be preached to the people so that the multitude of those who are uneducated or who are slower to understand think that it is in some sense refuted by its being preached, just as the foreknowledge of God—which they certainly cannot deny—also seems to be refuted if one says to people, "Whether you run or whether you sleep, you will be what he who cannot be deceived has foreknown that you will be." But it is an act of a deceitful or inexperienced physician to apply even a useful medicine in such a way that it either does no good or does harm. Rather, one should say, *Run in order that you may gain the prize* (1 Cor 9:24), and in order that you may know from your very running that you were foreknown to run in accord with the rules.[100] And the foreknowledge of God can perhaps be preached in other ways so that one wards off human laziness.

58. The definite decision of God's will concerning predestination, then, comes to this: Some, having received the will to obey, are converted from unbelief to the faith or persevere in the faith, while others who dally in the enjoyment of sins worthy of condemnation, even if they are predestined, have not yet risen up, because the help of merciful grace has not yet raised them up. For, if some are not yet called whom God has predestined by his grace to be chosen, they will receive the same grace by which they shall will to be chosen and shall be chosen. But if there are some who obey, but are not predestined for his kingdom and glory, they last only for a time and will not remain up to the end in the same obedience.

Although these statements are true, one should nonetheless not state them in the hearing of many people, so that this language is aimed at them, and those words of these brothers, which you included

---

100. See 2 Tm 2:5.

in your letter[101] and which I quoted above, are addressed to them: "The definite decision of God's will concerning predestination comes to this: Some of you, having received the will to obey, come from unbelief to the faith." What need is there to say "some of you"? For, if we are speaking to the Church of God, if we are speaking to believers, why should we say that some of them have come to the faith so that we seem to do an injury to the rest since we can more appropriately say, "The definite decision of the will of God comes to this: Having received the will to obey, you have come from unbelief to the faith, and having received perseverance, you continue in the faith."

59. Nor is it at all necessary to say what follows, namely, "The rest of you who dally in the enjoyment of sins have not yet risen up, because the help of merciful grace has not raised you up," though it could and ought to be phrased in a correct and suitable way as follows, "But if there are some of you who still dally in the enjoyment of sins worthy of condemnation, learn discipline which is most salutary.[102] But when you do this, do not be filled with pride as if over your own works or boast as if you had not received this. *For it is God who works in you both the willing and the action in accord with good will* (Phil 2:13), and your steps are directed by the Lord in order that you may will his way.[103] But learn from your good and correct course itself that you belong to the predestination of divine grace."

60. Likewise, the words which follow, "Yet, if some of you have not yet been called whom God has predestined by his grace to be chosen, you will receive the same grace by which you shall will to be chosen and shall be chosen," are stated more harshly than they need be, if we bear in mind that we are speaking not just to any human beings but to the Church of Christ. For why does one not rather put it this way, "And if any are not yet called, let us pray for them that they may be called? For they may perhaps be predestined in such a way that they are granted to our prayers and they receive the same grace by which they may will to be chosen and may become chosen." For God who accomplishes everything which he has predestined willed that we pray even for enemies of the faith in order that we might understand from this that he gives even to non-believers that they believe and makes them willing from unwilling.

---

101. This quotation is not taken from the Letter of Prosper or the Letter of Hilary which we possess.
102. See Ps 2:2.
103. See Ps 37:23.

61. But, as for that which is linked to the previous words, I wonder whether any weak persons in the Christian people can listen with patience when it is said to them, "And if some of you obey, but have been predestined to be rejected, the power to obey will be taken away so that you cease to obey." For what else does saying this seem to do but to curse[104] or somehow to foretell evil? But if one wants to or must say something about those who do not persevere, why does one not rather phrase it as I did a little before.[105] First of all, we should not say this concerning those who are listening to us in the people of God, but to these people concerning others. That is, we should not say, "If any of you obey, but are predestined to be rejected," but, "If any obey," with the rest in the third person, not in the second. For one does not speak of something desirable, but of something dreadful, and with great harshness and hatefulness it is thrown as if into the face of the listeners by compelling them when one who speaks to them says, "And if there are any of you who obey, but are predestined to be rejected, the power to obey will be withdrawn so that you cease to obey." For what does the statement lose if it is phrased as follows, "But if any obey, but are not predestined for his kingdom and glory, they last only for a time and will not remain up to the end in the same obedience"? Is the same point not stated with greater truth and fittingness so that we do not seem to desire so great an evil for them, but to report concerning others something our listeners hate and think does not pertain to them, since they hope and pray for a better end? But following the manner of speaking which our opponents think we should use, we can also express the same idea in almost the same words regarding the foreknowledge of God, which they certainly cannot deny. Then one would say, "And if you obey, but it is foreknown that you will be rejected, you will cease to obey." This is, of course, perfectly true; it is surely true, but most brutal, most inopportune, and most inappropriate, not because the statement is false but because it is not applied in a salutary manner to the frailty of human weakness.

A Further Addition to the Preaching of Predestination

62. I do not think that the manner of speaking which we have said should be used in preaching predestination can suffice for someone

---

104. Augustine plays upon "to say" (*dicere*) and "to curse" (*maledicere*).
105. See above 22, 58.

who is speaking before the people, unless he adds this or something of the sort and says, "And so, you ought to hope for this perseverance in obedience from the Father of lights from whom there comes down *every best gift and every perfect gift* (Jas 1:17). And you ought to ask for it by daily prayers and, in doing this, you ought to be confident that you are not strangers to the predestination of his people, because he himself also grants that you say these prayers and have this confidence. But heaven forbid that you despair about yourselves because you are commanded to place your hope in him, not in yourselves. *For cursed is* every *one who places his hope in a human being* (Jer 17:5), and *It is better to trust in the Lord than to trust in human beings* (Ps 118:8), for *blessed are they who trust in him* (Ps 2:13). Having this hope, *serve the Lord in fear, and exult before him with trembling* (Ps 2:11). For no one can be secure regarding the eternal life which God, who does not lie, has promised to the children of the promise before eternal times unless this life which is a temptation upon the earth[106] has come to an end. But he will make us persevere in himself up to the end of that life, for we say daily to him, *Bring us not into temptation*."

When these or such words are spoken whether to a few Christians or to the multitude of the Church, why do we fear to preach the predestination of the saints and the true grace of God, that is, the grace which is given not according to our merits but as the holy scripture preaches it? Or are we to fear that a human being will despair concerning himself when he is shown that he must place his hope in God, but that he will not despair if he has with great pride and to his great misfortune placed it in himself?

The Prayers of the Church Can Be Our Guide

23, 63. But I wish that the slow of heart and the weak who cannot or cannot as yet understand the scriptures or their explanations, whether they listen to our discussions on this question or not, would rather pay attention to their own prayers, which the Church has always had and always will have from her beginnings until this world comes to an end. For on this truth which we are now compelled not merely to mention but to protect and defend against the new heretics, was the Church ever silent in her prayers, even if at times she did not

---

106. See Job 7:1.

think that there was any need to insert it in her teachings when there was no pressing opponent? For when has the Church not prayed for non-believers and her enemies that they might come to believe? When has a believer had a non-believing friend, neighbor, or spouse and has not asked the Lord to grant him a mind obedient to the faith? But who has ever not prayed for himself that he might remain in the Lord? Or who has dared to reprehend, not merely aloud but even in thought, a priest who, while invoking the Lord upon the faithful, at some point said, "Grant, Lord, that they may persevere in you up to the end"? Has not such a person rather, both with a heart that believes and with lips that confess, responded "Amen" to such a blessing of the priest? For the faithful do not pray for anything else in the Lord's Prayer, especially when they say, *Bring us not into temptation*, but that they may persevere in holy obedience.

Just as, then, the Church was born, grew, and increased in these prayers, so the Church was also born, grew, and increased in this faith. By this faith the Church believes that the grace of God is not given according to our merits. For the Church would not pray that faith be given to non-believers unless she believed that God turns to himself the wills of persons which are turned away and opposed to him, nor would the Church pray to persevere in the faith of Christ, not deceived or overcome by the temptations of this world, unless she believed that the Lord has our heart in his power, so that the good which we have by our own will we would not have at all unless God also produces in us the willing. For, if the Church in fact asks this of him, but thinks that she gives it to herself, she does not have prayers that are genuine, but ones which are merely external formalities. Heaven forbid that this be so! For who sincerely groans, desiring to receive from the Lord what he prays for, if he thinks that he gets this from himself, not from the Lord?

Even Our Prayer Is God's Gift

64. This is especially true, since *we do not know what we should ask for in a way that is fitting, but the Spirit*, as the Apostle says, *makes intercession for us with indescribable groans. For he who searches hearts knows what the Spirit intends, for he makes intercession for the saints according to God.* (Rom 8:26-27) What does it mean that *the Spirit makes intercession* except that he makes us intercede *with indescribable*

groans, but truthful groans, since the Spirit is the truth? For he is the one of whom the Apostle says in another passage, *God sent the Spirit of his Son into our hearts, crying out, Abba, Father* (Gal 4:6). And what does *crying out* mean but "making us cry out," in that figure of speech by which we call the day happy which makes us happy? He shows this elsewhere where he says, *For you have not once more received a spirit of servitude in fear, but you have received the Spirit of adoption as children in whom we cry out, Abba, Father* (Rom 8:15). There he said *crying out*; here he said *in whom we cry out*, that is, revealing the sense in which he said *crying out*, that is, as I already explained, "making us cry out." There we understand that it is also a gift of God that we cry out to God with a truthful heart and in the Spirit.

Let them, therefore, notice how mistaken they are who think that we have from ourselves and are not given our asking, our seeking, and our knocking. And they say that the reason for this is that grace is preceded by our merit so that grace comes afterward when we receive by asking, find by seeking, and have the door opened by knocking.[107] Nor do they want to understand that it also belongs to the divine gift that we pray, that is, that we ask, seek, and knock. For we have received *the Spirit of adoption as children in whom we cry out, Abba, Father.* Blessed Ambrose also saw this, for he says, "And to pray to God pertains to spiritual grace, as scripture said, *No one can say, Jesus is Lord, except in the Holy Spirit* (1 Cor 12:6)."[108]

65. God therefore foreknew that he would give to those whom he called all these gifts which the Church asks for from the Lord and has asked for ever since she began to exist. He has, in fact, already given them in predestination itself, as the Apostle explains without any ambiguity. For, in writing to Timothy, he says, *Work with me for the gospel according to the power of God who saves us and calls us with his holy calling, not according to our works, but according to his plan and the grace which has been given to us in Christ Jesus before eternal times, but has now been made known through the coming of our savior, Jesus Christ* (2 Tm 1:8-10). Let that person, therefore, say that at some time the Church did not have in its faith the truth of this predestination and grace which is now being defended against the new heretics with greater care. Let that person, I repeat, say this

who dares to say that at some time the Church did not pray or did not sincerely pray either that non-believers would come to believe or that believers would persevere. But if she always prayed for these goods, she of course always believed that they were gifts of God, nor was she ever permitted to deny that he foreknew them. And for this reason the Church of Christ never lacked faith in this predestination which is now being defended with a new concern against the new heretics.

Summation and Conclusion of the Work

24, 66. But what more shall I say? I think that I have sufficiently, or rather more than sufficiently, taught that both to begin to believe in the Lord and to persevere in the Lord up to the end are gifts of God. But even these men on account of whom we are discussing these issues grant that the other goods which pertain to a pious life by which we correctly worship God are gifts of God. Moreover, they cannot deny that God foreknew all his gifts and those to whom he was going to give them.

Just as, then, we should preach the other gifts so that their preacher is heard with obedience, so we should preach predestination so that one who hears this with obedience may boast not in a human being and, for this reason, not in himself but in the Lord. For this too is God's commandment, and hearing this commandment with obedience, namely, *that one who boasts should boast in the Lord*, just as hearing the others, is a gift of God. I do not hesitate to say that one who does not have this gift has to no purpose whatever other gifts he has. We pray that the Pelagians may have this gift, but that these brothers of ours may have it more fully. Let us, then, not be quick in our arguments and lazy in our prayers. Let us pray, my beloved brothers, let us pray that the God of grace may give even to our enemies, but especially to our brothers and those who love us, that they may understand and confess that, after that great and indescribable fall by which all fell in the one, no one is set free except by the grace of God, and that grace is not a repayment as something owed in accord with the merits of those who receive it but is given as genuine grace with no preceding merits.

Christ as a Model of Our Predestination

67. But there is no more illustrious example of predestination than Jesus himself. I discussed this already in the first book,[109] and I have chosen to emphasize it at the end of this book. There is, I repeat, no more illustrious example of predestination than the mediator himself. Let any believer who wants to understand it well pay attention to him, and let him find himself in him. I mean a believer who believes and confesses in him a true human nature, that is, our nature, though raised up to the only Son of God by God the Word, who assumes it in a singular manner, so that he who assumed it and what he assumed is one person in the Trinity. For, when the man was assumed, a quaternity was not produced, but there remained a trinity, since that assumption ineffably produced the truth of one person in God and man. After all, we do not say that Christ is only God, like the heretical Manicheans, nor only a man, like the heretical Photinians,[110] nor do we say that he is man in such a way that he lacks something which certainly pertains to human nature, whether the soul or the rational mind in the soul or flesh, flesh taken from a woman, not made out of the Word which was transformed and changed into flesh. All these three false and vain views produced the three different and diverse sects of the Apollinarists,[111] but we say that Christ is true God, born of God the Father without any beginning of time and that the same Christ is true man born of a human mother at a certain fullness of time. Nor did his humanity by which he is less than the Father lessen something of his divinity by which he is equal to the Father. But the one Christ is both of these; as God he said most truly, *The Father and I are one* (Jn 10:30), and as man he said most truly, *The Father is greater than I* (Jn 14:28).

He, then, who made Christ a righteous man from the offspring of David, a man who was never not righteous, without any preceding merits of his will, makes righteous persons from unrighteous ones without any preceding merits of their will in order that Christ might be the head and they might be his members. He, then, who causes that man, without any preceding merits of that man, neither to contract by his origin

---

109. See The *Predestination of the Saints* 15, 30-31.
110. See *Heresies* 45 and 46 for the Photinians and the Manicheans.
111. See ibid. 55, where Augustine delineates the various positions which the Apollinarists adopted.

nor to commit by his will any sin which might be forgiven him, causes people, without any preceding merits of theirs, to believe in him, and he forgives them every sin. He who makes him such that he never had and never will have an evil will makes a good will from an evil will in his members. And he predestined both him and us, because he foreknew not our merits but his future works both in him, in order that he might be our head, and in us, in order that we might be his body.

68. Let those who read this thank God if they understand it, but let those who do not understand it pray that he may be their interior teacher, from whose face there comes knowledge and understanding.[112] But let those who think that I am mistaken carefully consider again and again what has been said lest they may perhaps themselves be mistaken. But since I not only receive more instruction, but also derive further correction from those who read my works, I acknowledge that the Lord is kind toward me, and I especially expect to receive this instruction and correction through the teachers of the Church, if what I write comes into their hands and they deign to come to know it.

112. See Prv 2:6 LXX.